DATE DUE

			PRINTED IN U.S.A.

ENCYCLOPEDIA
OF MORMONISM

EDITORIAL BOARD

ENCYCLOPEDIA OF MORMONISM

Edited by
Daniel H. Ludlow

Volume 4

The History, Scripture, Doctrine, and Procedure
of The Church of Jesus Christ of Latter-day Saints

Macmillan Publishing Company
New York

Maxwell Macmillan Canada
Toronto

Maxwell Macmillan International
New York   Oxford   Singapore   Sydney

Macmillan Publishing Company
866 Third Avenue, New York, NY 10022

Maxwell Macmillan Canada, Inc.
1200 Eglinton Avenue East, Suite 200, Don Mills, Ontario M3C 3N1

Library of Congress Catalog Card No.:91–34255

Printed in the United States of America

printing number
    4 5 6 7 8 9 10

Macmillan Inc. is part of the Maxwell Communication
Group of Companies.

Library of Congress Cataloging-in-Publication Data

Encyclopedia of Mormonism/edited by Daniel H. Ludlow.
        p.   cm.
      Includes bibliographical references and index.
      ISBN 0-02-879605-5 (4 vol. set).—ISBN 0-02-904040-X (5 vol.
    set).—ISBN 0-02-879600-4 (v. 1)
        1. Church of Jesus Christ of Latter-Day Saints—Encyclopedias.
    2. Mormon Church—Encyclopedias.   3. Mormons—Encyclopedias.
    I. Ludlow, Daniel H.
    BX8605.5.E62   1992
    289.3'03—dc20   91–34255
                                                              CIP

The paper used in this publication meets the minimum requirements
of American National Standard for Information Sciences—Permanence
of Paper for Printed Library Materials. ANSI Z39.48-1984.

T

TABERNACLE, SALT LAKE CITY

This dome-shaped building on TEMPLE SQUARE in SALT LAKE CITY is one of the most impressive achievements of Latter-day Saint architectural design and engineering skill. Since 1867, this unique pioneer structure has been the site of nearly all of the Church's General Conferences; addresses by prominent visitors, including several U.S. Presidents; and many significant cultural events. The site of weekly TABERNACLE CHOIR BROADCASTS since 1929, it is renowned for its organ. The Salt Lake Tabernacle culminated Latter-day Saint pioneer efforts to construct a very large auditorium for important meetings. On July 28, 1847, Brigham YOUNG designated Temple Square as the center of the new Latter-day Saint capital. By July 31, the first of a series of open-sided boweries had been erected on the square. With wood posts supporting a roof made of leafy boughs and dirt, this rough shelter provided some protection for religious worship and other public gatherings. In 1851–1852, the Old Tabernacle, the first major building on the block, was built in the southwest corner of Temple Square, later the site of the Assembly Hall. Truman O. Angell, architect of public works, designed the building with low adobe walls, a gabled roof, and a floor below ground level. Although it could accommodate 2,500 people, it was soon inadequate for conference crowds, and in 1854 the General Conferences were again held outdoors.

At the April 1863 conference, Daniel H. Wells, counselor to President Brigham Young, announced plans to build a new tabernacle "that will comfortably seat some ten thousand people" (*JD* 10:139). The construction of so large an auditorium in an isolated territory without railroad access to manufactured building materials was an extraordinary undertaking. Church architect William H. Folsom prepared the first plans under President Young's direction. The design called for a structure 150 feet wide and 250 feet long with semicircular ends and a peaked roof similar to that of the Old Tabernacle. The cornerstone was laid July 26, 1864, and forty-four sandstone piers to support the roof were begun that year.

The next year, President Young appointed an experienced bridge builder, Henry Grow, to superintend the construction. In consultation with the President, Grow modified a type of lattice truss used in bridge construction into huge elliptical arches that spanned the entire width of the structure without intermediate supports, an innovation without parallel for a building of these dimensions. The trusses were constructed of timbers pegged together with wooden dowels that were split and wedged at each end. Cracked timbers were wrapped with green rawhide, which contracted when dry and made a tight binding. When the building was completed, the roof structure was nine feet thick, and the plaster ceiling was 68 feet above the floor.

The tabernacle on Temple Square in Salt Lake City, under construction (c. 1866). The curved roof was built without metal or nails; beams were notched and fitted, then lashed with wet rawhide that shrunk as it dried to provide strong support. The roof's trestle-type design allowed for a 150-foot-wide, 80-foot-high and 250-foot-long unsupported interior space when the scaffolding was removed, resulting in exceptional acoustical qualities. Photographer: C. R. Savage.

Truman O. Angell, who replaced Folsom as Church architect early in 1867, designed the exterior cornice and the interior woodwork, including the gallery added in 1869–1870. This 3,000-seat balcony increased the building's seating capacity to approximately 10,000 and improved its acoustics by reducing echoes. Although the Tabernacle was used for the October 1867 conference, it was not formally dedicated until October 1875. A baptismal font was installed in 1890; the rostrum area was extensively remodeled in 1882, 1933, and 1977; the shingle roof was replaced with aluminum in 1947; and a basement was added in 1968. The building was designated as a National Historic Landmark in 1970 and as a National Civil Engineering Landmark in 1971.

BIBLIOGRAPHY

Anderson, Paul L. "William Harrison Folsom: Pioneer Architect." *Utah Historical Quarterly* 43 (Summer 1975):240–59.

Angell, Truman O. Journals. LDS Church Archives.

Grow, Stewart L. *A Tabernacle in the Desert*. Salt Lake City, 1958.

"The New Tabernacle." *Salt Lake Telegraph*, Oct. 6, 1867.

PAUL L. ANDERSON

TABERNACLE CHOIR

See: Mormon Tabernacle Choir

TABERNACLE ORGAN

While not the world's largest, the organ in the SALT LAKE TABERNACLE is one of the most famous musical instruments ever produced. Thanks to the widely disseminated "Music and the Spoken Word" weekly radio (and later TV) broadcast, this

The tabernacle on Temple Square c. 1873. In this view, looking west, the foundation of the Salt Lake Temple is in the foreground; construction equipment around the "old tabernacle" is to the left. Photographer: C. W. Carter.

organ has probably been heard by more people than any other. Year-round daily recitals (inaugurated in 1915 and attended by millions of visitors to TEMPLE SQUARE each year) and numerous performances at Church conferences and other public recitals and concerts add to the number of people whose lives have been enriched by this remarkable instrument.

The present organ was built in 1948 by the Aeolian-Skinner Company of Boston, under the supervision of its president and tonal director, G. Donald Harrison. However, the person most responsible for the project was Tabernacle organist Alexander Schreiner, who, with colleagues Frank Asper and Roy Darley, shared the goal of creating an organ for Temple Square to equal the greatest ever known. Given the enthusiastic acceptance of this instrument by organ experts and the general public, they did indeed succeed.

This organ is the most recent of a line of fine Tabernacle instruments. Pioneer organ builder Joseph Ridges (1827–1914) installed the first one in 1867. Some pipes and parts from that organ and its

successors have been incorporated into the present instrument not only to provide a link with the past but also to preserve the superb quality of those artifacts. The most notable feature from pioneer days is the central portion of the large organ case. The famous golden pipes, made of wood staves fashioned from Utah timber, still play today. Over the years, the case has been enlarged, but always following the style of the original, which was influenced by the Boston Music Hall organ (Walcker, 1863), the most sensational instrument of its day.

Neils Johnson enlarged the organ in 1885. Then an instrument incorporating some of the pioneer pipes and parts was built by the Kimball Company at the turn of the century. Much of that organ was replaced by the Austin Company in 1915. Essentially this is the instrument that was heard on the first radio broadcasts from the Tabernacle in 1930.

Most organ historians consider the present organ to be the most complete and perfect example of the American Classic style. The prime mover in developing the American Classic organ was G.

A widely recognized Mormon landmark, the Tabernacle Organ is one of the largest and finest in the world. It was originally built by Mormon pioneer Joseph Ridges for the newly completed Salt Lake Tabernacle in 1867. It was rebuilt 5 times over the next 124 years (shown here after the 1916 expansion). The current organ consists of 11,623 speaking pipes, ranging in length from 3/4 inch to 32 feet.

Donald Harrison, who brought this concept to maturity after World War II. Alexander Schreiner was impressed with this forward-looking approach and felt that an all-American instrument drawing on European and English traditions would be appropriate for the Tabernacle.

The organ presently contains 11,623 individual pipes organized into 147 voices (tone colors) and 206 ranks (rows of pipes). Grouped into 8 divisions, they are controlled from a console with five 61-note manuals (keyboards) and a 32-note pedalboard. All divisions of the organ are located behind the massive casework on the west end of the Tabernacle except the antiphonal division, which is in the lower attic at the east end and speaks through openings behind the center balcony seats. The longest pipe is 32 feet in speaking length; the shortest is three-quarters of an inch. Pipes are made of wood, zinc, and various alloys of tin and lead.

Between 1985 and 1989, Schoenstein and Co. of San Francisco directed a major renovation of the organ, regulating all pipework, rebuilding the console, and installing seventeen ranks of new pipes.

BIBLIOGRAPHY

Bethards, Jack M. "The Tabernacle Letters." *The Diapason* (June 1990):14–17; (July 1990):8–9; (Aug. 1990):10–11.

Callahan, Charles. *The American Classic Organ: A History in Letters.* The Organ Historical Society, Richmond, Virginia, 1989.

Owen, Barbara. *The Mormon Tabernacle Organ: An American Classic.* Salt Lake City, 1990.

JACK M. BETHARDS

TAYLOR, ELMINA SHEPARD

Elmina (Mina) Shepard Taylor (1830–1904), the first general president of the Young Ladies' Mutual Improvement Association (*see* YOUNG WOMEN), was born September 12, 1830, in Middlefield, New York. She was the eldest of three daughters of Methodist parents, David S. and Rozella (Rosella, Rozita) Bailey Shepard. Following her graduation from public school and Hardwick Academy, she left home in 1854 to teach school in Haverstraw, New York, where she met John Druce, a member of The Church of Jesus Christ of Latter-day Saints.

Elmina Shephard Taylor (1830–1904), first general president of the Young Ladies' Mutual Improvement Association, served from 1880 to 1904.

She was converted and baptized into the LDS Church on July 5, 1856. In a later account of her conversion, she wrote, "I fought against my convictions, for I well knew how it would grieve my dear parents . . . and I also thought I should lose my situation. . . . However, I could not silence my convictions, and . . . I went forth and was baptized" (Crocheron, p. 49).

On August 31, 1856, she married George Hamilton Taylor. They left New York for Utah on April 15, 1859, and arrived in Salt Lake City on September 16. They located in the Salt Lake Fourteenth Ward, where Elmina lived until her death. She was the mother of seven children, three of whom died in infancy.

Elmina Taylor was appointed secretary of the Fourteenth Ward RELIEF SOCIETY on December 12, 1867, and served in that capacity for twenty-six years. On September 23, 1874, she was called as president of the Young Ladies' Association of the ward. On December 22, 1879, she was chosen as a counselor to Salt Lake Stake Relief Society president Mary Isabella Horne, a position she held for sixteen years.

At a conference of women's organizations held June 19, 1880, in the Assembly Hall on Temple Square, Elmina Taylor, although shy and reserved, was appointed the first general president of the Young Ladies' Mutual Improvement Association. Originally organized to help teenage girls focus more on spiritual and less on worldly pursuits (see RETRENCHMENT ASSOCIATION), the association encouraged their study of gospel principles, development of individual talents, and service to those in need. Under her direction, the organization flourished. General, ward, and stake boards were appointed, lesson manuals produced, the *Young Woman's Journal* inaugurated (1889), and joint activities established with the Young Men's Association (see YOUNG MEN). President Taylor traveled thousands of miles yearly, giving instruction to ward and stake leaders. She became a member of the National Council of Women and, in 1891, three years after its organization, became an ex officio vice-president.

Elmina Taylor retained her office as president of the Young Ladies' Association through her last illness, reading reports in bed until the day of her death, December 6, 1904. Her funeral was held in the white-draped Assembly Hall. The choir and ushers were members of the Young Ladies' Association. President Joseph F. SMITH, one of the speakers, summarized her life's work: "She was one of the few in the world who had the light within her, and . . . power among her associates. . . . She was legitimately the head of the organization over which she was called to preside. . . . She was a strong character, . . . tempered and softened by the . . . spirit of kindness, of love, of mercy, and of charity" ("Death of Elmina S. Taylor," p. 221).

BIBLIOGRAPHY

Crocheron, Augusta Joyce. *Representative Women of Deseret.* Salt Lake City, 1884.

"Death of Elmina S. Taylor." *IE* 8 (Jan. 1905):218–22.

Jenson, Andrew. "Elmina Shepherd [*sic*] Taylor." *Latter-day Saint Biographical Encyclopedia*, Vol. 4, p. 267. Salt Lake City, 1971.

Romney, Thomas C. "Representative Women of the Church— Elmina Shepard Taylor." *Instructor* 85 (Aug. 1950):230–31.

FLORENCE SMITH JACOBSEN

TAYLOR, JOHN

John Taylor (1808–1887), the third President of The Church of Jesus Christ of Latter-day Saints, was born in Milnthorpe, Westmorland (now Cumbria), England, a son of James and Agnes Taylor. After John's formal schooling ended at the age of fourteen, he became a skilled woodturner and cabinetmaker. Much of his youth was spent in a picturesque region that inspired many of England's finest artists, poets, and writers. John himself would later be recognized for his cultural refinement and literary ability.

Although John was christened in the Church of England, he thought little of its creeds and at the age of sixteen joined the Methodist church. He was appointed a lay preacher a year later. He later remembered having a "strong impression on my mind" that he must "go to America to preach the gospel!" (Roberts, p. 28). He followed his parents

John Taylor (1808–1887), third President of the Church, was an articulate author, editor, publisher, and refined spokeman for the Church. He strengthened the priesthood organization and guided the Church during its darkest hours of legal persecution in the 1880s.

to Canada in 1832, where he met and married Leonora Cannon, a refined and intelligent young woman from the Isle of Man. In Toronto he preached for the Methodists, but told his wife that "this is not the work; it is something of more importance" (Roberts, p. 30). The Taylors belonged to a religious-studies group that prayed for the restoration of New Testament Christianity. They embraced Mormonism as the answer to their prayers and were baptized in 1836. Afterward, serving the Church became Taylor's life work. In 1837 the Taylors moved to Far West, Missouri, where Taylor was ordained an apostle on December 19, 1838. He played a prominent role in assisting the Saints as they fled from mob persecutions to a new gathering place at Commerce, Illinois. In 1839 he accompanied a number of his fellow apostles to the British Isles, where he opened Ireland and the Isle of Man for preaching the gospel and gained a reputation as a powerful debater (*see* MISSIONS OF THE TWELVE TO BRITISH ISLES). A bold advocate of the Church and the Prophet Joseph SMITH, John Taylor was called a "defender of the faith."

In Nauvoo he began a lifetime of community service. He served as a Nauvoo city councilman, a chaplain, a colonel, and a judge advocate for the NAUVOO LEGION, the city's militia. As a newspaper editor, he published the TIMES AND SEASONS (1842–1846) and the NAUVOO NEIGHBOR (1843–1846).

John Taylor was with Joseph and Hyrum SMITH in the CARTHAGE JAIL when the Smiths were martyred as they awaited a hearing regarding the destruction of an anti-Mormon newspaper. Severely wounded himself, Taylor became known as a living martyr. His tribute to the fallen brothers was later canonized as Section 135 of the Doctrine and Covenants.

Two years after the death of Joseph Smith, the Church moved westward from Nauvoo under the direction of Brigham YOUNG. While in Winter Quarters, Nebraska, Taylor was sent on a short-term mission to England to resolve problems in Church leadership there. Upon his return, he and Parley P. PRATT led 1,500 Saints to the Salt Lake Valley, arriving in the fall of 1847.

Taylor applied for U.S. citizenship in 1849, and in that year was appointed an associate judge under the provisional. state of DESERET (1849). Serving in the territorial legislature from 1853 to 1876, he was elected Speaker of the House for five consecutive sessions, beginning in 1857. For two years (1868–1870), he served as probate judge of Utah County, and in 1876 he was elected territorial superintendent of schools. In all of his offices, he felt dependent on the inspiration of God. "No man or set of men," he once declared, "of their own wisdom and by their own talents, are capable of governing the human family aright" (*JD* 9:10).

In 1849, Taylor returned to Europe, where he presided over missionary work in France and Germany and directed the translation and publication of a French-German edition of the Book of Mormon. He also wrote a short book, *The Government of God* (1852), in which he compared and contrasted the systems of God and man: "In God's government there is perfect order, harmony, beauty, magnificence, and grandeur; in the government of man, confusion, disorder, instability, misery, discord, and death" (p. 2). He described numerous examples of earthly societies that failed to resolve the problems of mankind, concluding that the only solution is "for his servants, to draw nigh to their Father, . . . throw themselves upon his guardianship, seek his wisdom and government, and claim a father's benediction" (p. 31).

While in Europe he founded the Deseret Manufacturing Company at the request of Brigham Young and purchased expensive sugar-processing equipment in Liverpool, that was shipped to Salt Lake City. It was his most notable failure. Lacking retorts, a key component, the assembled machinery produced only a good-quality molasses.

Following the death of Brigham Young in 1877, the Council of the Twelve governed the Church, with John Taylor as the senior apostle, presiding until he was set apart as the Church's third President in 1880. His motto as president was The Kingdom of God or Nothing. Although his most notable achievement was to hold the Church together under the intensifying pressure of the antipolygamy campaign, much else was achieved during his administration, especially in the early years. Under his direction, four new missions were organized; Mormon settlements were established in Colorado, Wyoming, and Arizona; construction continued on the Salt Lake and Manti temples; and the Logan Temple was dedicated. To encourage the Saints' economic independence, President Taylor established Zion's Central Board of Trade, a coordinating agency that encouraged cooperative economic activity in the Church's stakes.

On April 6, 1880, the fiftieth anniversary of the Church, President Taylor proclaimed a jubilee year, as observed in the Old Testament. "It occurred to me," he said, "that we ought to do something, as they did in former times, to relieve those that are oppressed with debt, to assist those that are needy, . . . and to make it a time of general rejoicing" (Roberts, p. 333). One-half of the debts owed by the Saints to the PERPETUAL EMIGRATING FUND, borrowed on migrating to Utah, was forgiven ($802,000), and one thousand cows and five thousand sheep were distributed to the poor, replacing many animals that had been lost in severe winter storms.

In October 1880, during President Taylor's administration, the Pearl of Great Price, a collection of ancient and modern scriptures, was canonized. A new edition of the Doctrine and Covenants, incorporating extensive cross-references and explanatory notes, was also published. The PRIMARY Association, a children's auxiliary, and the Young Ladies' Mutual Improvement Association (*see* YOUNG WOMEN), an organization for girls twelve through seventeen, were adopted Church-wide.

During the first years of his administration, while still President of the Quorum of Twelve Apostles, President Taylor continued work begun under Brigham Young in changing significant priesthood functions and defining important relationships. Members of the SEVENTY, one of the offices of the MELCHIZEDEK PRIESTHOOD, were organized into stake quorums. The relationship of the ward bishop to the priesthood and that of the AARONIC PRIESTHOOD to the Melchizedek Priesthood were clarified. Weekly bishopric meetings and monthly general stake priesthood meetings were inaugurated. Stake presidents were instructed to hold quarterly conferences under the direction of the First Presidency. President Taylor wrote a short work entitled *Items on Priesthood* (1881) to help the priesthood serve more effectively. He also wrote *The Mediation and Atonement of Our Lord and Savior Jesus Christ* (1882) as his witness of the preeminent role of the Son of God in the salvation of humankind; in it, he assembled scriptural passages pertaining to Christ's atonement and offered a commentary on their meaning.

Although he knew that obedience to authority brought strength and unity to the Church, President Taylor also stressed the importance of common consent: "The government of God is not . . . where one man dictates and everybody obeys without having a voice in it. We have our voice and agency, and act with the most perfect freedom" (1987, p. 321). A frequent theme expressed throughout his life was his love of liberty and hatred of slavery. "I'm God's free man," he said. "I cannot, will not be a slave!" (Roberts, p. 424). For such forthright determination he was called the "Champion of Liberty."

President Taylor was about six feet tall and weighed 180 pounds. He had large hands, an oval face, a high forehead, and deep-set gray eyes. As a young man, he had curly brown hair, which turned silver white in middle age. Erect in posture and fastidious in dress, he was polite, dignified, gracious, affable, and friendly. His speech was calm and deliberate, delivered in a voice that was clear, strong, and resonant. He enjoyed telling stories and had a keen sense of humor and a hearty laugh that shook his entire body. He generally did not prepare sermons ahead of time but depended upon inspiration as he spoke. He used gestures sparingly but with effect. An accomplished poet, his lyrics were used for several hymns published in the Church's hymnal.

In his private life, President Taylor was a kind and loving husband and father. He entered into PLURAL MARRIAGE, as counseled by Joseph Smith, and fathered thirty-five children by his seven wives. He went to great lengths to be fair and impartial with each of his families. The names and number of his wives are in dispute, but the women who were certainly married to him were Leonora Cannon, Elizabeth Haigham, Jane Ballantyne, Mary Ann Oakley, Sophia Whitaker, Harriet Whitaker, and Margaret Young.

During President Taylor's ministry, persecution of the Church grew in intensity. Three missionaries were killed in the southern states; and the U.S. secretary of state attempted to prevent Mormon immigrants from entering the United States, citing them as potential lawbreakers because of the Church's practice of polygamy. Congress passed the Edmunds Act in 1882, declaring polygamy to be a felony. Under its provisions, polygamists could not vote, hold public office, or serve on juries. The GENERAL AUTHORITIES discussed the Church's course of action as well as their hopes for achieving statehood. Wilford WOODRUFF later wrote that "President Taylor with the rest of us came to the conclusion that we could not swap of[f] the Kingdom of God or any of its Laws or Principles for a state government" (Wil-

John Taylor's watch was struck with a ball fired in Carthage Jail when he and others were attacked by the mob that killed Joseph Smith.

ford Woodruff Journal, Nov. 27, 1882). Mounting antipolygamy prosecution, known as "the Crusade," led to the arrest and imprisonment of hundreds of men and women. President Taylor instructed polygamous Saints to establish places of refuge in Mexico and Canada, and he and his counselors withdrew from public view to live in the "Underground." During his last public sermon he remarked, "I would like to obey and place myself in subjection to every law of man. What then? Am I to disobey the law of God? Has any man a right to control my conscience, or your conscience? . . . No man has a right to do it" (JD 26:152).

Persecution intensified in 1887 with the passage of the Edmunds-Tucker Act, which abolished women's suffrage, forced wives to testify against their husbands, disincorporated the Church, and escheated much of its property to the United States. For two and a half years, President Taylor presided over the Church in exile. The strain took a great toll on his health. He died on July 25, 1887, from congestive heart failure while living in seclusion at the farm home of Thomas F. Roueche in

Kaysville, Utah. He was eulogized as a "double martyr" for his near-fatal wounds in Carthage Jail and for his sacrifice for religious principles.

BIBLIOGRAPHY

Gibbons, Francis M. *John Taylor: Mormon Philosopher, Prophet of God.* Salt Lake City, 1985.

Roberts, B. H. *The Life of John Taylor.* Salt Lake City, 1963.

Smith, Paul Thomas. "John Taylor." In *Presidents of the Church*, ed. L. Arrington, pp. 74–114. Salt Lake City, 1987.

Taylor, John. *The Gospel Kingdom: Selections for the Writings and Discourses of John Taylor*, ed. G. Homer Durham. Salt Lake City, 1987.

Taylor, Samuel W., and Raymond W. Taylor. *The John Taylor Papers, Records of the Last Utah Pioneer: Vol. 1, 1836–1877, The Apostle*, and *Vol. 2, 1877–1887, The President.* Redwood City, Calif., 1984–1985.

PAUL THOMAS SMITH

TEA

Devout Latter-day Saints do not drink teas containing caffeine. This practice derives from an 1833 revelation known as the WORD OF WISDOM, which states that "hot drinks are not for the body or the belly" (D&C 89:9). Hyrum SMITH, Assistant President of the Church, later defined "hot drinks" as COFFEE and tea (*T&S* 3 [June 1, 1842]:800), thereby establishing the official interpretation for later generations (*see* DOCTRINE AND COVENANTS: SECTION 89). Caffeine, a cerebral and cardiovascular stimulant, has caused health concerns in recent years. The revelation has not been interpreted as proscribing herbal teas, for it states that "all wholesome herbs God hath ordained for the constitution, nature, and use of man" (D&C 89:10).

BIBLIOGRAPHY

Stratton, Clifford J. "The Xanthines: Coffee, Cola, Cocoa, and Tea." *BYU Studies* 20 (Summer 1980):371–88.

JOSEPH LYNN LYON

TEACHER, AARONIC PRIESTHOOD

A DEACON in the AARONIC PRIESTHOOD is, when worthy, advanced to the office of "teacher" at age fourteen and serves for a period of two years. Teachers meet together regularly for gospel instruction and other activities. Latter-day scriptures indicate that "the teacher's duty is to watch over the church always." His authority is "to warn, expound, exhort, and teach, and invite all to come unto Christ" (D&C 20:53–59). Teachers can function in all the duties of a deacon. In addition, they are to observe the counsel of the bishopric and teachers quorum president, prepare the SACRAMENT, perform HOME TEACHING, usher or speak in Church MEETINGS, be an example of moral integrity and uprightness, care for the poor, and help maintain the meetinghouse and grounds.

As the organization of the New Testament Church took form, teachers played a primary role (Acts 13:1; Eph. 4:11; 2 Tim. 1:11; James 3:1). The qualities teachers were to exhibit included reverence, temperance, and integrity (Titus 2:1–15). Postapostolic sources indicate that teachers served under prophets and later under bishops and that these higher offices comprehended the teaching function as well.

Teachers are organized into a PRIESTHOOD QUORUM of up to twenty-four members (D&C 107:86). Each quorum is headed by a presidency acting under the direction and supervision of the ward bishopric. To be ordained a teacher, candidates must be carefully interviewed by the bishop for personal worthiness and then approved in sacrament meeting by the members of the ward.

Teachers meet weekly on Sunday for instruction as a quorum and at other times for social activities or service projects, often with the YOUNG WOMEN or other YOUNG MEN. In the United States and other areas, some of these activities are organized around the SCOUTING program designed for young men of this age group.

The Book of Mormon mentions teachers frequently, but—unlike modern teachers—they evidently were adult leaders of their congregations and held the Melchizedek Priesthood with administrative powers (Mosiah 23:17; 25:19; 26:7; Alma 4:7; 15:13).

BIBLIOGRAPHY

Lowrie, Walter. *The Church and Its Organization in Primitive and Catholic Times: An Interpretation of Rudolph Sohm's Kirchenrecht.* New York, 1904.

Palmer, Lee A. *The Aaronic Priesthood Through the Centuries.* Salt Lake City, 1964.

JACK R. CHRISTIANSON

TEACHERS, TEACHER DEVELOPMENT

Latter-day Saints consider Jesus the master teacher who sets the example. He commissioned his disciples to teach, and still admonishes members of his Church to "teach one another the doctrine of the kingdom" (D&C 88:77). In the Church, therefore, lessons are taught regularly in ward and branch programs—PRIESTHOOD, RELIEF SOCIETY, SUNDAY SCHOOL, YOUTH organizations, HOME TEACHING and VISITING TEACHING, MISSIONARY work, SEMINARY classes, and FAMILY HOME EVENINGS. Instruction is intended to help members understand the principles Christ has taught in his life and through the prophets and apply them in their daily lives. This gospel-centered purpose of teaching was characterized by Joseph SMITH when he explained concerning Church members: "I teach them correct principles, and they govern themselves" (MS 13:339). Teachers are counseled to study, to seek, and to teach with the spirit (D&C 42:14).

Teaching the gospel is a duty implicit in Church membership. Responsibility for teaching, either directly or indirectly, is an element of virtually every Church calling. Each fully staffed ward requires more than thirty people in formal weekly teaching assignments, and so there are now an estimated 400,000 teachers Churchwide. Almost every active member will be called to serve at times as a teacher. Teaching is considered also as an opportunity to strengthen the teacher's own faith and knowledge through study and service to others.

A Teacher Development program designed to help teachers understand the principles of learning and gain confidence in their teaching ability is offered in most local units. This eight-week program advocates the use of learning objectives determined by preassessment of student needs and ability, and stresses the divine aspects of a Church teacher's calling.

Scripture-based lesson manuals are provided for each class. These bring a degree of consistency to the curriculum throughout the Church and offer teaching structures for the inexperienced teacher. The manuals suggest supporting resources from other Church publications and from a wide variety of materials produced by the Church Curriculum Department. These materials are generally made available in local meetinghouse or stake libraries.

Extensive catalogues of teaching resources are maintained and published regularly to encourage their use in the classroom and the home.

BIBLIOGRAPHY

Chidester, C. Richard. "Christ-Centered Teaching." *Ensign* 19 (Oct. 1989):6–9.

Church of Jesus Christ of Latter-day Saints, The. *Teaching: No Greater Call.* Salt Lake City, 1978.

——. *Teacher Development Basic Course.* Salt Lake City, 1980.

Dunn, Paul H. *You Too Can Teach.* Salt Lake City, 1962.

Packer, Boyd K. *Teach Ye Diligently.* Salt Lake City, 1975.

HARLEY K. ADAMSON

TEACHING THE GOSPEL

Among Latter-day Saints, the ultimate purpose of teaching the gospel is the transformation of lives. Neither the process of intensive study nor the knowledge gained is an end in itself. In addition to lecture and conceptual approaches, gospel teaching often follows a skill-learning model, in which a skill to be learned or quality to be developed such as prayer, kindness, or service is modeled or exemplified. Learners are encouraged to apply their new or renewed insight. As soon as possible, they become teachers themselves. Thus, teaching is the art of directing activities. Corrective responses from teacher and learner continue until the skill is incorporated into character. In the Church the gaps between priest and layman, teacher and learner, and leader and follower are all but erased. Teaching is a universal and inclusive mode of participation. Results are most impressive when family, church, and community cooperate and support each other's efforts.

Guidelines for teaching the gospel are often summarized in three imperatives:

1. Teach from the scriptures and teach the content of the scriptures. The STANDARD WORKS are studied systematically in recurring cycles, and this pattern is correlated for all age groups, AUXILIARIES, and PRIESTHOOD QUORUMS.

2. Teach by the Spirit, meaning under the influence of the HOLY GHOST. "If ye receive not the Spirit ye shall not teach" (D&C 42:14). "No man can preach the Gospel without the Holy Ghost" (TPJS, p. 112).

Classes such as this one, taught in the Hungarian branch in Vienna, Austria (1990), are integral parts of Sunday worship services. "And I give unto you a commandment that you shall teach one another the doctrine of the kingdom" (D&C 88:77). Courtesy Peggy Jellinghausen.

3. Teach by likening the scriptures to the lives of the learners (cf. 1 Ne. 19:23–24; 2 Ne. 11:2, 8).

These imperatives are reflected in teacher development manuals and courses, which reach hundreds of thousands of members each year in group efforts to inculcate, refresh, and improve teaching skills. They are implicit also in the teacher manuals that are published with student manuals for all classes and quorums of the Church.

Church leaders and teachers constantly emphasize the scriptures as the basis of personal and Church class study. Familiarity with the scriptures is viewed as basic to understanding the gospel and to the development of faith and testimony. Daily scripture study in the home and during FAMILY HOME EVENING is recommended for all members of all ages and in all Church callings.

Teaching the gospel is more than sharing knowledge. It also involves creating an atmosphere in which the spirit of the learner is touched and the intimate and ultimate strivings of the soul are related to truth. Latter-day Saints recognize that to teach knowledge and wisdom is a spiritual gift to be sought earnestly (D&C 46:16–18). Only when the Holy Ghost, or "spirit of truth"—enhancing the light of Christ (D&C 93:2)—is present is there genuine communication. Then teacher and learner "understand one another, and both are edified and rejoice together" (D&C 50:21–22).

Because of the multicultural base of the Church and its rapid growth, gospel teachers are asked to teach a wide array of members with radically different backgrounds, needs, and levels of understanding and spiritual preparation. This continues to be a major challenge to the Church.

ADRIAN P. VAN MONDFRANS

TELESTIAL KINGDOM

The telestial kingdom in Latter-day Saint understanding is the lowest of the three DEGREES OF GLORY to be inhabited by God's children in the AFTERLIFE following the RESURRECTION. The Doctrine and Covenants is the only known scriptural source for the word "telestial" (see D&C 76:88, 98, 109; 88:21). Paul spoke of the differing glories, comparing them to the differences in light we see from the sun, moon, and stars (1 Cor. 15:40–42), mentioning the celestial and terrestrial by name. Although the term "telestial" does not occur in biblical accounts, latter-day REVELATION cites telestial as the kingdom of glory typified by the lesser light we perceive from the stars (D&C 76:98). The CELESTIAL KINGDOM and TERRESTRIAL KINGDOM are typified by the light we perceive from the sun and moon, respectively.

Within the telestial glory there will be varying degrees of glory even as the stars vary in brightness as we see them. It embraces those who on earth willfully reject the GOSPEL of JESUS CHRIST, and commit serious SINS such as MURDER, ADULTERY, lying, and loving to make a lie (but yet do not commit the UNPARDONABLE SIN), and who do not repent in mortality. They will be cleansed in the postmortal SPIRIT WORLD or spirit prison before the resurrection (D&C 76:81–85, 98–106; Rev. 22:15). Telestial inhabitants as innumerable as the stars will come forth in the last resurrection and then be "servants of the Most High; but where God and Christ dwell they cannot come" (D&C 76:112). Although the least of the degrees of glory, yet the telestial kingdom "surpasses all understanding" (D&C 76:89).

[*See also* Degrees of Glory.]

CLYDE J. WILLIAMS

TEMPLE AND FAMILY HISTORY EXECUTIVE COUNCIL

See: Temples: Administration of Temples

TEMPLE GARMENTS

See: Garments

TEMPLE ORDINANCES

The ordinances performed only in the temple are baptisms for the dead, washings and anointings, endowments, and marriages or sealings for eternity. The privilege of entering the House of the Lord, the temple, and participating in its ordinances is a spiritual apex of LDS religious life. Through temple ordinances, one receives a ceremonial overview of and commitment to the Christlike life. Temple ordinances are instruments of spiritual rebirth. In the words of President David O. MCKAY, they are the "step-by-step ascent into the eternal presence." Through them, and only through them, the powers of godliness are granted to men in the flesh (D&C 84:20–22). Temple ordinances confirm mature discipleship; they are the essence of fervent worship and an enabling and ennobling expression of one's love for God (*see* TEMPLE WORSHIP).

All participants must be baptized and confirmed members of the Church, and must receive a temple recommend. However, children under eight years of age may participate in their own family sealings before being baptized. Members who are twelve years of age or older may serve as proxies in baptisms for the dead. Worthy adults may participate in the temple endowment ceremonies. All men must have been ordained to the Melchizedek Priesthood. Temple ordinances are performed in sequence.

WASHINGS AND ANOINTINGS. Washings and anointings are preparatory or initiatory ordinances in the temple. They signify the cleansing and sanctifying power of Jesus Christ applied to the attributes of the person and to the hallowing of all life. They have biblical precedents (*see* OIL; TEMPLES THROUGH THE AGES; WASHING AND ANOINTING). Women are set apart to administer the ordinances to women, and men are set apart to administer the ordinances to men. Latter-day Saints look forward to receiving these inspired and inspiring promises with the same fervent anticipation they bring to baptism. They come in the spirit of a scriptural command: "Cleanse your hands and your feet before me" (D&C 88:74; cf. 1 John 2:27). A commemorative garment is given with these ordinances and is worn thereafter by the participant (see GARMENTS).

TEMPLE ENDOWMENT. The temple endowment is spoken of in scripture as an "endowment," or outpouring, of "power from on high" (D&C 84:20–21; 105:11; 109:22, 26; cf. Luke 24:49). Participants in white temple clothing assemble in ordinance rooms to receive this instruction and participate in the unfolding drama of the PLAN OF SALVATION. They are taught of premortal life; the spiritual and temporal creation; the advent of Adam and Eve, and their transgression and expulsion into the harsh contrasts of the mortal probation; the laws and ordinances required for reconciliation through the atonement of Christ; and a return to the presence of God. The endowment is a series of symbols of these vast spiritual realities, to be received only by the committed and spiritual-minded (*TPJS*, p. 237; *see also* TEMPLES: MEANINGS AND FUNCTIONS OF TEMPLES). "All the ordinances," wrote Heber C. Kimball, "are signs of things in the heavens. Everything we see here is typical of what will be hereafter" ("Address to My Children," unpublished). The endowment increases one's spiritual power, based in part "on enlarged knowledge and intelligence—a power from on high, of a quality with God's own power" (Widtsoe, 1921, p. 55; Widtsoe, 1939, p. 335; *see also* ENDOWMENT).

During the endowment, solemn covenants are made pertaining to truthfulness, purity, righteous service, and devotion. In this way, the temple is the locus of consecration to the teaching of the law and the prophets and to the ways of God and his Son. One does not assume such covenants lightly. Modern commandments relating to temple building have been addressed to those "who know their hearts are honest, and are broken, and their spirits contrite, and are willing to observe their covenants by sacrifice—yea, every sacrifice which I, the Lord, shall command" (D&C 97:8–9). As with Abraham of old, latter-day revelation says that to obtain "the keys of the kingdom of an endless life" one must be willing to sacrifice all earthly things (*TPJS*, p. 322).

Before taking these solemn vows, new converts prepare for at least a year after baptism. Missionaries typically receive the temple blessings prior to their service. Couples receive them on, shortly before, or sometimes well in advance of the day of their temple marriage (*see* MARRIAGE:

ETERNAL MARRIAGE; TEMPLES: TEMPLE WORSHIP AND ACTIVITY).

This order of instruction and covenant making culminates in the celestial room, which represents the highest degree of heaven, a return to the presence of God, a place of exquisite beauty and serenity, where one may feel and meditate "in the beauty of holiness" (Ps. 29:2). Communal sensitivity in the presence of like-dedicated and like-experienced loved ones enhances deep fellowship. The temple is "a house of glory" and "a place of thanksgiving for all saints" (D&C 88:119; 97:13).

SEALING OF FAMILIES. Only after patrons make these unconditional covenants with and through Jesus Christ may they receive "the most glorious ordinances of the temple," the covenants of marriage and family sealing (Widtsoe, 1937, p. 128). Marriage and sealing covenants are performed in temple sealing rooms convenient to the celestial room. Officiators and close family and friends often attend the couple. Kneeling opposite each other at the altar, the bride and groom are placed under mutual covenants to each other, and are married through the sealing power of Jesus Christ; their children will thus be BORN IN THE COVENANT, and the family kingdom will become a nucleus of heaven. If the couple has been previously married under secular authority and now has children, the husband and wife are sealed in the temple under the new and everlasting covenant and their children are then brought to the altar and are sealed to them. All subsequent children born to this family are born in the covenant. By apostolic authority, the blessings of Abraham, Isaac, and Jacob are explicitly invoked upon all marriages and sealings. It is envisioned that eventually further sealings will link all the couple's progenitors and all of their descendants in an unbroken chain (see SEALING: TEMPLE SEALINGS). Thus, divine parenthood is imaged on earth. The saintly life is not in renunciation but in glorification of the family. The quest for happiness and completeness within the marital state is transformed from the banal and temporary toward the divine and eternal.

SEALING OF ADOPTED CHILDREN. If a couple elects to adopt children, those children are brought to the temple for a ceremony of sealing to their adoptive parents just as children born to them may be sealed.

PROXY ORDINANCES. All temple ordinances, beginning with baptism, may be performed by proxy for persons who died not having the opportunity to receive them for themselves (see BAPTISM FOR THE DEAD; SALVATION FOR THE DEAD).

BIBLIOGRAPHY

Madsen, Truman G. The Highest in Us, pp. 93–107. Salt Lake City, 1978.

Widtsoe, John A. "Temple Worship." In Utah Genealogical and Historical Magazine, 12 (Apr. 1921):55.

———. A Rational Theology, pp. 125–29. Salt Lake City, 1937.

———. Priesthood and Church Government, pp. 332–47. Salt Lake City, 1939, 1967 printing.

ALLEN CLAIRE ROZSA

TEMPLE PRESIDENT AND MATRON

Temple presidents and their wives, who serve as matrons, are appointed to specific LDS temples by the FIRST PRESIDENCY of The Church of Jesus Christ of Latter-day Saints, usually for three years. Their principal responsibilities are to set the spiritual tone of the temple, to supervise the performance of sacred ceremonies and ordinances therein, and to oversee the physical facility. Although instructions and ORDINANCES are the same in all LDS temples, the size of the temple and the number of patrons using it alter the procedures from temple to temple.

On a typical day in a fully operating temple, the president meets with the male supervisors and ordinance workers and the matron meets with the female supervisors and ordinance workers in prayer meeting before beginning each of the several daily shifts. They may also greet patrons, give preparatory instructions and guidance to those coming for the first time, and coordinate the performance of the ordinances. The president and matron may also answer personal inquiries of patrons and resolve procedural questions, by phone or correspondence, from BISHOPS, STAKE PRESIDENTS, RELIEF SOCIETY presidents, and other Church and community leaders within the temple district. Time is also spent consulting with counselors in the temple presidency, assistants to the president, and supervisors. In addition, the president and matron meet regularly with the temple executive council to resolve matters pertaining to the functioning of the temple.

The work in the temple is conducted prayerfully as befits the "House of the Lord." The phrase "Holiness to the Lord" appears prominently on the outside of each temple and symbolizes the spirit of temple worship (cf. Psalm 93:5). Although the temple ordinances are performed repetitiously, participating in them can be continuously revelatory and inspiring because of their rich symbolism and multiple applications. The temple president and matron are responsible for enhancing this spirit that all may "worship the Lord in the beauty of holiness" (Psalm 29).

DAVID H. YARN, JR.
MARILYN S. YARN

TEMPLE RECOMMEND

Temples have always been revered and reserved as sacred ground. Anciently, the prophet EZEKIEL declared, "Thus saith the Lord GOD; No stranger, uncircumcised in heart, nor uncircumcised in flesh, shall enter into my sanctuary" (Ezek. 44:9). The Prophet Joseph SMITH prayed that "[the temple] may be sanctified and consecrated to be holy, and that thy holy presence may be continually in this house" (D&C 109:12), "and that no unclean thing shall be permitted to come into thy house to pollute it" (D&C 109:20).

After construction and before a TEMPLE of The Church of Jesus Christ of Latter-day Saints has been dedicated to the Lord, an open house is held and the general public is invited to enter and view the rooms. But for participation in a TEMPLE DEDICATION and for all ORDINANCES performed in the temple thereafter, only members of the Church who have a current identification card, called a temple recommend, may enter.

Temple recommends are given to members of the Church who have completed the preliminary steps of FAITH, REPENTANCE, BAPTISM, and CONFIRMATION. Adult males must also have been ordained to the MELCHIZEDEK PRIESTHOOD. Temple recommends are usually issued by a BISHOP and countersigned by a member of the STAKE PRESIDENCY in interviews conducted in private. The bishop, who is responsible as a "judge in Israel" (D&C 107:72, 74, 76), conducts the initial

Approval from two priesthood leaders, including one's bishop, is required in order to enter the temple for most purposes. This 1879 "temple recommend" certified Martha Laughton to be a Church member in good standing and worthy to go to the temple to receive her endowment.

interview. He seeks to discern personal worthiness and standards of Christlike living and counsels appropriately with those whose lives are in need of any change or repentance. It is considered a serious matter to become prepared to receive the COVENANTS, ordinances, and BLESSINGS of the temple. Questions are asked to ascertain one's faith in God the Eternal Father, in his Son Jesus Christ, and in the Holy Ghost; and inquiry is made regarding the person's TESTIMONY of the restored gospel and loyalty to the teachings and leaders of the Church. Worthiness requirements include being honest, keeping the COMMANDMENTS, such as CHASTITY—sexual continence before marriage and fidelity within marriage—obeying the laws of TITHING and the WORD OF WISDOM, fulfilling family responsibilities and avoiding affiliation with dissident groups. The FIRST PRESIDENCY often emphasizes that it is a solemn responsibility for a bishop or stake president to conduct a temple recommend interview. An equal responsibility rests upon the person who is interviewed to respond to questions fully and honestly (*Ensign* 8 [Nov. 1978]:40–43). One practical purpose of the recommend interview is to help the applicant be adequately prepared to commit to the way of life the temple covenants will require.

Currently three different types of recommends are given: (1) for members to receive their own ENDOWMENT, to be sealed to a spouse, or to be married in the temple for time only; (2) for members who have received their endowment to participate in all temple ordinances for the dead (*see* SALVATION FOR THE DEAD); and (3) for unendowed members to (*a*) be baptized on behalf of the dead, (*b*) be sealed to their parents, or (*c*) witness SEALINGS of their living brothers and sisters to their parents. The same standards of worthiness apply for all recommends.

BIBLIOGRAPHY

Packer, Boyd K. *The Holy Temple*, pp. 11, 26–28, 50–53. Salt Lake City, 1980.

ROBERT A. TUCKER

TEMPLES

[*The articles included under this entry are:*

Latter-day Saint Temple Worship and Activity
History of LDS Temples from 1831 to 1990
LDS Temple Dedications
Administration of Temples
Meanings and Functions of Temples
Temples Through the Ages

The first four articles pertain to temples in The Church of Jesus Christ of Latter-day Saint tradition. See also Endowment Houses; Kirtland Temple; Freemasonry and the Temple; Nauvoo Temple; *and* Salt Lake Temple. *The fifth article treats the meanings and functions of temples in world religions generally, and the concluding article discusses ancient temples in particular, including the continuities between ancient Israelite and Latter-day Saint temples.*

See also Baptism for the Dead; Endowment; Family History; Garments; Holy of Holies; Marriage: Eternal; Prayer Circle; Salvation of the Dead; Sealing; Temple Ordinances; *and* Washings and Anointings.]

LATTER-DAY SAINT TEMPLE WORSHIP AND ACTIVITY

Performing ordinances and seeking the will of the Lord in the temple are a sacred and meaningful form of worship in Latter-day Saint religious life. In the temple, holy truths are taught and solemn covenants are made in the name of Jesus Christ, both by the individual members on their own behalf and as proxies on behalf of others who have died (the latter have the choice in the spirit world to accept or reject such vicarious service). Obedience to temple covenants and reverence in doing temple ordinances give peace in this world and the promise of eternal life in the world to come.

There are special areas inside each temple for the various ordinances. A large baptismal font supported on the backs of twelve sculpted oxen (cf. 1 Kgs. 7:25) is used for BAPTISM FOR THE DEAD. In other areas are cubicles in which individuals are ritually WASHED AND ANOINTED before endowments can be performed. In the older temples, larger rooms are decorated to represent the Creation, the Garden of Eden, this world, and the terrestrial kingdom, and in such endowment rooms, participants watch and hear figurative presentations in which scenes are acted out, depicting by whom and why the earth was created and how one may come to dwell again in God's presence. The participants make covenants and receive promises and blessings. This is known as receiving one's ENDOWMENT. The Prophet Joseph Smith taught that this endowment was necessary to empower one "to overcome all things" (*TPJS*, p. 91). A veil symbolically divides the terrestrial room from the celestial room, which suggests through furnishings and decor the peace, beauty, and glory of the highest degree of heaven. Also in the temple are smaller SEALING rooms, where temple marriages and sealings are solemnized for the living and vicariously for the dead. A temple may also have an upper room where SOLEMN ASSEMBLIES can be convened.

The first visit to the temple for one's own endowment is a major event in the life of a Latter-day Saint. (Children enter the temple only to be sealed to their parents or, after age twelve, to be baptized for the dead.) Full-time missionaries receive their endowment shortly before they begin to serve; other members generally do so shortly before temple marriage or, if unmarried, at a mature time in life. All Latter-day Saints attending a temple must

TEMPLE	LOCATION	DEDICATED		TEMPLE	LOCATION	DEDICATED		TEMPLE	LOCATION	DEDICATED
1- Kirtland	Kirtland, Ohio	Mar 1836		16- Ogden	Ogden, Utah	Jan 1972		31- Manila Philippines	Quezon City, Philippines	Sep 1984
2- Nauvoo	Nauvoo, Illinois	Apr 1846		17- Provo	Provo, Utah	Feb 1972		32- Dallas Texas	Dallas, Texas	Oct 1984
3- St. George	St. George, Utah	Apr 1877		18- Washington	Kensington, Maryland	Nov 1974		33- Taipei Taiwan	Taipei, Taiwan	Nov 1984
4- Logan	Logan, Utah	May 1884		19- São Paulo	São Paulo, Brazil	Oct 1978		34- Guatemala City	Guatemala City, Guat.	Dec 1984
5- Manti	Manti, Utah	May 1888		20- Tokyo	Tokyo, Japan	Oct 1980		35- Freiberg Germany	Freiberg, Germany	Jun 1985
6- Salt Lake	Salt Lake City, Utah	Apr 1893		21- Seattle	Bellevue, Washington	Nov 1980		36- Stockholm Sweden	Västerhaninge, Swed.	Jul 1985
7- Hawaii	Laie, Oahu, Hawaii	Nov 1919		22- Jordan River	South Jordan, Utah	Nov 1981		37- Chicago Illinois	Glenview, Illinois	Aug 1985
8- Alberta	Cardston, Alberta	Aug 1923		23- Atlanta Georgia	Sandy Springs, Ga.	Jun 1983		38- Johannesburg S. Africa	Johannesburg, S. A.	Aug 1985
9- Arizona	Mesa, Arizona	Oct 1927		24- Apia Samoa	Apia, West. Samoa	Aug 1983		39- Seoul Korea	Seoul, Korea	Dec 1985
10- Idaho Falls	Idaho Falls, Idaho	Sep 1945		25- Nuku'alofa Tonga	Nuku'alofa, Tonga	Aug 1983		40- Lima Peru	Lima, Peru	Jan 1986
11- Swiss	Zollikofen, Switzerland	Sep 1955		26- Santiago Chile	Santiago, Chile	Sep 1983		41- Buenos Aires Argentina	Buenos Aires, Argen.	Jan 1986
12- Los Angeles	Los Angeles, California	Mar 1956		27- Papeete Tahiti	Pirae, Tahiti	Oct 1983		42- Denver Colorado	Littleton, Colorado	Oct 1986
13- New Zealand	Hamilton, New Zealand	Apr 1958		28- Mexico City	Mexico City, Mexico	Dec 1983		43- Frankfurt Germany	Friedrichsdorf, Germ.	Aug 1987
14- London	Newchapel, England	Sep 1958		29- Boise Idaho	Boise, Idaho	May 1984		44- Portland Oregon	Portland, Oregon	Aug 1989
15- Oakland	Oakland, California	Nov 1964		30- Sydney Australia	Carlingford, Australia	Sep 1984		45- Las Vegas Nevada	Las Vegas, Nevada	Dec 1989
								46- Toronto Ontario	Toronto, Ontario	Aug 1990

be worthy, and the men must hold the MEL-CHIZEDEK PRIESTHOOD.

After receiving his or her personal endow-ment, a Church member is encouraged to return often to re-experience the same ordinances on behalf of persons who have died without receiving them. The temple goer stands as a proxy for a per-son of his or her gender on each visit to the temple. This selfless service of "saviours . . . on mount Zion" (cf. Obad. 1:21) is rooted in faith in the literal resurrection and afterlife of all human beings.

After being dedicated, LDS temples are not open to the public but are restricted to Latter-day Saints. Even among themselves, Latter-day Saints do not talk about the details of the temple cere-mony outside the Temple, because they are sa-cred. In the temple, worshipers go through several steps that symbolize withdrawal from the world and entrance into the abode of deity. They present their TEMPLE RECOMMEND to enter, change from street clothes to all-white clothing, and communi-cate only in quiet voices while in the holy building. Temples are not open on Sunday, because the Sabbath day is dedicated to worshiping the Lord in homes and in Church gatherings at MEETINGHOUSES.

For those who enter the house of the Lord with "clean hands, and a pure heart" (Ps. 24:4), with a "broken heart and a contrite spirit" (3 Ne. 9:20; cf. Ps. 51:17), and with no ill feelings toward others (Matt. 5:23–24), the temple is an ideal place to worship through meditation, renewal, prayer, and quiet service. The Lord described his house as "a house of prayer, a house of fasting, a house of faith, a house of learning, a house of glory, a house of order, a house of God" (D&C 88:119). The rev-erence in the temple is hospitable to the spirit of humble worship and holiness. In the stillness of the Lord's house, those who yearn to hear the word of the Father and to be heard by him pray silently or join in solemn supplications on behalf of the sick and afflicted and those seeking inspiration and guidance (cf. 1 Kgs. 8:30–49; *see also* PRAYER CIRCLES).

Words spoken in the temple endowment give "the answers of eternity" (Hinckley, p. 37) lodged in the perspective of all God's children. The words set forth eternal principles to be used in solving life's dilemmas, and they mark the way to become

A couple leaving the Logan Temple after serving for a day as temple workers, assisting those who come to the temple to participate in religious ordinances such as temple marriages, baptisms for the dead, anointings, and endowments. The Logan Temple (dedicated 1884 by John Taylor) is in a castellated style designed by Truman O. Angell. Courtesy Craig Law.

more Christlike and progressively qualify to live with God. There, the laws of the new and everlast-ing covenant are taught—laws of obedience, sacri-fice, order, love, chastity, and consecration. In the temple, one learns the sacred roles of men and women in the eternal plan of God the Father and toward each other, receives a stable perspective on the repeating pattern of life, and gains a greater love for ancestors and all mankind.

←——LDS Temples around the world, 1990.

The Manti Temple, dedicated in 1888, was the third temple completed in Utah. The temple grounds have been the site of the summer "Mormon Miracle Pageant."

This refuge from the world is part of the fulfillment for Latter-day Saints of the ancient prophecy that "in the last days . . . the Lord's house shall be established . . . and all nations shall flow unto it" (Isa. 2:2). In the house of the Lord, faithful Church members seek to understand whom they worship and how to worship, so that in due time they may come to the Father in Christ's name and receive of the Father's fulness (D&C 93:19).

BIBLIOGRAPHY

Derrick, Royden G. *Temples in the Last Days*. Salt Lake City, 1987.

Edmunds, John K. *Through Temple Doors*. Salt Lake City, 1978.

Hinckley, Gordon B. "Why These Temples?" *Ensign* 4 (Aug. 1974):37–41.

Leone, Mark P. "The New Mormon Temple in Washington, D.C." In *Historical Archaeology and the Importance of Material Things*. Charleston, S.C., 1977.

Madsen, Truman G. "The Temple and the Restoration." In *The Temple in Antiquity*, ed. Truman G. Madsen. Provo, Utah, 1984.

Packer, Boyd K. *The Holy Temple*. Salt Lake City, 1980.

Talmage, James E. *The House of the Lord*. Salt Lake City, 1976.

IMMO LUSCHIN

HISTORY OF LATTER-DAY SAINT TEMPLES FROM 1831 TO 1990

Latter-day Saints are a temple-building people. Theirs is a history of temples projected and built, often under intense opposition. An early REVELATION declared that "my people are always commanded to build [temples] unto my holy name" (D&C 124:39–40). In the last weeks of his life, the Prophet Joseph SMITH affirmed: "We need the temple more than anything else" (Journal History of the Church, May 4, 1844).

The functions of latter-day temples parallel in some aspects those of the ancient Tabernacle and biblical temples, which were dedicated as sacred places where God might reveal himself to his people (Ex. 25:8, 22), and where sacrifices and holy priesthood ORDINANCES might be performed (D&C 124:38). Although the Bible does not clarify the precise nature and extent of these rites, it is clear that sacrifice by the shedding of blood anticipated the supreme sacrifice of Jesus Christ.

The New Testament uses two words that are translated as temple: *naos* for the sanctuary, and *hieron* for the general grounds and courtyards. Although Jesus vigorously condemned abuses in the temple courts, he nevertheless held the holy sanctuary in highest esteem as "my Father's house" (John 2:16) or as "my house" (Matt. 21:13). His cleansing of the temple and condemnation of abuses (John 2:13–16; Matt. 21:12–13) related to the *hieron* rather than the *naos*.

RESTORATION OF TEMPLE WORSHIP AND ORDINANCES. Latter-day Saints built their first temple at KIRTLAND, OHIO. A solemn cornerstone-laying ceremony in 1833 marked the beginning of construction. Over a period of about three years, the SAINTS sacrificed their means, time, and energies to build the House of the Lord (the word "temple" was not generally used at that time). Even though the temple's exterior looked much like a typical New England meetinghouse, its interior had some unique features. A revelation specified that the building should include two large rooms, the lower hall being a chapel, while the upper was for educational purposes (D&C 95:8, 13–17). There were no provisions for the sacred ceremonies that were yet to be revealed.

Notable spiritual blessings followed the years of sacrifice. The weeks just preceding the KIRTLAND TEMPLE dedication witnessed remarkable spiritual manifestations. On January 21, 1836, when Joseph Smith and others met in the nearly completed temple, they received WASHINGS AND ANOINTINGS and saw many VISIONS, including a vision of the CELESTIAL KINGDOM. They learned that all who had died without a knowledge of the gospel, but who would have accepted it if given an opportunity, were heirs of that kingdom (D&C 137:7–8). This was the earliest latter-day revelation on the subject of SALVATION OF THE DEAD, a major doctrinal principle related to ordinances in LDS temples.

On Sunday, March 27, 1836, the Kirtland Temple was dedicated. Toward the conclusion of the daylong service, Joseph Smith read the dedicatory prayer that he had previously received by revelation (D&C 109). Following this prayer, the choir sang "The Spirit of God," a hymn written for the occasion by William W. Phelps (see Appendix, "Hymns"). After the SACRAMENT was administered and several TESTIMONIES were borne, the congregation stood and rendered shouts of "Hosanna, Hosanna; Hosanna, to God and the Lamb!" Formal dedicatory prayers, the singing of this hymn, and the Hosanna Shout have characterized all temple DEDICATIONS since (see HOSANNA SHOUT).

Significant manifestations occurred in the Kirtland Temple on April 3, one week after its dedication. Jesus Christ appeared and accepted the temple. Moses, Elias, and Elijah then appeared and restored specific PRIESTHOOD powers (D&C 110). Through the SEALING keys restored by Elijah, priesthood ordinances performed on earth for the living and the dead could be bound or sealed in heaven, thus helping to turn the hearts of the fathers and children to one another (Mal. 4:5–6).

At the time when Joseph Smith was planning the temple in Kirtland, he was also giving attention to developments in Missouri. In 1831 he had placed a cornerstone for a future temple at INDEPENDENCE in Jackson County, which had been designated as the "center place" of ZION (D&C 57:3). In June 1833 he drew up a plat for the city of Zion, specifying that twenty-four temples or sacred buildings would be built in the heart of the city to serve a variety of priesthood functions. When the Latter-day Saints were forced to flee from Jackson County that fall, plans to build the city of Zion and its temples were postponed.

In 1838 cornerstones were laid for a temple at FAR WEST in northern Missouri. This structure was to be for the gathering together of the Saints for worship (D&C 115:7–8). However, persecution prevented construction.

One of the spiral staircases inside the Manti Temple. "And they went up with winding stairs into the middle chamber [in the temple of Solomon]" (1 Kings 6:8).

The NAUVOO TEMPLE, dedicated in 1846, was the first temple designed for the recently restored sacred ordinances for the living and the dead. Vicarious BAPTISMS FOR THE DEAD were inaugurated in 1840. They were first performed in the Mississippi River until a font was completed in the basement of the temple. In 1842 the Prophet gave the first ENDOWMENTS in the assembly room above his red brick store (TPJS, p. 237). Given at this time only to living persons, this ceremony reviewed the history of mankind from the CREATION, emphasizing the lofty standards required for returning to God's presence. The first sealings or MARRIAGES of couples for eternity were also performed at about this time. Then all such ordinance work was stopped until the temple was completed.

The main outside walls of the temple were only partially completed when Joseph Smith and his brother Hyrum were murdered in 1844. The martyrdom, however, caused only a temporary lull in temple construction. Even though the Saints knew they would soon be forced to leave Nauvoo and lose access to the temple, they were willing to spend approximately one million dollars to fulfill their Prophet's vision of erecting the House of the Lord. By December 1845, the rooms in the temple were sufficiently completed that endowments could be given there. During the next eight weeks 5,500 persons received these blessings even as they were hurriedly preparing for their exodus to the West. Brigham YOUNG and other officiators stayed in the temple day and night. To maintain order, Heber C. KIMBALL insisted that only those with official invitations be admitted to the temple, which perhaps marked the beginning of issuing TEMPLE RECOMMENDS.

TEMPLES IN THE TOPS OF THE MOUNTAINS. Temple building remained a high priority for the Mormon PIONEERS as they made their trek to the Rocky Mountains. Only four days after entering the Salt Lake Valley, Brigham Young selected the site for the temple there. Temporary provisions were made for giving the endowment until this temple could be completed, and an adobe ENDOWMENT HOUSE opened on TEMPLE SQUARE in 1855. President Young explained that not all ordinances could appropriately be performed there, however, so in the mid-1870s he encouraged the Saints to press forward with the construction of other temples in Utah.

The site for the temple at St. George was swampy, but Brigham Young insisted that it be built there because the spot had been dedicated by ancient BOOK OF MORMON prophets (statement by David H. Cannon, Jr., Oct. 14, 1942, quoted in Kirk M. Curtis, "History of the St. George Temple," Master's thesis, Brigham Young University, 1964, pp. 24–25). An old cannon, filled with lead, became an improvised pile driver to pound rocks into the soggy ground. In 1877 the St. George Temple was completed, the first in Utah. Endowments for the dead were inaugurated there in January of that year, enabling the Saints to perform these important rites as proxies on behalf of their forebears.

As the number of endowments for the dead increased, the basic design of temples was modified to accommodate the ordinance. The Logan and Manti temples (dedicated in 1884 and 1888, respectively) contain large upper assembly rooms and a series of smaller lower rooms especially designed for presenting the endowment instructions. Murals on the walls depict different stages in man's eternal progression. Because of outside political

hostility in 1888, Church leaders dedicated the Manti Temple first in private ceremonies. At the public dedication a short time later, members of the congregation reported unusual spiritual experiences including hearing heavenly choirs.

Completion of the Salt Lake Temple lifted the Saints' spirits during dark days of persecution. Symbolic stones on the great temple's exterior represent the degrees of eternal glory and other gospel principles. The east center spire is topped by a statue of the angel MORONI, symbolic of John's PROPHECY of a heavenly herald bringing the gospel to the earth (Rev. 14:6). The interior includes council rooms for the GENERAL AUTHORITIES. On the afternoon prior to its dedication on April 6, 1893, visitors of many faiths were invited to tour the temple. Such prededication open houses have grown in importance and become the norm during the twentieth century.

TWENTIETH–CENTURY TEMPLES. During the first third of the twentieth century, temples were built more and more distant from Church headquarters, reflecting Church expansion and growth. President Joseph F. SMITH spoke of the need to provide temple blessings to scattered Saints without requiring them to travel often thousands of miles to the intermountain West to receive them. The temples built at this time were comparatively small, without towers or large assembly halls.

President Smith, who had served a MISSION to Hawaii as a young man, selected the temple site at Laie on the island of Oahu. Because traditional building materials were scarce on the island, the temple was built of reinforced concrete. It was dedicated in 1919, one year after President Smith's death. Meanwhile, construction had also begun on a temple at Cardston, Alberta, Canada. Following its dedication in 1923, Church members from Oregon and Washington organized annual caravans to attend that temple, the forerunners of temple excursions that became an increasingly important facet of religious activity for members not living close to these sacred structures.

At the 1927 dedication of the Arizona Temple in Mesa, President Heber J. GRANT petitioned divine blessings for the American Indians and other modern-day descendants of BOOK OF MORMON PEOPLES. In 1945 the endowment and other temple blessings were presented there in Spanish, the first time these ceremonies were offered in a language other than English. In subsequent decades, members in the southwestern United States, Mexico, and as far away as Central America traveled to attend Spanish temple sessions in Mesa.

President Grant also approved sites for temples in California and Idaho. Although construction of the Idaho Falls Temple began in 1937, shortages of materials during World War II delayed its completion until 1945.

The rapid growth of Church membership in southern California during and following World War II led to the construction of the Los Angeles Temple, the largest in the Church at that time. Dedicated in 1956, it was the first in the twentieth century to include a large upper hall for priesthood leaders to conduct SOLEMN ASSEMBLIES, as well as an angel Moroni statue on its 257-foot tower. Architectural plans called for the angel to face southeast, as did the temple itself. President David O. MCKAY, however, insisted that the statue be turned to face due east. Most (but not all) LDS temples face east, symbolic of the anticipated second coming of Christ, which Jesus compared to the dawning in the east of a new day (Matt. 24:27). Members in California regarded this temple as the fulfillment of Brigham Young's prophecy that the shores of the Pacific would one day be overlooked from the Lord's house, and that temples would have a central tower and would feature reflecting ponds and have plantings on their roofs.

THE FIRST OVERSEAS TEMPLES. The decision to build temples abroad signaled a new emphasis. Although for decades Church leaders had counseled the overseas Saints not to gather to America, but to build up the Church where they were, the blessings of the temple were not available in their homelands. The Swiss Temple near Bern in 1955 and the New Zealand and London temples in 1958 partially met this need. The use of film and projectors allowed the endowment ordinance to be presented in one place of instruction rather than in a series of muraled rooms. President McKay had announced that future temples would be smaller, so that more of them could be built around the world. Furthermore, on film, these ceremonies could be presented in several languages with only a small group of attending temple ordinance workers.

Those responsible for locating these temples were convinced that they had divine assistance. Swiss Mission officials experienced prolonged difficulties in acquiring a site they had selected and petitioned the Lord for help. Immediately they found a larger site at half the cost; they soon learned that the original site was rendered useless by the unexpected construction of a highway through one portion of the lot. When the original price asked for the New Zealand temple plot seemed excessive, attorneys representing the owners and the Church reviewed the matter and independently arrived at exactly the same lower figure. Engineers cautioned against building the London Temple on the ground selected by President McKay because it was too swampy, but bedrock was discovered at the proper depth to support the foundations.

MODERN TEMPLES IN NORTH AMERICA. During the decade 1964–1974, four more temples were dedicated in the United States. The Oakland Temple (1964) had been eagerly anticipated by the Saints in northern California. Forty years earlier, Elder George Albert SMITH had spoken while in San Francisco of the day when a beautiful temple would surmount the East Bay hills and be a beacon to ships sailing through the Golden Gate. During World War II property became available high in the Oakland Hills. However, two decades passed before Church growth in the area warranted construction of a temple. The Oakland Temple now uses film projection to present the endowment ceremony. Three spacious rooms allow large groups to receive these instructions simultaneously.

The entrance to the Garden Room in the Salt Lake Temple. This room represents the Garden of Eden.

Even though early leaders had spoken of future temples in Ogden and Provo, the 1967 announcement of these two Utah temples came as a surprise to many Latter-day Saints. Church leaders explained that the Salt Lake Temple was being used beyond its capacity, so building two new nearby temples would ease the pressure and also reduce travel time for the Saints in Ogden and Provo. When the temples were completed five years later, each featured six endowment rooms, enabling a new group to begin the presentation every twenty minutes for up to sixty sessions daily.

The Washington D.C. Temple not only met the needs of Saints living in the eastern United States and Canada but, located close to the U.S. capital, became a monument to the restored Church. Architects designed it as a modern and easily recognizable adaptation of the familiar six-towered pattern of the Salt Lake Temple. Its 289-foot east central spire is tallest of any LDS temple in the world. The Washington Temple included a complex of six endowment rooms, and it became the second twentieth-century temple to have the large upper-level priesthood assembly room.

During the 1970s, the Arizona Temple and several other temples were remodeled to utilize film projection in presenting the endowment. Because these renovations were extensive, open houses were held for visitors prior to rededication of the temples. During this same decade, construction began on three other large temples in North America: the Seattle Temple (dedicated in 1980), first in the U.S. Pacific Northwest; the Jordan River Temple (1981), second in the Salt Lake Valley; and the Mexico City Temple (1983), which features a Mayan architectural style. While at the dedication of the Mexico City Temple, Elder Ezra Taft BENSON was impressed to emphasize the Book of Mormon—a theme that later characterized his administration as President of the Church.

WORLDWIDE EXPANSION. In 1976 two revelations (now D&C 137 and 138) were added to the STANDARD WORKS. One recorded Joseph Smith's 1836 vision of the celestial kingdom. The other was an account of President Joseph F. Smith's 1918 vision of the Savior's organizing the righteous to preach his gospel in the world of departed spirits. Both contributed to the Saints' comprehension of salvation for the dead, and provided new stimulus for unprecedented temple building.

Plans had already been announced for temples in São Paulo and Tokyo—the first in South America and Asia, respectively. Then, in 1980, a dramatic acceleration came when the FIRST PRESIDENCY announced that seven new temples were to be built. These included the first temple in the southeastern United States, two more temples in South America, and four in the Pacific. The following year, plans for nine more temples were announced—two each in the United States, Europe, and Latin America; plus a temple each in Korea, the Philippines, and South Africa. By 1984, plans to build ten additional temples were announced, including one in the German Democratic Republic. These temples were smaller than most built in earlier decades. Since many were built at the same time, they are of similar design.

Most of these new temples were located where they could make temple blessings available to the living even though they might not contribute large numbers of ordinances for the dead. More than ever before, temples were within the reach of Latter-day Saints living around the world, who greeted the construction of these temples with gratitude and joy. When President Spencer W. KIMBALL announced the intention to build the São Paulo Temple, for example, there was an audible gasp that swept the huge congregation gathered for the Brazil area conference; tears flowed freely as families throughout the hall embraced one another at the news. Church leaders suggested that rather than sacrificing lifetime earnings to reach a distant temple, members would now need to make a different kind of sacrifice—finding time for regular attendance at their temple.

Latter-day Saints expect that this rapid expansion of temple building will continue. Sacred temple ordinances are to be made available to all. Brigham Young prophesied that during the MILLENNIUM there would be thousands of temples dotting the earth. At that time, tens of thousands of the faithful are to enter and perform sacred ordinances around the clock.

TEMPLE BLESSINGS FOR THE DEAD. When the Saints in Nauvoo performed vicarious baptisms for close relatives, information on them was readily accessible. More difficult genealogical research became necessary, however, as Church members met their responsibility to provide temple blessings for all deceased ancestors as far back as they could trace them. The introduction of endowments for the dead in 1877, which took far more time than baptisms, represented a significant expansion in Church members' temple commitment.

Heretofore the Saints had performed vicarious ordinances only for their own deceased relatives or friends. While directing the unfolding of the vicarious service at the St. George Temple, however, Elder Wilford WOODRUFF declared that the Lord would allow members to help one another in this important work.

A further innovation came during the early twentieth century when those living in faraway mission fields were allowed to send names of deceased loved ones to the temple where other proxies would perform the ordinances. Church leaders then exhorted members living near a temple to take time to perform this unselfish service. In the Salt Lake Temple, for example, there had been at first only one endowment session per day. By 1921, however, that increased to four, and in 1991 to ten.

With the growing number of temples, the number of endowments performed increased. Beginning in the 1960s, therefore, Church leaders directed GENEALOGICAL SOCIETY OF UTAH employees to obtain names from microfilmed vital records and make them available for temple work. By the early 1970s, three-fourths of all names for temple ordinances were being submitted in this manner.

To facilitate the members assuming a greater share in providing names for the temples, in 1969 they were permitted to submit names individually rather than only in family groups. Computers could then assist in determining family relationships. Beginning in 1978, small groups of Church members were called to spend a few hours each week in the NAME EXTRACTION PROGRAM copying names and data from microfilm records. In this way most names for temple work were supplied by members rather than by professionals at Church headquarters. In 1988 the 100 millionth endowment for the dead was performed; over five million were accomplished that year.

THE HOUSE OF THE LORD.   As did ancient Israel, Latter-day Saints regard temples as sacred places set apart where they can go to draw close to God and receive revelations and blessings from him (D&C 97:15–17; 110:7–8). The physical structure

as such is not the source of its holiness. Rather, the character of those who enter and the sacred ordinances and instructions received there nurture the spiritual atmosphere found in the temple. When members enter this holy house and center their thoughts on serving others, their own understandings are clarified and solutions to personal problems are received.

Because of the spiritual nature of temple activity, personal preparation is essential. Latter-day Saints insist that temple ceremonies are sacred. This is consistent with ancient practice when, for example, only specifically qualified persons were admitted into the holiest precincts of the Tabernacle. The function of local Church leaders in issuing temple recommends is not only to establish the individual's worthiness and preparation but also to assure the sanctity of the temple.

BIBLIOGRAPHY

For a scholarly treatise of temples and their ordinances, see James E. Talmage, *The House of the Lord* (Salt Lake City, 1962); Boyd K. Packer in *The Holy Temple* (Salt Lake City, 1980) explains the spirit and importance of temple work; Richard O. Cowan in *Temples to Dot the Earth* (Salt Lake City, 1989) traces the history of LDS temples and temple service. For an in-depth discussion of some of the ancient background, see Hugh Nibley, *Message of the Joseph Smith Papyri: An Egyptian Endowment* (Salt Lake City, 1975); N. B. Lundwall, *Temples of the Most High* (Salt Lake City, 1971) includes dedicatory prayers and descriptive data about individual temples; Royden G. Derrick in *Temples in the Last Days* (Salt Lake City, 1987) has a collection of essays on temple-related topics; and Laurel B. Andrew explains architectural influences in her *Early Temples of the Mormons* (Albany, N.Y., 1989).

RICHARD O. COWAN

LDS TEMPLE DEDICATIONS

A temple dedication is a supremely sacred ceremonial enactment in the Church, which consecrates the building to the Lord before the beginning of temple ordinance work. From the time of the dedication of the KIRTLAND TEMPLE in 1836 until 1990, forty-six LDS temples have been dedicated.

The dedication of a temple is a time of great rejoicing and spiritual celebration. Men, women, and sometimes children who live within the area to be served by the temple and have temple recommends are invited to sessions held within, or adjacent to, the temple. These ceremonies are repeated several times to accommodate all who can participate. Most come in the spirit of fasting and

Two murals in the Telestial Room (or World Room) in the Manti Temple depict the fallen state of mortal life on this earth. Photographer: Craig Law.

prayer. The ceremonies include sacred choral anthems, such as Evan Stephens's "Holiness Becometh the House of the Lord," and special addresses from the GENERAL AUTHORITIES. A formal dedicatory prayer is offered under apostolic authority. Historically these prayers encompass the whole sweep of the modern dispensation, invoking divine blessings on all mankind, living and dead. They have often been prophetic of world events (see D&C 109).

At some point in all temple dedications the congregation rises and, while waving white handkerchiefs, unites in the shout "Hosanna, hosanna, hosanna, to God and the Lamb" three times (see HOSANNA SHOUT). This solemn expression was introduced by Joseph Smith at KIRTLAND (see D&C 19:37; 36:3; 39:19). It is reminiscent of the praise of the followers of Jesus as he descended the Mount of Olives (Matt. 21:1–11), and of the outcry of the multitudes in America while surrounding the temple in the land Bountiful: "Blessed be the name of the Most High God" (3 Ne. 11:17); it also parallels the "praising and thanking the Lord" by voices and instruments at the dedication of Solomon's temple (2 Chr. 5:11–14).

The dedication of a temple is ultimately the dedication of people. In the spirit of sacrifice, they build it, and in the same spirit they perform sacred ordinances within it. The dedication sets the building apart from all other Church edifices. It be-

comes a consecrated sanctuary not for regular Sabbath worship sessions but for daily performances of temple ordinances.

All the gifts of the Spirit and of the holy priesthood mentioned in scripture have been manifest at one time or another in the spiritual outpourings attending temple dedications, including visions, revelations, healings, discernment, and prophecy; and likewise the fruits of the Spirit—love, joy, peace, long-suffering, gentleness, meekness, faith. For Latter-day Saints on such occasions it is as if the earthly and heavenly temples meet and as if the rejoicing of ancient worthies mingles with that of mortals. These experiences and subsequent service in the temples lead to "the communion and presence of God the Father, and Jesus the mediator of the new covenant" (D&C 107:19). They are earthly demonstrations of celestial unity. President Wilford WOODRUFF wrote, "The greatest event of the year [1893] was the dedication of the Great Salt Lake Temple. The power of God was manifest . . . and many things revealed" (Journal of Wilford Woodruff, Dec. 31, 1893, HDC).

BIBLIOGRAPHY

Woodbury, Lael. "The Origin and Uses of the Sacred Hosanna Shout." *Sperry Lecture Series*. Provo, Utah, 1975.

D. ARTHUR HAYCOCK

ADMINISTRATION OF TEMPLES

The administration and internal working of a temple are designed to reflect the FAITH of members of The Church of Jesus Christ of Latter-day Saints that each temple is in every way "The House of the Lord." Only in dedicated temples can certain sacred ORDINANCES be performed, certain COVENANTS between man and God be made, and the promise of certain BLESSINGS be conveyed. Through them a person may more fully comprehend the PURPOSE OF EARTH LIFE, the ultimate destinies of MANKIND, and the importance of developing Christlike attributes here in MORTALITY.

ENTERING THE TEMPLE. All who enter the temple must come as worthy members duly certified by ecclesiastical leaders—the BISHOP and the STAKE PRESIDENT. The individual's TEMPLE RECOMMEND or certification to enter the temple is presented upon arrival to the recommend desk attendant. The signatures are verified and the expiration date is checked. A recommend is issued annually and is valid for one year.

Everyone in the temple, temple workers and patrons alike, is dressed in white clothing and is free of worldly ornamentation. All are encouraged to speak with soft voices and guard against extraneous thoughts and conversations, which detract from the spiritual tone of the sanctuary.

The temple is not used for Sunday worship but is rather a sacred edifice where ordinances may be performed and covenants may be made in quiet dignity, away from the cares and din of the outside world. The temple is closed on Sunday, the day in which members worship and learn in their ward meetinghouses. The temple is normally closed on Monday as well, for cleaning and maintenance work in preparation for the scheduled days of operation.

GENERAL SUPERVISION. All temples are administered under the direction of the FIRST PRESIDENCY OF THE CHURCH and the QUORUM OF THE TWELVE APOSTLES. The Temple Department under the direction of the First Presidency and with the guidance of the Temple and Family History Executive Council is the agency responsible for the supervision of all temples. Special attention is given to the following:

- Proper performance of all ordinances of the temple following scriptural patterns as approved by the First Presidency
- Upkeep, maintenance, and security of temples and grounds
- Technical facilities of all temples, especially audiovisual equipment and computers
- Personnel relationships in all temples
- Budgetary matters
- Monitoring temple clothing inventories
- Operation of laundries and cafeterias in temples

TEMPLE PRESIDENCY AND WORKERS. The TEMPLE PRESIDENT is selected and called to his position by the First Presidency of the Church. This is a Church CALLING of usually two to three years. Normally the wife of a temple president serves as the matron of the temple. The president is assisted by two counselors, and the matron by two assistants. Each temple has a temple recorder.

THE TEMPLE EXECUTIVE COUNCIL. The temple president, his counselors, the temple matron, and the recorder constitute the temple executive council. They meet weekly to do all master planning. As needed, other key personnel are invited into this meeting.

VOLUNTEER WORKERS. Each temple relies heavily on volunteer workers to assist in administering the TEMPLE ORDINANCES. A large temple may have as many as two thousand volunteer workers. These ordinance workers, usually assigned two six-hour shifts each week, assist the patrons as they participate in BAPTISMS, CONFIRMATIONS, the ENDOWMENT, and temple SEALINGS.

All of these workers are recommended by their local priesthood leaders. Each person recommended is cleared by the First Presidency of the Church, name by name. This procedure emphasizes the importance of those selected to assist in the temple. Each ordinance worker is finally interviewed carefully by the temple president or one of his counselors who, when satisfied as to personal worthiness, attitude, and ability, sets the person apart by the LAYING-ON OF HANDS, thus conveying the authority essential to officiate in temple ordinances.

TRAINING TEMPLE WORKERS. The temple president is anxious that all that transpires in the temple is in complete harmony with the desires and specifications outlined by SCRIPTURE and the First Presidency of the Church. The temple is a "House of glory," "of order," "of God" (D&C 88:119). Each ordinance worker undergoes an initial training program wherein the actions and words of the ordinances and covenants to be administered are memorized and rehearsed. In addition to the initial instructions, there is a continuation training to make sure all is carried out in an acceptable manner each day. All training is performed in a quiet and gentle manner.

Each shift (forty to eighty workers) begins the day with a prayer meeting that sets a spiritual tone and permits instruction for the work to follow. Usually, a few minutes of each prayer meeting are given to follow-up training. All persons assigned to train others are carefully and prayerfully selected by the temple presidency and the matron.

TEMPLE SEALERS. A sealer in the temple has authority to seal families for time and for all eternity—husbands and wives to each other and children to parents. The process of sealing families together for time and for eternity is the very essence of temple work, and an important foundation stone of

The Terrestrial Room in the Manti Temple. Receiving "of the presence of the Son, but not of the fulness of the Father," the terrestrial glory "excels in all things the glory of the telestial" (D&C 76:77, 91). Photographer: Craig Law.

Latter-day Saint THEOLOGY. Worthy male members of demonstrated faithfulness, ability, and integrity may be called to be sealers in the temple. All such calls and authorization come from the First Presidency of the Church.

THE BAPTISTRY.   The temple baptistry is used for proxy baptisms, living persons being baptized for and in behalf of deceased individuals who have lived through mortality without the opportunity of receiving this sacred ordinance.

The fundamental program encouraged is for members of the Church to perform this work for their deceased ancestors; however, a proven kindred relationship is not essential for the work to be valid. Males are proxies for males; females for females.

Baptisms for the dead often involve young people, ages twelve to seventeen. By appointment, they will spend two to three hours in the temple baptistery area, each person being baptized typically, for a score or more deceased persons. They dress in all-white baptismal clothing, attend a brief worship service, and then participate in the proxy baptisms. Those performing the baptism often include the adult male supervisors traveling with the group.

It is understood that in the spirit world all persons for whom temple work by proxy is performed will have heard of the gospel and its ordinances (*see* SALVATION OF THE DEAD; TEMPLES: MEANINGS AND FUNCTIONS OF TEMPLES).

BIBLIOGRAPHY
Packer, Boyd K. *The Holy Temple.* Salt Lake City, 1980.
Talmage, James E. *The House of the Lord.* Salt Lake City, 1968.

ROBERT L. SIMPSON

MEANINGS AND FUNCTIONS OF TEMPLES

The temple is the primal central holy place dedicated to the worship of God and the perfecting of his covenant people. In the temple his faithful may enter into COVENANTS with the Lord and call upon his holy name after the manner that he has ordained and in the pure and pristine manner restored and set apart from the world. The temple is built so as to represent the organizing principles of the universe. It is the school where mortals learn about these things. The temple is a model, a presentation in figurative terms, of the pattern and journey of life on earth. It is a stable model, which makes its comparison with other forms and traditions, including the more ancient ones, valid and instructive.

THE COSMIC PLAN.   From earliest times, temples have been built as scale models of the universe. The first known mention of the Latin word *templum* is by Varro (116–27 B.C.), for whom it designated a building specially designed for interpreting signs in the heavens—a sort of observatory where one gets one's bearings on the universe. The root *tem-* in Greek and Latin denotes a "cutting," or intersection of two lines at right angles and hence the place where the four regions of the world come together, ancient temples being carefully oriented to express "the idea of pre-established harmony between a celestial and a terrestrial image" (Jeremias, cited in *CWHN* 4:358). According to Varro, there are three temples: one in heaven, one on earth, and one beneath the earth (*De Lingua Latina* 7.8). In the universal temple concept, these three are identical, one being built exactly over the other, with the earth temple in the middle of everything, representing "the Pole of the heavens, around which all heavenly motions

The Celestial Room in the Manti Temple, symbolizing the highest degree of the Celestial Kingdom in heaven. "These are they who are just men made perfect through Jesus the mediator of the new covenant, who wrought out this perfect atonement through the shedding of his own blood" (D&C 76:69). Photographer: Craig Law.

revolve, the knot that ties earth and heaven together, the seat of universal dominion" (Jeremias, cited in *CWHN* 4:358). Here the four cardinal directions meet, and here the three worlds make contact. Whether in the Old World or the New, the idea of the three vertical levels and four horizontal regions dominated the whole economy of such temples and of the societies they formed and guided.

The essentials of Solomon's temple were not of pagan origin but a point of contact with the other world, presenting "rich cosmic symbolism which was largely lost in later Israelite and Jewish tradition" (Albright, cited in *CWHN* 4:361). The twelve oxen (1 Kgs. 7:23–26) represent the circle of the year, and the three stages of the great altar represent the three worlds. According to the Talmud, the temple at Jerusalem, like God's throne and the law itself, existed before the foundations of the world (*Pesahim* 54a–b). Its measurements were all sacred and prescribed, with strict rules about it facing the east.

Its nature as a cosmic center is vividly recalled in many passages of the Old Testament and in medieval representations of the city of Jerusalem and the Holy Sepulcher. These show the temple as the exact center, or navel, of the earth. It was in conscious imitation of both Jewish and Christian ideas that the Muslims conceived of the Kaaba in Mecca as "not only the centre of the earth, [but] the centre of the universe. . . . Every heaven and every earth has its centre marked by a sanctuary as its navel" (von Grunebaum, cited in *CWHN* 4:359). What is bound on earth is bound in heaven. From the temple at Jerusalem went forth ideas and traditions that are found all over the Jewish, Christian, and Muslim worlds.

THE PLACE OF CONTACT. As the ritual center of the universe, the temple was anciently viewed as the one point on earth at which men and women could establish contact with higher spheres. The earliest temples were not, as once supposed, permanent dwelling places of divinity but were places at which humans at specific times attempted to make contact with the powers above. The temple was a building "which the gods transversed to pass from their celestial habitation to their earthly residence. . . . The ziggurat is thus nothing but a support for the edifice on top of it, and the stairway that leads between the upper and lower worlds"; it resembled a mountain, for "the mountain itself was originally a place of contact between this and the upper world" (Parrot, cited in *CWHN* 4:360).

Investigation of the oldest temples represented on prehistoric seals concludes that these structures were also "gigantic altars," built both to attract the attention of the powers above (the burnt offering being a sort of smoke signal) and to provide "the stairways which the god, in answer to prayers, used in order to descend to the earth, . . . bringing a renewal of life in all its forms" (Amiet, cited in *CWHN* 4:360). From the first, it would seem, towers and steps for altars were built in the hope of establishing contact with heaven (Gen. 11:4).

At the same time, the temple is the place of meeting with the lower world and the one point at which passage between the two is possible. In the earliest Christian records, the gates and the keys are closely connected with the temple. Some scholars have noted that the keys of Peter (Matt. 16:19) can only be the keys of the temple, and many studies have demonstrated the identity of tomb, temple, and palace as the place where the powers of the other world are exercised for the eternal benefit of the human race (cf. *CWHN* 4:361). The gates of hell do not prevail against the one who holds these keys, however much the church on earth may suffer. Invariably temple rites are those of the ancestors, and the chief characters are the first parents of the race (see, for example, Huth, cited in *CWHN* 4:361, n. 37).

THE RITUAL DRAMA. The pristine and original temple rites are dramatic repetitions of the events that marked the beginning of the world. This creation drama was not a simple one, for an indispensable part of the story is the ritual death and resurrection of the king, who represents the founder and first parent of the race, and his ultimate triumph over death as priest and king, followed by some form of *hieros gamos*, or ritual marriage, for the purpose of begetting the race. This now familiar "year-drama" is widely attested—in the Memphite theology of Egypt, in the Babylonian New

Year's rites, in the great secular celebration of the Romans, in the *panagyris* and beginnings of Greek drama, in the temple texts of Ras Shamra, and in the Celtic mythological cycles. These rites were performed "because the Divinity—the First Father of the Race—did so once in the beginning, and commanded us to do the same" (Mowinckel, cited in *CWHN* 4:362).

The temple drama is essentially a problem play, featuring a central combat, which may take various mimetic forms—games, races, sham battles, mummings, dances, or plays. The hero is temporarily beaten by the powers of darkness and overcome by death, but calling from the depths upon god, "he rises again and puts the false king, the false Messiah, to death" (Weinsinck, cited in *CWHN* 4:363). This resurrection motif is essential to these rites, whose purpose is ultimate victory over death. These rites are repeated annually be-

Idaho Falls Temple, dedicated in 1945. A mixture of white quartz aggregate and white cement covers the exterior. Photograph, 1987; courtesy Floyd Holdman.

cause the problem of evil and death persists for the human race.

INITIATION. The individuals who toiled as pilgrims to reach the waters of life that flowed from the temple were not passive spectators. They came to obtain knowledge and regeneration, the personal attainment of eternal life and glory. This goal the individual attempted to achieve through purification (washing), initiation, and rejuvenation, which symbolize death, rebirth, and resurrection.

In Solomon's temple, a large bronze font was used for ritual washings, and in the Second Temple period, people at Jerusalem spent much of their time in immersions and ablutions. Baptism is one specific ordinance always mentioned in connection with the temple. "When one is baptized one becomes a Christian," writes Cyril, "exactly as in Egypt by the same rite one becomes an Osiris" (*Patrologiae Latinae* 12:1031), that is, by initiation into immortality. The baptism in question is a washing rather than a baptism, since it is not by immersion. According to Cyril, this is followed by an anointing, making every candidate, as it were, a messiah. The anointing of the brow, face, ears, nose, breast, etc., represents "the clothing of the candidate in the protective panoply of the Holy Spirit," which however does not hinder the initiate from receiving a real GARMENT on the occasion (*CWHN* 4:364). Furthermore, according to Cyril, the candidate was reminded that the whole ordinance is "in imitation of the sufferings of Christ," in which "we suffer without pain by mere imitation his receiving of the nails in his hands and feet: the antitype of Christ's sufferings" (*Patrologiae Graecae* 33:1081). The Jews once taught that Michael and Gabriel will lead all the sinners up out of the lower world: "they will wash and anoint them, healing them of their wounds of hell, and clothe them with beautiful pure garments and bring them into the presence of God" (R. Akiba, cited in *CWHN* 4:364).

LOSS OF THE TEMPLE ORDINANCES. The understanding of the temple and its ancient rites was eventually corrupted and lost for several reasons.

Both Jews and Christians suffered greatly at the hands of their enemies because of the secrecy of their rites, which they steadfastly refused to discuss or divulge because of their sanctity. This caused misunderstanding and opened the door to unbridled fraud: Gnostic sects claimed to have the lost rites and ordinances of the apostles and patri-archs of old. Splinter groups and factions arose. A common cause of schism, among both Jews and Christians, was the claim of a particular group that it alone still possessed the MYSTERIES OF GOD.

The rites became the object of various schools of interpretation. Indeed, mythology is largely an attempt to explain the origin and meaning of rituals that people no longer understand. For example, the Talmud tells of a pious Jew who left Jerusalem in disgust wondering, "What answer will the Israelites give to Elijah when he comes?" since the scholars did not agree on the rites of the temple (*Pesahim* 70b; on the role of Elijah, see A. Wiener, *The Prophet Elijah in the Development of Judaism* [London, 1978], pp. 68–69).

Ritual elements were widely copied and usurped. The early Christian fathers claimed that pagan counterparts had been stolen from older legitimate sources, and virtually every major mythology tells of a great usurper who rules the world.

Comparative studies have discovered a common pattern in all ancient religions and have traced processes of diffusion that spread ideas throughout the world. The task of reconstructing the original prototype from the scattered fragments has been a long and laborious one, and it is far from complete, but an unmistakable pattern emerges (*CWHN* 4:367).

Reconstructions of great gatherings of people at imposing ceremonial complexes for rites dedicated to the renewal of life on earth are surprisingly uniform. First, there is tangible evidence, the scenery and properties of the drama: megaliths; artificial giant mounds or pyramids amounting to artificial mountains; stone and ditch alignments of mathematical sophistication correlating time and space; passage graves and great *tholoi*, or domed tombs; sacred roads; remains of booths, grandstands, processional ways, and gates—these still survive in awesome combination, with all their cosmic symbolism.

Second is the less tangible evidence of customs, legends, folk festivals, and ancient writings, which together conjure up memories of dramatic and choral celebrations of the Creation, culminating in the great Creation Hymn; ritual contests between life and death, good and evil, and light and darkness, followed by the triumphant coronation of the king to rule for the new age, the progenitor of the race by a sacred marriage; covenants; initiations (including washing and clothing); sacrifices and scapegoats to rid the people of a year of guilt and pollution; and various types of divination and oracular consultation for the new life cycle.

OTHER FUNCTIONS OF THE TEMPLE. Many things surrounding the temple were not essential to its form and function, but were the inevitable products of its existence. The words "hotel," "hospital," and "Templar" go back to those charitable organizations that took care of sick and weary pilgrims traveling to the holy places. Banking functions arose at the temple, since pilgrims brought offerings and needed to exchange their money for animals to be sacrificed, and thus the word "money" comes from the temple of Juno Moneta, the holy center of the Roman world. Along with that, lively barter and exchange of goods at the great year rites led to the yearly fair, when all contracts had to be renewed and where merchants, artisans, performers, and mountebanks displayed their wares.

Actors, poets, singers, dancers, and athletes were also part of temple life, the competitive element (the *agonal*) being essential to the struggle with evil and providing the most popular and exciting aspects of the festivals. The temple's main drama, the *actio*, was played by priestly temple actors and royalty. Creation was celebrated with a creation hymn, or *poema*—the word "poem" meaning "creation"—sung by a chorus that, as the Greek word shows, formed a circle and danced as they sang (*CWHN* 4:380).

The temple was also the center of learning, beginning with the heavenly instructions received there. It was the *Museon*, or home of the Muses, representing every branch of study: astronomy, mathematics, architecture, and fine arts. People would travel from shrine to shrine exchanging wisdom with the wise, as Abraham did in Egypt. Since the Garden of Eden, or "golden age" motif, was essential to this ritual paradise, temple grounds contained trees and animals, often collected from distant places. Central to the temple school was the library, containing sacred records, including the "Books of Life," the names of all the living and the dead, as well as liturgical and scientific works.

The temple rites acknowledged the rule of God on earth through his agent and offspring, the king, who represented both the first man and every man as he sat in judgment, making the temple the ultimate seat and sanction of law and government. People met at the holy place for contracts and covenants and to settle disputes.

THE TEMPLE AND CIVILIZATION. All this indicates that the temple is the source, and not a derivative, of the civilizing process. If there is no temple, there is no true ISRAEL; and where there is no true temple, civilization itself is but an empty shell—a material structure of expediency and tradition alone, bereft of the living organism at its center that once gave it life and made it flourish.

Many secular institutions today occupy structures faithfully copied from ancient temples. The temple economy has been perverted along with the rest: feasts of joy and abundance became orgies; sacred rites of marriage were perverted; teachers of wisdom became haughty and self-righteous, demonstrating that anything can be corrupted in this world, and as Aristotle notes, the better the original, the more vicious the corrupted version.

THE RESTORATION AND THE TEMPLE. Latter-day Saint temples fully embody the uncorrupted functions and meanings of the temple. Did the Prophet Joseph SMITH reinvent all this by reassembling the fragments—Jewish, Orthodox, Masonic, Gnostic, Hindu, Egyptian, and so forth? In fact, few of the fragments were available in his day, and those poor fragments do not come together of themselves to make a whole. Latter-day Saints see in the completeness and perfection of Joseph Smith's teachings regarding the temple a sure indication of divine revelation. This is also seen in the design of the SALT LAKE TEMPLE. One can note its three levels; eastward orientation; central location in ZION; brazen sea on the back of twelve oxen holding the waters through which the dead, by proxy, pass to eternal life; rooms appointed for ceremonies rehearsing the creation of the world; and many other symbolic features.

The actual work done within the temple exemplifies the temple idea, with thousands of men and women serving with no ulterior motive. Here time and space come together; barriers vanish between this world and the next, between past, present, and future. Solemn prayers are offered in the name of Jesus Christ to the Almighty. What is bound here is bound beyond, and only here can the gates be opened to release the dead who are awaiting the saving ordinances. Here the whole human family meets in a common enterprise; the records of the race are assembled as far back in time as research has taken them, for a work performed by the present generation to assure that they and their kindred dead shall spend the eternities together in the future. Here, for the first time in many centuries, one may behold a genuine temple, functioning as a temple in the fullest and purest sense of the word.

BIBLIOGRAPHY

Nibley, Hugh W. "Christian Envy of the Temple." In *CWHN* 4:391–434.

———. "What Is a Temple?" In *CWHN* 4:355–87.

———. "The Hierocentric State." *Western Political Quarterly* 4 (June 1951):226–53.

———. *Message of the Joseph Smith Papyri.* Salt Lake City, 1975.

Packer, Boyd K. *The Holy Temple.* Salt Lake City, 1980.

Talmage, James E. *The House of the Lord.* Salt Lake City, 1962.

For a lengthy bibliography on temples, see Donald W. Parry, Stephen D. Ricks, and John W. Welch, *Temple Bibliography*, Lewiston, N.Y., 1991.

HUGH W. NIBLEY

TEMPLES THROUGH THE AGES

The center of the community in ancient Israel and in other parts of the ancient Near East was the temple, an institution of the highest antiquity. Its construction regularly represented the crowning achievement in a king's reign. Thus, it was the central event in the reign of king Solomon, far overshadowing any of his other accomplishments (1 Kgs. 6–8), and it was a crucial event in the establishment of the Nephite monarchy (2 Ne. 5:16–18). The presence of the temple represented stability and cohesiveness in the community, and its rites and ceremonies were viewed as essential to the proper functioning of the society. Conversely, the destruction of a temple and the cessation of its rites presaged and symbolized the dissolution of its community and the withdrawal of God's favor. The fall of Jerusalem and its temple (586 B.C.), along with the rifling of its sacred treasures, symbolized, like no other event, the catastrophe that befell Judah. Following the return of the Jews from exile in Babylon (c. 500 B.C.), the prophets Haggai and Zechariah persistently reminded their people that no other achievement would compensate for their failure to reconstruct a temple. Temples were so important that, when distance or other circumstances made worship at the Jerusalem temple

Provo Temple, in Provo, Utah, dedicated in 1972. Photograph, 1988; courtesy Floyd Holdman.

impractical, others were built. Thus, Israelite temples were built at Arad near Beersheba, at Elephantine and Leontopolis in Egypt, and a Nephite temple was erected in the land of Nephi.

Several studies have shown that certain characteristics regularly recur in the temples of the ancient Near East. Among the features that have been identified that distinguish the temple from the meetinghouse type of sacred structure such as synagogue or church are: (1) the temple is built on separate, sacral, set-apart space; (2) the temple and its rituals are enshrouded in secrecy; (3) the temple is oriented toward the four world regions or cardinal directions; (4) the temple expresses architecturally the idea of ascent toward heaven; (5) the plans for the temple are revealed by God to a king or prophet; and (6) the temple is a place of sacrifice (Lundquist, pp. 57–59).

Latter-day Saints recognize among these features several that are characteristic of ancient Israelite temples as well as their own. For example, the sites of ancient Israelite and modern Latter-day Saint temples are viewed as holy, with access restricted to certain individuals who are expected to have "clean hands and a pure heart" (Ps. 24:3–6; cf. Ps. 15; Isa. 33:14–16; *see* TEMPLE RECOMMENDS). Like the tabernacle and temple in ancient Israel, many Latter-day Saint temples are directionally oriented, with the ceremonial main entrance (indicated by the inscription "HOLINESS TO THE LORD" on modern temples) facing east. Ancient Israelite temples were divided into three sections, each representing a progressively higher

Model of the temple in Jerusalem at the time of Herod. Courtesy Paul A. Cheesman.

stage, reaching from the netherworld to heaven; similar symbolism can be recognized in the LDS temples as well. The plans for the temple of Solomon were revealed to King Solomon. Likewise, plans for many Latter-day Saint temples were received through revelation.

What occurred within temples of antiquity? The temple is a place of sacrifice, a practice that is well attested in ancient Israel. Animal sacrifice is not to be found in temples of the Latter-day Saints because blood sacrifice had its fulfillment in the death of Jesus (3 Ne. 9:19). Still, Latter-day Saints learn in their temples to observe the eternal principles of sacrifice of a broken heart and contrite spirit (3 Ne. 12:19). In addition, inside the temples of the ancient Near East, kings, temple priests, and worshippers received a washing and anointing and were clothed, enthroned, and symbolically initiated into the presence of deity, and thus into eternal life. In ancient Israel—as elsewhere—these details are best seen in the consecration of the priest and the coronation of the king. LDS TEMPLE ORDINANCES are performed in a Christian context of eternal kingship, queenship, and priesthood.

The features of temple worship described above are also found among many other cultures from ancient to modern times. Several explanations of this can be offered. According to President Joseph F. SMITH, some of these similarities are best understood as having spread by diffusion from a common ancient source:

Undoubtedly the knowledge of this law [of sacrifice] and of the other rites and ceremonies was carried by the posterity of Adam into all lands, and continued with them, more or less pure, to the flood, and

through Noah, who was a "preacher of righteousness," to those who succeeded him, spreading out into all nations and countries. . . . If the heathen have doctrines and ceremonies resembling . . . those . . . in the Scriptures, it only proves . . . that these are the traditions of the fathers handed down, . . . and that they will cleave to the children to the latest generation, though they may wander into darkness and perversion, until but a slight resemblance to their origin, which was divine, can be seen [JD 15:325–26].

When Jesus drove the moneychangers from the temple—which he referred to as "my Father's house" (John 2:16)—it reflected his insistence on holiness for the sanctuaries in ancient Israel. Neither Stephen's nor Paul's statements that "the most High dwelleth not in temples made with hands" (Acts 7:48; 17:24; cf. Isa. 66:1–2) imply a rejection of the temple, but rather an argument against the notion that God can be confined to a structure. Solomon, at the dedication of the temple in Jerusalem, said similarly, "The heaven of heavens cannot contain thee; how much less this house that I have builded?" (1 Kgs. 8:27; 2 Chr. 6:18). As late as the fourth century A.D., Christians were able to point to the spot on the Mount of Olives "where they say the sanctuary of the Lord, that is, the Temple, is to be built, and where it will stand forever . . . when, as they say, the Lord comes with the heavenly Jerusalem at the end of the world" (Nibley, p. 393).

While the idea of the temple was somewhat submerged in the later Jewish–Christian consciousness, it was never completely forgotten. As Hugh Nibley points out, the Christian church sensed that it possessed no adequate substitute for the temple. Jerusalem remained at the center of medieval maps of the world, and the site of the temple was sometimes indicated on such maps as well. When the Crusaders liberated the holy places in Jerusalem, the site of the temple was visited immediately after that of the Holy Sepulcher, even though no temple had been there for over 1,000 years (Nibley, pp. 392, 399–409).

Jews and Christians who take the vision of the reconstruction of the temple in Ezekiel seriously—and literally—anticipate the place in God's plan of rebuilding a future temple, as well as the reconstitution of distinct tribes of Israel (Ricks, pp. 279–80). While Jewish life proceeded without the temple following its destruction by the Romans in A.D. 70, it retained a significant role in their thought and study. In the modern period, the temple remains important to some Jews, who continue to study their sacred texts relating to it.

BIBLIOGRAPHY

Lundquist, John M. "The Common Temple Ideology in the Ancient Near East." In *The Temple in Antiquity*, ed. T. Madsen, pp. 53–74. Provo, Utah, 1984.

Nibley, Hugh W. "Christian Envy of the Temple." In *CWHN* 4:391–433.

Ricks, Stephen D. "The Prophetic Literality of Tribal Reconstruction." In *Israel's Apostasy and Restoration: Essays in Honor of Roland K. Harrison*, ed. A. Gileadi, pp. 273–81. Grand Rapids, Mich., 1988.

STEPHEN D. RICKS

TEMPLE SQUARE

Temple Square is the architectural center of Salt Lake City, sacred ground for The Church of Jesus Christ of Latter-day Saints, and a primary point of interest for millions of visitors annually. Within the square are the SALT LAKE TEMPLE, the TABERNACLE (home of the MORMON TABERNACLE CHOIR), the Assembly Hall, two VISITORS CENTERS, several historical statues, and well-kept grounds. Its appearance today differs sharply from that of the treeless desert that greeted the first Mormon pioneers in 1847.

Only days after arriving in the SALT LAKE VALLEY, President Brigham YOUNG identified the site for the temple. It was originally planned as a 40-acre block but was reduced to ten acres "for convenience." The ground-breaking ceremony for the temple was held on February 14, 1853, even though the ground was frozen and covered with snow. Construction continued for forty years, and the temple was dedicated on April 6, 1893.

Construction of the Tabernacle began in 1863. It was in use four years later and dedicated in 1875. A decade later the Assembly Hall was built to accommodate smaller gatherings. This building holds approximately 3,000 people and is often used for overflow of the Church's general conferences.

Almost from the beginning, keen interest in Temple Square and the Church made it an attrac-

Prior to the construction of the domed tabernacle, Church members gathered in the "Old" Tabernacle shown here (c. 1863). To the right is the North Bowery, which accommodated larger crowds in good weather. Construction on the first Tabernacle began in 1851; it was dedicated April 6, 1852, by President Willard Richards and was used until 1870. It was replaced by the Assembly Hall. Photographer probably C. R. Savage.

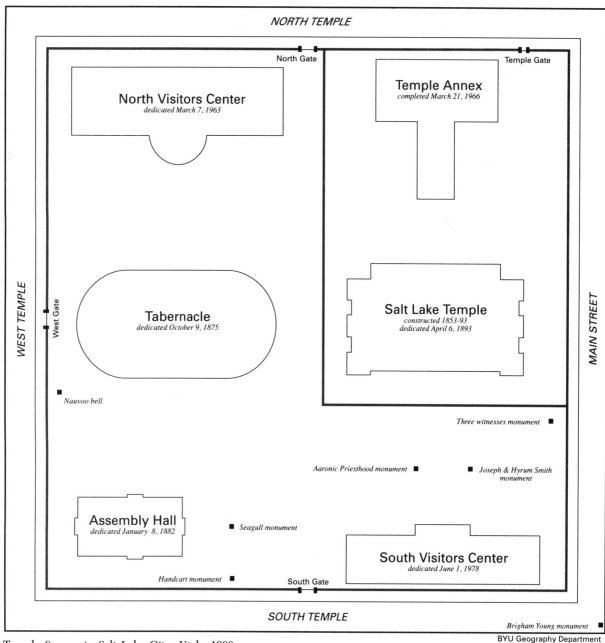

Temple Square in Salt Lake City, Utah, 1990.

BYU Geography Department

tion for those visiting the "Crossroads of the West." In 1875 Charles J. Thomas was appointed the first official guide to Temple Square. In 1876 he greeted 4,000 visitors. The first visitors center, called the "Bureau of Information," was built in 1902, followed by larger buildings in 1904 and 1910. However, when the number of visitors increased, the depiction of the story and beliefs of the Church required additional exhibit areas. In 1963 the large visitors center at the northwest cor-

ner of the square was opened to the public. It houses theaters, artwork, displays, and dioramas. Its focal point is a copy of the 11-foot CHRISTUS STATUE originally carved by the Danish sculptor Bertell Thorvaldsen. It depicts the Savior with arms outstretched inviting all to come to him. The Christus represents the central focus of the Church's beliefs and worship: Jesus Christ.

An additional visitors center was built in the southeast corner of the square and dedicated on

The spires of the Salt Lake Temple and the oval dome of the tabernacle dominate this view of Temple Square (1990). To the left of the Temple is the Annex; to the right, the South Visitors Center. The former Hotel Utah and the LDS Church Office Building are behind the Temple. To the left of the tabernacle is the North Visitors Center, and the Assembly Hall is in the lower right.

June 1, 1978. Its displays include an exact replica of the baptismal font of the Salt Lake Temple, like the biblical "molten sea" on the backs of twelve life-size oxen (see 2 Chr. 4:2–5).

Many monuments and statues adorn the square. They represent people and entertain the story of the beginnings of the Church and of the pioneers. The first statues to become a permanent part of the square were those of the Prophet Joseph SMITH and his brother Hyrum in 1911. In 1913, the Seagull Monument was placed on the square memorializing the gulls' providential intervention in 1848 that saved the Mormon pioneers' early crops from being devoured by crickets.

Other monuments include a statue honoring the three witnesses to the BOOK OF MORMON: Oliver COWDERY, David WHITMER, and Martin HARRIS; the Handcart Monument representing approximately 3,000 pioneers who walked either from Iowa City, Iowa, or from the Missouri River near Florence, Nebraska, to the Salt Lake Valley; a small bronze and granite sundial provided by the young women of the Church in 1940; the AARONIC PRIESTHOOD Memorial Monument, which depicts JOHN THE BAPTIST bestowing the Aaronic Priest-

hood on Joseph Smith and Oliver Cowdery; and the RELIEF SOCIETY Memorial Campanile, a 35-foot tower in which the NAUVOO bell is preserved

Temple Square has been the most popular tourist attraction in Utah for over a century. In the mid-1880's, Grant Brothers Stages took visitors around the temple construction site as part of their tour of Salt Lake City. Blocks of granite for the temple are visible in the foreground. Photographer: Charles Ellis Johnson.

and displayed and upon which a tone is struck on the hour each hour of the day. The bell had originally hung in the NAUVOO TEMPLE and was brought to Utah by oxteam in 1847.

Visitors may choose to walk through the grounds and visitors centers at their leisure or may request a guide to accompany them. Guides are familiar with the state's pioneer history as well as the teachings and culture of the Church. Foreign visitors are provided, when possible, with guides who speak their language.

At every season, the temple grounds are colorful. Long before spring, workmen are trimming, planting, and cultivating flowers, shrubs, and trees. Since 1969, the limbs of almost every tree have been wrapped in lights for the Christmas season. On the day after Thanksgiving, a special program inaugurates the celebration and the lights are turned on. They remain on until New Year's Day.

BIBLIOGRAPHY

Grant, Carter E. "Zion's Ten Acres." *IE* (June 1970):16–19.

Johnson, Melvin Kay. "A History of the Temple Square Mission of The Church of Jesus Christ of Latter-day Saints to 1970." Master's thesis, Brigham Young University, 1971.

CAROLYN J. RASMUS

TEMPTATION

"Temptation" and related terms in the Old Testament are translated from the Hebrew *nasah*, meaning "to try" or "to test." Such a test elicits responses demonstrating a person's disposition and will rather than abilities. In this sense God is said to "tempt" human beings. Thus did "God tempt" Abraham by commanding him to sacrifice Isaac (Gen. 22:1). In Abraham's account of creation in the Pearl of Great Price, the Lord indicates that mortal experience constitutes such a test (Abr. 3:25). In other latter-day scriptures, temptation usually refers to the enticement of human beings into attitudes and actions that alienate them from God and jeopardize their salvation. The Lord taught people to shun this kind of temptation: "And lead us not into temptation" (Luke 11:4; cf. JST). Although in this kind of temptation the individual is usually enticed from without (whether by human or nonhuman agents), the scriptures make clear the individual's responsibility and accountability:

> Let no man say when he is tempted, I am tempted of God: for God cannot be tempted with evil, neither tempteth he any man. But every man is tempted, when he is drawn away of his own lust, and enticed. Then when lust hath conceived, it bringeth forth sin: and sin, when it is finished, bringeth forth death [James 1:13–16].

Latter-day Saints believe that though God does not tempt human beings to do evil, he does, for benevolent purposes, allow them to be tempted. If people were not confronted with opposing possibilities and inclinations, they would not be able to exercise their AGENCY, and, thus, their opportunity for moral and spiritual growth would be diminished. The prophet Lehi explained:

> To bring about [God's] eternal purposes in the end of man, after he had created our first parents, . . . it must needs be that there was an opposition; even the forbidden fruit in opposition to the tree of life; the one being sweet and the other bitter. Wherefore, the Lord God gave unto man that he should act for himself. Wherefore, man could not act for himself save it should be that he was enticed by the one or the other [2 Ne. 2:15–16].

Though confronting temptation is an essential and unavoidable element of mortal experience, God mercifully limits the extent to which people can be tempted. For example, he does not allow Satan or his hosts to tempt little children until they begin to be accountable (D&C 29:47), nor anyone beyond his or her capacity to endure (1 Cor. 10:13). During the Millennium, Satan and his angels will be bound so that they cannot tempt humankind (1 Ne. 22:26; 4 Ne. 1:15). Satan will be loosed for "a little season" following the Millennium, and will finally be banished with his angels as part of the final judgment (D&C 88:110–15).

Since God knew that all humans would yield in some degree to temptation and become sinners, he planned from the beginning and carried out through Jesus Christ an ATONEMENT whereby people can be forgiven of their SINS and obtain power to resist temptation in the future, when they accept and follow his gospel.

The language of temptation in the scriptures can also refer to the various trials that humans experience in mortality. While these trials may become stumbling blocks, they may also become opportunities for moral and spiritual growth. Regarding such temptations, James counsels,

> My brethren, count it all joy when ye fall into divers temptations; knowing this, that the trying of your

faith worketh patience. But let patience have her perfect work, that ye may be perfect and entire, wanting nothing. . . . Blessed is the man that endureth temptation: for when he is tried, he shall receive the crown of life, which the Lord hath promised to them that love him [James 1:2–4, 12].

Sometimes the scriptures speak of people tempting God or of sinful human ways of responding or relating to God. People may "tempt God" by complaining against him or by challenging him in unbelief (cf. Ex. 17:1–7; 1 Cor. 10:9), by defying him in disobedience (Heb. 3:8), or by demanding signs or miracles from him for an unworthy motive, such as to exalt themselves or to satisfy their curiosity (Matt. 12:39). Compare also Satan's temptations of Jesus in the wilderness and the Lord's rebuke: "Thou shalt not tempt the Lord thy God" (Matt. 4:1–11).

BIBLIOGRAPHY

Madsen, Truman G. "The Better Music." *IE* 66 (June 1963):554–55.

McKay, David O. "The Temptations of Life." *IE* 71 (July 1968):2–3.

DAVID L. PAULSEN

TEN COMMANDMENTS

The Ten Commandments or "decalogue," literally "ten words" (Ex. 34:28; Deut. 4:13; 10:4), are usually understood to be the divine injunctions revealed to Moses and recorded in Exodus 20:1–17 and Deuteronomy 5:6–21. These basic standards of behavior, part of the COVENANT made on Sinai between the Lord and the children of ISRAEL, have relevance transcending the DISPENSATION of MOSES, and have been quoted (Mosiah 12:34–35; 13:12–24) and elaborated throughout later scripture (Matt. 5:21–37; D&C 42:18–28; 59:6).

The Ten Commandments encapsulate the basic tenets of the Torah, or LAW OF MOSES. Refugees from Egyptian bondage, the Israelites agreed to keep the law (Ex. 19:8), and in return the Lord promised to make them "a peculiar treasure . . . a kingdom of priests, and an holy nation" (Ex. 19:5–6). Moses, realizing that keeping this covenant was essential to Israel's successful establishment in Canaan, used the decalogue to remind his people of their covenant as they prepared to enter the PROMISED LAND (Deut. 5:6–21).

In response to the Israelites' worship of the golden calf, Moses shattered the original tablets on which the commandments were engraved (Ex. 32:19). Though a second set was produced (Ex. 34:1), the JOSEPH SMITH TRANSLATION OF THE BIBLE (JST) indicates that the accompanying law was diminished. The second law was "not . . . according to the first . . . [but] after the law of a carnal commandment" (JST Ex. 34:1–2; JST Deut. 10:1–2).

Each set was made up of two stone "tables of testimony" (Ex. 31:18), reflecting the two classes of instructions they contained. The first group, or "table," consists of commandments dealing with the relationship between God and his children. They forbid the worship of other gods and of idols, the misuse of the Lord's name, and the desecration of the SABBATH DAY. These are elaborated with explanations and consequences. The second table, written in short, direct statements, deals with relationships among God's children, containing commands to honor parents, and not to kill, commit adultery, steal, bear false witness, or covet.

These standards have been known in all DISPENSATIONS (*MD*, p. 782), but in the form received by Moses they were an important influence on later scripture. In the Book of Mormon, ABINADI, in his defense before King Noah, quotes the entire decalogue from Exodus (Mosiah 12:34–35; 13:12–24). Christ, who fulfills the law, expands upon the terse second table in the SERMON ON THE MOUNT (Matt. 5:21–37; 3 Ne. 12:21–37). He warns of attitudes that lead to misdeeds, forbidding not only adultery, but lust, not only killing, but anger. The second table is likewise expanded in latter-day REVELATION. The Doctrine and Covenants forbids stealing, adultery, killing, or "anything like unto it" (59:6), while D&C 42:18–28 details the consequences of such actions.

Finally, Christ not only expands upon applications of the commandments, but reduces the two principal focuses of the decalogue to their essence. Each of the two great commandments, to love the Lord (Matt. 22:37; Deut. 6:5) and to love one's neighbor (Matt. 22:39; Lev. 19:18; Rom. 13:9), encapsulates one of the two tables of the Ten Commandments.

BIBLIOGRAPHY

Fuller, Reginald H. "The Decalogue in the New Testament." In *Interpretation: A Journal of Bible and Theology* 43 (1989):43–55.

Wells, Robert E. "We Are Christians Because. . . ." *Ensign* 14 (Jan. 1984):16–19.

BRUCE T. VERHAAREN

TERRESTRIAL KINGDOM

The Church of Jesus Christ of Latter-day Saints teaches of three DEGREES OF GLORY or kingdoms of HEAVEN in the AFTERLIFE: the CELESTIAL KINGDOM, terrestrial kingdom, and TELESTIAL KINGDOM. Paul likened these kingdoms to the relative radiance of the sun, moon, and stars (1 Cor 15:40–41; cf. D&C 76:50–98). Further evidence of a heaven with multiple kingdoms is found in Jesus' statement, "In my Father's house are many mansions" (John 14:2). On February 16, 1832, the Prophet Joseph SMITH and Sidney RIGDON saw in vision the three degrees of glory, identifying the glory of the terrestrial kingdom as typical "of the moon [which] differs from the sun in the firmament" (D&C 76:71).

The terrestrial glory is for those who lived honorable lives on the earth but "were blinded by the craftiness of men" and were "not valiant in the testimony of Jesus." Those who did not receive a TESTIMONY of Jesus while on earth, but who could have done so except for their neglect, are also heirs to the terrestrial kingdom (D&C 76:72–74, 79). They obtain not "the crown over the kingdom of our God" (D&C 76:79) and remain without EXALTATION in their saved condition (D&C 132:17). They "receive of the presence of the Son, but not of the fulness of the Father," and their kingdom differs from the celestial "as the moon differs from the sun" (D&C 76:77–78).

[*See also* Degrees of Glory.]

SUSAN EASTON BLACK

TESTATOR

A testator is one who at death leaves a valid will or testament. In certain usages, the word is synonymous with witness. The term appears twice in scripture, retaining the strictly legal sense in Hebrews 9:16–17, where the death of Jesus Christ makes valid the new testament, or covenant. In Doctrine and Covenants 135:5–6, testator includes the additional connotation of "martyr" when referring to the deaths of the Prophet Joseph SMITH and his brother Hyrum. The outline of Joseph Smith's

accomplishments in verse 3 underscores why Latter-day Saints regard him as a valid testator.

ROBERT L. MARROTT

TESTIMONY

[*Testimony is a generic term among Latter-day Saints for the assurance of the reality, truth, and goodness of God, of the teachings and atonement of Jesus Christ, and of the divine calling of latter-day prophets. It is the core of LDS religious experience. It reaches beyond secondhand assent, notional conviction, or strong belief. It is knowledge buttressed by divine personal confirmation by the Holy Ghost and is interrelated with authentic faith and trust in God as demonstrated by dedication and discipleship. Fundamental in the Church is the doctrine that "no man can be a minister of Jesus Christ except he has the testimony of Jesus; and this is the spirit of prophecy. Whenever salvation has been administered, it has been by testimony" (TPJS, p. 160).*

Articles that relate to this theme and its connections with other aspects of Latter-day Saint spiritual life include Faith in Jesus Christ; Fast and Testimony Meeting; Inspiration; Knowledge; Light of Christ; Religious Experience; Revelation; Testimony Bearing; Testimony of Jesus Christ; Truth; *and* Witnesses, Law of.]

TESTIMONY BEARING

Testimony bearing among members of The Church of Jesus Christ of Latter-day Saints is a person's verbal expression of what he or she knows to be true concerning the divinity of Jesus Christ, the RESTORATION of the fulness of his gospel in our time, and the blessings that come from living its principles. By divine mandate, bearing testimony is to be done "in my name, in solemnity of heart, in the spirit of meekness, in all things" (D&C 100:7). Latter-day Saints often bear testimony when teaching in Church services, when explaining gospel principles to members of other faiths, and in the FAST AND TESTIMONY MEETING, held monthly in each congregation.

Bearing testimony while teaching the gospel of Jesus Christ is pervasive in the Church and is based on two central beliefs. The first is that the primary responsibility of members is to "teach one another" (D&C 88:118) rather than to depend upon one formal teacher or minister only. The second is that the power that motivates individuals to live as Christ taught is the power of the HOLY GHOST, rather than the power of logic or the eloquence of gospel teachers: "For when a man speaketh by the power of the Holy Ghost the power of the Holy Ghost carrieth it unto the hearts of the children of men" (2 Ne. 33:1). Testimony bearing complies with the Lord's instruction through Isaiah: "Ye are my witnesses, saith the Lord, that I am God" (Isa. 43:12).

Latter-day Saints who speak in SACRAMENT MEETING or teach classes in the organizations of the Church (i.e., SUNDAY SCHOOL, PRIMARY, RELIEF SOCIETY, YOUNG WOMEN AND YOUNG MEN, and PRIESTHOOD) are urged to conclude their presentations by bearing personal testimony that the things which they have said are true. Hearing testimony borne under the influence of the Holy Spirit enables those listening under the Spirit's influence to understand the message both intellectually and spiritually (1 Cor. 2:11; D&C 50:17–24; 100:6–10).

Latter-day Saint missionaries, in particular, rely on testimony bearing, rather than on logic or artifice, to reach their listeners. The impact of this faith and practice is illustrated by Brigham YOUNG's account of his own conversion to the gospel when as LDS missionary, Eleazar Miller, bore his testimony:

> If all the talent, tact, wisdom and refinement of the world had been sent to me with the Book of Mormon, and had declared, in the most exalted of earthly eloquence, the truth of it, undertaking to prove it by learning, and worldly wisdom, they would have been to me like the smoke which arises only to vanish away. But when I saw a man without eloquence, or talents for public speaking, who could only say, "I know, by the power of the Holy Ghost, that the Book of Mormon is true, that Joseph Smith is a prophet of the Lord," the Holy Ghost proceeding from that individual illuminated my understanding, and light, glory, and immortality were before me. I was encircled by them, filled with them, and I knew for myself that the testimony of the man was true [JD 1:90].

Fast and testimony meetings, usually held in each congregation of the Church as part of the SACRAMENT meeting on the first Sunday of each month, provide all members the opportunity to bear testimony. In these meetings, no one is assigned in advance to prepare a sermon. Rather, any member who desires may stand before the congregation and testify of the things he or she has learned to be true through trying to live in the manner Christ has taught. Members typically come to these meetings fasting, abstaining from food and drink for at least two meals. Opportunities to bear testimony are also given to young children in Primary, to young people in youth conferences or FAMILY HOME EVENINGS, to missionaries in various conferences, and to all members in a wide variety of settings.

Spoken testimony is the foundation of faith and with written testimony becomes the essence of scripture. Faith comes by hearing—as well as by reading—"the word of the Lord." The Doctrine and Covenants says, "Whatsoever they shall speak when moved upon by the Holy Ghost . . . [whether or not it is recorded or written] shall be scripture" and "the power of God unto salvation" (D&C 68:4). Said the Prophet Joseph SMITH, "No generation was ever saved or destroyed upon dead testimony neither can be; but by Living" (WJS, p. 159). He taught further that the living word of the Lord "has such an influence over the human mind—the logical mind—that it is convincing without other testimony" (WJS, p. 159). "Faith cometh by hearing the word of God through the testimonies of the servants of God," he said, and is "always attended by the spirit of prophecy and revelation" (WJS, p. 3). These principles are the background of the constancy of the mode of testimony bearing in Church life.

Patterns of testimony bearing in ancient churches closely parallel today's practice. The apostle Paul, for example, said that he was "determined not to know anything among you, save Jesus Christ, and him crucified," and spoke "not with enticing words of man's wisdom, but in demonstration of the Spirit" (1 Cor. 2:2–5). In early Christian sources (e.g., the Didache) one reads of sacrament meetings or feasts where hymn singing was followed by an opportunity for individual testimonies (Davies, pp. 342–43). The Book of Mormon prophet ALMA₂ concluded that the only way to reclaim his people from selfishness and pride was "in bearing down in pure testimony against them" (Alma 4:19). Amulek testified in a manner similar to Latter-day Saint testimony bearing today: "And now, behold, I will testify unto you of myself that these things are true. Behold, I say unto you, that I do know that Christ shall come among the children of men, to take upon him the transgressions of his people, and that he shall atone for the sins of the world; for the Lord God hath spoken it" (Alma 34:8).

BIBLIOGRAPHY

Davies, J. G., ed. *The Westminster Dictionary of Liturgy and Worship*. Philadelphia, 1986.

Stoker, H. Steven, and Joseph C. Muren, comps. *Into Your Heart Like Fire*. Ogden, Utah, 1975.

CLAYTON CHRISTENSEN

TESTIMONY OF JESUS CHRIST

For Latter-day Saints, the FIRST PRINCIPLE OF THE GOSPEL is FAITH in Jesus Christ. This faith is intertwined with "the testimony of Jesus," which is received from God, "for the testimony of Jesus is the spirit of prophecy" (Rev. 19:10). Joseph Smith said, "No man can *know* that Jesus is the Lord, but by the Holy Ghost" (*TPJS*, p. 223; 1 Cor. 12:3). The essence of a TESTIMONY is a personal inward assurance of Jesus Christ's divinity, and it provides the fundamental basis for a Christian life. One becomes a disciple of Christ in the fullest spiritual sense only when a personal testimony of Jesus is received.

To have such a testimony is to be conscious that God has borne witness within one's soul by the power of the Holy Ghost that Jesus is the Christ (D&C 46:13). How is this witness obtained? As Paul wrote, "faith cometh by hearing, and hearing by the word of God" (Rom. 10:17). The testimony of Jesus Christ comes to those who hear of him. But to hear the GOSPEL OF JESUS CHRIST preached is not yet to have a testimony of him. Divine confirmation must also be received, usually in answer to sincere prayer. These three elements usually occur in a sequence: hearing, praying, receiving the divine witness by the Spirit. They can also occur simultaneously. Following Peter's earnest declaration, "Thou art the Christ, the Son of the living God," Jesus replied, "Blessed art thou . . . for flesh and blood hath not revealed it unto thee, but my Father which is in heaven" (Matt. 16:16–17). Like Peter, PROPHETS and APOSTLES of all ages have testified of Jesus Christ (see John 20:31).

Praying for a testimony of Jesus Christ or for any other truth of the gospel does not assume the presence of the faith being sought. The common phrase, "acting in good faith," may offer insight here. It suggests a willingness to approach a matter not with suspicion but with trust. The Book of Mormon prophet ALMA₂ asks his listeners to "awake and arouse your faculties, even to an experiment upon my words . . . even until ye believe in a manner that ye can give place for a portion of my words" (Alma 32:27). To those willing to open their hearts at least this much, a testimony may come,

but hardly to those without a fervent desire to obtain it. Most Latter-day Saints treasure the spiritual experiences that awaken and confirm testimony.

The gaining of a testimony is best viewed not as a single event but as a continuing process. Just as spiritual indolence and disobedience to the commandments of Christ constantly weaken a testimony, so close communion with God and selfless Christian service progressively strengthen it. Because Latter-day Saints view religion as an active as well as a contemplative way of life, they stress the unity of these two ends. Drawing close to God and serving others are aspects of a single purpose, following Christ. Only those who seek to do this may come to truly know him. "For how knoweth a man the master whom he has not served, and who is a stranger unto him, and is far from the thoughts and intents of his heart?" (Mosiah 5:13). But to all who follow him, the testimony of Jesus Christ gives an assurance of his presence, his all-enveloping care, and his love.

BIBLIOGRAPHY

Muren, Joseph C., and H. Stephen Stoker, comps. *Testimony*. Salt Lake City, 1980.

DENNIS RASMUSSEN

THANKFULNESS

From time immemorial those who believe in God have expressed their thankfulness to him. Giving humble thanks is also among the most basic religious expressions of members of The Church of Jesus Christ of Latter-day Saints, as with religious people everywhere. It is also a prescribed element of prayer (D&C 46:32).

In ancient times MOSES offered sacrifices of thanksgiving (Lev. 7:11–13) and King Hezekiah gave "thank offerings" (2 Chr. 29:30–31). Ascribed to David are the Talmud's One Hundred Daily Benedictions that begin with "Blessed are thou, O Lord, our God, King of the Universe!" and express gratitude for common as well as exceptional activities, enjoyments, natural phenomena, and encounters with remarkable persons. Upon receiving good news or blessings, the Hebrews uttered appreciation for God's munificence; when experiencing trials they thanked God because he is just.

Jesus memorably taught the appropriateness of gratitude after he healed ten lepers on his way to Jerusalem. When only one of the ten, a Samaritan, gave earnest thanks, Christ commented, "Were there not ten cleansed? but where are the nine?" (Luke 17:11–19). Later, Paul emphasized that the righteous should "in every thing give thanks: for this is the will of God in Christ Jesus concerning you" (1 Thes. 5:18).

In the Book of Mormon the prophet ALMA2 admonished Christ's followers to acquire his attributes, among them, "asking for whatsoever things ye stand in need, both spiritual and temporal; always returning thanks unto God for whatsoever things ye do receive" (Alma 7:23). Modern scripture promises that "he who receiveth all things with thankfulness shall be made glorious" (D&C 78:19), and that "in nothing doth man offend God, or against none is his wrath kindled, save those who confess not his hand in all things, and obey not his commandments" (D&C 59:21). Thankfulness is to be offered for "all things" received from the Lord whether or not, from limited human understanding, they initially appear to be blessings.

Although thankfulness is most commonly communicated through prayer, a revelation given to Brigham YOUNG counsels, "If thou art merry, praise the Lord with singing, with music, with dancing, and with a prayer of praise and thanksgiving" (D&C 136:28). Additional appropriate means for expressing thanksgiving include singing hymns (the Latter-day Saints Hymnal lists twenty-seven titles under the topic of "gratitude"); participating in regular Church worship services; commemorating such religious holidays as Easter, Christmas, and Thanksgiving; having a devout personal life characterized by a repentant spirit and righteous works; and showing love toward others.

BIBLIOGRAPHY

Faust, James E. "Gratitude as a Saving Principle." *Ensign* 20 (May 1990):85-87.

GARY L. BROWNING

THEODICY

Theodicy is the attempt to explain God's goodness and power and reconcile these with the evident evil in the created world. Since most theologians and religious philosophers in the West have assumed both God's unconditional power and his absolute goodness, the existence and persistence of evil are often held to be inexplicable. In recent centuries the absence of a convincing theodicy and

the frequent theological resort to mystery as an explanation have led many to atheism.

Latter-day Saint scriptural sources have reshaped certain dimensions of the problem and its resolution.

SELF-EXISTENCE AND OMNIPOTENCE. Traditionally, the affirmation of God's sovereign power is expressed philosophically by the concept of "omnipotence," which means that God can do absolutely anything at all, or at least anything "logically possible." This often accompanies the dogma that all that is was created ex nihilo (from nothing) by God. The conclusion follows that all forms of evil, even the "demonic dimension," must be directly or indirectly God-made.

In Latter-day Saint sources, God is not the only self-existent reality. The CREATION ACCOUNTS and other texts teach that God is not a fiat creator but an organizer and life-giver, that the "pure principles of element" can be neither created nor destroyed (D&C 93; *TPJS*, p. 351), and that the undergirdings of eternal law, with certain "bounds and conditions," are coexistent with him (cf. D&C 88:34–45). "Omnipotence," then, means God has all the power it is possible to have in a universe—actually a pluriverse—of these givens. He did not create evil.

APPEARANCE AND REALITY. Often omnipotence is taken to mean that God is able to overrule or overcome whatever lesser powers interfere with his sovereign will. This view still leaves God responsible for everything that occurs, just as it occurs. It follows that if God is truly good, then, despite appearances, all that happens must be good, however horrible the "good" may seem for human beings. "Evil" then is held to be privative (an absence), simply in the human mind, or a matter of perspective. The conclusion follows that this is the best of all possible worlds. But the problem then arises all over again, for why does not God exercise his power to remove the pain that arises from mortal misunderstanding?

Latter-day Saint scripture teaches unmistakably that such things as sin and sinfulness, ignorance, deformity, disease, and death are real. As they and their effects continue to increase and prevail, then even from the perspective of God, this is a less than perfect world. Another realm is conceivable where these evils in individual and community life have been overcome.

INVIOLATE FREEDOM. Traditional thought has often held that God limits his own power for the greater good. Usually this view is associated with insistence on the importance of human freedom. Character and personality, it is argued, can develop only if human beings are genuinely free. Likewise, God's love, if authentic, must be voluntary. These goods are held to outweigh the evil introduced by free agents into the world, even when the consequences are terribly destructive. Mormon thought concurs. Creation is indeed a "vale of soul making." Experiences of contrast are indispensable to knowledge and growth (2 Ne. 2; D&C 122). God's self-limitation is essential to the attainment of his purpose. Moreover, God not only will not but cannot ultimately coerce men to choose life over death. "All intelligence . . . is free to act for itself in that sphere in which God has placed it. . . . Behold, here is the agency of man and here is the condemnation of man" (D&C 93:30–31). God can bring good out of the experience of evil to the degree that his creatures harmonize their will with his and continue to seek, affirm, and embrace him. In that cooperative mode, he can, and will, enable all his creatures to become what they have it in them to become (D&C 88:14–40).

NATURAL EVIL AND THE NATURE OF POWER. It is commonly observed that not all evil is caused by human beings. Earthquakes, epidemics, plagues, volcanic eruptions, and other natural disasters occur. Furthermore, these and some evils caused by human aberration are of such magnitude as to call for divine intervention. The Holocaust is a glaring modern instance. Such considerations underscore the scriptural teaching that although God has power over the elements, and though there is divine intervention, divine influence over human beings is never "controlling" or "manipulating"; it is liberating, empowering, and persuading. This is the power continuously exercised by God, even in the midst of tragedy and affliction. It is the power most to be sought and most to be emulated.

"No power or influence," says the Doctrine and Covenants of the uses of authority, "can or ought to be maintained . . . [except] by persuasion, by long-suffering, by gentleness and meekness, and by love unfeigned" (D&C 121:41). Indeed, in the exercise of power "without compulsory means," it is not enough to say that man needs God. It is also the case, and eternally, that God needs man.

CREATIVE COMPLICITY. Some contemporary movements affirm either that human beings emerged from a long and mindless process of evolution or that they have been "thrown" or thrust into the world. Either way, creatures exist without their permission in a predicament not of their own making. Latter-day Saint thought returns to the oft-forgotten scriptural thesis that all mankind participated in the original plan of life and prepared for the hazards and traumas waiting in this world. In an act of faith and foresight, the entire human family elected to enter mortality. For Latter-day Saints the cumulative witness of sacred texts, ancient and modern, is that, with rare exceptions, every person who ever lived will have benefited from the mortal sojourn and from embodiment.

JOHN COBB, JR.
TRUMAN G. MADSEN

THEOGONY

Theogony refers to the origin of God and has been a subject of religious inquiry throughout the ages. Ancient peoples, notably Sumerians, Egyptians, Greeks, and Romans, developed elaborate genealogies for their various gods, rationalizing and mythologizing the birth and characteristics of each. This is in contrast to the monotheistic, Judeo-Christian view that God is eternal, uncaused, and without origin. The traditional argument states that if every effect has a cause, there must be a first cause that has always existed, and that is God.

The LDS theogonic view is unlike all others. It is based on a doctrine of eternal existence of all intelligent beings (D&C 93:29) coupled with a belief in their eternal progression (see D&C 93:13–14). By embracing truth and light, uncreated intelligence is capable of growing in knowledge, power, and organization until it arrives at the glorified state of GODHOOD, being one with God (see DEIFICATION). This process known as eternal progression is succinctly expressed in the LDS aphorism, "As man is, God once was. As God is, man may become" (Lorenzo SNOW). Adam was told by God, "Thou art after the order of him who was without beginning of days or end of years, from all eternity to all eternity. Behold, thou art one in me, a son of God; and thus may all become my sons" (Moses 6:67–68).

CHARLES R. HARRELL

THEOLOGY

The traditional task of theology (from the Greek *theos*, god, and *logos*, study of) is to seek understanding of God's reality, to describe divine things rationally, and to elaborate the present meaning of past manifestations of God, whether theoretically, practically, descriptively, or critically. Since scriptures and specific REVELATIONS supply Latter-day Saints with authoritative answers to many of the traditional concerns of faith, members of the Church tend to devote little energy to theoretical, speculative, or systematic theology. For Latter-day Saints, faith is anchored in revelations that occurred in history (*see* HISTORY, SIGNIFICANCE OF). From the perspective of the restored gospel, what can be known about divine things must be revealed by God. Though rationally structured, coherent, and ordered, the content of Latter-day Saint faith is not the fruit of speculation, nor has it been deduced from premises or derived from philosophical or scientific inquiries into the nature of things.

The word "theology" and much of what it describes originated with Plato, Aristotle, and the Orphics. The word is not found in the Bible or other LDS scriptures. What is typically understood as theology within Christianity was introduced by Origen (A.D. 185–254) and developed by Augustine (A.D. 354–430). Latter-day Saints have little interest in theology in the sense of trying to discover divine things with the unaided resources of the human mind. Even when theology is seen as essentially descriptive or apologetic, it is not entirely at home in the LDS community.

Not having what has traditionally been understood as theology, Latter-day Saints instead have texts that describe theophanies and special revelations and contain inspired teachings, along with several accounts of God's establishing his covenant people, usually coupled with accounts of a dialectic of obedience and disobedience that followed such events. These accounts may be said to contain "theology," but not in the sense that their meaning is discovered by human ingenuity instead of disclosed through the proclaimed word and will of God.

The core of faith is not a confession to a creed but a personal witness that Jesus of Nazareth is the Christ (*see* RELIGIOUS EXPERIENCE; TESTIMONY). Events such as the Prophet Joseph Smith's FIRST VISION and belief in continuing contact between God and his prophets anchor Latter-day Saint beliefs, allowing those beliefs to be both clearly identified and adapted to changing circumstances. This leaves little room for systematic treatises intended to fix, order, and settle the understanding of the believers, though it does allow room for reason as a tool for attaining coherence and for working out implications in the revelations (*see* REASON AND REVELATION).

Nor is the Book of Mormon a theological treatise. Instead, it is a long and tragic history, filled with prophetic warnings about deviations from covenants with God. In this sacred text, the gospel of Jesus Christ—beginning with faith, repentance, baptism, and the gift of the HOLY GHOST—provides the foundation for all other beliefs. According to the plan of God, those who genuinely comply and endure to the end will eventually be saved in the kingdom of God. As both ground and substance of LDS faith, these points of doctrine are understood as realities, not as matters of conjecture. It is a mistake to see them (or what is built upon them "line by line" through additional divine revelation) as "theology," as that term is generally understood among Christians. Since the texts setting forth the gospel or doctrine of Jesus Christ are rooted in events that Latter-day Saints believe actually happened, it is in exegetical and historical work that both the explication and the defense of the faith usually take place.

Latter-day Saints can scarcely be said to have much in the way of a dogmatic theology, though they sometimes informally borrow a Christian tendency to designate the whole of their beliefs and dogma by the label "theology." Some of the early leaders, coming as they did from sectarian backgrounds, seem to have felt a need for something approaching an orderly and authoritative setting forth of their beliefs. What they produced were initially called theological lectures (*see* LECTURES ON FAITH), and they seem to have been modeled after formal treatises like those by Charles G. Finney (1792–1875) or Alexander Campbell (1788–1866). But the formal methodology of these seven lectures has not been much adopted by other LDS writers.

The early Latter-day Saints were fond of the word "theology," and it turns up conspicuously in some of their writings. A well-known example is Parley P. Pratt's *A Key to the Science of Theology* (1855), in which he defined theology as "the science of communication, or of correspondence, between God, angels, spirits, and men, by means of visions, dreams, interpretations, conversations, inspirations, or the spirit of prophecy and revelation." For Pratt, theology embraced all principles and powers upon which the worlds are organized, sustained, reformed, and redeemed: "It is the science of all other sciences and useful arts" (pp. 1–2). Such books have filled a need for a seemingly orderly explication of what was believed to have been revealed through Joseph Smith and for an indication of how to apply those revelations "in the duties of life" (AF, p. 5). To some extent, such works approach systematic theology, in that they are concerned with identifying truth, its structure, correspondences, and unity. These volumes have dogmatic dimensions with respect to the attributes and roles of God, his government, the creation, redemption, eschatology, and the like. They are also concerned with scrutinizing moral aspects of human life, free actions, suffering, ignorance, and sin. But their authors do not approach these topics by the use of reason unaided by revelation, nor are they considered officially authoritative by Latter-day Saints.

The desire for definitive answers to a host of vexing and unsettled questions has been satisfied in the present era by books like Bruce R. McConkie's *Mormon Doctrine*. This book did not derive from a philosophical culture, as did much of traditional Christian theology. It is more nearly an instance of what those outside of Mormon circles would label as dogmatic, rather than formal or systematic, theology. Such compendia have no official standing and represent the opinions of their authors. Their pronouncements, however, are popular among some in the Church.

Some LDS teachings have been set forth in a seemingly philosophical framework by Sterling M. McMurrin, who has attempted to show how classical philosophy and Christian theology might be accommodated to what he defines as the metaphysics inherent in LDS teachings. Still, he discounts divine revelation, does not take the LDS approach to EPISTEMOLOGY seriously, and looks instead for signs of naturalism and humanism. Thus, his views are incomprehensible to many Latter-day Saints, since he diverts attention away from historical matters and the crucial prophetic claims upon which the Latter-day Saint faith rests.

Elements of McMurrin's stance have been appropriated by a few historians interested in trying to show that there has been a radical reconstruction of Mormon theology in its first 150 years, and that it has shifted from a pessimistic orthodoxy to an optimistic liberalism and back again toward a pessimistic neo-orthodoxy. Such explicitly theological literature seems selective, if not contrived or forced, and it has had virtually no impact on the life of believers. Instead, the influential scholarly works among Latter-day Saints tend to be either strictly historical or exegetical, though these works also have no official standing.

BIBLIOGRAPHY

For an elaboration of some of the themes addressed above, see Louis Midgley, "Prophetic Messages or Dogmatic Theology?" *Review of Books on the Book of Mormon* 1 (1989):92–113. For investigations from a Latter-day Saint perspective of the differences between the prophetic and theological approaches to matters of faith, see Hugh W. Nibley, *The World and the Prophets*, in CWHN 3; likewise, M. Gerald Bradford, "On Doing Theology," *BYU Studies* 14 (Spring 1974):345–58. For an attempt to cast LDS beliefs in traditional theological terminology and then to compare and contrast those formulations with the views of various philosophers and theologians, see Sterling M. McMurrin, *The Theological Foundations of the Mormon Religion* (Salt Lake City, 1965). The historical grounds and tendencies of early Latter-day Saints to eschew systematic treatises and formal theology are discussed by Richard L. Bushman, *Joseph Smith and the Beginnings of Mormonism* (Urbana, Ill., 1984).

For a fine brief introduction to theology, see Yves Congar, "Christian Theology," in *Encyclopedia of Religion*, Vol. 14, pp. 455–64 (New York, 1987). For more detailed treatments, see Brian Hebblethwaite, *The Problems of Theology* (Cambridge, 1980); Theodore W. Jennings, Jr., *Introduction to Theology* (Philadelphia, 1976); and Wolfhart Pannenberg, *Theology and the Philosophy of Science* (Philadephia, 1976).

LOUIS C. MIDGLEY

"THIS IS THE PLACE" MONUMENT

This monument depicts a dramatic moment in western and Church history. Brigham YOUNG entered the Great Salt Lake Valley on July 24, 1847, and said, according to Church tradition, "This is the right place."

In 1915 a committee including George Albert Smith, an apostle, and Church historians B. H. Roberts and Andrew Jenson identified the approximate spot at the mouth of Emigration Canyon where Brigham Young might have first seen the Salt Lake Valley and made his famous pronouncement. They placed a small board as a marker there that July.

One year later, a larger wooden marker was erected with the inscription "This is the place." In

The figures on the "This Is the Place" monument overlook the Salt Lake Valley from the mouth of Emigration Canyon. The monument, sculpted by Mahonri M. Young, was dedicated in 1947. On the monument are statues of Brigham Young, Wilford Woodruff, and Heber C. Kimball (top), along with sculptures of other pioneers and trail blazers. Courtesy Special Collections Department, University of Utah Libraries.

1921 the Young Men's Mutual Improvement Association dedicated a cast stone marker at the same location and denominated the area Pioneer View.

In 1937 a more imposing monument was conceived and created by a state commission composed of persons of various faiths, in anticipation of the 1947 centennial celebration. Mahonri M. Young, a grandson of Brigham Young, was selected as sculptor. The monument is built of Utah granite, the rectangular base is 206 feet long and supports a centered 60-foot-high pylon surmounted by the bronze figures of Brigham Young, Heber C. Kimball, and Wilford Woodruff, each 12.5 feet high. On the pylon and base are seventeen bronze friezes depicting an Indian chief, Spanish and U.S.

government explorers, trappers, groups of pioneers, and a wagon train. Two statuary groups, one at either end, symbolize the Dominguez-Escalante exploring party of 1776 and a group of mountainmen and trappers.

The monument, which cost $450,000, was dedicated on July 24, 1947, by Church President George Albert Smith. Today it is part of Pioneer Memorial State Park, a 221-acre area at the mouth of Emigration Canyon.

BIBLIOGRAPHY

Lyon, T. Edgar. *This Is the Place Monument, Story and History* (pamphlet). Salt Lake City, 1955.

Roberts, B. H. "Monument at Pioneer View." *IE* 24 (Sept. 1921):958–78.

"'This Is the Place' Monument Dedication." *IE* 50 (Sept. 1947):570–71, 627.

JAMES L. KIMBALL, JR.

THREE NEPHITES

LDS stories of the Three Nephites comprise one of the most striking religious legend cycles in the United States. Bearing some resemblance to stories of the prophet Elijah in Jewish lore, or of the Christian saints in the Catholic tradition, Three Nephite accounts are nevertheless distinctly Mormon. Part of a much larger body of LDS traditional narratives (*see* FOLKLORE), these stories are not official doctrine and are not published in official literature. They are based on the Book of Mormon account of Christ's granting to three Nephite disciples, during his visit to the New World following his death and resurrection, the same wish he had earlier granted to JOHN the Beloved—to "tarry in the flesh" in order to bring souls to him until his second coming (John 21:22; 3 Ne. 28:4–9). The Book of Mormon account states: "And they [the Three Nephites] are as the angels of God, and . . . can show themselves unto whatsoever man it seemeth them good. Therefore, great and marvelous works shall be wrought by them, before the great and coming day [of judgment]" (3 Ne. 28:30–31; *see also* BOOK OF MORMON: THIRD NEPHI).

As the newly founded Church grew in numbers, an ever-increasing body of stories began circulating among the people, telling of kindly old men, usually thought to be these ancient Nephite disciples, who had appeared to individuals in physical or spiritual distress, helped them solve their problems, and then suddenly disappeared.

Because they span a century and a half of LDS history, these narratives mirror well the changing physical and social environments in which Latter-day Saints have met their tests of faith. For example, in pre–World War II agrarian society, the stories told of Nephites' guiding pioneer trains to water holes, saving a rancher from a blizzard, providing herbal remedies for illnesses, plowing a farmer's field so that he could attend to Church duties, or delivering food to starving missionaries. In the contemporary world, the stories tell of Nephites' leading LDS genealogists to difficult library resources, pulling a young man from a lake after a canoeing accident and administering artificial respiration, stopping to fix a widow's furnace, guiding motorists lost in blizzards, comforting a woman who has lost her husband and daughter in an airplane crash, and pulling missionaries from a flaming freeway crash.

Even though the settings of the newer stories have moved from pioneer villages with a country road winding past to urban settings with freeways sounding noisily in the background, some circumstances have remained constant. In the stories, the Three Nephites continue to bless people and, in telling these stories, Latter-day Saints continue to testify to the validity of Church teachings and to encourage obedience to them. The stories continue to provide the faithful with a sense of security in an unsure world, persuading them that just as God helped righteous pioneers overcome a hostile physical world, so will he help the faithful endure the evils of urban society. Taken as a whole, then, the stories continue to provide understanding of the hearts and minds of Latter-day Saints and of the beliefs that move them to action.

BIBLIOGRAPHY

Lee, Hector. *The Three Nephites: The Substance and Significance of the Legend in Folklore.* University of New Mexico Publication in Language and Literature, no. 2. Albuquerque, N.M., 1949.

Wilson, William A. "Freeways, Parking Lots, and Ice Cream Stands: The Three Nephites in Contemporary Society." *Dialogue* 21 (Fall 1988):13–26.

WILLIAM A. WILSON

TIME AND ETERNITY

In Latter-day Saint understanding, time and eternity usually refer to the same reality. Eternity is time with an adjective: It is endless time. Eternity is not, as in Platonic and Neoplatonic thought, supratemporal or nontemporal.

In religions where eternity is radically contrasted with time, time is seen as an illusion, or utterly subjective, or an ephemeral episode. God and the higher realities are held to be "beyond." This is still the premise of much classical mysticism, Christian and non-Christian, as it is of absolutistic metaphysics. It is written into many Christian creeds.

But scriptural passages that ascribe eternity to God do not say or imply that God is independent of, or outside of, or beyond time. Nor do they say, with Augustine, that God created time out of nothing. In context they stress that he is everlasting, that he is trustworthy, that his purposes do not fail.

The view that time and eternity are utterly incompatible, utterly irreconcilable, has taxing consequences for theology. If God is supratemporal, for example, he could not have been directly related to the Creation because being out of time— and also beyond space and not subject to change— he could not enter this or any process. Theories of emanation were thus introduced to maintain God as static Being, and intermediaries were postulated as agents of creation, for example, intelligences, hosts, pleromas, etc.

In LDS understanding, God was and is directly involved in creation. The creative act was a process (the book of Abraham speaks of creation "times" rather than of "days"). His influence on creation, then and now, is not seen as a violation of his transcendence or of his glory and dominion but a participative extension of them.

The dogma of a supratemporal eternity led to another set of contradictions in postbiblical thought, the paradoxes of incarnation. The coming of Jesus Christ was recast within the assumptions of Greek metaphysics: God the universal became particular; God the nontemporal became temporal; God, superior to change, changed; God, who created time, now entered it. Most Christian traditions have embraced these paradoxes, but LDS thought has not. In LDS Christology, Jesus was in time before he entered mortality, is in time now, and will be forever.

Whatever the subtleties of the ultimate nature of time, or of scientific postulates on the relativity of time, and of the modes of measuring time, several assurances are prominent features of LDS understanding:

1. Time is a segment of eternity. One may distinguish eternities, long epochs of time, within eternity. Influenced by passages in the writings of Abraham and Enoch, some early LDS leaders speculated on the length of an eternity. One (W. W. Phelps) suggested that time "in our system" began two billion five hundred million years ago (*T&S*, Vol. 5, No. 24, p. 758). In any case, time itself had no beginning and will have no end.

2. Time unfolds in one direction. It extends rather than repeats precisely. The view of eternal recurrence common in the Far East that leads, for example, to the pessimism of Schopenhauer, is rejected. Worlds and world systems may come and go, as civilizations may rise and fall, but history does not exactly repeat itself. Individual creative freedom modifies the outcomes.

3. Eternity, as continuing time, is tensed: past, present, and future. God himself, eternal in identity, self-existent, and therefore without beginning or end, is nevertheless related to time. At his own supreme and unsurpassable level, he has a past, a present, and a future. Neither he nor his creations can return to or change the past. He has become what he is through eons of time gone by. He is now in relation to, and responsive to, his creations. Response implies time and change.

4. In a cosmic sense, the reckoning of time is according to the rotations of the spheres. It is presumed that God, angels, men, and prophets reckon time differently (see Abr. 3; D&C 130:4). There is some connection between time and space, for example, "one day to a cubit" (*see* BOOK OF ABRAHAM: FACSIMILES FROM THE BOOK OF ABRAHAM, Facsimile 2, Figure 1).

5. The eternal is sometimes contrasted to time as the permanent is contrasted to the transitory. "Every principle proceeding from God is eternal" (*TPJS*, p. 181). The phrase "for time and eternity" is equivalent to "now and forever." LDS thought is uncommon in the Christian world in its affirmation that intelligence, truth, the "principles of element," priesthood, law, covenants, and ordinances are eternal.

6. Time is occasionally used in scripture as a synonym for mortality. In this sense, the time will come when "time shall be no longer" (D&C 84:100; 88:110). The mortal probation will end. But another segment of measurable existence will follow, namely, the Millennium. Time and eternity also function as place names or situations as in such expressions as "not only here but in eternity," or "the visions of eternity" (heaven). Eternal is also the name of God—"endless and eternal is my name"—hence, eternal life is God's life, as it is also everlasting life (*HC* 1:136; cf. D&C 19:10–12; Moses 1:3; 7:35).

The thesis that God is beyond time has sometimes been introduced to account for God's omniscience or foreknowledge. Only if God is somehow transtemporal, it is argued, can he view past, present, and future as "one eternal now." This position is assumed by much postbiblical theology. But, again, this leads to contradiction: What will happen in the infinite future is now happening to God. But "now" and "happening" are temporal words that imply both duration and change. For Latter-day Saints, as for the Bible, God's omniscience is "in time." God anticipates the future. It is "present" before him, but it is still future. When the future occurs, it will occur for the first time to him as to his creatures. The traditional concept of "out-of-time" omniscience does not derive either from the Old or the New Testament but is borrowed from Greek philosophy.

BIBLIOGRAPHY

Kenney, Anthony. "Divine Foreknowledge and Human Freedom." In *Aquinas*, pp. 255–70. Garden City, N.Y., 1967.

Robson, Kent E. "Omnipotence, Omnipresence, and Omniscience in Mormon Theology." In *Line Upon Line: Essays on Mormon Doctrine*, ed G. J. Bergera. Salt Lake City, 1989.

KENT E. ROBSON

TIMES AND SEASONS

The journalistic voice of The Church of Jesus Christ of Latter-day Saints in Nauvoo, Illinois, the *Times and Seasons*, was published in 135 issues of sixteen pages each between November 1839 and February 1846. It was a monthly from November 1839 to October 1840, then a biweekly, issued, about the first and the fifteenth of each month, until February 15, 1846. It was the fourth major semiofficial newspaper published by the Church. During the seven months in 1842 that the Prophet Joseph SMITH was the editor, he published several important documents of Mormon history in its pages: the translation and facsimiles of the BOOK OF ABRAHAM, the WENTWORTH LETTER, and the early segments of the HISTORY OF THE CHURCH.

The *Times and Seasons* was first established and edited by Don Carlos Smith, Joseph Smith's youngest brother, and Ebenezer Robinson for the Saints who had been scattered by the MISSOURI CONFLICT and were anxious "to learn of the condition and welfare of the Church." They proposed to publish "all general information respecting the Church" (*T&S* 1 [Nov. 1839]:16). This included Church news and history, world news and history, political and literary materials, Nauvoo city news, obituaries, announcements, doctrinal expositions, conference reports, mission reports, letters from missionaries, and notices and trial minutes of excommunications. The *Times and Seasons* also responded to polemic and apologetic treatment of Mormonism by other newspapers in an attempt to establish goodwill and understanding.

In Nauvoo the press offices were first located in a warehouse basement at Water and Bain (Fifth) streets. The operations of the newspaper later moved to the new, brick *Times and Seasons* Printing Office building at Kimball and Main (Seventh) streets, which is now restored in Nauvoo.

John TAYLOR and Wilford WOODRUFF, both apostles and later Presidents of the Church, edited the paper from late 1842 until April 1844, and then John Taylor edited it alone until its last issue on February 15, 1846, just before the Saints left Nauvoo on their exodus west.

BIBLIOGRAPHY

Bray, Robert T. "*Times and Seasons*: An Archaeological Perspective on Early Latter Day Saints Printing." *Historical Archaeology* 13 (1979):53–119.

Sorensen, Parry D. "Nauvoo *Times and Seasons*." *Journal of the Illinois State Historical Society* 55 (1962):117–35.

REED C. DURHAM, JR.

TITHING

Tithing is the basic contribution by which Latter-day Saints fund the activities of the Church. By revelation to the Prophet Joseph SMITH, the Lord stated that members should pay "one-tenth of all

Printing Office Complex in Nauvoo, Illinois. In 1907, the Times and Seasons building (left) was used as an LDS meetinghouse. It has been restored as a part of the restoration of historic Nauvoo. Photographer George E. Anderson.

their interest [increase] annually; and this shall be a standing law unto them forever" (D&C 119:4).

The law of tithing has ancient origins. The word "tithe" means "tenth" and connotes a tenth part of something given as a voluntary contribution. Abraham paid tithes to Melchizedek (Gen. 14:18–20; Alma 13:14–15). Jacob also covenanted to pay a tenth of everything the Lord gave him (Gen. 28:20–22). Tithing was a fundamental part of the law of Moses (Lev. 27:30–32; Num. 18:25–28; Deut. 26:12–14) and was used in support of priests, holy edifices, and sanctuaries (Amos 4:4).

The prophet Malachi underscored the seriousness of paying tithes:

> Will a man rob God? Yet ye have robbed me . . . in tithes and offerings. Ye are cursed . . . for ye have robbed me. . . . Bring ye all the tithes into the storehouse . . . and prove me . . . if I will not open you the windows of heaven, and pour you out a blessing, that there shall not be room enough to receive it [Mal. 3:8–10].

The Deseret Store and Tithing Office of Salt Lake City, located east of Temple Square, in 1861. At this time, Brigham Young encouraged Church members to pay tithing in U.S. currency whenever possible, but tithing often had to be paid in produce or labor. Tithing offices served at this time somewhat as general stores. Photographer: Marsena Cannon.

The collection of tithing is the responsibility of the BISHOP in each ward. Tithes are presented confidentially to him or his counselors. He forwards the tithes collected locally to Church headquarters, where a committee consisting of the FIRST PRESIDENCY, the PRESIDING BISHOPRIC, and the QUORUM OF THE TWELVE APOSTLES supervises the distribution and expenditure of tithing funds (D&C 120). These funds are used for such purposes as the building and maintenance of meetinghouses, temples, and other facilities, as well as for the partial support of the missionary, educational, and welfare programs of the Church.

At the end of each year, ward members meet individually with their bishop in a tithing settlement interview to verify Church records of their individual contributions and to declare confidentially to the bishop whether or not the amount contributed is a "full tithe."

The common mode of tithing payment is by cash. However, when income has been received in some other form, the member may pay accordingly, as was done anciently (Lev. 27:30, 32). In its early years the Church maintained "tithing houses" to receive payments in grain, livestock, vegetables, and fruits.

A 1970 letter from the First Presidency stated that notwithstanding the fact that members should pay one-tenth of their income, "every member of the Church is entitled to make his own decision as

to what he thinks he owes the Lord and to make payment accordingly" (Mar. 19, 1970; cf. Doxey, pp. 16, 18). Hence, the exact amount paid is not as important as that each member feels that he or she has paid an honest tenth.

As part of the latter-day restoration of the gospel, the law of tithing was reestablished. Joseph Smith and Oliver COWDERY initiated implementation of the principle in 1834, when they pledged one-tenth of all the Lord should give them as an offering for the poor (HC 2:174–75). In 1838 the Prophet inquired about tithing for the Church (HC 3:44) and received the law, now published as Section 119 of the Doctrine and Covenants. The term "tithing" had been used in some revelations before 1838 (e.g., D&C 64:23; 85:3; 97:11–12) but connoted all free-will offerings or contributions, whether they were less or more than 10 percent.

Prior to the revelation on tithing, an adaptation of the law of CONSECRATION of property was practiced by the Church to care for the poor, to purchase lands, and to build Church facilities (D&C 42:30–39). The declared spiritual object of that law was to "advance the cause" of "the salvation of man" (D&C 78:4–7) by creating equality in both "earthly things" and "heavenly things." This proved too difficult at the time, especially under the disruptive conditions suffered by Church members in Missouri, and the practice was temporarily suspended in 1840 (HC 4:93). The law of tithing was given in part to fulfill material needs and to prepare the membership of the Church to live the material aspects of the law of consecration at some future time. Tithing has variously been described as the donation of (1) a tenth of what people owned when they converted; (2) a tenth of their "increase" or income each year; and (3) one workday in ten of their labor, teams, and tools to public projects. Today, tithe payers pay a tenth of their "increase," or income.

Although many in the early decades of the Church were slow to obey the principle and practice of tithing, leaders continued to affirm the obligatory nature of the commandment. In January 1845 the Quorum of the Twelve Apostles under the direction of President Brigham YOUNG issued an epistle reminding the Saints of their duty to pay tithing (*HC* 7:358). In 1881 obedience to the law of tithing became a requirement for temple attendance (*JD* 22:207–208) for those with an income. In May 1899 a manifestation was given to President Lorenzo SNOW that even though the Church was beleaguered by financial difficulties, it was nonetheless bound by the law of tithing, as were its members individually, and all would be blessed materially and spiritually by heeding it (Snow, p. 439).

As with all commandments, there is a correlation between observance of the law of tithing and blessings or punishments. The promises to the obedient are great, but the revelation also warns, "It shall come to pass that all . . . shall observe this law, or they shall not be found worthy to abide among you" (D&C 119:5). President Joseph F. SMITH taught that the disobedient "have cut themselves off from the blessings of Zion," but added that the Lord will fulfill his rich promises to the faithful tithe payers of the Church (*GD*, pp. 225–27). "A host of testimonies might be secured of the joy in life that follows obedience to this important law of the Lord" (Widtsoe, Vol. 1, p. 228). President Heber J. Grant counseled the Church that obedience to the law of tithing provides a protective shield (D&C 64:23–24) from economic distress (pp. 59–60).

[*See also* Bishop, History of the Office.]

BIBLIOGRAPHY

Doxey, Roy W. *Tithing: The Lord's Law.* Salt Lake City, 1976.

Grant, Heber J. *Gospel Standards.* Salt Lake City, 1941.

Kimball, Spencer W. "Tithing." In *Faith Precedes the Miracle*, pp. 281–90. Salt Lake City, 1975.

Snow, LeRoi C. "The Lord's Way Out of Bondage." *IE* 41 (July 1938):400–401, 439–42.

Widtsoe, John A. *Evidences and Reconciliations*, 3 vols. Salt Lake City, 1943.

HOWARD D. SWAINSTON

TOBACCO

Devout Latter-day Saints do not use tobacco in any of its forms. They abstain because of an 1833 revelation known as the WORD OF WISDOM, which states that tobacco is "not for the body, neither for the belly, and is not good for man," except as a poultice for bruises and treating "all sick cattle" (D&C 89:8).

The Word of Wisdom was originally given to show the will of God, but not as a commandment. Abstinence from tobacco was expected of all fully participating Church members by the early twentieth century (*see* DOCTRINE AND COVENANTS: SECTION 89).

Tobacco contains nicotine, which is a cerebral and vascular stimulant. The burning of the tobacco leaf also releases and produces a large number of chemicals, many of which are absorbed by the body and are known to cause cancer and other serious diseases.

BIBLIOGRAPHY

U.S. Department of Health and Human Services, Public Health Service, Centers for Disease Control, Center for Chronic Disease Prevention and Health Promotion, Office on Smoking and Health. *Reducing the Health Consequences of Smoking: 25 Years of Progress. A Report of the Surgeon General.* DHHS Publication No. (CDC) 89-8411. Rockville, Md., 1989.

Wilson, J. D., et al., eds. *Harrison's Principles of Internal Medicine*, 12th ed., pp. 2158–61. New York, 1991.

JOSEPH LYNN LYON

TOLERANCE

The LDS principles of tolerance are rooted in the teaching that all who have lived, now live, and will yet live on this earth are spirit children of God and are responsible only to God for their religious beliefs and practices. "We claim the privilege of worshipping Almighty God according to the dictates of our own conscience," says Article of Faith 11, "and allow all men the same privilege, let them worship, how, where or what they may."

A corollary of this statement is a declaration of belief regarding governments and law, adopted by the Church in 1835. It affirms that governments have no power to prescribe rules of worship to bind the consciences of men or to dictate forms for public or private devotion. In matters of religion, the declaration asserts, "men are amenable to God and to Him only for the exercise of their religious beliefs, unless their religious opinions prompt them to infringe upon the rights and liberties of others" (D&C 134). The Church has maintained these principles while accommodating to secular authority: "We believe in being subject to kings, presidents, rulers, and magistrates, in obeying, honoring and sustaining the law" (A of F 12; cf. D&C 134:1–12).

Related to this is a doctrine of primordial individual freedom. For Latter-day Saints agency is indestructible. All truth is "independent in that sphere in which God has placed it, to act for itself, as all intelligence also" (D&C 93:30). The individual's freedom to search for this truth should not be contravened, and in the last analysis it cannot be. Even God cannot coerce belief. The only power justified on earth or in heaven is loving persuasion (D&C 121:41).

Intolerance often arises from sectarian conviction. But contrary to stereotypes, The Church of Jesus Christ of Latter-day Saints is neither a SECT nor a CULT. It has an extensive scriptural foundation, but no formalized CREEDS and no closed canon. As the Prophet Joseph SMITH said to Stephen A. Douglas, Latter-day Saints are "ready to believe all true principles that exist, as they are manifest from time to time" (HC 5:215). They are taught to "gather all the good and true principles in the world and treasure them up" (TPJS p. 316). Commitment to truth in this inclusive sense is commitment to the view that all philosophies, religions, and ethical systems have elements of truth and that all persons have a portion of light. This is a buttress for tolerance, goodwill, and fellowship on a worldwide scale (see WORLD RELIGIONS [NON-CHRISTIAN] AND MORMONISM). "If ye will not embrace our religion," Joseph Smith said, "embrace our hospitalities" (WJS 162).

The crucial need for tolerance has been impressed upon Latter-day Saints by the buffetings, persecutions, and drivings of their own history. In various places in the world they have sometimes been denied civil and even survival rights.

The Church itself has a long history of forbearance. The Prophet Joseph Smith taught that "the same principle that would trample upon the rights of the Latter-day Saints would trample upon the rights of the Roman Catholics, or of any other denomination. . . . If it has been demonstrated that I have been willing to die for a Mormon I am bold to declare before heaven that I am just as ready to die for a presbyterian, a baptist or any other denomination. It is a love of liberty which inspires my soul, civil and religious liberty. . . . " He added, "If I esteem mankind to be in error shall I bear them down? No. I will lift them up and in their own way, too, if I cannot persuade them my way is better" (TPJS, p. 313).

Within the Church two principles taught by Joseph Smith have prevailed: "I teach the people correct principles and they govern themselves" (JD 10:57–58), and, "It does not prove that a man is not a good man because he errs in doctrine" (HC 5:340).

Latter-day Saints today face the challenge of being a religious majority in some areas of the world and a minority in others. Tolerance is reinforced by its converts, who come from diverse religious and cultural backgrounds and by its hundreds of thousands of returned missionaries, who have, early in their lives, learned the languages, customs, and religious concerns of multiple cultures and peoples. Today as the Church grows in Latin America, Asia, and Africa, it faces new challenges to its commitment to tolerance and goodwill.

BIBLIOGRAPHY

Hunter, Howard W. "All Are Alike Unto God." In *Devotional Speeches of the Year, 1989*, pp. 32–36. Provo, Utah.

GEORGE ROMNEY

TOPICAL GUIDE

The Latter-day Saint edition of the Bible, first published in 1979, includes a 598-page "Topical Guide with Selected Concordance and Index." It is designed to aid SCRIPTURE STUDY and is considered by Latter-day Saints to be a major, unique reference tool.

The Topical Guide provides 3,495 categories citing about 50,000 verses from the Bible, the Book of Mormon, the Doctrine and Covenants, and the Pearl of Great Price. By bringing together references from all four STANDARD WORKS, the Topical Guide enables readers to see the unity and harmony of all these scriptures. It also shows how latter-day REVELATIONS bring greater clarity to the understanding of the word of God.

A preliminary topical guide, listing the main supporting scriptures for over 600 topics, which were selected initially with seminary students and young missionaries in mind, was published in 1977. Scripture references at first were gathered by about one hundred teachers in the CHURCH EDUCATIONAL SYSTEM, along with the same number of returned missionaries at BRIGHAM YOUNG UNIVERSITY, who were called to render this Church service. The original number of scriptural topics grew to about 750, and over 2,500 other concordance or index categories were also added. Several committees then collated, evaluated, and selected entries to be included in the current version.

All entries are arranged alphabetically. Parenthetical cross-references to related entries and to the BIBLE DICTIONARY follow the heading in many entries.

Citations within entries are listed in the following order: Bible, Book of Mormon, Doctrine and Covenants, Pearl of Great Price. Each citation gives the specific chapter and verse and a brief excerpt from the passage, with the key word italicized. If the key word is identical to the entry heading, only the initial letter appears. Each citation refers to a single verse, but readers are also alerted that surrounding verses may contribute to understanding.

After certain references, cross-references to other passages containing similar wording may appear in parentheses. This allows students to see relationships among similarly worded passages. If a student cannot find a citation in its expected sequence, it may be necessary to look back through earlier references for parenthetical cross-references. Some entries conclude with a brief list of additional passages.

As a concordance and index, the Topical Guide helps readers to locate specific verses on subjects of interest. (For people and places, the Topical Guide generally refers students to the Bible Dictionary). The Topical Guide goes beyond standard concordances with its topical dimension, bringing together pertinent references on common topics of interest to Latter-day Saints (such as "Faith," "Resurrection," or "Jesus Christ, Atonement through"), whether or not the relevant passages share the same specific key word. For example, the entry "Prayer, Pray" contains 176 references not only to verses with variations of *prayer* and *pray* but also to passages with such words as *call upon, inquire, ask,* and *seek*; in addition, cross-references are given to entries on "Communication," "Faith," "God, Access to," "Meditation," and "Supplication," as well as to the Bible Dictionary entry on prayer.

The Topical Guide is not exhaustive, however, either as a concordance or as a listing of all passages on given topics. Although by necessity it is selective and somewhat interpretive, its purpose is not to define or limit thinking but to stimulate scripture study and suggest profitable directions that study may take. It strives to offer not only a quick path to specific destinations but also a gateway to deeper acquaintance with the word of God.

The combined edition of the Book of Mormon, Doctrine and Covenants, and Pearl of Great Price published in 1981 also contains an expanded index, constructed on principles similar to those governing the Topical Guide.

BIBLIOGRAPHY

Anderson, Lavina Fielding. "Church Publishes First LDS Edition of the Bible." *Ensign* 9 (Oct. 1979):9–18.

Horton, George A. "I Have a Question." *Ensign* 16 (Apr. 1986):41.

Ludlow, Daniel H. *Marking the Scriptures*, pp. 41–43. Salt Lake City, 1980.

BRUCE T. HARPER

TRANSFIGURATION

Transfiguration for mortals consists of a temporary physical and spiritual change, allowing them not only to behold the glory of God but to enter his presence. It is characterized by illumination of countenance such as MOSES experienced (Moses 1:11; Ex. 34:29–35) and comes about by an infusion of God's power (*MD*, p. 725). Because God is a being of transcendent glory, it is impossible for men and women to enter his presence without their physical bodies being spiritually "quickened." The Prophet Joseph SMITH explained that God "dwells in eternal fire; flesh and blood cannot go there, for all corruption is devoured by the fire. 'Our God is a consuming fire'" (*TPJS*, p. 367; cf. Heb. 12:29; Deut. 4:24). Transfiguration bestows on individuals a temporary condition compatible to that of deity and allows them to see God face-to-face.

Modern REVELATION says that "no man has seen God at any time in the flesh, except quickened by the Spirit of God" (D&C 67:11). Soon after Moses' call, for example, he was transfigured so that he could withstand God's power; he later wrote: "His glory was upon me; and I beheld his face, for I was transfigured before him" (Moses 1:11). After God's spirit withdrew, Moses returned to his normal mortal condition and testified that he had beheld God with his own eyes, not however with his natural but with his spiritual or transfigured eyes. He explained that his "natural eyes could not have beheld; for I should have withered and died in [God's] presence" (Moses 1:10–11).

From time to time, other worthy persons have been transfigured. Jesus was transfigured before PETER, JAMES, and JOHN on the MOUNT OF TRANSFIGURATION so that "his face did shine as the sun, and his raiment was white as the light" (Matt. 17:2). On the same occasion, the APOSTLES were similarly changed, enabling them to remain in his transfigured presence (*TPJS*, p. 158). At the opening of the present DISPENSATION, Joseph Smith was spiritually quickened so that he could see both God the Father and his Son Jesus Christ and receive instruction from them. After seeing a transcendent brilliance descend upon him, the Prophet wrote: "When the light rested upon me I saw two Personages, whose brightness and glory defy all description, standing above me in the air" (JS—H 1:16–17). When the VISION of the three DEGREES OF GLORY was received, he and Sidney RIGDON were "in the Spirit," with the result that they "were enlightened, so as to see and understand the things of God" (D&C 76:11–12, 113–119; cf. D&C 110:1–4).

Transfiguration should not be confused with translation of the body, though both possibly affect the body in similar ways. Transfiguration describes a momentary change, whereas TRANSLATED BEINGS experience a long-term change that ends only when they pass from mortality to immortality (3 Ne. 28:8). Among those translated are ENOCH and the city ZION (Moses 7:18–23, 27; *MD*, p. 727), ELIJAH, the apostle JOHN (D&C 7), and the three Nephite disciples (3 Ne. 28:4–11, 15–40).

The EARTH itself will be transfigured at Christ's second coming. While on the Mount of Transfiguration the three apostles saw not only God's divine glory but also the earth in its transfigured state (cf. D&C 63:21; *TPJS*, p. 13). Modern revelation says that, through obedience and enduring to the end, faithful Saints will receive an inheritance upon the transformed earth when the millennial day arrives (D&C 63:20–21).

BIBLIOGRAPHY

McConkie, Bruce R. *The Mortal Messiah*, Vol. 4, pp. 392–96. Salt Lake City, 1981.

Turner, Rodney. "The Visions of Moses." In *Studies in Scripture*, ed. K. Jackson and R. Millet, Vol. 2, pp. 43–61. Salt Lake City, 1985.

DALE C. MOURITSEN

TRANSLATED BEINGS

Latter-day Saint scriptures speak of a unique class of beings, persons whom the Lord has "translated" or changed from a mortal state to one in which they are temporarily not subject to death, and in which they experience neither pain nor sorrow except for the sins of the world. Such beings appear to have much greater power than mortals. All translated beings will eventually experience physical death and RESURRECTION (*MD*, p. 807–808). Translation is a necessary condition in special instances to further the work of the Lord.

Translated beings are not resurrected beings, though all translated beings either have since been or yet will be resurrected or "changed in the twinkling of an eye" to a resurrected state (3 Ne. 28:8). In effect, this last change is their death, and they therefore receive what amounts to an instantaneous death and resurrection. Resurrection is a step beyond translation, and persons translated prior to the resurrection of Christ were resurrected with him (cf. D&C 133:54–55); it is expected that those translated since Christ's resurrection will be resurrected at his second coming.

During the period from Adam to MEL-CHIZEDEK, many faithful persons were translated. Enoch and the righteous residents of his city of Zion were translated not many years after Adam's death (Moses 7:18–21, 31, 63, 69; D&C 38:4; 45:11–14; 84:99–100; Gen. 5:22–24; Heb. 11:5). During the period from Enoch to Noah, it appears that faithful members of the Church were translated, for "the Holy Ghost fell on many, and they were caught up by the powers of heaven into Zion" (Moses 7:27).

After the Flood, others were also translated. In his inspired rendition of the Bible, Joseph SMITH tells of many who "were translated and taken up into heaven" (JST Gen. 14:32–34). Fewer translations apparently occurred in the New Testament era, though JOHN THE BELOVED (John 21: 20–23; D&C 7) and the THREE NEPHITES were translated (3 Ne. 28).

Translated beings are assigned special ministries, some to remain among mortals, as seems to be the case of John and the Three Nephites, or for other purposes, as in the case of MOSES and ELIJAH, who were translated in order to appear with physical bodies hundreds of years later on the MOUNT OF TRANSFIGURATION prior to the resurrection of Christ. Had they been spirits only, they could not have laid hands on the mortal Peter, James, and John (cf. D&C 129:3–8). Why those of Enoch's city were translated, we are not specifically informed, although the Prophet Joseph Smith explained the role of translated beings thus: "Many have supposed that the doctrine of translation was a doctrine whereby men were taken immediately into the presence of God, and into an eternal fullness, but this is a mistaken idea. Their place of habitation is that of the terrestrial order, and a place prepared for such characters He held in reserve to be ministering angels unto many planets, and who as yet have not entered into so great a fullness as those who are resurrected from the dead" (TPJS, p. 170).

The scriptures do not define differences between TRANSFIGURATION and translation, but it appears that transfiguration is more temporary, as in Matthew 17:1–9 and Moses 1:11, occurring primarily to permit one to behold spiritual things not possible in the mortal condition.

BIBLIOGRAPHY

Pratt, Orson. "The Doctrine of Translation." JD 17:146–49.

MARK L. MCCONKIE

TREE OF LIFE

Four images of the Tree of Life are significant for Latter-day Saints: in the GARDEN OF EDEN; in LEHI's vision (1 Ne. 8); the parable of ALMA₂ comparing the word to a seed that can grow to be "a

Izapa Stela 5, discovered in 1935 in southwestern Mexico near the Guatemalan border. This preclassic Mayan monument (c. 300 B.C. to A.D. 50) and parts of its imagery have been linked by some archaeologists to Lehi's dream (1 Ne. 8). Standing behind the stone with a native boy are (left to right) Ernest L. Wilkinson (president of Brigham Young University), Thomas S. Ferguson, Mark E. Petersen, Marion G. Romney, and one other person. Courtesy Rare Books and Manuscripts, Brigham Young University.

tree springing up unto everlasting life" (Alma 32:28–43); and the so-called Tree of Life Stone from pre-Hispanic Mexico.

From earliest times, people in many cultures have venerated trees because they are majestic and, compared to a person's life span, seemingly immortal. Groves were among the first places used for sacred rites, and many cultures envisioned the heavens supported by the branches of a giant tree whose roots led to the underworld and whose sturdy trunk formed the link between the two realms. The most important attribute ascribed to the Tree of Life by those for whom such a symbol existed was its ability to provide immortality to those who ate its fruit. The Tree of Life was present in the Garden of Eden (Gen. 2:9) and is a standard symbol in ancient TEMPLES, as well as in temples of The Church of Jesus Christ of Latter-day Saints. It will be present at the end and its fruit available to eat "for him that overcometh" (Rev. 2:7).

Lehi's vision conveys an unforgettable message of the need to "give heed to the word of God and remember to keep his commandments always in all things" (1 Ne. 15:25). In his vision, Lehi saw by a fountain of living waters a tree "whose fruit was desirable to make one happy" (1 Ne. 8:10). The tree represented "the love of God" (1 Ne. 11:25). A path led to the tree, and great numbers of people walked the path, but many became lost in a mist of darkness. A "rod of iron" ran along the path, and only those in the multitude who pressed "their way forward, continually holding fast to the rod" (1 Ne. 8:30), reached the tree and partook of the desired fruit.

Alma used the Tree of Life image to teach about the acquisition of faith in the word of God, which he compared to a seed. When planted in one's heart and "nourished with much care," it would grow in the believer to yield the same sweet and pure fruit described by Lehi. By diligence and patience, one can "feast upon [this fruit] even until ye are filled, that ye hunger not, neither shall ye thirst" (Alma 32:42). Other ancient texts also describe the faithful as trees in God's paradise (Ps. 1:3; Odes of Solomon 11).

Interest was generated among Latter-day Saints in the 1950s by the discovery of a pre-Columbian sculpture that bore a complex Tree of Life scene similar to those found in the ancient Near East. Izapa Stela 5, carved sometime between 100 B.C. and A.D. 100, portrays a large tree in full leaf, laden with fruit, and surrounded by several persons and objects, including water. Some investigators are convinced that the scene is a depiction of Lehi's vision; others are less certain, since the scene also contains items that are difficult to understand, such as triangles and U-shaped elements. The elaborate clothing and headdresses worn by the people, the various objects they hold, and an array of other elements make this carving, which is one of the most complex from this period in Mexico, exceptionally difficult to interpret.

Another intricate Tree of Life carving discovered in Mexico is the beautiful sarcophagus lid from the tomb in the Temple of the Inscriptions at Palenque. Once thought to depict a deity, it is now thought to portray a king named Pacal (meaning "shield") at the moment of his death. As he falls to the earth (represented by the monster face), the sacred ceiba tree rises toward the heavens, topped by the divine serpent-bird, and flanked by two oval cartouches emblematic of the sun.

This sarcophagus cover from the tomb of king Pacal in the Mayan Temple of Inscriptions, Palenque (c. 683 A.D.) shows a ceiba tree emerging from the center of the reclining ruler as he is about to be reborn as a god. Similar imagery may be seen in Alma 32:41–42, which speaks of the tree of God's goodness taking root in the believer and growing up to eternal life. Courtesy Merle Greene Robertson.

Whether or not such artworks are related to the Book of Mormon, the remains of cultures from the Near East (*CWHN* 6:254–55; 7:189–92) and Mesoamerica show that the Tree of Life was a significant image in many areas of the world.

BIBLIOGRAPHY

Christensen, Ross, ed. *The Tree of Life in Ancient America.* Provo, Utah, 1968; on Izapa Stela 5 research up to 1965.

James, E. O. *The Tree of Life: An Archaeological Study.* Leiden, 1966.

Norman, V. Garth. *Izapa Sculpture*. Provo, Utah, 1973; for the most complete description of Izapa Stela 5.

Robertson, Merle G. *The Sculpture of Palenque*, Vol. 1, fig. 99. Princeton, 1983.

MARTIN RAISH

TRIALS

Encountering trials, or testing, is one of the purposes of mortality. A key verse of Latter-day Saint understanding is from the Book of Abraham: "And we will prove them herewith, to see if they will do all things whatsoever the Lord their God shall command them" (Abr. 3:25). Although often painful and difficult, trials are an essential and expected part of life and provide experiences necessary for developing Christlike qualities and spiritual strength (Abr. 3:25; D&C 98:12–14; Mosiah 23:21–22).

Abraham's trials provide a prototype for man's dilemma in the world. Early in life he was placed on an altar amidst idol worshippers and delivered by divine intervention (Abr. 1). Later, God commanded him to offer his son Isaac for a burnt offering. Prophets have said that if Abraham's feelings could have been touched more deeply in any other way than by the instruction to offer up his own son (Gen. 22:1–19), that way would have been followed. Modern scripture says that all must eventually be "chastened and tried even as Abraham" (D&C 101:4; 132:37, 51). For Latter-day Saints, trials are not evidence of an indifferent God who allows his children to suffer, but rather evidence of a loving Father who honors the desire of his children to grow (Zech. 13:9; Heb. 12:6; Prov. 3:11–12).

Adversity may be a test of faithfulness and endurance. These tests allow persons to demonstrate to God and to themselves that they will love and trust him "at all hazards" (*TPJS*, p. 150). Ironically, God's love is often felt more closely and abundantly during times of adversity, when prayers are intensified and thoughts are turned to God, than during times of prosperity, when it seems easy to forget the need for divine help. Thus, the Lord has said: "In the day of their peace they esteem lightly my counsel" (D&C 101:8). Prosperity itself can therefore be viewed as a type of trial. Faith grows as one recognizes that, whether or not divine intervention modifies circumstances, God's power may change persons, enabling them to endure well (Mosiah 24:13–15; John 9:1–3). In a very real sense, whatever one's circumstances, life is a trial, a test of faithfulness (Hel. 12:1–3; D&C 101:4; Rom. 5:3–5). Adversity also may generate and perfect attributes of godliness, such as patience, empathy, sacrifice, and compassion.

Like all persons of faith, Latter-day Saints sometimes struggle to reconcile their acceptance of adversity with another important concept: that God has promised to bless and prosper the righteous. Latter-day Saints believe still in this ancient Deuteronomic covenant, renewed in modern times. During times of adversity, often the greatest anguish comes not from dealing with the difficult circumstances, but from introspectively determining whether they came as a result of personal unworthiness. In these situations, adversity can provide the motivation needed to repent (Deut. 11:26–28; 2 Ne. 1:20).

Even with this understanding, faithful Latter-day Saints often find the vicissitudes of life challenging. Nevertheless, they derive great strength and comfort from the teachings and example of Jesus Christ, and the promise that God will never test them beyond their ability to withstand (1 Cor. 10:13). Jesus' own mortal life was a perfect example of trials well endured. Latter-day Saints believe that Christ suffered every feeling of temptation, pain, sorrow, and despair that anyone has ever felt in the darkest hours of adversity so that he would be able to give comfort (D&C 122:5–8). In addition, they find hope in his assurance that these difficult times are a small moment in the span of eternity with great blessings to follow for those who, without bitterness or despair, prove worthy and endure to the end (D&C 98:3; 121:7–8; 122:5–9; Alma 7:11–13).

BIBLIOGRAPHY

Holland, Jeffrey R. *However Long and Hard the Road*. Salt Lake City, 1985.

Kimball, Spencer W. *Faith Precedes the Miracle*, pp. 95–110. Salt Lake City, 1972.

Madsen, Truman G. "Power from Abrahamic Tests." In *The Highest In Us*, pp. 49–57. Salt Lake City, 1978.

Maxwell, Neal A. *All These Things Shall Give Thee Experience*. Salt Lake City, 1980.

———. *We Will Prove Them Herewith*. Salt Lake City, 1982.

CHRISTIE H. FRANDSEN

TRIALS OF JOSEPH SMITH

See: Smith, Joseph: Legal Trials of Joseph Smith

TRUE AND LIVING CHURCH

"The only true and living church upon the face of the whole earth" is a phrase from a REVELATION given to the Prophet Joseph SMITH (D&C 1:30) often used by members of The Church of Jesus Christ of Latter-day Saints when they testify to the truthfulness of the restored gospel in testimony meetings, MISSIONARY presentations, or other settings. The phrase echoes Paul's "the living and true God" (1 Thes. 1:9), which also occurs elsewhere in the scriptures.

Latter-day Saints speak of "the only true and living church" because of their belief that Jesus Christ and his apostles organized the Church during their ministry on the earth. This organization included prophets and apostles at its head, along with various other offices such as bishop, elder, seventy, and so on. The holders of these offices were given authority to preach the gospel, perform ORDINANCES, and govern the Church.

However, as Christ and his apostles had prophesied, the "true" Church they established was lost from the earth through APOSTASY (JS—M 1:7–9, 22; 2 Thes. 2:3). Therefore there was a need for a RESTORATION. Guided by angelic messengers and by revelation from God, Joseph Smith and his successors have reestablished Christ's Church in these "latter days." Members bear testimony that the Church is true because they believe it is the restored Church of Christ, with the same authority, teachings, organization, and spirit found in the Church that the Savior originally established.

The Church is a "living" church with "living" scripture, not only because it has been restored by a "living God" who continues to reveal his will to his living prophets and people to lead them to life eternal, but also because it is a growing, dynamic organization that plays an important role in the way of life of active members. The Church has a lay ministry; therefore its offices are filled by the general membership. Many young men and women begin early in life to serve in Church positions as teachers and leaders, and continue to serve throughout their lives. Being involved in a significant way in an organization that is directed by continuing revelation and is dramatically growing leads its members to speak of it as a true and living church.

To its members, as President Spencer W. KIMBALL has stated, the LDS Church "is not *a* church. [It] is *The* Church of Jesus Christ" (*The Teachings of Spencer W. Kimball*, ed. E. L. Kimball, p. 421, Salt Lake City, 1982).

BIBLIOGRAPHY

Romney, Marion G. "We, The Church of Jesus Christ of Latter-day Saints." *Ensign* 9 (May 1979):50–52.

Stapley, Delbert L. "What Constitutes the True Church." *Ensign* 7 (May 1977):21–23.

SOREN F. COX

TRUTH

The LDS conception of truth does not fit any of the categories in which it has been discussed in the Western philosophical tradition. For Latter-day Saints, truth is found in living the type of life exemplified by JESUS CHRIST.

In the Western philosophical tradition, truth is the characteristic or quality of an idea or statement that justifies belief in it. What this characteristic might be has been the subject of long-standing philosophical debate; some have said it is the correspondence with reality that true statements possess; some, their "tie-in" or coherence with other statements; some, their consequences or practical usefulness. So devastating have been the attacks upon each of these theories that in recent times many philosophers have abandoned altogether the traditional assumption that a firm or absolute kind of truth is possible. These philosophers say that because our knowledge of the world is heavily conditioned by the peculiarities of the particular language in which it is expressed, it is an interpretation at best; we have no basis for claiming we can ever know "how things really are," they argue, and therefore, whatever truth exists is relative to the speaker's language, culture, and situation. Absolute truth, thought of as a property of ideas or statements, is a concept that has fallen on hard times.

Commonly it is supposed that for Latter-day Saints truth is absolute in a way that makes it vulnerable to the relativist's arguments. But for Latter-day Saints, as their scriptures and everyday discourse reveal, truth is not primarily a matter of the correctness of ideas or statements, and consequently their view is not to be found among the traditional alternatives or any combination of them. Though they do speak of the truth of statements, they most often use the word "truth" to signify an entire way of life—specifically, the way of life exemplified, prescribed, and guided by Jesus Christ.

This conception of truth preserves senses attached to the word from the earliest times of which we have record. For example, central to the original idea of being true was "steadfast . . . adherence to a commander or friend, to a principle or cause, . . . faithful, loyal, constant, trusty," "honest, honourable, upright, virtuous, . . . free from deceit, sincere" ("True," *Oxford English Dictionary*). And among the main original senses of "truth" was "troth"—a pledge or covenant of faithfulness made uprightly and without deceit ("Truth," *OED*). It is in the spirit of these ancient etymologies that Latter-day Saints believe that to walk in truth is to keep one's commitments to follow Christ's way uprightly.

Because Christ perfectly embodies the virtue of being true and faithful (in his case, to the life his Father required of him), there is a crucial sense in which he himself is the truth. "I am the way," he said, "the truth, and the life" (John 14:6). He "received a fulness of truth" (D&C 93:26). His cosmic influence, called "the light of Christ," is also the light of truth, giving life to everything and enlightening human minds. By means of this light, he is "in all and through all things" (D&C 88:6), a permeating presence. Given this sense of the word "truth," it is not odd, as it otherwise would appear, to say, as does a key doctrinal REVELATION, that "truth shineth" (D&C 88:6–13).

Latter-day Saint scriptures indicate that people can come to "know the truth of all things" by the power of the HOLY GHOST (Moro. 10:5). The relevant contexts suggest this means to enjoy that comprehension of things that comes to the person who receives the light of truth and walks obediently in it. "He that keepeth his commandments receiveth truth and light, until he is glorified in truth and knoweth all things" (D&C 93:28). To the BROTHER OF JARED, a Book of Mormon figure of extraordinary FAITH, the Lord showed "all the inhabitants of the earth . . . even unto the ends of the earth. For he had said unto him . . . that if he would believe in him that he could show unto him

all things" (Ether 3:25–26). Other prophets have had similar experiences (Moses 1:8, 27–29; 7:21; Abr. 3:12).

A certain scriptural definition of "truth" is especially familiar to Latter-day Saints: "Truth is knowledge of things as they are, and as they were, and as they are to come" (D&C 93:24). Taken out of context (as it often is), this definition sounds like a statement of the correspondence theory of truth; but in context it expresses the morally richer idea of the comprehensive vision of reality that comes to those who walk in truth faithfully.

Understood in this way, disobedience and unfaithfulness are rejections of the light of truth. Satan "was a liar from the beginning" (D&C 93:25) and seeks always to "turn . . . hearts away from the truth" (D&C 78:10), partly by enticing people to become liars and deceivers themselves (D&C 10:25). The reason "men [love] darkness rather than light" is "because their deeds [are] evil. For every one that doeth evil hateth the light, neither cometh to the light, lest his deeds should be reproved" (John 3:19–20). It is not for being mistaken that people are damned, but for their resistance to the truth they could receive if they would.

For Latter-day Saints, salvation is a matter of growing in truth and particularly in KNOWLEDGE of the GOSPEL OF JESUS CHRIST. Joseph SMITH taught that "a man is saved no faster than he gets knowledge" (*HC* 4:588) and that "it is impossible for a man to be saved in ignorance" (D&C 131:6). In context these statements mean that one cannot be saved in ignorance of the gospel of Jesus Christ. Latter-day Saints who recognize that truth is not merely a property of language but is central to a life of obedience to the Savior do not interpret these passages to mean that the learned—the scholars and scientists—have a better chance of being saved. Gaining knowledge and becoming more godlike are two aspects of a single process, which helps explain the Latter-day Saint emphasis on EDUCATION and personal scriptural mastery as well as on righteous living.

The prophets of the present dispensation, from Joseph Smith onward, have championed the idea that the Latter-day Saints have no exclusive access to truth. God enlightens people everywhere, and therefore, as Presidents of the Church have all insisted, insofar as other peoples have any principle of truth (and they do), "whether moral, religious, philosophical, or of any other kind, that is calculated to benefit mankind, . . . [we] will embrace it" (John Taylor, *JD* 1:155). However, these same prophets also claim that the truths of the gospel of Jesus Christ that are necessary for salvation have been revealed in modern times exclusively through them.

BIBLIOGRAPHY

Hinckley, Gordon B. "The Continuing Pursuit of Truth." *Ensign* 16 (Apr. 1986):2–6.

Roberts, B. H. *Excerpts from The Truth, the Way, the Life: An Elementary Treatise on Theology.* Provo, Utah, 1985.

Tanner, N. Eldon. "Ye Shall Know the Truth." *Ensign* 8 (May 1978):14–16.

C. TERRY WARNER

U

UNITED ORDERS

"United orders" refers to the cooperative enterprises established in LDS communities of the Great Basin, Mexico, and Canada during the last quarter of the nineteenth century in an effort to better establish ideal Christian community and group economic self-sufficiency. The roots go back to Joseph Smith's 1831 revelations outlining the law of CONSECRATION and STEWARDSHIP as the foundation for the ideal community. Economic goals of consecration included relative income equality, group self-sufficiency, and the elimination of poverty (*see* ECONOMIC HISTORY OF THE CHURCH). Under this plan, the head of each family would consecrate or deed all real and personal property to the Presiding Bishop of the Church and would receive, in turn, a stewardship, or "inheritance," from consecrated property. Thereafter, Church members would consecrate annually all surplus production from their stewardships to the bishop's storehouse. This system functioned briefly in a few LDS communities in the Midwest during the 1830s; in the Great Basin, Church members prepared deeds of consecration in 1855–1858, but they were never acted upon.

During the 1860s President Brigham Young reemphasized economic cooperation and self-sufficiency, and a network of more than 150 cooperative mercantile and manufacturing enterprises was established in the region (*see* PIONEER ECONOMY). Designed to promote unity and to reduce dependence on non-Mormon merchants and traders, the cooperatives did not require consecration of property but issued and sold shares of stock and paid wages and dividends. Among the most successful cooperatives was the Brigham City Mercantile and Manufacturing Association, which operated forty departments and encompassed the economic activity of the entire community. President Young saw this cooperative movement as an important step toward the ideal society but recognized that a more comprehensive system was necessary to reach his political and economic goals.

Three events undoubtedly influenced Brigham Young to introduce the United Order system in 1874. First, completion of the transcontinental railroad in 1869 led to an influx of Gentiles into the territory. The accompanying individualistic and competitive attitudes and institutions of nineteenth-century American capitalism seriously threatened to erode the bonds of selflessness and cooperation that held the LDS social fabric together. Second, congressional bills designed to reduce LDS political and economic power and individual rights led to persecution, including the arrest of Brigham Young in 1871. Third, the Panic of 1873 brought depression to Utah's mining industry and loss of jobs and markets to Mormon laborers, farmers, and merchants. Faced with general disruption of social, political, and economic life, Brigham Young introduced The United Order of Enoch.

He organized the first united order at St. George, Utah, on February 9, 1874. The last known Church-authorized united order was organized at Cave Valley, Chihuahua, Mexico, on January 9, 1893. In the interim more than 200 united orders were organized in LDS communities in several mountain states, including Utah, Idaho, Wyoming, Arizona, and Nevada, mostly in 1874 and 1875. This ambitious attempt to establish a utopian society was both a direct response to the forces that threatened LDS economic and political independence and a final effort by Brigham Young to build the ideal community envisioned by Joseph Smith (*see* CITY PLANNING).

Brigham Young saw the united order as an intermediate step between the cooperatives of the 1860s and Joseph Smith's ideal community based on consecration and stewardship. Though they differed from one another in form, nearly all united orders were organized as voluntary producer cooperatives where, rather than working for fixed wages, members shared the net income of the enterprise. United orders used two main types of producer cooperatives. In the St. George type, members contributed their economic property to the order and received dividends and labor income according to the relative amounts of capital and labor contributed. A governing board directed the enterprise.

The second category of united orders was communal. Members contributed all their property to the order, shared more or less equally in the common product, and functioned, ate, and worked as a well-regulated family. This system is called the Orderville type, after the most famous of the united orders. Established in southern Utah in 1875, the Orderville united order attained almost complete self-sufficiency. It produced its own food, fuel, fiber, and nearly all needed manufactured items, some of which it exported to other parts of the territory. The most successful of the communal-type orders, it disbanded in 1885. In addition to Orderville, communal united orders were established in several LDS communities in southern Utah, Nevada, Arizona, and Mexico.

The few united orders that were not producer cooperatives were patterned after the Brigham City united order (formerly the Brigham City Mercantile and Manufacturing Association), a joint-stock company with significant cooperative characteristics. The Brigham City–type united orders were intended to strengthen and reinforce existing cooperative arrangements. Such orders did not require consecration of all one's property and labor but operated much like a profit-sharing capitalist enterprise, issuing dividends on stock and hiring labor. There was no necessary connection between owning stock in the united order and working for the order, although workers were encouraged to take part of their wages in stock. Several Brigham City–type united orders were established in northern Utah and southern Idaho. Wards in larger cities in the territory used a modified Brigham City plan in which members pooled their capital to establish a needed cooperative or corporate enterprise. These enterprises were similar in many respects to stake welfare projects organized in the twentieth century as part of the Church welfare system.

Brigham Young believed that pooling capital and labor would not only promote unity and self-sufficiency but would also provide increased production, investment, and consumption through specialization, division of labor, and economies of scale. In spite of some notable successes, however, the united order movement was relatively short-lived. Most of the St. George–type orders never fully operated or operated only briefly. When President Young died in 1877, most of the united orders had already failed. Some, like those in Orderville and Brigham City, functioned successfully for a decade, and a very few continued in some form into the 1890s. At least one, a joint enterprise of the Logan Second and Third wards, survived into the twentieth century, selling out to private interests in 1909. Many factors combined to hamper the united order movement, including uncertainty as to operating rules, influx of immigrants with no capital to contribute, internal disputes, difficulties surrounding legal incorporation, and persecution and federal prosecution of united order leaders.

In spite of the short life of the movement, the united order was important to the development of LDS pioneer society and economy in several ways. First, the united order was an important vehicle for COLONIZATION of the inhospitable southern part of the Great Basin, where cooperation and organization were essential for survival. Second, the united order provided a mechanism through which Church leaders were able to promote economic self-sufficiency. The diversification of Utah's economy that resulted from this process helped Utah avoid the mineral-based economic colonialism experienced by other mountain states during the late nineteenth century. Finally, for Latter-day Saints of the time, the united order was a symbol of separateness from the world, a means of maintaining group identity in a hostile society, and a way of meeting their religious commitment to individual and group perfection. Today, the united order experience remains in Mormon historical consciousness as a symbol of the more perfect society that Latter-day Saints believe will one day be achieved.

BIBLIOGRAPHY

Arrington, Leonard J. *Great Basin Kingdom: An Economic History of the Latter-day Saints, 1830–1900.* Cambridge, Mass., 1958.

———; Feramorz Y. Fox; and Dean L. May. *Building the City of God: Community and Cooperation Among the Mormons.* Salt Lake City, 1976.

Israelsen, L. Dwight. "An Economic Analysis of the United Order." *BYU Studies* 18 (Summer 1978):536–62.

L. DWIGHT ISRAELSEN

UNITED STATES OF AMERICA

The Church of Jesus Christ of Latter-day Saints was first organized in the United States. It is now known worldwide as one of the most distinctive and successful religions organized in America. Its members acknowledge that its American origins made possible much of its contemporary success. They also believe that the United States of America is a divinely blessed land of promise and that it will continue to play a pivotal role in important events of the Restoration and the LAST DAYS.

ROLE IN THE RESTORATION OF THE GOSPEL. Latter-day Saints believe that the United States was divinely prepared as a suitable place for the prophesied RESTORATION OF THE GOSPEL OF JESUS CHRIST. Their scriptures teach that God kept the Americas hidden from the rest of the world until the time had come when he could accomplish his purpose and prepare the way for the American Republic (2 Ne. 1:8–9), that COLUMBUS was inspired in his discovery of the Western Hemisphere (1 Ne. 13:12), and that the Lord governed and controlled the settling of the continent (1 Ne. 13:13–19). The War of Independence, the ultimate victory of the colonies, the establishment of representative political institutions, and the peace and prosperity that prevailed in early nineteenth-century America were all divinely inspired and guided.

By 1820, at the time the Restoration commenced, political domination of the American continents by European nations had ceased. The established state religions that had prevailed in the majority of the English colonies had been replaced by constitutional guarantees of the separation of CHURCH AND STATE. Representative political institutions and a commitment to individual liberty, freedom of speech and religion, and freedom of assembly sustained unprecedented religious toleration and a spirit of inquiry. Economic arrangements largely free of the direction of governments or guilds contributed to a sense of freedom and a cascade of innovations. A vast, sparsely inhabited continent encouraged mobility and attracted the restless and those seeking a new life. This combination of conditions provided fertile ground for establishing a new church and enabling it to grow and flourish.

A PROMISED LAND WITH RESPONSIBILITIES. Latter-day Saints view the American continent as a land "choice above all other lands" (1 Ne. 13:30). It is the land in which the NEW JERUSALEM will be established (3 Ne. 20:22). It is also a land whose security, prosperity, potential, and stature are conditioned by the actions of its inhabitants. Further, the land of America was designated to be a land of liberty for the Gentiles. It has been a land of liberty for the righteous. The Book of Mormon teaches that no king shall be raised up here and that those who seek to establish a king in this land shall perish (2 Ne. 10:11).

Latter-day Saints believe that the United States is guaranteed protection against all other nations only on the condition of righteousness. It is a blessed land for all the inhabitants of the earth who will act righteously, but it is, and will be, cursed to those who will not act righteously (2 Ne. 1:7; Ether 2:9–12).

Not only is the United States a land of great promises, it is also a land with special responsibilities. It serves as a standard of liberty to the world, as a warning to oppressors, and as a star of hope to the oppressed (cf. O. Hyde, *JD* 6:368). The United States has a mission to be a benefactor to all nations. Moreover, it is to provide an example of righteousness and good government to all people. It has a mission to teach the principles of freedom and religious liberty (Benson, pp. 588, 655).

REVERENCE FOR THE U.S. CONSTITUTION.   Latter-day Saints respect and revere the Declaration of Independence and the CONSTITUTION OF THE UNITED STATES as documents framed by the hands of wise men who were raised up and inspired by God (D&C 101:80). They recognize that the Constitution and the law of the land are the four.dation of the people's freedom (D&C 98:8; *see also* CONSTITUTIONAL LAW) and that its principle of freedom, which maintains "rights and privileges, belongs to all mankind, and is justifiable before" God (D&C 98:5). As a matter of loyalty to the message of God and in the service of their fellow citizens, Latter-day Saints are taught to uphold, defend, and cherish the Constitution.

Speaking in the Doctrine and Covenants, the Lord instructs the Saints to observe the constitutional laws of the land, to uphold them by their votes, and to sustain good, wise, and honest officials to administer them. In this sense, the Saints carry on much of an older American civil religion (*see* POLITICS: POLITICAL TEACHINGS).

ATTITUDE TOWARD THE UNITED STATES. During the first two decades following the organization of the Church in 1830, the Latter-day Saints suffered much PERSECUTION within the boundaries of the United States. They were driven from Ohio to Missouri, to Illinois, and finally to the Rocky Mountains, which were not a part of the United States at that time (*see* POLITICS: POLITICAL HISTORY).

When expelled from the state of Missouri under an EXTERMINATION ORDER of its governor, they held that the federal government, by virtue of the Constitution, had the responsibility and power to protect and reinstate them in their rights. President Martin Van Buren, when confronted with this request, replied, "Your cause is just, but I can do nothing for you" (*HC* 4:40, 80).

That We May Be Redeemed, by Harold I. Hopkinson (1988, oil on canvas, 4' × 5'). This painting hangs in the St. George Temple, where in 1877 the Founding Fathers of the United States appeared to Wilford Woodruff in a vision, asking that baptisms be performed on their behalf. Latter-day Saints believe that righteous men were raised up by God to establish a government of liberty and justice under the Constitution of the United States of America.

In 1845, following the martyrdom of Joseph SMITH, Brigham YOUNG addressed letters to all the governors of the states and territories in the Union, asking for asylum within their borders for the Latter-day Saints. All either were silent or flatly refused. Three members of Congress negotiated with the Saints to have them leave the confines of the United States. Ultimately, the main body of the Church left Nauvoo, the city they had founded and then the second-largest city in the state of Illinois, and, beginning in 1847, settled in the Great Basin in an area then governed by Mexico.

This pattern of persecution did not weaken the Latter-day Saints' attachment to the principles of free government. Upon arriving in the valley of the Great Salt Lake, they raised the American flag and announced their determination to live under the U.S. Constitution.

Notwithstanding the martyrdom of the Prophet Joseph Smith and the sustained persecution suffered by the Saints as a whole, they were able to differentiate the Constitution and the laws of the United States consistent with it from the cruel and illegal deeds committed against Church members in various states of the Union. The Church and its members have continued to see the Constitution and laws of the United States as a potential and real source of protection for their worship, as is reflected in a number of court cases involving these issues (see LEGAL AND JUDICIAL HISTORY).

LATTER-DAY SAINTS IN THE UNITED STATES. During the early period of the Church's history, the United States was a place of GATHERING. Tens of thousands of converts, principally from England and Europe, journeyed across the Atlantic Ocean and the American continent to the headquarters of the Church, first in Nauvoo and then in Salt Lake City.

The economic opportunity and relative prosperity enjoyed by members of the Church in the United States helped provide a strong financial base that has sustained a growing global missionary effort, the establishment and support of congregations in developing countries, and humanitarian relief programs. By the middle of the twentieth century, the Church had become virtually a worldwide faith, a trend that accelerated sharply during the last half of the century.

LDS wards and branches exist in all fifty states, with a heavy Latter-day Saint population in several Rocky Mountain and western states. By 1990, Church membership in the United States had grown to more than 4 million, making it the sixth-largest religious denomination in the nation.

BIBLIOGRAPHY

Allen, James B., and Glen M. Leonard. *The Story of the Latter-day Saints.* Salt Lake City, 1976.

Benson, Ezra Taft. *The Teachings of Ezra Taft Benson*, pp. 569–705. Salt Lake City, 1988.

Cowan, Richard O. *The Church in the Twentieth Century.* Salt Lake City, 1985.

ROGER B. PORTER

UNITY

The LDS concept of unity focuses primarily on three doctrinal issues: the nature of the GODHEAD, relations among members of the Church, and the relation between a person and God, although it differs at some points from the tenets of traditional Christianity.

LDS scriptures usually emphasize the separate identities of the members of the Godhead, but sometimes describe them as one. This unity is understood to mean oneness of purpose and testimony—not identity of being. With respect to the Godhead, this means that although God the Father, his son Jesus Christ, and the Holy Ghost are three distinct beings, they are united in purpose. This precept was one of the first to be given to the Prophet Joseph Smith when, in 1820, he beheld both the Father and Son in his first vision (JS—H 1:14–20). In that vision, the Father appeared and bore witness of the Son. LDS scriptures emphasize that the oneness of the Godhead derives partly from the fact that each member of the Godhead bears witness of the others (3 Ne. 11:35–36; 28:10–11; D&C 20:27–28). To the faithful in the New World, Christ taught the same doctrine that he had taught his disciples in the Old World—namely, that the members of the Godhead were one in purpose, glory, joy, and witness, and that this same oneness could be shared with his faithful followers (3 Ne. 19:29; 28:10; cf. John 17:20–22). This LDS understanding is at variance with the traditional concept of a mystical union of the members of the Godhead.

For the members of the Church, "unity" refers to common aspirations, beliefs, and purposes, not to mystical or substantial union. In the Book of

Mormon, for example, the Savior explained that to become "one," members must end disputations and CONTENTION (3 Ne. 11:22–28, 36). Latter-day Saints are taught that they must mitigate any condition that undermines unity among members, including significant economic and social distinctions (3 Ne. 6:10–16; 4 Ne. 1:24–35). Unity among members begins with the family (D&C 38:26–27). The concluding words of the Old Testament (Mal. 4:5–6) describe how the earth must prepare for the second coming of the Savior by binding the hearts of the children to the fathers and the hearts of the fathers to the children. In fulfillment of this prophecy and under divine direction, Latter-day Saints perform ORDINANCES in the temples of God that seal parents and children together, not only for the living but also for all those who have ever lived on this earth. The goal is not limited to family unity but includes the unity of all believing and worthy human beings.

Jesus taught that unity among his followers witnesses to the world that he is the Christ (John 17:20–26). Paul exhorts all to become "fellowcitizens with the saints, and of the household of God" (Eph. 2:19) and to "come in the unity of the faith" (Eph. 4:13). Zion refers to the community of believers who, through their unity in Christ, have become "of one heart and one mind" (Moses 7:18). Such unity of faith is achieved through individual obedience to the laws of God and through common dedication to the promotion of faithfulness among all human beings.

The unity of God and human beings refers to the eventual personal reassociation of worthy men and women with God. Entry into mortal life brings about a separation from God, while compliance with the GOSPEL OF JESUS CHRIST enables persons to overcome this separation and return to God through the at-one-ment mediated by Jesus Christ. Latter-day Saints believe that by progressing in knowledge and righteousness, human beings bring their lives into harmony with Christ's and that upon resurrection the body and soul will be inseparably reunited and the exalted person will dwell with God forever.

[See also Common Consent; Equality.]

BIBLIOGRAPHY

Talmage, James E. AF, pp. 40–41. Salt Lake City, 1949.

F. NEIL BRADY

UNIVERSITY OF DESERET

On February 28, 1850, two and a half years after the PIONEERS entered Great Salt Lake Valley, the General Assembly of the State of DESERET chartered the University of Deseret, which eventually became the University of Utah. The founding of the university in the early years of Utah settlement, the first such institution west of the Mississippi, indicates the value Latter-day Saints placed on education.

Although chartered as a university, the school had a humble beginning and slow and interrupted development in its early years. Its first term opened for men on November 11, 1850, in a private home in Salt Lake City. The second term opened in 1851 for both women and men and was held in the State House, known later as the Council House. After the third term, held in 1852, lack of funds closed the school.

In 1867 the University of Deseret reopened, primarily as a business school, and in 1884 its first

The old main building (University Hall) of the University of Deseret on Union Square in Salt Lake City (c. 1920), on the later site of West High School. The University of Deseret became the University of Utah in 1892.

building was constructed on the site now occupied by West High School. The first commencement exercises, in 1886, conferred ten normal (teaching) and two bachelor degrees. By the 1890s 400 students were enrolled, and B.A. and B.S. degrees were offered in classical, scientific, and normal programs.

In 1892, four years before statehood, an amendment to the University of Deseret charter changed the name to the University of Utah. In 1894, Congress granted sixty acres of land from Fort Douglas on the east bench of Salt Lake Valley to the university, which established its campus there.

In the 1890s, a nationwide financial crisis and the competition of other institutions for students and funds threatened the fledgling state university. Responding to the crisis, the LDS Church discontinued its support of its own recently founded university in Salt Lake City and urged Latter-day Saints to "faithfully devote their influence and energy . . . to the University of Utah."

BIBLIOGRAPHY

Chamberlin, Ralph V. *The University of Utah: A History of Its First Hundred Years, 1850–1950.* Salt Lake City, 1960.

GRETHE BALLIF PETERSON

UNPARDONABLE SIN

The gravest of all sins is BLASPHEMY against the HOLY GHOST. One may speak even against Jesus Christ in ignorance and, upon repentance, be forgiven, but knowingly to sin against the Holy Ghost by denying its influence after having received it is unpardonable (Matt. 12:31–32; Jacob 7:19; Alma 39:6), and the consequences are inescapable. Such denial dooms the perpetrator to the hell of the second SPIRITUAL DEATH (*TPJS*, p. 361). This extreme judgment comes because the person sins knowingly against the light, thereby severing himself from the redeeming grace of Christ. He is numbered with the SONS OF PERDITION (D&C 76:43).

The Prophet Joseph SMITH explained, "No man can commit the unpardonable sin after the dissolution of the body, nor in this life, until he receives the Holy Ghost" (*TPJS*, p. 357). To commit the unpardonable sin, a person "must receive the Holy Ghost, have the heavens opened unto

him, and know God, and then sin against Him. After a man has sinned against the Holy Ghost, there is no repentance for him. . . . he has got to deny Jesus Christ when the heavens have been opened to him, and to deny the plan of salvation with his eyes open to the truth of it" (*TPJS*, p. 358; cf. Heb. 10:26–29).

If people have such knowledge and willfully turn altogether away, it is a sin against light, a sin against the Holy Ghost, and figuratively "they crucify to themselves the Son of God afresh, and put him to an open shame" (Heb. 6:4–6; D&C 76:35). Such remain as though there were no ATONEMENT, except that they shall be resurrected from the dead (Alma 11:41).

RODNEY TURNER

URIM AND THUMMIM

The Urim and Thummim is mentioned in the Bible and, with added details about its use and significance, in latter-day scriptures. It is an instrument prepared by God through which revelation may be received. Abraham learned about the universe through the Urim and Thummim (Abr. 3:1–4). The Prophet Joseph Smith "through the medium of the Urim and Thummim . . . translated the [Book of Mormon] by the gift and power of God" (*HC* 4:537; D&C 10:1; JS—H 1:62). Servants of God who are allowed to use the Urim and Thummim have been known as SEERS (Mosiah 8:13), among whom were Abraham, Moses, the brother of Jared, Mosiah$_2$, Alma$_1$, Helaman$_1$, Moroni$_2$, and Joseph Smith.

In Antiquity at least two different Urim and Thummim existed, and possibly three. Chronologically, the brother of Jared received the first known one (D&C 17:1). This same set came into the hands of Mosiah$_2$ and other Book of Mormon prophets, subsequently being deposited with the GOLD PLATES (JS—H 1:35). The fate of the second set, given to Abraham (Abr. 3:1), remains unknown. Unless Abraham's Urim and Thummim had been passed down, Moses received a third set mentioned first in Exodus 28:30. The Urim noted in 1 Samuel 28:6, probably an abbreviated form of Urim and Thummim, was most likely the one possessed by Moses (cf. Num. 27:18–21). What happened to this one is also unknown, though certainly by postexilic times the Urim and Thummim were no longer extant (Ezra 2:63; Neh. 7:65).

Joseph Smith described the Urim and Thummim as "two transparent stones set in the rim of a [silver] bow fastened to a breast plate" (*HC* 4:537; JS—H 1:35). Biblical evidence allows no conclusive description, except that it was placed in a breastplate over the heart (Ex. 28:30; Lev. 8:8).

Urim and Thummim is the transliteration of two Hebrew words meaning, respectively, "light(s)" and "wholeness(es)" or "perfection(s)." While it is usually assumed that the -*im* ending on both words represents the Hebrew masculine plural suffix, other explanations are possible.

The Urim and Thummim to be used during and after the Millennium will have a functional similarity to the Urim and Thummim mentioned above. God's dwelling place is called a Urim and Thummim; and the white stone of Revelation 2:17 is to become a Urim and Thummim for inheritors of the CELESTIAL KINGDOM (D&C 130:8–10).

PAUL Y. HOSKISSON

UTAH EXPEDITION

The Utah War of 1857–1858 was the largest military operation in the United States between the times of the Mexican War and the Civil War. It pitted the Mormon militia, called the NAUVOO LEGION, against the army and government of the United States in a bloodless but costly confrontation that stemmed from the badly handled attempt by the administration of President James Buchanan to replace Brigham YOUNG as governor of UTAH TERRITORY. It delayed, but did not prevent, the installation of Governor Alfred Cumming, and it had a significant impact on the territory, its predominantly Latter-day Saint inhabitants, and the Church itself. Because the conflict resulted from misunderstandings that were distorted by time and distance, had the transcontinental telegraph been completed in 1857 instead of 1861, the expedition almost certainly would not have occurred.

The decision to replace Governor Young was inevitable, given the national reaction to the Church's 1852 announcement of PLURAL MARRIAGE and Republican charges in the campaign of 1856 that the Democrats favored the "twin relics of barbarism"—polygamy and slavery. The method chosen to implement that decision, however, is still puzzling. Apparently influenced by reports from Judge W. E. Drummond and other

former territorial officials, Buchanan and his cabinet decided that the Latter-day Saints would reject a non-Mormon governor. So, without investigation, mail service to Utah was suspended and 2,500 troops led by Albert Sidney Johnston were ordered to accompany Cumming to Great Salt Lake City.

Remembering earlier difficulties with troops and perhaps swayed by the ardor of the recent reformation movement (*see* REFORMATION [LDS] OF 1856–1857), Church leaders interpreted the army's unannounced coming as religious persecution and decided to resist. Brigham Young, still acting as governor, declared martial law and deployed the Nauvoo Legion to delay the troops with "scorched earth" tactics. Harassing actions, including burning three supply trains and capturing hundreds of government cattle, forced Johnston's expedition and the accompanying civil officials into winter quarters at Camp Scott and Eckelsville, near burned-out Fort Bridger, some 100 mountainous miles east of Salt Lake City.

During the winter both sides strengthened their forces. Congress, over almost unanimous Republican opposition, authorized two new volunteer regiments, and Buchanan, Secretary of War John B. Floyd, and Army Chief of Staff Winfield Scott assigned 3,000 additional regular troops to reinforce the Utah Expedition. Meanwhile, Utah communities were called upon to equip a thousand men for a spring campaign. Predictions of hostilities came from LDS pulpits, Camp Scott, and the national press.

There is persuasive evidence, however, that Brigham Young never intended to force a military showdown. He and other leaders often spoke of abandoning and burning their settlements rather than permitting their occupation by enemies, as had happened in Missouri and Illinois.

That Brigham Young hoped for a diplomatic solution is clear from his early appeal to Thomas L. KANE, the influential Pennsylvanian who had for ten years been a friend of the Mormons. Soon after Christmas, Kane received Buchanan's permission to go to Utah, via Panama and California, as an unofficial mediator. Reaching Salt Lake City late in February, he found Church leaders ready for peace but distrustful. When the first reports of Kane's contacts with General Johnston were discouraging, the apprehension was reinforced.

The "Move South" resulted. President Young announced on March 23, 1858, that all settlements in northern Utah must be abandoned and prepared

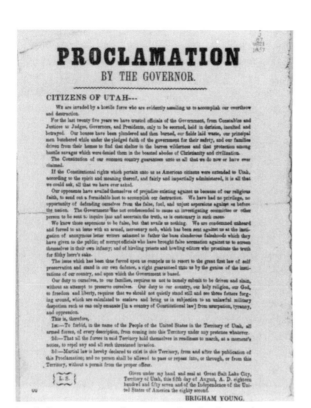

In defense against the approach of Johnston's army, Brigham Young posted this proclamation throughout Utah Territory on August 5, 1857, declaring martial law and forbidding any person to pass in or through the territory without permission from an authorized officer. Courtesy Special Collections Department, University of Utah Libraries.

for burning if the army came in. The evacuation started immediately. Though at first perceived as likely to be permanent, the Move South was transformed into a tactical and temporary maneuver soon after word came that Kane had persuaded Cumming to come to Salt Lake City without the army. Still, in numbers at least, it dwarfed the earlier Mormon flights from Missouri and Illinois: about 30,000 people moved fifty miles or more to Provo and other towns in central and southern Utah. There they remained in shared and improvised housing until the Utah War was over.

When Kane and Cumming arrived early in April, Young surrendered his political title and soon formed an amiable working relationship with his successor. However, the Move South continued, probably because the government representatives insisted that Johnston's troops must be admitted but were unable to guarantee that they would come in peacefully.

Meanwhile, President Buchanan responded to rising criticism by appointing Lazarus Powell and Ben McCulloch to carry an amnesty proclamation to Utah. Arriving early in June, they found Church leaders willing to accept Cumming and a permanent army garrison in exchange for peace and amnesty. Johnston's army marched through a largely deserted Salt Lake City on June 26, 1858, and went on to build Camp Floyd forty miles to the southwest. Soon the refugees returned home; the Utah War was over.

From this episode the Buchanan administration reaped an unbalanced defense budget and some political embarrassment. With a fair and impartial approach, Governor Cumming soon became more popular with the Latter-day Saints than with the military. Camp Floyd and the nearby civilian town of Fairfield represented the first sizable non-Mormon resident population in Utah. Though the troops left Utah at the outbreak of the Civil War, the presence for three years of thousands of troops and camp followers ended the Latter-day Saint dream of a Zion geographically separate and distant from the world of unbelievers.

As for the LDS community in Utah, the exertions and expenditures strained both capital and morale. Defense efforts terminated some of the Mormon outpost settlements in present-day California, Nevada, Wyoming, and Idaho, interrupted and weakened the missionary effort in Europe, curtailed immigration, and dissipated much of the enthusiasm and discipline generated by the Reformation of 1856. Unsympathetic, if not hostile, troops and camp followers influenced economics, politics, and lifestyles. The Move South won media sympathy, but it also disrupted Latter-day Saint community and religious life and did little to increase the toleration for Mormon differences from mainstream American ideas and institutions.

In spite of the posturing and bumbling of those involved, what seemed like an inevitable military confrontation was ultimately resolved peacefully. The tensions, differences, and misunderstandings that preceded the resolution, however, remained, and it would be nearly forty years before Utah would be accepted as a state (*see* UTAH STATEHOOD).

BIBLIOGRAPHY

Furniss, Norman F. *The Mormon Conflict, 1850–1859.* Westport, Conn., 1977.

Poll, Richard D. *Quixotic Mediator: Thomas L. Kane and the Utah War.* Ogden, Utah, 1985.

———. "The Move South." *BYU Studies* 29 (Fall 1989):65–88.

RICHARD D. POLL

UTAH GENEALOGICAL AND HISTORICAL MAGAZINE

Printed from 1910 to 1940 by the Genealogical Society of Utah, *Utah Genealogical and Historical Magazine* provided instruction for local Church leaders and members on how to do genealogy and submit names of ancestors for temple ordinances. It often contained material for ward genealogical classes and reports about stake activities in genealogy and temple work. For serious genealogists it contained articles on sources and methodology. It also printed genealogies, biographies, and news about activities of the Genealogical Society of Utah and its library.

In 1940 the role of the Utah Genealogical Society in directing genealogical and temple activities among the Latter-day Saints was changed, and with it, the need for its magazine as a separate publication. Its last issue (October 1940) announced that the First Presidency had assigned responsibility for genealogical and temple activities to local priesthood leaders. From this time on, genealogy columns began to appear as regular features in the *Instructor* and the *Improvement Era*, and later in the *Church News*, which became the new forum for official Church statements about genealogy and temple activities.

RAYMOND S. WRIGHT III

UTAH STATEHOOD

By 1847, experience had clearly taught the Latter-day Saints the importance of obtaining more political autonomy and protection than was offered by a territorial government, whose federally appointed officials would have little sympathy for the LDS way of life (*see* POLITICS: POLITICAL HISTORY). Therefore, from the time the Mormon pioneers arrived in the Great Basin, they fervently sought statehood and self-government. In 1850, 1856, 1862, 1867, 1872, and 1882, LDS representatives made appeals for statehood to the U.S. Congress,

all to no avail. In fact, statehood seemed to become more elusive as time went on, because those opposed to Utah statehood could generate emotional opposition through the issue of PLURAL MARRIAGE. In 1865, Schuyler Colfax, Speaker of the U.S. House of Representatives, visited Utah and pointedly warned Brigham YOUNG that his territory could never become a state so long as the Church upheld polygamy. Latter-day Saints persisted in the practice, which for another generation blocked Utah's admission as a state.

After the U.S. Supreme Court ruled decisively against plural marriage in 1879 (*see* REYNOLDS V. UNITED STATES), federal officials began to enforce laws more firmly during what became known as the antipolygamy raid (*see* ANTIPOLYGAMY LEGISLATION). The Edmunds-Tucker Act of 1887, intended to bar polygamists from voting, was still pending in Congress when LDS agents secured approval from President Grover Cleveland's administration and from President of the Church John TAYLOR for a strategy of seeking statehood by accepting a Utah constitution prohibiting plural marriage. President Taylor's belief in plural marriage remained unaltered, but he recognized that elected state officials would likely enforce marriage laws more leniently than appointed federal officials had done. In mid-1887 such a constitution was framed and ratified in Utah. Despite these efforts, congressional Democrats balked at delivering statehood until the Church gave up polygamy.

Soon thereafter, the First Presidency of the Church, acting as a committee on statehood, began working with members of the Republican party. Some Republicans had been hostile to the Church and its marriage practices; others recognized the value of the Mormon vote throughout the West. With the assistance of friendly Republican party leaders, George Q. Cannon, counselor in the First Presidency, and others thwarted a proposed law that would have disfranchised all LDS voters, not just the polygamists. Yet, the threat of such legislation persisted, along with the even more ominous peril that the four Utah TEMPLES stood in danger of being confiscated under provisions of the Edmunds-Tucker Act.

Church leaders early faced the irony that the statehood and home rule desired as an additional protection for the Church and its institutions could seemingly be obtained only by yielding a part of the religious life they wished to protect. With ever harsher legislation, they now faced the necessity of bending on less central matters in order to protect the core mission and essential ordinances of the Church. In these circumstances, Church President Wilford WOODRUFF fervently sought and received divine direction. Accordingly, he publicly announced in his 1890 MANIFESTO that he would no longer permit plural marriages in opposition to the laws of the United States, thus removing the main obstacle to Utah statehood and protecting the temples and other matters central to the faith.

Perhaps the most important remaining problem to be resolved before Utah could gain statehood was normalizing political affairs within the territory. Up to that time, non-LDS voters had mainly backed the so-called Liberal party, while Church members belonged to the People's party, primarily associated in national affairs with the Democrats. LDS leaders recognized the necessity of convincing party members in Congress that Utah voters were not irretrievably aligned with the Democrats. It was time for Utah politics to mirror the federal, with the Democratic and Republican parties both being strong. This took place with impressive dispatch through determined efforts by John Henry Smith, an apostle, and others. At their urging, local LDS leaders—and in some cases entire congregations—were divided along national party lines.

However, as Republican party members became more convinced that admission of Utah as a state might give them two more U.S. senators in the closely balanced upper house, Democratic lawmakers became less committed to the cause of statehood, necessitating complex and intense behind-the-scenes lobbying efforts. The chief agents in these negotiations were Bishop Hiram B. Clawson and his relative Colonel Isaac Trumbo, a close friend of President Wilford Woodruff, whose effective lobbying with Republican lawmakers was of critical importance. Through a series of discussions and agreements, Trumbo and Clawson finally regained the cooperation of key Democratic leaders, partly by agreeing that actual admission of the state would not take place until 1896, after Democrats had an opportunity to complete their congressional agenda without the possible opposition of Republican senators from Utah.

The enabling act for admission was passed in July 1894, allowing a state constitutional convention to meet in early 1895. Once the constitution was approved by the U.S. Congress, it was submit-

ted to Utah citizens for ratification at the same time that they elected their first state officers. Finally, on January 4, 1896, President Grover Cleveland proclaimed Utah a state, the forty-fifth, and the new government went into effect two days later.

BIBLIOGRAPHY

Larson, Gustave O. *The "Americanization" of Utah for Statehood.* San Marino, Calif., 1971.

Lyman, Edward Leo. *Political Deliverance: The Mormon Quest for Utah Statehood.* Urbana, Ill., 1986.

Wolfinger, Henry J. "A Reexamination of the Woodruff Manifesto in the Light of Utah Constitutional History." *Utah Historical Quarterly* 39 (Fall 1971):328–49.

EDWARD LEO LYMAN

UTAH TERRITORY

The arrival of the Latter-day Saints in the SALT LAKE VALLEY in July 1847 preceded by only a few months the transfer of the Utah area and much more of the American Southwest from Mexico to the United States. The Treaty of Guadalupe Hidalgo was signed on February 2, 1848, making the transfer final. A petition requesting the United States to grant statehood to the Utah area was delivered in 1849, but statehood was not granted. Instead, Utah Territory was created as part of the national Compromise of 1850. The compromise

Celebrating Utah's admission to the United States in 1896, the Salt Lake Temple is draped with a huge flag of the United States. Courtesy Special Collections Department, University of Utah Libraries.

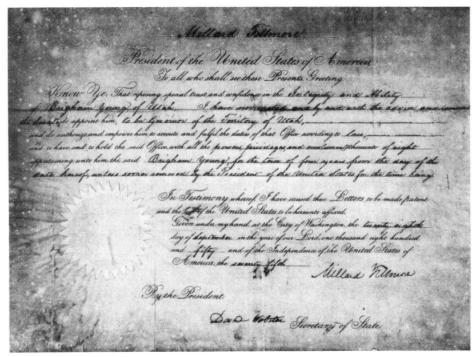

Brigham Young's certificate of appointment as governor of Utah Territory (1850), signed by Millard Fillmore, President of the United States. Courtesy Utah State Historical Society.

admitted California into the Union as a free state and designated Utah and New Mexico as territories with the right to decide whether to permit slavery or not.

Beyond the complications of the slavery issue, the petition for statehood was weakened by several other factors. The first was the tremendous size of the proposed State of Deseret (*see* DESERET, STATE OF) with boundaries extending into southern California. In addition, the small population of Deseret (less than 12,000 in 1850 excluding Native Americans) was far short of the 60,000 required for statehood by the Northwest Ordinance of 1785. And Anti-Mormon sentiment in Congress added further weight to these reasons for organizing Utah Territory rather than admitting Deseret into the Union as a state.

The act creating Utah Territory was signed by President Millard Fillmore on September 9, 1850. The boundaries of the territory were the forty-second parallel on the north, the thirty-seventh parallel on the south, the summits of the Rocky Mountains to the east, and the Sierra Nevada Mountains to the west. In 1861, Utah Territory was significantly reduced when Nevada was admit-

ted to the Union (with a smaller population than Utah), the western slope of the Rockies became part of the Colorado Territory, and the northeastern corner of Utah Territory was included in Wyoming Territory.

The 1850 act provided for a territorial legislature and a delegate to Congress, and established the following major offices to carry out governmental activities: territorial governor, secretary of the territory, U.S. marshal, U.S. attorney, chief justice, associate justice, and superintendent of Indian affairs. The president of the United States filled these offices by appointment—a situation fraught with problems, for territorial residents were excluded from electing their own governing officials. Federal appointees were often considered incompetent and malicious.

The transition from an autonomous government under the direction of Church authorities to one administered under provisions of the territorial organic act was made easier by the appointment of Brigham YOUNG as the first territorial governor and the superintendent of Indian affairs. Difficulties arose, however, as Brigham Young's forceful methods and local popularity rankled non-

As second counselor to Brigham Young, Jedediah Morgan Grant (1816–1856) was one of the main figures in the Utah Reformation during the early years of the Utah Territory. At age eighteen he served in Zion's Camp, and later he became Salt Lake City's first mayor. The father of Heber J. Grant, he died at age forty.

Mormon carpetbag appointees—especially the chief justice and associate justices. For their part, some of these non-Mormon imports from the East acted in ways that offended local sensibilities.

Conflicts also developed between territorial judges and locally elected county officials—especially the probate judges, who, in Utah, had unusually broad jurisdiction. Elected by popular vote and often serving concurrently as local BISHOPS, the probate judges also served as chairmen of the county court, which included three other selectmen, and oversaw timber and water resources. In addition, they supervised the establishment of districts for roads, schools, voting, and other purposes; the levying of taxes; the construction of public buildings; the care of orphans, the insane, and stray animals; and the election or appointment of lesser officials. They also exercised original jurisdiction in both civil and criminal cases

(see COURTS, ECCLESIASTICAL, NINETEENTH CENTURY).

In 1850 the territory consisted of only seven counties: Salt Lake, Davis, Weber, Tooele, Utah, Sanpete, and Iron. While these counties still existed in 1896, when statehood was granted, their size had been reduced. When Utah became a state, twenty-eight of the present twenty-nine counties were functioning.

The election of James Buchanan as U.S. president in 1856 and his decision to put down the alleged Mormon rebellion and appoint a new territorial governor in place of Brigham Young led to the UTAH EXPEDITION of 1857–1858. At its peaceful conclusion, federal troops established Camp Floyd, forty miles south of Salt Lake City, and Alfred Cumming became territorial governor. During the ensuing years, eleven individuals were appointed territorial governor, and five territorial secretaries served briefly as acting governor. Most of the appointed officials were sincere in their efforts, though a few appeared to be political scoundrels. All were challenged by the task of interpreting, administering, and enforcing federal laws that went against the beliefs and practices of Utah's majority population (see ANTIPOLYGAMY LEGISLATION).

The fundamental conflict was resolved and the way to statehood opened when Church President Wilford WOODRUFF issued the 1890 MANIFESTO ending the practice of PLURAL MARRIAGE. In July 1894 U.S. President Grover Cleveland signed an enabling act to permit the people of Utah to prepare a state government. On January 4, 1896, President Cleveland proclaimed UTAH STATEHOOD, formally ending Utah's territorial period.

BIBLIOGRAPHY

Cooley, Everett L. "Carpetbag Rule—Territorial Government in Utah." *Utah Historical Quarterly* 26, no. 2 (Apr. 1958):107–129.

LaMar, Howard R. *The Far Southwest, 1846–1912: A Territorial History.* New Haven, Conn., 1966.

Larson, Gustive O. *The "Americanization" of Utah for Statehood.* San Marino, Calif., 1971.

Lyman, Edward Leo. *Political Deliverance: The Mormon Quest for Utah Statehood.* Urbana, Ill., 1986.

ALLAN KENT POWELL

V

VALUES, TRANSMISSION OF

Like other religious organizations, The Church of Jesus Christ of Latter-day Saints is concerned about transmitting its values to its young people. Its youth are viewed as future leaders, teachers, and parents who will one day influence the growth and success of other Church members, including their own children. Of central interest to the Church is helping young people gain a foundation of basic values that will have vital influence on later behavior and future religious development.

The process of transmitting these values is neither simple nor easy. It focuses on the conditions and experiences of home and family. Domestic factors have the greatest potential for positive or negative influence in a child's life. In addition, the Church provides a multi-faceted support program in the form of the second-strongest influences—leaders, teachers, and advisers seen by youth as credible, respected, and approachable adults.

The Lord has commanded parents, first and foremost, to teach their children the gospel (D&C 68:25–28; cf. Deut. 6:7; 2 Ne. 25:23–27; Jacob 3:10; 4:2–5). This obligation cannot be delegated. President David O. MCKAY taught, "The home is the first and most effective place for children to learn the lessons of life. . . . No other success can compensate for failure in the home" (*Family Home Evening Manual*, p. iii; also quoting J. E. McCul-

loch, *Home: The Savior of Civilization* [Washington, D.C., 1924], p. 24). Church leaders continue to stress the need for parents to teach values in the home.

Church support for parental duties was apparent as early as President Brigham YOUNG: "Let the keynote of your work be the establishment in the youth of an individual testimony of the truth and magnitude of the great Latter-day work, and the development of the gifts within them" (*GD*, p. 391).

Well-documented trends throughout the world give ample reason for concern about young people. Although the level and intensity of problematic social behaviors are lower among active, involved LDS youth (*see* SOCIAL CHARACTERISTICS), there are so many negative influences that the reinforcement of traditional Christian values has become a persistent concern of the Church.

Prevention is the preferred mode of addressing potential problems among the youth of the Church, and the best preventative efforts are those that do indeed inculcate values. Such efforts take several approaches: formal and informal, and systematic, localized, and individualized.

The Church regularly provides its youth with educational instruction, service opportunities, social activities, role models, leadership experiences, speaking opportunities, teaching assignments, and frequent personal interviews with ecclesiastical leaders. The settings for these efforts are PRIMARY for children, YOUNG WOMEN for girls twelve to eighteen, AARONIC PRIESTHOOD quorums and YOUNG MEN for boys twelve to eighteen. Church-sponsored sports programs, Sunday School classes, summer camps, youth conferences, FIRESIDES, SCOUTING, and SEMINARY also supplement the efforts of parents through FAMILY HOME EVENING and other interaction. The Church also publishes the *Friend* and the *New Era*, monthly magazines for young children and for youth to age eighteen. Lessons, speeches, and magazine articles designed for the youth of the Church are usually based on personal experiences, scriptural models, or values stressed by the Presidents of the Church.

Youth growing up in the Church advance through a series of stages in their maturation that give some structure to their formation of religious values. At the age of eight, girls and boys are prepared by their parents and teachers for BAPTISM and are interviewed by their bishop before they are baptized and confirmed. Baptism and confirmation are occasions for individual attention, as well as family participation and celebration. From a young age children are encouraged to bear their TESTIMONY in Church meetings and in the home, and are asked to memorize the ARTICLES OF FAITH in order to graduate from Primary. Young men typically are ordained deacons, teachers, and priests in the Aaronic Priesthood at the ages of twelve, fourteen, and sixteen, respectively. They are inducted into service and leadership experiences in these ordinations. They also advance through the ranks of the Scouting program, where the values of the Scout Law are taught. Young women from twelve to eighteen, similarly advance through a program of study and activity that involve the setting and achieving of many value-shaping goals. In addition, most young people in the Church receive a PATRIARCHAL BLESSING during their teenage years. This may serve as an influential personal guide to the values and goals they will adopt for the rest of their lives.

In the late 1970s and early 1980s, the Church conducted studies of the process of value acquisition and program effectiveness, first within the Young Women organization and later within a U.S. sample of young men (Weed, Condie, Hafen, and Warner; "Key to Strong Young Men"). These studies validated the Church's placing emphasis on the family as the most important agent for the transmission of values. Home religious observance was the strongest predictor of positive outcomes and

explained more of the difference between young men's religious intention and behavior than all other factors combined. Home religious observance included the examples set by parents, experiences, and activities such as FAMILY PRAYER, family home evening, scripture study, and informal discussions about religion. Indicators of value acquisition included one's intention to be active in the Church, to be morally clean, and to serve as a full-time missionary (*see* ACTIVITY IN THE CHURCH; MISSION; MORALITY).

A second important factor noted in transmitting values was the nature and quality of interpersonal relationships between the youth and their adult Church leaders. This factor became more significant as boys grew older, with sixteen- to eighteen-year-old boys strongly influenced by Church leaders whom they trusted, respected, and admired, as people in whom they felt they could confide. Having trusted leaders can be especially important to young LDS converts in combining the basic values taught in their homes with Church doctrines and principles.

Home and family, combined with high-quality relationships with Church leaders, were more influential than any particular programs or activities. These results comprised not just a simple tabulation of expression by youth of important influences in their lives but empirical data confirming the relationship between what youth valued and what they actually did.

The implications of the study are both reassuring and disconcerting. It is reassuring to the Church to know that its emphasis on parental responsibility contributes directly and significantly to the goals of the Church for its young people; that its young people, even in the challenging teenage years, are influenced by caring adult leaders; and that value acquisition and religious SOCIALIZATION do not require great expense and elaborate facilities. Less reassuring is the knowledge that many of the programs, activities, and lessons are not as productive by themselves as had been hoped. For the youth, a particular lesson's content may not be as important as who presents it and the mutual relationships of trust, confidence, respect, and admiration that are built between the youth and the presenter. The leader's personality and example of faith apparently carry more weight than the carefully planned curriculum prepared at Church headquarters.

Peers and the CHURCH EDUCATIONAL SYSTEM are also strong value-transmission factors as young people mature. These factors build on the relationships and activities experienced by teenagers, but as these young people leave home, institutes of religion near college campuses, wards composed of students and singles, and Church institutions of higher learning, such as BRIGHAM YOUNG UNIVERSITY, provide young adults with additional opportunities to develop relationships with dedicated leaders and teachers and with peers who have similar values.

For many young men and women, service as a full-time missionary is a powerful experience in the transmission of spiritual values from the Church to the individual. Working as a full-time missionary for eighteen months (for women) or two years (for men) becomes for many a rite of passage from a culturally based religious identity to one that is spiritually based, or internalized. During this time, many benefits of gospel instruction, the BAPTISMAL COVENANT, PRIESTHOOD ORDINATIONS and blessings, and the temple ENDOWMENT are realized and become securely embedded as one's ideals for life.

This religious identity gives the young adult an image of what it means to be a religious person, a son or daughter of God, a disciple of Jesus Christ, a member of the Church. Seeing oneself as wanting and striving to be consistent with those images gives much of the meaning and purpose to LDS life. Church members often describe the experience of receiving a witness or testimony from the Holy Ghost as a sacred moment, which contributes to, or further solidifies, their commitment to the gospel of Christ and their personal identity within the community of Saints.

[See also Individuality; Leadership Training.]

BIBLIOGRAPHY

Family Home Evening Manual. Salt Lake City, 1968.

Fife, Austin E. "Folk Elements in the Formation of the Mormon Personality." BYU Studies 1 (Autumn 1959):1–17.

"Key to Strong Young Men: Gospel Commitment in the Home." Ensign 14 (Dec. 1984):66–68.

Kimball, Spencer W. "Therefore I Was Taught." Ensign 12 (Jan. 1982):3–5.

Oaks, Dallin H. "Parental Leadership in the Family." Ensign 15 (June 1985):7–11.

Smith, Joseph F. "Auxiliary Organizations." In GD, p. 391.

Weed, Stan; Spencer Condie; Bruce Hafen; and Keith Warner. Young Women Study. A Technical Report. Research and Evaluation Division, The Church of Jesus Christ of Latter-day Saints. Salt Lake City, 1977.

STAN E. WEED

VIEW OF THE HEBREWS

Ethan Smith's View of the Hebrews (Poultney, Vt., 1823; second enlarged edition, 1825) combines scriptural citations and reports from various observers among American Indians and Jews to support the claim that the Indians were the descendants of the Lost Ten Tribes of Israel. It is one of several books reflecting the popular fascination at the time of Joseph Smith with the question of Indian origins. While some have claimed it to be a source for the Book of Mormon, no direct connections between this book and the Book of Mormon have been demonstrated.

The full title of the 1825 edition is View of the Hebrews; or the Tribes of Israel in America. Exhibiting the Destruction of Jerusalem; the Certain Restoration of Judah and Israel; the Present State of Judah and Israel; and an Address of the Prophet Isaiah to the United States Relative to Their Restoration. The author, Ethan Smith (no relation to Joseph Smith), was pastor of the Congregational church in Poultney, Vermont.

The first chapter deals with the destruction of Jerusalem in A.D. 70 by the Romans, as referred to in scriptural prophecy and historical sources. The second chapter tells of the literal expulsion of the Ten Tribes of Israel in 721 B.C. and the establishment of the kingdom of Judah; it also maintains that their restoration will be literal, and it quotes heavily from Isaiah. The third chapter summarizes the outcast condition of Israel in 1823; it also argues that the natives of America are "the descendants of Israel" and propounds that all pre-Columbian Americans had one origin, that their language appears originally to have been Hebrew, that they had an ark of the covenant, that they practiced circumcision, that they acknowledged one and only one God, that their tribal structure was similar to Hebrew organization, that they had cities of refuge, and that they manifest a variety of Hebraic traits of prophetic character and tradition. These claims are supported by citations from James Adair and Alexander von Humboldt. The fourth chapter emphasizes the restoration of Israel, quoting from Isaiah and using Isaiah chapter 18 to create an "Address" to the United States to save Israel. In conclusion, Ethan Smith pleads that the "suppliants of God in the West" be faithful and helpful in bringing scattered Israel "to the place of the name of the Lord of hosts, the Mount Zion."

Alleged relationships of View of the Hebrews to the Book of Mormon have attracted interest periodically through the years. Ethan Smith's book was published in the adjoining county west of Windsor County, where Joseph Smith was born and lived from 1805 to 1811. Nevertheless, there is no evidence that Joseph Smith ever knew anything about this book. Detractors have pointed to several "parallels" between the two books, but others point to numerous "unparallels"; as two of many examples, the Book of Mormon never mentions an ark of the covenant or cities of refuge.

I. Woodbridge Riley in 1902 was the first author to suggest a relationship between *View of the Hebrews* and the Book of Mormon (*The Founder of Mormonism*, New York, 1902, pp. 124–26). In 1921, LDS Church authorities were asked to reply to questions posed by a Mr. Couch of Washington, D.C., regarding Native American origins, linguistics, technology, and archaeology. B. H. Roberts, a member of the First Quorum of Seventy, undertook a study of Couch's issues; he received some assistance from a committee of other General Authorities. Roberts's first report, in December 1921, was a 141-page paper entitled "Book of Mormon Difficulties." However, he was not satisfied with that work and later delved more deeply into other critical questions about Book of Mormon origins, which led him to a major analysis of *View of the Hebrews*.

Around March–May 1922, Roberts wrote a 291-page document, "A Book of Mormon Study," and an eighteen-point summary entitled "A Parallel." In the "Study" Roberts looked candidly at the possibility that Joseph Smith could have been acquainted with Ethan Smith's book and could have used it as a source of the structure and some ideas in the Book of Mormon. He cited some twenty-six similarities between the two books. In all his writings, Roberts did not draw any conclusions that Joseph Smith used Ethan Smith's work to write the Book of Mormon, but rather posed questions that believers in the Book of Mormon should be aware of and continue to find answers for. Roberts's faith in the Book of Mormon as divinely revealed scripture was unshaken by his studies.

Roberts's papers were published in 1985. This again stirred an interest in the relationship of *View of the Hebrews* and the Book of Mormon, especially since the editorial "Introduction" concluded that "the record is mixed" as to whether Roberts kept his faith in the authenticity of the Book of Mormon after making his studies (B. D. Madsen, p. 29). Subsequent research, however, strongly indicates that Roberts remained committed to the full claims of the origin and doctrine of the Book of Mormon to the end of his life (Welch, pp. 59–60), and substantial evidence favors the position that there is little in common between the ideas and statements in *View of the Hebrews* and the Book of Mormon.

BIBLIOGRAPHY

Madsen, Brigham D., ed. *B. H. Roberts: Studies of the Book of Mormon.* Urbana, Ill., 1985.

Madsen, Truman G., comp. *B. H. Roberts: His Final Decade.* Provo, Utah, 1985.

Welch, John W. "B. H. Roberts: Seeker After Truth." *Ensign* 16 (Mar. 1986):56–62.

RICHARD C. ROBERTS

VIRGIN BIRTH

Mary, mother of Jesus Christ, was a virgin at the time of Jesus' birth. Of Old Testament prophets, ISAIAH alone foretold this circumstance (Isaiah 7:14), but Book of Mormon prophets also foresaw the virgin birth. NEPHI$_1$ described Mary as "a virgin, most beautiful and fair" and "mother of the son of God, after the manner of the flesh" (1 Ne. 11:15, 18). ALMA declared that Christ "shall be born of Mary . . . a virgin . . . who shall . . . conceive by the power of the Holy Ghost and bring forth a son, yea, even the Son of God" (Alma 7:10).

In fulfillment of these prophecies, Gabriel "was sent from God . . . to a virgin . . . and the virgin's name was Mary," and Gabriel announced to her that she would "bring forth a son, and . . . call his name Jesus." To her question, "How shall this be?" Gabriel answered, "The Holy Ghost shall come upon thee . . . therefore [the child] . . . born of thee shall be called the Son of God" (Luke 1:26–35). Thereafter, Joseph married Mary but "knew her not till she had brought forth her firstborn son" (Matt. 1:25). Thus, Jesus was born of a mortal mother who was a virgin.

[See also Immaculate Conception; Mary, Mother of Jesus.]

BIBLIOGRAPHY

McConkie, Bruce R. *The Promised Messiah*, pp. 465–66. Salt Lake City, 1978.

ELEANOR COLTON

VISIONS

A vision from God is a form of revelation whereby God discloses himself and his will. It is a visual mode of divine communication, in contrast with hearing words spoken or receiving impressions to the mind. LDS experience is consistent with biblical precedent in affirming that visions constitute a mark of divine approval. Such heavenly manifestations informed and directed Old Testament prophets (e.g., Daniel, Isaiah) and New Testament apostles (e.g., Peter, Paul). They have similarly been part of the foundation of revelation upon which Latter-day Saint prophets and apostles have asserted their testimony of the Lord. The visions of Joseph SMITH and of the Book of Mormon prophets are comparable with those of the other testamental epochs. These historic periods of testimony—the Old, the New, the Book of Mormon, and the Latter-day—show similar patterns of revelation from God. Each of these dispensations of the gospel has included visions that communicated the mind and will of the Lord for that time.

An experience of a vision in Old Testament times is "The Lord spake unto Moses face to face, as a man speaketh with his friend" (Ex. 33:11). Similarly, Moses "saw God face to face, and he talked with him, and the glory of God was upon Moses; therefore Moses could endure his presence" (Moses 1:2). The vision of Stephen in Acts 7:55–56 is no less vivid: "He, being full of the Holy Ghost . . . said, Behold, I see the heavens opened, and the Son of man standing on the right hand of God." Comparable is the vision of Joseph Smith and Sidney RIGDON recorded in D&C 76:19: "The Lord touched the eyes of our understandings and they were opened. . . . And we beheld the glory of the Son, on the right hand of the Father." Each vision is unequivocal and is accompanied by the Spirit of the Lord (see VISIONS OF JOSEPH SMITH).

These distinctive testimonies anchor all the rest of God's communion by a visual link with an ordinarily unseen world that directs the destiny of humankind. They provide a vivid sense of the nature of God and his design for the world that gives coherence to all other scripture and inspiration. Spiritual illumination, visual and otherwise, is contingent upon faith and trust in the Lord and obedience to him. When people reject or stray from the will of the Lord, they withdraw from his spirit (Mosiah 2:36), and visions cease. And, as declared in Proverbs 29:18: "Where there is no vision, the people perish."

In LDS doctrine visions are perceptions, aided by the Spirit, of something ordinarily invisible to human beings. The things disclosed are viewed as part of general reality. This process is according to natural law and is not "supernatural," in the usual sense of that term. It is analogous to the fact that some physically real phenomena, such as X rays and atomic particles, are not discerned by the ordinary senses but may be detected by scientific instruments. In the case of visions, the instrument is the person, and the mechanism of observation is faith aided by the Spirit of God.

It is vital to distinguish authentically revealed visions from self-induced imaginings, wish-fulfilling dreams, errors of perception, satanic deceptions, and pathological hallucinating, all of which have been abundant in human history. Spurious visions result from seeking "signs"; authentic visions usually come unbidden. "He that seeketh signs shall see signs, but not unto salvation. . . . Faith cometh not by signs, but signs follow those that believe" (D&C 67:7, 9).

Certain criteria assist in judging the authenticity of any revelation, including a vision:

- It strengthens faith in Jesus Christ, the Son of God, and in his divine mission and doctrine.

- It is confirmed by the witness of the Holy Ghost to the sincere seeker.

- It is usually experienced and reported by an ordained servant of the Lord, often in the name of the Lord. It is declared clearly and unequivocally, and has general application for a people or a time, or for all people and all time. Inspired visions may be experienced by others, but they have specific application to those persons or situations.

- The witness is usually supported by additional testimony, such as accompaniment of the Spirit of God, other manifestations, or the word of additional testators.

- It is consistent with scriptural principles and established doctrine.

- The one receiving and conveying the message is morally upright, honest, and humbly obedient to the commandments of God.

- The content revealed and the behavior admonished are comprehensible as good and true.

- The consequences of following the information or direction are beneficial to the individual and to others, except in cases where the vision contains a rebuke of iniquity or a prophecy of destruction.
- Feelings of enlightenment, edification, and peace, rather than of anxiety or confusion, follow the receiving or awareness of the vision.
- It is not induced by drugs, eroticism, violent or hyperemotional ritual, or worship of false spirits.

While it is often asserted that visions are merely the natural outcome of psychology, biology, culture, or drugs, this viewpoint has never been adequately supported. Such interpretations are helpful for a narrow range of explainable phenomena but do not reach the transcendent and inspirational realm of true visions. Theories from the time of Freudian psychoanalysis to the modern psychobiology of dreams and altered states of consciousness fall short of comprehending divinely given concepts.

BIBLIOGRAPHY

Flusser, David. "Visions." In *Encyclopaedia Judaica*, Vol. 16, pp. 166–68. Jerusalem, 1972.

Nibley, Hugh W. *Enoch the Prophet.* In *CWHN*, Vol. 2.

ALLEN E. BERGIN

VISIONS OF JOSEPH SMITH

Ancient prophets were typically called through a revelatory process—visions and/or revelations: "If there be a prophet among you, I the Lord will make myself known unto him in a vision, and will speak unto him in a dream" (Num. 12:6). The prophet Joel anticipated that visions would increase in the last days, saying, "Old men shall dream dreams, [and] young men shall see visions" (Joel 2:28–32).

The Prophet Joseph Smith had his first vision at the age of fourteen while praying in a grove of trees in western New York (see FIRST VISION). The appearance of the Lord to him, like that to Saul of Tarsus, was attended by a shining light from heaven (Acts 9:3). The Lord spoke face-to-face with Joseph and called him to service. This was the first of a series of visions Joseph SMITH received, many of which were shared with other persons. Blessed like John on the isle of Patmos and Paul who spoke of the third heaven, the Prophet Joseph Smith affirmed, "Could you gaze into heaven five minutes, you would know more than you would by reading all that ever was written on the subject" (*TPJS*, p. 324; cf. *HC* 6:50). He also declared that "the best way to obtain truth and wisdom is not to ask it from books, but to go to God in prayer, and obtain divine teaching" (*TPJS*, p. 191).

President John TAYLOR said that Joseph Smith had contact with prophets from every dispensation:

Because he [Joseph] stood at the head of the dispensation of the fulness of times, which comprehends all the various dispensations that have existed upon the earth, and that as the Gods in the eternal worlds and the Priesthood that officiated in time and eternity had declared that it was time for the issuing forth of all these things, they all combined together to impart to him the keys of their several missions [*JD* 18:326].

A new dispensation requires the conferral of priesthood and keys, in accordance with the law of witnesses: "In the mouth of two or three witnesses shall every word be established" (2 Cor. 13:1). During the restoration sequence when priesthood and keys were conferred by angelic ministrants, the Prophet was accompanied by one or more witnesses. Oliver COWDERY was a principal figure in the fulfillment of this law of witnesses (see WITNESSES, LAW OF); others were David WHITMER, Martin HARRIS, and Sidney RIGDON. Distinguishing dreams from visions and associating visions and visitations, Joseph said, "An open vision will manifest that which is more important" (*TPJS*, p. 161). Crucial visions received by the Prophet Joseph Smith are the source of many cardinal doctrines and teachings of the Latter-day Saints.

THE FIRST VISION. Lucy Mack SMITH recalled that as the Joseph Smith, Sr., family worked their Manchester, New York, farm in the period of 1820, "there was a great revival in religion, which extended to all denominations of Christians in the surrounding country." Lucy and three of the children joined the Western Presbyterian Church in Palmyra, but Joseph remained "unchurched." He later wrote, "It was impossible . . . to come to any certain conclusion who was right and who was wrong" (JS—H 1:8). In answer to a biblical prompting that "if any of you lack wisdom, let him ask of God" (James 1:5), Joseph retired to the woods and uttered what he termed his "first vocal prayer." His prayer of faith was answered. Joseph recorded, "I saw two Personages, whose brightness and glory defy all description, standing above me in the air. One of them spake unto me, calling me by name and said, pointing to the other—*This is My Beloved Son. Hear Him!*" Responding to his inquiry concerning which church he should join, the Lord instructed Joseph to join none of them, saying that he must continue as he was "until further directed" (JS—H 1:17–19, 26). When Joseph left the grove, he possessed the knowledge that God and his Son were actual personages, that the Godhead was composed of separate individuals, and that God hears and answers prayers. He also knew that he must not affiliate with the existing denominations (Backman, 1971, pp. 206–208). This vision set in motion a train of visitations by angelic ministrants directing the young prophet in the process of restoring the gospel of Jesus Christ.

VISITATIONS OF MORONI. The Prophet continued to pursue his common vocations until September 21, 1823, while "suffering severe persecution at the hands of all classes of men," in part as a result of his claims concerning his first vision (JS—H 1:27). As he prayed that evening that he might know his standing before God, an angel appeared at his bedside, saying that he had been sent from the presence of God and that his name was Moroni. He explained "that God had a work for [Joseph] to do; and that [his] name should be had for good and evil among all nations" (JS—H 1:33). He instructed Joseph concerning a book that was written on gold plates, giving an account of the former inhabitants of the continent. The fulness of the everlasting gospel was contained in the record as delivered by the Savior to these people. Joseph was also shown a vision of a nearby hill and the place where the plates containing this record were deposited.

The next day, Joseph went to the hill, subsequently known by his followers as Cumorah, removed a stone covering, and viewed the contents of the box beneath, the plates, the URIM AND THUMMIM, and a breastplate. The angel reappeared and informed him that the time for the removal of the plates had not arrived and that he was to meet him for further instruction at that same site over a succession of four years (JS—H 1:53). A further vision was opened to Joseph's view, and he saw the "prince of darkness, surrounded by his innumerable train of associates." The heavenly messenger said, "All this is shown, the good and the evil, the holy and impure, the glory of God and the power of darkness, that you may know hereafter the two powers and never be influenced or overcome by that wicked one" (*Messenger and Advocate* 2:198).

From 1824 to 1827, Joseph returned to the hill each year as specified. On September 22, 1827, he met the angel and received final instructions regarding the record. Moroni gave the record to the Prophet to translate. Joseph said, "The same heavenly messenger delivered them up to me with this charge: that I should be responsible for them; that if I should let them go carelessly, or through any neglect of mine, I should be cut off; but that if I would use all my endeavors to preserve them, until he, the messenger, should call for them, they should be protected" (JS—H 1:59). The messenger did not limit his instruction solely to these annual meetings, but made contact with Joseph on numerous occasions (Peterson, pp. 119–20). In all, the angel Moroni visited Joseph Smith at least twenty times (*see* MORONI, VISITATIONS OF). Joseph informed associates that other Book of Mormon prophets also visited him, including Nephi, son of Lehi (Cheesman, pp. 38–60). Lucy Mack Smith recalled that her son Joseph was enabled from this tutoring to describe "with much ease" the ancient inhabitants of America, "their dress, mode of traveling, and the animals upon which they rode; their cities, their buildings, with every particular; their mode of warfare; and also their religious worship" (p. 83).

JOHN THE BAPTIST. While translating the Book of Mormon at Harmony, Pennsylvania, on May 15, 1829, Joseph Smith and Oliver COWDERY became concerned about baptism for the remission of sins as described in 3 Nephi 11. They went into the woods to pray for enlightenment. Both record that a messenger from heaven, identifying himself as John the Baptist, laid hands on them and ordained them to the Aaronic Priesthood, saying, "Upon you my fellow servants, in the name of Messiah, I confer the Priesthood of Aaron, which holds the keys of the ministering of angels, and of the gospel of repentance, and of baptism by immersion for the remission of sins; and this shall never be taken again from the earth until the sons of Levi do offer again an offering unto the Lord in righteousness" (JS—H 1:69; D&C 13; cf. *TPJS*, pp. 172–73).

PETER, JAMES, AND JOHN. John the Baptist also informed Joseph and Oliver that "this Aaronic Priesthood had not the power of laying on hands for the gift of the Holy Ghost, but that this should be conferred on us hereafter." John stated "that he acted under the direction of Peter, James and John, who held the keys of the Priesthood of Melchizedek, which Priesthood, he said, would in due time be conferred on us" (JS—H 1:70, 72).

This restoration occurred during the latter part of May or early June 1829, someplace between Harmony and Colesville on the Susquehanna River (see MELCHIZEDEK PRIESTHOOD: RESTORATION OF). Of this visitation, Joseph Smith later testified, "The Priesthood is everlasting. The Savior, Moses, & Elias—gave the Keys to Peter, James & John on the Mount when they were transfigured before him. . . . How have we come at the priesthood in the last days? It came down, down in regular succession. Peter, James & John had it given to them & they gave it up [to us]" (WJS, p. 9).

THREE WITNESSES OF THE BOOK OF MORMON. By revelation Oliver Cowdery, David Whitmer, and Martin Harris were selected to be witnesses of the plates and the authentic translation of the Book of Mormon (2 Ne. 11:3; 27:12; Ether 5:2–4; D&C 5:11–18; D&C 17). During the latter part of June 1829, in company with Joseph Smith, these three men went into the woods adjacent to the Whitmer home in Fayette, New York, and knelt in prayer. When the promised revelation was not immediately received, Martin Harris stated that he felt he might be the cause of their failure. After Martin Harris withdrew, the others knelt in prayer again. David Whitmer described the visitation of Moroni:

> The angel stood before us. He was dressed in white, and spoke and called me by name and said "Blessed is he that keepeth His commandments. . . ." A table was set before us and on it the Records of the Nephites, from which the Book of Mormon was translated, the breast plates [and also the Urim and Thummim], the Ball of Directors [Liahona], the Sword of Laban and other plates. While we were viewing them the voice of God spoke out of heaven saying that the Book was true and the translation correct [quoted in "Letter from Elder W. H. Kelley," Saints' Herald 29 (Mar. 1, 1882):68].

Afterward, Joseph found Martin Harris, and together they experienced a similar manifestation. The Three Witnesses later endorsed a statement describing their experience that has been appended to all copies of the Book of Mormon. They swore that they had seen the angel and the plates and that "we also know that they have been translated by the gift and power of God, for his voice hath declared it unto us" (see BOOK OF MORMON WITNESSES). Subsequently, eight others were privileged to see and handle the plates, but without the presence of the angel or having heard the voice of God.

VISION OF GLORIES. While preparing the text of his translation of the Bible, Joseph Smith, with Sidney Rigdon, moved to the John Johnson home in Hiram, Ohio, on September 12, 1831. As the two men worked on the Gospel of John, it became apparent to them that many important points concerning the salvation of individuals had been lost from the Bible. Joseph wrote, "It appeared self-evident from what truths were left, that if God rewarded every one according to the deeds done in the body the term 'Heaven,' as intended for the Saints' eternal home must include more kingdoms than one" (HC 1:245). On February 16, 1832, in an upper room of the Johnson home, while he and Sidney Rigdon were examining the passage from John 5:29, they saw a multifaceted vision (D&C 76), commencing with a vision of the Father and the Son in the highest glory. This scene was followed by a series of visions, including Perdition and the sons of Perdition and then the celestial, terrestrial, and telestial kingdoms of glory. One witness, Philo Dibble, present in the room recalled that the two men sat motionless for about an hour. One would say, "What do I see," and describe it, and the other would say, "I see the same" (Juvenile Instructor 27 [May 15, 1892]:303–304).

It is apparent that the Prophet Joseph Smith did not impart all that he saw in vision, for he later said, "I could explain a hundred fold more than I ever have of the glories of the kingdoms manifested to me in the vision, were I permitted, and were the people prepared to receive them" (TPJS, p. 305).

KIRTLAND TEMPLE VISIONS. From January 21 to May 1, 1836, many of the Saints in Kirtland experienced an outpouring of the Spirit, a "Pentecostal season." On January 21, the Prophet assembled with others in the west schoolroom on the third story of the Kirtland Temple. Here Joseph beheld a vision of the celestial kingdom of God (D&C 137). He beheld the Father and the Son and several ancient worthies, including Adam, Abraham, and his own mother and father (both still living), and his brother Alvin, who had died in 1823 (verse 5). As Joseph marveled over Alvin's station in the celestial kingdom, the voice of the Lord declared, "All who have died without a knowledge of this gospel, who would have received it if they had been permitted to tarry, shall be heirs of the celestial kingdom of God" (verse 7). He was also instructed concerning the destiny of little children. The Prophet recorded, "I also beheld that all children who die before they arrive at the years of accountability are saved in the celestial kingdom of heaven" (verse 10).

During the dedication of the Kirtland Temple on March 27, 1836, many testified of the presence of angels. The Prophet specifically identified the ancient apostles Peter and John as present among them (Backman, *The Heavens Resound*, 1983, pp. 299–300; cf. *JD* 9:376).

One week later, on April 3, 1836, Joseph Smith and Oliver Cowdery had retired to the Melchizedek Priesthood pulpits on the west side of the first floor of the temple. The curtains were dropped around the pulpit area as the men prayed. "The veil was taken from our minds, and the eyes of our understanding were opened" (D&C 110:1). The Lord stood before them on the breastwork of the pulpit. "His eyes were as a flame of fire; the hair of his head was white like the pure snow; his countenance shone above the brightness of the sun; and his voice was as the sound of the rushing of great waters, even the voice of Jehovah" (D&C 110:3). The Savior accepted the newly completed structure and promised that his name and glory would be present and that thousands of persons would receive an outpouring of blessings because of the temple and the endowment received by his servants in that house (D&C 110:6–9).

Following the Savior's appearance, three other messengers presented themselves. Each bestowed specific priesthood keys on the two leaders. Moses came and "committed [to them] the keys of the gathering of Israel" (verse 11). As Moses departed, Elias, possessing the keys of "the gospel of Abraham," appeared and administered the keys of this dispensation, saying "that in us and our seed all generations after us should be blessed" (verse 12). Further priesthood keys were restored by Elijah, who declared, "Behold, the time has fully come, which was spoken of by the mouth of Malachi—testifying that he [Elijah] should be sent

. . . to turn the hearts of the fathers to the children, and the children to the fathers" (verses 14–15; *see also* ABRAHAMIC COVENANT; GOSPEL OF ABRAHAM).

OTHER HEAVENLY MANIFESTATIONS. A variety of accounts affirm that other persons also witnessed such appearances not only in association with the Kirtland Temple but in an earlier period during meetings in the log schoolhouse on the Isaac Morley farm and in the SCHOOL OF THE PROPHETS, held in the Newel K. WHITNEY STORE (K. Anderson, pp. 107–113, 169–77; Backman, *The Heavens Resound*, 1983, pp. 240, 264–68, 284–309).

The visions discussed herein are but a few of the myriad manifestations that gave the Prophet direction. Joseph mentions having seen others in vision, including Michael, Gabriel, and Raphael, but does not detail their association (D&C 128:20–21). President John Taylor identified yet others who ministered to the Prophet, notably Adam, Seth, Enoch, Noah, Abraham, Isaac, and Jacob (*JD* 17:374; 18:325–26; 21:65, 94, 161; 23:48).

One writer has commented, "He had visions of the past as well as of the future. As a seer, he knew things about the past that are not part of our own scripture, but which he spoke of in discourse" (Madsen, p. 44). "I saw Adam in the valley of Adam-ondi-Ahman" (*TPJS*, p. 158). To Joseph Knight, Sr., the Prophet commented on the vistas opened to him through the Urim and Thummim, which he found deposited with the gold plates. Knight explained, "He seemed to think more of the glasses or Urim and Thummim . . . says he, 'I can see anything; they are marvelous'" (Jessee, 1976, p. 33). Accordingly, after reading Foxe's *Book of the Martyrs*, Joseph remarked that he had "seen those martyrs, and they were honest, devoted followers of Christ, according to the light they possessed, and they will be saved" (Stevenson, p. 6). He saw in vision marchers in ZION'S CAMP who had perished from cholera in Clay County, Missouri. He related their condition, observing to the survivors, "Brethren, I have seen those men who died of the cholera in our camp; and the Lord knows, if I get a mansion as bright as theirs, I ask no more" (*HC* 2:181n). The organizations of the Quorum of the Twelve Apostle and the First Quorum of the Seventy were made known to him "by vision and by the Holy Spirit," and he established those priesthood offices in February 1835 (*HC* 2:182). In an earlier vision, he "saw the Twelve Apostles of the Lamb, who are now upon the earth, who hold the keys of this last ministry, in foreign lands, standing together in a circle, much fatigued, with their clothes tattered and feet swollen, with their eyes cast downward, and Jesus standing in their midst, and they did not behold Him. The Savior looked upon them and wept" (*HC* 2:381). He saw a vision enabling him to designate the "central place" in Independence, Missouri (*TPJS*, p. 79). Of a vision of the resurrection of the dead, he explained, "So plain was the vision, that I actually saw men, before they had ascended from the tomb, as though they were getting up slowly" (*TPJS*, pp. 295–96). He also saw the Kirtland and Nauvoo temples in vision before their construction and gave detailed instructions to the architects, describing the windows and their illumination (*JD* 13:357; 14:273; *HC* 6:196–97). He foresaw the struggles of the Saints in crossing the plains, their establishment in the Rocky Mountains, and the future condition of the Saints (*HC* 5:85n–86n).

He remarked late in his life, "It is my meditation all the day & more than my meat & drink to know how I shall make the saints of God to comprehend the visions that roll like an overflowing surge, before my mind" (*WJS*, p. 196).

BIBLIOGRAPHY

Anderson, Karl Ricks. *Joseph Smith's Kirtland.* Salt Lake City, 1989.

Anderson, Richard Lloyd. *Investigating the Book of Mormon Witnesses.* Salt Lake City, 1981.

Andrus, Hyrum. *Joseph Smith, the Man and the Seer.* Salt Lake City, 1960.

Backman, Milton V., Jr. *Joseph Smith's First Vision.* Salt Lake City, 1971.

———. *Eyewitness Accounts of the Restoration.* Orem, Utah, 1983.

———. *The Heavens Resound.* Salt Lake City, 1983.

Bushman, Richard L. *Joseph Smith and the Beginnings of Mormonism.* Urbana, Ill., 1984.

Cheesman, Paul R. *The Keystone of Mormonism.* Provo, Utah, 1988.

Ehat, Andrew F., and Lyndon W. Cook. *The Words of Joseph Smith.* Salt Lake City, 1980.

Jessee, Dean C. "Joseph Knight's Recollection of Early Mormon History." *BYU Studies* 17 (Autumn 1976):29–39.

———. *The Papers of Joseph Smith,* Vol. 1. Salt Lake City, 1989.

Ludlow, Daniel H. *A Companion to Your Study of the Doctrine and Covenants,* Vol. 1. Salt Lake City, 1978.

Madsen, Truman G. *Joseph Smith the Prophet.* Salt Lake City, 1989.

Peterson, H. Donl. *Moroni, Ancient Prophet, Modern Messenger.* Bountiful, Utah, 1983.

Porter, Larry C. "Dating the Restoration of the Melchizedek Priesthood." *Ensign* 9 (June 1979):4–10.

———. "The Priesthood Restored." In *Studies in Scripture,* ed. R. Millet and K. Jackson, Vol. 2, pp. 389–409. Salt Lake City, 1985.

Smith, Lucy Mack. *History of Joseph Smith,* ed. Preston Nibley. Salt Lake City, 1958.

Sperry, Sidney B. *Doctrine and Covenants Compendium.* Salt Lake City, 1960.

Stevenson, Edward. *Reminiscences of Joseph, the Prophet.* Salt Lake City, 1893.

LARRY C. PORTER

VISITING TEACHING

Visiting teaching is an organized means whereby the women of the Church receive regular instructional and compassionate service visits—usually by personal contact in the home—from other female members of the Church. The purpose is to promote SISTERHOOD, present inspirational messages, and note instances of need wherein the temporal and spiritual resources of the Church might be helpful.

In practice, the ward RELIEF SOCIETY president or those assisting her assign pairs of visiting teachers to keep in contact with specific families over a period of several months or even years. More frequent contact is made with women and families exhibiting special needs, such as those new to the Church, the less active, single parents, the divorced, the widowed, the aged, and those faced with illness, death, or other difficulties.

The need for such visitors was recognized soon after the founding of the Relief Society in 1842. At the second meeting of the society on March 24, Emma SMITH, wife of the Prophet Joseph SMITH, suggested appointing persons to wait upon the poor. On July 28, 1843, a Necessity Committee of sixteen was named "to search out the poor and suffering, to call upon the rich for aid, and thus as far as possible, relieve the wants of all." The original functions of this committee were twofold: "to ascertain the condition of the families visited, and to accept contributions for charitable purposes" (General Board, 1942, pp. 43–44; 1966, p. 68).

In the early years of the Church in Nauvoo, Illinois, visiting teachers reported their visits at the regular Relief Society meeting before all members present, citing specific instances of need. It was also customary for visiting teachers during this period to apportion and distribute to needy families the commodities donated to the society.

In 1921 visiting teachers were relieved of the personal responsibility of both ascertaining and meeting the material needs of families, but since then they have continued to report confidentially (to the ward Relief Society president) any instances of illness or need requiring attention. Upon hearing such reports, the Relief Society president either visits the family herself or designates the visiting teachers or someone else to give aid as a representative of the society. In cases of economic need, the Relief Society president and ward bishop confidentially inquire concerning the family's condition to arrange for any needed assistance from Church resources and for means to remedy the situation causing need. This modification of assignment brought visiting teachers into the more agreeable role of friendly visitors carrying messages from the society to the home, yet still fulfilling the original assignment from the Prophet Joseph Smith to "provoke the brethren to good works in looking after the wants of the poor—searching after objects of charity, and in administering to their wants" (General Board, 1966, p. 18).

An observation of Eliza R. snow, an early president of the Relief Society organization, encapsulates the spirit of visiting teaching: "Many times a kind expression—a few words of counsel, or even a warm or affectionate shake of the hand—will do more good and be better appreciated than a purse of gold" (General Board, 1966, p. 40).

The importance of visiting teaching has been consistently reemphasized by Church Presidents. Spencer W. KIMBALL exhorted visiting teachers to do as the priesthood teachers do:

"Watch over the Church always"—not twenty minutes a month but always—"and be with and strengthen them"—not a knock at the door, but to be *with* them, and *lift* them, and strengthen them, and empower them, and fortify them—"and see that there is no iniquity, . . . neither hardness, . . . backbiting, nor evil speaking" (D&C 20:53–54). . . . How glorious is the privilege of two sisters going into a home, soft-pedaling anything that could be detrimental, and instead, building up all the authorities of the Church, the Church itself, its doctrines, its policies, its practices—"And see that [they] meet together often, and . . . do their duty" (D&C 20:55) [*Ensign*, June 1978, p. 24].

Visiting teaching allows every sister to serve in the Church. Whether active or inactive, single or married, newly baptized or a member of long standing, each can serve effectively as a visiting teacher.

Because of their sensitivity to the home and family and their consequent ability to identify needs that might otherwise go unobserved, visiting teachers give complementary support to the bishop and Relief Society president. They can also become a readily organized corps in times of emergency, crisis, or death. Countless recorded stories demonstrate the effectiveness of the visiting teaching program in extending essential service, love, and compassion to members, particularly the sisters of the Church.

[*See also* Compassionate Service.]

BIBLIOGRAPHY

General Board of the Relief Society. *A Centenary of Relief Society*. Salt Lake City, 1942.

———. *History of Relief Society—1842–1966*. Salt Lake City, 1966.

Relief Society Handbook, pp. 3–4. Salt Lake City, 1988.

MARIAN R. BOYER

VISITORS CENTERS

The Church maintains and staffs several HISTORICAL SITES and visitors centers. Their main functions are to introduce visitors to the history and doctrine of the Church, to help them understand the blessings of the restored gospel, and to strengthen the members and provide them with missionary opportunities.

Most tour guides at visitors centers and historic sites are volunteers, called to serve from six months to two years. They are taught specific information to present to visitors individually or in guided tours, and they are encouraged to meet the needs of their guests, answer questions, and have friendly personal interaction with them. Visitors are taught that the Church is a Christian religion and that Jesus is the Christ. An atmosphere of goodwill and positive public relations is sought for and fostered by the attendants and tour guides.

Visitors centers typically feature visual displays, films, photographs or paintings, replicas, and artifacts regarding the local site, as well as presentations about the Savior Jesus Christ, the Prophet Joseph Smith, the Bible and the Book of

The North Visitors Center welcomes more than 4.5 million visitors annually to Temple Square, the most-visited attraction in Utah. Located next to the Tabernacle (foreground), the building centers on the Christus statue, a large replica by Aldo Rebichi of the sculpture by Bertel Thorvaldsen in the Cathedral Church of Our Lady in Copenhagen. The statue is set among murals of planets, stars, and other elements of the universe, symbolic of Christ's infinite works and atonement.

Mormon, and the purpose of life on earth. Books and pamphlets are also made available.

As of 1990, ten visitors centers were located near Church temples. These centers are open to the public and explain the purposes of temples, but the temples themselves are not open to the public once they have been dedicated to sacred services. Visitors centers are located near the temples in Mesa, Arizona; Laie, Hawaii; Idaho Falls, Idaho; Los Angeles and Oakland, California; Mexico City, Mexico; Hamilton, New Zealand; St. George and Salt Lake City, Utah; and Washington, D.C.

As of 1990, seven other visitors centers were also maintained by the Church. They are located in New York City; at the hill CUMORAH, near Palmyra, New York; in NAUVOO, Illinois; in

INDEPENDENCE, MISSOURI; in San Diego, California (*see* MORMON BATTALION); at WELFARE SQUARE in Salt Lake City; and in Montevideo, Uruguay. Fifteen additional historical sites are likewise maintained and staffed by the Church, offering tours and historical information to all who are interested. Several other historical sites are owned and maintained by the Church but are not staffed.

[*See also* Historical Sites.]

GARETH W. SEASTRAND

VITAL STATISTICS

The membership of The Church of Jesus Christ of Latter-day Saints has undergone dramatic growth and increased geographic dispersion, and its composition is unusual in several respects. This discussion of LDS demographics will focus on (1) size, growth, and distribution of the population; (2) sources of growth and redistribution, including fertility, mortality, migration, conversion, and disaffiliation; and (3) composition of the membership in terms of age, gender, race, marital status, household structure, and socioeconomic status. Several of the statistics will be summarized for major geographical regions.

The Church implemented record-keeping procedures from its organization in 1830 (*see* RECORD KEEPING). Its records provide several sources of information. First, such vital events as the blessing of children (soon after birth) and baptism (after age eight) are recorded, and summary statistics are compiled. Second, a membership record is created and updated with information on marriages, ordinations to the lay priesthood, and geographic relocation. In the United States and an increasing number of other countries, membership records are computerized and some summary statistics are compiled. Third, every ward and branch is instructed to compile quarterly and annual reports that include information on the size of the congregation, numbers in attendance at church services, and group composition. Fourth, sample surveys of the membership have been conducted in the United States and some other countries by the Church's Research Division. These surveys provide up-to-date information comparable to demographic data available at the national level, and provide a basis for comparison between

Latter-day Saints and the host societies in which they live. Fifth, Latter-day Saints are encouraged to compile information on their ancestors. These genealogies provide interesting historical information on LDS demographics. Finally, some sources of data for national populations in the United States and Canada include religion, and these populations contain a sufficient number of Latter-day Saints to allow separate analysis and comparison between them and other groups.

The accuracy of data is limited by several factors. Record keeping is often assigned to lay members with insufficient time, resources, and training to ensure a high level of accuracy. Changing procedures and personnel also create inconsistencies in collection procedures. Undercounts, missing reports, delays in recording change, and computational errors detract from data quality. Despite these problems, it is assumed that official data sources generally mirror demographic changes in actual Church membership.

SIZE, GROWTH, AND DISTRIBUTION

SIZE AND GROWTH. From its inception, the Church has viewed missionary work as divinely mandated and thus has been committed to increas-ing its membership. Beginning with the six people who officially organized the Church in 1830, the membership exhibits a classic pattern of exponential growth (Fig. 1). Since 1860, the membership has grown at a relatively steady rate, doubling approximately every nineteen years. Growth was slower in the first half of the twentieth century, but picked up again after 1950. Membership stood at 7.76 million at the end of 1990.

The size of the LDS population by the end of 1990 is presented for all countries in the Appendix. In addition to the United States, with 4.27 million members, nine other countries have more than 100,000 members. Thirty-eight countries have at least 10,000 members. The ratio of Latter-day Saints per 1,000 in the national population varies widely, from a low of .1 in Nigeria to more than 300 in Tonga. Eight countries have at least 1 percent of their population belonging to the LDS Church. Recent growth rates also vary widely, from a low of 0.0 in Scotland to a high of .23 in Portugal. With some exceptions, growth rates are relatively low in Europe and the South Pacific, while Latin America and some areas of Asia and Africa have relatively high rates of growth.

Although projections based on current growth rates are usually not precise predictions of the fu-

Figure 1

GROWTH IN TOTAL MEMBERSHIP

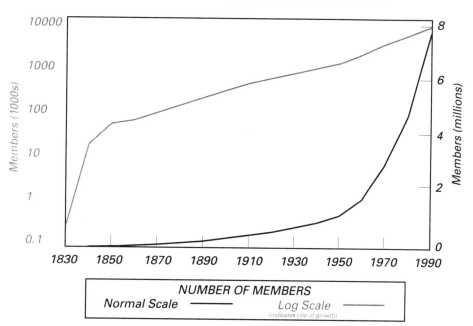

NUMBER OF MEMBERS
Normal Scale ——— Log Scale ———
(indicates rate of growth)

ture, such projections do indicate future possibilities. Using past patterns of growth as a baseline, religious sociologist Rodney Stark has projected an LDS population of 265 million by the year 2080. Using this projection, Stark has predicted that the LDS Church will become the next major world religion. If growth rates for the total membership observed between 1980 and 1989 remain constant, the membership will increase to 12 million by the year 2000, to 35 million by 2020, and to 157 million by the mid-twenty-first century (Fig. 2). But some regions are growing faster than others. If regional rates of growth remain constant, growth will be even more dramatic in some areas.

GEOGRAPHIC DISTRIBUTION.   Growth has been accompanied by shifting distribution of the population. The first few decades were marked by several relocations of a core LDS community and by a substantial infusion of new convert immigrants from Great Britain and northern Europe. By the turn of the century, the core of the Church was firmly established in Utah (Fig. 3). In 1930 one of every two Latter-day Saints resided in Utah, an additional 30 percent lived in the western United States, and another 11 percent lived in the rest of the United States or Canada. In short, the membership was

largely in the United States (90 percent) and concentrated in the Great Basin.

By 1960, 90 percent of the membership still lived in the United States; but Utah's share had declined by 10 percent, and the other western states had gained 10 percent. After 1960, significant expansion of the international membership is evident. The share of members in South America increased from 1 percent in 1960 to 16 percent in 1989. In the same period, Mexico and Central America increased from 1 percent to 11 percent, and an Asian population appeared with 5 percent of the total. The share of the population has remained fairly stable for Europe (4–5 percent) and the South Pacific islands (3–4 percent). Although a majority of the membership still resides in the United States (57 percent), an increasingly international mix is evident. Rapid growth between 1980 and 1989 in countries such as the Philippines (from 57,000 to 213,000), Mexico (from 237,000 to 569,000), and Brazil (from 102,000 to 311,000), along with potential new sources of growth in Africa, East Europe, and Asia, implies dramatic shifts in the distribution of Church membership.

Another way to consider growth is to focus on the distribution of new members. Between 1987 and 1989, nearly a million new members were

Figure 2

PROJECTIONS OF CHURCH MEMBERSHIP

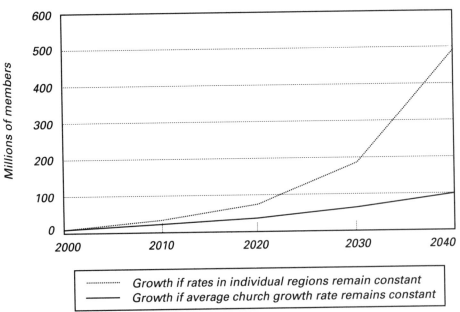

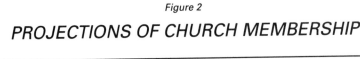

Figure 3

DISTRIBUTION OF CHURCH MEMBERS

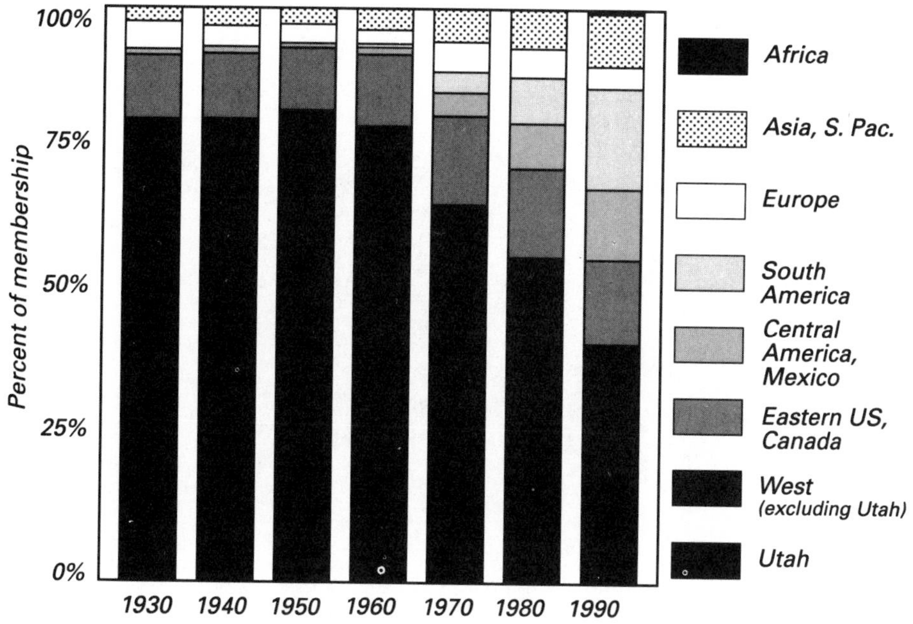

added. Figure 4 shows the geographic location of this growth. South America, Central America, and Mexico contain more than 60 percent of these new members. Another 9 percent comes from Asian countries. Three percent of new growth is occurring in Utah, and other western states continue to be a solid source of new adherents. The total contribution of the United States and Canada amounts to one-fifth of the growth. The remaining 10 percent comes from Europe, the South Pacific, and Africa.

Membership projections based on the assumption that each area will continue to grow at the same rate observed between 1980 and 1989 indicate that geographic shifts may become even more dramatic. The membership in the United States, Canada, and Europe is growing at a relatively slow pace, such that their percentage would drop to 40 percent in the year 2000, to 22 percent in 2010, and to about 11 percent by 2020. Although the African membership is growing at a high rate (14 percent annually), it has such a small base that it would constitute less than 3 percent by 2020. Asia would grow to more than 13 percent of the membership by 2020. But the biggest gains would be in Mexico and Central and South America. Col-

lectively, these areas would increase their share to 46 percent in 2000, to 62 percent in 2010, and to 71 percent in 2020.

SOURCES OF POPULATION CHANGE

The basic demographic equation states that population change equals births minus deaths plus net migration. For religious institutions, conversion and disaffiliation must also be discussed.

FERTILITY. Fertility refers to actual childbearing rather than to the biological capacity to give birth. LDS theology supports attitudes and behaviors that directly influence fertility (Bean, Mineau, and Anderton; see also CHILDREN; MARRIAGE). Consistent with a pronatalist doctrine, LDS fertility in the United States has been higher than the U.S. average, probably since the inception of the Church.

Genealogical records of persons living in Utah show a high average family size throughout the nineteenth century (Fig. 5). Family size is lower, however, for the earliest members of the Church (those born before 1830) than for those who reached the prime years of childbearing during the period of Utah settlement. This rise in fertility is

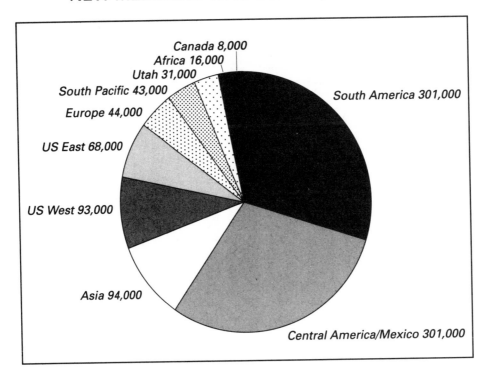

Figure 4

GEOGRAPHIC DISTRIBUTION OF THE MILLION NEW MEMBERS WHO JOINED, 1987-1989

Canada 8,000
Africa 16,000
Utah 31,000
South Pacific 43,000
Europe 44,000
US East 68,000
US West 93,000
Asia 94,000
South America 301,000
Central America/Mexico 301,000

consistent with the frontier hypothesis that low population density and easy access to new land promotes early marriage and larger families. As population growth and economic development led to a more urbanized, secularized society, family size declined. Family size also was larger for those who evidenced greater attachment to the LDS Church (lifetime-committed and converts) than for nonactive LDS and for non-LDS residents. This difference is consistent with LDS teachings favoring increased birthrate.

In the twentieth century, the LDS and Utah birthrates generally have been parallel with, but substantially higher than, birthrates in the United States (Fig. 6). After 1965, the United States birthrate continued to decline, but Utah experienced another baby boom while the total LDS birthrate leveled off at a relatively high level. Since 1980, both Utah and total LDS birthrates have declined precipitously, though still remaining above total U.S. levels. As an increasingly larger share of the LDS population in the United States resides out-

side of Utah and the LDS population grows in other countries, neither the Utah nor the total LDS fertility rate provides an accurate measure of LDS fertility in the United States. Trends do, however, support the conclusion that Latter-day Saints respond to many of the same historical forces that affect family size of broader populations, and that LDS families have persistently been larger than the U.S. national average.

A comparison of LDS family size in the United States with family size in other major religious groups shows that LDS families are substantially larger, especially for Mormons who attend church regularly (Fig. 7). Latter-day Saints who regularly attend church average one child more per family than Catholics, and the difference is even greater in comparison with both liberal and conservative Protestants. Larger LDS family size is sustained by pronatalist religious beliefs, by contact with a reference group sharing similar values, and by socialization into the LDS subculture (Heaton). As the Church spreads into other cul-

Figure 5

AVERAGE NUMBER OF CHILDREN BORN TO WOMEN
Utah Genealogies

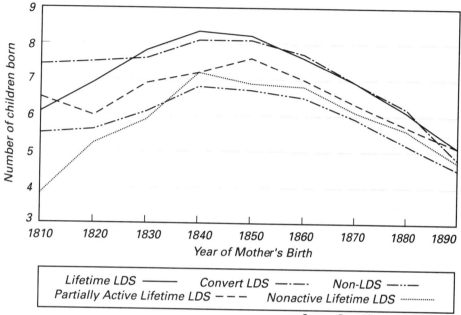

Lifetime LDS ——— Convert LDS —·—· Non-LDS ——··—
Partially Active Lifetime LDS ——— Nonactive Lifetime LDS ············

Source: Bean, Mineau, and Anderton

Figure 6

BIRTHRATES: LDS, UTAH, and U.S., 1920-1985

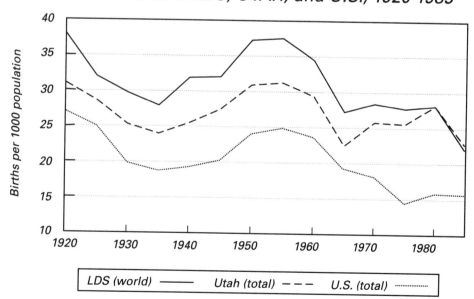

LDS (world) ——— Utah (total) ——— U.S. (total) ············

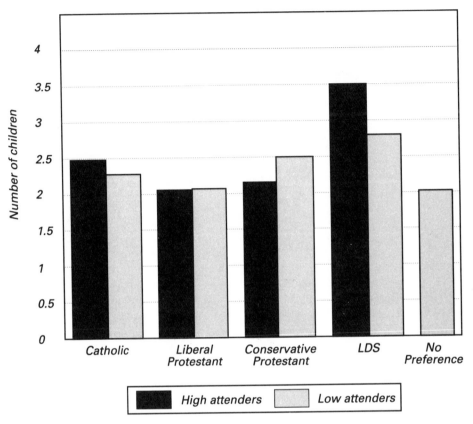

Figure 7

CHILDREN EVER BORN IN THE U.S.A.
By Religion and Church Attendance, 1981

Source: Heaton & Goodman

tural contexts, it remains to be seen how the interplay between religious pronatalism and broader societal trends will be resolved. LDS fertility appears to be above the national average in Britain and Japan but below average in Mexico (Heaton). Commitment to the LDS Church does not have uniform influence on family size in these three countries. These cross-cultural differences suggest that converts will be flexible in adapting to the pronatalist beliefs of their new religion.

High birthrates have been an important source of growth throughout LDS history. In the frontier era, high fertility was necessary to fuel population expansion. After 1900, conversion rates for several decades were relatively low, and fertility was the major source of growth. As LDS birthrates dropped in the United States in the late twentieth century, conversions in various coun-

tries became the major source of growth. Although LDS family size will most likely adjust to broader social trends, it seems that emphasis on childbearing will remain a distinctive feature of the religious tradition.

MORTALITY. The LDS code of health, known as the WORD OF WISDOM, prohibits the use of alcoholic beverages, tobacco, coffee, and tea. Conformity to this code should reduce death rates. Utah death rates are below rates in the nation at large and in the mountain states for most major causes of death, including heart disease, cancer, cerebrovascular disease, accidents, pulmonary disease, pneumonia/flu, diabetes, liver disease, and atherosclerosis. Utah suicide rates are higher than the national average, but lower than in the mountain states as a whole (Smith). Unfortunately, the accuracy of such reports of death are difficult to verify. Deaths of nonparticipating members can go unrecorded on Church records for years, thus creating imprecise estimates of respective death rates.

Studies of specific LDS populations in California (Enstrom), Utah (Gardner and Lyon; Lyon, Gardner, and West), and Alberta, Canada (Jarvis) show that LDS men are about half as likely to die of cancer as other men. LDS women also have lower cancer mortality, but the difference is not as great as for men. Latter-day Saints also have a lower risk of dying from cardiovascular and respiratory diseases. Death rates are lower for Latter-day Saints who have higher levels of religious participation. In short, adherence to the Mormon code of health appears to lower death rates from several diseases. But lower mortality is not as important as high fertility or conversion in creating high rates of growth in the LDS membership.

MIGRATION. Migration was a common experience for early Latter-day Saints as the central settlement shifted from New England to Kirtland, Ohio; to Missouri; to Nauvoo, Illinois; and finally to Utah. During this early period, a major missionary effort was launched in Britain and western Europe (see BRITISH ISLES, THE CHURCH IN; EUROPE, THE CHURCH IN; MISSIONS OF THE TWELVE TO THE BRITISH ISLES; SCANDINAVIA, THE CHURCH IN). Converts were encouraged to gather to the center of Mormon activity, and the Church established a fund to support IMMIGRATION from Europe. Indeed, the infusion of new members from Europe was crucial to expansion and possibly even survival of the Utah Church. In some years, the number of new baptisms reported by the British mission exceeded the total reported growth in LDS membership. Of the women in the Utah genealogical data base who were born between 1820 and 1849, more than 20 percent were born in Scandinavia, more than 40 percent in Great Britain, and an additional 2–4 percent in other European countries (Bean, Mineau, and Anderton). Although the LDS Church had its beginnings in the United States, there was a significant period when a majority of the membership was foreign-born. By the turn of the century, however, more than 90 percent of members were born in Utah. Immigration had virtually ceased as a source of growth.

Gathering to Utah is no longer encouraged; indeed, members have been encouraged to remain and build the Church wherever they reside. LDS migration trends in the United States between 1976 and 1981 suggest, however, some persistent attraction to Utah (Larson). Utah Mormons are somewhat less likely to move to another state, and those born in Utah are more likely to return to their state of birth in a subsequent move than are Mormons born elsewhere. Between 1976 and 1981, there was also a net flow of migrants into Utah. It appears that Utah, as the center of LDS culture, still has some power to draw migrants from other areas. There is virtually no information on migration patterns of Latter-day Saints outside of the United States.

CONVERSION. As a result of missionary efforts, 330,877 convert baptisms were reported in 1990, up from 210,777 in 1980. In 1987–1989, Church membership grew at approximately 4 percent per year because of convert baptisms (Fig. 8). Conversion rates tend to be higher in areas where the LDS presence is relatively recent than in areas with more extended contact. Growth due to conversion during this period varied from a high of 13 percent in Africa to a low of .5 percent in Utah. Latin America and Asia had rates a little under 10 percent, Europe was a little above 5 percent, the eastern United States and the South Pacific were around 3 percent, and Canada and the western United States were between 1 and 2 percent.

Reporting procedures render it impossible to get exact data on whether new members are children of members or new converts. An approximation can be made, however, by comparing the reported number of convert and eight-year-old baptisms. For the entire membership the ratio of convert baptisms to eight-year-old baptisms increased slightly from 2.59 for 1980–1984 to 2.72 for 1985–1989. The ratio varies dramatically from region to region (Fig. 9). In Asia and South America there are roughly fifteen converts for every eight-year-old baptized. The figure for Mexico and Central America is somewhat lower, with about ten converts per eight-year-old. Europe, Africa, the eastern United States, and the South Pacific have values between two and ten converts per eight-year-old, while Canada falls between one and two converts per eight-year-old baptized. In the western United States, converts and children are about evenly numbered, but in Utah, children baptized outnumber converts by about five to one. In most parts of the world, a majority of Latter-day Saints

Figure 8

GROWTH FROM CONVERT BAPTISMS
1987-1990

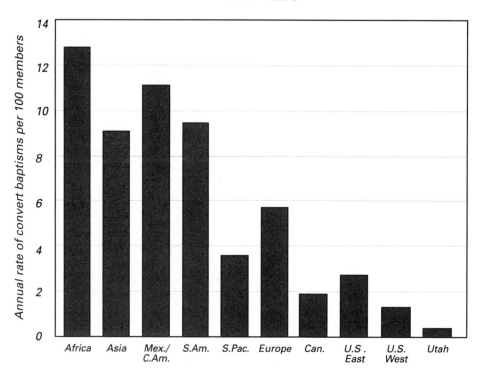

Figure 9

CONVERT BAPTISMS and CHILD BAPTISMS
(age 8), 1980-1990

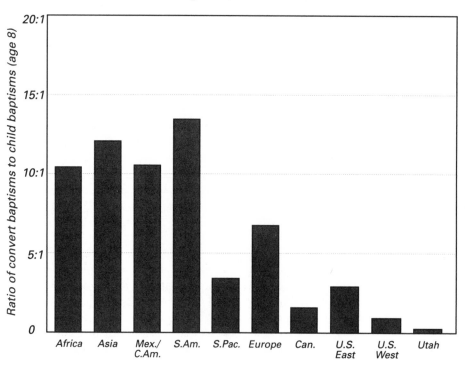

join the Church through conversion rather than family socialization. This trend stands in contrast to the late nineteenth and early twentieth centuries, when a majority of Mormons had been raised in an LDS family.

DISAFFILIATION. Not all whose names are on the Church records as members would consider themselves to be so. In the 1981 Canadian census, for example, 82,000 people stated Mormon as their religious preference, yet LDS records reported 85,006 members. The difference implies that 3–4 percent of members on the records do not consider themselves to be Latter-day Saints. Official statistics on excommunication are not published, but formal excommunication or removal of names from the records is rare, probably affecting less than 1 percent of the membership. More common is the experience of disaffiliation or disengagement. A recent study of LDS members in the United States indicates that 44 percent experience a period of inactivity at some time and then resume religious involvement (regularly attending meetings), while 22 percent remain active throughout their entire lives (Fig. 10). Eight out of 10 current members will become disengaged for a period of at least one year. About 1 of every 5 members retains his or her religious belief but does not attend meetings (disengaged believers); and only 14 percent remain disengaged nonbelievers.

Evidence of net change in membership comes from national social surveys of self-reported religious affiliation. One such survey reports a 36 percent net gain for Mormons among people who switch religions (Roof and Hadaway).

In areas outside the United States where the Church is less well established and where most growth is from recent conversion, retention of members may not be as high. Attendance at sacrament meeting varies substantially. Asia and Latin America have weekly attendance rates of about 25 percent, Europe averages about 35 percent, and Africa, Canada, the South Pacific, and the United States average between 40 percent and 50 percent. Integration of new members is more difficult in areas of high growth due to conversion because there are fewer established members to help converts become acculturated.

DEMOGRAPHIC CHARACTERISTICS

GENDER RATIOS. LDS gender ratios are similar to those of national populations, except they are also greatly influenced by the conversion process.

Figure 10

PROJECTIONS OF CHURCH ACTIVITY BY AGE 65
LDS Membership in the U.S.A.

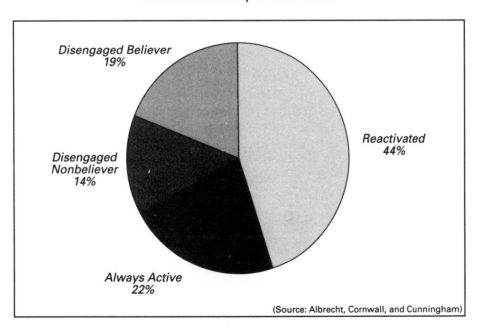

Disengaged Believer
19%

Disengaged Nonbeliever
14%

Reactivated
44%

Always Active
22%

(Source: Albrecht, Cornwall, and Cunningham)

In most populations, there are slightly more male than female births, but males experience a higher mortality rate, such that females predominate at older ages. It can be problematic within the Church if gender ratios in certain areas are substantially unequal, since Latter-day Saints are encouraged to marry within their own faith and because a majority of higher-level leadership positions are not available to women, who do not hold the PRIESTHOOD required to fill these positions (see MEN, ROLES OF; SINGLE ADULTS; WOMEN, ROLES OF). The ratio of males to females for geographic areas is shown in Figure 11. Africa is unusual because there are substantially more men than women who are members of the Church. This indicates that African men are more likely to be converted than are African women. Latter-day Saints in Utah, other western states, and the South Pacific have gender ratios of approximately 95 males per 100 females, which is the value for the total U.S. population. Ratios in the Church are somewhat below the U.S. average in the eastern United States, Canada, and Asia, and females outnumber males by a large margin in Latin America and Europe.

Information from the 1981 Church Membership Survey of the United States and Canada indicates that gender ratios become smaller for older age groups, for singles, and for those who attend church regularly (Goodman and Heaton). For example, among singles over age 30 who attend church weekly, there are only 19 men for every 100 women.

AGE. Church membership statistics are reported separately for children under twelve, youth aged twelve to eighteen, and adults. The ratio of children to adults gives some indication of age structure (Fig. 12). This ratio ranges from more than sixty children per one hundred adults in the South Pacific to about thirty children per one hundred adults in Europe. Ratios for young children (under twelve) are particularly high in Utah and the South Pacific, where fertility contributes a larger share of growth, but relatively low in areas where conversion rates are highest. On the other hand, ratios of children aged twelve to eighteen to adults are greater in areas where conversion rates are high. This is probably because a substantial number of converts join in late adolescence. Thus, the overall ratio is lowest in Europe because of relatively low fertility and conversion rates. Differences in ratios suggest substantial variability in the types of activities and programs that would be most beneficial to the membership in each locale.

Figure 11

GENDER RATIOS BY REGION
Males per 100 Females, 1990

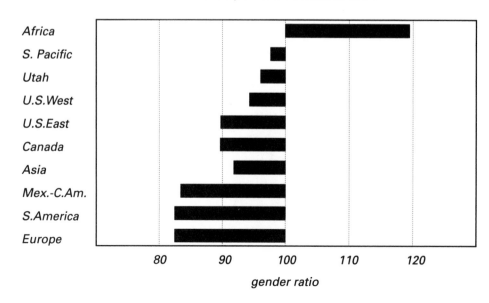

gender ratio

Figure 12

CHILD DEPENDENCY RATIOS
Children per 100 Adults, 1990

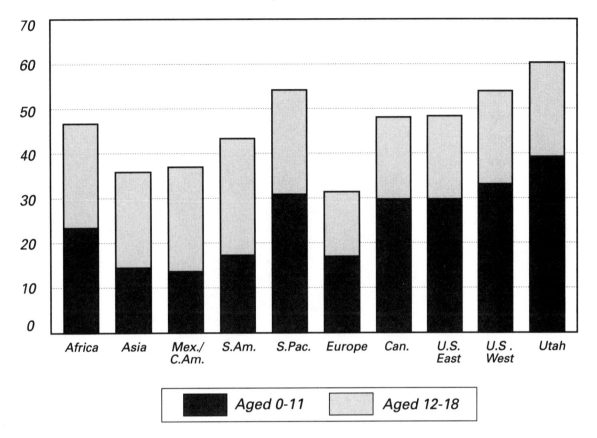

More detailed age categorization is possible where membership records have been computerized. The age-sex structure of the U.S. membership reflects several trends (Fig. 13). Smaller numbers in the two youngest age groups are a consequence of declining fertility in the 1980s. Smaller numbers in successive age groups over age fifteen are created by (1) the past history of high birthrates, which result in greater numbers at each younger age; (2) new converts, who tend to join in the late teens and twenties; and (3) mortality, which creates declining numbers at older ages. The shape of the age pyramid also suggests that the near future will bring declining numbers of young children, temporarily growing numbers who may serve missions or want to enroll in Church universities, a larger number available for marriage, and

possibly a high fertility "echo" when the large ten-to-fifteen age group reaches childbearing age.

At the youngest ages, males outnumber females by a slight margin in the U.S. membership. A higher percentage of females converting to the Church creates a more equal gender ratio in the twenties. Higher female conversion and higher male mortality rates shift the numbers in favor of females in the thirties. At older ages, females outnumber males by a substantial margin.

Another way to think of age from an organizational perspective is to focus on years of experience in the organization. Using membership totals for past years, one may estimate the percent of current members with various amounts of experience (Fig. 14). Consistent with patterns of growth, Africa, Asia, Mexico, and Central America have high

Figure 13

DISTRIBUTION BY AGE and SEX
1000s of Members (U.S.), 1990

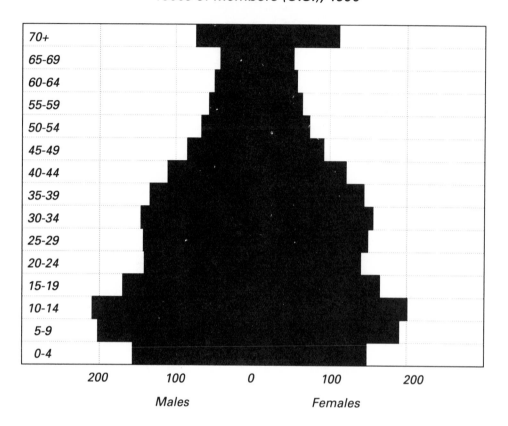

percentages of members with limited experience as Latter-day Saints: Roughly two-thirds of the members have been LDS less than nine years, and between a third and a half have less than four years' experience. Between one-fifth and one-third of those in the South Pacific, Europe, Canada, and the United States (excluding Utah) have fewer than nine years' experience. In Utah, 84 percent of the membership has belonged for at least nine years. As one would expect, rapidly growing areas have only a small pool of well-seasoned Church members, while the opposite is the case for the membership of more established areas.

RACE-ETHNICITY. Ethnic MINORITIES are underrepresented in many LDS congregations. In the United States, where about 77 percent of the population were non-Hispanic whites in 1980, 95 percent of the LDS population were non-Hispanic whites. About 12 percent of the U.S. population and only 0.4 percent of the LDS population were

black (see BLACKS). Hispanics and Asians constituted about 8 percent of the U.S. population and less than 3 percent of the LDS population. American Indians (see NATIVE AMERICANS) had a higher percentage in the LDS Church (1.1 percent) than in the U.S. population (0.6 percent).

The spread of the Church in Asia, the South Pacific, and Africa signals an increasingly diverse ethnic membership. Straight-line growth projections discussed above suggest the possibility of a Hispanic majority by 2010. In any event, international expansion implies a decline in the dominance of white North Americans.

MARRIAGE RATES AND HOUSEHOLD COMPOSITION. LDS teachings on marriage continue to be a distinguishing feature of belief and practice. In the early Church, PLURAL MARRIAGE was one of the LDS family's most widely noticed features. After it was taught openly in Utah, this practice increased quite rapidly. Of the Utah women born

Figure 14

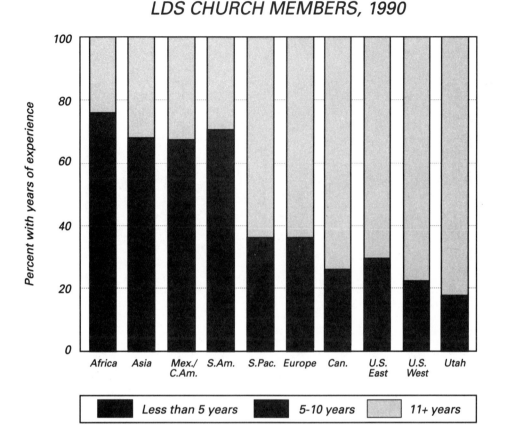

YEARS OF EXPERIENCE AS LDS CHURCH MEMBERS, 1990

Less than 5 years   5-10 years   11+ years

between 1830 and 1840 who ever married (they would have reached the prime marriage ages in the 1860s, when plural marriage was at its peak), about 30 percent entered into such marriages (Bean, Mineau, and Anderton). The practice faded in the face of national pressures. Only about 12 percent of the women born between 1855 and 1859 entered polygynous marriages, and the practice was rare among women born after 1880.

In the United States in the late twentieth century, LDS members have higher rates of marriage and lower rates of marital dissolution than the national population (*see* DIVORCE; MARRIAGE). Marriage patterns vary in different areas of the Church (Fig. 15). Marriages performed in LDS TEMPLES are the LDS ideal. The percentage of adults in a temple marriage varies from about 45 percent in Utah to less than 2 percent in Mexico and Central America. Temple marriage is relatively common among Latter-day Saints throughout the United

States and Canada but is relatively rare in other areas of the world. Marriage outside the temple is about as frequent as temple marriage and is the most common form of marriage outside the United States and Canada. In some areas, a significant minority of marriages involve one partner who is LDS and another who is not. These interfaith marriages involve only about 5 percent of the membership in Utah, Mexico, and Central America, but reach nearly 20 percent in other parts of the United States and in Canada. There are more than twice as many LDS women as LDS men married to spouses of another faith.

The total percent married ranges from just over 40 percent in Asia to almost 70 percent in Utah. Differences in the percent married are attributable to (1) high conversion rates among young people who have not yet married; (2) regional variation in the age at which people marry; and (3) regional variation in divorce rates and in

Figure 15

PERCENT MARRIED AND TYPE OF MARRIAGE, 1990

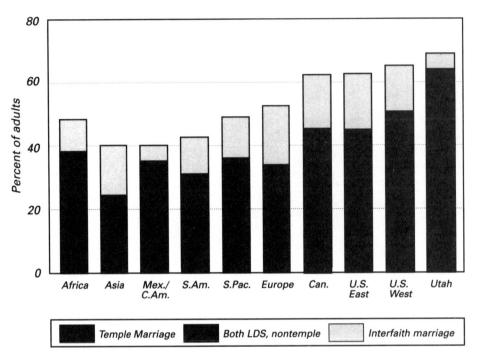

the propensity for divorced people to convert to Mormonism.

Less information is available on LDS household composition, but sample surveys show characteristics of the United States, Britain, Mexico, and Japan in the early 1980s. In Figure 16, three types of households are distinguished: (1) married couples with one or both being LDS; (2) households headed by LDS singles (never married, divorced, or widowed); and (3) households with LDS children but in which neither husband nor wife nor single head is LDS. Married-couple households are the majority in the United States and Britain and form a slight majority in Mexico. Single households constitute 20–30 percent. Japan and, to a lesser degree, Mexico are characterized by many households in which children are the only LDS Church members. Married-couple households are further divided into both-member and one-member couples. Both-member marriages predominate in the United States, Britain, and Mexico, but one-member marriages are more common in Japan. A significant portion of both-member marriages have not been solemnized in a temple, especially outside of the United States.

Regarding the presence of children (under age eighteen) in households, a majority of married-couple LDS households in each country have children, but the percent of married-couple households without children living at home is substantial (43 percent in the United States, 35 percent in Britain, 24 percent in Mexico, and 33 percent in Japan). In many of these cases, the children are grown and have left their parents' home. Although a majority of single-headed households do not have children, a proportion (ranging from 0.9 percent in Japan to 9.7 percent in Britain) are single-parent families.

The distribution of households does not fit any uniform pattern across countries. The idealized vision of a family with a husband and wife married in the temple and children present describes only one out of five LDS families in the United States and less than 3 percent of LDS families in Japan. Information for these four countries suggests that the household composition of the LDS membership is diverse.

SOCIOECONOMIC STATUS. Membership records and statistical reports from local areas do not in-

Figure 16

COMPOSITION OF HOUSEHOLDS WITH AT LEAST ONE LDS MEMBER

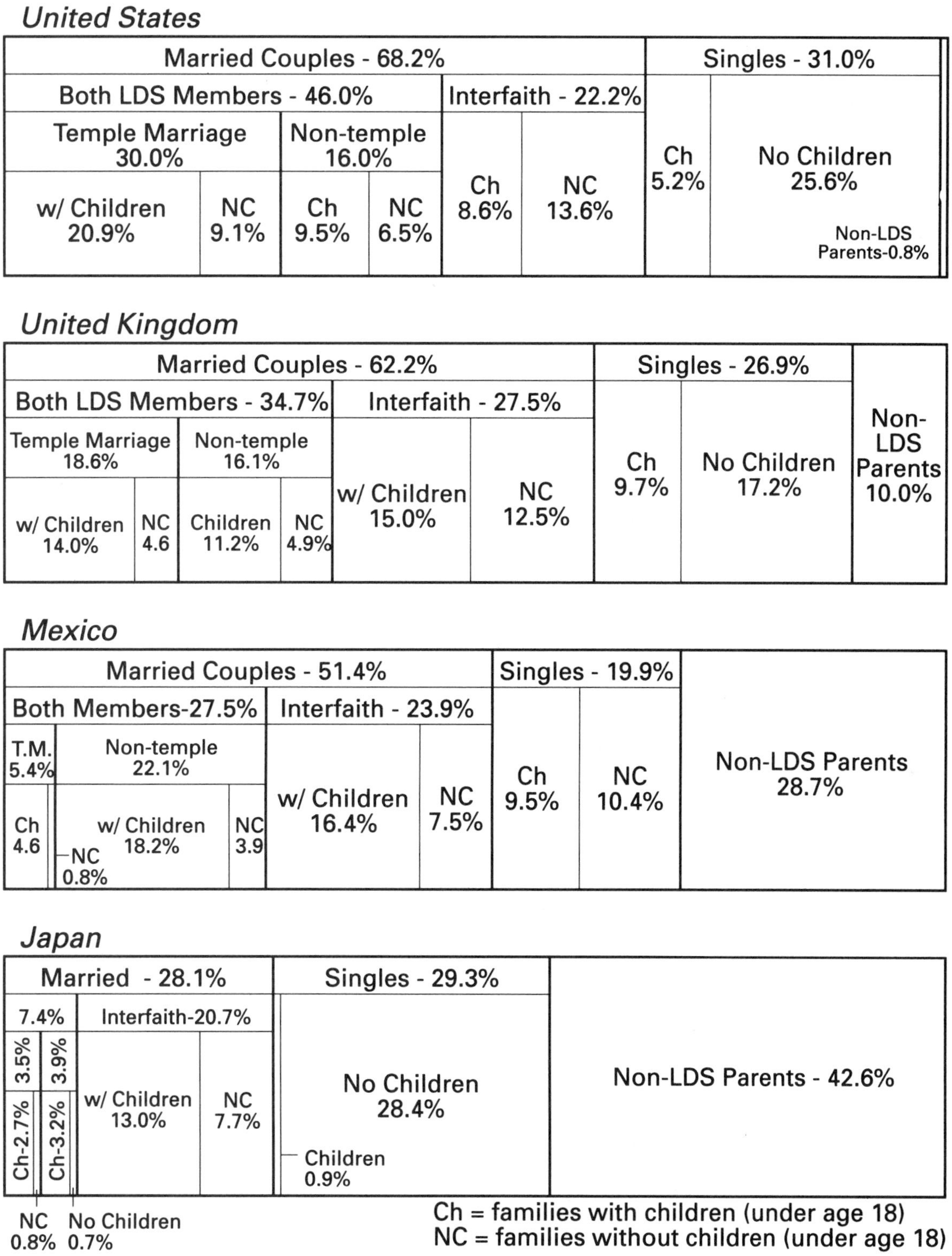

United States

Married Couples - 68.2%						Singles - 31.0%		
Both LDS Members - 46.0%				Interfaith - 22.2%				
Temple Marriage 30.0%		Non-temple 16.0%				Ch 5.2%	No Children 25.6%	
w/ Children 20.9%	NC 9.1%	Ch 9.5%	NC 6.5%	Ch 8.6%	NC 13.6%			Non-LDS Parents-0.8%

United Kingdom

Married Couples - 62.2%						Singles - 26.9%		Non-LDS Parents 10.0%
Both LDS Members - 34.7%				Interfaith - 27.5%				
Temple Marriage 18.6%		Non-temple 16.1%				Ch 9.7%	No Children 17.2%	
w/ Children 14.0%	NC 4.6	Children 11.2%	NC 4.9%	w/ Children 15.0%	NC 12.5%			

Mexico

Married Couples - 51.4%						Singles - 19.9%		Non-LDS Parents 28.7%
Both Members-27.5%			Interfaith - 23.9%					
T.M. 5.4%	Non-temple 22.1%			w/ Children 16.4%	NC 7.5%	Ch 9.5%	NC 10.4%	
Ch 4.6	w/ Children 18.2% ⌐NC 0.8%		NC 3.9					

Japan

Married - 28.1%				Singles - 29.3%	Non-LDS Parents - 42.6%
7.4%	Interfaith-20.7%				
3.5% Ch-2.7%	3.9% Ch-3.2%	w/ Children 13.0%	NC 7.7%	No Children 28.4% ⌐ Children 0.9%	

NC 0.8%   No Children 0.7%

Ch = families with children (under age 18)
NC = families without children (under age 18)

clude information on socioeconomic status. Sample survey data are available from a few countries, but the data must be interpreted with caution because survey response rates favor those who participate in Church activities most frequently. Socioeconomic information may be more indicative of participating members than of all members.

Studies in the United States indicate that LDS educational attainment is above the national average and that, compared to the population as a whole, Latter-day Saints are more likely to be both highly educated and religiously involved (Albrecht and Heaton). Possible explanations for the positive role of EDUCATION are that the Church has emphasized the importance of gaining knowledge and that education facilitates participation in an organization staffed by lay volunteers.

A similar orientation toward educational achievement can also be observed in other countries. Figure 17 shows that in Japan, Latter-day Saints are more than twice as likely as the national population to have college experience. In Britain,

Church members are only slightly above the national average in educational experience. In Mexico, where the comparison standard is postprimary rather than college experience, Church members exceed that national rate by a factor of two. The percentage with postsecondary education is higher among Canadian Saints than the national population. Less-representative samples also show above-average LDS educational attainment in some African countries (Heaton and Jacobson).

Adult male employment rates are quite high and relatively uniform throughout most countries of the world, and available evidence indicates that averages for LDS males are similar to national averages. Female employment is much more variable. In the early 1980s, about half of LDS adult women were in the labor force in the United States, Canada, and Britain (Fig. 18). These percentages were virtually identical to the national averages. LDS women in Mexico were less likely to be in the labor force when compared with LDS women in the United States, but were still slightly

Figure 17

PERCENT OF ADULTS WITH COLLEGE EXPERIENCE
1981-1983

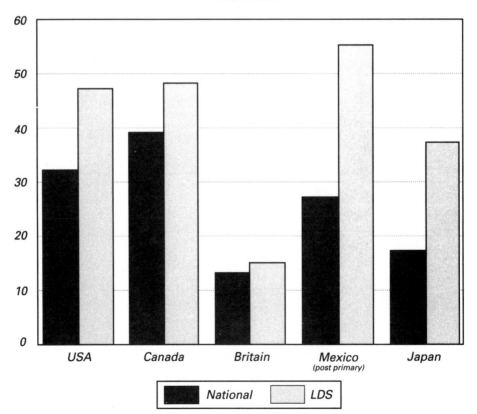

National   LDS

Figure 18

PERCENT OF WOMEN IN
THE LABOR FORCE, 1981-1983

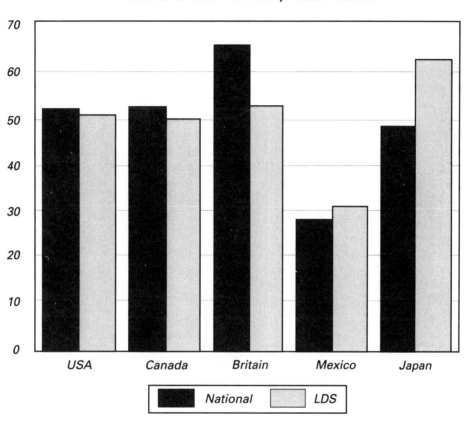

above the national average for Mexico. Japan presents a contrast, as 63 percent of LDS women are in the labor force. This is notably higher than the rate for LDS women in other countries or for Japanese women as a whole.

A comparison of the OCCUPATIONAL STATUS of Latter-day Saints with national populations shows that within each country Church members are at least as likely to have professional occupations (Fig. 19). In Japan and Mexico the LDS percentages are substantially higher than those for the total population (the Mexico comparisons are based only on six cities where the LDS survey was conducted). African data also suggest that Church members have above-average occupational attainment (Heaton and Jacobson).

Although information on education, employment, and occupation is limited to a few countries, patterns suggest that Mormons have average or above-average socioeconomic attainment. In some

Third World countries, joining an American-based church may be associated with upward mobility. Missionary efforts may also focus, either intentionally or unintentionally, on middle- or upper-level socioeconomic groups. Finally, an emphasis on achievement and SELF-SUFFICIENCY may promote and develop higher socioeconomic attainment within the membership.

Information on income is more difficult to obtain than for education and employment because of national differences in reporting and individual reluctance to divulge income. Surveys conducted in the early 1980s indicate that LDS income is about the same as the national average in some countries. In the United States, reported average household income of Church members was $22,294, slightly above the national average of $21,063. In Britain, 33 percent of Latter-day Saints and 32 percent of the national population had incomes below £5,000, while 3 percent of Church members and 4 percent

Figure 19

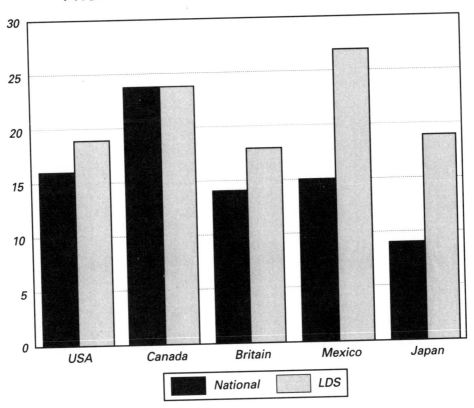

PERCENT OF LDS IN LABOR FORCE IN
PROFESSIONAL OCCUPATIONS, 1981-1983

of the national population had incomes above £10,000. In the 1981 Canadian census, LDS men were a little above the national average ($17,222, compared to $16,918), but LDS women were a little below average ($7,243, compared to $8,414). In Mexico and Japan the percentage of income going to the poorest and richest fifths of the population were approximately equal for Latter-day Saints and the national population. Although LDS family income may be slightly above the national average in the United States, LDS per-capita income is lower, due in part to larger family size.

Measures of poverty, which take into account household size, show that 13 percent of U.S. LDS households fell below the poverty level in 1981, compared to a national figure of 14 percent. As in the U.S. population as a whole, female-headed LDS households with children are especially prone to fall below the poverty level (Goodman and Heaton).

As the LDS Church expands in developing countries, the economic status of the membership will continue to change. A rough approximation of economic status of the membership can be computed by multiplying the per-capita gross national product (GNP) of each country by the proportion of all LDS membership in that country and summing the product across all countries. For 1974 this procedure yields a per-capita LDS GNP of $6,044, or 88 percent of the U.S. national per-capita GNP. By 1987, the LDS figure had become only 75 percent of the national GNP. Projections of Third World growth presented above suggest even greater decline in the average income of the total LDS membership in the coming years.

BIBLIOGRAPHY

Albrecht, Stan L., and Tim B. Heaton. "Secularization, Higher Education, and Religiosity." *Review of Religious Research* 20 (Sept. 1984):43–58.

Bean, Lee L.; Geraldine P. Mineau; and Douglas L. Anderton. *Fertility Change on the American Frontier.* Berkeley, Calif., 1990.

Enstrom, James E. "Health Practices and Cancer Mortality Among Active California Mormons." *Journal of the National Cancer Institute* 81 (1989):1807–1814.

Gardner, John W., and Joseph L. Lyon. "Cancer in Utah Mormon Men by Lay Priesthood Level." *American Journal of Epidemiology* 116 (1982):243–57.

Goodman, Kristen L., and Tim B. Heaton. "LDS Church Members in the U.S. and Canada: A Demographic Profile." *AMCAP Journal* 12 (1986):88–107.

Heaton, Tim B. "Religious Influences on Mormon Fertility: Cross-National Comparisons." *Review of Religious Research* 30 (1989):401–411.

Heaton, Tim B., and Kristen L. Goodman. "Religion and Family Formation." *Review of Religious Research* 26 (1985): 343–59.

Heaton, Tim B., and Cardell K. Jacobson. "The Globalizing of an American Church: Mormonism in the Third World." Unpublished paper, Aug. 1990.

Jarvis, George K. "Mormon Mortality Rates in Canada." *Social Biology* 24 (1977):294–302.

Larson, Don C. "A Descriptive Analysis of United States Mormon Migration Streams." Unpublished paper presented to the Western Social Science Association, Albuquerque, N.M., Apr. 1989.

Lyon, J. L.; J. W. Gardner; and D. W. West. "Cancer Incidence in Mormons and Non-Mormons in Utah During 1967–75." *Journal of the National Cancer Institute* 65 (1980):1055–61.

Roof, W. C., and C. K. Hadaway. "Review of the Polls: Shifts in Religious Preference: The Mid-Seventies." *Journal for the Scientific Study of Religion* 16 (1977):409–412.

Smith, James E. "Mortality." In *Utah in Demographic Perspective,* ed. Thomas K. Martin, Tim B. Heaton, and Stephen J. Bahr, pp. 59–69. Salt Lake City, 1986.

Stark, Rodney. "The Rise of a New World Faith." *Review of Religious Research* 26 (1984):18–27.

TIM B. HEATON

VOCABULARY, LATTER-DAY SAINT

Although Latter-day Saints share with other Christian faiths a general Judeo-Christian linguistic heritage, "Mormon language" includes many words and phrases that have distinctive meanings. Also, many words commonly used in other branches of Christianity are not common in LDS language.

From scripture and the religious vocabulary of the western world, LDS language inherits such words as "angel," "apostle," "atonement," "baptism," "covenant," "damnation," "deacon," "exaltation," "the Fall," "glory," "God," "heaven," "hell," "Israelite," "judgment," "Messiah," "oath," "patriarch," "priesthood," "prophet," "redemption," "repentance," "resurrection," "sacrament," "saint," "salvation," "sin," "soul," "tabernacle," "temple," "Urim and Thummim," and "Zion." Even though these words come from a common heritage, most of them have significantly different connotations in LDS vocabularies, as do many other words.

Conspicuously absent from LDS language, or used infrequently, are many terms of other Christian cultures, such as "abbot," "archbishop," "beatification," "cardinal," "catechism," "creed," "diocese," "eucharist," "host," "limbo," "outward sign," "inward grace," "minister," "parish," "pastor," "preacher," "purgatory," "radio or television evangelist," "rapture," "rectory," "sanctuary," and "Trinity."

LDS language is likewise distinctive in terms of address and titles. Members address one another as "Brother" and "Sister" in preference to "Mister" or "Mrs.," or a professional title such as "Professor" or "Doctor." Aaronic and Melchizedek Priesthood offices are almost never used as titles of address, with the notable exception of "Bishop" and "Elder," and the latter term may apply to any male Church leader (but is usually reserved for missionaries and members of presiding councils— the Twelve and the Seventy). The only other frequently used title is "President," a term widely used for both men and women in a presiding position in many of the units of the Church.

Unique names found in the Book of Mormon have been carried over into given names for places and persons, such as Abinadi, Ammon, Ether, Korihor, Laman, Lehi, Moroni, Nephi, and Zoram. Alma, usually a woman's name in English and Spanish, is a man's name in the Book of Mormon and in many older LDS families. LDS colonizers honored settlements with Book of Mormon names such as Lehi, Moroni, and Nephi. Other unique or uniquely used LDS words include "Deseret," "Kolob," "Liahona," "disfellowship," and "telestial." Some terms also have specialized meanings in reference to LDS temples, such as "baptism by proxy," "celestial room," "temple recommend," "sealings," "endowment," and "garment."

Problems with the transfer of English connotations into other languages are extensive. Distinctions in LDS theology have led some LDS translators to avoid literal transliteration of commonly used terms in favor of coining a new word, borrowing the English word, or reviving an archaic term.

Because of the worldwide missionary program of the Church and the immigration of converts from many lands to the United States, there is a high level of language-consciousness among Church members. Brigham Young University has among its 27,000 students an unusually high percentage (up to one-third) who speak and read languages learned during missionary service. The "gift of tongues" is often spoken of in reference to missionaries' ability to learn languages rapidly, although the term is also used in reference to biblical modes of speaking in tongues and interpretation of tongues (cf. D&C 46:24–25).

Since its organization in 1973, the Deseret Language and Linguistics Society has solicited papers for its annual symposium on all aspects of LDS language, and a selection of these papers has been published annually since 1974.

BIBLIOGRAPHY

Harris, John B., and William A. Wilson. "And They Spake with a New Tongue (on Missionary Slang)." In *Conference on the Language of the Mormons*, ed. Harold S. Madsen and John L. Sorenson, pp. 46–48. Provo, Utah, 1974.

McNaughton, Patricia T. "Ordinary Language for Special Purposes." *DLLS Annual Symposium* (Brigham Young University). Provo, Utah, 1979.

Monson, Samuel C. "Some Observations on the Language of Hymns." *DLLS Annual Symposium* (Brigham Young University). Provo, Utah, 1979.

ROBERT W. BLAIR

"VOICE FROM THE DUST"

For Latter-day Saints, the phrase "voice from the dust" speaks of the coming-forth of the BOOK OF MORMON (cf. 2 Ne. 25:18; 26:16), which was translated from metal PLATES buried in the ground for fourteen centuries. As early as Joseph SMITH, LDS leaders have consistently indicated that this phrase applies to the Book of Mormon (*PJS*, p. 307; Hinckley, p. 10). This distinctive phrase and others like it usually appear in a context that speaks of the need for repentance and of an accompanying VOICE OF WARNING that will "whisper out of the dust" (Isa. 29:4).

Latter-day Saints believe prophets foresaw that in the latter days a book, a companion to the Bible, would come forth as another testament of Jesus Christ (Ezek. 37:15–19; 2 Ne. 29:1–14). This other testament is the Book of Mormon. The Lord foretold the coming-forth of such a record to ENOCH: "And righteousness will I send down out of heaven; and truth will I send forth out of the earth, to bear testimony of mine Only Begotten" (Moses 7:62; cf. Ps. 85:11; *TPJS*, p. 98). According to the Book of Mormon, JOSEPH OF EGYPT also prophesied that one of his descendants would write words from the Lord that "shall cry from the dust; yea, even repentance unto their brethren, even after many generations have gone by them" (2 Ne. 3:18–20; cf. 33:13; Morm. 8:16, 23, 26; Moro. 10:27).

BIBLIOGRAPHY

Hinckley, Gordon B. *Faith, The Essence of True Religion*. Salt Lake City, 1989.

WILLIAM SHEFFIELD

VOICE OF WARNING

The concept of a divine warning is part of the Judeo-Christian tradition and is a primary focus in The Church of Jesus Christ of Latter-day Saints. Section 1 of the Doctrine and Covenants, which by revelation is designated as a preface (verse 6), proclaims the voice of warning to be an essential thrust of the restored gospel of Jesus Christ: "And the voice of warning shall be unto all people, by the mouths of my disciples, whom I have chosen in these last days" (verse 4). The gospel of Jesus Christ is by nature a voice of warning because it calls people to repentance.

In LDS theology the voice of warning has four components: (1) deity, who originates the message; (2) the message, which is the gospel of Jesus Christ; (3) an authorized messenger, who delivers the message; and (4) mankind, to whom the message is delivered.

The voice is the voice of God, whether by his Spirit (D&C 88:66), his servants (D&C 1:38), or inspired writings (2 Ne. 33:13–15). The warning is for mankind to prepare by repentance for the great day of the Lord (D&C 1:11–12). The warning voice is a proclamation of revealed truth to the inhabitants of the earth so "that all that will hear may hear" (D&C 1:11). Eventually all will be persuaded or left without just excuse (D&C 88:81–82; 101:91–93; 124:3–10).

In modern time as in antiquity, a solemn responsibility envelops both the messengers and those to whom the message is delivered. The Lord informed Ezekiel, "I have made thee a watchman unto the house of Israel: therefore hear the word at my mouth and give them warning from me" (Ezek. 3:17). Only those who hearken to the warning are spared the punishments and receive the blessings. The messengers who deliver the message also save their own souls; if they fail to deliver the message they acquire responsibility for those whom they failed to warn—"[their] blood will I require at thine hand" (Ezek. 3:18–21).

It is a covenant obligation of all who are baptized into the Church of Jesus Christ to "stand as witnesses of God at all times, and in all things, and in all places" (Mosiah 18:9). Once warned, "it becometh every man . . . to warn his neighbor" (D&C 88:81). The messengers who deliver the warning will be present at the day of JUDGMENT as witnesses (D&C 75:21; 2 Ne. 33:11; Moro. 10:34). The essence of missionary work is for each member of the Church to become a voice of warning to those who have not been warned (see *DS* 1: 307–311).

NEIL J. FLINDERS

VOLUNTEERISM

Latter-day Saint doctrine teaches that basic tenets of a Christ-centered life are CHARITY, LOVE, and JOY through service. Volunteerism in the Mormon COMMUNITY strives to implement the principles of service and concern for one's neighbor as taught in the GOSPEL OF JESUS CHRIST. The volunteering of time, energy, talents, and other resources for the betterment of the community and individual lives is a daily occurrence, primarily inside but also often outside a formal ecclesiastical setting. Church members are taught that cultivating the attribute of service is a spiritual obligation. This responsibility is reflected in the motto of the women's RELIEF SOCIETY organization, "Charity Never Faileth," from 1 Corinthians 13:8.

WARD and STAKE organizations are staffed by members with CALLINGS to serve in various capacities in carrying out the programs of the Church (*see* LAY PARTICIPATION AND LEADERSHIP). In this manner MISSIONARIES, TEACHERS, leaders, and many others voluntarily donate their time and tal-

ents. A balance exists in Mormon volunteerism between the spontaneous actions of members and organized Church initiatives. Some Church programs have begun at the grass-roots level through volunteer-member initiative; however, most Church operations are centrally approved and implemented under the guidance of the GENERAL AUTHORITIES. Members strive to govern themselves and voluntarily find ways to serve within the principles, objectives, and guidelines taught by the Church. While all members are commanded to be "anxiously engaged in a good cause, and do many things of their own free will" (D&C 58:27), it is not customary for members to offer unsolicited advice, to intervene in the responsibilities of others, or to suggest themselves for specific Church callings. Most members accept whatever callings are extended to them, and few request to be released except under difficult circumstances.

In areas with concentrated Latter-day Saint populations, Mormons traditionally organize themselves to help members and, where possible, all others in the community in times of need. Local Church leaders often use PRIESTHOOD QUORUMS, the Relief Society, and Church YOUTH groups as vehicles for volunteer efforts. Latter-day Saints are also encouraged to volunteer their efforts in civic service. Examples of volunteer service extend to the national and international levels, as when members rally together to help in times of crisis. Latter-day Saints in many parts of the world have joined with others in the aftermath of natural disasters, famine, and war to donate and deliver goods and services, to perform clean up, and to rebuild communities.

Many types of volunteer service are seen in LDS congregations and communities. Typical activities include refurbishing homes of the elderly or the cleanup of public parks or buildings. Handicapped individuals are visited by members who assist them with their rehabilitation efforts. Visits to hospitals, nursing centers, or prisons with programs or projects for the patients or inmates are typical services. Groups of members frequently work together to raise money to help ease heavy medical bills for neighborhood families. Food and clothing are donated to charitable organizations, including the DESERET INDUSTRIES. A call for help in such diverse activities as harvesting crops or moving a family usually generates willing volunteers. Many members spend hours of volunteer service translating materials for the deaf and the blind. Others work to preserve cultural or genealogical records. Returned missionaries offer their language skills when foreign visitors or immigrants are in the community. In addition, other professionally trained members teach the application of home nursing or agricultural technology in cross-cultural settings. Although not all members find themselves in circumstances permitting extensive service both inside and outside the Church, charitable service is highly admired and valued in the Mormon lifestyle.

Whether living in a community having few or many Latter-day Saints, Church members are taught and encouraged to render acts of kindness to their neighbors. Some charitable acts are done as a result of HOME TEACHING, VISITING TEACHING, or COMPASSIONATE SERVICE assignments. These Church callings bring to those who render unselfish service the joy of Christlike love for one's fellow beings. Many other deeds of service occur as the result of a need seen by an individual who is willing to fulfill that need. Hot meals, shoveled winter sidewalks, visits to the sick, the lonely, or the elderly, child care in times of despair, tutoring, painting, yard work, housekeeping, the sharing of musical talents, the remaking of clothing or home furnishings, and donating food from family garden plots are all small acts of volunteer kindness given, sometimes anonymously, to those in need.

BIBLIOGRAPHY

Cuthbert, Derek A. "The Spirituality of Service." *Ensign* 20 (May 1990):12–13.

For numerous references concerning Church counsel on volunteerism and service, or specific stories of individual or group volunteer efforts, see *Index to the Periodicals of The Church of Jesus Christ of Latter-day Saints*, Salt Lake City, 1961–present. Key Words: Volunteers, Service, Compassionate Service, Community Service, and Service Projects.

MARIBETH CHRISTENSEN

WARD

The ward is the basic ecclesiastical unit in The Church of Jesus Christ of Latter-day Saints. It is comparable to a Protestant congregation or a Roman Catholic parish. Normally, its membership ranges between 300 and 600 people. A ward is part of a larger unit called a STAKE, which usually includes between five and ten wards. When a ward or stake grows beyond the usual size in membership and in number of active MELCHIZEDEK PRIESTHOOD holders, it is divided, creating a new ward or a new stake, usually determined by geographical boundaries.

The ward is presided over by a BISHOP and his two counselors. Assisted by several CLERKS, these men comprise the BISHOPRIC. All are laymen and serve without monetary compensation. Bishops of wards extend CALLINGS to men and women in the ward so that each may serve in one of numerous offices or teaching positions in the ward.

The first wards were organized early in the history of the Church in the 1840s in NAUVOO, ILLINOIS. By 1844 the city was divided into ten wards, with three more in the surrounding rural neighborhood. The name "ward" was borrowed from the term for political districts of the frontier municipality. Joseph SMITH, who was simultaneously mayor of the city and President of the Church, assigned a bishop to preside over each

ward. The bishop's chief responsibility to begin with was temporal rather than spiritual leadership. To prevent hunger, he surveyed the physical needs of the members living within his ward boundaries. Second, the bishop organized his members for Church work assignments, particularly to serve one day in ten as laborers on the NAUVOO TEMPLE. This was a form of paying tithing.

Many of the Saints who fled Nauvoo under persecution in 1846 gathered at WINTER QUARTERS, located near present-day Florence, Nebraska. There Brigham YOUNG and other leaders again set up ward organizations. Their function was similar—to look after the temporal welfare of the people.

Soon after the first group of pioneer immigrants arrived in the valley of the Great Salt Lake, Brigham Young divided the area into several wards and called a bishop to preside over each. The temporal well-being of the people was still the bishop's chief concern. Soon bishops were assigned to collect tithes from the members and deliver them to the central tithing office. At this time, most of the tithes were paid in produce and livestock because of a lack of circulating currency.

Initially, worship meetings in the Salt Lake Valley were held in the Bowery, erected in the block now occupied by TEMPLE SQUARE. But soon the population increased until the various wards started building their own meetinghouses and holding separate worship services.

Brigham Young determined quickly to move the immigrants beyond the limits of Salt Lake City. Thus, he established small agricultural settlements throughout the Rocky Mountain valleys in the Great Basin. Through this colonization effort nearly four hundred Mormon villages were founded during his lifetime, built on nearly every available water source. Each village was eventually organized into a ward, and several wards into a stake. The bishop of each village ward was essentially the community leader, serving as the judge and mayor as well as the bishop. In the villages the bishops out of necessity became the temporal as well as ecclesiastical leader. Each ward also tried to support an elementary school.

Gradually, the activities and programs of several organizations were added to the normal weekly worship meetings. Sunday Schools, priesthood quorums, the Relief Society, and youth groups emerged in the rural areas as well as in the cities. All were nominally guided by the bishopric, but each received some encouragement from stake and central Church leaders.

In 1890 the MANIFESTO was published, which ended Church support for the performance of plural marriages and the Manifesto was also an important landmark in the separation of the church and state in Utah. Gradually the wards and the villages turned many secular functions over to non-reli-

Members of a student ward partake of the sacrament during a sacrament meeting (1975). Local members of the Church are organized into wards (usually about 200–600 members) for purposes of religious, social, educational, and service activities. Courtesy Doug Martin.

gious leaders. Bishops withdrew from being mayors and judges. Ward schools gave way to public schools. Water companies took over the administration of pioneer irrigation systems. Church-run cooperative stores were gradually replaced by private commercial enterprises. As this separation occurred, the ward became more and more an exclusively ecclesiastical organization rather than both a religious and political-economic one. Nonetheless, the resulting ward was more than just a congregation; it still retained much of the spirit of a close-knit community that it had so long been.

In the nineteenth century, wards and stakes were organized mainly in the intermountain United States, in Alberta, CANADA, and in northern MEXICO. Most members outside these regions were organized into missions and branches, the name given to small dependent units within the mission. By the outbreak of World War II, a few wards and stakes were organized in states beyond the intermountain region, particularly California and Hawaii. Then following the war, as the Church became established all over the United States, wards and stakes were organized throughout the country. By the 1960s, wards and stakes were organized in Europe and the Pacific. Asian and Latin American wards soon followed. In 1991 wards exist in many parts of the world. This means that these units are essentially able to provide their own leadership. On January 1, 1991, the Church had a total

Salt Lake 11th Ward chapel (erected 1911; photo c. 1934). Beginning in Nauvoo, Illinois, the Church divided its membership into local ward units. They served a wide variety of functions: economic, cultural, social, and educational, as well as religious. Photographer: Acme Photo Co.

of 18,090 wards and branches in 1,784 stakes, and 497 districts.

Today LDS wards continue many of the community functions of pioneer times. The Sunday meetings are just an outer evidence of the unit. Social life and friendship among members are largely developed within the ward. Youth programs bind teenagers and their parents to the ward. Education of children is supplemented by teachers of the youth and primary programs. Family education is furthered through training parents in the ward programs. Sports and other activities are promoted in the ward.

Great diversity exists among wards. Many are located in Mormon communities. Others are in areas where Mormons are a distinct minority. Some have an overabundance of leadership and talent. Others suffer from lack of leadership or lack of youth involvement. Some cover a small neighborhood; others, a widespread area. But wherever located, wards have much similarity, following the same curriculum, working under equitable budget allocations, and adhering closely to central authority from Church headquarters. Increasingly, materials such as videotapes or satellite broadcasts from the GENERAL AUTHORITIES in Salt Lake City are received in all wards, promoting uniformity and commitment.

As Latter-day Saints move throughout the world, they typically transfer from one ward to another with ease, finding acceptance, responsibility, and similarity of doctrine and practice everywhere. The ward system is successful partly because wards are kept small and because, ideally, everyone in them is needed and asked to accept a calling. Serving one another, bearing each other's burdens, is the norm. Socializing the young is everywhere a mainstream activity, and the youth also contribute much to the dynamics of the ward.

BIBLIOGRAPHY

Alder, Douglas D. "The Mormon Ward: Congregation or Community?" *Journal of Mormon History* 5 (1978):61–78.

Allen, James B., and Glen M. Leonard. *The Story of the Latter-day Saints.* Salt Lake City, 1976.

Arrington, Leonard J. *From Quaker to Latter-day Saint: Bishop Edwin D. Woolley.* Salt Lake City, 1976.

———; Feramorz Fox; and Dean May. *Building the City of God: Community and Cooperation Among the Mormons.* Salt Lake City, 1976.

The Hollywood Stake tabernacle and Wilshire Ward chapel was one of the most imposing church buildings of its day in Los Angeles. Built as a solid piece of reinforced concrete, it was dedicated in 1929. In the early 1900s, the Church expanded significantly in California.

Beecher, Dale. "The Office of Bishop." *Dialogue* 15 (Winter 1982):103–115.

Nelson, Lowry. *The Mormon Village: A Pattern and Technique of Land Settlement.* Salt Lake City, 1952.

DOUGLAS D. ALDER

WARD BUDGET

A WARD budget is the fund from which local congregations (wards) finance their activities. Historically, the ward budget was raised through voluntary donations. Since January 1, 1990, ward and stake budgets in the United States and Canada are funded entirely from general tithing without additional local contributions. (Before 1990, bishops and ward members agreed privately on voluntary annual contributions. Wards sometimes organized supplementary fundraising activities.) Building operation and maintenance costs are reimbursed from Church headquarters. The quarterly allowance for each stake and ward is based on average meeting attendance. Additional fund raising is discouraged, and expenditures are carefully monitored. Donations are not solicited in worship services.

In parts of the world other than the United States and Canada, some local costs are still financed by voluntary contributions, although building rentals, maintenance, and some other expenses are reimbursed from central funds.

The ward budget continues to cover costs of general operations, materials, and activities of the wards and stakes. Each unit of the ward organization prepares annually a detailed estimate of needs, which the BISHOPRIC then uses to develop a ward budget proposal. The BISHOP presents this for a sustaining vote of the ward membership at a special meeting, and then submits the proposal to the stake, from which it goes to Church headquarters.

ROBERT J. SMITH

WARD COUNCIL

The ward council (formerly known as the Ward Correlation Council) is the meeting of local leaders wherein the doctrines of the gospel are turned into plans of action. The shared activities that help turn ward members into a community of Saints are coordinated by the ward council. This council is composed of the ward PRIESTHOOD EXECUTIVE COMMITTEE and the presidents of the ward AUXILIARY ORGANIZATIONS, and the chair of the Activities Committee. These leaders coordinate the efforts of all ward quorums and organizations to support the families of the Church, meet the needs of individuals from all age groups, and provide Christian service. The BISHOP presides in this monthly meeting, where ward programs are reviewed and activities are proposed. The bishop may invite other individuals to participate in the ward council as necessary. Approval of activities is based on such matters as their appropriateness, the ability to conduct them without additional cost to ward members (see TITHING), and how well an activity will strengthen ward members. For example, if HOME TEACHERS were to discover that a group of elderly members felt neglected, and if youth leaders reported that they were searching for a service project, an activity could be planned that would place the youth in the service of the elderly.

BIBLIOGRAPHY

Benson, Ezra Taft. "Church Government Through Councils." *Ensign* 9 (May 1979):86–89.

General Handbook of Instructions. Salt Lake City, 1989.

DENNIS L THOMPSON

WARD ORGANIZATION

A WARD is a geographically defined Church unit organized to provide every member the opportunity to find fellowship with the Saints and give service to others. The ward is led by a BISHOP and two counselors (see BISHOPRIC). An executive secretary and ward CLERKS assist the bishopric with the tasks of RECORD KEEPING and management. PRIESTHOOD and AUXILIARY presidencies (a president and two counselors) are assigned to attend to various needs of ward members. Other leaders supervise missionary activities, provide gospel instruction, and help ward members with temporal needs, such as searching for employment. Frequent social and service activities involve adults and youth.

Typically, the administration of the ward is carried out in a weekly bishopric meeting attended by the bishop, his two counselors, and his executive secretary. These same men hold a weekly ward PRIESTHOOD EXECUTIVE COMMITTEE meeting with the HIGH PRIEST group leader, the ELDERS quorum president, the ward mission leader, and the YOUNG MEN president. They consider such matters as ward TEMPLE attendance, FAMILY HISTORY activity, missionary work, HOME TEACHING, and member activation. When the female RELIEF SOCIETY president attends this meeting (at least monthly) for a discussion of the temporal needs of ward members, it becomes the ward welfare services committee. The Relief Society president helps the bishop coordinate appropriate assistance and COMPASSIONATE SERVICE to the sick, the aged, the lonely, and the needy. Under her direction, monthly home visits are made to each adult woman in the ward in which brief gospel instruction and encouragement are given (see VISITING TEACHING). Once each month this ward welfare services group becomes the WARD COUNCIL when joined by the SUNDAY SCHOOL president, the YOUNG WOMEN president, the PRIMARY president, and the activities committee chairman. The ward council discusses and plans all ward activities and correlates the services and programs of the Church in relation to individuals and families. Historically, youth usually have been given leadership roles in planning their own activities and in helping with events to which all ward members are invited. Since the mid-1970s, youth leadership has been nurtured on a monthly basis by the bishopric in the bishopric youth committee meeting, where youth activities and service projects are planned. Often members of a ward activities committee are called to supervise and carry out special wardwide events as requested by the bishopric.

Since 1980, when the Church adopted the consolidated meeting schedule, each ward holds three general meetings during a three-hour block of time on Sunday. In SACRAMENT MEETING family members worship together, renew covenants through partaking of the sacrament, and listen to talks and sermons based on the scriptures. During a second hour, Sunday School classes are held in age groups from twelve to adult. Each year in the adult classes, one of the standard works of scripture is studied: OLD TESTAMENT, NEW TESTAMENT, the BOOK OF MORMON, the DOCTRINE AND COVENANTS, and the PEARL OF GREAT PRICE. During a third hour Priesthood quorums, Young Women, and Relief Society meet separately, where youth, men, and women are taught how to put gospel principles into action in everyday life. Priesthood quorums and the Relief Society are the service arms of the ward. Their members provide the volunteer help necessary to implement the plans made by the bishopric and auxiliary leaders. Adult holders of the priesthood attend quorum meetings according to whether they are HIGH PRIESTS or ELDERS. Young men (ages twelve to eighteen) meet in AARONIC PRIESTHOOD quorums for DEACONS (ages twelve and thirteen), TEACHERS (ages fourteen and fifteen), and PRIESTS (ages sixteen to eighteen). The Young Women are organized in age groups similar to the Young Men: Beehives (ages twelve and thirteen), Mia Maids (ages fourteen and fifteen), and Laurels (ages sixteen and seventeen). From age eighteen, women are members of the Relief Society, a benevolent society dedicated to caring for the needy and to assisting in spiritual, social, and personal development. Relief Society lessons focus on spiritual living, home and family education, compassionate service, and social relations.

Concurrent with the Sunday School and the men's and women's activities, the PRIMARY organization holds a nursery for children from ages eighteen months to three years, and classes for those three through eleven years of age, where children are taught lessons about Jesus Christ and the scriptures and are involved in singing and speaking.

Special activities (service projects and socials) are held for the women and youth on a day other than Sunday. The Relief Society holds a monthly evening meeting in which the sisters are taught home management techniques and skills.

The bishop is responsible for the finances of the ward, and is assisted in this matter by a financial clerk. Ward activities are either financed locally by individual contributions of ward members, or by a system wherein each ward receives an operating budget from general tithing funds based on the number and level of activity of its members. There are to be no other fund-raising activities.

The ward organization is a tool to help assure that Church activities complement, rather than compete with, family activities; that social activities are inclusive, rather than exclusive; and to nurture those who feel that geographic boundaries are artificial and thus exclude them from Sabbath day association with longtime Church friends.

Ideally, the ward organization becomes the means of creating an intimate religious community where the work of the kingdom of God on earth is carried out by every member in a lay ministry. Through the ward organization members teach the gospel, perform the ordinances, provide fellowship with the saints, and in all ways nurture one another in the faith.

BIBLIOGRAPHY

Alder, Douglas D. "The Mormon Ward: Congregation or Community?" *Journal of Mormon History* 5 (1978):61–78.

Arrington, Leonard J., and Davis Bitton. "The Nineteenth Century Ward." In *The Mormon Experience: A History of the Latter-day Saints*, pp. 206–219. New York, 1979.

L. ROBERT WEBB

WARD WELFARE COMMITTEE

Certain officers of each WARD form the ward welfare committee, headed by the BISHOP. Through his priesthood CALLING, the bishop is entrusted with the sacred responsibility to know the temporal circumstances of his ward members and to ensure that proper care is given to those in need (D&C 84:112).

The bishop is assisted in these efforts by his two counselors, the HIGH PRIESTS quorum group leader, the ELDERS quorum president, the YOUNG MEN president, the RELIEF SOCIETY presidency, the ward executive secretary, the ward CLERK, and others. The bishop convenes the ward welfare committee at least monthly. These leaders report and confidentially discuss any welfare needs in the ward that they have become aware of, either personally or by reports from HOME TEACHERS and VISITING TEACHERS. Where possible, the priesthood quorums and the Relief Society serve as the first Church source of assistance to members who need help beyond what the family can provide (D&C 52:39–40). When these ward resources have been exhausted, the committee may suggest that additional help be sought from the "Lord's storehouse" (D&C 51:13; 83:5–6) or from other people or services.

In addition, the committee may also help ward members in learning to provide for themselves and their families, to live the principle of the monthly fast, and to contribute a generous monetary FAST OFFERING, and in preparing for unexpected adversity, rendering service in return for Church assistance, and preparing for emergencies in the community.

BIBLIOGRAPHY

The Church of Jesus Christ of Latter-day Saints. *Caring for the Needy*, pp. 4–5. Salt Lake City, 1986.

Romney, Marion G. "The Role of Bishops in Welfare Services." *Ensign* 7 (Nov. 1977):79–81.

Welfare Services Resource Handbook, pp. 8–10. Salt Lake City, 1980.

JOHN H. COX

WAR IN HEAVEN

When Latter-day Saints speak of the "war in heaven," they generally mean the conflict in the PREMORTAL LIFE that began when Lucifer, in a rebellion against God the Father and his Son Jesus Christ, sought to overthrow them. The result was that Lucifer and his followers were cast out of heaven. The prophet Isaiah (Isa. 14:12–15) and John the Revelator (Rev. 12:4–9) both referred to the war, and Jesus himself spoke of having "beheld Satan as lightning fall from heaven" (Luke 10:17–18). Latter-day revelation gives additional insight, which is supplemented by the teachings of latter-day prophets.

To "bring to pass the immortality and eternal life of man" (Moses 1:39), God the Father insti-

tuted the eternal PLAN OF SALVATION, which centered on mankind's AGENCY, anticipated the fall of man, and provided a savior. Although previously known in the heavenly realm, the plan was formally presented to the spirit children of God at a COUNCIL IN HEAVEN. "Whom shall I send?" (Abr. 3:27) was the Father's call for someone to be the redeemer. His eldest Son (D&C 93:21; Col. 1:15), known also as JEHOVAH, one "like unto God" (Abr. 3:24), and chosen from the beginning (Moses 4:2), officially accepted this role and responded, "Here am I, send me" (Abr. 3:27). He also stated, "Father, thy will be done, and the glory be thine forever" (Moses 4:2). With this formal acceptance and selection of the future Messiah, the spirit children of God "shouted for joy" (Job 38:7). It was also a time to signify individual commitment to the Father's plan.

Not all accepted, however. The scriptures state that Lucifer, an "angel of God who was in authority in the presence of God" (D&C 76:25), rebelled and offered himself as the proposed redeemer, saying to the Father, "Behold, here am I, send me" (Moses 4:1). His offer was not well-intentioned and was a defiance of the Father and his Only Begotten Son. Lucifer's proposal was couched in his own interests: "I will be thy son, and I will redeem all mankind, that one soul shall not be lost, and surely I will do it; wherefore give me thine honor" (Moses 4:1). His proposal, if accepted, would have destroyed mankind's agency (Moses 4:3). Lucifer possessed character flaws, which finally manifested themselves in jealousy of the Christ and rejection of the Father's plan. Just how he proposed to save every soul is not explained but it apparently allowed either no opportunity for sin or, if sin did occur, no condemnation for sin. As his reward for saving everyone, Lucifer demanded that God surrender his honor and power to Lucifer (Isa. 14:13; D&C 29:36; Moses 4:3).

Although Lucifer made a false offer of salvation without individual responsibility, he gained many followers, and "war in heaven" ensued. Michael, the archangel (who later was Adam), led the "forces" of Jehovah in a battle for the loyalties of the Father's spirit children. The exact nature of this war is not detailed in the scriptures, but there can be little doubt that it involved the principles of the gospel of Jesus Christ and how mankind was to be saved. The Prophet Joseph Smith explained, "The contention in heaven was—Jesus said there would be certain souls that would not be saved; and the devil said he could save them all, and laid his plans before the grand council, who gave their vote in favor of Jesus Christ. So the devil rose up in rebellion against God, and was cast down, with all who put up their heads for him" (*TPJS*, p. 357).

Lucifer and his followers, who were "a third part of the hosts of heaven" (Rev. 12:4; D&C 29:36), made open warfare against the Father, the Son, the Holy Ghost, and the eternal Plan of Salvation and were cast down to earth (cf. Jude 1:6), eternally deprived of being born into mortality with physical bodies, and never to have salvation (*TPJS*, pp. 181, 297–98). So tragic was the fall of Lucifer that "the heavens wept over him" (D&C 76:26).

Known on earth as Satan or the devil, Lucifer and his followers still continue the war against the work and the people of God, being permitted to do so to give people opportunity to exercise agency, being "enticed by the one or the other" (2 Ne. 2:16–25). They will persist until the day of judgment, when Michael, the archangel, and his armies will ultimately prevail and cast them out forever (D&C 88:111–15).

BIBLIOGRAPHY

McConkie, Bruce R. *Doctrinal New Testament Commentary*, Vol. 3, pp. 513–19. Salt Lake City, 1973.

Top, Brent L. "The War in Heaven." In *The Life Before*. Salt Lake City, 1988.

BRENT L. TOP

WAR AND PEACE

LDS ideas about war and peace are complex. They synthesize a number of basic values. First are the ideals of finding peace in Christ (John 14:27), turning the other cheek and loving one's enemies (Matt. 5:39, 44), repeatedly forgiving one's enemies (D&C 64:10; 98:23–27, 39–43), and renouncing war and proclaiming peace (D&C 98:16). Next are the goals of establishing a perfect community of righteous, harmonious people (*see* ZION) and of welcoming the millennial reign of Jesus for a thousand years of peace. Third is a fundamental aversion to any use of force or violence that denies personal AGENCY (D&C 121:41–44). Next is the recognition that war was the tactic Satan used in the premortal existence (*see* WAR IN HEAVEN) and

that he continues to reign with violence on this earth (Moses 6:15). Then there is acknowledgment that it is appropriate and sometimes required to take up arms in defense of one's family, religion, and freedom (Alma 43:45–47; 46:12). Next are the ethical and legal distinctions between deliberate murder and the killing of opposing soldiers in the line of combat duty. There is an obligation of all citizens to honor and obey the constitutional law of their land (*see* CIVIC DUTIES), together with the belief that all political leaders are accountable to God for their governmental administrations (D&C 134:1). And finally, there is the role of the UNITED STATES OF AMERICA as a nation of divine destiny with a mission to lead the way in establishing international peace and individual freedom on earth. Under the extreme pressures and agonies that may arise from differing circumstances, an individual must have personal faith, hope, charity, and revelation to implement all these principles in righteousness.

Countries may define their interests differently and hence make reliance on force more or less salient, with various political and ethical consequences. For example, a group may adopt a radical pacifist position, but its survival then depends on the attitudes of others. Thus, in the Book of Mormon, the survival of the converted Lamanites who vowed never to shed blood was vouchsafed by the Nephites and by their own sons, who were not bound by their oath of pacifism (Alma 27:24; 56:5–9).

War also has some legal status in international law: "War is a fact recognized, and with regard to many points regulated, but not established by International Law" (L. Oppenheim, *International Law*, London, 1952, p. 202). In the exercise of their sovereignty, states may limit the initiation or conduct of war, but the present political system of self-help grants the right to make war as one's safety, vital interests, or sense of justice may dictate. Over time peaceful conditions may emerge, but as long as separate independent entities exist, the likelihood of resort to armed conflict remains, and in any sovereign state wherein LDS citizens reside they are pledged to "being subject to kings, presidents, rulers, and magistrates, etc., obeying, honoring, and sustaining the law" (A of F 12).

TEACHINGS OF THE BOOK OF MORMON AND THE DOCTRINE AND COVENANTS. The LDS response to the political realities of war is largely condi-

Troops marching through Salt Lake City to join the United States forces in the Spanish-American War (1898), two years after Utah statehood. Photographer: C. W. Carter.

tioned by the concept of the justification of defensive war provided in the Book of Mormon and in modern revelation. The main statements come from accounts of MORONI₁ (a Nephite commander, c. 72–56 B.C.), from the prophet MORMON (final commander of the Nephite armies, c. A.D. 326–385), and from guidance given to the Church in 1833, when persecutions were mounting in Missouri (see D&C 98).

Captain Moroni raised a banner on which he laid out the principal Nephite war aims: the defense of "our God, our religion, and freedom, and our peace, our wives, and our children" (Alma 46:12). Legitimate warfare is described here in defensive terms. Moroni established a forward defense perimeter, constructed protective fortifications for some cities, and deployed his main armies as mobile striking forces to retake captured towns. His purpose was "that they might live unto the Lord their God" (Alma 48:10), giving no support for war as an instrument to expand territorial or political control (Morm. 4:4–5). He taught the Nephites to defend themselves but "never to give

an offense, yea, and never to raise the sword except it were against an enemy, except it were to preserve their lives. And this was their faith, that by so doing God would prosper them in the land" (Alma 48:14–15). They sought the guidance of prophets before going to battle (Alma 16:5; 43:23; 3 Ne. 3:19–20). Moroni "glor[ied]" in this position—"not in the shedding of blood but in doing good, in preserving his people, yea, in keeping the commandments of God" (Alma 48:16). Even in the conduct of war itself, indiscriminate slaughter, plunder, and reprisal were prohibited (see *CWHN* 8:328–79).

Four centuries later, when the Nephite forces "began to boast in their own strength, and began to swear before the heavens that they would avenge themselves of the blood of their brethren who had been slain by their enemies" (Morm. 3:9), Mormon, their leader, withdrew from command. Vengeance belonged only to the Lord (Morm. 3:15). When Mormon's sense of duty caused him again to lead the armies, he knew that the Nephite turn to aggression and bloodthirsty reprisal betrayed a deeper corruption that ultimately spelled their doom. As his people drifted into barbaric acts of torture, rape, and enslavement, Mormon lamented the depravity of his people: "They are without order and without mercy" (Moro. 9:18); and they were destroyed (*see* BOOK OF MORMON, HISTORY OF WARFARE IN).

Even if the sword is taken up in self-defense, it is a fearful choice. It should be undertaken only if God commands (D&C 98:33) and after "a standard of peace" has been offered three times (98:34–38). Great rewards are promised to those who warn their enemies in the name of the Lord, who patiently bear three attacks against themselves or their families, and who repeatedly forgive their enemies (98:23–27, 39–43). If an enemy "trespass against thee the fourth time, . . . thine enemy is in thine hands, and if thou rewardest him according to his works thou art justified"; but if forgiveness is again extended, "I, the Lord, will avenge thee of thine enemy an hundred-fold" (98:31, 44–45). Accordingly, in the Missouri persecutions (*see* MISSOURI CONFLICT) and in Nauvoo at the time of the 1844 MARTYRDOM OF JOSEPH AND HYRUM SMITH, the posture of the Church was strictly defensive; likewise, the 1857 military threat of the UTAH EXPEDITION was defused without the occurrence of bloodshed.

HISTORICAL PERSPECTIVES. In several respects, the LDS response to the subsequent historical realities of war has paralleled the experience of Christianity in general. As long as the early Christians had no responsibility for government, they were obliged only "to obey magistrates, to be ready to every good work" (Titus 3:1), to render unto Caesar "the things which are Caesar's, and unto God the things that are God's" (Matt. 22:21); Paul saw the real battle as being one with evil spiritual forces (Eph. 6:12). Once it became clear in early Christianity that the second coming of Jesus was not at hand and that the Roman Empire had become Christian, responsibility for political order became a Christian duty. There then developed a theory of war culminating in the doctrine of "just war" formulated by theologians such as Thomas Aquinas.

Likewise, millennial enthusiasm initially focused Latter-day Saints more on the gathering of Israel than on accommodation to the world. An early and continuing LDS theme was that the hour was drawing near for the end of worldly states.

With the collapse of "Babylon" would come intense conflicts and the wrath of God (D&C 63:32–33). Bloody war would arise at home and abroad (D&C 38:29). The CIVIL WAR PROPHECY in 1832 foretold increasing turmoil until the "full end of all nations" (D&C 87:6). War in this perspective is the harbinger of the apocalyptic end of the world, and the Church is to raise the voice of warning "for the last time" and gather the faithful together to "stand in holy places, and be not moved, until the day of the Lord come" (D&C 88:74–88; 87:8).

Animated by this vision, President Brigham Young counseled the Saints to "flee to Zion . . . that they may dwell in peace" (*MFP* 2:107). Little hope was given for the reclamation of the secular society. This tendency toward withdrawal, however, was counterbalanced by the LDS perspective on the divine inspiration undergirding the Constitution of the United States and the fact that the Church was inevitably drawn into national politics (*see* UNITED STATES OF AMERICA; CHURCH AND STATE). Although the attempt to establish Zion attracted the hostility of many politicians, Church leaders took an active role in national affairs, supporting the Mexican War (*see* MORMON BATTALION), immediately responding to a request by President Lincoln to protect the mail and telegraph route east of Fort Bridger during the Civil War (1862), and proving their loyalty in the Spanish-American War (1898). After the MANIFESTO OF 1890, the division between the Church and the larger society declined, leading to a reconciliation with the existing political order.

World Wars I and II impelled the Church to speak about the religious duties of citizens of warring states, balancing the condemnation of war with statements about civic duties and the relative justice of the causes and conduct of particular combatants. In 1939, the First Presidency asserted that the commandment "Thou shalt not kill" (Ex. 20:13) applies both to individuals and to political entities and condemned the notion of war as an instrument of state policy (*MFP* 6:88–93). Later in 1940 and 1942 they warned against the self-righteous justifications of the belligerents, which could cloak genocidal acts of mass destruction (*MFP* 6:115–17), putting distance between the Church and the state: "The Church itself, as such, has no responsibility for these policies, as to which it has no means of doing more than urging its members fully to render that loyalty to their country and to free institutions which the loftiest patriotism calls for"

(*MFP* 6:156). The combatants are "the innocent instrumentalities of the war," who cannot be held responsible for their lawful participation (*MFP* 6:159). At the same time, reference to "free institutions" and the observation that "both sides cannot be wholly right; perhaps neither is without wrong" (*MFP* 6:159) point out that there are other grounds on which to evaluate one's participation in war, just cause and just conduct.

Echoing the concerns of the Book of Mormon for just war, the First Presidency warned people not to convert a legitimate war of self-defense into a bloody search for vengeance or the killing of innocent civilians. President J. Reuben Clark, Jr., held that "to be justified in going to war in self-defense, a nation must be foreclosed from all other alternatives" (Firmage and Blakesley, p. 314). President Joseph F. SMITH identified wickedness in the whole system of states as the root of world war: "I presume there is not a nation in the world today that is not tainted with this evil more or less. It may be possible perhaps, to trace the cause of the evil, or the greatest part of it, to some particular nation of the earth; but I do not know" (*MFP* 5:71). At the same time, he also affirmed "that the hand of God is striving with certain of the nations of the earth to preserve and protect human liberty, freedom to worship him according to the dictates of conscience, freedom and the inalienable right of men to organize national governments in the earth" (*MFP* 5:71). Accordingly, the Church supported the war "to free the world from the domination of monarchical despotism" (*MFP* 5:71).

Although some used the global threat of nazism, fascism, and communism to justify war beyond a reaction to direct and immediate threat to American territorial integrity or political independence, others such as J. Reuben Clark in the 1940s continued to plead for a neutral, unarmed United States: "Moral force is far more potent than physical force in international relations. I believe that America should again turn to the promotion of peaceful adjustment of international disputes" (cited in Firmage and Blakesley, p. 298). Since World War II, the LDS stance toward just cause and just conduct in war has provided guides by which to evaluate participation in specific conflicts without departing either from the obligation of civic obedience or the generalized condemnation of war. These attitudes accommodate the cross-cultural and millennial aspirations of a worldwide church and the demands placed on citizens in a world of competing secular states whose ultimate demise is inevitable.

[*See also* Military and the Church.]

BIBLIOGRAPHY

Berrett, William E. "The Book of Mormon Speaks on War." In *A Book of Mormon Treasury*, pp. 275–84. Salt Lake City, 1959.

Blais, Pierre. "The Enduring Paradox: Mormon Attitudes toward War and Peace." *Dialogue* 17 (Winter 1984):61–73.

Firmage, Edwin Brown. "Violence and the Gospel: The Teachings of the Old Testament, the New Testament, and the Book of Mormon." *BYU Studies* 25 (Winter 1985):31–53.

———, and Christopher L. Blakesley. "Clark, Law and International Order." *BYU Studies* 13 (Spring 1973):273–346.

Garrett, H. Dean. "The Book of Mormon on War." In *A Symposium on the Book of Mormon*, pp. 47–53. Salt Lake City, 1986.

Oaks, Dallin H. "World Peace." *Ensign* 20 (May 1990):71–73.

Packer, Boyd K. "The Member and the Military." *IE* 71 (June 1968):58, 60–61.

Roy, Denny; Grant P. Skabelund; and Ray C. Hillam, eds. *A Time to Kill: Reflections on War.* Salt Lake City, 1990.

Walker, Ronald W. "Sheaves, Bucklers, and the State: Mormon Leaders Respond to the Dilemmas of War." *Sunstone* 7 (July–Aug. 1982):43–56.

ROBERT S. WOOD

WASHING OF FEET

The ordinance of washing of feet performed by Jesus Christ after the Last Supper with his apostles was a gesture of humility. Amidst discussion of who would be the greatest in the kingdom, Jesus, demonstrating what he had taught, removed his outer robe and performed this menial task, teaching that one who would be a leader must be a servant (John 13:1–8; cf. D&C 88:141). The Joseph Smith Translation adds this explanation about this incident: "Now this was the custom of the Jews under their law; wherefore, Jesus did this that the law might be fulfilled" (JST John 13:10). By this clarification it appears that the washing of feet was an ordinance of the law of Moses.

There is no clear explanation of the washing of feet in the Old Testament, although it is evident that it was a social custom for administering kindness to a guest. The washing of feet is not mentioned in the Book of Mormon, and it is spoken of only briefly in the Doctrine and Covenants in 88:138–41.

DOUGLAS A. WANGSGARD

WASHINGS AND ANOINTINGS

Ritual anointings were a prominent part of religious rites in the biblical world. Recipients of the anointing included temple officiants (Ex. 28:41), prophets (1 Kgs. 19:16), and kings (1 Sam. 16:3; 1 Kgs. 1:39). In addition, sacral objects associated with the Israelite sanctuary were anointed (Ex. 30:22–29). Of equal importance in the religion of the Israelites were ablutions or ceremonial washings (Ex. 29:4–7). To ensure religious purity, Mosaic law required that designated individuals receive a ritual washing, sometimes in preparation for entering the temple (Ex. 30:17–21; Lev. 14:7–8; 15:5–27).

The washings and anointings of the biblical period have a parallel today in The Church of Jesus Christ of Latter-day Saints. In response to a COMMANDMENT to gather the SAINTS and to build a house "to prepare them for the ordinances and endowments, washings, and anointings" (*TPJS*, p. 308), these ordinances were introduced in the KIRTLAND TEMPLE on January 21, 1836 (*HC* 2:379–83). In many respects similar in purpose to ancient Israelite practice and to the washing of feet by Jesus among his disciples, these modern LDS rites are performed only in temples set apart and dedicated for sacred purposes (D&C 124:37–38; *HC* 6:318–19).

Many symbolic meanings of washings and anointings are traceable in the scriptures. Ritual washings (Heb. 9:10; D&C 124:37) symbolize the cleansing of the soul from sins and iniquities. They signify the washing-away of the pollutions of the Lord's people (Isa. 4:4). Psalm 51:2 expresses the human longing and divine promise: "Wash me thoroughly from mine iniquity, and cleanse me from my sin" (cf. Ps. 73:13; Isa. 1:16).

The anointing of a person or object with sacred ointment represents SANCTIFICATION (Lev. 8:10–12) and CONSECRATION (Ex. 28:41), so that both become "most holy" (Ex. 30:29) unto the Lord. In this manner, profane persons and things are sanctified in similitude of the MESSIAH (Hebrew "anointed one"), who is Christ (Greek "anointed one").

BIBLIOGRAPHY

McConkie, Joseph Fielding, and Donald W. Parry. *A Guide to Scriptural Symbols.* Salt Lake City, 1990.

DONALD W. PARRY

WEALTH, ATTITUDES TOWARD

[*For related articles, see* Business; Consecration; Equality; Financial Contributions; Poverty, Attitudes Toward; Zion. *The blessings of eternal wealth are discussed in* Riches of Eternity.]

Latter-day Saints view wealth as a blessing and also as a test. The Lord has repeatedly promised his people, "Inasmuch as ye shall keep the commandments of God ye shall prosper in the land" (Alma 36:30). But wealth can lead to pride and inequality: "Woe unto the rich, who are rich as to the things of the world. For because they are rich they despise the poor, and they persecute the meek, and their hearts are upon their treasures" (2 Ne. 9:30). Therefore, attitudes toward wealth and the use of material abundance reveal a person's priorities: "Before ye seek for riches, seek ye for the kingdom of God. And after ye have obtained a hope in Christ ye shall obtain riches, if ye seek them; and ye will seek them for the intent to do good" (Jacob 2:18–19). To those who will inherit the celestial kingdom, God has promised the RICHES OF ETERNITY.

LDS beliefs about the nature and purpose of life influence Church members' attitudes toward wealth. Thus, the concept of wealth has both materialistic and spiritual dimensions: wealth is an accumulation of worldly possessions; it is also an acquisition of knowledge or talents. Since MATTER and SPIRIT are of the same order, material wealth can become refined and sanctified by the influence of God's spirit as it is consecrated to his purposes. Latter-day Saints are encouraged to increase in all honorable forms of wealth, knowledge, and obedience, which increase the "wealth" or worth of the human soul and to "lay up . . . treasures in heaven" (Matt. 6:20; D&C 18:10; 130:19; *see* EDUCATION, ATTITUDES TOWARD).

The world and its resources belong to the Creator. Material blessings may be delivered from heaven if the recipient conforms to the Christian ideals of integrity, honesty, and charity. All people are of divine origin and have come to earth to know good and evil and to be tested to see if they will choose the good. By the grace of God and by their diligent labors consistent with divine law, both the earth and mankind can be perfected and glorified.

If the earth's resources are not wisely and carefully husbanded, however, wealth can become a curse. It is the "love of money," not money itself, that is identified as the root of all evil (1 Tim. 6:10).

Christ and the Rich Young Man, by Heinrich Hofmann (1889). Jesus counsels a rich young man who has asked how to obtain eternal life: "Sell that thou hast, and give to the poor" (*see* Matt. 19:16–22).

President Brigham Young warned that wealth and perishable things "are liable to decoy the minds of [the] saints" (*CWHN* 9:333). Wealth may result in misuse and un-Christian conduct, immoral exploitation, or dishonesty. Greed and harmful self-indulgence are sins, and the pursuit of materialistic goals at the expense of other Christian duties is to be avoided. People with materialistic wealth draw special warnings regarding responsibility toward the poor; riches can canker the soul and make entrance into heaven exceedingly difficult (Matt. 19:24; D&C 56:16).

Thus, the accumulation and utilization of wealth confront the human family with some of its major challenges in determining the righteousness of goals and the correctness of behavior. "In many respects the real test of a man is his attitude toward his earthly possessions" (F. Richards, p. 46). The prosperity that results from honest and intelligent work is not necessarily repugnant to the spiritual

quality of life, but the Church consistently warns of the risks of "selfishness and personal aggrandizement" that lurk in accumulating wealth (S. Richards, *CR* [Apr. 1928]:31).

Personal reflection, prayer, and inspiration are needed in deciding how to use one's wealth. Fairness, justice, mercy, and social responsibility are individual requirements; improper behavior is not to be excused by the behavior of others, reflected in market forces or windfall accumulations. The responsibility of each human being is to think and act in ways that ennoble the divine nature. President N. Eldon Tanner outlined five principles that epitomize the Church's counsel on personal economic affairs: pay an honest TITHING, live on less than you earn, distinguish between needs and wants, develop and live within a budget, and be honest in all financial affairs (*Ensign* 9 [Nov. 1979]:81–82).

While not taking vows of poverty, Latter-day Saints covenant to use their wealth, time, talents, and knowledge to build up the kingdom of God on earth (D&C 42:30; 105:5). Providing for a family is a sacred requirement (1 Tim. 5:8). The mission of the Church in many countries of the world requires considerable resources to sustain Church members in seeking the spiritual growth and perfection of themselves and others. Ignorance, disease, and poverty can be overcome only with the assistance of material assets that result from the wise use of human talent and the resources abundant in nature. Thus the Church and its members seek to obtain the material resources that are needed to build the kingdom of God.

The principles taught in the STANDARD WORKS concerning the accumulation and use of wealth are sufficiently broad to permit an ongoing dialogue among Church members about what is pleasing in the sight of the Lord. Some emphasize that man must work and that the fruits of his labor are his due and right (D&C 31:5). Others point out that although man must work, God makes life and its abundance possible, and thus everything rightly belongs to him (Mosiah 2:21–25) and comes to man "in the form of trust property" to be used for God's purposes (S. Richards, *CR* [Apr. 1923]:151). Some suggest that there are no limits on the profits one may gather provided the pursuit is legal and the ultimate utilization is appropriate. Others see business and legal standards of secular society as falling short: "Except your righteousness shall exceed the righteousness of the scribes and Pharisees, ye shall in no case enter into the kingdom of heaven. . . . Ye cannot serve God and mammon" (Matt. 5:20; 6:24). Having taught correct principles in the scriptures and through his priesthood leaders, the Lord leaves it to Church members to govern themselves through individual righteousness, with knowledge that all will be held personally accountable for the choices they make.

BIBLIOGRAPHY

Johnson, Richard E. "Socioeconomic Inequality: The Haves and the Have Nots." *BYU Today* 44 (Sept. 1990):46–58.

Nibley, Hugh W. *Approaching Zion*, Vol. 9 in *CWHN*. Salt Lake City, 1989.

Richards, Franklin D. "The Law of Abundance." *Ensign* 1 (June 1971):45–47.

R. THAYNE ROBSON

WELFARE

[It is a major concern of The Church of Jesus Christ of Latter-day Saints to care for the physical, as well as the spiritual, welfare of its own members, and of others as far as possible. There are theological foundations for LDS attitudes toward such subjects as Blessings; Community; Love; Matter; Physical Body; Poverty; Righteousness; and Wealth.

Institutionally, the Church operates an extensive program that delivers food, clothing, and other essentials of life to those in need. See Bishop's Storehouse; Compassionate Service; Deseret Industries; Elders; Fast Offerings; Hospitals; Relief Society; Social Services; Ward Welfare Committee; Welfare Farms; Welfare Services; and Welfare Square.

It encourages and assists members in finding suitable employment. See Business; Deseret Industries; Education; Occupational Status; Social Services; and Work.

For specialized services to the disabled, see Blind, Materials for and Deaf, Materials for.

The Church counsels all its members to store food and commodities in preparation for possible disasters. See Emergency Preparedness and Self-sufficiency.

It also extends aid and assistance to other peoples of the world in times of emergency. See Calamities and Disasters; Economic Aid; and Humanitarian Service.]

WELFARE FARMS

The purchase of farmlands by the Church began in the late 1930s. The intent was to give unemployed people an opportunity to work and to produce

commodities to help the poor and needy. In the 1940s, stakes and groups of stakes began purchasing farms as approved welfare projects. Sometimes the Church would purchase a farm, and the local unit would repay the Church loan from farm revenues. In the 1970s, farms were purchased on a shared basis, with half of the funds coming from the local unit and half from Church headquarters. All new farmlands are now purchased solely by the Church. In 1990 the Church owned and operated about 160 localized welfare farms, which raised many kinds of produce for its welfare program. In addition, it had extensive farm holdings in its welfare reserve system and investment portfolio.

Produce from the welfare farms is canned in local Church canneries and transferred to the BISHOP'S STOREHOUSES. Surpluses are sold on the open market, and the revenues from these sales are used to help pay for the production overhead of the farm. Under the supervision of a stake president, a stake farm committee from the local priesthood units involved directs the local welfare farm

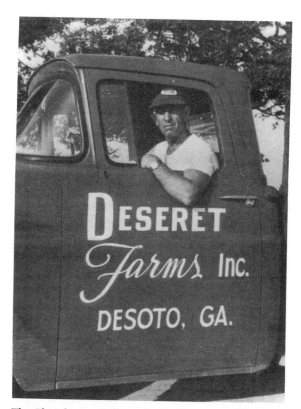

The Church owns and operates farms as a part of its charitable welfare program and as reserve investments. Most of these farms are in Utah, Arizona, Idaho, and California. Photo c. 1959.

operations, including its finances. Day-to-day business matters are handled by a farm manager, who is usually a full-time employee. Where feasible, donated farm labor from Church members is utilized, which is counted as a contribution to the stake's welfare program. Local ward units organize crews of volunteers who work different shifts at the farms. As modern agricultural work becomes more sophisticated, the welfare farms are relying increasingly on hired farm labor.

Currently, Church farm properties fall into three categories. First, there are about 160 Church welfare farms, which are operated by a farm committee as described above, transferring their products to Church canneries and bishop's storehouses. Second, the Church owns about 250 reserve farms, which are held by the Church primarily for possible future welfare needs. These properties are assigned to the Church-owned Farm Management Corporation. They have been acquired over the years for a variety of reasons and are not always the best-quality agricultural lands. They tend to be concentrated in areas where Church populations are located. Their products are sold on the open market. Third, the Church owns other properties for various purposes, such as investment diversification (*see* FINANCES OF THE CHURCH). These farms are leased to private individuals or companies which operate them as private enterprises.

Church farms are tax-exempt only to the extent that they fill Church welfare needs. Above their welfare function, these farms pay taxes as regular businesses. In 1983 the Church sold more than 200 farms that exceeded its welfare needs.

Farm projects vary according to locale, need, climate, and soil conditions. Welfare farms produce grain, fruit, and vegetables. There are also beef, pork, and poultry projects, as well as such specialized projects as honey production. The first priority of all farm production is to supply the needs of welfare canneries and bishop's storehouses, and to use as much donated labor as possible, giving opportunities for charitable service.

Farms may vary in size from just a few acres to several thousand. Most are located in the United States, primarily in Utah, Arizona, California, and Idaho. The largest reserve farm is in California. A notable investment farm is a 300,000-acre ranch in Florida that raises livestock and citrus fruit and is used as a hunting and forestry reserve.

T. GLENN HAWS

WELFARE SERVICES

The basic philosophy underlying the welfare services system of The Church of Jesus Christ of Latter-day Saints was succinctly stated by the Church's sixth President, Joseph F. SMITH: "It has always been a cardinal teaching with the Latter-day Saints, that a religion which has not the power to save the people temporally and make them prosperous and happy here cannot be depended upon to save them spiritually, and exalt them in the life to come" (quoted in L. Arrington, *Great Basin Kingdom*, 1958, p. 425, n. 16).

This Christlike objective of caring for the physical well-being of humans has been pursued throughout the history of the Church, involving a wide variety of activities undertaken in radically different circumstances, but all based on the same set of principles drawn from ancient and modern scripture:

- Self-sufficiency and family support are seen as a spiritual as well as a temporal obligation (1 Tim. 5:8; D&C 42:42). The Church is responsible for teaching principles and providing necessary assistance to enhance self-reliance.

- Those who are economically deprived for reasons either within or beyond their control (Mark 14:7) are to be provided with short-term emergency help, then assisted to a state of self-reliance, if possible, and provided with support if not.

- Assistance provided should exalt, rather than demean, the poor (D&C 104:16).

- The salvation of a person who is not poor depends to a substantial degree upon the care that person gives to the poor (Mosiah 4:16–22; D&C 56:16; 104:18).

- The salvation of the poor depends in part on the spirit in which they receive assistance (Mosiah 4:24–25; D&C 56:17–18).

HISTORY OF WELFARE SERVICES. During its first century, the modern Church applied these principles primarily by assisting Church members to gather at central locations—Kirtland, Ohio; western Missouri; Nauvoo, Illinois; the Great Basin—and to obtain land on which they could become self-sufficient. But all were not able to support themselves as farmers or in other pursuits, so other employment opportunities were created for the poor. They helped to build temples and other Church buildings and assisted in public works projects, receiving pay out of contributions given by those who had regular incomes. As early as 1896, forty years before the inauguration of a public employment service in America, the Church had an employment bureau, gathering and publishing information on employment opportunities as well as compiling data about those needing employment.

The present-day system for helping the poor had its roots in the Great Depression of the 1930s, which hit urban Church members hardest. Though often struggling in the 1930s, farm-owning Latter-day Saints usually were self-sufficient, while city-dwellers deprived of employment were in the most serious straits. Stake presidents in urban areas contacted nearby farmers who faced prices so low that it was not profitable to harvest their crops. Arrangements were made so that idle urban members could harvest the crops in return for a share thereof. The produce thus obtained was stored in Church-controlled warehouse facilities and distributed according to need. Drawing upon that experience, welfare farms were soon established under Church ownership in areas surrounding Mormon-populated cities. Other Church units undertook processing and manufacturing projects based on the rural produce. BISHOP'S STOREHOUSES were created for storage and distribution, and products were moved from location to location by a Church-sponsored transportation system. A sheltered workshop program, DESERET INDUSTRIES, was introduced in 1938 to create jobs for the unemployed and the handicapped, refurbishing used clothing, furniture, and household goods for retail sale at low cost.

With the return of prosperity in the United States following World War II, these facilities were expanded to offer short-term emergency work and commodities during recessions, strikes, and natural disasters, as well as employment assistance to the aged, the handicapped, and others with limited ability for self-support. As the complexities of urban life increased and other obstacles such as unemployment and the need for various types of counseling became more evident, a social services agency was added. When needs became apparent, other welfare service functions were also added, growing into the system that currently operates, primarily in the United States and Canada. Meanwhile, the rapid growth of the international membership of the Church, especially in less developed lands, poses new challenges, which the welfare services system is adapting to meet.

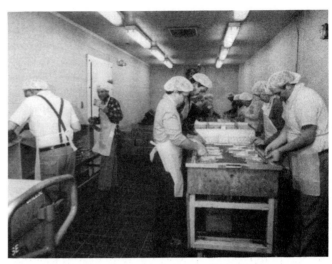

Church members wrapping cheese at the Church cheese factory in Logan, a dairy region of Utah (1987). Local areas produce different kinds of commodities depending on geographical abilities and contribute them to the centralized distribution network of the Church Welfare system. Courtesy Craig Law.

WELFARE PRINCIPLES AND PRACTICES. Emphasizing family self-reliance, the Church welfare obligation begins with the teaching of principles of provident living, encouraging the use of appropriate community services, and then filling in with Church assistance when other resources prove to be inadequate.

Individuals and families are expected to live prudently, providing for their own needs and when possible, producing a surplus to use in helping others. Organizations within the Church such as the RELIEF SOCIETY, PRIESTHOOD QUORUMS, the SUNDAY SCHOOL, and youth programs teach the appropriate principles, while the Relief Society and the priesthood, through VISITING TEACHING and HOME TEACHING, encourage self-reliance and identify individual and family needs. Areas of emphasis are literacy and education; career development and counseling; financial and resource management; home production and storage; physical health; and social, emotional, and spiritual support.

Latter-day Saints view education as a spiritual, as well as a temporal, obligation. All members are expected to take advantage of available educational opportunities. Church leaders counsel parents to read to their children, teach them, and encourage them to study the scriptures and other good literature and to communicate well in writing and speaking. Church organizations reinforce these family efforts. Instruction in family relations strengthens the family's ability to meet its challenges. People are given counsel to help them select careers in which their talents and skills can be used in meaningful employment. Adults and youth are expected to become proficient through appropriate training. The Church accepts responsibility for arranging for career counseling, encouraging access to training, providing assistance as necessary, and motivating members to assist each other in finding employment.

Church directives teach members to establish financial goals, pay tithing and fast offerings, avoid excessive debt, pay their obligations, use their resources wisely, and pursue a regular savings program. Keeping property in good repair is also encouraged. LDS families are taught to grow and preserve fruits and vegetables, sew clothing, and make household items. Every family is urged to be prepared for emergencies and to maintain a year's supply of food, clothing, and, if possible, fuel. The WORD OF WISDOM obliges members to avoid tobacco, alcohol, tea, coffee, and harmful drugs. Church organizations teach principles and skills of nutrition, physical fitness, immunization, sanitation, health, accident prevention, medical care, and the maintenance of a healthy home environment. Members are also advised to carry adequate health and life insurance when feasible and to avoid questionable medical practices.

It is assumed that, barring the unforeseen, most members and their extended families will be self-sufficient and able to give, rather than need to receive, assistance. Nevertheless, the Church stands ready to assist whatever needs exist. The *Welfare Services Handbook* states:

> No true Latter-day Saint, while physically or emotionally able, will voluntarily shift the burden of his own or his family's well-being to someone else. So long as he can, under the inspiration of the Lord and with his own labors, he will work to the extent of his ability to supply himself and his family with the spiritual and temporal necessities of life. As guided by the Spirit of the Lord and through applying these principles, each member of the Church should make his own decisions as to what assistance he accepts, be it from governmental or other sources. In this way, independence, self-respect,

dignity and self-reliance will be fostered, and free agency maintained (1980, p. 5).

Latter-day Saints are encouraged to avoid "unearned" public assistance programs insofar as possible. They are also encouraged to take full advantage of all available education and training programs and, as appropriate, to draw upon public insurance programs established for the benefit of employees, such as unemployment insurance and social security pensions.

ADMINISTRATION. While all members of the Church have the duty to "succor those that stand in need" (Mosiah 4:16) and to "bear one another's burdens" (Mosiah 18:8), the institutional responsibility for the welfare of others in the WARDS belongs to BISHOPS, Relief Society presidencies, priesthood quorum leaders, and home and visiting teachers. These Church leaders are admonished to be alert to the condition of each family and to offer assistance when needs exceed family resources and extended families are unable or unwilling to assist. Assignments are made to "succor the weak, lift up the hands which hang down, and strengthen the feeble knees" (D&C 81:5; Heb. 12:12).

Marshaling the resources of the Church on behalf of needy families is then the primary responsibility of the bishop. For this purpose, he can use cash from fast offering funds and direct the personal help of members (*see* VOLUNTEERISM) or can refer members to community resources or give temporary assistance from the storehouse resource system.

Members receiving Church assistance are expected to work to the extent of their ability to compensate for the help received. The local ward leadership has responsibility to provide work opportunities, which may be on a Church welfare project, in Church building maintenance, or in behalf of another needy member. Following short-term emergency assistance, a rehabilitation program is developed to bring the member back to self-sufficiency.

Faithful members of the Church are deemed to have a right to assistance, and the bishop can aid inactive members and nonmembers at his discretion. Help is to be extended graciously without embarrassment to the recipient and with complete confidentiality.

Within a year of the organization of the Church in 1830, Latter-day Saints in Ohio and Missouri were instructed through revelation to consecrate their surplus properties to the Church for the care of the poor. The bishop allocated properties to the members as STEWARDSHIPS, through which the people were to become self-supporting. Properties and commodities over and above immediate needs were "kept in [the Lord's] storehouse, to administer to the poor and the needy" (D&C 42:34); such accumulated assets were called "storehouse resources." Today these resources include fast offerings, production projects and commodities, the Church employment system, Deseret Industries, and LDS Social Services.

PRODUCTION. The Church welfare production system, as of 1985, consisted of 199 agricultural production projects, 51 canneries, and 27 large and 36 small grain-storage facilities feeding into 12 central, 69 regional, and 32 branch storehouses. These storehouses are essentially a combination of warehouses and outlet stores. The commodities in them are distributed after Relief Society leaders meet with families to determine their needs and bishops sign written orders for the needed commodities, which the family can pick up or have picked up for them at the storehouses or at Deseret Industries outlet stores. Also available in the storehouses are the products of a meat-packing plant, a milk-processing facility, a bakery, a soap factory, a pasta factory, and a number of Relief Society sewing projects. Items not produced in the Church system can be purchased at the bishop's discretion from outside sources. The bulk of the production occurs in the western United States, with a fleet of trucks moving commodities to the storehouses scattered around the country for distribution. As of the late 1980s, commodities conservatively valued at $30 million were dispersed in response to approximately 350,000 bishops' orders a year. The production system provides service opportunities as well: 872,000 hours of volunteer labor were donated in 1987. Recipients are encouraged to provide as much of this labor as possible, but about half of the volunteer hours are donated by nonrecipients. Longer-term recipients are also given meaningful training through production projects.

EMPLOYMENT SERVICES. The most visible components of the Church employment system are the thirty-six employment centers staffed with full-time professionals and the fifty-one centers operated by Church service volunteers. These are located in the United States in areas of membership concentration, with a few abroad. The volunteer-run centers function as satellites under the direction of the professional centers. However, the bulk of the employment activity occurs at the ward and stake levels. Each ward and stake has an employment specialist who contacts ward officers to identify any employment needs and job openings of which they are aware. Possible matches are made, and unfilled job openings are reported to the stake specialist, who disseminates the information to other wards and to the employment centers. Employment specialists are expected to be familiar with the workings of local labor markets and to counsel jobseekers on improving their job search skills and their employability. Professionals from the employment centers hold periodic seminars to train the stake and ward specialists and provide them on an ongoing basis with lists of current job openings. The specialists are encouraged to refer needy people to an employment center for career counseling, training in job search skills, information on the local and national labor markets, and referral to community job agencies.

DESERET INDUSTRIES. In the western United States there are twenty-one parent and twenty-seven branch Deseret Industries installations. Through periodic donation drives in the wards and stakes, clothing, furniture, appliances, toys, and other items are collected to be refurbished and sold by Deseret Industries' employees in sheltered workshops and stores. In addition, new products are manufactured in a mattress and furniture factory. A homecraft program offers productive opportunities for the homebound. Deseret Industries provides kits, patterns, materials, and supplies for items, which are then manufactured at home and picked up for sale through Deseret Industries retail stores.

WELFARE SERVICES MISSIONS. A welfare services missionary program responds to requests from Church units around the world with special needs that exceed local resources. Primarily young women and older persons with special skills are called to go, at their own expense, to these areas to train people in basic child development, family relations, nutrition, sanitation, health care, social work, counseling, and agriculture or vocational

Ezra Taft Benson and his wife, Flora (on the left), and many members of the Church give volunteer services at LDS canneries and welfare projects. The food raised and preserved is distributed to the needy through the Bishop's Storehouses and Church welfare services. In recent times, these projects have been increasingly automated and professionally staffed.

training. In 1990 there were about 280 welfare services missionaries.

Few social phenomena are more challenging to cope with than widespread poverty. Nevertheless, in all geographical areas where the Church program is established, members have some Church resources to assist them. Church welfare projects supply commodities to prevent serious deprivation. Since teaching self-sufficiency and counseling are unending one-on-one tasks, the fellowship of the Church provides a personal and reassuring support system to help members confront the problems of poverty.

The Church now faces the challenge of establishing its program in developing nations. Not since its early years has the Church struggled with situations in which a majority of members in some areas are plagued with poverty in conditions that arise from severe economic and social circumstances. To meet these challenges, programs are beginning, first with the teaching of self-reliance principles and the wise use of fast offerings, then with projects in conjunction with experienced Third World economic development agencies and with the establishment of Church employment centers. What will happen and what patterns or institutions will emerge cannot be foreseen; but that the effort will be made to establish the welfare

system of ZION in all parts of the world is inherent in LDS doctrine.

BIBLIOGRAPHY

Arrington, Leonard J., and Wayne K. Hinton. "Origin of the Welfare Plan of the Church of Jesus Christ of Latter-day Saints." *BYU Studies* 5 (1965):67–85.

Barton, Betty L. "Mormon Poor Relief: A Social Welfare Interlude." *BYU Studies* 18 (1977):66–68.

Blumell, Bruce D. "Welfare Before Welfare: Twentieth-Century LDS Church Charity Before the Great Depression." *Journal of Mormon History* 6 (1979):89–106.

Child, Paul C. "Physical Beginnings of the Church Welfare Program." *BYU Studies* 14 (1974):383–85.

GARTH L. MANGUM

WELFARE SQUARE

Welfare Square in Salt Lake City is the largest and most complete facility in the Church welfare system. It produces and delivers food and clothing and provides other services to needy people in the Salt Lake area. It also supplies and coordinates welfare efforts of the Church in other areas.

The first structures built on Welfare Square, in 1938, were a BISHOP'S STOREHOUSE, a root cellar (now used as a storage building), and a cannery. A milk-processing plant and a 300,000-bushel grain elevator were built in 1941. A new milk-processing plant replaced the old one in 1960, and a new cannery replaced the old one in 1963. The original Bishop's Storehouse was replaced with a larger facility in 1976. In 1981 a DESERET INDUSTRIES plant and its affiliated store were built on Welfare Square, and an office building to house the Social Services Department and employment services was added in 1983. A bakery was added in 1986.

Welfare Square provides regular employment for about fifty people, and volunteer assistance to run its operations and services is provided on a regular basis by about 200 people from fifty surrounding stakes. Financial support for Welfare Square comes largely from the FAST OFFERINGS of local members.

Most of the recipients of food and services at Welfare Square are members of The Church of Jesus Christ of Latter-day Saints, but there is also a transient service center associated with the Bishop's Storehouse that gives temporary assistance to the homeless of all faiths.

Welfare Square became functionally and symbolically important to the Church in the 1930s and 1940s. It was the flagship of the Church welfare program initiated in the Pioneer Stake in Salt Lake City in 1932. Over the years, the pattern established at Welfare Square has been replicated in more than a hundred Bishop's Storehouse facilities. Welfare Square continues to be the central supplier and coordinator for many of these other locations.

Welfare Square stands for all the principles of welfare advocated and practiced by the Church—industry, work, and caring for the poor and needy. A VISITORS CENTER is located on Welfare Square to distribute information about the Church welfare program and to teach the principles of the gospel of Jesus Christ concerning social and religious obligations toward those in need.

[*See also* Poverty, Attitudes Toward.]

T. GLENN HAWS

WELLS, EMMELINE B.

Emmeline Blanche Woodward Wells (1828–1921) was a strong advocate for women's rights and advancement as editor of the WOMAN'S EXPONENT for nearly four decades, as general president of the RELIEF SOCIETY for over a decade, as a national suffrage leader, and as a Utah political activist.

Born to David and Deiadama Hare Woodward on February 29, 1828, at Petersham, Massachusetts, Emmeline experienced early the extremes of private tragedy and public triumph that would recur throughout her life. The death of her father when she was four years old and the controversy in her community occasioned by her conversion to The Church of Jesus Christ of Latter-day Saints ten years later were harrowing to the young girl. Yet Emmeline had opportunities for education not widely available to girls of her time. While still in her early teens she started teaching, but her teaching career was cut short by her marriage on July 29, 1843, at age fifteen, to James H. Harris, only two months her senior, and their subsequent move the following spring with his parents and other Latter-day Saints to Nauvoo, Illinois. However, within sixteen months of their marriage, James's parents abandoned both the Church and Nauvoo after Joseph Smith's assassination; the young couple's son, Eugene Henri Harris, died shortly after

Emmeline B. Wells (1828–1921), writer, editor, and suffrage leader, was the fifth general president of the Relief Society (1910–1921). Photographer: C. M. Bell.

birth; and James left Nauvoo to look for work, never to return. Many years later, Emmeline discovered he had died in a sailing accident in the Indian Ocean.

She found refuge by returning to teaching, and among her pupils were the children of Bishop Newel K. and Elizabeth Ann Whitney. In February 1845, Emmeline became a plural wife to Whitney, who was thirty-three years older than she. He died in 1850, two years after they had arrived in the Salt Lake valley, leaving her with two young daughters.

Emmeline's third marriage in 1852 proved more enduring, but not always satisfying. Seeking protection and stability, she petitioned Whitney's friend and prominent Church leader Daniel H. Wells to marry her. He already had six other wives, and, because of numerous business and ecclesiastical obligations, he and Emmeline rarely saw each other. Although three daughters were born to the union (two of them died in young adulthood), only in the later years of their marriage did Emmeline find the love and companionship that she had so long desired, but had found so elusive.

Emmeline Wells turned to civic affairs for ful-fillment and found her cause in the fight for suf-frage and women's rights. "I desire," she pro-claimed, "to do all in my power to help elevate the condition of my own people especially women" (Journals, January 4, 1878). Her writing talent blossomed as she submitted articles to the *Woman's Exponent*, a feminist Mormon publication es-tablished in 1872. In 1877 she became its editor, a position she held for thirty-seven years.

In 1879 Emmeline was appointed one of two representatives from Utah to the suffrage conven-tion in Washington, D.C., the first of many such meetings she would attend and address. She soon became friends with national suffrage leaders Eliz-abeth Cady Stanton and Susan B. Anthony, who were impressed with her abilities. Election to sev-eral offices in the National Woman Suffrage Associ-ation, the National Council of Women, the Inter-national Council of Women, and as president of the Utah Woman Suffrage Association followed. In 1899 she was invited by the International Council of Women to speak at its London meeting as a rep-resentative from the United States.

Emmeline Wells was nearly eighty-three years old when she was called as general president of the Relief Society in 1910, an organization she had previously served for twenty years as general secretary and as head of its grain storage program in the 1870s. Her tenure proved, like her life, to be bittersweet. In 1912 she was awarded an honor-ary doctorate of literature from Brigham Young University, yet two years later she suspended pub-lication of *Woman's Exponent*, upon which she had labored for almost half her life, when the Relief Society declined her proposal to make it the official organ of the Relief Society. In 1919 she was hon-ored by a visit to her home by U.S. President Woodrow Wilson and his wife; the occasion com-memorated the sale of over 205,000 bushels of Re-lief Society wheat to the U.S. government during World War I, and, ironically, the loss of the Relief Society's autonomy over its grain-storage program.

Finally, in 1921 at age ninety-three and suffer-ing from serious illness, Emmeline was released as President of the Relief Society, the first since Emma Smith not to die in office. Upon hearing of her release, she suffered a stroke and then died three weeks later on April 25, 1921. In death, she continued to receive honors: a funeral in the TABERNACLE (the second woman to be so com-memorated) and the installation of a marble bust in the Utah State Capitol from the women of Utah engraved, "A Fine Soul Who Served Us."

BIBLIOGRAPHY

Madsen, Carol Cornwall. "A Mormon Woman in Victorian America." Ph.D. diss., University of Utah, 1985.

———. "Emmeline B. Wells: Romantic Rebel." In *Supporting Saints: Life Stories of Nineteenth-Century Mormons*, ed. D. Cannon and D. Whittaker, pp. 305–341. Provo, Utah, 1985.

Wells, Emmeline B. Journals. Division of Archives and Manu-scripts, Harold B. Lee Library, Brigham Young University, Provo, Utah.

CAROL CORNWALL MADSEN
MARY STOVALL RICHARDS

WELLS, JUNIUS F.

Junius Free Wells (1854–1930) was the organizer of the Young Men's Mutual Improvement Associa-tion (YMMIA, in 1977 YOUNG MEN). Born June 1, 1854, in Salt Lake City, a son of Daniel H. and Hannah C. Free Wells, Junius attended school at the Union Academy and graduated from the UNIVERSITY OF DESERET at the age of seventeen. He was known as an exceptionally intelligent young man. As a youth, he managed his father's lumberyard and was a sales clerk for Zion's Coop-erative Mercantile Institution (ZCMI).

He was called to serve a mission to Great Brit-ain (1872–1874), and in 1874 he accompanied Eld-ers George A. Smith, Lorenzo SNOW, Relief Soci-ety President Eliza R. SNOW, and others to Palestine, where, on the Mount of Olives, near JERUSALEM, they dedicated the land for the resto-ration of the gospel. Immediately upon his return, Wells was asked by President Brigham YOUNG to organize the first YMMIA in the Thirteenth WARD in Salt Lake City, which he did on June 10, 1875. Wells married Helena Middleton Fobes on June 17, 1879. They were the parents of two children.

The YMMIA, counterpart to the previously organized association for young women, was charged to help boys develop intellectually and spiritually and to enjoy recreation under proper supervision. A central committee was formed on December 6, 1876, with Wells as president, to coordinate all associations organized throughout the Church. He served as president of the board for four years. In October 1879 he founded the *Contributor*, a monthly magazine that served both

Junius F. Wells was the first general superintendent of the Young Men's Mutual Improvement Association, serving in that role for four years.

the young men and young women groups. Its motto was The Glory of God Is Intelligence (D&C 93:36). The publication featured articles written by young LDS men and women on a variety of literary and gospel themes. Wells served for thirteen years as its editor and publisher. In October 1899 the magazine was replaced by the *Improvement Era*.

Wells served a mission in the United States, laboring in the Midwest and New England. In 1919–1921, he served as associate editor of the *Millennial Star*, a Church magazine published in Liverpool, England, and accompanied the European MISSION PRESIDENT on visits to the Scandinavian, Swiss, and German missions.

Acting as agent for the Church, Junius purchased the Solomon Mack farm, the birthplace of the Prophet Joseph Smith. A Church-history enthusiast, Wells designed a hundred-ton granite monument, with a shaft 38.5 feet tall, commemorating the thirty-eight and a half years of the Prophet Joseph SMITH's life. Erected near Sharon

and South Royalton, Vermont, near the site of Joseph Smith's birthplace, the monument was dedicated by President Joseph F. SMITH on December 23, 1905, the centennial of the Prophet's birth. In 1918 Wells made a smaller replica, which was erected in the Salt Lake Cemetery in honor of Hyrum SMITH, the Prophet's brother.

Sustained as an assistant Church historian in 1921, Wells collected and preserved paintings and photographs of persons and scenes connected with the early history of the Church. In 1928 he was instrumental in purchasing thirty thousand dryplate negatives of Church history scenes taken by LDS photographer George Edward Anderson.

He died of a cerebral hemorrhage in Salt Lake City on April 15, 1930. At his funeral on Easter Sunday, he was memorialized as a kind and thoughtful man of dignity who made friends easily, "a polished gentleman, a fearless servant of God" (Smith, p. 15).

BIBLIOGRAPHY

Jenson, Andrew. *Latter-day Saint Biographical Encyclopedia*, Vol. 1, p. 714; Vol. 4, p. 249. Salt Lake City, 1901.

Smith, George A. *Funeral Services for Junius Free Wells*. Salt Lake City, 1930.

PAUL THOMAS SMITH

WENTWORTH LETTER

John Wentworth, editor of the *Chicago Democrat*, wrote Joseph SMITH in 1842 to request information about the Church for a friend who was writing a history of New Hampshire. The "Wentworth Letter" was written by the Prophet Joseph Smith in response to this inquiry.

The letter contains a brief history of the Church to 1842, including the key events in the restoration of the gospel. It states that the purpose of the Church is to take the gospel to every nation and prepare a people for the MILLENNIUM. The letter also describes concisely the origin, contents, and translation of the Book of Mormon. It concludes with thirteen doctrinal statements that have since become known as the ARTICLES OF FAITH and are published in the Pearl of Great Price (*HC* 4:535–41).

The contents of this letter were published March 1, 1842, in the Nauvoo *Times and Seasons*. There is no evidence that Wentworth or his friend,

George Barstow, ever published it. In response to other inquiries in 1844, Joseph Smith sent revised copies of this letter to several publishers of works about various churches and religious groups. It has been published several times over the years (for the complete text of the letter, see Appendix item "Wentworth Letter" in Vol. 4).

BIBLIOGRAPHY

Jessee, Dean C., ed. "'Church History,' 1842." In *PJS* 1:427–37.

EDWARD J. BRANDT

WEST INDIES, THE CHURCH IN

The Church of Jesus Christ of Latter-day Saints took root in the West Indies as English-speaking members moved from the United States to Puerto Rico. Finding no organized group of the Church there, they organized a branch and shared the gospel message with the local population, some of whom joined the Church and later became leaders themselves. Membership in the West Indies grew from 104 members in 1960 to over 50,000 in 1990, with seven STAKES and six MISSIONS. It grew fastest in Puerto Rico and the Dominican Republic, and Spanish quickly became the language of the Church. The first Caribbean district of the Church was organized in 1963, the first MEETINGHOUSE was dedicated in 1970, and the first stake was organized in Puerto Rico by Elder Ezra Taft BENSON on December 14, 1980, in Puerto Rico, with Herminio De Jesus as president. In 1990 Church units were functioning throughout the West Indies in such additional places as Antigua, the Bahamas, Barbados, Bermuda, the Cayman Islands, Cuba (Guantanomo U.S. Naval Base), Curaçao, Grenada, Haiti, Jamaica, Martinique, the Netherlands Antilles, and Trinidad.

PUERTO RICO.   In the early 1950s, as a few LDS families moved to Puerto Rico on business and to work or to serve in the military at Ramey Air Force Base, they organized the first branch, which met in a member's home in Guajataca. A second branch was organized in San Juan, and the first Puerto Rican converts were baptized there in the early 1950s. Puerto Rico led the way for the Church in the West Indies, receiving the first district, meetinghouse, stake, and mission. In 1990 it had almost 13,000 members attending more than fifty wards and branches in four stakes and one mission.

DOMINICAN REPUBLIC.   The Church began in the Dominican Republic in 1978, when the John Rappeley family from Utah and the Eddie Amparo family from New York met in the customs office in Santo Domingo and initiated regular Church meetings. Two months later, Rodolfo Bodden and his family became the first LDS baptisms in the country. In 1986, Brother Bodden was ordained the first STAKE PATRIARCH of the new Santo Domingo Dominican Republic Stake. In 1990 there were almost twenty thousand members in over seventy Church units, including one stake and two missions.

HAITI.   The first LDS missionaries went to Haiti in 1980 and organized a branch of the Church in Port-au-Prince. In 1984 the Haiti mission was es-

Baptizing in the Waters of Mormon, by Henri-Robert Bresil (1987, oil on canvas, 36″ × 24″). The Book of Mormon prophet Alma taught and baptized at a place called Mormon in the wilderness, depicted in a Haitian setting by LDS artist Henri-Robert Bresil of Haiti. "The place of Mormon, the waters of Mormon, the forest of Mormon, how beautiful are they to the eyes of them who there came to the knowledge of their Redeemer" (Mosiah 18:30). Church Museum of History and Art.

tablished, and by 1990 there were 3,000 members in eighteen branches, and the Book of Mormon was being translated into Haitian.

JAMAICA. The Church sent missionaries to Jamaica in 1841, but they were soon recalled because the prejudice against them made their efforts futile. However, the Church was finally established there in 1970 when several LDS families went to Jamaica to work. Victor Nugent and his family became converts in Jamaica in 1974. Brother Nugent was called as president of the Kingston District when the Jamaica Kingston Mission was organized in 1985. The Church in Jamaica is primarily Jamaican, and it had almost 2,000 members in thirteen branches in 1990.

EDWIN O. HAROLDSEN

WESTWARD MIGRATION, PLANNING AND PROPHECY

For Brigham Young and his associates, the 1846 exodus from NAUVOO, far from being a disaster imposed by enemies, was foretold and foreordained—a key to understanding LDS history and a necessary prelude for greater things to come. From a later perspective, too, scholars of the Mormon experience have come to see the exodus and COLONIZATION of the Great Basin as the single most important influence in molding the Latter-day Saints into a distinctive people. Popular histories invariably attribute the Saints' exodus from Nauvoo to increasing violence, mob action, and persecution. This view, that the exodus was forced upon a people who had no choice, is simplistic and fails to account for more complex reasons for the exodus or to explain its importance in LDS belief.

From its beginnings and with each successive move, the Church was seemingly drawn toward the West. As early as 1832, LDS publications connected the destiny of the Church with the American Far West. An 1840 letter preserves Joseph SMITH's prophecy about "a place of safety preparing for [the Saints] away towards the Rocky Mountains" (Esplin, p. 90); and throughout the Nauvoo period the Prophet collected information and prepared for a latter-day ZION to be established in the tops of the Rocky Mountains (see Isa. 2:2–3). Several diaries record Joseph Smith's February 1844 instructions to the QUORUM OF THE TWELVE

APOSTLES to lead an expedition to the West to locate a new home for the Saints.

Though the Prophet put the plan on hold and his murder three months later further delayed implementation, Brigham YOUNG and his fellow apostles firmly believed that their responsibility was to lead the Church to the West once the NAUVOO TEMPLE was completed and the Saints had received the ENDOWMENT ordinances therein. Therefore, even had there been no violence against the Church in Illinois, there still would have been an exodus, a western migration, and western colonization.

Though most of the Saints, comfortable in a prosperous Nauvoo and not anxious to leave, knew little about the plans or the prophecy, some outside the Church were aware. In 1845, Illinois Governor Thomas Ford, anxious to solve the "Mormon problem" by having the Saints leave, chided Brigham Young for remaining when Joseph Smith had spoken of going west. Committed though they were to the West, however, Church leaders would not consider departing until the Saints were endowed in the Nauvoo Temple. Not until late summer 1845, with temple construction nearly completed, did they quietly resume preparations for the West.

When violence broke out in September 1845, Brigham Young had already announced that ordinance work would begin in December. He therefore "capitulated" to mob pressures and proclaimed to the Saints and to the world that he and his people would leave for the West the following spring. That announcement bought a peaceful interlude for ordinance work and preparation, while the threat of violence if they did not leave "put the gathering spirit" in the Saints, in Brigham Young's words, encouraging the entire community to depart.

In meetings that fall, Brigham Young and the Twelve explained to the Saints the reasons for the exodus. They presented it as the will of God and as a God-given opportunity—a necessary step toward their destiny. They also saw the exodus as an unfolding of scriptural PROPHECY, including Isaiah's vision of the last days when "the mountain of the Lord's house shall be established in the top of the mountains, and shall be exalted above the hills; and all nations shall flow unto it" (Isa. 2:2). Orson PRATT pronounced the proposed movement "a direct and literal fulfillment of many prophecies, both ancient and modern" (*MS* 6 [Dec. 1, 1845]:192). His brother, Parley P. PRATT, agreed that it was the event that "ancient prophets have long since pointed out" (T&S 6 [Nov. 1, 1845]:1011).

Therefore, while the sermons reflected a sense of urgency, their tenor was clearly optimistic. If the Saints were being driven, it was to their destiny. President Young spoke of "a crisis of extraordinary and thrilling interest," and admonished the Saints to "wake up, wake up" and accept "the present glorious emergency" (T&S 6 [Nov. 1, 1845]:1019). Orson Pratt saw the approaching exodus as "long looked for, long prayed for, and long desired." They were on the threshold, he declared, of "one of the grandest and most glorious events yet witnessed" in the Church (MS 6 [Dec. 1, 1845]:191–92).

Numerous extant sermons from Nauvoo also suggested additional reasons for the exodus. A move west would permit greater expansion and continued growth. In the western wilderness the Church could more easily fulfill a divine commitment to take the gospel to the LAMANITES. The mass migration would be a test separating the wheat from the chaff, a purifying furnace bringing greater unity and strength to the Church.

Later, in the Rocky Mountains, pioneer Latter-day Saints came to see the exodus from Nauvoo as a key to who they were and what they could become.

[See also History of the Church: c. 1844–1877.]

BIBLIOGRAPHY

Christian, Lewis Clark. "Mormon Foreknowledge of the West." BYU Studies 21 (Fall 1981):403–415.

Esplin, Ronald K. "A Place Prepared": Joseph, Brigham and the Quest for Promised Refuge in the West." Journal of Mormon History 9 (1982):85–111.

Leonard, Glen M. "Westward the Saints: The Nineteenth-Century Mormon Migration." Ensign 10 (Jan. 1980):6–13.

REED C. DURHAM, JR.

WHITMER, DAVID

David Whitmer (1805–1888) was one of the Three Witnesses to the Book of Mormon whose testimony has been printed in all published copies of the book (see BOOK OF MORMON WITNESSES). Although Whitmer was excommunicated from the Church in 1838, he never repudiated his testimony

David Whitmer (1805–1888), the most interviewed of the Three Witnesses to the Book of Mormon. An individualist who was doggedly unwavering in his testimony of the spiritual manifestations received in June 1829, he was known as an honest, conscientious, and guileless man. Courtesy Library-Archives, Reorganized Church of Jesus Christ of Latter Day Saints.

of the Book of Mormon, reaffirming it thereafter on at least seventy recorded occasions.

David Whitmer was born to Peter Whitmer, Sr., and Mary Musselman Whitmer near Harrisburg, Pennsylvania, on January 7, 1805. In 1809 the family moved to Fayette, New York, where they worked a large farm. He learned about the Book of Mormon from Oliver COWDERY, who was scribe for Joseph SMITH during the translation. When persecution grew severe in Harmony, Pennsylvania, where the two were working, Whitmer invited Joseph, Oliver, and Joseph's wife, Emma, to his family's house in Fayette. The translation of the Book of Mormon was completed there in June 1829.

In the same month, Joseph Smith told David Whitmer that he, along with Cowdery and Martin HARRIS, another supporter of the work, were to be witnesses of the Book of Mormon. In answer to their prayers, an angel appeared to them near the Whitmer house and showed them the gold plates from which the Book of Mormon was translated. An account of this experience comprises the Testimony of the Three Witnesses in the Book of Mormon. David's brothers, Christian, Jacob, John, and Peter, Jr., were four of the Eight Witnesses to whom Joseph Smith showed the plates without an angelic visitation and whose testimony also appears in the book.

In 1829, David, John, and Peter, Jr., received revelations through Joseph Smith calling them to missionary work (D&C 14:6; 15:6; 16:6). In April 1830 the Church was organized in Peter Whitmer, Sr.'s, house (see ORGANIZATION OF THE CHURCH, 1830). However, David's close association with Joseph Smith did not prevent occasional chastisement. A revelation in 1830 warned Whitmer, "Your mind has been on the things of the earth more than on the things of me, your Maker, and the ministry whereunto you have been called; and you have not given heed unto my Spirit, and to those who were set over you, but have been persuaded by those whom I have not commanded" (D&C 30:2). In view of Whitmer's later separation from the Church, this statement seems prophetic.

When the Church moved from New York in 1831, the Whitmers went with the Saints to Kirtland, Ohio, and then to Jackson County, Missouri, which had been designated as Zion, a gathering place for the Saints. By July 1832, the Whitmers had settled along the Big Blue River in Kaw Township (now Kansas City). To their great disappointment, the hopes for Zion were short-lived. The differences between the Latter-day Saints and the local settlers erupted into open conflict. On one occasion, a mob threatened to kill Whitmer and other Church leaders if they did not admit that the Book of Mormon was a fraud. Whitmer absolutely refused.

Driven from Jackson County, the Whitmers settled in adjacent Clay County, Missouri, along with other Latter-day Saint refugees. As their numbers grew, a STAKE was organized and Whitmer became the stake president in July 1834, making him the leading figure in Church administration in the area. By October 1834, David and John Whitmer had moved back to Kirtland, Ohio, to prepare for the spiritual blessing promised to the Saints when the KIRTLAND TEMPLE was completed. In February 1835, in accord with an earlier commission received by revelation, David Whit-

mer with Oliver Cowdery and Martin Harris selected the twelve men who constituted the first Quorum of Twelve Apostles in the Church (D&C 18:37–38). Whitmer was also a member of the committee that drafted rules for the regulation of the temple. On the day of its dedication, March 27, 1836, he testified of an outpouring of the Spirit from on high, as the Lord had promised (HC 2:427).

In spite of all their great contributions to the work, by 1838 David and the remainder of the Whitmers had left the Church (Christian and Peter, Jr., had previously died in Clay County). The year 1837 was a time of disillusion and financial trial for the Saints in Kirtland. To help shore up the local economy, Joseph Smith and other leaders organized a banking society (see KIRTLAND ECONOMY). When it failed, many members who lost their savings were embittered. Brigham Young said it was a time when the "knees of many of the strongest men in the Church faltered" (Elden Jay Watson, ed., Manuscript History of Brigham Young, 1801–1844, Salt Lake City, 1968, p. 16). Even earlier, in February 1837, some dissenters wanted to depose Joseph Smith and replace him with David Whitmer. Whitmer, a proud and stubborn man, was still smarting from conflicts over his leadership in Missouri. In the disciplinary council that excommunicated Whitmer, on April 13, 1838, one of the main charges brought against him was "possessing the same spirit with the Dissenters" (Donald Q. Cannon and Lyndon W. Cook, eds., Far West Record, Minutes of The Church of Jesus Christ of Latter-day Saints, 1830–1844, Salt Lake City, 1983, p. 177; see DISCIPLINARY PROCEDURES).

After Whitmer left the Church, he moved to Richmond, Missouri, and opened a livery stable, which he ran until 1888. A respected citizen in the community, he served on fair boards, was a member of the city council, and was elected mayor. Over his lifetime, hundreds of visitors inquired about and heard his testimony of the Book of Mormon.

A year before his death Whitmer wrote a pamphlet, An Address to All Believers in Christ (1887), apparently to justify his separation from the Church. In the pamphlet, he again gave witness to the truth of the Book of Mormon, but claimed that Joseph Smith drifted into errors after completing the translation. Whitmer rejected many later developments in the Church, such as the offices of HIGH PRIEST and PROPHET, SEER, AND REVELA-

TOR; the DOCTRINE AND COVENANTS; and the doctrines of GATHERING and of PLURAL MARRIAGE.

Shortly before his death, Whitmer repeated once more, for the *Richmond Conservator*, what he had written in the *Address*: "I have never at any time denied that testimony or any part thereof, which has so long since been published with that Book, as one of the three witnesses. Those who know me best, well know that I have always adhered to that testimony." He died in Richmond, Missouri, on January 25, 1888, bearing testimony again on his deathbed of the authenticity of the Book of Mormon.

BIBLIOGRAPHY

Anderson, Richard Lloyd. *Investigating the Book of Mormon Witnesses*. Salt Lake City, 1981.

Cook, Lyndon W., and Matthew K. Cook, eds. *David Whitmer Interviews: A Restoration Witness*. Orem, Utah, 1991.

Nibley, Preston, comp. *The Witnesses of the Book of Mormon*. Salt Lake City, 1973.

Perkins, Keith W. "True to the Book of Mormon: The Whitmers." *Ensign* 19 (Feb. 1989):34–42.

KEITH W. PERKINS

WHITNEY STORE

The Newel K. Whitney store played a major role in the history of the Latter-day Saints in KIRTLAND, OHIO, during the years 1831–1838. When the Prophet Joseph SMITH arrived in Kirtland on February 1, 1831, he strode up to the counter where Whitney was clerking and extended his hand: "Newel K. Whitney, . . . I am Joseph, the Prophet. . . . You've prayed me here; now what do you want of me?" (*HC* 1:146).

The Prophet later received a number of significant revelations in the Whitney store, including the WORD OF WISDOM (D&C 89) and two important revelations on PRIESTHOOD (D&C 84, 88). Jo-

Newel K. Whitney Store, at the four corners area in Kirtland (built 1826–1827; photo 1907; restored 1979–1984). Joseph and Emma Smith lived here beginning in the fall of 1832. It became the headquarters of the Church, home of the School of the Prophets in 1833, and the venue of Doctrine and Covenants 84, 87–89, 95, 98, and much of the Joseph Smith Translation of the Bible. Photographer: George E. Anderson.

seph Smith also worked on his translation of the Bible in an upstairs room.

The store started in a log cabin in 1823. The present frame structure was built in the flats of Kirtland, Ohio, by 1827. Operating the N. K. Whitney & Co. store as a mercantile establishment and as a post office, Whitney and his partner Sidney Gilbert maintained as large an inventory as any store in northeastern Ohio.

One of the first adult education programs in the United States, the SCHOOL OF THE PROPHETS, was held in the store during the winter of 1833 in accord with revelation (D&C 88:127–41). The school's purpose was to prepare missionaries to take the gospel to the world. Many people told of receiving visions in the store's upper room. The UNITED ORDER, the predecessor of the current welfare system of the Church, had its beginning in the store, which was also used as the BISHOP'S STOREHOUSE (D&C 72:8–10; 78:3).

Today the building is owned by The Church of Jesus Christ of Latter-day Saints and has been restored to its 1830s form as a historical site for visitors. President Ronald Reagan awarded the restored store the President's Historic Preservation Award on November 18, 1988.

BIBLIOGRAPHY

Anderson, Karl Ricks. *Joseph Smith's Kirtland: Eyewitness Accounts.* Salt Lake City, 1989.

Backman, Milton V., Jr. *The Heavens Resound: A History of the Latter-day Saints in Ohio, 1830–1838.* Salt Lake City, 1983.

KEITH W. PERKINS

WILLIAMS, CLARISSA

Clarissa Smith Williams (1859–1930) served as the sixth general president of RELIEF SOCIETY from 1921 to 1928, a period in which the Relief Society focused on health care and other social issues. She began her Relief Society activity as a visiting teacher at age sixteen and later served as secretary and president of both the Salt Lake Seventeenth Ward and Salt Lake Stake Relief Societies. In 1901 she was appointed treasurer and a member of the general board. Ten years later she became first counselor to President Emmeline WELLS. In April 1921, President Heber J. GRANT appointed her general president of the Relief Society and editor of its magazine.

Clarissa Smith Williams (1859–1930), sixth general president of the Relief Society, served from 1921 to 1928.

Clarissa was born April 21, 1859, in the residential wing of the Church Historian's Office in Salt Lake City, Utah. She was the first of five daughters born to George A. Smith, an APOSTLE and Church historian, and his seventh and last wife, Susan Elizabeth West Smith. This family shared the residential apartment in the Historian's Office with the apostle's first wife, Bathsheba W. SMITH, and her children. The polygamist wives and their families lived amicably in their comfortable pioneer residence.

Clarissa and her sisters received the best education available in the territory at that time. In 1875 she received a teaching certificate from the Normal Department of the UNIVERSITY OF DESERET (later the University of Utah).

Clarissa married William Newjent Williams on July 17, 1877, the day before he left on a mission to Wales. They had eleven children and lived to celebrate their fiftieth wedding anniversary. William was a successful businessman, regent of the University of Utah, and state senator. In spite of their busy schedules, their family was always their first concern.

William supported Clarissa in her Relief Society activities. She later wrote: "After I was married and had seven children, I was asked to be secretary of the Seventeenth Ward Relief Society. I felt that I could not do this with all my little babies. But my husband said, 'My dear, you must do it; it is the very thing you need; you need to get away from the babies, and I will help you all I can, either by taking care of the children or making out your reports or copying your minutes, or any other thing I can do'" (*Relief Society Magazine* 15 [Dec. 1928]:668–69).

As general Relief Society president, Clarissa Williams concentrated on social problems. During her presidency, the Relief Society funded loans for training public health nurses, distributed free milk to infants, provided health examinations for preschool children, and operated summer camps for underprivileged children. She encouraged ward Relief Societies to prepare layettes for new mothers and distribute them according to need. In 1924 under her supervision the Relief Society established the Cottonwood Maternity Hospital, which continued in operation until 1963 (*see* HOSPITALS).

A member of the National Council of Women, Clarissa was one of nine U.S. delegates to the International Council of Women in Rome, Italy, in May 1914. She was appointed chairwoman of the Utah Women's Committee of the National Council of Defense during World War I. She died March 8, 1930, at her home in Salt Lake City.

BIBLIOGRAPHY

Lyman, Amy Brown. "Clarissa S. Williams." *Relief Society Magazine* 15 (Dec. 1928):639–43.

Peterson, Janet, and LaRene Gaunt. *Elect Ladies: Presidents of the Relief Society.* Salt Lake City, 1990.

EVALYN DARGER BENNETT

WINTER QUARTERS

Brigham YOUNG's original plan for the LDS exodus from NAUVOO, Illinois, envisioned a quick journey across Iowa in the spring of 1846 and, at least for some, a journey "over the mountains" by fall. That plan called for small winter camps in Iowa, at the Missouri River, and at Grand Island, whence later

encampments could depart in the spring of 1847 for their mountain home. As the first wagons took over three months just to cross windblown and storm-drenched Iowa, this plan could not be carried out. By the time advance companies had reached the Missouri River, it was mid-June and too late for them or the 12,000 following to attempt a mountain crossing that season. A layover place had to be found.

The term "winter quarters," often used by trappers and explorers to describe a place of refuge from the hazards of winter, took on special significance in Mormon pioneer history. Built on Indian lands on the west bank of the Missouri River—now

A *Tragedy of Winter Quarters*, by Avard T. Fairbanks (1936, bronze sculpture), erected at Winter Quarters, in present Omaha, Nebraska. Commemorating the deaths of 340 Latter-day Saints at Winter Quarters between the fall of 1846 and the spring of 1848, and sculpted by a descendant of pioneers buried here, this statue depicts a couple huddled together in sorrow over the death of their child. It bears the inscription: "That the struggles, the sacrifices and the sufferings of the faithful pioneers and the cause they represented shall never be forgotten." Courtesy Brigham Young University.

Florence, a suburb of Omaha, Nebraska—their Winter Quarters became a vital new center for planning, regrouping, preparing, and religious renewal. Surveyed in October 1846 and subsequently laid out in a grid with 14 streets, 38 blocks, and over 760 lots and stockyards, and with houses ranging from two-story brick homes to sod huts, Winter Quarters housed almost 4,000 Latter-day Saints by December 1846. For the next two years, the name was also loosely applied to scores of much smaller settlements on the river's east side, home for another 8,000 LDS immigrants.

After the establishment of SALT LAKE CITY in 1847 and upon orders from government officials concerned about settlement on Indian lands, the Saints vacated Winter Quarters in 1848 to go either to the Salt Lake Valley or back east across the river, where they created the city of Kanesville, Iowa (*see* COUNCIL BLUFFS).

Winter Quarters was more than a resting spot on the way to the West: It became a place of implementation and experimentation in Church practice and government. It was there, for example, that the LAW OF ADOPTION and PLURAL MARRIAGE were first openly practiced, though they had been taught in Nauvoo. Also at Winter Quarters Brigham Young and the QUORUM OF THE TWELVE APOSTLES deliberated at length about leadership and Church government before reorganizing the FIRST PRESIDENCY at Kanesville, December 1847. The role of BISHOP was also refined. Because of the needs created by the July 1846 departure of 500 able-bodied men to serve in the MORMON BATTALION, Winter Quarters became the first community divided into small WARDS (congregations) of 300 to 500 people, with a bishop responsible for each.

Winter Quarters also represents the tragic side of Mormon history: Some 2,000 Latter-day Saints died there and across the river between June 1846 and October 1848. This high death rate is attributable to excessive fatigue, heavy spring storms, generally inadequate provisions, the malaria then common along the river lowlands, improvised shelters, and the weakened condition of the "poor camp" refugees driven out of Nauvoo in the fall of 1846.

Winter Quarters tested Brigham Young's remarkable leadership abilities and the faith of thousands who followed him through sickness and wilderness to their eventual mountain refuge. In Latter-day Saint chronicles, Winter Quarters will be forever remembered as a place of suffering and of faith.

BIBLIOGRAPHY

Bennett, Richard E. *Mormons at the Missouri, 1846–1852.* Norman, Okla., 1987.

Brooks, Juanita, ed. *On the Mormon Frontier: The Diary of Hosea Stout, 1844–1861,* 2 vols. Salt Lake City, 1964.

Bryson, Conrey. *Winter Quarters.* Salt Lake City, 1986.

Stegner, Wallace. *The Gathering of Zion: The Story of the Mormon Trail.* New York, 1964.

RICHARD E. BENNETT

WITNESSES, BOOK OF MORMON

See: Book of Mormon Witnesses

WITNESSES, LAW OF

The scriptural law of witnesses requires that in the mouth of two or three individuals shall every word be established (Deut. 19:15; 2 Cor. 13:1; 1 Tim. 5:19). This law applies in divine as well as human relations, for members of the Godhead bear witness of one another (John 5:31–37; 3 Ne. 11:32), and books of holy writ give multiple witness to the work of God in the earth (2 Ne. 29:8–13). The law of witnesses is prominent in the history and practice of The Church of Jesus Christ of Latter-day Saints.

A witness gives personal verification of, or attests to the reality of, an event. To "witness" in the scriptural sense is much the same as in the legal sense: to give personal testimony based on firsthand evidence or experience. To bear false witness is a very serious offense (Deut. 5:20; 19:16–21). When prophets have an experience with the Lord, often he commands them to "bear record" of him and of the truths that have been revealed (1 Ne. 10:10; 11:7; D&C 58:59; 112:4; 138:60). In legal affairs, testimony is usually related to what a person knows by the physical senses. In spiritual matters there is additional knowledge or information received through the Holy Spirit.

The Bible illustrates that God often works with mankind through two or more witnesses (Num. 35:30; Deut. 17:6; 19:15; Matt. 18:15–16). Likewise, latter-day scripture teaches the need for witnesses (D&C 6:28; 42:80–81; 128:3). One person's word alone, even though it may be true, may not be sufficient to establish and bind the hearer to the truth. Witnesses provide the means of establishing faith in the minds of people, for faith comes by hearing the word of God through the power of human testimony accompanied by the Holy Ghost (Rom. 10:17; *TPJS*, p. 148; *Lectures on Faith*, 2). In the BOOK OF MORMON, the prophet NEPHI₁ combined his brother Jacob's testimony with Isaiah's testimony to reinforce and verify his own witness of the divine sonship of the Redeemer (2 Ne. 11:2–3). Likewise, Alma₂ called upon the words of ZENOS, ZENOCK, and MOSES to corroborate his own testimony of the Son of God (Alma 33:2–23).

When the keys of the PRIESTHOOD were restored to the Prophet Joseph SMITH and often when visions were received, the Prophet was accompanied by a witness. This is the case with the restoration of the AARONIC PRIESTHOOD, the MELCHIZEDEK PRIESTHOOD, the keys given in the KIRTLAND TEMPLE (Ohio), and the vision of the DEGREES OF GLORY (D&C 13; 76; 110). Subsequent to the translation of the Book of Mormon and prior to its publication, three men on one occasion, and eight men on a separate occasion, in addition to Joseph Smith, became witnesses of the Book of Mormon PLATES (*see* BOOK OF MORMON WITNESSES). The Prophet Joseph was likewise accompanied in his martyr's death by his brother Hyrum, a second martyr or witness, making their testimony valid forever (D&C 135:3; 136:39). The meaning of the Greek word *martyr* is "witness."

The scriptures also indicate other ways in which the law of witnesses applies:

THE DIVINITY OF JESUS CHRIST. JOHN THE BAPTIST testified of the divinity of Jesus (John 1:15; 3:26; 5:32–39), the Father testified of Christ (Matt. 3:17; 17:5; John 8:18), and Christ himself bore record of his own divinity as the Son of God (Matt. 26:63–64; John 11:4; 13:31). The theme of John 5–8 illustrates the principle of witnesses. When Jesus spoke in his own behalf, some Jews, referring to the law of witnesses, said, "Thou bearest record of thyself; thy record is not true" (John 8:13). Jesus had earlier explained that both John the Baptist and the Father in Heaven had borne record of him (John 5:31–39; 8:18) and his testimony was therefore valid and binding. He declared that his works testified that he was the Son of God (John 5:

31–38). Peter also bore testimony that Jesus was the Son of God, a fact he had learned by revelation (Matt. 16:16).

JESUS' RESURRECTION FROM THE DEAD. Witnesses to the RESURRECTION of Christ included groups of women, two disciples on the road to Emmaus, and the apostles (Matt. 28; Luke 24; Acts 4:33; 5:32). Paul records that there were in Galilee over 500 witnesses to Jesus' resurrected body (1 Cor. 15:6). The Book of Mormon reports that about 2,500 people in America witnessed the resurrected body of Jesus Christ by seeing and touching it, and did "bear record" of it (3 Ne. 11:14–16; 17:25).

AUTHENTICATION OF RITES AND CEREMONIES. In the Church, witnesses are officially present for all baptisms and marriages. Witnesses also confirm proxy baptisms, endowments, marriages, and sealings in the temples on behalf of the dead (D&C 127:6). Missionaries travel in pairs as witnesses for one another (Mark 6:7; Luke 10:1; D&C 42:6; 52:10; 61:35; 62:5).

ON JUDGMENT DAY. In the final judgment that God will render to all mankind, the fact of the gospel having been taught on the earth by multiple witnesses will be important. Nephi₁ has written, "Wherefore, by the words of three, God hath said, I will establish my word. Nevertheless, God sendeth more witnesses, and he proveth all his words" (2 Ne. 11:3; cf. 27:14).

In a very fundamental way, the Bible and the Book of Mormon are witnesses to each other. Each record establishes the truth found in the other, and the DOCTRINE AND COVENANTS establishes the truth of them both (1 Ne. 13:20–40; 2 Ne. 3:12; 29:8–14; Morm. 7:8–9; D&C 17:6; 20:11–12; 42:12). The written testimony of two nations, the Jews and the Nephites, is a witness to the world that there is a God (2 Ne. 29:8).

BIBLIOGRAPHY

McConkie, Bruce R. *A New Witness for the Articles of Faith*, pp. 446–47. Salt Lake City, 1985.

Trites, Allison A. *The New Testament Concept of Witness.* Cambridge, 1977.

Van Orden, Bruce A. "The Law of Witnesses in 2 Nephi." In *The Book of Mormon: Second Nephi, The Doctrinal Structure*, ed. M. Nyman and C. Tate, pp. 307–321. Provo, Utah, 1989.

ROBERT L. MARROTT

WOMAN'S EXPONENT

The *Woman's Exponent* (1872–1914) was the first publication owned and published by Latter-day Saint women. An eight-page, three-column, quarto (10 inch x 13½ inch) newspaper, it was issued bimonthly, or in later years, monthly. During the forty-two years of its publication, Louisa Lula Greene (1872–1877) and Emmeline B. WELLS (1877–1914) served as editors. Although not owned by the Church, the *Exponent* had the approval and encouragement of the GENERAL AUTHORITIES of the Church.

First discussed among RELIEF SOCIETY leaders, the idea of a newspaper exclusively for women came to the attention of Edward L. Sloan, editor of the *Salt Lake Herald*. Not only did he agree with the prospect, but he actively promoted it, suggesting twenty-two-year-old Louisa Lula Greene as editor and the Woman's Exponent as a possible name, and offered help in the form of editorial advice and actual printing until the paper could become established. Reluctant to become the editor because of her lack of experience, Greene said she would consent if her great-uncle, President Brigham YOUNG, would call her to the position as a mission. This he did and gave her a blessing as well.

The number of *Exponent* subscribers is uncertain (perhaps reaching to one thousand or more). However, its influence within, and sometimes outside, the Church was greater than its circulation figures would suggest. One writer declared that it wielded more power in state politics "than all the newspapers in Utah put together" (*Tullidge's Quarterly Magazine*, p. 252). If not quite that important, the paper was widely read and much quoted. Without question, it was a forceful voice for women.

Loyal to the Church and its leaders, the *Exponent* often carried editorials defending the practice of POLYGAMY. The paper's independence made its case the more persuasive since, as one outsider observed, the writers were obviously not "under direction" or "prompted by authority" (Bennion, p. 223).

To the editor of a Chicago paper who wrote of her "amiable and liberal spirit," then-editor Greene responded, "Had we treated it in any other spirit than that of womanly frankness and courtesy we should have done discredit to our home education as well as to the religion we profess, and consequent injustice to our own conscience" (*Woman's Exponent* 2 [Aug. 15, 1873]:44). While this reply may have been of some benefit to Chicago readers, such editorials undoubtedly had their greatest value among LDS women who, reading their own feelings articulated with such surety, were fortified in their sometimes difficult roles.

Principally under the direction of Emmeline B. Wells, the paper vigorously supported WOMAN SUFFRAGE and often wrote about it, although the women of Utah had initially been granted voting rights two years before the *Woman's Exponent* began publication. The *Exponent* was also a force in the successful effort to have the voting franchise included in the 1896 Utah constitution. Many other items also found their place, but the topic most often discussed was women's roles, with a closely allied subject of education for women: "the brain should also be instructed how to work, and allowed to expand and improve" (*Woman's Exponent* 1 [Oct. 1, 1872]:69).

Woman's Exponent was not a single-cause paper, unless that cause might have been women and their families. The first edition stated: "The aim of this journal will be to discuss every subject interesting and valuable to women" (*Woman's Exponent* 1 [July 15, 1872]:32). A detailed index of items published during its forty-two years in print reveals how remarkably this purpose was followed.

Along with editorials and articles, the paper published original poems, short stories, and essays written by LDS women and others. It carried regular reports of the PRIMARY, RETRENCHMENT/ M.I.A., and Relief Society activities throughout the Church, and published a number of the Society's histories, one written by Emmeline Wells.

Just before the turn of the century, the *Exponent* began having financial problems. In 1914, Wells offered the paper to the Relief Society as its official organ, but was turned down, and the *Exponent* ceased publication in February of that year. It had fulfilled its role in "speaking for women," as it promised it would in the first issue. For forty-two years, *Woman's Exponent* was the voice for women in the Church. The *Bulletin*, and subsequently the *Relief Society Magazine* (1915), became the official organ of the Relief Society.

BIBLIOGRAPHY

Bennion, Sherilyn Cox. "The *Woman's Exponent*: Forty-two Years of Speaking for Women." *Utah Historical Quarterly* 44 (Summer 1976):222–39.

"Emmeline B. Wells." *Tullidge's Quarterly Magazine* 1 (Jan. 1881):250–53.

History of Relief Society, 1842–1966, pp. 95–96. Salt Lake City, 1966.

Robinson, Phil. *Sinners and Saints*. Boston, 1883.

SHIRLEY W. THOMAS

WOMAN SUFFRAGE

Though far removed from the centers of agitation for woman suffrage, LDS women were neither strangers to it nor indifferent about it. They were aware of efforts for a national suffrage act and of several unsuccessful congressional bills between 1867 and 1869 that urged adoption of woman suffrage in the territories. The first organized effort to secure woman suffrage in Utah occurred on January 6, 1870, when a group of LDS women met in the Salt Lake City Fifteenth Ward to protest a proposed congressional antipolygamy bill. Asserting their right to "rise up . . . and speak for ourselves," the women voted to demand of the territorial governor "the right of franchise" and voted also to send representatives to Washington with a memorial defending the free exercise of their religion (Fifteenth Ward Relief Society minutes, Jan. 6, 1870; *Deseret News*, Jan. 11, 1870). This preliminary meeting precipitated a mass rally of more than five thousand women in Salt Lake City a week later to protest publicly against proposed ANTIPOLYGAMY LEGISLATION. Spurred by congressional inaction on woman suffrage and no doubt impressed by this demonstration of female political acumen, the legislature of Utah Territory, with the approval of the acting non-Mormon governor, enfranchised Utah women a month later, on February 12, 1870.

The response of LDS women to their new political status varied. One comment expressed at a subsequent Fifteenth Ward RELIEF SOCIETY meeting was that women were already surfeited with rights. Another urged caution to avoid "abusing" their new political power. Sarah M. KIMBALL, president of the ward Relief Society, rejoiced in announcing that she had always been a "woman's rights woman" (Fifteenth Ward Relief Society minutes, Feb. 19, 1870; Tullidge, pp. 435–36). Imme-

diately thereafter, the Relief Societies initiated programs of instruction to educate women in the political process. In reviewing these events some years later, Eliza R. SNOW distinguished Latter-day Saint women from women activists elsewhere who "unbecomingly clamored for their rights." Asserting that Mormon women "had made no fuss about woman suffrage," she explained that they were given the vote only when God "put it in the hearts of the brethren to give us that right" (Senior and Junior Cooperative Retrenchment Association minutes, Aug. 8, 1874).

Mormon women did fuss in 1880, however, about extending their political rights to include holding public office, and they lobbied the legislature to amend the voting act accordingly. Though the legislature approved, the governor refused to sign the amendment. This action was followed by several attempts by local non-Mormons to disfranchise Utah women, whom they viewed as so oppressed by the Church patriarchy that they would vote as their husbands instructed. This, they argued, would further entrench Mormon political hegemony and perpetuate PLURAL MARRIAGE. These efforts were similarly unsuccessful.

An alliance of LDS and eastern suffragists was forged in 1879 when Emmeline B. WELLS and Zina Young Williams represented Mormon women at the national woman suffrage convention in Washington. From the time of the first congressional attempt in the 1860s to repeal woman suffrage in Utah as an antipolygamy measure, eastern suffragists had lobbied against each congressional effort to do so. Though strongly opposed to POLYGAMY, eastern suffragists were equally opposed to linking suffrage with attempts to eradicate polygamy. With help from prosuffrage congressmen, their effort delayed federal antipolygamy legislation and earned them a measure of condemnation for their support of the unpopular Latter-day Saints.

The Edmunds Act of 1882 withdrew the vote from polygamists, and the Edmunds-Tucker Act of 1887 disfranchised all Utah women. The false logic and injustice of disfranchising all women in Utah territory in order to attack polygamy were repeatedly asserted by the suffragists and other sympathizers. For Utah women, this withdrawal of rights after they had had them for seventeen years ignited their determination to regain the vote permanently with UTAH STATEHOOD.

In 1889 Utah women for the first time initiated a campaign to obtain the ballot. Within four

Susan B. Anthony (center first row) with a group of Utah women and other woman suffrage leaders, May, 1895. Sarah M. Kimball, behind Anthony; Emmeline B. Wells, on Kimball's left; Zina D. H. Young, second row, second from right. Courtesy Utah State Historical Society.

months of an organizational meeting in January 1889, the Woman Suffrage Association of Utah had fourteen branches. When President Wilford WOODRUFF officially ended plural marriage with the 1890 MANIFESTO, statehood was imminent, and Utah suffragists prepared to put woman suffrage into the law of the new state. By the time the constitutional convention convened in 1895, both political parties had agreed to support woman suffrage. Unexpected dissent in the convention, however, almost derailed passage of the measure, evoking high-flown rhetoric on both sides. B. H. Roberts, leader of the opposition, posed the traditional argument that women would defile themselves if they entered the "filthy stream of politics," while Orson F. Whitney countered that women would help refine the political process and bring their own special capabilities to the betterment of society (Official Report of the Proceedings and Debates of the Convention, Vol. 1, pp. 469, 473, 505–513). Utah suffragists immediately gathered petitions and lobbied to hold delegates to their original pledge. The measure finally passed, and in January 1896 Utah became the third state to join the Union with equal suffrage.

BIBLIOGRAPHY

Beeton, Beverly. "Woman Suffrage in Territorial Utah." *Utah Historical Quarterly* 46 (Spring 1978):100–120.

Carter, Kate B., comp. *Woman Suffrage in the West*. Salt Lake City, 1943.

Tullidge, Edward M. *The History of Salt Lake City*. Salt Lake City, 1886.

White, Jean Bickmore. "Woman's Place Is in the Constitution: The Struggle for Equal Rights in Utah in 1895." *Utah Historical Quarterly* 42 (Fall 1974):344–69.

CAROL CORNWALL MADSEN

WOMEN, ROLES OF

[Two articles appear under this entry and reflect the evolving nature of women's roles in the context of Church doctrine and culture:

Historical and Sociological Development
Gospel Principles and the Roles of Women

The first article discusses the roles of women as they emerged during significant periods of the Church. The second article describes the impact of gospel principles on the roles, and eventually, the lives of women in the Church.]

HISTORICAL AND SOCIOLOGICAL DEVELOPMENT

LDS beliefs create a unique feminine identity that encourages women to develop their abilities as potentially Godlike individuals, while at the same time asserting that the most important activities for both men and women center around the creation and maintenance of family relationships.

The eternal potential for women has always been based on doctrinal canon, which has remained essentially unaltered since the Church was organized. However, women's temporal roles have taken different forms depending on the situations confronting the Church at various times in its history. Across all the historical periods, the application of the LDS theological perspective on women to pragmatic circumstances has meant that the Church's female membership always played a central role in ensuring the success of Mormonism as a religion and as a society.

WOMEN'S ROLES IN THE CHURCH'S FORMATIVE PERIOD (1830–1847). Typical of most adherents to newly formed and struggling religions, the early Latter-day Saints reacted to stresses by emphasizing an intensely spiritual orientation to everyday living. Although the authority to administer most ordinances and preside over most gatherings was restricted to a male PRIESTHOOD, the gifts of the Spirit were not considered to belong to men alone. Women received personal revelation, healed the sick, prophesied future events, and performed various other actions that required spiritual gifts. The faith of these women and their ability to develop spiritual qualities were essential for keeping the Church alive during its difficult first years. They voted on Church matters, assisted in temple ceremonies, and contributed to welfare activities. As a group, women obtained an ecclesiastical identity through the formation of the Relief Society,

viewed by the Prophet Joseph SMITH as an integral and essential part of the Church. Additionally, the women provided much of the physical labor, doctored the sick and injured, assisted in reestablishing a succession of new communities, and cared for the needs of members whose families had faced hardships.

WOMEN'S ROLES IN THE CONSOLIDATION PERIOD (1847–1920). The broad-scale migration of the Latter-day Saints from the Midwest of the United States to the sparsely populated Great Basin region of the West marked the beginning of the consolidation of the LDS religion. Separated from the larger Anglo-American civilization by hundreds of miles of forbidding and unsettled terrain, the Latter-day Saints were able to set up their community under guidelines dictated by their religion. Among the social practices that became prominent after the migration to the West, and that significantly influenced women's lives, were PLURAL MARRIAGE and the assignment of adult men to extensive tours of duty as Church missionaries. A woman whose husband divided his time between multiple wives and/or missionary service was often obliged to provide single-handedly both material and emotional support for herself and her children.

The growth of the population and its socialization in the Church were important factors in consolidating and strengthening the LDS organization; and much of this responsibility fell to the women. Because of the absence of their husbands, women enlarged their role as "mothers in Zion" with aspects not generally associated with nineteenth-century feminine domesticity. President Brigham YOUNG encouraged the education of both girls and boys in "the manners and customs of distant kingdoms and nations, with their laws, religions, geographical location, . . . their climate, natural productions, the extent of their commerce, and the nature of their political organization" (*JD* 9:188–89; Widtsoe, p. 211). He also suggested that women should "keep books and sell goods" (*JD* 12:374–75; Widtsoe, p. 218), and exhorted them to "vote . . . because women are the characters that rule the ballot box" (*JD* 1:218; Widtsoe, p. 367). Some LDS women participated in political action concerning their gender, as evidenced by their being the second female population, after that of Wyoming, to vote in a national election.

The admonitions of President Young reflect an image of female responsibility drawn both from the belief that women and men are eligible for the same "eternal progression" and from the dependency of the early Utah Church on maintaining a capable and resourceful female membership. The women's response to the necessity of developing broad practical abilities and to an intense devotion to family forged the image of LDS women that emerged from practical as well as religious factors during this period.

WOMEN'S ROLES IN THE EXPANSIONIST ERA (1920–PRESENT). Throughout the early 1900s, the ideal of LDS converts flocking to Utah from all corners of the globe to build up an isolated "Zion" was gradually transformed into one of establishing the Church in many different countries and cultures. This change, accompanied by the encroachment of non-LDS settlers into "Mormon country," confronted the Church with the social issues of integrating its membership into non-LDS societies. Delimiting and articulating the position of LDS women was one of those issues; however, the role of women was not a topic that aroused much controversy.

The centrality of the family in LDS culture and doctrine fit easily into the popular nineteenth-century Victorian ideal of a highly, not to say exclusively, domestic role for women. The necessity of consolidating the Church as a community and as an organization was replaced by the desire to form a stable population that could fit comfortably into ambient cultures, particularly the culture of the United States.

Until the latter half of the twentieth century, the traditional role of women presented few obstacles to achieving this goal. As industrialization pushed the sphere of American males progressively out of the home, and that of females increasingly into it, most Latter-day Saints simply followed the pattern of secular society. In accordance with its family-centered doctrines, the Church readily endorsed the ideal of women as homemakers, wives, and mothers. The popularization of feminism in the 1970s presented LDS women with a complex set of expectations and competing priorities. Secular analyses set the attainment of an individual's personal goals or advancement in opposition to dedication to the family; LDS belief defines the two as inextricably intertwined.

The divergence of LDS religious beliefs from the theoretical basis of secular society presents modern-day LDS women with a perplexing set of role dilemmas. In the first place, they are inculcated by LDS doctrine and the historical examples

of other LDS women with the twin beliefs of developing their personal abilities and centering their lives in their families. On the other hand, like all women, they operate in the larger societal context of legal, political, and economic systems in which these two ideals are sometimes seen as mutually exclusive.

BIBLIOGRAPHY

Arrington, Leonard J., and Davis Bitton. "Marriage and Family Patterns." In *The Mormon Experience: A History of the Latter-day Saints*, pp. 185–205. New York, 1979.

Beecher, Maureen, and Lavinia F. Anderson, eds. *Sisters in Spirit: Mormon Women in Historical and Cultural Perspective*. Chicago, 1987.

LeCheminant, Ileen Ann Waspe. "The Status of Women in the Philosophy of Mormonism, 1830–1845." Master's thesis, Brigham Young University, 1942.

Shipps, Jan. *Mormonism: The Story of a New Religious Tradition*. Chicago, 1985.

Young, Brigham. *The Discourses of Brigham Young*, ed. John A. Widtsoe, pp. 194–218. Salt Lake City, 1977.

MARTHA NIBLEY BECK

GOSPEL PRINCIPLES AND THE ROLES OF WOMEN

The present role of women in LDS society is singular to the degree that it reflects the teachings and doctrines of the Church. Among the most fundamental of these is individual AGENCY, or the right to choose. Consistent with this doctrine, a woman's role varies with her circumstances and the choices that she makes within the context of LDS belief; she may fill many roles simultaneously.

One function of women is the consistent attention to the needs of others—not only family but all within reach of their help. Most render care personally in times of illness, death, or other life crises, but often they work in a coordinated effort with other members of the RELIEF SOCIETY. To "share one another's burdens, that they may be light" (Mosiah 18:8) is a principle and expectation associated with the very essence of a woman's membership in the Church (*see* BAPTISM; SISTERHOOD).

Caring for those in need often leads women to develop better ways of handling problems and to acquire specialized skills. Early in the history of the Church, women became nurses, midwives, and doctors; some established hospitals and baby clinics, while others started schools for young people (*see* DESERET HOSPITAL, MATERNAL AND CHILD HEALTH CARE). They also developed HOME

INDUSTRIES, carried out a thriving SILK CULTURE, and established a large grain-storage program (*see* WELFARE).

The Latter-day Saint community in the mountain West, perhaps because of polygamy, perhaps because men were often away on missions, provided an unusual independence for women—and an interdependence among polygamous wives. These conditions offered both the impetus and the practicality for women to acquire education and training uncommon to many women of their day. No less typical, LDS women today continue to take part in helping to "bring forth and establish the cause of my Zion" (D&C 6:6). They care for the poor and sick; serve proselytizing, welfare, and humanitarian missions; and teach children and youth, realizing their contribution to the temporal and spiritual welfare of the Saints.

The companionship role is the one most often identified for women in the Church. Adam "began to till the earth," and "Eve, also, his wife, did labor with him" (Moses 5:1). President Spencer W. KIMBALL pointed out that women are "full partners" with men (Kimball, p. 42). This companionship is not limited to the husband and wife partnership but includes women serving cooperatively with men (e.g., Priesthood and Relief Society) to carry out the work of the Church. From the early days, "the women of the Church have voted side by side with the men on all questions submitted to the Church membership for vote, . . . an advanced concept in 1830 when no women and few men voted in any church and few women had political franchise" (*History of the Relief Society*, p. 102).

Underlying the companionship role is the inherent EQUALITY of men and women as suggested by the creation account: "In the image of his own body, male and female, created he them, and blessed them" (Moses 6:9). Spiritual gifts, promises, and blessings of the Lord are given to those who qualify, without regard to gender. The receipt of spiritual gifts is conditional on obedience, not gender (D&C 46:9–25).

Bruce R. McConkie of the Council of the Twelve emphasized the equality of men and women in things of the spirit:

> Where spiritual things are concerned, as pertaining to all of the gifts of the Spirit, with reference to the receipt of revelation, the gaining of testimonies, and the seeing of visions, in all matters that pertain to godliness and holiness and which are brought to pass as a result of personal righteousness—in all

these things men and women stand in the position of . . . equality before the Lord [*Ensign* 9 (June 1979):61].

Temple ordinances are further evidence that "neither is the man without the woman, neither the woman without the man, in the Lord" (1 Cor. 11:11).

> It is to be noted that the highest blessings therein [the temple] available are only conferred upon a man and woman jointly. Neither can receive them alone. In the Church of Christ woman is not an adjunct to but an equal partner with man [Widtsoe, p. 373].

Women and men, although equal in status, fulfill some separate and different roles in the work of the Church. To men is given the responsibility of holding the priesthood, with many prescribed duties. The role for women is less precisely defined, though no less real. According to Neal A. Maxwell of the Quorum of the Twelve:

> We know so little about the reasons for the division of duties between womanhood and manhood as well as between motherhood and priesthood. These were divinely determined in another time and another place. We are accustomed to focusing on the men of God because theirs is the priesthood and leadership line. But paralleling that authority line is a stream of righteous influence reflecting the remarkable women of God who have existed in all ages and dispensations, including our own [Maxwell, p. 94].

Wielding an influence for good, women fill myriad assignments in the Church: They preside over, direct, and staff the organizations for women (Relief Society), young women (YOUNG WOMEN), and children (PRIMARY) at WARD, STAKE, and general levels; they teach doctrinal study classes for adults, youth, and children; they direct choirs and dramatic productions; they officiate in temple ceremonies; they serve as members of welfare committees at all levels of the Church; and they organize cultural and recreational events in which all members participate.

LDS women also fulfill societal roles such as physicians, lawyers, professors, homemakers, administrators, teachers, writers, secretaries, artists, and businesswomen. Additionally, many serve in community, political, and volunteer capacities. Consistent with the LDS belief that the greatest good that parents do is in their own home and that no other involvement ought to have precedence over their concern for family, members are encouraged to make pivotal decisions with regard to their effect on the family. This priority of family unavoidably influences the role expectations for women, including that of mother, wife, homemaker, and teacher. Latter-day Saint women are taught from their youth to prepare for marriage and homemaking, as well as for a vocation. Camilla Kimball, wife of President Spencer W. KIMBALL, counseled every girl and woman to: "qualify in two vocations—that of homemaking, and that of preparing a living outside the home, if and when the occasion requires. A married woman may become a widow without warning. . . . Thus a woman may be under the necessity of earning her own living and helping to support her dependent children" (*Ensign* 7 [Mar. 1977]:59).

Church leaders have long urged women, individually and as a group, to obtain all the education available to them, to "be given to writing, and to learning much" (D&C 25:8). Schooling for women has been encouraged not only for their own fulfillment and achievement but also for its value in helping them make the home a place of learning and refinement and for its importance in the lives of children. Even though training and education may open many career opportunities for women, the role of mother is dominant for those who have young children, and they are urged to use their training to benefit their children.

The Church does not oppose women working outside the home per se, and recognizes the contributions that they make in government, professions, business, and in creative fields. Marvin J. Ashton of the Quorum of the Twelve explained that "a woman should feel free to go into the marketplace and into community service on a paid or volunteer basis if she so desires when her home and family circumstances allow her to do so without impairment to them" (Ashton, p. 93). It is understood that some mothers are required to work for the support of their children, but it is hoped that whenever possible, mothers with children in the home will make home their priority career.

All women are daughters of "glorious mother Eve" (D&C 138:39) who, as the "mother of all living" (Moses 4:26), left a legacy that is the inheritance of every woman. This role transcends the care of an immediate family. It describes a nature and attitude that is basic for all women. President Harold B. LEE expressed this when he addressed the women of the Church assembled in the Tabernacle: "Now you mothers over the Church. . . ." (*see* MOTHERS IN ISRAEL). Every woman, whatever her family status, calling, or occupation, is involved in the roles of one who nurtures, lifts, consoles; who tenders love; and who protects and preserves families.

BIBLIOGRAPHY

Ashton, Marvin J. "Woman's Role in the Community." In *Woman*. Salt Lake City, 1979.

History of the Relief Society, 1842–1966. Salt Lake City, 1966.

Kimball, Spencer W. "Privileges and Responsibilities of Sisters." *New Era* 9 (Jan. 1979):42.

Maxwell, Neal A. "The Women of God." In *Woman*. Salt Lake City, 1979.

Widtsoe, John A. "The 'Mormon' Women." *Relief Society Magazine* 30 (June–July 1943):372–75.

BARBARA B. SMITH
SHIRLEY W. THOMAS

WOMEN IN THE BOOK OF MORMON

Some general conclusions about Book of Mormon women can be drawn from the book's fragmentary material about marriage, family, and religious organization. Six women are mentioned by name: Sariah, Isabel, Abish, EVE, SARAH, and MARY. Since no women are mentioned as religious or military leaders and only a few as political leaders, it appears that males held virtually all leadership positions in this society. Also, since the Book of Mormon was written primarily to remind future readers of the goodness of God and to persuade them to believe in Christ, it contains no law books and little intellectual or social history discussing the meshing of familial and religious practices. It is reasonable to assume, however, that these people began with many customs similar to their ancestral Semitic cultures and that their practices changed somewhat over the years.

In Nephite society, marriage and childbearing were expected, carrying religious significance and responsibilities (1 Ne. 7:1; Mosiah 4:14–15; 4 Ne. 1:11). Marriages may have been arranged within ethnic groups (1 Ne. 16:7; Alma 17:24) and were restricted outside certain groups (Alma 3:8). Polygamy and concubinage were prohibited and scorned; monogamy was expected, except as the Lord might command otherwise to "raise up seed" unto himself (Jacob 2:27–30).

Husbands and wives were expected to be faithful and loyal to each other (Jacob 3:7). One case shows that a wife was valued, even if unable to conceive. The righteous Jaredite king Coriantum remained with his barren wife until her death at age 102. He then married a young maid and fathered sons and daughters (Ether 9:23–24). It was, likewise, a sign of great wickedness that the priests of king Noah deserted their families. While in hiding, they abducted twenty-four Lamanite women for wives. When Lamanite kinsmen discovered and sought to kill the priests several years later, however, these women faithfully pleaded for the lives of their husbands (Mosiah 23:33).

Men were expected to support their wives and children, as well as the widows and children of men killed in war (Mosiah 21:17). Men were to pray for their households (Alma 34:21), and many took up arms to defend their families.

Both parents were concerned about their offspring (1 Ne. 5:1–7; 8:37). LEHI blessed and counseled his granddaughters and grandsons (2 Ne. 4:3–9). Children were taught to honor their mother and father. HELAMAN₁ and his 2,000 young warriors credited their Ammonite mothers with instilling in them the faith that "if they did not doubt, God would deliver them" (Alma 56:47).

In religious life, women participated in assemblies at the temple (Jacob 2:7; Mosiah 2:5–8), in teaching their children about God (Alma 56:46–47), and in offering sacrifice (1 Ne. 5:9). Evidently they were not excluded from, or segregated during, worship (2 Ne. 26:28–33); nor is there any indication that they were considered ritually unclean during menstruation. The gospel taught by the NEPHITES and Christ in the Book of Mormon is addressed to all, regardless of gender, age, or descent (2 Ne. 26:33; Mosiah 27:25; Alma 11:44; 32:23; 3 Ne. 17:25). BAPTISM was offered to all men and women who believed (Mosiah 18:16; Moro. 9:10). Women demonstrated profound faith and were tested by great sacrifice. In Ammonihah, women were burned to death with their children for refusing to renounce their faith in Christ (Alma 14:7–11). Apparently the LIAHONA responded to the collective faith and diligence of the entire group, men and women (1 Ne. 16:28).

During the years in the wilderness, the Lehite women toiled and were strong, but little is known about their activities, other than pregnancy and childbirth. Spinning is the only work specifically attributed to women (Mosiah 10:5; Hel. 6:13).

Women's dancing is associated with leisure and sometimes with wickedness (1 Ne. 18:9; Mosiah 20:1; Ether 8:10–11). Harlots provided immoral sexual activity in return for sustenance (Mosiah 11:14).

Politically, women had rights of succession to the Lamanite throne, for when Amalickiah murdered a Lamanite king, rule passed to the queen, whom Amalickiah then married to gain the throne (Alma 47:32–35). In extreme crises women took up arms in war alongside their men (Alma 54:12; 55:17; Ether 15:15).

Assignment of tasks in the family or in the whole economy—trade, planting and harvesting crops, and tending animals—is not apparent. Cycles of colonization, agriculture, urbanization, war, destruction, and renewal, as well as differing belief systems, certainly affected family and work patterns.

The Book of Mormon women Sariah, Abish, and Isabel can be viewed not only as historical figures but also as archetypal figures of, respectively, the righteous mother, the godly servant, and the attractive but sexually impure outsider.

Sariah was the faithful mother of the Nephite and Lamanite nations. She left a comfortable home near Jerusalem with Lehi and their family to suffer the rigors of desert and ocean travel, bearing two more sons, JACOB and JOSEPH, late in life while in the wilderness (1 Ne. 18:7, 17–19). She complained against Lehi when she thought their sons were dead, but affirmed his calling and the power of God when they returned unharmed (1 Ne. 5:2–8). With Lehi she gave sacrifice in thanksgiving. She was the mother of six sons and at least two daughters (2 Ne. 5:6).

Abish, a Lamanite convert of surpassing faith, servant to the queen of king Lamoni, recognized that the power of God had overcome the king, queen, and Ammon when they fell to the ground unconscious; she gathered people to witness the event and then raised the queen with her touch when the confusion of the crowd led to contention. Many believed the testimonies of the revived queen, who then raised the king, who also testified of Jesus (Alma 19:16–36).

Isabel, according to ALMA₂ (Alma 39:3–4), was a harlot who stole the hearts of many, including that of Alma's son Corianton, who for a time forsook the ministry to go after her (Alma 39:3).

The other three named women are biblical figures: Eve (e.g., 2 Ne. 2:15–20; cf. several references to "our first parents," e.g., 2 Ne. 9:9); Sarah (2 Ne. 8:2); and Mary, the mother of Jesus (e.g., Mosiah 3:8). Eve is mentioned in the context of an explication of the doctrine of the FALL OF ADAM as the precursor of the salvation of mankind. Sarah is recognized as the faithful mother of nations. Mary is called "a virgin, most beautiful and fair above all other virgins" (1 Ne. 11:15).

Other women are known in the Book of Mormon only by their individual deeds: the wife of NEPHI₁ a daughter of Ishmael, tried to soften wicked hearts with her tears (1 Ne. 7:19; 18:19); Ishmael's wife and three of their daughters supported Nephi (1 Ne. 7:6); a maidservant fled from Morianton's camp, after being severely beaten by him, to warn MORONI₁ of the plans of her rebel master (Alma 50:30–31); a daughter of Jared originated a plot to regain the kingdom for her father through enticement, violence, and deceit (Ether 8–9); two Lamanite queens were converted by the sons of Mosiah₂ (Alma 19:29–30; 22:19–24). Perhaps, as in some Semitic cultures today, the formal or more polite way of referring to a woman was not by her given name, but by describing her position in the family, such as "the daughter of Jared." Others so designated include Ishmael's wife, Ishmael's daughters, Ishmael's eldest daughter and wife of Zoram, Lehi's daughters and Nephi's sisters, Lamoni's daughter; and Coriantumr's unrepentant daughters.

The behavior and treatment of women were seen as an index of social and spiritual health. Many references to women concern their suffering during war, captivity, and hardship. Nephi and his brothers measure the difficulty of their travels in terms of the suffering of their wives, though Nephi emphasizes that the women were made strong like the men, while his brothers describe their wives' sufferings as being worse than death (1 Ne. 17:1, 20). Jacob sharply contrasts male infidelity with the tenderness of the women (Jacob 2–3); immorality is described as precipitating the collapse of both family and society. The inhumanity and depravity of dying civilizations are also described in terms of the suffering of women: Lamanites fed to women and children the flesh of their dead husbands and fathers (Moro. 9:8); Nephite women were sacrificed to idols (Morm. 4:15, 21); Nephites raped captured Lamanite women, tortured them to death, and then ate their flesh as a token of their bravery (Moro. 9:9–10).

Much of the imagery involving women in the

Widow of King Lehonti, Minerva K. Teichert (1935, oil on canvas, 36″ × 48″). After assassinating the Lamanite king Lehonti, the treacherous Amalickiah married the queen, legitimating his accession to the throne (Alma 47:18–35). The paintings of Minerva Teichert are particularly sensitive to the extensive but understated importance of women in the Book of Mormon. Courtesy Museum of Fine Arts, Brigham Young University.

Book of Mormon parallels that in the Bible. For example, Christ compares his gathering of the repentant to a mother hen gathering her chicks under her wing. As in Proverbs 3:13–20, wisdom is female (Mosiah 8:20), as is mercy (Alma 42:24). Sometimes female imagery is applied to the Lord, as when the mother nursing her child is the image used of the Lord comforting and remembering his covenant children (1 Ne. 21:15).

In a sense, the woman is the image of God's people. The biblical imagery of God as husband and his people as wife is continued in the Book of Mormon, mostly from the writings of Isaiah. Decadent Israel is described as devoid of honorable men, in that they valued women as decorative sex objects (2 Ne. 13:16–26; Isa. 3:16–26). When God's people become unfaithful to him, they are called "the whore of all the earth" (2 Ne. 10:16). When he calls his people to repentance, the Lord asks rhetorically, "Have I put thee away? . . . Where is the bill of your mother's divorcement?" (2 Ne. 7:1; Isa. 50:1). The images of a mother too weak to nurse her child and a pregnant woman so near term she is unable to flee destruction are used to motivate the Nephites to repent (Hel. 15:1–2); the woman whose children are lost is the image of desolation (1 Ne. 21:20–21). Those who accept "marriage" with the Lord are to experience joy as abundant as that of a barren woman who becomes a mother of many children, and the Lord consoles his people by saying, "For thy maker, thy husband, the Lord of Hosts is his name; . . . For a small moment have I forsaken thee, but with great mercies will I gather thee" (3 Ne. 22:1, 5–8; Isa. 54:1, 5–8).

BIBLIOGRAPHY

Spencer, Majorie Meads. "My Book of Mormon Sisters." *Ensign* 7 (Sept. 1977):66–71.

DONNA LEE BOWEN
CAMILLE S. WILLIAMS

WOMEN'S TOPICS

[Women; their roles in the family, in The Church of Jesus Christ of Latter-day Saints, and in the community; and other issues of concern to them are the subjects of several articles in this encyclopedia. Also included are the biographies of women who have figured prominently in the history of the Church.

For a discussion of both doctrinal perspectives and historical influences on women's roles, see Feminism; Mother in Heaven; Mother in Israel; Motherhood (*cf.* Fatherhood); Single Adults; Sisterhood (*cf.* Brotherhood); *and* Women, Roles of (*cf.* Men, Roles of). *Related articles include* Family; Marriage; *and* Plural Marriage.

For issues related to sexuality and reproduction, see Abortion; Birth Control; Maternity and Child Health Care; Sex Education; *and* Sexuality.

Articles discussing women in the scriptures include Eve; Mary, Mother of Jesus; Ruth; Sarah; *and* Women in the Book of Mormon.

Among Church Auxiliary Organizations, three are headed by women: Primary; Relief Society; *and* Young Women. *See also* Retrenchment Association. *For biographies of individual women, including many who served as auxiliary presidents, see* Fox, Ruth May; Gates, Susa Young; Horne, Mary Isabella; Kimball, Sarah Granger; Lyman, Amy Brown; Parmley, LaVern Watts; Robison, Louise Yates; Rogers, Aurelia Spencer; Smith, Bathsheba Bigler; Smith, Emma Hale; Smith, Lucy Mack; Smith, Mary Fielding; Snow, Eliza R.; Spafford, Belle Smith; Taylor, Elmina Shephard; Wells, Emmeline B.; Williams, Clarissa Smith; *and* Young, Zina Huntington.

Publications by and for LDS women have included Relief Society Magazine; Woman's Exponent; *and* Young Woman's Journal.

[See also Abuse, Spouse and Child; Divorce; Silk Culture; *and* Woman Suffrage.]*

WOODRUFF, WILFORD

Wilford Woodruff (1807–1898), the fourth President of the Church, is especially remembered for his 1890 MANIFESTO, which led to the discontinuance of PLURAL MARRIAGE among the Latter-day Saints and to the assimilation of Utah into the political and economic mainstream of America. Prior to that event he led a strenuous life, notable for his remarkable success as a missionary and his diligence as one of the Church's premier diarists.

Wilford was born in Farmington, Hartford County, Connecticut, on March 1, 1807. His father, a miller, worked hard to support a family of eight sons and one daughter. Wilford was fifteen months old when his mother died of spotted fever at age twenty-six. During his early years Wilford worked as a miller, attended school, fished with his brother Thompson, and engaged in the social life of the community. At an early age he became con-

Wilford Woodruff (1807–1898) was a stout, hard-working man who escaped a score of life-threatening injuries. In his extensive daily journal he once wrote: "The repeated deliverances from all these remarkable dangers I ascribe to the mercies of my Heavenly Father." Photograph c. 1853; attributed to Marsena Cannon.

cerned about religion and looked for a denomination whose doctrines and practices agreed with biblical Christianity. He spent much of his leisure time in reading, meditation, and prayer. Not far from a mill where he worked was a tree-covered island in a stream of rapid water. "I spent many a midnight hour alone upon that island in prayer before the Lord," he recalled ("Autobiography of Wilford Woodruff," Ms., p. 13). His quest eventually led him to Richland, Oswego County, New York, where he was baptized by Latter-day Saint missionaries on December 31, 1833. In April of 1834 he arrived at Kirtland, Ohio, where he met the Prophet Joseph Smith for the first time.

A month later, Woodruff participated in the march of ZION'S CAMP, a military company organized to help the Saints who had been driven from their homes in Jackson County, Missouri. Soon afterward, he began missionary work for the Church in Arkansas, Tennessee, and Kentucky in 1835–1836 and on the Fox Islands, off the coast of Maine, in 1837. His mission there ended in 1838 when, at age thirty-one, he was called to the Church's QUORUM OF THE TWELVE APOSTLES. On his return from Maine to the new headquarters of the Church in Nauvoo, Illinois, he led a company of fifty-three converts in ten wagons nearly 2,000 miles. Brigham Young ordained him an apostle on April 26, 1839, at Far West, Missouri.

A short time later, he was among the missionaries sent to England. He traveled there twice, first with other members of the Twelve in 1839 (D&C 118) and then to take charge as president of the mission in 1844. During his first mission in England, some 1,800 people, including 200 ministers, were baptized under his direction.

After embracing the restored gospel, Woodruff found himself in touch with the heavenly powers he had sought as a youth. As a missionary in the southern states in 1835, he went into a small room to meditate one evening and was overwhelmed by the appearance of a heavenly messenger who unfolded a panorama of events that would transpire on the earth before the second coming of Christ. In London one night, as he contemplated teaching the people of that city, he was beset by an evil spirit that nearly choked him to death before he was freed from its power by "three personages dressed in white" ("Autobiography of Wilford Woodruff," 1883–1884, p. 302).

He was also beset with an unusual number of accidents during his life. He suffered broken bones in his arms and legs, split his foot with an ax, was bitten by a rabid dog, and was crushed and pinned by falling trees. He nearly lost his life from blood poisoning when he accidentally cut his arm while skinning an ox that had died of poison. He survived the wreck of a speeding train, nearly drowned, was frozen and scalded, and suffered several severe illnesses. Woodruff believed that the promptings of the Holy Spirit saved his life on several occasions. He explained his preservation as a divine approval of his record keeping. He had prayed to know why the force of evil harassed him all his life. "The only answer I could ever get . . . was: 'The devil knew you would write, if you lived'—and I guess he did" ("Address to YMMIA Officers," Apr. 8, 1883, HDC).

One of Woodruff's most enduring legacies is his diary, a meticulous multivolume work covering nearly the entire history of the Church in the nineteenth century: "I have been inspired and moved upon to keep a Journal and write the affairs of this Church as far as I can. . . . You may say that this is a great deal of trouble. Very well it has been. . . . It has occupied nearly every leisure moment of my time. . . . But what of it? I have never spent any of my time more profitably for the benefit of mankind than in my journal writing" ("Wilford Woodruff Diary," Mar. 17, 1857, HDC). His diary contains the only record of many events and speeches of Church leaders. Although he was not a polished writer, his dedication, candid observations, and accurate reporting of speeches established his reputation as a devoted chronicler and brought his colleagues to his door to seek his services. In 1852 Woodruff was appointed clerk and historian of the Quorum of the Twelve Apostles, and in 1856 he commenced thirty-three years of service as a CHURCH HISTORIAN. In addition to his diary, he left an extensive autobiographical record and some 12,000 items of correspondence.

Following his appointment to the Quorum of the Twelve in 1839, Woodruff was engaged in a variety of ecclesiastical and secular labors. He assisted in publishing the *Times and Seasons* and *Nauvoo Neighbor* in Illinois and the *Millennial Star* and Doctrine and Covenants in England. He was a member of the Nauvoo City Council, chaplain of the Nauvoo Legion, and a member of the Council of Fifty. He was a member of the pioneer company of Latter-day Saints to arrive in the Great Basin on July 24, 1847. He served in the Utah territorial legislature for twenty-two years and the territorial council for twenty-one; served on the

Wilford Woodruff was ordained an apostle at age 32. He served missions in the southern United States (1834–1836), eastern United States and to the Fox Islands (1837–1838), England (1839–1841), the eastern states (1843–1844), was Church Historian and presided over several Church areas and territorial boards. He became fourth President of the Church in 1889. Photo, c. 1888, by Charles R. Savage.

board of directors of Zion's Co-operative Mercantile Institution (ZCMI); and was foreman of a Salt Lake City grand jury, president of the Cooperative Stock Company Association, president of the Universal Scientific Society, and chairman of the territorial Medical Board of Examiners.

Despite responsibilities that often took him away from home, Woodruff cared for a large family. Living during the years when PLURAL MARRIAGE was an authorized practice among the Latter-day Saints, he married five women: Phoebe Whittemore Carter, Mary Ann Jackson, Emma Smoot Smith, Sarah Brown, and Sarah Delight Stocking. They bore him thirty-three children. He was not immune from the heartaches and frailties of domestic life. His marriage to Mary Ann Jackson ended in divorce, and another wife and thirteen

children preceded him in death. His philosophy of family living is reflected in words he wrote to a daughter: "We are all expecting to live together forever after death. I think we all as parents and children ought to take all the pains we can to make each other happy as long as we live that we may have nothing to regret" (letter to Blanche Woodruff, Sept. 16, 1894).

In addition to his public and domestic labors, Woodruff was a devoted farmer. His Salt Lake City farm, consisting of a garden, an orchard, and herds of cattle and sheep, did more than sustain his family; he worked at farming as a calling and profession. For fourteen years he presided over the Deseret Agricultural and Manufacturing Society, which sponsored the annual territorial fair, and in 1855 was appointed president of the Utah Territorial Horticultural Society. He exchanged information and samples with horticulturists in the United States and Europe, seeking to improve a species of tree or crop, or to develop plants suited to the arid conditions of the Great Basin. Products from his land repeatedly won awards at the territorial fair. Not a large man (Woodruff weighed 135 pounds in his prime), he nevertheless had a reputation as a hard worker. He continued tilling the soil, when not away on Church assignments, until he was nearly ninety.

Among his few leisure pursuits, Woodruff was an avid outdoorsman. He enjoyed fishing and hunting from his Connecticut days until his later years in the Great Basin. In August 1892 he wrote to *Forest and Stream* magazine about a fishing and hunting trip on the Weber River in the Uinta Mountains, where in four hours he caught twenty trout, four of which weighed over four pounds, and noted that he lost a ten-pounder because the bank was too steep to land it.

At the death of Church President John TAYLOR in 1887, Wilford Woodruff first led the Church as President of the Quorum of the Twelve Apostles and was then sustained as President of the Church at the General Conference in April 1889, at the age of eighty-two. He had not expected to outlive his predecessor, who was younger, and saw his appointment as a case of the Almighty choosing "the weak things of the world" to perform his work ("Wilford Woodruff Diary," July 25, 1887). One observer noted that "he was not so learned, nor so eloquent a man as President John Taylor, but there was an earnest, honest zeal about him that convinced his hearers" (Cowley).

Woodruff's ordination as President came at a crucial time in the Church's history. Like other leaders, he had gone into seclusion to avoid imprisonment under provisions of federal ANTIPOLYGAMY LEGISLATION before word came of President Taylor's death. By the summer of 1890, legislation had been enacted that dissolved the Church as a legal entity, confiscated much of its property, and drove many of its leaders into hiding or prison. Federal legislation against polygamy had almost totally destroyed the effectiveness of the Church. For weeks President Woodruff "wrestled mightily with the Lord," and then, on September 24, 1890, after seeing in vision the consequences of inaction, he issued his now-famous Manifesto of 1890, which announced the end of the official practice of plural marriage (D&C, Official Declaration–1). On September 25 he wrote in his diary, "I have arrived at a point in the history of my life as the president of the Church . . . where I am under the necessity of acting for the temporal salvation of the Church. . . . and after praying to the Lord and feeling inspired by his spirit I have issued the following Proclamation." He then declared his intention to submit to the laws of the land "and to use my influence with the members of the Church over which I preside to have them do likewise" ("Wilford Woodruff Diary," Sept. 25, 1890).

While this action opened the door to a resolution of the issues that divided the Church from the nation, it did not relieve the pressures on the aging Church president. The financial burden incurred by the antipolygamy crusade, the completion of the SALT LAKE TEMPLE, demands of Church education, increased welfare expenditures due to the 1893 depression, and costs of funding local industries created apparently insurmountable financial difficulties. In 1893 he wrote to a friend, "I never saw a day in my life when I was so overwhelmed in business care and responsibility as I am today" (letter to W. H. Atkins and family, Aug. 10, 1893). He did not live to see the financial relief he had hoped for. He died on September 2, 1898, at the age of ninety-one, in San Francisco, California, where he had occasionally gone to seek relief from the ailments of old age.

Although Woodruff's leadership was somewhat eclipsed by colleagues who were more articulate and astute in matters of finance and politics, his pen produced the instrument that led to UTAH STATEHOOD in 1896 and opened the door for the twentieth-century progress and growth of the

Wilford Woodruff was called to be the first president of the St. George Temple in 1877 and commenced endowment work for the dead. This view shows the lower half of the sandstone being prepared for a whitewash coating, symbolizing purity and light. The main tower was not according to Brigham Young's plan; when it was damaged by lightning, it was replaced with the taller one.

Church. During his administration, other milestones were reached. In 1890 he inaugurated weekday religious education classes, a precursor to the later seminary and institute programs of the Church. He supervised the completion of the Salt Lake Temple and presided at its dedication in 1893. He placed temple recommends, which certify a Latter-day Saint's worthiness to enter the Church's temples, formerly issued only by the President of the Church, under the responsibility of bishops and stake presidents. Fast Day, formerly held on the first Thursday of each month, was changed to the first Sunday. In 1896 he signed a "political manifesto" that required all general Church officials, before they accepted any political position, to discuss the prospective appointment with presiding Church authorities.

A statement written while he was presiding over the Saints in England is a fitting epitaph to his life: "I am overwhelmed as it were in Mormonism for it is my life, meat, and drink and I do not expect to be anything else but a Mormon either in life or death. . . . It certainly looks like a marvelous work and a wonder that an obscure unlearned miller should stand . . . at the head of ten thousand saints" (letter to Aphek Woodruff, Apr. 18, 1845).

BIBLIOGRAPHY

Cowley, Matthias F. "President Wilford Woodruff." Address at University Branch, Chicago, Ill., Oct. 4, 1925, Ms., HDC.

Jessee, Dean C. "Wilford Woodruff." In *The Presidents of the Church*, ed. L. Arrington, pp. 117–43. Salt Lake City, 1986.

Woodruff, Wilford. "History of Wilford Woodruff." *Deseret News* 8 (July–Aug. 1858).

——. "The Autobiography of Wilford Woodruff." Ms., HDC.

——. "The Autobiography of Wilford Woodruff." *Tullidge's Quarterly Magazine* 3 (Oct. 1883–July 1884):1–25, 121–37, 302–311.

——. "Wilford Woodruff's Journal, 1833–1898," ed. Scott G. Kenny, typescript, 9 vols. Midvale, Utah, 1983–1984.

DEAN C. JESSEE

WORD OF WISDOM

Word of Wisdom is the common title for a revelation that counsels Latter-day Saints on maintaining good health and is published as DOCTRINE AND COVENANTS: SECTION 89. The practice of abstaining from all forms of ALCOHOL, TOBACCO, COFFEE, and TEA, which may outwardly distinguish active Latter-day Saints more than any other practice, derives from this revelation.

Called "a word of wisdom" in the introduction, the revelation was given to Joseph SMITH at KIRTLAND, OHIO, on February 27, 1833, when the School of the Prophets was meeting at his home in the Whitney Store. It came in response to the Prophet's inquiry about tobacco, which was being used by some of the men attending the school. The revelation states that it is specifically for the latter days because of "evils and designs which do and will exist in the hearts of conspiring men" (D&C 89:4). The Word of Wisdom limited alcohol use to wine for the sacrament and hard liquor for washing the body. It noted tobacco as useful only for treating bruises and sick cattle. Hot drinks (later defined as coffee and tea) were not for "the body or belly" (D&C 89:9). Additional advice was given permitting the use of meat, but suggesting that it be restricted to winter or times of famine (D&C 89:12–13). The revelation places strong emphasis on the use of grains, particularly wheat, as the staple of the human diet (D&C 89:14, 16–17), and upon fruits and vegetables ("herbs" verse 11; cf. 59:17–18) in season. The Word of Wisdom also states that some "herbs" are present on the earth for the healing of human ailments (D&C 89:8–11). Church members should not consume alcohol, tobacco, tea, or coffee and should use moderation in eating other foods.

Those who follow this counsel and keep the other commandments of God are promised that they will have "health in their navel and marrow to their bones," "shall run and not be weary, and shall walk and not faint," "shall find wisdom and great treasures of knowledge, even hidden treasures," and "the destroying angel shall pass by them . . . and not slay them" (D&C 89:18–21; cf. Dan. 1:3–20; 2:19–30).

The promises associated with the Word of Wisdom are considered both temporal and spiritual. The temporal promise has been interpreted as better health, and the spiritual promise as a closer relationship to God. These promises reflect the concern of the Church with both the temporal and spiritual welfare of its members. They also reflect God's concern with the condition of the PHYSICAL BODY of every person, paralleling aspects of other religious health codes defining types of foods forbidden for health and spiritual reasons.

The introduction to the 1835 printing of the revelation in the Doctrine and Covenants indicated that it was given as counsel or advice rather than as a binding COMMANDMENT, though the revelation states that it was "adapted to the capacity of the weak and the weakest of all saints" (D&C 89:3). Compliance with its teachings was sporadic from the late 1830s until the early years of the twentieth century. The Church encouraged leaders to be an example to the people in abstaining from alcohol, tobacco, tea, and coffee; but no binding Church policy was articulated during this time.

The PROHIBITION movement, spearheaded by the Protestant Evangelical churches in America, focused on alcohol consumption as a political rather than a moral issue. The movement intensified the Church's interest in the Word of Wisdom. There is evidence that Church Presidents John TAYLOR, Joseph F. SMITH, and Heber J. GRANT wanted to promote adherence to the Word of Wisdom as a precondition for entering LDS temples or holding office in any Church organization; and indeed, by 1930 abstinence from the use of alcohol, tobacco, coffee, and tea had become an official requirement for those seeking TEMPLE RECOMMENDS. While abstinence from these substances is now required for temple attendance and for holding priesthood offices or other Church callings, no other ecclesiastical sanctions are imposed on those who do not comply with the Word of Wisdom.

Other dietary aspects of the Word of Wisdom have not received the stress that the abstinence portions have. While some leaders, such as John A. Widtsoe, have emphasized the benefits of eating whole grains, no distinctive dietary practices have emerged that distinguish Mormons from non-Mormons, though the use of whole-grain cereals is often assumed to be higher among Latter-day Saints than other people.

With the appearance of cola drinks in the early 1900s, the Church was confronted with cold beverages containing caffeine, a harmful substance believed to make coffee and tea unacceptable. While no official Church position has been stated, leaders have counseled members to avoid caffeine and other addictive chemicals.

Church leaders universally caution against any use of such DRUGS as marijuana and cocaine and the abuse of prescription drugs. While none of these substances are mentioned specifically in the Word of Wisdom, the concept of the sanctity of the body and the deleterious effects of chemical substances on it have been emphasized as an extension of the Word of Wisdom.

Many of the health benefits associated with abstinence from the substances mentioned in the Word of Wisdom did not become clear until the latter part of the twentieth century. During World War I use of cigarettes among men became widespread, and during World War II, among women. The association of cigarette smoking with lung cancer was documented in the early 1950s, but official statements by scientific bodies accepting this relationship as causal did not occur until the mid-1960s. Since that time, many other diseases have been associated with cigarette smoking, including cancers of the oral cavity, larynx, esophagus, kidney, bladder, and pancreas; peptic ulcers; coronary heart disease; chronic bronchitis; infant mortality; and chronic obstructive airway disease.

Studies have found that Latter-day Saints have substantially lower risk for all of these illnesses (30–80 percent below that of non-Mormons living in Utah or in other areas of the United States) and that people who abstain from these substances are at much lower risk of these diseases than those who do not. Few health risks have been clearly identified with the use of tea and coffee, though some evidence suggests that those who abstain from coffee may be at lower risk for peptic ulcers, cancer of the pancreas, and coronary heart disease. Some studies estimate that those complying with the Word of Wisdom increase their life expectancy up to seven years.

BIBLIOGRAPHY

Alexander, Thomas G. *Mormonism in Transition*, pp. 258–71. Urbana, Ill., 1986.

Arrington, Leonard J. "An Economic Interpretation of the 'Word of Wisdom.'" *BYU Studies* 1 (Winter 1959):37–49.

Backman, Milton V., Jr. *The Heavens Resound: A History of the Latter-day Saints in Ohio 1830–1838*, pp. 234–36, 257–61. Salt Lake City, 1983.

Bush, Lester E., Jr. "The Word of Wisdom in Early Nineteenth-Century Perspective." *Dialogue* 14 (Autumn 1981): 47–65.

———. "The Mormon Tradition." In *Caring and Curing: Health and Medicine in the Western Religious Traditions*, ed. R. Numbers and D. Amundsen, pp. 397–419. New York, 1986.

Enstrom, James E. "Cancer Mortality Among Mormons." *Cancer* 36 (1975):825–41.

———. "Health Practices and Cancer Mortality Among Active California Mormons." *Journal of the National Cancer Institute* 81 (1989):1807–1814.

Gardner, John W., and Joseph L. Lyon. "Cancer in Utah Mormon Men by Lay Priesthood Level." *American Journal of Epidemiology* 116 (1982):243–57.

———. "Cancer in Utah Mormon Women by Church Activity Level." *American Journal of Epidemiology* 116 (1982):258–65.

Lyon, Joseph L., et al. "Cancer Incidence in Mormons and Non-Mormons in Utah, 1966–1970." *New England Journal of Medicine* 294 (1976):129–38.

———, and Steven Nelson. "Mormon Health." *Dialogue* 12 (Fall 1979):84–96.

———; John W. Gardner; and Dee W. West. "Cancer Incidence in Mormons and Non-Mormons in Utah during 1967–1975." *Journal of the National Cancer Institute* 65 (1980):1055–61.

Peterson, Paul H. "An Historical Analysis of the Word of Wisdom." Master's thesis, Brigham Young University, 1972.

Widtsoe, John A., and Leah D. Widtsoe. *The Word of Wisdom: A Modern Interpretation*. Salt Lake City, 1937.

Woolley, F. Ross; Katharina L. Schuman; and Joseph L. Lyon. "Neonatal Mortality in Utah." *American Journal of Epidemiology* 116 (1982):541–46.

JOSEPH LYNN LYON

WORK, ROLE OF

The role of work, as it has been consistently explained in the scriptures and taught by The Church of Jesus Christ of Latter-day Saints, involves four principles: Work is a universal obligation; work enhances the quality of life on earth; daily work has eternal consequences; and work will continue in the eternities.

A UNIVERSAL AND LIFELONG OBLIGATION. In the Church no individual who is able to work is excused from working. This principle refers to more than paid employment; it also means worthwhile activities that provide useful products or services for one's family and others.

The obligation to work was stated when the Lord commanded Adam and Eve to dress the Garden of Eden (Gen. 2:15) and was reemphasized later, when they were driven out. The ground was cursed for their ultimate benefit (Gen. 3:17–19), and work is viewed as a blessing and an opportunity: "God has blessed us with the privilege of working. When he said, 'Earn thy bread by the sweat of thy brow,' he gave [us] a blessing. Men and women have so accepted it. Too much leisure is dangerous. Work is a divine gift" (McKay, p. 4).

The Ten Commandments instruct, "Six days shalt thou labour" (Ex. 20:9). Other scriptures explain that life is to be a rhythm of work and worship (Ex. 31:15; Neh. 13:15–22).

Latter-day Saints do not view work as drudgery, as though its only purpose is to sustain life. Although the use of technological equipment and labor-saving devices is encouraged, their value lies in making work more efficient, not in eliminating it. Work is the natural lot of all people, and they are enjoined to be diligent in their labors (Prov. 6:6–8; 1 Thes. 4:11; 2 Thes. 3:10–15).

THE QUALITY OF LIFE. Work is necessary for personal development and represents a major source of happiness and fulfillment. "Our Heavenly Father loves us so completely that he has given us a commandment to work. This is one of the keys to eternal life. He knows that we will learn more, grow more, achieve more, serve more, and benefit more from a life of industry than from a life of ease" (Hunter, p. 122).

Individuals are encouraged to work with a happy, cheerful attitude. "Learn to like your work. Learn to say, 'This is my work, my glory, not my doom' " (McKay, p. 4). Enthusiasm for labor is especially extolled in such LDS hymns as "Today, While the Sun Shines," "Improve the Shining Moments," "Let Us All Press On," "I Have Work Enough to Do," and "Put Your Shoulder to the Wheel."

Work can also serve as a rehabilitative or therapeutic activity. The apostle Paul directed, "Let him that stole steal no more: but rather let him labour, working with his hands" (Eph. 4:28). This application of work is consistent with modern work-therapy programs that have helped ex-convicts return to society, mental patients function more effectively, students improve their academic performance, the disabled obtain greater self-esteem, and drug abusers conquer their chemical dependencies.

ETERNAL CONSEQUENCES. Work has lasting implications beyond the temporary reimbursement received in this life. Dedicated work helps to develop attributes of godliness: self-discipline, perseverance, accountability, and integrity (see GRACE). Idleness is condemned in the scriptures: "Cease to be idle" (D&C 88:124; 1 Tim. 5:8, 13; D&C 42:42; 60:13). The curse of idleness is not an arbitrary penalty imposed on those who use their time unproductively but a natural consequence of acting contrary to humanity's divine nature (Maxwell, p. 26). The final judgment, we are assured and warned, will be unto every one according to his work (e.g., Rev. 22:12; see also WORKS).

WORK IN THE HEREAFTER. Work will not cease with death. "Work with faith is a cardinal point of our theological doctrine and our future state—our heaven, is envisioned in terms of eternal progression through constant labor" (Richards, pp. 10–11; cf. Rev. 13:14; D&C 59:2). Detailed information about the nature of work in the hereafter has not been revealed. However, "what little information we have of a tactical nature suggests that we will be intelligently involved doing specific things which are tied to the eternal purposes of our Father in heaven" (Maxwell, p. 26; cf. Sill, p. 7).

The Latter-day Saint work ethic is similar to the Protestant work ethic regarding the central role of work in a devout life; however, the Latter-day Saint view maintains a strict distinction between work and worship. Although dedicated work builds character and is a form of service to God, it alone is not sufficient to express worship for God. No matter how much service humans render, they still remain "unprofitable servants" overwhelmingly blessed by God (Mosiah 2:21). Other sacred activities such as prayer; attending meetings; making and renewing covenants through baptism, the sacrament, and temple ordinances; and serving the needy are more direct and explicit forms of worship and are a ritual dimension of the LDS pattern of life.

Some measures in the Church are taken to keep the commandment to work from being misconstrued to encourage "workaholism," or a frantic compulsion to be constantly busy. Church members are encouraged to use judgment in how much they undertake and are counseled not to run faster than they have the strength (Eccl. 9:11; Mosiah 4:27; D&C 10:4).

The importance of work is to be balanced with other worthwhile pursuits. Members are exhorted to be anxiously engaged in a good cause (D&C 58:26–28), including the fine arts, music, dance, and literature (D&C 88:118; 136:28). Brigham YOUNG taught the need for a balance between physical and mental labor: "Some think too much, and should labor more, others labor too much, and should think more, and thus maintain an equilibrium between the mental and physical members of the individual; then you will enjoy health and vigor, will be active, and ready to discern truly, and judge quickly" (JD 3:248).

The Latter-day Saint work ethic was clearly evident during the settlement of the western United States. After the Mormon pioneers entered the Salt Lake Valley, they immediately began turning the desert into fertile farms and thriving cities. Their motto became "Industry," and their symbol, the beehive. During the first decade there, the Mormons colonized approximately ninety-six communities, and before the end of the century at least 500 more (see COLONIZATION). Opinion surveys indicate that Latter-day Saints continue to accept the moral importance of work and take pride in craftsmanship.

[See also Occupational Status.]

BIBLIOGRAPHY

Arrington, Leonard J. Great Basin Kingdom. Lincoln, Neb., 1958.

Cherrington, David J. The Work Ethic: Working Values and Values That Work. New York, 1980.

Hunter, Howard W. "Prepare for Honorable Employment." Ensign 5 (Nov. 1975):122-24.

Maxwell, Neal A. "I Have a Question." Ensign 6 (Aug. 1976):26.

McKay, David O. "Man Is That He Might Have Joy." Church News (Aug. 8, 1951):2, 4.

Nibley, Hugh W. "Work We Must, But the Lunch Is Free." In CWHN 9:202–251.

Richards, Stephen L. "The Gospel of Work." IE 43 (Jan. 1940):10-11, 60-61, 63.

Sill, Sterling W. "In the Sweat of Thy Face." Church News (May 8, 1965):7.

DAVID J. CHERRINGTON

WORKS

[God has made provision through the atonement of Jesus Christ for the salvation of the human family. Those things that God does for mankind are called "grace." Those things that people have to do for themselves are called "works." Both are necessary.

The Lord requires all persons to do all that they can do for themselves to obtain salvation. For instance, James said, "Faith without works is dead" (James 2:26), and John wrote that the dead are judged "according to their works" (Rev. 20:12). Paul emphasized grace, but did not exclude works: "By grace are ye saved through faith; and that not of yourselves: it is the gift of God: not of works, lest any man should boast. For we are his workmanship, created in Christ Jesus unto good works, which God hath before ordained that we should walk in them" (Eph. 2:8–10). Also, "as ye have always obeyed, . . . work out your own salvation with fear and trembling" (Philip. 2:12). Likewise, Nephi₁ wrote, "We know that it is by grace that we are saved, after all we can do" (2 Ne. 25:23).

Latter-day Saint doctrine teaches that works alone can never bring salvation, but good works accompany both faith and grace. Articles pertaining to this topic are Atonement; Commandments; Enduring to the End; Faith; Grace; Judgment Day; Justification; Obedience; Righteousness; Salvation; Second Estate.]

WORLDLY, WORLDLINESS

Latter-day Saints use the term "world" to refer to the planet Earth as well as to the social conditions created by those who live carnal, sensuous, and lustful lives (MD, p. 847). Worldly refers to people whose thoughts and interests are engrossed in fleeting, temporal pursuits of mortality such as power, success, gain, or pleasure.

Jesus said, "My kingdom is not of this world" (John 18:36), and "I have overcome the world" (John 16:33). In endeavoring to follow his example, Latter-day Saints seek to overcome the world as he did by valuing spiritual wealth and eternal treasures above earthly goods and attainments.

The apostle PAUL defined worldly pursuits as "adultery, fornication, uncleanness, lasciviousness, idolatry, witchcraft, hatred, variance, emulations, wrath, strife, seditions, heresies, envyings, murders, drunkenness, revellings, and such like: . . . they which do such things shall not inherit the kingdom of God" (Gal. 5:19–21). In contrast, the things of God or the fruits of the spirit are "love, joy, peace, longsuffering, gentleness, goodness, faith, meekness, temperance" (Gal. 5:22-23).

Just as the Father sent Jesus into the world, the Savior sent his disciples into the world (John 17:18). Latter-day Saints, therefore, do not believe in asceticism—a withdrawal from the world in an effort to avoid worldliness and to obtain spirituality. Their commission is to be in the world but not of the world, to improve the quality of life on earth by such things or activities as rearing good children, pursuing education, expanding their knowledge of all truth, contributing to the well-being of members of their communities, and sharing the gospel with others. Through example and precept, they seek to encourage all people to put off worldliness and become spiritually reborn by obedience to the laws and ordinances of the gospel. In summary, LDS doctrine cautions that "Men drink damnation to their own souls except they humble themselves and become as little children, . . . putteth off the natural man and becometh a saint through the atonement of Christ the Lord" (Mosiah 3:18–19).

BIBLIOGRAPHY

Nibley, Hugh W. *Approaching Zion.* In *CWHN* 9. Salt Lake City, 1989.

C. RICHARD CHIDESTER

WORLD CONFERENCES ON RECORDS

Two World Conferences on Records have been sponsored by The Church of Jesus Christ of Latter-day Saints in SALT LAKE CITY, UTAH. In celebration of the Diamond Jubilee of the FAMILY HISTORY LIBRARY and to exhibit the newly constructed GRANITE MOUNTAIN RECORD VAULT, the GENEALOGICAL SOCIETY OF UTAH hosted the first world conference, August 5–8, 1969. The theme, "Records Protection in an Uncertain World," emphasized that, since no one organization can preserve all the valuable records of the world, each nation or society must preserve its own records from wear, deterioration, neglect, and natural or man-created disasters.

Sessions combined two types of meetings: records preservation, usage, and accessibility; and genealogical research. For the first time on a world scale, a conference brought together genealogists, archivists, demographers, and technical experts on microfilming and other methods of preserving records. Two hundred and eighty specialists in these fields presented 180 seminars during the four days to an audience of both amateurs and professionals from national and governmental bodies, private institutions and societies, and individuals from every state in the United States and forty-five nations.

The second World Conference on Records was held August 12–15, 1980. The theme, "Preserving Our Heritage," was stimulated by Alex Haley's, 1976 book *Roots.* Much of the conference focused on gathering, preparing, and preserving personal and individual family histories—writing "the history of the heart"—in addition to factual genealogical data. The featured speaker, Alex Haley, said: "In all of us there is a hunger . . . to know who we are and where we come from." Attendance of 11,500 more than doubled that of the previous conference, including representatives from each of the United States and from fifty nations. Printed copies of the sessions of the conferences were made available at the Genealogical Society headquarters in Salt Lake City.

BIBLIOGRAPHY

Jolley, Joann. "The World Conference on Records—Writing the History of the Heart." *Ensign* 10 (Oct. 1980):72–75.
"The World Conference on Records." *IE* 72 (Jan. 1969):22–24.

DORIS BAYLY BROWER

WORLD RELIGIONS (NON-CHRISTIAN) AND MORMONISM

[*This entry consists of seven articles:*

Overview

Buddhism

Confucianism

Hinduism

Islam

Judaism

Shinto

The articles gathered under this title generally explain the relationships between Latter-day Saints and persons of other faiths, and illustrate differences and similarities in belief between non-Christian religions and the LDS religion. On the former subject, see also Interfaith Relationships: Jewish and Interfaith Relationships: Other.]

OVERVIEW

Latter-day Saints believe that God has inspired not only people of the Bible and the Book of Mormon, but other people as well, to carry out his purposes. Today God inspires not only Latter-day Saints but also founders, teachers, philosophers, and reformers of other Christian and non-Christian religions. Since LDS belief is grounded in a theistic biblical faith, it has been relatively easy for scholars and believers to perceive parallels between it and traditional Christianity, Judaism, and Islam. Now that the Church has become a global movement extending into Asia, comparisons between the gospel of Jesus Christ and the principal religions of India, China, Korea, and Japan are increasingly significant.

The gospel does not hold an adversarial relationship with other religions. Leaders of the Church have said that intolerance is a sign of weakness (R. Lindsay, "A Mormon View of Religious Tolerance," Address to the Anti-defamation League of B'nai B'rith, San Francisco, February 6, 1984). The LDS perspective is that "we claim the privilege of worshiping Almighty God according to the dictates of our own conscience, and allow all men the same privilege, let them worship how, where, or what they may" (A of F 11). The Church teaches that members must not only be kind and loving toward others but also respect their right to believe and worship as they choose.

George Albert SMITH, eighth President of the Church, publicly advocated the official Church policy of friendship and TOLERANCE: "We have come not to take away from you the truth and virtue you possess. We have come not to find fault with you nor to criticize you. . . . We have come here as your brethren. . . . Keep all the good that you have, and let us bring to you more good, in order that you may be happier and in order that you may be prepared to enter into the presence of our Heavenly Father" (pp. 12–13).

On February 15, 1978 the FIRST PRESIDENCY of the Church issued the following declaration:

> The great religious leaders of the world such as Mohammed, Confucius, and the Reformers, as well as philosophers including Socrates, Plato, and others, received a portion of God's light. Moral truths were given to them by God to enlighten whole nations and to bring a higher level of understanding to individuals. . . . Our message therefore is one of special love and concern for the eternal welfare of all men and women, regardless of religious belief, race, or nationality, knowing that we are truly brothers and sisters because we are sons and daughters of the same Eternal Father [Palmer, 1978].

In the words of Orson F. Whitney, an apostle, the gospel "embraces all truth, whether known or unknown. It incorporates all intelligence, both past and prospective. No righteous principle will ever be revealed, no truth can possibly be discovered, either in time or in eternity, that does not in some manner, directly or indirectly, pertain to the Gospel of Jesus Christ" (*Elders' Journal* 4, no. 2 [Oct. 15, 1906]:26). "If there is anything virtuous, lovely, or of good report or praiseworthy, we seek after these things" (A of F 13).

BIBLIOGRAPHY

Palmer, Spencer J. *The Expanding Church.* Statement of the First Presidency, Feb. 15, 1978, frontispiece. Salt Lake City, 1978.

———, and Roger R. Keller. *Religions of the World: A Latter-day Saint View.* Provo, Utah, 1989.

Smith, George Albert. *Sharing the Gospel with Others,* ed. Preston Nibley. Salt Lake City, 1948.

SPENCER J. PALMER

BUDDHISM

"Buddhism has been the most important religious force in Asia for nearly two thousand years. No other religion has affected the thought, culture, and politics of so many people. In aesthetics, architecture, dance, drama, handicrafts, literary arts, and music Buddhism has also been the single most important civilizing influence in the Eastern world" (Palmer and Keller, p. 49).

Siddhartha Gautama (563–483 B.C.), the founder of Buddhism, acknowledged no God, no soul, and no future life; he taught of the bliss of nirvana, which involves the extinction of ego and lust. Caught in the legacy of karma, one's life is bequeathed to another who falls heir to it—a continuation that is sometimes called "stream of consciousness," the "aggregates of character," or the "skandas." Consequently, the historical Buddha did not advocate worship or prayer, but practiced introspective meditation as a form of spiritual discipline.

The philosophy of Gautama (Gotama, in Pali), sometimes called Theravada Buddhism, with its emphasis upon the worthlessness of the physical body, of individuality, of this phenomenal mortal life, of faith in God, and of judgment, disagrees with LDS doctrine. In the restored gospel, mankind is the literal, personal offspring of God. It is a privilege to be born into mortality to gain a PHYSICAL BODY, so that one can become more like the Heavenly Father, who is a personal, tangible being (cf. D&C 130:22). Self-fulfillment, not self-negation, is the PURPOSE OF EARTH LIFE. Latter-day Saints seek to emulate Christ and, through the power of his divine atonement, to be personally exalted into the presence of God after death, and to become like him (see GODHOOD).

This is not to say that the gospel and Buddhism contradict one another in every way. The LDS religion, like Buddhism, advocates meditation, REVERENCE, INSPIRATION, and moderation. Latter-day Saints embrace elements similar to those of the Eightfold Middle Path, which advocate freedom from ill will and cruelty, and abstinence from lying, talebearing, harsh and vain thought, violence, killing, stealing, and sexual immorality (see COMMANDMENTS).

Other dimensions of Buddhist doctrine and practice, in the schools of Mahayana Buddhism in northern Asia, are similar to LDS doctrine and practice. Both LDS belief and Mahayana Buddhism are theistic. The Bodhisattva ideal of benevolence and compassionate service, of helping others who cannot by themselves reach the highest realms of spirituality, is not only largely consistent with the vicarious sacrifice and redeeming love of Jesus Christ, but also is expressed in wide-ranging, loving service on behalf of the living and the dead carried out within Latter-day Saint temples (see TEMPLE ORDINANCES).

BIBLIOGRAPHY

Palmer, Spencer J., and Roger R. Keller. *Religions of the World: A Latter-day Saint View*. Provo, Utah, 1989.

SPENCER J. PALMER

CONFUCIANISM

The Confucian focus upon moral example as the basis of harmony in society, government, and the universe is consistent with LDS views. However, Confucius was not interested in METAPHYSICS or THEOLOGY; he did not advocate belief in God, nor did he talk about life after death. He was concerned with humans in their social setting.

Arguments that Confucianism is not a religion have often been answered by references to its sacred text. One could also point to the lives of millions who have sought to practice its teachings by honoring parents and deceased ancestors through acts of affection and piety in the home or through performances at tombs, shrines, and temples that convey spiritual belief as well as moral affirmations (Palmer, p. 16). For Latter-day Saints, morality is based upon the individual's relationship with God as an expression of one's faith in God and upon obedience to his will.

Confucian morality is generally expressed in social and cultural ways. Values of loyalty, virtue, respect, courtesy, learning, and love are preserved primarily through outward courtesies and formalities, including traditional family ceremonies. Filial piety is the ultimate virtue. It includes honoring the spirits of one's ancestors not only by observances at graves and family tombs but also by striving to achieve acclaim in learning, in the mastery of sacred texts, and in aesthetic arts such as music, poetry, and painting.

The Confucian quest for sagehood, for refinement and cultivation of the ideal human, has its counterpart in the Latter-day Saint quest for ETERNAL LIFE. Both the sage and the true Latter-day Saint personify the transforming power of righteous behavior (see RIGHTEOUSNESS). In LDS scripture it is sometimes referred to as putting off "the natural man" and becoming a saint, one characterized as being "submissive, meek, humble, patient, full of love, willing to submit to all things which the Lord seeth fit to inflict" (Mosiah 3:19).

Latter-day Saints and Confucians share a mutual concern for the SALVATION of the extended family. Though the focus differs, both carry out devotional ceremonies in sacred places on behalf of departed ancestors. In this respect, both the LDS Church and Confucianism may be called family-centered religions. Both place importance upon genealogical research, the preservation of family records, and the performance of vicarious holy ordinances on behalf of their dead. In both instances, there exists a commitment to the idea that the living can serve the needs of departed loved ones (see TEMPLE ORDINANCES).

Church members believe that ELIJAH, the Old Testament prophet, personally appeared to Joseph SMITH in the KIRTLAND TEMPLE in 1836 and conferred priesthood KEYS, or authority, by means of which the hearts of children could turn to their ancestors and to the promises of salvation made to the fathers and the hearts of forebears could turn to their children (D&C 110:13–16), with the result that families and generations can be joined together "for time and for all eternity." Joseph Smith's remark concerning the dead "that they without us cannot be made perfect—neither can we without our dead be made perfect" (D&C 128:15; cf. Heb. 11:40) also resonates in the Confucian world.

BIBLIOGRAPHY

Palmer, Spencer J. *Confucian Rituals in Korea.* Berkeley, Calif., 1984.

———, and Roger R. Keller. *Religions of the World: A Latter-day Saint View.* Provo, Utah, 1989.

SPENCER J. PALMER

HINDUISM

Unlike the LDS Church, Hinduism has no founder, no central authority, no hierarchy, no uniformly explicated or applied moral standards. However, Hindus and Latter-day Saints share at least two fundamental beliefs—the continuing operation of irreversible cosmic law and the importance of pursuing ultimate union with the divine—though these principles may be understood differently (see UNITY).

Hinduism and the gospel of Jesus Christ differ in their perceptions of deity. In Hinduism there exist many gods, of thunder, drink, fire, sky, mountains, and the like, who are variously playful, capricious, vindictive, loving, and law-abiding. During the period of classical Hinduism, Brahma, Vishnu, and Shiva emerged to represent, respectively, the three primary functions of creation, preservation, and destruction. However, among the gods there is no generally recognized order.

For Latter-day Saints, God the Father, his son Jesus Christ, and the Holy Ghost form a tritheistic group of individuals of unified purpose and power, always systematic and ethical. The Father and the Son have bodies of flesh and bones, and the Holy Ghost is a personage of SPIRIT (D&C 130:22). The physical world was organized by the Father, through the instrumentality of the Son, who is the only Savior of the world, having willingly submitted to the suffering in Gethsemane and to crucifixion as an atoning sacrifice so that humankind could be delivered from death and sin. Several ORDINANCES of the Church are similitudes of the life, death, and redemption of Christ.

LDS belief and Hinduism both subscribe to a belief in an antemortal existence (see PREMORTAL LIFE). Hindus believe that premortal experiences determine inequalities of earthly life, including the caste system. In LDS cosmology, eternal laws of cause and effect were applicable in the premortal existence, as they are for inhabitants of the current temporal world: "There is a law, irrevocably decreed in heaven before the foundations of this world, upon which all blessings are predicated—and when we obtain any blessing from God, it is by obedience to that law upon which it is predicated" (D&C 130:20–21). Valiant souls from the pre-earth life may be ordained to be leaders here (Abr. 3:23; cf. Jer. 1:4; see FOREORDINATION).

In Hindu terminology, the cosmic law of justice is called "karma." Hindus believe that individual spirits are reincarnated repeatedly on earth in accordance with the effects of karma. Those who have not yet merited release from this wheel of rebirth are in a state of negative karma. If they improve their deeds during the next incarnation, they can improve their karmic condition and may even gain freedom to reach Nirvana (see REINCARNATION).

To Latter-day Saints, mortality is considered an extension and continuation of premortal performance in proving and preparing persons for exaltation in life after death. Humans are born only once on earth, and all mortal beings at birth are candidates for exaltation in the CELESTIAL KINGDOM. Hindus believe that the accumulated prebirth experiences have more consequence in determining one's future state than the actions of mortality. For Church members, birth is not an indication of failure to achieve release from the wheel of birth but rather a positive step forward along the path from premortal life to mortal life to IMMORTALITY and ETERNAL PROGRESSION. In this connection, the FALL OF ADAM was no accident. It was an essential event in the plan of reunion with God (cf. 2 Ne. 2:25).

At the philosophical level, Hinduism sees the phenomenal world as an illusion, but within the manifold appearances there is Brahman, the World Soul. Individual life is an invisible aspect of Universal Life. The ultimate object of all works, devotion, and knowledge is to gain release from egotistical lustful attachments to this physical world so as to achieve a state of peace that comes from identity with the impersonal Universal Soul, or Nirvana.

Gaining a conscious union with God is also a prime objective of LDS belief, although it is perceived differently. Jesus not only declared that he and his Father were one but also prayed that his disciples would likewise become one with them (John 10:30; 17:11), both in mind and will, as well as in heightened states of celestial consciousness, that is, to develop thoroughly Christlike and godlike qualities (D&C 35:2; 76:58; 1 Cor. 6:17; Heb. 2:11; Rom. 12:2). In purpose, power, and personality, and even in the glorification of the body, humankind can become perfect (Matt. 5:48; 3 Ne. 12:48; *see also* PERFECTION). Unlike Hinduism, the LDS faith does not seek the relinquishment of INDIVIDUALITY. Free AGENCY and personal responsibility are not impaired but ultimately honored and enhanced.

BIBLIOGRAPHY

Palmer, Spencer J., and Roger R. Keller. *Religions of the World: A Latter-day Saint View.* Provo, Utah, 1989.

SPENCER J. PALMER

ISLAM

Interest in the Church's associations with Islam has appeared in literary comparisons, within LDS teachings, and through historical contacts. The initial comparison was perhaps made in 1834, when the anti-Mormon Pastor E. D. Howe suggested that Joseph SMITH matched Muhammad's "ignorance and stupidity," thereby coining an analogy that experienced polemical and "scientific" phases. The polemical phase entailed American Protestants vilifying the Church and its prophet by likening them to Islam and Muhammad, long presumed fraudulent by Christians. This disputative tactic had been used against Protestants during the Counter-Reformation, and emphasized such allegations as sensuality, violence, and deception. These polemics yielded a literary corpus—for example, "The Yankee Mahomet" and books by Joseph Willing and Bruce Kinney. The scientific phase began when the explorer and Arabist Richard Francis Burton visited Utah in 1860 and rephrased in academic discourse the analogy, subsequently elaborated by David Margoliouth, Eduard Meyer, Hans Thimme, and Georges Bousquet. These Orientalists and sociologists of religion apparently felt they could study fully documented Mormonism as a proxy for underdocumented Islam.

The Church's doctrinal posture toward Islam has also gone through phases. Islam is not mentioned in either the Book of Mormon or the Doctrine and Covenants. Yet articles in *Times and Seasons* suggest that some LDS spokesmen initially echoed medieval Christian views of Islam as fanatical heresy (Editorial, 3 [15 Apr. 1842]; "Last Hour of the False Prophet," 5 [Apr. 1, 1844]; "Mahometanism," 6 [Jan. 15, 1845]). But speeches by apostles George A. Smith and Parley P. PRATT in 1855 evoked more positive traditional interpretations: that Islam, fulfilling biblical promises made to Ishmael (Gen. 21), was divinely instigated to "scourge" apostate Christianity and to curb idolatry. Perhaps unknowingly paraphrasing Muhammad ibn Abd al-Wahhab (d. 1792), George A. Smith applied historical judgment to Islam's experience: "As they abode in the teachings which Mahomet gave them, . . . they were united and prospered; but when they ceased to do this, they lost their power and influence" (pp. 34–35). More recently, perhaps in the context of the Church's growth to global dimensions, Muslim cultures have figured prominently in dicta—such as those by President Spencer W. KIMBALL and Elders Howard W. Hunter, Bruce R. McConkie, and Carlos E. Asay—stressing that God is no respecter of persons on grounds of race or color. In the "Easter Message" of February 15, 1978, the LDS FIRST PRESIDENCY wrote that Muhammad and other nonbiblical religious leaders and philosophers "received a portion of God's light. Moral truths were given to them by God to enlighten whole nations." On balance, Mormon teachings thus seem to have cast Islam in a positive historical role.

Latter-day Saints' historical contacts with Islam include missions in countries with Muslim populations. Some LDS proselytizers have expressed sentiments articulated earlier by such Catholic and Protestant missionaries as Cardinal Lavigerie and Samuel Zwemer: that Islam's own doctrinal claims (e.g., God is one not three; Jesus was a prophet, not God's son; apostates from Islam merit death), Islamic society's holistic character, and the sad legacy of Muslim–Christian relations make difficult the converting of Muslims to Christianity. Since World War II many LDS professionals have lived in Muslim communities. Some have chronicled their experience in terms that are human (Marion Miller) or historical-theological (Arthur Wallace). At least one has engaged in radical syncretism (Ibn Yusuf/Lloyd Miller; see Green, 1983). Governments of Islamic countries, most of which ban proselytizing, such as Egypt and Saudi Arabia, have allowed discreet worship by LDS families. In 1989 Jordan permitted the establishment of an LDS cultural center in Amman.

BIBLIOGRAPHY

For general reviews of the literature, see A. H. Green, "Joseph Smith as an American Muhammad," *Dialogue* 6 (Spring 1971):46–58; and "The Muhammad-Joseph Smith Comparison: Subjective Metaphor or a Sociology of Prophethood," in *Mormons and Muslims*, ed. Spencer J. Palmer, Provo, Utah, 1983. This latter volume constitutes a collection of essays on the subject. For recent authoritative LDS statements, see Spencer W. Kimball, "The Uttermost Parts of the Earth," *Ensign* 9 (July 1979):2–9; and Howard W. Hunter, "All Are Alike Unto God," *BYU Devotional Speeches*, Provo, Utah, 1979, pp. 32–36.

ARNOLD H. GREEN

JUDAISM

The views of The Church of Jesus Christ of Latter-day Saints and its members toward Jews and Judaism have been shaped chiefly by LDS teachings and by historical contacts with Jewish communities. These teachings include regarding the Jews as an ancient covenant people with a prophesied role in the contemporary gathering of Israel and in events of the last days, and the contacts include educational activities in Israel and LDS proselytizing efforts outside of Israel.

Latter-day Saints share some traditional Christian positions toward Judaism, such as acknowledging debts for ethical foundations and religious terminology. Moreover, they have adopted stances expressed in Paul's mildly universalistic writings: Bible-era Judaism, based on the law of Moses and embodying the Old Testament or covenant, was essentially "fulfilled" in Jesus Christ (cf. 3 Ne. 15:4–8), so Christianity became the New Covenant and therefore spiritual "Israel." However, they have tended not to share the anti-Semitic postures of some Christian eras or groupings. Reflecting a more positive view, the Book of Mormon contains such passages as "Ye shall no longer hiss, nor spurn, nor make game of the Jews, . . . for behold, the Lord remembereth his covenant unto them" (3 Ne. 29:8), and President Heber J. GRANT stated, "There should be no ill-will . . . in the heart of any true Latter-day Saint, toward the Jewish people" (*GS*, p. 147).

Mormons consider themselves a latter-day covenant people, the divinely restored New Testament Church. In this light, they have interpreted literally the Lord's mandate to them to regather Israel. While seeing historical judgment in Assyrian, Babylonian, and Roman treatment of biblical peoples, they have viewed the "scattering" as having beneficially diffused the "blood of Israel" worldwide. As a result, the Prophet Joseph SMITH said that the Church believes in the "literal gathering of Israel" (A of F 10). This is done principally by missionary work searching for both biological and spiritual "Israelites" among the Gentile nations.

In LDS eschatology, the first Israelite tribe thus being gathered is EPHRAIM, with which most Latter-day Saints are identified through PATRIARCHAL BLESSINGS. To this "Semitic identification" has been attributed the substitution of Judeophilia for anti-Semitism among Mormons (Mauss). Indeed, LDS doctrine has envisaged a partnership both in promulgating scripture—in Ezekiel 37:16, Latter-day Saints find allusions to the Bible and Book of Mormon—and in erecting millennial capitals: Ephraim will build the NEW JERUSALEM in an American ZION, Jews ("Judah") will gather in "the land of their fathers" (3 Ne. 20:29) to rebuild (old) Jerusalem, a prominent theme in the Book of Mormon (see 2 Ne. 6, 9–10, 29; Ether 13) and the Doctrine and Covenants (sections 39, 42, 45, 110, 133). Like several post-Reformation evangelical groups, Latter-day Saints have anticipated a return of Jews to Palestine as part of Israel's gathering. Indeed, the Prophet Joseph Smith sent Orson Hyde, an apostle, to Jerusalem, where in October 1841 he dedicated the land and prayed "for the gathering together of Judah's scattered remnants" (*HC* 4:456). On grounds that "the first shall be last," Brigham Young said that the conversion of the Jews would not occur before Christ's second coming (Green; cf. Ether 13:12). Yet Palestine was subsequently rededicated for the Jews' return by several apostles in the Church: George A. Smith (1873), Francis M. Lyman (1902), James E. Talmage (1921), David O. MCKAY (1930), and John A. Widtsoe (1933).

The creation by modern Zionism (secular Jewish nationalism) of a Jewish community and then a state in Palestine tested LDS doctrine's equating the Jews' "return" with Israel's "gathering" (i.e., conversion, but in different locations). While Rabbi Abraham Kook's disciples viewed Zionism's success from Jewish eschatalogical perspectives, some Latter-day Saints began regarding it from LDS perspectives: a secular preparatory stage for the messianic era. A latter-day apostle, LeGrand

Richards, and some others in effect identified Zionism and the State of Israel as the expected "return," the physical prelude to the spiritual "gathering." Others, such as Elder Bruce R. McConkie, wrote that the Zionist ingathering was not that "of which the scriptures speak. . . . It does not fulfill the ancient promises." He saw it as a "gathering of the unconverted" but "nonetheless part of the divine plan" (*Millennial Messiah*, Salt Lake City, 1982, p. 229).

Pre–World War I contacts with Jewish communities were apparently influenced by Brigham Young's dictum. Jews immigrated into Utah after 1864, aligning politically with non-LDS "Gentiles." Yet they related well to the LDS majority, which did not proselytize them. Indeed, to the earliest Jewish settlers in Utah, the LDS Church provided meeting places for services and donated land for a cemetery. Utahans have also elected several Jews to public office, including a judge, state legislators, and a governor (see Brooks, 1973).

An LDS Near East mission (from 1884) was based temporarily at Haifa, where a cemetery contains graves of missionaries and German converts. Teaching mostly Armenians and German colonists, this mission ignored the longtime resident Jews of the Old Yishuv and had few contacts with new Zionist immigrants. After World War I some LDS leaders felt impressed to begin "gathering" Jews. New York Mission President (1922–1927) B. H. Roberts wrote pamphlets later consolidated into *Rasha—The Jew*, Mormonism's first exposition directed at Jews. In this same vein, Elder LeGrand Richards composed *Israel! Do You Know?* and then received permission to launch experimental "Jewish missions," the largest being in Los Angeles. This and smaller Jewish missions (Salt Lake City; Ogden; San Francisco; Portland, Oreg.; New York; Washington D.C.) were disbanded in 1959, when the First Presidency directed that Jewish communities not be singled out for proselytizing.

Noteworthy interaction has accompanied Brigham Young University's foreign study program in Jerusalem (begun 1968), based first at a hotel and then at a kibbutz. Seeking a permanent facility, BYU leaders were granted a location on Mount Scopus by Jerusalem's municipal authorities. Construction began in 1984 on the Jerusalem Center for Near Eastern Studies and, because it was such a prominent facility on such a choice site, drew opposition; ultra-Orthodox Jews, suspecting a "missionary center" under academic cover, warned of "spiritual holocaust." However, anti-Mormon campaigns failed to halt construction of the center, partly because U.S. congressmen and Jewish leaders, as well as Israeli liberals, defended it. The controversy reached Israel's Knesset, which obliged BYU to strengthen its non-proselytizing pledge. This contest was linked to the larger debate between Israel's secularists, who valued pluralism, and its militant Orthodox, who feared a new alien presence.

LDS contacts with Judaism have led to an exchange of converts. Salt Lake's synagogue Kol Ami has been attended by some ex-Mormons. Perhaps a few hundred Jews have become Latter-day Saints. Like Evangelical Jews, most have continued to emphasize their Jewishness, and fellow Mormons have welcomed them and considered them "of Judah." Convert memoirs have appeared; for honesty and literary quality probably none surpasses Herbert Rona's *Peace to a Jew*. Jewish Mormons formed B'nai Shalom in 1967 to function as a support group and to facilitate genealogical research.

BIBLIOGRAPHY

For Mormon activities in Palestine/Israel, see Steven W. Baldridge and Marilyn Rona, *Grafting In: A History of the Latter-day Saints in the Holy Land*, Salt Lake City, 1989. On LDS attitudes and behavior toward Jews, see Herbert Rona, *Peace to a Jew*, New York, 1952; Armand L. Mauss, "Mormon Semitism and Anti-Semitism," *Sociological Analysis*, 29 (Spring 1968):11–27; Arnold H. Green, "A Survey of LDS Proselyting Efforts to the Jewish People," *BYU Studies* 8 (1968):427–43; and Juanita Brooks, *History of the Jews in Utah and Idaho*, Salt Lake City, 1973. For theological dimensions, see Truman G. Madsen, ed., *Reflections on Mormonism: Judeo-Christian Parallels*, Provo, Utah, 1978.

ARNOLD H. GREEN

SHINTO

Shinto, the earliest and largest native religion of Japan, has no known founder, no sacred scriptures, no systematized philosophy, no set of moral laws, no struggle between good and evil, no eschatology or life after death, no ecclesiastical organization. Shinto is "the way of the gods." It is folkways and spiritual feeling toward the awesomeness, the purity, the beauty of unspoiled nature.

In the Japanese view, the ever-present powers and spirits within nature are the *kami*, or gods, but they are neither transcendent nor omnipotent.

Shinto has a rich mythology. Its luxuriant polytheism is dominated by Amaterasu, the goddess of the Sun, and by her brother Susano, who is most often frivolous and rude.

The LDS Church, on the other hand, has a founder, a set of sacred scriptures, a philosophical basis, a declared body of ethics and doctrine, and a structured church organization, and accepts a tritheistic godhead through obedience to whom mankind can overcome the evils of this world. The Father, Son, and Holy Ghost are the supreme godhead, perfect, tangible beings whose light and love emanate from their presence "to fill the immensity of space" (D&C 88:12; cf. 130:22).

Latter-day Saints believe that God's work and glory are to "bring to pass the immortality and eternal life of man" (Moses 1:39). But Shinto is concerned with the here and now. It expresses a "joyful acceptance of life and a feeling of closeness to nature" (Reischaur, in D.B. Picken, *Shinto: Japan's Spiritual Roots*, Tokyo, 1980, pp. 6–7).

No counterpart to the central tenet of LDS faith—the crucifixion and atonement of Christ—exists in Shinto. While the LDS Church and many other world religions concentrate on the theology of death and sin, the importance of holy writ, and the responsibilities of parenting and church service, Shinto values and attitudes are transmitted through festive celebrations of the powers within mountains, waterfalls, trees, and other aspects of nature.

BIBLIOGRAPHY

Palmer, Spencer J., and Roger R. Keller. *Religions of the World: A Latter-day Saint View.* Provo, Utah, 1989.

SPENCER J. PALMER

WORLDS

Latter-day Saint prophets and scripture teach that other worlds similar to this earth have been and will be created and inhabited in fulfillment of God's eternal designs for his children. As explained in REVELATIONS to the Prophet Joseph SMITH, God has in operation a vast plan for the eternal progress of his children. In a vision given to MOSES, the Lord said, "Worlds without number have I created; and I also created them for mine own purpose, . . . there are many (worlds) that now stand, and innumerable are they unto man" (Moses 1:33, 35). This same many-worlds view is echoed in other scriptures (see Heb. 1:2; D&C 76:24; Moses 7:30; Abr. 3:12).

Joseph Smith's version of pluralism shared some similarities with ideas of his religious contemporaries and of modern science. But the pluralistic cosmology that emerged from his revelations and the interpretations of the early generation of LDS leaders taught by him were distinctive. Unlike other religious pluralists, Joseph Smith evidenced no interest in using pluralism for proselytizing purposes, but only to unfold a fuller understanding of God's purposes for people in this life and in the hereafter. The full and coherent picture painted in these Mormon teachings is not plausibly derived from any contemporary view, but is generally compatible with ancient cosmologies, and particularly with ideas attributed anciently to Enoch (Crowe, pp. 245–46; Paul, pp. 27–32; see also *CWHN* 1:180–88; 2:236–40).

Like contemporary pluralists, Joseph Smith's system implied innumerable stellar systems with inhabited planets. In addition (see Paul, p. 28), Joseph taught that old physical worlds pass away while new ones are being formed (Moses 1:35, 38); worlds are governed hierarchically (Abr. 3:8–9); each system of worlds has its own laws (D&C 88:36–38); Jesus Christ is the creator of all these worlds (D&C 76:24; 93:9–10); people assigned to different levels of glory inhabit different worlds (D&C 76:112); the earth has been the most wicked of all worlds (Moses 7:36); resurrected beings also reside on worlds (D&C 88:36–38); and these other worlds exist in both time and space (Moses 1:35, 38; D&C 88:36–38, 42–47; 93:9–10).

Mormons therefore accept the existence of other worlds created by God for a divine purpose that is the same as the PURPOSE OF EARTH LIFE—"to bring to pass the immortality and eternal life" of God's children (Moses 1:39). The inhabitants of these other planets are understood by Latter-day Saints to be children of God and created in his image, though they might differ from the earth's inhabitants in unspecified ways (Moses 1:33; D&C 76:24). The means of SALVATION through the GOSPEL OF JESUS CHRIST is the same for all of God's creations. CREATION is continual and expansive and is directed toward the eternal happiness of all intelligent beings, for the Lord told Moses, "As one earth shall pass away, and the heavens thereof even so shall another come; and there is no end to my works, neither to my words" (Moses 1:38). For

Latter-day Saints the gospel of Jesus Christ has universal validity, in both time and space. God's PLAN OF SALVATION operates on a universal scale. Latter-day Saints believe that there are now countless planets whose inhabitants—children of God—are progressing, as are human beings on this earth, according to eternal principles towards a Godlike life.

BIBLIOGRAPHY

Crowe, Michael J. *The Extraterrestrial Life Debate 1750–1900: The Idea of a Plurality of Worlds from Kant to Lowell.* Cambridge, Eng., 1986.

Johnson, H. R. "Civilizations Out in Space." *BYU Studies* 11 (Autumn 1971):3–12.

Paul, Robert. "Joseph Smith and the Plurality of Worlds Idea." *Dialogue* 19 (Summer 1986):13–36.

HOLLIS R. JOHNSON

WORSHIP

Latter-day Saint worship is defined as coming unto the Father in the name of Jesus Christ, in spirit and truth (D&C 93:19; cf. JST John 4:24). All of life may be worshipful, as manifest in prayer and in devotion, in the ordinances of the gospel, including the sacrament, in selfless service to mankind, and in the culmination of all worship in the temples of God.

The Lord spoke to the Prophet Joseph SMITH, "I give unto you these sayings that you may understand and know how to worship, and know what you worship, that you may come unto the Father in my name, and in due time receive of his fulness" (D&C 93:19). Worship is idolatry unless it is reverent homage and devotion to the living God.

A modern revelation warns against the worship of false gods: "They seek not the Lord to establish his righteousness, but every man walketh in his own way, and after the image of his own God, whose image is in the likeness of the world, and whose substance is that of an idol" (D&C 1:16). Modern prophets have counseled Latter-day Saints against the worship of idols under new names: success, money, prestige, lavish pleasure, fashion (see Kimball, p. 4).

Much traditional religion assumes that only if God is "utterly other," that is, mysterious and unknowable, can he be properly reverenced. For Latter-day Saints, the foundation of worship is not the radical contrast but the intimate kinship of the Father and his children. Christ was near unto God because he was "the brightness of his glory and the express image of his person" (Heb. 1:2). By keeping his commandments and walking in the way of his ordinances, every person walks in the path of the Master. In inspired worship, "truth embraceth truth; virtue loveth virtue; light cleaveth unto light; mercy hath compassion on mercy" (D&C 88:40). The outcome for Christ was that he could pray, "as thou, Father, art in Me, and I in thee" (John 17:21). Beyond this, worship cannot reach.

The restoration of Christ's Church began with the lament from on high, "They draw near to me with their lips but their hearts are far from me" (JS—H 1:19). Worship involves the heart and the whole of man. Unified worship—which occurs when those assembled are of one heart and one mind and are "agreed as touching all things whatsoever ye ask of me" (D&C 27:18)—prevails with the heavens. "By union of feeling, we obtain power with God" (Relief Society Minutes, June 9, 1842, Church Archives; cf. *TPJS*, P. 91).

Worship also involves the mind. "Love the Lord thy God with all thy . . . mind" (Matt. 22:37). The living God has a "fulness of truth," is "glorified in truth and knoweth all things," and is "more intelligent than they all" (D&C 93; Abr. 2, 3). As Elder B. H. Roberts wrote, worship is the soul's surrender to God: "This submission of the mind to the Most Intelligent, Wisest—wiser than all—is worship" (*TPJS*, p. 353, n). Thus, daily prayer and study, penetrating, pondering study of the gospel and the scriptures, are commended to all Latter-day Saints. "It is not wisdom," said Joseph Smith, "that we should have all knowledge at once presented before us; but that we should have a little at a time; then we can comprehend it" (*TPJS*, p. 297). Jacob Neusner has compared this linkage of worship with the mind to Jewish study-worship of the Torah (Neusner, p. 55). Such communion with God leads one through and beyond the written and the spoken word to the source of Light.

WORSHIP AND SERVICE. For Latter-day Saints, the life of consecrated labor surpasses the life of withdrawal. Thus, although proper worship may require fasting, self-denial, discipline, and sacrifice, the religious life is in the context of the natural and social life. Daily labor is the fulcrum of religion and the locus of holiness. One may bring the spirit of worship to every aspect of life and community life, of which the dedicated family is the apex and paradigm. Nothing is so menial, so servile, so trivial that it is irreligious, as long as it is the way of duty and as long as it is done "in the name of the Son." "Thou shalt love the Lord thy God with all thy heart, with all thy might, mind, and strength; and in the name of Jesus Christ thou shalt serve him" (D&C 59:5).

WORSHIP AND THE TEMPLE. The Hebrew verb *la-avodh*, "to worship," also means "to work" and "to serve" and is associated with the temple. Early in Church history, "the house [Kirtland Temple] was constructed to suit and accommodate the different orders of priesthood and *worship peculiar to the Church*" (John Corrill, *A Brief History of the Church of Christ of Latter Day Saints*, 1839, p. 22, italics added), and it has been so with all LDS temples since. The Spirit of the Lord and the descent of his glory are promised the Saints in the House of the Lord, which is defined as a "house of fasting and a house of prayer" and a "house of worship" (D&C 88:119; *HC* 4:205). Anciently, the temple was the locus of feast and provided the joy of sacred place (Hebrew *simha makom*). An Aramaic link of the Hebrew word for joy (*hdw*) connotes both inner and outer joy and relates to temple service. Today, in LDS spiritual life, the temple is a place of the most "solemn assemblies" and the administration of ordinances on behalf of the living and the dead. Within the precincts of the temple, one experiences this shared joy in its most complete form. In Judaism after the destruction of the temple in Jerusalem in A.D. 70, the home became the surrogate temple, the table an altar, and the study of the Torah, especially on Shabbat, the focus of worship and rejoicing. Worship was centered in prayer and sacrificial service. In Christendom the sacraments and private devotion were thought to replace the temple. In the LDS experience, all these forms of worship are regained, renewed, and confirmed in the temples (*see* TEMPLES: TEMPLE WORSHIP AND ACTIVITY).

In their modern history, Latter-day Saints have worshiped in sobriety and solemnity as well as with rejoicing and gladness. And they have also worshiped in the midst of affliction. Modern revelation commends worship "with a glad heart and a cheerful countenance," especially in the midst of "fasting and prayer," which is defined as "rejoicing and prayer" (D&C 59:14). Thus, on the eve of their exile from Nauvoo, the Saints assembled in the Nauvoo Temple and prayed, feasted, sang, and danced in rejoicing. They crossed the river in the dead of winter, but still were admonished, "If thou art merry, praise the Lord with singing, with music, with dancing, and with a prayer of praise and thanksgiving. If thou art sorrowful, call on the Lord thy God with supplication, that your souls may be joyful" (D&C 136:28–29). They were not too exhausted after the day's travel to build a fire and share songs of the heart, testimonies, and spiritual gifts. In the same spirit, a century and a half later, amidst the Teton Dam disaster (1975), the Latter-day Saints were counseled by their leaders to end each day by bringing out the violins and rejoicing, acknowledging the hand of the Lord in all things (*Ensign* 6 [Oct. 1976]:95; cf. D&C 59:21).

"The song of the righteous is a prayer unto me, and it shall be answered with a blessing upon their heads" (D&C 25:12). In the last days, it has been prophesied, "all shall know me who remain, even from the least unto the greatest, and shall be filled with the knowledge of the Lord, and shall see eye to eye, and shall lift up their voice, and with the voice together sing this new song, saying:

The Lord hath brought again Zion;
The Lord hath redeemed his people, Israel,
According to the election of grace,
Which was brought to pass by the faith
And covenant of their fathers.
The Lord hath redeemed his people;
And Satan is bound and time is no longer.
The Lord hath gathered all things in one.
The Lord hath brought down Zion from above.
The Lord hath brought up Zion from beneath.
The earth hath travailed and brought forth her strength;
And truth is established in her bowels;
And the heavens have smiled upon her;
And she is clothed with the glory of her God;
For he stands in the midst of his people.
Glory, and honor, and power, and might,
Be ascribed to our God; for he is full of mercy,
Justice, grace and truth, and peace,
Forever and ever, Amen [D&C 84:98–102].

When Zion is finally established in the last days, "all who build thereon are to worship the true and living God" (*TPJS*, p. 80). Each year people from many lands will come up to worship at the Feast of Tabernacles in Jerusalem. Eventually, "all nations whom thou hast made shall come and worship before thee, O Lord; and shall glorify thy name" (Ps. 86:9).

BIBLIOGRAPHY

Hatch, Verena U. *Worship in the Church of Jesus Christ of Latter-day Saints.* Provo, Utah, 1968.

Heidenreich, John. "An Analysis of the Theory and Practice of Worship in The Church of Jesus Christ of Latter-day Saints." Master's thesis, Brigham Young University, 1963.

Kimball, Spencer W. "The False Gods We Worship." *Ensign* 6 (June 1976):3–6.

Neusner, Jacob. *The Glory of God Is Intelligence.* Salt Lake City, 1978.

JOHANN A. WONDRA

WRATH OF GOD

The "wrath of God" is a term usually indicating his disapproval of the deeds of the wicked and justifying the inevitable punishments that will befall them if they do not repent. Latter-day Saints believe that his response is a natural application of the law of justice (Mosiah 3:26), which requires that punishments be exacted when God's laws have been violated or the blood of innocent Saints has been shed (Morm. 8:21–41; D&C 77:8). The scriptures state that God sends cursings, judgments, and destruction upon the unbelieving and the rebellious, including all who reject the Savior or his prophets and are not willing to confess his hand in all things (D&C 1:6–13; 59:21; 63:6; 88:85; 104:8; 124:48, 52; Moses 7:1). The scriptures assert that those who attempt to destroy the righteous can expect to give an account to an offended God (1 Ne. 22:16). The Lord has sometimes chastened his disobedient children through war, plague, famine, and earthquake (1 Ne. 14:15–16; D&C 63:33; 87:1–6; 112:24–26). Not all natural calamities, however, are the direct result of the wrath of God, although the scriptures clearly indicate that God has used these for his purposes.

God's wrath may come upon individuals or nations or civilizations when they have "ripened in iniquity" (Gen. 15:16; Deut. 9:4–5; 1 Ne. 17:35; Ether 2:9). His wrath manifests itself most completely when a majority of the people desire that which is contrary to the laws of God and have already chosen iniquity for themselves (Mosiah 29:25–27). The people of NOAH's day (Gen. 6–8), the people of Ammonihah (Alma 16:9–11), the JAREDITES (Ether 14–15), the NEPHITES (3 Ne. 8–9; Morm. 6), and, to a small degree, the Latter-day Saints in Missouri (D&C 105:2–9; 124:48) all experienced God's wrath in their time (see *MD*, p. 771).

The severest form of punishment will be dealt to the SONS OF PERDITION, who are known as "vessels of wrath" (D&C 76:33). These will suffer God's rejection and exclusion throughout eternity (D&C 76:31–37), for they have committed an UNPARDONABLE SIN against the light and knowledge obtained through the HOLY GHOST.

While the Lord may chasten his people in mortality, chastisement will be tempered with his mercy and compassion as his children heed and obey him (D&C 101:2–9; 3 Ne. 22:8–10). Those who escape the wrath of God will include all persons who repent and keep the commandments, and prepare themselves for the hour of judgment that is to come, gathering "together upon the land of Zion, and upon her stakes" as a place of refuge (D&C 115:6; cf. Alma 12:33–37; 13:30; D&C 88:76–88; 98:22). Even God's wrath is intended to be beneficent, for whom he loves, he chastens (D&C 95:1; cf. Heb. 12:6–11; *see also* CHASTENING).

BIBLIOGRAPHY

McConkie, Bruce R. *The Millennial Messiah*, pp. 500–505. Salt Lake City, 1982.

DONALD B. GILCHRIST

WYOMING, PIONEER SETTLEMENTS IN

Beginning in 1855, LDS settlements were located in western Wyoming on the eastern approach to Utah. Fort Bridger was purchased and Fort Supply was founded in part to control the Oregon-California Trail entrance into the Great Basin. The MORMON PIONEER TRAIL crossed the breadth of Wyoming from Fort Laramie on the east to Fort Bridger on the west. Across Wyoming the Oregon, California, and Mormon trails were one and the same, with the exception of Sublette's Cutoff, until they reached Fort Bridger, where the Mormon Trail turned southwest along the Hastings Cutoff.

Fort Bridger, near present-day Evanston, was founded in 1843 by mountainmen Jim Bridger and Louis Vasquez. Brigham Young and the original pioneers of 1847 stopped there en route to the Salt Lake Valley, and in 1855 the Church purchased the fort from Vasquez. Church leaders desired it as a supply station for the thousands of converts coming into the Great Basin and, because of its strategic location, as a base for missionary work among the Indians. When the men sent to occupy Fort Bridger encountered armed mountain men who refused to vacate, they established Fort Supply twelve miles to the southwest. Eventually Latter-day Saints took possession of Fort Bridger, but with the approach of the UTAH EXPEDITION in 1857, they abandoned and destroyed both forts.

Individual LDS families began to resettle in the vicinity of Fort Bridger beginning in 1890, and a branch of the Church was organized there in 1894, eventually becoming headquarters for a stake.

LDS settlements were also established in western Wyoming's Star Valley (1879) and in north central Wyoming's Big Horn basin (1893, 1900). The latter was one of the last colonizing efforts conducted under official Church auspices (*see* COLONIZATION).

Prayer Rock, by LDS western artist Harold I. Hopkinson (1982, oil on canvas, 40″ × 36″), in the LDS Visitors Center, Cody, Wyoming. In 1900 thirty-five families were called by President Lorenzo Snow to settle in northern Wyoming. A large rock blocked their effort to dig the Sidon irrigation canal. Following a prophetic prediction, prayer, and a poignant instruction to move men and horses out of the way, the rock split cleanly from top to bottom.

BIBLIOGRAPHY

Campbell, Eugene E. "Brigham Young's Outer Cordon: A Reappraisal." *Utah Historical Quarterly* 41 (Summer 1973):221–53.

Gowans, Fred R., and Eugene E. Campbell. *Fort Bridger: Island in the Wilderness*. Provo, Utah, 1975.

———. *Fort Supply: Brigham Young's Green River Experiment*. Provo, Utah, 1976.

TED J. WARNER

Y

YOUNG, BRIGHAM

[*This entry consists of two articles:*

    Brigham Young

    Teachings of Brigham Young

Brigham Young is a biography of the famed pioneer leader and second President of the Church; Teachings of Brigham Young *provides a glimpse of the variety and significance of his teachings as preserved in his discourses. The overviews* History of the Church: c. 1831–1844 *and* c. 1844–1877 *review LDS history during Brigham Young's lifetime and the period of his presidency. He was a central figure in the subjects dealt with in* Westward Migration; Pioneers; Immigration and Emigration; *and* Colonization.]

BRIGHAM YOUNG

Colonizer, territorial governor, and President of The Church of Jesus Christ of Latter-day Saints, Brigham Young (1801–1877) was born in Whitingham, Vermont, on June 1, 1801, the ninth of eleven children born to John Young and Abigail (Nabby) Howe. Following service in the Revolutionary Army of George Washington, John Young settled on a farm in Hopkinton, Massachusetts. After sixteen years in Hopkinton, John and Nabby moved to southern Vermont, where Brigham was born. When Brigham was three the family moved to central New York state, and when he was ten, to Sherburne, in south-central New York. Brigham helped clear land for farming, trapped for fur animals, fished, built sheds and dug cellars, and helped with planting, cultivating, and harvesting crops. He also cared for his mother, who was seriously ill with tuberculosis.

Brigham's mother died in 1815, when he was fourteen. Not long after, in search for someone to look after his younger children, John Young married a widow, Hannah Brown, who brought her own children into the family. Brigham decided to leave home. Living for a period with a sister, he became an apprentice carpenter, painter, and glazier in nearby Auburn. Over the next five years he assisted in building in Auburn the first marketplace, the prison, the theological seminary, and the home of "Squire" William Brown (later occupied by William H. Seward, who served as governor of New York and Lincoln's secretary of state). As a master carpenter, Brigham built door fittings and louvered attic windows, and carved ornate mantelpieces for many homes. Many old homes in the region to this day have chairs, desks, staircases, doorways, and mantelpieces made by Brigham Young.

Brigham left Auburn in the spring of 1823 to work in Port Byron, New York, where he repaired furniture and painted canal boats. He developed a device for mixing paints, and turned out many chairs, tables, settees, cupboards, and doors. He also helped organize the local forensic and oratori-

Brigham Young (1801–1877), leader, builder, father, governor, preacher, and colonizer, was the President of the Church for 29 years, longer than any other man. His wisdom was expansive and practical, with a spontaneous power and compelling charisma. Courtesy Utah State Historical Society.

cal society. On October 5, 1824, at the age of twenty-three, Brigham married Miriam Works. They established a home in Aurelius township, where they joined the Methodist Church. Within a year their first child, Elizabeth, was born.

After four years in Port Byron, Brigham and Miriam moved to Oswego, a port on Lake Ontario, where he added to his reputation for good craftsmanship, trustworthiness, and industry. He joined a small group of religious seekers, offering fervent prayers and singing enlivening songs. An Oswego associate testified that his conduct was exemplary, humble, and contrite.

Near the end of 1828 Brigham took his family to Mendon, New York, forty miles from Port Byron, near his father and other relatives. At Mendon, Miriam gave birth to a second daughter, Vilate, but contracted chronic tuberculosis and became a semi-invalid. Brigham prepared the

meals, dressed the children, cleaned the house, and carried Miriam to a rocking chair in front of the fireplace in the morning and back to bed in the evening. In Mendon he built a shop and mill, made and repaired furniture, and put in window-panes, doorways, staircases, and fireplace mantels.

In the spring of 1830 Samuel Smith, brother of Joseph SMITH, passed through Mendon on a trip to distribute the Book of Mormon. He left a copy with Brigham's oldest brother, Phineas, an itinerant preacher. Phineas was favorably impressed with the book and lent it to his father, then to his sister Fanny, who gave it to Brigham. Though impressed, Brigham nevertheless counseled caution: "Wait a little while . . . I [want] to see whether good common sense [is] manifest" (JD 3:91; cf. 8:38). After nearly two years of investigation, Brigham, moved by the testimony of a Mormon elder, was baptized in the spring of 1832. All of Brigham's immediate family were also baptized, and they all remained loyal Latter-day Saints throughout their lives. Miriam, who also joined, lived only until September 1832.

One week after his baptism, Brigham gave his first sermon. He declared "[After I was baptized] I wanted to thunder and roar out the Gospel to the nations. It burned in my bones like fire pent up, so I [commenced] to preach. . . . Nothing would satisfy me but to cry abroad in the world, what the Lord was doing in the latter days" (JD 1:313). Brigham felt the impulse to "cry abroad" so strongly that he enlisted the assistance of Vilate and Heber C. KIMBALL to care for his daughters and abandoned his trade to devote himself wholeheartedly to building the "kingdom of god." That fall, after Miriam's death, he, Heber Kimball, and several relatives traveled to KIRTLAND, OHIO, where he first met the twenty-six-year-old Prophet Joseph Smith. Invited to evening prayer in the Smith home, Brigham was moved by the Spirit and spoke in tongues, the first speaking in tongues witnessed by the Prophet.

Brigham's subsequent missionary tours carried him north, east, west, and south of Mendon. He and his brother Joseph Young made several preaching trips into the New York and Ontario, Canada, countryside. In the summer of 1833 he traveled to Kirtland with several of his Canadian converts, where he heard Joseph Smith teach about the GATHERING, emphasizing that building the kingdom of God required more than just preaching. Thus instructed, Brigham returned to

Brigham Young with his brothers (c. 1870). Left to right, Lorenzo, Brigham, Phineas, Joseph, and John. Photographer: C. R. Savage.

New York and, with the Kimballs, moved his household to Kirtland so he could participate in building a new society.

Among those whom Brigham met in Kirtland was Mary Ann Angell, a native of Seneca, Ontario County, New York, who had worked in a factory in Providence, Rhode Island, until her conversion to the Church and move to Kirtland. Brigham married her on February 18, 1834. She looked after Brigham's two daughters by Miriam and subsequently had six children of her own.

In 1834 Brigham and his brother Joseph served with ZION'S CAMP, a small army that walked from Ohio to Missouri in the summer of 1834 to assist those driven from their homes by hostile mobs. Brigham regarded the difficult trek, which was led by Joseph Smith, as superb education and later called it "the starting point of my knowing how to lead Israel" (Arrington, pp. 45–46).

Dedication and potential, more than accomplishments, qualified Brigham Young to be selected in February 1835 as a member of the Church's original QUORUM OF THE TWELVE APOSTLES. The Twelve were a "traveling high council" charged to take the gospel "to all the nations, kindreds, tongues, and people." They presided not "at home" but "abroad," where no local STAKES were established. This group later became

the leading quorum in the Church after the FIRST PRESIDENCY.

Each summer Brigham undertook proselytizing missions in the East; each winter he cared for his family and helped build up Kirtland. He helped construct the KIRTLAND TEMPLE, attended the SCHOOL OF THE PROPHETS, participated in the Pentecostal outpouring that accompanied the dedication of the Kirtland Temple in the spring of 1836, and engaged in Church-related business activities assigned to him by Joseph Smith. When the Kirtland community became divided over Joseph Smith's leadership, Brigham Young's strong defense of the Prophet so enraged the critics that Brigham had to flee Kirtland for his safety.

By the summer of 1838 most of the Kirtland faithful, including Brigham and his family, had moved to Caldwell County, in northern Missouri. Growing numbers of Latter-day Saint arrivals rekindled antagonisms with old settlers, and violence erupted (see MISSOURI CONFLICT). Disarmed, violated, and robbed of most of their holdings, the Latter-day Saints were driven from the state. With Joseph Smith, his brother Hyrum, Sidney RIGDON, and other Church leaders imprisoned, Brigham Young, senior member of the Quorum of the Twelve, directed the evacuation of the Saints to Quincy and other Illinois communities. To ensure that members without teams and wagons would not be left behind, he drew up the Missouri Covenant. All who signed it agreed to make their resources available to remove every person to safety.

In the spring of 1839 Joseph Smith designated Commerce (renamed NAUVOO), Illinois, the new central gathering place of the Saints. Brigham's family were hardly settled in the area when he and other members of the Twelve left to fulfill their calls to Great Britain as missionaries. Despite poverty and poor health all around, Brigham left his wife and children in September, determined to go to England or to die trying. He and his companions finally docked at Liverpool in April 1840 (*see* MISSIONS OF THE TWELVE TO THE BRITISH ISLES).

As quorum president, Brigham directed the work of his quorum in Britain during an astonishing year in which they baptized between 7,000 and 8,000 converts; printed and distributed 5,000 copies of the Book of Mormon, 3,000 hymn books, 1,500 volumes of the MILLENNIAL STAR, and 50,000 tracts; and established a shipping agency and assisted nearly 1,000 to emigrate to Nauvoo. Brigham traveled to the principal cities in England and took time to visit Buckingham Palace, St. Paul's Cathedral, Westminster Abbey, the Lake district, factory towns, the Potteries, museums, art galleries, and, of course, the homes of converts, both rich and poor. In later years he often commented on what he had seen and learned in England.

Such striking success, the first such experience of a united quorum, prepared the Twelve for additional responsibilities. Back in Nauvoo, Brigham was given the assignment of directing the Twelve in their supervision of missionary work, the purchase of lands and settling of immigrants, and various construction projects. Along with others, Brigham was also taught the principle of PLURAL MARRIAGE; he accepted it after much reluctance and considerable thought and prayer. With Mary Ann's consent, he married Lucy Ann Decker Seeley in June 1842, and later other plural wives. He was among the first to receive the full temple ENDOWMENT in 1842 and, later, with Mary Ann, participated with others who had received temple ordinances in sessions during which Joseph Smith gave additional instructions on gospel principles.

Because Brigham Young was now the president of the quorum, which came second only to the First Presidency in authority and responsibility, he was highly prominent and influential in Nauvoo. Nonetheless, though he helped direct everything from the construction of the NAUVOO TEMPLE to missionary work abroad, he also continued the pattern established in Kirtland of personally undertaking preaching missions each summer. In February Joseph Smith further instructed Brigham Young and others of his quorum about a future move to the Rocky Mountains. In March 1844 Brigham participated in the creation of the COUNCIL OF FIFTY—an organization suggesting a pattern of government for a future theocratic society and the last such organizational pattern left by Joseph Smith. Soon after, as if in foreboding of his impending death, Joseph Smith gave Brigham and other members of the Twelve a dramatic charge to "bear off this kingdom," telling them that they now had all the keys and instruction needed to do so successfully (*CR* [Apr. 1898]:89; *MS* 5 [Mar. 1845]:151).

In May 1844, Brigham and other apostles left on summer missions. While they were gone, events in Nauvoo deteriorated. Joseph Smith was arrested and, on June 27, was killed with his brother Hyrum when a mob stormed the jail where they were being held (*see* CARTHAGE JAIL; MARTYRDOM OF JOSEPH AND HYRUM SMITH). Brigham was in the Boston area and did not hear definite word of the assassination until July 16. He and his companions immediately rushed back to Nauvoo, arriving August 6. After a dramatic confrontation with Sidney RIGDON on August 8, Brigham and the Twelve were sustained to lead the Church (*see* SUCCESSION IN THE PRESIDENCY). Brigham remained the leader until his death in 1877.

Although privately committed to leaving Nauvoo, Brigham and his associates were determined to complete the Nauvoo Temple so that the Saints could receive their temple ordinances. Even as they labored to defend themselves and finish the temple, they held meetings to decide on when and where to move farther west. Soon after violence erupted in September 1845, they publicly announced their intention to leave by the following spring. By December the temple was ready for ordinance work, and by February nearly 6,000 members had received temple blessings therein. The Saints had also spent the fall and winter preparing for the exodus. Committees were appointed, and a Nauvoo Covenant was signed, helping to ensure that those with property would assist those without.

Partly because of concerns about governmental intervention, Brigham Young began the migration in the cold and snow of February 1846 rather than await spring. By hundreds, then by thousands, people, animals, and wagons crossed the Mississippi River and trudged across Iowa mud to a WINTER QUARTERS (now Florence, Nebraska) on the Missouri River. In late spring nearly 16,000 Saints were on the road.

Brigham personally directed this massive odyssey, which involved the allocation of foodstuffs, wagons, oxen, and Church property to organized companies setting out on the trail. The preparation and the move through Iowa took so long that none of the companies could reach the Rocky Mountains that year, as was hoped. This demanding Iowa experience taught Brigham Young valuable lessons about men and organization that he used throughout his years of leadership. He also learned anew that when human resources prove inadequate, one must turn in faith to God. That winter Brigham announced "The Word and Will of the Lord" (D&C 136) to help organize the Saints and prepare them for the westward trek.

Brigham Young set out with an advance group of 143 men, 3 women, and 2 children on April 5, 1847. Delayed by illness, he arrived in the SALT LAKE VALLEY on July 24, a few days behind the advance party. Once he saw the valley with his own eyes, he announced it as the right place for a new headquarters city and confirmed that the region would be the new gathering place. He also identified the exact spot for a temple. He directed the exploration of the region; helped survey and apportion the land for homes, gardens, and farming; named the new settlement "Great Salt Lake City, Great Basin, North America"; held meetings where he appointed John Smith religious leader of the new colony and agreed on basic policies of cooperative work and sharing. On August 26, Brigham joined the return party to Winter Quarters.

In Winter Quarters, in December 1847, Brigham and other members of the Twelve reorganized the First Presidency of the Church, with Brigham as president. The following April he, his family, and approximately 3,500 other Saints headed for the Salt Lake Valley. Brigham's activities in organizing companies, building bridges, repairing equipment, and training oxen developed abilities that would be in evidence the rest of his life.

A series of problems confronted Brigham, now forty-seven, as he established his permanent home in the Salt Lake Valley. The first problem was to provide housing for his family. On a lot adjoining City Creek in what is now the center of SALT LAKE CITY, he built a row of log houses for his wives and children that, collectively, were called Harmony House. To the south of this he later built the White House, a sun-dried adobe structure covered with white plaster. Still later, he built a large, two-story adobe house faced with cement that fronted on what came to be known as Brigham Street (now South Temple Street). Sporting a tower surmounted by a gilded beehive, this building was known as the Beehive House and was Brigham's official residence as governor and President of the Church. In 1856, Brigham added an impressive three-story adobe structure, which came to be called the Lion House from the statue of a crouching lion on the portico. Several of his families lived in this building, just west of the Beehive House. He later built homes in south Salt Lake City, Provo, and St. George. Brigham's homes were all well constructed and finely appointed.

A central public problem was finding places to accommodate the incoming Saints. Salt Lake City was divided into ten-acre blocks, and each family head was allotted by community drawing a one-and-one-fourth-acre lot on one of the blocks in the city. There people would keep their livestock, gar-

Brigham Young's home, the Lion House, in 1858. Known as the "Lion of the Lord," Brigham Young laid out the city of Salt Lake, commenced the construction of the Salt Lake Temple, and oversaw the building of the Salt Lake Tabernacle, other temples, schools, roads, hospitals, theatres, canals, and mills. Photograph by surveyor D. A. Burr.

Brigham Young with pictures of 21 of his wives. Permission from the first wife was sought and approval from the appropriate priesthood leader was required to practice plural marriage. Many had only one or two wives; it was unusual to have more than four. The Manifesto of 1890 officially ended the Church practice of plural marriages. Photograph created 1901, Johnson Co.

dens, and other "home" properties (*see* CITY PLANNING). A ten-acre block just west of Brigham's was designated the Temple Block (*see* TEMPLE SQUARE), and on this were located the Bowery, a temporary shelter built of tree boughs, where the Saints first held religious services; the TABERNACLE; and various shops used in constructing public buildings. Construction of the SALT LAKE TEMPLE was begun in 1853.

Outside the city, five-acre and ten-acre plots were apportioned to those who wanted to farm. Under Brigham Young's direction, cooperative teams were assigned to dig ditches and canals to irrigate crops and to furnish water to homes. Other brigades fenced residential areas, built roads, cut timber, and set up shops. Other groups selected new locations for settlements and helped place people in the best areas. Still others were called on missions to proselytize in the United States, Europe, or the Pacific.

In the spring of 1849 Brigham Young organized Salt Lake City into nineteen WARDS; organized wards in other settlements; set up the state of Deseret with himself as governor; and established the PERPETUAL EMIGRATING FUND as a device for assisting with the emigration of Saints from Great Britain, Scandinavia, and continental Europe.

With thousands of Saints arriving from the eastern United States and Europe, COLONIZATION demanded Brigham Young's attention. Under his direction, four kinds of colonies were established: first, settlements intended to be temporary places of gathering and recruitment, such as Carson Valley in Nevada; second, colonies to serve as centers for production, such as iron at Cedar City, cotton at St. George, cattle in Cache Valley, and sheep in Spanish Fork, all in Utah; third, colonies to serve as centers for proselytizing and assisting Indians, as at Harmony in southern Utah, Las Vegas in southern Nevada, Lemhi in northern Idaho, and present-day Moab in eastern Utah; fourth, permanent colonies in Utah and nearby states and territories to provide homes and farms for the hundreds of new immigrants arriving each summer. Within ten years, nearly 100 colonies had been planted; by 1867, more than 200; and by the time of his death in 1877, nearly 400 colonies. Clearly, he was one of America's greatest colonizers.

As President of the Church, Brigham conducted regular Sunday services in Salt Lake City and each year visited as many outlying communities as possible. He appointed BISHOPS for each

ward and settlement and encouraged each ward to provide cultural opportunities for its members, such as dances, theater, music recitals, and, above all, schools. He listened to people with complaints, responded to myriad questions about personal and family affairs as well as religion, and dictated thousands of letters with instruction, counsel, friendly advice, and casual comment about Church and national affairs. He was a firm Latter-day Saint and a wise counselor.

Brigham gave some 500 sermons in pioneer Utah that were recorded word for word by a stenographer. These, all delivered without a prepared text, may have seemed rambling in organization, but they were well thought out and suggest remarkable mental power. They were well adapted to his audiences. His discourses were like "fireside chats," an informal "talking things over" with his audiences. Interweaving subjects as diverse as women's fashions, the atonement of Christ, recollections of Joseph Smith, and how to make good bread, Brigham kept his audiences enthralled,

President George Albert Smith greets guests at the unveiling of Brigham Young's statue by Mahonri M. Young in the National Statuary Hall in Capitol Building, Washington, D.C. (1950). Brigham Young is recognized as one of the great Americans of the nineteenth century.

amused, and in tears, sometimes for hours. He inspired, motivated, taught, and encouraged.

The Latter-day Saints had settled among various tribes of NATIVE AMERICANS. Intent upon helping them, converting them, and avoiding bloodshed, Brigham established Indian farms, took Indians into his own home, advocated a policy of "feeding them is cheaper than fighting them," and held periodic meetings with chiefs. His policies were not always successful, but he consistently sought peaceful solutions and firmly opposed the all-too-common frontier practice of shooting Indians for petty causes.

In 1851, Brigham was appointed governor and superintendent of Indian Affairs of UTAH TERRITORY by U.S. President Millard Fillmore. His principal problem as governor was dealing with the "outside" federal appointees, many of whom were, from any point of view, both unsympathetic to the Church and inexcusably incompetent. There were problems over the small federal expenditures, the failure of Saints to use federal judges in cases of civil disputes, the lack of tact of the federally appointed officials in discussing the Church, their opposition to the union of church and state, and their assumption that Latter-day Saints were immoral because of their tolerance of plural marriage. [For other events that occupied Brigham Young's attention in 1856 see HANDCART COMPANIES; REFORMATION (LDS) OF 1856–1857.]

This continuing controversy eventually led to the decision of U.S. President James Buchanan in 1857 to replace Brigham Young with an "outside" governor, Alfred Cumming of Georgia. At the same time, President Buchanan, who had been (wrongly) informed that the Mormons were "in a state of substantial rebellion against the laws and authority of the United States," sent a major portion of the U.S. Army to Utah to install the new governor and to ensure the execution of U.S. laws (see UTAH EXPEDITION). Though Governor Young was not notified of this action, armed forces were observed secretly heading for Utah. Fearful of a repetition of the "mobocracy" of Missouri and Illinois, he called people home from outlying colonies and mobilized the Saints to defend their homes. Eventually, with the assistance of Thomas L. KANE, he arranged a peaceful settlement whereby the Army occupied Camp Floyd, a post some forty miles from Salt Lake City. The U.S. Army was an irritant, but not a hindrance, to continued Church expansion and development. President Young

remained, as his colleagues boasted, governor of the people, while his replacements merely governed the territory. The Army left Utah in 1861 with the start of the Civil War.

A believer in adapting the newest technology to the advantage of LDS society, Brigham Young contracted in 1861 to build the transcontinental telegraph line from Nebraska to California, and then proceeded to erect the 1,200-mile Deseret Telegraph line from Franklin, Idaho, to northern Arizona. This connected nearly all Mormon villages with Salt Lake City and, through that connection, with the world. While the transcontinental railroad was under construction, he negotiated for contracts with Union Pacific and Central Pacific for LDS contractors to build the roadbeds east of Salt Lake City into part of Wyoming and west well into Nevada. He then organized the Utah Central, Utah Southern, and Utah Northern railroads to extend the line south from Ogden to Frisco in southern Utah and north to Franklin, Idaho, and eventually to Montana.

Aware that the completion of the railroad would imperil the independent social economy of his people, President Young inaugurated a protective movement that sought to preserve, as much as possible, their unique way of life. He organized cooperatives to handle local merchandising and manufacturing; initiated several new enterprises to develop local resources; promoted RELIEF SOCIETIES in each ward in order to provide opportunities for self-development, socialization, and COMPASSIONATE SERVICE for women; opened the doors of the UNIVERSITY OF DESERET (later the University of Utah) for both young men and women; encouraged women to become professionally trained, especially in medicine; and gave women the vote. In 1875 he established Brigham Young Academy (later BRIGHAM YOUNG UNIVERSITY), in 1877 Brigham Young College (Logan, Utah) and the Latter-day Saints College (see LDS BUSINESS COLLEGE). In 1874 he also promoted the UNITED ORDER movement in an effort to encourage cooperation and home production and consumption (see ECONOMIC HISTORY OF THE CHURCH).

Brigham Young remained vigorous until his death in August 1877. Just before his death, he dedicated the St. George Temple and launched there the full scope of LDS temple ordinances, something he had anticipated since Nauvoo; and he overhauled Church organization at every level, formalizing for the first time practices that would characterize the Church for nearly a century.

Brigham was a well-built, stout (in later years, portly) man of five feet, ten inches, somewhat taller than average for his day. His light brown hair, often described as "sandy," had very little gray. Visitors noticed his penetrating blue-gray eyes lined by thin eyebrows. Though he later wore a full beard, Brigham was clean-shaven until the 1850s, when he first sported chin whiskers. His mouth and chin were firm, bespeaking, visitors thought, his iron will. He was generally composed and quiet in manner, but he could thunder at the pulpit. Sometimes called the "Lion of the Lord," he could also roar when aroused.

Brigham Young's manner was pleasant and courteous. His dress, generally neat and plain, was often homespun. He combined vibrant energy and self-certainty with deference to the feelings of others and a complete lack of pretension. By the time of his death, Brigham Young had married twenty women, sixteen of whom bore him fifty-seven children. He died on August 29, 1877, of peritonitis, the result of a ruptured appendix.

Brigham's most obvious achievements were the product of his lifelong talent for practical decision making. He instituted patterns of Church government that persist to this day. In leading the Saints across Iowa, he issued detailed instructions that were followed by the hundreds of companies that crossed the plains to the Salt Lake Valley in succeeding years. In the Great Basin he directed the organization of several hundred LDS settlements; set up several hundred cooperative retail, wholesale, and manufacturing enterprises; and initiated the construction of meetinghouses, tabernacles, and temples. While doing all this, he carried on a running battle with the United States government to preserve the unique LDS way of life.

But for Brigham Young these were means, not ends. His overriding concern was to build on the foundation begun by Joseph Smith to establish a commonwealth in the desert where his people could live the gospel of Jesus Christ in peace, thereby improving their prospects in this life and in the next. He loved the Great Basin because its harshness and isolation made it an ideal place to "make Saints."

BIBLIOGRAPHY

Arrington, Leonard J. *Brigham Young: American Moses.* New York, 1985.

Bringhurst, Newell G. *Brigham Young and the Expanding American Frontier.* Boston, 1986.

Palmer, Richard F., and Karl D. Butler. *Brigham Young: The New York Years.* Provo, Utah, 1982.

Walker, Ronald W., and Ronald K. Esplin. "Brigham Himself: An Autobiographical Recollection." *Journal of Mormon History* 4 (1977):19–34.

LEONARD J. ARRINGTON

TEACHINGS OF BRIGHAM YOUNG

In leading the Latter-day Saints for over thirty years, Brigham Young wrote comparatively little, except for his letters, but he spoke frequently and on numerous subjects. He was constantly obliged to speak ex cathedra on many topics relative to life in this world and the next. His discourses were vigorous and forthright, filled with candid realism and common sense, and many of his speeches were recorded in shorthand by scribes. Along with his practical attainments and mechanical skills, he was one of the most discursive and lucid of men. Here was a man tested by fire (e.g., he was actually driven from his home five times) and who knew all the trials of life, from the corridors of power to the roughest frontiers. He sometimes made statements that surprised or even offended those who tended to accept his every utterance as doctrine, but with a New Englander's passion for teaching and learning, he plunged ahead.

All the commentators concede that Brigham Young was one of the ablest and most dynamic leaders in American history. He was one of the supremely practical men of his age, a hardheaded, even-keeled, no-nonsense realist who got things done. But, for him, all of that was incidental. The important thing was that the people should know what they were doing and why. His orders and recommendations came with full and persuasive explanations.

His teachings begin with faith in Jesus Christ: "My faith is placed upon the Lord Jesus Christ, and my knowledge I have received from him" (*JD* 3:155). "Jesus is our captain and leader; Jesus, the Savior of the world—the Christ we believe in" (*JD* 14:118). "Our faith is placed upon the son of God, and through him in the Father, and the Holy Ghost is their minister to bring truths to our remembrance" (*JD* 6:98).

Brigham Young gained much of his knowledge of Jesus Christ through his constant association with the Prophet Joseph SMITH: "What I have re-

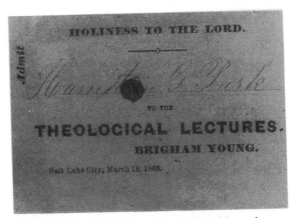

Brigham Young was a popular and forceful speaker on many practical and inspiring subjects. This nontransferable ecclesiastical ticket admitted the holder to one of Brigham Young's lectures in the School of the Prophets, Salt Lake City, 1868. Courtesy Rare Books and Manuscripts, Brigham Young University.

ceived from the Lord, I have received by Joseph Smith" (*JD* 6:279). To the end of his life, Young testified of the mission of Joseph Smith in restoring knowledge of Christ to earth. "I love his doctrine," he said. "I feel like shouting Hallelujah, all the time, when I think that I ever knew Joseph Smith, the Prophet whom the Lord raised up and ordained" (*JD* 13:216; 3:51). His dying words were "Joseph, Joseph, Joseph."

On this foundation, Brigham Young emphatically taught the law of eternal progression. This life is a part of eternity. Eternal knowledge and glory are to be obtained and promoted on this earth. Improvement, learning, training, building, and expanding are the joy of life: "We do not expect to cease learning while we live on earth; and when we pass through the veil, we expect still to continue to learn" (*JD* 6:286). And eternal progression leads to GODHOOD: "The faithful will become gods, even the sons of God" (*JD* 6:275).

Brigham Young recognized that many people were not prepared to understand the mysteries of God and godhood. "I could tell you much more about this," he said, speaking of the role of ADAM, but checked himself, recognizing that the world would probably misinterpret his teaching (*JD* 1:51).

All of the descendants of Adam (men, women, and children) must work. "What is this work?" Brigham asks. "The improvement of the condition of the human family. This work must continue

until the people who live on this earth are prepared to receive our coming Lord" (*JD* 19:46).

For Brigham, improvement meant "to build in strength and stability, to beautify, to adorn, to embellish, to delight, and to cast fragrance over the House of the Lord; with sweet instruments of music and melody" (*MS* 10:86). More specifically, the one way man can leave his mark on the face of nature without damage is to plant. President Young ceaselessly counseled his people to do as Adam was commanded to do in the Garden of Eden when he dressed and tended the garden: Our work is "to beautify the face of the earth, until it shall become like the Garden of Eden" (*JD* 1:345).

In caring for the world, "every accomplishment, every polished grace, every useful attainment in mathematics, music, and in all science and art belongs to the Saints, and they should avail themselves as expeditiously as possible of the wealth of knowledge the sciences offer to every diligent and persevering scholar, and that's our duty. . . . It is the duty of the Latter-day Saints, according to the revelation, to give their children the best education that can be procured, both from the books of the world and the revelations of the Lord" (*JD* 10:224). "If an elder shall give a lecture on astronomy, chemistry, or geology, our religion embraces it all. It matters not what the subject be if it tends to improve the mind, exalt the feelings, and enlarge the capacity. The truth that is in all the arts and sciences forms part of our religion" (*JD* 2:93–94).

President Young's fascination with the things of the mind extended to mundane experience. The enjoyment of the senses, he said, is one of our notable privileges upon the earth and a wonderful source of enjoyment.

Although Brigham Young's destiny led him to the desert barrenness of the West, he sensed a spiritual beauty in that land. "You are here commencing anew," he told the people. "The soil, the air, the water are all pure and healthy. Do not suffer them to become polluted with wickedness. Strive to preserve the elements from being contaminated by the filthy wicked conduct of those who pervert the intelligence God has bestowed upon the human family" (*JD* 8:79). For Brigham, moral and physical cleanliness and pollution are no more to be separated than mind and body: "Keep your valley pure, keep our towns as pure as you possibly can, keep your hearts pure, and labor what you can consistently, but not so as to injure yourselves" (*JD* 8:80).

Brigham Young also had a Yankee passion for thrift, but it rested on a generous respect for the worth of material things, not on a mean desire simply to possess them. When he said, "I do not know that during thirty years past, I have worn a coat, hat, or garment of any kind, or owned a horse, carriage, &c, but what I have asked the Lord whether I deserved it or not—Shall I wear this? Is it mine to use or not?" (*JD* 8:343), he was expressing the highest degree of human concern and responsibility.

Brigham Young often spoke of ZION and of building up the kingdom of God. He used the name Zion to describe the intended state of affairs and constantly had Zion in his view: "There is not one thing wanting in all the works of God's hands to make a Zion upon the earth when the people conclude to make it" (*JD* 9:283). He recognized that the ideal of Zion stood in the face of contemporary economic values: "It is thought by many that the possession of gold and silver will produce for them happiness; . . . in this they are mistaken" (*JD* 11:15). "If, by industrious habits and honorable dealings, you obtain thousands or millions of dollars, little or much, it is your duty to use all that is put in your possession, as judiciously as you have knowledge, to build up the Kingdom of God on the earth" (*JD* 4:29).

Zion was to be established on the basis of co-operation: "The doctrine of uniting together in our temporal labors, and all working for the good of all is from the beginning, from everlasting, and it will be for ever and ever" (*JD* 17:117). In this there was no room for debate or contention, least of all rancor: "Cast all bitterness out of your own hearts—all anger, wrath, strife, covetousness, and lust, and sanctify the Lord God in your hearts, that you may enjoy the Holy Ghost" (*JD* 8:33).

The contrast between light and darkness was vivid to President Young: "Whence comes evil? It comes when we make an evil of good. Speaking of the elements in the creation of God, their nature is as pure as the heavens, and we destroy it. I wish you to understand that sin is not an attribute in the nature of man, but is an inversion of the attributes God has placed in him" (*JD* 10:251). He recognizes a conscious, active agent in the spreading of evil: "Satan never owned the earth; he never made a particle of it; his labor is not to create, but to destroy" (*JD* 10:320).

The true stature of Brigham Young emerges if one seeks to compose a list of his peers. He led a ragged and impoverished band, stripped of virtually all their earthly goods, into an unknown territory. His critics and biographers note that the man was unique among the leaders of modern history, for he alone, without any political and financial backing, established from scratch in the desert an ordered and industrious society, having no other authority than the priesthood and the spiritual strength with which he delivered his teachings. By constant exhortations and instructions, he drew his people together and inspired them in carrying out the divine mandate to build up the kingdom of God on earth.

BIBLIOGRAPHY

The *Journal of Discourses* contains more than 350 of Brigham Young's speeches. For a selection of passages organized topically, see John A. Widtsoe, comp., *Discourses of Brigham Young*, Salt Lake City, 1954.

Melville, J. Keith. "The Reflections of Brigham Young on the Nature of Man and the State." *BYU Studies* 4 (1962):255–67.

———. "Brigham Young's Ideal Society: The Kingdom of God." *BYU Studies* 5 (1962):3–18.

Nibley, Hugh W. "Educating the Saints—A Brigham Young Mosaic." *BYU Studies* 11 (Autumn 1970):61–87.

———. "Brigham Young on the Environment." In *To the Glory of God*, ed. T. Madsen and C. Tate, pp. 3–29. Salt Lake City, 1972.

Walker, Ronald W. "Brigham Young on the Social Order." *BYU Studies* 28 (Summer 1988):37–52.

HUGH W. NIBLEY

YOUNG, ZINA D. H.

Zina Diantha Huntington Young (1821–1901), third general president of the RELIEF SOCIETY, possessed great faith and compassion. Sometimes called "the heart of the women's work in Utah" (Susa Young Gates, *History of the Young Ladies' Mutual Improvement Association* [Salt Lake City, 1911], p. 21), "Aunt Zina" led the Relief Society from 1888 to 1901.

Born January 31, 1821, in Watertown, New York, Zina Diantha was the eighth of William and Zina Baker Huntington's ten children. Her father served in the War of 1812, and his father, William Huntington, Sr., in the Revolutionary War. Zina's great-great-uncle, Samuel Huntington, was a signer of the Declaration of Independence.

Zina Diantha Huntington Young (1821–1901) was the third general president of the Relief Society (1888–1901). A plural wife of Brigham Young, she became known for her medical skills. Photographed with her sons, Zebulon William Jacobs and Henry Chariton Jacobs and her daughter, Zina Presendia Young. Courtesy Rare Books and Manuscripts, Brigham Young University.

Zina spent her childhood on the family farm learning the skills taught girls of that time—spinning, weaving, soap making, candle dipping, and other household skills. She attended school intermittently and acquired a basic education.

When Zina was fourteen, LDS missionaries, including Hyrum SMITH and David WHITMER, visited the Huntington home in Watertown. The family listened, prayed, and believed, and all but the oldest son, Chauncey (Chancy), joined the Church.

Zina was a spiritually sensitive young woman. She later wrote that soon after her conversion, "the gift of tongues rested upon me with overwhelming force." Somewhat awed, she endeavored to repeat the experience but discovered that the gift had left her, and she feared she had offended the Holy Spirit. "One day while mother and I were spinning together, I took courage and told her of the gift . . . and how . . . I had lost it entirely. Mother appreciated my feelings, and told me to make it a matter of earnest prayer, that the gift might once more be given to me" (Young, pp. 318–19). Zina thereafter spoke in or interpreted unknown tongues on many occasions throughout her life (see GIFTS OF THE SPIRIT).

Counseled by Joseph SMITH, Sr., father of the Prophet Joseph SMITH, to unite with the Latter-day Saints in KIRTLAND, OHIO, the Huntingtons sold their home and property in New York and moved to Ohio in October 1836. Their nineteen months in Kirtland were a period of great physical privation but rich spiritual experiences.

In May 1838 the Huntington family joined the Saints' migration to Far West, Missouri, arriving at the height of bitter mob persecution, which resulted in the infamous EXTERMINATION ORDER issued by Missouri governor Lilburn Boggs. Zina's father helped coordinate the Saints' evacuation. The family then settled with other Saints in NAUVOO, Illinois, where Zina's mother died of cholera in July 1839. Joseph and Emma SMITH cared for Zina and others of the sick in their home.

On March 7, 1841, Zina married Henry Bailey Jacobs. She later married Joseph Smith and, after Joseph's death, Brigham YOUNG. She had two sons, Zebulon William and Henry Chariton Jacobs, and one daughter, Zina Presendia (Prescindia, Precindia) Young.

Following the expulsion from Nauvoo, Zina migrated with the Saints to the West. In the 1850s she studied obstetrics and subsequently helped deliver the babies of many women, including those of some of the other plural wives of Brigham Young. At their request, she anointed and blessed many of these sisters prior to their deliveries. Other women in need of physical and emotional comfort also received blessings under her hands.

Zina helped establish DESERET HOSPITAL, built in Salt Lake City in 1872, and served as its vice-president. She also organized a nursing school and instructed in a school for obstetrics.

In 1876 the Deseret Silk Association was organized, and Zina was appointed president by her prophet-husband Brigham Young. She traveled extensively throughout the territory to promote this home industry.

In 1880 the general organization of Relief Society, encompassing all local Relief Societies, was formed. Eliza R. SNOW, the president, selected Zina as her first counselor. They were instrumental in the development of the Relief Society, the Young Ladies' RETRENCHMENT ASSOCIATION, and the Primary Association for children.

In the winter of 1881–1882, the FIRST PRESIDENCY sent Zina to the East to advocate women's suffrage and dispel misinformation about the Church. She attended the Women's Congress in Buffalo and the National Suffrage Association Convention in New York. She also addressed many temperance societies.

Following the death of Eliza R. Snow in 1887, President Wilford WOODRUFF appointed Zina general president of the Relief Society. She continued in that capacity until her death August 28, 1901.

In her later years she wrote of her hope to have accomplished some lasting good: "As the mantle of time is fast draping its folds around many of us [w]hen we go hence to our rest, after our sacrifices may it be . . . that many in the future may have reason to praise God for the noble Women of this generation" (Zina Card Brown family collection). Inscribed on her gravestone is the Relief Society motto: Charity Never Faileth.

BIBLIOGRAPHY

Beecher, Maurine Ursenbach, ed. "'All Things Move in Order in the City': The Nauvoo Diary of Zina Diantha Huntington Jacobs." *BYU Studies* 19 (Spring 1979):285–320.

Young, Zina D. H. "How I Gained My Testimony of the Truth." *Young Woman's Journal* 4 (Apr. 1893):317–19.

Zina Card Brown family collection, LDS Archives.

MARY FIRMAGE WOODWARD

YOUNG MEN

The AARONIC PRIESTHOOD is the basic organization for the young men of the Church, ages twelve through eighteen. The Young Men organization is an auxiliary to the PRIESTHOOD and includes SCOUTING and other programs designed to help with the full development of young male members of the Church, including spiritual, social, and physical aspects. Its purpose is to help each young man come to Christ through conversion to the gospel of Jesus Christ, understand the priesthood he holds, learn to give service to others, prepare to advance to the MELCHIZEDEK PRIESTHOOD, and live in such a way that will qualify him to enter the temple and become a worthy husband and father. Through PRIESTHOOD QUORUM instruction and activities, including combined Young Men and YOUNG WOMEN activities, young men learn fundamental principles and have opportunities to apply them in their lives. The Young Men organization serves hundreds of thousands of young men in

most parts of the world. Its literature is published in many languages and is adapted for use in various cultures.

The organization is under the direction of the BISHOPRIC or branch presidency in wards and BRANCHES, with assistance from a Young Men presidency comprised of adult advisers to the PRIESTS, TEACHERS, and DEACONS quorums or others as the bishop may call. Young Men presidencies also function at the stake and general levels. The Young Men general presidency is comprised of members of the QUORUMS OF SEVENTY and is assisted by a general board to develop programs and materials.

The Young Men groups are the priesthood groups, determined by age. Twelve- and thirteen-year-olds constitute the deacons quorum (Scouts); fourteen- and fifteen-year-olds, the teachers quorum (Venturers); and sixteen- seventeen- and eighteen-year-olds, the priests quorum (Explorers). Each deacons and the teachers quorum is presided over by a three-member presidency. The president from the group is selected by the BISHOP and he then selects his two counselors. The priests quorum is presided over by the bishop, and he selects assistants from the quorum.

Quorums meet individually or collectively, depending on the type of activity and the purpose of their gathering. On Sundays the quorums usually meet separately for lessons on gospel subjects. On one evening during the week, they may meet for activities, such as scouting, sports, service projects, or career education. Occasionally, all three groups meet together to perform service or to enjoy athletic or cultural events, either as participants or spectators. All activities are designed to help the young men become well-rounded and well-prepared individuals with self-confidence, motivation, and a desire to make a significant contribution to their communities.

Once each month, all three age groups meet together with young women from their ward or branch who are organized into similar age-group categories. These joint activities are designed to help young men and young women learn to work together, to respect one another, and to develop social and communication skills that will help them regard one another as individuals. In addition to the traditional activities of dancing and socializing, they solve problems together and overcome stereotypical gender images, while maintaining strong, independent gender identities. Individuality, creativity, teamwork, a sense of belonging, and unity are stressed by adult Young Men and Young Women advisers.

Primarily in the United States, but in several other countries as well, the Young Men organization uses the scouting movement as part of its activity program. Young men register and participate in scouting and embrace its values and principles while adhering to their own religious and moral code. They are encouraged to earn the Eagle Scout Award (or its international equivalent). In Great Britain and in other Commonwealth countries, many young men participate in the Duke of Edinburgh Award Scheme or its equivalent. The Church also encourages young men to earn the LDS Duty to God and On My Honor awards, which are religious service recognitions.

LDS young men participate in a wide range of competitive and noncompetitive athletics as part of their quorum experience. Most Church buildings in the United States, for example, are equipped with facilities for playing basketball, and many have adjoining softball diamonds. In Europe, South America, and parts of Asia, soccer is a major part of the Young Men athletic program. Tennis, swimming, racquetball, squash, handball, golf, volleyball, and other popular sports are pursued as tournament events in many Young Men organizations.

In addition to athletic participation, young men are encouraged to develop interest in cultural events by participating in or attending theatrical productions or musical programs. Occasionally wards and stakes sponsor "road shows," in which the young men and young women of each ward write, produce, and perform short plays or skits. Young men may also participate in choral groups, comprised either entirely of young men or, more often, combined with young women, or with youth and adults, such as in a ward or stake choir.

In the decades since its founding, the Young Men organization has undergone many changes in structure, format, frequency of meeting, and leadership, but it has, for the most part, maintained its original purpose and direction: to provide for "the establishment in the youth of individual testimony of the truth and magnitude of the great latter-day work; the development of the gifts within them" (IE 1 [Nov. 1897]:3).

Associations for the spiritual and cultural growth of the youth began in the early days of the Church. In February 1843 the Prophet Joseph SMITH authorized the formation of a Young Gentlemen's and Young Ladies' Relief Society, and in 1854, Elder Lorenzo Snow organized the Polysophical Society. As Church membership increased, various types of youth societies were organized. President Brigham YOUNG, aware that these organizations were individually good but lacked unity and structure, organized the young men into one association, the Young Men's Mutual Improvement Association (YMMIA), in 1875 (CHC 5:480). President Young instructed YMMIA leaders to help the young men develop the gifts within them, stand up and speak, and bear testimony.

With the growth of the association, a central committee (later general board) was formed in December 1876 to oversee all ward YMMIAs, conduct missionary work among the young people, receive reports, and issue general instructions. The central committee recommended that an advisory committee be appointed with some General Authority members. In 1880, Church President John Taylor proposed that a general YMMIA superintendency (later presidency) be formed.

From 1876 to 1905, young men were called to serve full-time YMMIA missions to increase membership and assist local superintendencies. Because of rapid Church growth, this program was discontinued in 1905.

In the first YMMIA meetings, before class study was formalized, all of the young men met together, without regard to age, to hear the lesson. In 1900 a preliminary program of prayer, announcements, and singing was added. In 1901 the YMMIA was divided into junior and senior classes, and social and cultural activities were added to theological studies. An athletic committee, formed in 1909, brought outdoor activities into the junior program by fostering athletic meets. As the programs developed and as needs of the youth changed, Church leaders divided the YMMIA into smaller classes.

Until around 1900 the YMMIA met separately from the Young Women's Mutual Improvement Association (YWMIA). Joining the YWMIA with the YMMIA to form the Mutual Improvement Association (MIA) was another step in strengthening youth programs.

In 1911 the Church formed the YMMIA Scouts, patterned after the Boy Scouts of America (BSA), for young men ages twelve through eighteen. The YMMIA Scouts were later invited to be affiliated with BSA and were issued a national charter on May 21, 1913.

By the 1950s the activities of YMMIA, which included sports, dance, drama, music, and public speaking, were often conducted with the YWMIA as well. Athletics had become a major part of the program. From local stake tournaments, winners progressed to all-Church finals held annually in Salt Lake City. The All-Church tournaments were discontinued in the early 1970s.

The young men ages twelve and older were divided into five classes or age groups, including a Special Interest class for those twenty-six and older. The general level organization at this time consisted of a superintendency of five men and a general board of sixty to seventy men. The general level was financed by a general fund (paid by stakes based on YMMIA membership), sale of YMMIA materials, and investments. General board members instructed local YMMIA and YWMIA leaders.

The 1960s brought changes for both the general and local organizations. The responsibility of training local leaders gradually shifted to local priesthood leaders, significantly reducing the size of the general board and simplifying its responsibilities. The general fund was discontinued, and all finances were handled by the Church. Production and sales of materials were also centralized.

Early in the 1970s the YMMIA was divided into separate youth and adult organizations. In November 1972 the Church organized two priesthood-oriented MIAs: the Aaronic Priesthood—MIA for young men ages twelve through seventeen, and the Melchizedek Priesthood—MIA, or Special Interests, for unmarried men ages eighteen and older. At this time, the MIA became part of the priesthood and was no longer an auxiliary. The Aaronic Priesthood—MIA conducted lessons, service projects, and activities centered around the Aaronic Priesthood quorums.

In June 1974 the name Aaronic Priesthood—MIA was shortened to Aaronic Priesthood. For a time, the organization was under the jurisdiction of the Presiding Bishopric and there was no general presidency. However, in May 1977 the name was changed to Young Men and a general presidency was reinstated. In October 1979 the Church announced that the Young Men general presidency would be comprised of three General Authorities from the First Quorum of the Seventy. Since 1989,

the small general board has been made up of the deacon, teacher, and priest committees.

BIBLIOGRAPHY

Anderson, Edward H. "The Past of Mutual Improvement." *IE* 1 (Nov. 1897):1–10.

Strong, Leon M. "A History of the Young Men's Mutual Improvement Association 1875–1938." Master's thesis, Brigham Young University, 1939.

Williams, John Kent. "A History of the Young Men's Mutual Improvement Association 1939 to 1974." Master's thesis, Brigham Young University, 1976.

CHARLES E. MITCHENER
MARK E. HURST

YOUNG WOMAN'S JOURNAL

A monthly magazine published in Salt Lake City from 1889 to 1929, *Young Woman's Journal* served the young female members of The Church of Jesus Christ of Latter-day Saints and their leaders. Susa Young GATES conceived the idea of a magazine for girls and was encouraged by the FIRST PRESIDENCY and the YOUNG WOMEN's general presidency to publish one.

The first issue appeared in October 1889, with Susa Young Gates as managing editor, business manager, subscription manager, art director, and manager of all the other details. Although the Church encouraged publication, it did not provide financial assistance, and the *Journal* was plagued with financial problems for the first ten years. However, printing the 1899 lessons for the Young Women classes increased the number of subscribers, thus reducing the financial strains. Because the subscription of the magazine was $1 per year, very few young women could actually subscribe; additionally, it was directed mostly to their teachers and leaders. Initially published privately, and only later by the Church, the *Journal* was nonetheless the official organ of the Young Women's Mutual Improvement Association (in 1977 YOUNG WOMEN). Succeeding editors included May B. Talmage (1900–1902), Ann M. Cannon (1902–1907), Mary Connelly Kimball (1907–1923), Clarissa Beesley (1923–1929), and Elsie Talmage Brandley (1929).

The publication featured articles on theology, fashion, literature, marriage, housekeeping, hygiene, gardening, and ethics, and talks by GENERAL AUTHORITIES and Young Women leaders. It also printed recipes and patterns for sewing and handiwork, as well as short stories, poems, and lesson guides.

At the June 1929 conference, the decision was made to combine the *Young Woman's Journal* and the Young Men's IMPROVEMENT ERA into one publication to serve both youth organizations. Elsie Talmage Brandley, the last editor of the *Journal*, became an associate editor of the *Improvement Era*.

BIBLIOGRAPHY

Josephson, Marba C. *A History of YWMIA*, pp. 109–121. Salt Lake City, 1955.

PETREA GILLESPIE KELLY

YOUNG WOMEN

The Young Women program of the Church in 1990 reached an international membership of one million young women between the ages of twelve and eighteen. It sponsored weekly meetings and classes with prepared manuals. It extended a full range of activity programs for young women that relate to their intellectual and spiritual growth, physical fitness, speech, drama, music, dance, vocational and homemaking talents, outdoor and camping skills, and leadership development.

The Young Women organization began as the Cooperative RETRENCHMENT ASSOCIATION in November 1869. President Brigham YOUNG organized the society in the Lion House, his official residence in Salt Lake City, with his daughters as charter members. He challenged them to grow spiritually, to resist idleness and gossip, to retrench from the styles of the world in dress and deportment, and thus to be proper examples of Latter-day Saints. They were not to give in to rude or harsh frontier ways. The poet and Relief Society President Eliza R. SNOW became the supervisor of the new association, and Ella V. Empey, age twenty-three, was chosen as president.

The leaders designed a retrenchment costume, conservative in comparison to the high fashion of the day (no furbelows, flounces, or ruffles), with skirts to boot tops, pantaloons beneath, and necklines to the base of the throat.

By 1870 each ward in Salt Lake Valley had its own similar young women's organization with its own stated resolutions. The "one central thought" in all resolutions was "electing a greater simplicity of dress and of living; and . . . cultivating the mind rather than ministering to the pleasure of the body" (Gates, pp. 60–61). For example, the Fourteenth Ward resolved: "Feeling that we have worshipped at the shrine of fashion too long [we] do solemnly pledge ourselves to retrench in our dress, and to wear only that which is becoming to women professing to be Saints" (Gates, p. 61). And the Eighth Ward resolved: "Inasmuch as order is the first law of heaven, we will endeavor to learn the law by making ourselves acquainted with the principles of life and salvation. We will study the Bible, Book of Mormon, Doctrine and Covenants, and all works pertaining to our holy religion. . . . We will also study all literature that will qualify us to become ornaments in the kingdom of God, that we may merit the approbation of our brethren and sisters and of God. . . . We will not speak evil of anyone, but will be kind to all, especially the aged and infirm, the widow and orphan. We will en-

Ardeth G. Kapp, from Alberta, Canada, was sustained as general president of the Young Women in 1984.

deavor to become acquainted with the laws of nature, that we may become strong, healthy and vigorous" (Gates, pp. 64–65).

In 1871 the leaders renamed the society "YL," short for Young Ladies Retrenchment Association. They focused on the teenage girls by sponsoring weekly meetings, charitable deeds, instruction in public speaking, and lively discussions of the gospel and current events. A modest exercise program consisted of ball bouncing and throwing, knee bends, and side stretches. Later they introduced croquet.

The program expanded and flourished. Eliza R. Snow and her women companions traveled throughout the territory of Deseret in wagons pulled by oxen, and usually acted as their own teamsters. Fervent prayer, a few candles, baskets of bread and molasses, and personal enthusiasm for the cause kept them going.

Following Ella Empey, the presidents of the organization were as follows: Elmina S. TAYLOR (1880–1904), Martha Horne Tingey (1905–1929), Ruth May FOX (1929–1937), Lucy Grant Cannon (1937–1948), Bertha S. Reeder (1948–1961), Florence S. Jacobsen (1961–1972), Ruth Hardy Funk (1972–1978), Elaine Anderson Cannon (1978–1984), and Ardeth G. Kapp (1985–).

In 1875 an organization similar to YL was established for young men. It was called The Young Men's Mutual Improvement Association, and the goal was "personal improvement rather than entertainment." The two organizations soon began monthly conjoint meetings. In 1877 the YL name was changed to Young Ladies National Mutual Improvement Association to correlate with the Young Men's group and to reflect the growth of many units in many places across the nation. The first general conference for the YLNMIA was held April 4, 1880. Leaders admonished those attending to find new ways to teach girls how to develop every gift and grace of true womanhood.

Supportive efforts were developed. Susa Young Gates had personally published a magazine called *Young Woman's Journal* and now gave one-third of its space to the YL organization. A guide for all YL groups was printed, containing lessons and instructions for the girls and leaders and even ideas for beautifying the meeting places with pretty cloths and flowers. Typical lesson outlines included "What is the meaning of the word 'Chastity'?" and "Why have you not the right to take the pin comb out of your sister's drawer?" A favorite

couplet became: "One cheerful face in a household will keep everything bright—put envy, selfishness, despondency to shame and flight." Tuesday night became "Mutual" night for both boys and girls. The weekly talent programs, preceding separate lesson sessions for Young Ladies and Young Men, attracted large groups of young people, including many of other faiths.

In 1880 several prominent Utah women attended the first National Suffrage Convention in Washington, D.C. Church President John TAYLOR sent them with his blessing and the reminder that the Mormon women enjoyed voting and other rights afforded few other women in the country. Both the YL and Relief Society organizations became charter members of the National Council of Women of the United States and of the International Council of Women.

In 1886 and 1887, semi-annual training conferences for YL were held at the time of general conferences of the Church in April and October. In 1888, the first annual June Conference for young Women and Young Men organizations was held. Leaders provided special training in physical activity, story-telling, and music and class instruction. Four decades later, in 1929, they launched a new camping program for girls. In 1929 they combined *Young Woman's Journal* and *Improvement Era*, to make one magazine for young men and young women. President Heber J. GRANT was editor, with Elsie Talmage Brandley as associate editor and Hugh J. Cannon as managing editor. During this period they introduced the hymn "Carry On" as the anthem for LDS youth. Ruth May Fox wrote the words and Alfred M. Durham the music. They adopted the scriptural statement, "The glory of God is intelligence" (D&C 93:36) as the motto for both groups.

The Lion House, birthplace of the retrenchment association, became a cultural and social center for many young women. Young women received cultural enrichment through reviews and lessons in charm. Their service projects included wrapping bandages for soldiers and knitting baby clothing and shawls for the Primary Children's Hospital. At the National Council of Women exhibit at the Century of Progress Fair in Chicago in 1932, LDS Young Women leaders gave a demonstration on the monumental accomplishments of women in the previous one hundred years.

In the 1930s, leaders gave new emphasis to music, dance, and the performing arts. They published a recreational song book, and sociable singing became popular. They sponsored ten-minute musical programs or "road shows" that were locally created and rehearsed and then presented in successive wards in each LDS stake. They sent instructions in music and dance from Church headquarters to all MIA units, many of which then participated in an annual June Conference dance festival, a spectacle of choreography with up to 2,000 participants each year. Social dancing was also featured in the ward and stake houses, and "Gold and Green Balls," featuring the MIA colors, became popular events throughout the Church.

In 1937 Lucy Grant Cannon became president of the YWMIA. She organized the youth according to age and interest, with special manuals, incentive programs, and symbols that fostered development and recreation for all girls twelve years of age and over. She introduced an annual theme to be memorized and recited at every MIA meeting throughout the world. For example, in 1941 the theme was, "I, the Lord, am bound when ye do what I say; but when ye do not what I say, ye have no promise" (D&C 82:10). Manuals were written in Salt Lake City but adapted to the needs and customs of non-English speaking members of the Church. By 1948, during the administration of President Bertha S. Reeder, coordination, translation, and communication with the youth presidencies worldwide were a great challenge and new programs were created. Increasingly general board members were sent on weekend convention tours to present programs in activities, dance, drama, music, athletics, and camping.

In the late 1940s and 1950s, the First Presidency turned over to the YWMIA the girls enrollment incentive program that had been previously administered by the Presiding Bishopric. It was designed to increase attendance at all Church meetings. Individual awards were presented annually to qualifying youth at ward sacrament meetings.

In this period the Young Men and Young Women leaders initiated stake youth conferences that grew into major events. Sometimes they combined youth from multiple stakes for workshops, discussion groups, or meetings with keynote speakers from Church headquarters. They reinforced dress and dating standards and stressed morality. They generated a series of posters with full color illustrations called "Be Honest With Yourself." These included such admonitions as "Virtue Is Its Own Reward," "Great Men Pray,"

and "Temple Marriage Is Forever." They distributed wallet and purse-size reproductions to the Church youth. In 1960 they launched *Era of Youth*, an insert for youth in the monthly *Improvement Era*, with Elaine Cannon and Marion D. Hanks as editors. They prepared and announced musical productions from Church headquarters. In 1960 hundreds of stakes sponsored and produced the musical pageant "Promised Valley" by Crawford Gates, which celebrated the 1847 trek of the Mormon pioneers across the plains and into the Salt Lake Valley.

By the 1960s work for sixty or more women on the general board became a full-time Church assignment. Subcommittees prepared new manuals, programs, leadership training, and special youth conferences.

Youth leaders sponsored the restoration and full renovation of the Lion House for the centennial celebration of the organization of the first Young Ladies' group, November 18, 1869. The new Young Women general president, Florence Smith Jacobsen, placed a prayer bell in a niche in the front hall of the Lion House with a brass plaque describing how Brigham Young used it to call his daughters together to form the Retrenchment Association. A historical publication, *A Century of Sisterhood*, was also prepared. New full-color manuals were introduced to lead the girls forward from Beehives, named to symbolize industry and dedication, to Gleaner Girls, whose biblical model was Ruth. Girls sixteen to eighteen had been named Junior Girls, but were soon called Laurels with appropriate symbols, songs, and motto.

An elaborate June Conference was held in 1969, with many foreign countries represented. An early morning reception on Temple Square was followed by banquets, dance festivals, musicals, dramatic readings, road show presentations, camp training in the nearby mountains, athletic seminars, and testimony meetings. The final general session was held in the Tabernacle on Sunday.

Church President Harold B. LEE in the early 1970s introduced a correlation program designed to integrate many Church programs for youth. The new Young Women president, Ruth H. Funk, and the general presidencies and boards of other Church auxiliary organizations began to meet with priesthood leaders to formulate and initiate the best possible spiritual and social experiences for youth. Coordinated with departments of instructional development, audiovisual materials, library resources, and translation, they subordinated all other activities to the quest for spirituality. From this effort came the personal progress program and the young womanhood achievement awards. June Conference was replaced by regional training meetings under the direction of the priesthood. Under the aegis of Church correlation, a special magazine was introduced: *New Era*, a magazine for youth twelve to eighteen.

Elaine Anderson Cannon, as Young Women president in 1978, called twelve women with daughters between the ages of twelve and eighteen to serve on a governing board. Young women were encouraged to "prepare themselves to perform": to develop a personal testimony of Jesus, study the scriptures, and share the truth. They were to keep personal diaries, gather family histories and genealogy, set educational goals, and strengthen their families.

In 1980, at the Church's sesquicentennial celebration, a Days of '47 parade opened with 1,500 Young Women in white dresses forming a phalanx a full city block long and marching to the beat of 100 young trumpet and drum instrumentalists. Each girl carried her own three-by-five-foot banner mounted on a tall staff. Each banner was embroidered, quilted, appliqued, or painted to depict the girl's personal goals. This activity was repeated by other young women across the world in local celebrations.

During this period Sunday classes for Young Women began to be held at the same time as priesthood meeting for Young Men. This focus on gospel principles was carried into activity programs on weekday evenings. The consolidated schedule of all Sunday meetings required new manuals that featured units of study and in-depth training on principles and practices relevant to a girl's life. Preparation for the temple endowment was stressed for Young Women. Teachers of Sunday classes applied the manuals to timely local needs. Leadership training was conducted through special prototype discussion groups. "Open house" displays during general conference allowed for one-on-one conversations between stake Young Women leaders and priesthood leaders across the Church. Special helps were given leaders to assist in spiritual presentation of Sunday lessons. General board representatives held area conferences combining many stakes and regions in two-day sessions, and training sessions were given for Young Women and Relief Society leadership.

In this same period the presidency introduced semi-annual General Women's meetings. Under the direction of the First Presidency, these meetings were held shortly before general conference week. Representative women leaders and General Authorities spoke. Women and girls from age ten were invited to attend, and some participated in special choruses. The meetings were held in the Tabernacle in Salt Lake City and were broadcast via satellite.

President Ardeth Kapp introduced the Young Women motto, "We stand for truth and righteousness." She made a presentation to the U.S. Attorney General's program against pornography and continued this effort as a member of a national task force. In the tradition of Brigham Young's challenge, she encouraged girls to become "bell-ringers" or special examples to others in word, conversation, charity, faith, and purity. Her presidency focused on seven values for the Young Women program, each with a symbolic color and definitive direction: Faith, Divine Nature, Individual Worship, Knowledge, Choice and Accountability, Good Works, and Integrity. On the same day and at the same time, a special program sponsored Churchwide the release of helium-filled balloons carrying the testimony and commitment to these ideals of the young women of the Church.

Over the years, whatever the variations in programs and organizational structure, the emphasis among young women on being true daughters of God in appearance, demeanor, and testimony has not changed. Young Women units worldwide welcome nonmembers to participate in the personal progress program, to draw closer to Jesus Christ, and to increase their knowledge of eternal principles and appreciation for the worth and potential of their own souls.

BIBLIOGRAPHY

Evans, Joyce O., et al. *A Century of Sisterhood, 1869–1969.* Salt Lake City, 1970.

Gates, Susa Young. *History of the Young Ladies' Mutual Improvement Associations.* Salt Lake City, 1911.

Josephson, Marba C. *History of YWMIA.* Salt Lake City, 1956.

ELAINE ANDERSON CANNON

YOUTH

The Church defines "youth" as all men and women ages twelve to eighteen. Church policies and programs for youth are designed to help them make the transition from childhood to young adulthood

Deacon's quorum snow outing of the Holladay Ward, Salt Lake City, 1976. Each youth age group in the Church is led by a volunteer adult adviser under the direction of the ward bishop. Studies indicate that the most important influence in the religious growth of teenagers in the Church, after the influence of religious observance in the home, is the personal relationship developed between the youth and their adviser. Courtesy Craig Law.

with feelings of confidence and well-being, avoiding the pitfalls of adolescence, gaining more mature testimonies of the gospel of Jesus Christ, and drawing closer to their families and the Church.

The Church expects full participation from youth, who plan and administer many of their own activities, share the gospel with others, serve as examples of LDS teachings to their friends, render Christian service in the Church and community, and participate in BAPTISMS FOR THE DEAD in the TEMPLE. They also receive leadership and speaking assignments and are taught to be examples to other members of their families and WARDS.

Young people in the Church sometimes are referred to as "youth of the noble birthright," sons and daughters of God, born at this time in the earth's history for a sacred purpose. Although the moral climate and religious values of society seem to be weakening, the youth of the Church are asked to be "standard bearers" and lights to guide others to Jesus Christ. Each individual is considered by the Church to have a purpose for and mission in life, and adolescents are asked to draw near to the Lord to learn how best to fulfill that purpose (see PATRIARCHAL BLESSINGS). LDS youth are taught that they can function in and contribute to

society without participating in its ills (John 17:15).

Not all LDS youth desire the same level of participation in Church programs, although the level of activity is high as compared to youth in many other religious traditions. Most LDS youth organizations try to understand and accommodate individual differences and competing claims for young people's time. However, if an individual seems to be drifting from the Church or to be involved with undesirable or dangerous activities, Church resource care is made available to aid the family in helping the youth find a healthier and happier path.

Young men and young women of the Church are guided by adult advisers, who also teach the quorums and classes. Each quorum and class has a youth presidency that conducts meetings, involves group members in class experiences, and helps plan and carry out activities. Each group follows a prescribed course of study, and group members are encouraged to build friendships with each other and to encourage and strengthen each other in keeping the standards of the Church.

Church programs for youth are designed to support parents in preparing their children to live responsible adult lives as faithful Christians (see VALUES, TRANSMISSION OF). Parents and youth often are involved in events and activities together. Youth are encouraged to seek parental counsel, share experiences with parents and siblings, and help strengthen family bonds.

The AARONIC PRIESTHOOD and the YOUNG MEN and YOUNG WOMEN organizations provide the major avenues for Church-sponsored youth activity. The purpose of the Aaronic Priesthood and Young Men organizations is identical: to help each young man come to Christ, become converted to the gospel, respect and fulfill his priesthood callings, give meaningful service, and prepare to receive the Melchizedek Priesthood, serve a full-time mission, and become an honorable husband and father.

The purpose of the Young Women program is similar: Each young woman is to become converted to the gospel, strengthen her testimony of the Heavenly Father and Jesus Christ, recognize her identity as a daughter of God, and be a witness for God by living the Young Women Values: Faith, Divine Nature, Individual Worth, Knowledge, Choice and Accountability, Good Works, and Integrity. Each young woman is encouraged to keep covenants that she made at baptism, prepare spiritually for temple ordinances, and appreciate the importance of service as a wife and mother.

The missions and purposes of the youth programs are mutually supportive. As young men and women meet together to be taught, to share activities, and to give service, they gain leadership experience. This combined youth program helps young men and women learn to appreciate each other, to understand and value strengths and differences, and to prepare for responsible adulthood. Their shared values help them reinforce the commitment of all to the gospel.

Young Men–Young Women combined activities are regularly planned by the BISHOP or BRANCH PRESIDENT and Ward Youth Council. Youth leaders represent their peers and counsel with their leaders in making the decisions and solving the problems associated with planning and implementing activities. The Church youth programs include a range of wholesome activities in addition to lessons, speakers, discussion groups, and service projects. Sports and physical fitness, camping, Boy Scouts of America, socials, conferences, skills training, and opportunities in drama, dance, and music are encouraged. Sharing such experiences helps youth to meet the social, physical, cultural, and emotional/spiritual needs. Additional study of the scriptures is provided to high school students through the Church Educational System seminary program.

Because the standards of the Church are different from the standards acceptable to much of the world, LDS youth face many significant decisions, expectations, and pressures. They are encouraged to seek all things good and virtuous both inside and outside the Church (see A of F 13) and to decide early in life to build their testimonies and remain faithful to the teachings of Jesus Christ.

BIBLIOGRAPHY

Aaronic Priesthood-Young Men Handbook. Salt Lake City, 1977.

Benson, Ezra T. *To Young Men of the Priesthood.* Salt Lake City, 1986.

New Era 18 (March, 1988):5–67.

Young Women Handbook. Salt Lake City, 1988.

ARDETH G. KAPP

Z

ZENOCK

Zenock was a preexilic Israelite prophet whose words were found on the PLATES of brass, a record carried from Jerusalem to the new promised land in the Western Hemisphere by the Book of Mormon prophet LEHI c. 600 B.C. Zenock is not known from the Hebrew Bible or other sources and is noted in only five passages in the Book of Mormon. It is possible that he was of the lineage of JOSEPH OF EGYPT and an ancestor of the NEPHITES (3 Ne. 10:16).

Each reference to Zenock refers to his teaching of either the coming or redemptive mission of Jesus Christ. NEPHI₁, son of Lehi, in teaching from the words of previous prophets, stated that the God of Abraham, Isaac, and Jacob (Jesus Christ) would be "lifted up, according to the words of Zenock" (1 Ne. 19:10), referring to his crucifixion. Alma 33:16 contains the only direct quotation of Zenock's words, citing him as one of many Israelite prophets who foretold the mission of the Son of God (Alma 33:14–17; cf. 34:7) and quoting him on the mercies that God grants because of his Son. ALMA₂ noted, however, that because the people "would not understand" Zenock's words, they "stoned him to death" (Alma 33:17). NEPHI₂ cited Zenock and others who testified of the coming of the Son of God (Hel. 8:20). In the last reference to his work, MORMON wrote that ZENOS and Zenock foretold the destruction that preceded the coming of Christ to the remnant of their posterity (3 Ne. 10:16).

KENT P. JACKSON

ZENOS

Zenos is one of four Israelite prophets of Old Testament times cited in the BOOK OF MORMON whose writings appeared on the PLATES of brass but who are not mentioned in the Old Testament (*see also* ZENOCK; NEUM; and EZIAS). Zenos is quoted or mentioned by NEPHI₁ (1 Ne. 19:10–17), JACOB (Jacob 5:1–77; 6:1), ALMA₂ (Alma 33:3–11, 13, 15), Amulek (Alma 34:7), NEPHI₂ (Hel. 8:19–20), and MORMON (3 Ne. 10:14–17).

Although specific dates and details of Zenos' life and ministry are not known, the Book of Mormon provides considerable information about him from his teachings and related facts. Evidently he lived sometime between 1600 and 600 B.C. because he was apparently a descendant of JOSEPH OF EGYPT and his writings were on the plates of brass taken from JERUSALEM to the Americas by Nephi₁ about 600 B.C. He may also have been a progenitor of the Book of Mormon prophet LEHI (cf. 3 Ne. 10:16). Zenos spent time "in the wilderness" (Alma 33:4), but also preached "in the midst" of the "congregations" of God (Alma 33:9). Some of his enemies became reconciled to him through the power of God, but others were visited "with speedy destruction" (Alma 33:4, 10). Finally, he was slain because of his bold testimony of the coming of the "Son of God" (Hel. 8:13–19).

A major theme in the teachings of Zenos was the destiny of the house of Israel. His allegory or parable comparing the house of Israel to a tame olive tree and the Gentiles to a wild olive tree constitutes the longest single chapter in the Book of Mormon, Jacob chapter 5 (see BOOK OF MORMON: BOOK OF JACOB). The allegory refers to major events in the scattering and gathering of the house of Israel (see ALLEGORY OF ZENOS; ISRAEL: GATHERING OF ISRAEL; ISRAEL: SCATTERING OF ISRAEL).

The second-longest quotation from Zenos in the Book of Mormon is his hymn of thanksgiving and praise recorded in Alma 33:3–11, which emphasizes prayer, worship, and the mercies of God. A careful comparison of the style and contents of this hymn with *Hymn* H (or 8) and *Hymn* J (or 10) of the *Thanksgiving Hymns* of the DEAD SEA SCROLLS, noting certain striking similarities, suggests that the three may have been written by the same person. Further, the life situations of the author (or authors) are very similar (*CWHN* 7:276–83). Some LDS scholars anticipate that other evidences of Zenos' writings may appear as additional ancient manuscripts come to light.

Book of Mormon prophets frequently quoted Zenos because of his plain and powerful testimony of the future life, mission, atonement, death, and resurrection of the Son of God. Alma₂ recorded part of Zenos' prayer to God, recounting that "it is because of thy Son that thou hast been thus merciful unto me, therefore I will cry unto thee in all mine afflictions, for in thee is my joy; for thou hast turned thy judgments away from me, because of thy Son" (Alma 33:11). Nephi₁ recalled Zenos' knowledge that after the Son of God was crucified, he would "be buried in a sepulchre" for three days, and a sign of darkness should be "given of his death unto those who should inhabit the isles of the sea, more especially given unto those who are of the house of Israel" (1 Ne. 19:10). AMULEK quoted Zenos' words to show "that redemption cometh through the Son of God" (Alma 34:7). Mormon included Zenos as one of the prophets who spoke of events associated with "the coming of Christ" (3 Ne. 10:15), as did Nephi₂, who stated, "Yea, be-

hold, the prophet Zenos did testify boldly; for the which he was slain" (Hel. 8:19).

Elder Bruce R. McConkie of the QUORUM OF THE TWELVE APOSTLES summarized some of the teachings of Zenos and evaluated his contributions as follows:

It was Zenos who wrote of the visit of the Lord God to Israel after his resurrection; of the joy and salvation that would come to the righteous among them; of the desolations and destructions that awaited the wicked among them; of the fires, and tempests, and earthquakes that would occur in the Americas; of the scourging and crucifying of the God of Israel by those in Jerusalem; of the scattering of the Jews among all nations; and of their gathering again in the last days "from the four quarters of the earth" (1 Ne. 19:11–17). I do not think I overstate the matter when I say that next to Isaiah himself—who is the prototype, pattern, and model for all the prophets—there was not a greater prophet in all Israel than Zenos [p. 17].

BIBLIOGRAPHY

McConkie, Bruce R. "The Doctrinal Restoration." In *The Joseph Smith Translation, The Restoration of Plain and Precious Things*, ed My. Nyman and R. Millet. Provo, Utah, 1985.
Nibley, Hugh. "Prophets in the Wilderness." *CWHN* 7:264–90.

DANIEL H. LUDLOW

ZION

Latter-day Saints use the name Zion to signify a group of God's followers or a place where such a group lives. Latter-day scriptures define Zion as the "pure in heart" (D&C 97:21). Other uses of the name in scripture reflect this one. For example, Zion refers to the place or land appointed by the Lord for the gathering of those who accept his gospel (D&C 101:16–22; 3 Ne. 20–22). The purpose of this gathering is to raise up a committed society of "pure people" who will "serve [God] in righteousness" (D&C 100:13, 16). Hence, the lands of Zion are places where the pure in heart live together in RIGHTEOUSNESS. Geographical Church units are called "stakes . . . of Zion" (D&C 101:21–22). The Church and its STAKES are called Zion because they are for gathering and purifying a people of God (D&C 43:8–11; Eph. 4:11–13). Scripture also refers to Zion as a "City of Holiness" (Moses 7:19), because the "sanctified" or "pure" live there (Moro. 10:31–33; Alma 13:11–12), and a "city of refuge" where the Lord protects them from the peril of the world (D&C 45:66–67).

"Pure in heart" may be explained in terms of the gospel of Jesus Christ. Jesus said that to be saved a person must believe in him, repent of sins, and be born of water and of the Spirit (John 3:5, 16; 3 Ne. 27:20). Scripture describes the rebirth to which Jesus refers as a "mighty change in your hearts" or being "born of God" (Alma 5:13, 14). It means that the person puts off the "natural man" and puts on a new nature that has "no more disposition to do evil, but to do good continually" (Mosiah 5:2; 3:19). A person pure of heart is one who has died to evil and awakened to good. Thus "pure people," being alive to good, dwell together in righteousness and are called Zion (Moses 7:18). Zion, then, is the way of life of a people who live the gospel of Jesus Christ.

Since love comprehends all righteousness (Matt. 22:36–40), the people of Zion live together in love as equals (*see* EQUALITY; D&C 38:24–27). They have "all things common" (4 Ne. 1:3). They labor together as equals, each contributing to the good of all and to the work of salvation according to their individual talents (D&C 82:3; Alma 1:26). As equals, all receive the things that are necessary for survival and well-being, according to their circumstances, wants, and needs (D&C 51:3, 9). Consequently, among a people of Zion there are no rich or poor (4 Ne. 1:3). It is written of the ancient people of Enoch that "the Lord called his people Zion, because they were of one heart and one mind, and dwelt in righteousness; and there was no poor among them" (Moses 7:18).

People of Zion enjoy fulness of life, or happiness, in the highest degree possible in this world and, if they remain faithful, in the world to come (4 Ne. 1:3, 16; Mosiah 16:11). According to LDS belief, persons may attain different degrees of "fulness" of life, ranging from "celestial" to "telestial," depending on the level of "law" they "abide" (D&C 88:22–35; 76). By living the principles of Zion, the people live together according to the celestial law that governs the highest order of heaven and partake of the life it promises (D&C 105:4–5). Fulness of life in the celestial degree consists in being filled with God's love, or being alive to all that is good—a state of happiness that reaches full fruition only in eternity (Eph. 3:17–19; Moro. 7:16–25, 44–48). The capacity of people to live ce-

lestial law and enjoy life in its fulness results from the purifying rebirth already mentioned.

The prophets always labor to prepare people to become a people of Zion. Sometimes people embrace Zion; most often they do not. For example, the followers of Enoch (the son of Jared and father of Methuselah; Gen. 5:18–24; Luke 3:37) built Zion, and because of their righteousness, "God received [them] up into his own bosom" (Moses 7:69; Heb. 11:5). Later, Noah declared the word of life unto "the children of men, even as it was given unto Enoch" (Moses 8:19). Still later, Moses "sought diligently" that his people might be purified and enter the rest of God, as did Enoch's people (D&C 84:23–45). But the people of Noah and, to a lesser degree, the people of Moses "hardened their hearts" (D&C 84:24) and refused to accept the ways of Zion. On the other hand, "the people in the days of Melchizedek" were "made pure and entered into the rest of the Lord their God" (Alma 13:10–14). Before 125 B.C. in ancient America, king BENJAMIN's people, and the Nephites who followed the prophet ALMA₁ underwent that mighty change of heart that makes a people pure (Mosiah 2–5; Alma 5:3–14). When Jesus Christ visited his "other sheep" in ancient America after his crucifixion (John 10:16; 3 Ne. 15:21), he established Zion among them. It is said of them that "there was no contention in the land, because of the love of God which did dwell in the hearts of the people. . . . Surely there could not be a happier people among all the people who had been created by the hand of God" (4 Ne. 1:3, 15–16). The Bible also describes early Christians who experienced purification and lived the order of Zion (Acts 2:44; 4:32; 15:9).

Hand of God, by Maynard Dixon (1940, oil on masonite). God's guiding and protecting hand, depicted in a cloud formation, rests over a group of pioneers laboring to establish a home in the wilderness. Courtesy Museum of Fine Arts, Brigham Young University.

In the RESTORATION, Joseph Smith taught his people that they can, and must, become people of Zion. That vision inspires the labors and programs of the Church to this day. In establishing Zion, Latter-day Saints believe they may be a light to humankind (D&C 115:4–6) and usher in the millennial reign of Christ (Moses 7:60–65; D&C 43:29–30). During the MILLENNIUM, Zion will have two great centers—JERUSALEM of old and a NEW JERUSALEM in America—from which "the law" and the "word of the Lord" will go forth to the world (Isa. 2:3; Ether 13:2–11).

BIBLIOGRAPHY

Zion as explained here is much more detailed than, but bears certain social similarities to, the idea of Zion found in the work of Martin Buber in *On Zion: The History of an Idea* (New York, 1973). An LDS work that applies the idea of Zion to contemporary life is Hugh W. Nibley's *Approaching Zion* (*CWHN* 9).

A. D. SORENSEN

ZIONISM

Zion (Hebrew, early the Jerusalem mountain on which the City of David was built) is employed in LDS scripture both geographically and spiritually: the land of Zion and "the pure in heart" (D&C 84:99; 97:21; 100:16; cf. Moses 7:18–21). The declaration that "we believe in the literal gathering of Israel and the restoration of the ten tribes" refers to a new Zion in America as well as a renewed Jerusalem in the Old World. Latter-day scripture declares that Jerusalem will become the spiritual-temporal capital of the whole Eastern Hemisphere, "One Great Centre, and one mighty Sovereign" (*MFP* 1:259), while Zion will be the place of refuge and divine direction in the Western Hemisphere.

In 1831, less than two years after the organization of the Church, Joseph SMITH received a revelation that included the imperative "Let them who be of Judah flee unto Jerusalem, unto the mountains of the Lord's house" (D&C 133:13). In 1833 he wrote that the tribe of Judah would return and obtain deliverance at Jerusalem, citing Joel, Isaiah, Jeremiah, Psalms, and Ezekiel (cf. *TPJS*, p. 17).

In March 1836, the dedicatory prayer given by Joseph Smith at the KIRTLAND TEMPLE—since canonized and used as a pattern in later LDS temple dedications—pleaded that "Jerusalem, from this hour, may begin to be redeemed; and the yoke of bondage may begin to be broken off from the house of David" (D&C 109:62–63). In 1840–1841, Orson Hyde, an apostle, was commissioned by the Prophet to go to Jerusalem and dedicate the land. His prayer petitioned for the gathering home of the exiles, the fruitfulness of the earth, the establishing of an independent government, the rebuilding of Jerusalem, and "rearing a Temple in honor of thy name" (Heschel, p. 18). Two years later, Joseph Smith prophesied that the gathering and rebuilding would occur "before the Son of Man will make his appearance" (*TPJS*, p. 286). These prayers and prophecies have been frequently reiterated by other apostolic authorities, both on the Mount of Olives and on Mount Carmel in the Holy Land and in official convocations of the Saints throughout the world.

Jewish tradition warns that commitment to "sacred soil" without faith in the living God is a form of idolatry. Early in the twentieth century the Zionist movement advocated a compromise between secular Zionists, who envisioned a state without traditional Judaism, and religious Zionists, who argued that the state must be grounded in traditional Judaism. History in the modern political state of Israel has thus far implemented that compromise.

Spiritual Zionism among Latter-day Saints is advocated in the setting of concern for all of the children of God. It does not pronounce on specific geopolitical struggles or endorse speculations on the exact "when" and "how" of the fulfillment of ancient and modern prophecy. Many LDS leaders see events of the past 160 years as a preface. They continue to plead for peace and for coexistence with all the peoples who lay claim to old Jerusalem and the Holy Land: Jewish, Christian, Islamic, and others.

The term Zion, pertaining to a spiritually significant New Jerusalem in America, is one of the central themes of the Doctrine and Covenants (*see* NEW JERUSALEM).

BIBLIOGRAPHY

Davis, Moshe, ed. *With Eyes Toward Zion*, Vol. 2. New York, 1986.

Heschel, Abraham J. *Israel, an Echo of Eternity*. New York, 1968.

Madsen, Truman G. *The Mormon Attitude Toward Zionism*, ed. Yaakov Goldstein. Haifa, 1980.

TRUMAN G. MADSEN

ZION'S CAMP

Zion's Camp was a Latter-day Saint expedition from Kirtland, Ohio, to Clay County, Missouri, during May and June 1834. The Mormon settlers in adjacent Jackson County, Missouri, had been driven out in the fall of 1833 by hostile non-Mormon elements, and the initial objective of Zion's Camp was to protect those settlers after the Missouri militia escorted them back to their homes. The camp was to bring money, supplies, and moral support to the destitute Saints.

A revelation to Joseph SMITH in July 1831 (D&C 57) designated Independence, Jackson County, Missouri, as the site of ZION, a gathering place for the Saints and the location for the NEW JERUSALEM spoken of in the Bible and the Book of Mormon. By the summer of 1833, the Latter-day Saints numbered about one-third of the population in Jackson County. Their increasing numbers and distinctive beliefs troubled the other settlers, who shortly demanded that the Church members leave. When these demands were not immediately complied with, the Missourians attacked the settlements, compelling the Saints to flee. Most went north across the Missouri River to Clay County in November 1833.

Lyman Wight and Parley P. PRATT brought word of their plight to Joseph Smith and the main body of Saints in Kirtland, Ohio, on February 22, 1834. Wight and Pratt informed the Prophet that after their conversation with Governor Daniel Dunklin, Attorney General Robert W. Wells of Missouri promised to supply a force to escort the exiles back to their homes. With this in mind, Joseph Smith saw the wisdom of sending a force to protect his people from further attacks once they were safely back in Jackson County.

A revelation on February 24, 1834 (D&C 103), commanded the Saints to send to Missouri a relief force consisting of at least 100 and as many as 500 volunteers. Eight Church leaders were told to recruit participants for the march, which later was called Zion's Camp. Four teams of two men each went east to obtain men, money, and supplies. A fifth pair, Lyman Wight and Joseph Smith's brother Hyrum SMITH, went to Michigan and Illinois. The northern group was to join the marchers from Kirtland at the house of James Allred, a Church member living on the Salt River in eastern Missouri about one hundred miles northwest of St. Louis.

Zion's Camp marched from eastern Ohio in 1834 to come to the aid of the beleaguered Saints in western Missouri. Its most enduring legacy was the dedication and loyalty it instilled in those who served in the ranks. Many of the nineteenth-century Church leaders who remained faithful to Joseph Smith and Brigham Young were in this camp. Engraving from T.B.H. Stenhouse, *The Rocky Mountain Saints* (New York, 1873), p. 52. Courtesy the Utah State Historical Society.

An advance party of 20 left Kirtland on May 1, 1834, to prepare the first camp at New Portage, near present-day Akron, Ohio, and the main group of about 85 joined them on May 6. When Joseph and Hyrum's contingents rendezvoused at the Allred settlement, east of Paris, Monroe County, Missouri, there were approximately 200 men, 11 women, and 7 children. Included in these figures were the 20 men, women, and children comprising Hyrum's company from the Pontiac, Michigan, area.

The marchers were well armed, carrying muskets, pistols, swords, and knives, and they attempted to prevent the Missourians from knowing of the expedition. But Jackson County residents learned of their coming and burned down virtually all the remaining Mormon buildings. Lacking in military training, the members of Zion's Camp conducted military exercises and sham battles along the way of the 900-mile journey. They were organized into groups of ten and fifty, with a captain over each. After the rendezvous at the Salt River on June 8, Lyman Wight, a veteran of the War of 1812, was elected general of the camp, and William Cherry, a British dragoon for twenty years, was made drill master.

Contrary to the attempted military discipline, the men sometimes quarreled among themselves.

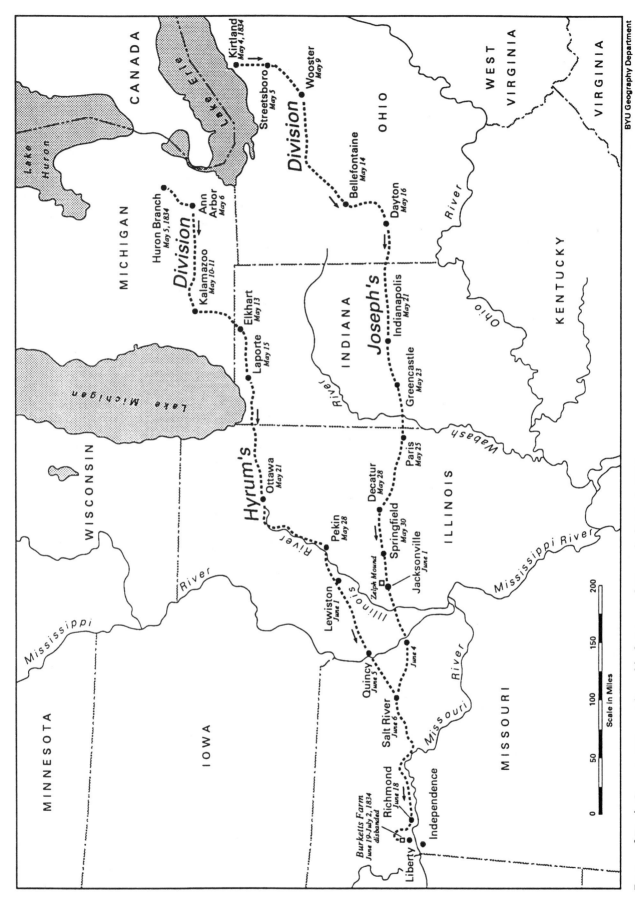

Routes of Zion's Camp to Missouri (Joseph's division and Hyrum's division), 1834.

On June 3, as the group approached the Mississippi, Joseph warned them that in consequence of their misconduct a scourge would strike the camp. His words proved prophetic when, at the conclusion of their journey on June 23 at Rush Creek in Clay County, Missouri, cholera struck the camp. Some sixty-eight men were afflicted, and thirteen of them and one woman died of the disease. Earlier at Fishing River a band of about 300 armed Missourians threatened to invade the camp, but a fierce hailstorm drove them off and prevented a conflict.

In the meantime, negotiations were conducted between the Zion's Camp leaders, Missouri State officials, and the citizens of Jackson County. Joseph Smith learned that, contrary to expectations, Governor Dunklin would not provide troops to escort the Mormons into Jackson County, fearing a civil war if he did. The two sides exchanged proposals for buying out each other's property in Jackson County, but these efforts broke down.

On June 22, 1834, while still at Fishing River, the Prophet received a revelation that rebuked some members of the Church for not sufficiently supporting Zion's Camp, but accepted the sacrifice of the camp members. They were not to fight but to wait for the Lord to redeem Zion (D&C 105). The experience had been intended to test their faith. The revelation directed the Saints to build goodwill in the area in preparation for the time when Zion would be recovered by legal rather than military means. Since there was little more to be done to help the displaced Jackson County Saints, the remaining Zion's Camp supplies were distributed to the refugees, and the camp disbanded on June 30, 1834. Most of the troops soon returned to Ohio.

Zion's Camp failed to achieve its ostensible purpose of protecting the Jackson County Saints. In retrospect, however, Brigham Young and other participants felt that they learned valuable lessons. In subsequent migrations, the Mormons used the organizational experience gained in Zion's Camp. Most importantly, they had answered the Lord's call (D&C 103). Nine of the first twelve apostles and all of the first Quorum of Seventy (seven presidents and sixty-three members) were later called from the ranks of Camp members.

BIBLIOGRAPHY

Crawley, Peter, and Richard L. Anderson. "The Political and Social Realities of Zion's Camp." *BYU Studies* 14 (1974):406–20.

Launius, Roger D. *Zion's Camp*. Independence, Mo., 1984.

Talbot, Wilburn D. "Zion's Camp." Master's thesis, Brigham Young University, 1973.

LANCE D. CHASE

ZORAM

Three men named Zoram are noted in the Book of Mormon. The first Zoram was the servant of Laban, a Jewish commander in Jerusalem about 600 B.C. (1 Ne. 3:31). This Zoram gave the disguised NEPHI₁ the plates of brass thinking he was Laban. Offered freedom if he would become part of Nephi's group in the wilderness, Zoram accepted Nephi's offer and made an oath to stay with them from that time on (1 Ne. 4:20–38). He married one of the daughters of Ishmael (1 Ne. 16:7), was a true friend to Nephi, was blessed by Nephi's father Lehi (2 Ne. 1:30–32), and went with Nephi when the Nephite colony separated after Lehi's death (2 Ne. 5:5–6). His descendants were called Zoramites.

A second Zoram was the chief captain over the armies of the Nephites in 81 B.C. He consulted with Alma₂, the high priest over the church, regarding his military actions (Alma 16:5–8).

The third Zoram was the leader of a group called Zoramites who separated themselves from the Nephites about 24 B.C. and apostatized from the established church. These Zoramites killed Korihor, the antichrist (Alma 30:59). Alma₂ led a missionary contingent among them to try to reclaim them from their apostasy and to prevent them from entering into an alliance with the Lamanites. While several of their poor were reconverted, the majority continued in their wicked ways (Alma 31:35), eventually joining the Lamanites and becoming antagonists to the Nephites. Some Zoramites served as Lamanite military commanders and even as kings (Alma 43:4–44; 48:5; 3 Ne. 1:29).

BIBLIOGRAPHY

Nibley, Hugh. *CWHN* 6:127–30; 8:543–44.

MONTE S. NYMAN

ZORAMITES

See: Book of Mormon Peoples

Appendix 1

Biographical Register of General Church Officers

This register contains basic biographical information on all persons sustained as General Church Officers in the general Church conferences since the Church was organized on April 6, 1830. The entries are listed alphabetically for ease of reference. For a list of general officers of the Church in the chronology of their being called *see* Appendix 5, General Church Officers, A Chronology.

Where the information is available, the entry includes general Church calling(s) and date(s); birth and death dates and places; family information such as spouse and number of children; vocation at time of calling; former Church service positions (stake, mission, or temple president, regional representative, or general board office). Although the names of some of the auxiliary organizations have changed through the years, references use only the current names. Because public records for many plural marriages do not exist, it was decided to list only that the man practiced plural marriage when that is known rather than give partial or incomplete marriage information.

ABREA, Angel. Seventy, April 4, 1981; b. Sept. 13, 1933, Buenos Aires, Argentina; married Maria Victoria Chiapparino, three children; certified public accountant; regional representative, temple and mission president.

ALDRICH, Hazen. Seventy, Feb. 28, 1835; released April 6, 1837, having previously been ordained a high priest.

AMADO, Carlos H. (Humberto). Seventy, April 7, 1989; b. Sept. 25, 1944, Guatemala City, Guatemala; m. Mayavel Pineda, six children; Church Educational System area director; regional representative, mission and stake president.

ANDERSEN, H. (Hans) Verlan. Seventy, April 6, 1986–Oct. 5, 1991; b. Nov. 6, 1914, Logan, Utah; m. Shirley Hoyt Anderson, eleven children; emeritus educator; stake president.

ANDERSON, Joseph. Asst. to the Twelve, April 6, 1970; Seventy, Oct. 1, 1976; Emeritus General Authority, Dec. 31, 1978; b. Nov. 20, 1889, Salt Lake City, Utah; m. Norma Peterson, three children; secretary to the First Presidency.

ANDERSON, May. First counselor to general president Louie B. Felt, Primary, Dec. 29, 1905–Oct. 6, 1925; General president, Oct. 6, 1925–Sept. 11, 1939; b. June 8, 1864, Liverpool, England; d. June 10, 1946, Salt Lake City, Utah; editor, *Children's Friend,* 1902–1940.

ARRINGTON, Leonard J. (James). Church historian, Jan. 14, 1972–June 26, 1980; b. July 2, 1917, Twin Falls, Idaho; m. Grace Fort (d. 1983), three children; m. Harriet Ann Horne; educator.

ASAY, Carlos E. (Egan). Seventy, April 3, 1976; b. June 12, 1926, Sutherland, Utah; m. Colleen Webb, seven children; educator; regional representative, mission president.

ASHTON, Marvin J. (Jeremy). Asst. to the Twelve, Oct. 3, 1969; Apostle, Dec. 2, 1971; b. May 6, 1915, Salt Lake City, Utah; m. Norma Bernston, four children; businessman; Boy Scouts of America national committee member.

ASHTON, Marvin O. (Owen). First counselor to Presiding Bishop LeGrand Richards, April 6, 1938–Oct. 7, 1946; b. April 8, 1883, Salt Lake City, Utah; d. Oct. 7, 1946, Salt Lake City; m. Rae Jeremy, seven children; businessman; stake president.

AYALA, Eduardo. Seventy, Mar. 31, 1990; b. May 3, 1937, Coronel, Chile; m. Blanca Ester Espinoza, three children; business management; regional representative, mission and stake president.

BACKMAN, Robert L. (LeGrand). Second counselor to general president W. Jay Eldredge, Young Men, June 25–Nov. 9, 1972; general president, Nov. 9, 1972–June 23, 1974; Seventy, April 1, 1978; b. Mar. 22, 1922, Salt Lake City, Utah; m. Virginia Pickett, seven children; attorney and state legislator; regional representative, mission and stake president.

BADGER, Rodney C. (Carlos). Second counselor to general president Junius F. Wells, Young Men, 1876–1880; b. Sept. 8, 1848, Salt Lake City, Utah; d. April 12, 1923, Salt Lake City; m. Harriet Ann Whitaker Taylor;

children; business management; regional representative, mission and stake president.

BACKMAN, Robert L. (LeGrand). Second counselor to general president W. Jay Eldredge, Young Men, June 25–Nov. 9, 1972; general president, Nov. 9, 1972–June 23, 1974; Seventy, April 1, 1978; b. Mar. 22, 1922, Salt Lake City, Utah; m. Virginia Pickett, seven children; attorney and state legislator; regional representative, mission and stake president.

BADGER, Rodney C. (Carlos). Second counselor to general president Junius F. Wells, Young Men, 1876–1880; b. Sept. 8, 1848, Salt Lake City, Utah; d. April 12, 1923, Salt Lake City; m. Harriet Ann Whitaker Taylor; practiced plural marriage, seventeen children on record; businessman.

BAIRD, J. (Joseph) Hugh. Second counselor to general president Richard L. Warner, Sunday School, Aug. 1979–Oct. 1979; b. July 25, 1929, Salt Lake City, Utah; m. Florence Richards, nine children; educator; Sunday School general board member.

BALLARD, M. (Melvin) Russell, Jr. Seventy, April 3, 1976; Apostle, Oct. 10, 1985; b. Oct. 8, 1928; m. Barbara Bowen, seven children; businessman; mission president.

BALLARD, Melvin J. (Joseph). Apostle, Jan. 7, 1919–July 30, 1939; b. Feb. 9, 1873, Logan, Utah; d. July 30, 1939, Salt Lake City; m. Martha Annabelle Jones, eight children; businessman, civic leader; mission president.

BANGERTER, William Grant. Asst. to the Twelve, April 4, 1975; Seventy, Oct. 1, 1976; b. June 8, 1918, Granger, Utah; m. Mildred Schwantes (d. 1952), three children; m. Geraldine Hamblin, seven children; building contractor; regional representative, mission president.

BANKS, Ben B. (Berry). Seventy, April 7, 1989; b. April 4, 1932, Murray, Utah; m. Susan Kearnes, seven children; businessman; mission and stake president.

BARKER, Kate Montgomery. Second counselor to general president Louise Yates Robinson, Relief Society, April 3, 1935–Dec. 1939; b. May 30, 1881, North Ogden, Utah; d. Feb. 13, 1972, Salt Lake City; m. James L. Barker, three children.

BARRATT, Matilda Morehouse W. First counselor to general president Louie B. Felt, Primary, June 19, 1880–Oct. 1888; b. Jan. 17, 1837, Stockport, England; d. April 14, 1902; m. John Barratt, four children.

BEEBE, Clara M. Woodruff. Second counselor to general president Louie B. Felt, Primary, Dec. 29, 1906–Oct. 6, 1925; b. July 23, 1868, Salt Lake City, Utah; d. Dec. 27, 1927; m. Ovando C. Beebe, eight children.

BEESLEY, Clarissa Alice. Second counselor to general president Ruth May Fox, Young Women, Mar. 30, 1929–Oct. 1937; b. Nov. 13, 1878, Salt Lake City, Utah; d. July 7, 1974, Salt Lake City.

BENNETT, Emily Higgs. First counselor to general president Bertha S. Reeder, Young Women, June 13,

1948–Sept. 30, 1961; b. June 27, 1896, Salt Lake City, Utah; d. Mar. 19, 1985, Salt Lake City; m. Harold H. Bennett, eight children; homemaker; Young Women general board member.

BENNETT, John C. (Cook). Assistant President with the First Presidency, April 8, 1841; disfellowshipped, May 25, 1842; excommunicated 1842; b. Aug. 3, 1804, Fair Haven, Massachusetts; d. Aug. 5, 1867, Polk City, Iowa.

BENNETT, William H. (Hunter). Asst. to the Twelve, April 6, 1970; Seventy, Oct. 1, 1976; Emeritus General Authority, Dec. 31, 1978; b. Nov. 5, 1910, Taber, Alberta, Canada; d. July 23, 1980, Bountiful, Utah; m. Patricia June Christiansen, six children; educator; regional representative, stake president.

BENNION, Adam S. (Samuel). Apostle, April 9, 1953–Feb. 11, 1958; b. Dec. 2, 1886, Taylorsville, Utah; d. Feb. 11, 1958, Salt Lake City; m. Minerva Young, five children; educator, general superintendent of Church Schools; Sunday School general board member.

BENNION, Milton. First asst. to general superintendent George D. Pyper, Sunday School, Oct. 1934–May 1943; general superintendent, May 1943–Sept. 1949; b. June 7, 1870, Salt Lake City, Utah; d. April 5, 1953, Salt Lake City; m. Cora Lindsay, eleven children; educator; Sunday School general board member.

BENNION, Samuel O. (Otis). Seventy, April 6, 1933–Mar. 8, 1945; b. June 9, 1874, Taylorsville, Utah; d. Mar. 8, 1945, Salt Lake City; m. Charlotte Trowler, two children; newspaper executive; mission president.

BENSON, Ezra T. (Taft). Apostle, July 16, 1846–Sept. 3, 1869; b. Feb. 22, 1811, Mendon, Massachusetts; d. Sept. 3, 1869, Ogden, Utah; m. Pamelia Andrus; practiced plural marriage, thirty-four children on record; businessman-contractor; mission president.

BENSON, Ezra Taft. Apostle, Oct. 7, 1943; President of the Quorum of the Twelve Apostles, Dec. 30, 1973; President of the Church, Nov. 10, 1985; b. Aug. 4, 1899, Idaho; m. Flora Smith Amussen, six children; farm bureau executive, U.S. Secretary of Agriculture in President Eisenhower's cabinet; mission and stake president. (*See biography*, Benson, Ezra Taft.)

BENTLEY, Joseph T. (Taylor). General superintendent, Young Men, July 21, 1958–Oct. 6, 1962; b. Mar. 6, 1906, Colonia Juárez, Chihuahua, Mexico; m. Kathleen Bench, six children; certified public accountant, educator; mission president.

BILLINGS, Titus. Second counselor to Presiding Bishop Edward Partridge, Aug. 1, 1837; released at the death of Bishop Partridge, May 27, 1840; b. Mar. 24 or 25, 1793, Greenfield, Massachusetts; d. Feb. 6, 1866, Provo, Utah; m. Diantha Morely; practiced plural marriage, nineteen children on record; carpenter.

BOWEN, Albert E. (Ernest). Apostle, April 8, 1937–July 15, 1953; b. Oct. 31, 1875, Henderson Creek, mary, July 20, 1943–April 14, 1951; b. April 21, 1886, Liverpool, England; d. Sept. 18, 1970, Salt Lake City, Utah; m. Ashby D. Boyle, five children.

BOYNTON, John F. (Farnham). Apostle, Feb. 15, 1835–Sept. 3, 1837; disfellowshipped, Sept. 3, 1837; excommunicated same year; b. Sept. 20, 1811, Bradford, Massachusetts; d. Oct. 20, 1890, Syracuse, New York; m. Susannah (Susan) Lowell (d.), five children; m. Caroline Foster Harriman; businessman.

BRADFORD, William R. (Rawsel). Seventy, Oct. 3, 1975; b. Oct. 25, 1933, Springville, Utah; m. Mary Ann Bird, six children; businessman; mission president.

BREWERTON, Ted E. (Eugene). Seventy, Sept. 30, 1978; b. Mar. 30, 1925, Raymond, Alberta, Canada; m. Dorothy Hall, six children; pharmacist; regional representative, mission and stake president.

BROCKBANK, Bernard P. (Park). Asst. to the Twelve, Oct. 6, 1962; Seventy, Oct. 1, 1976; Emeritus General Authority, Oct. 4, 1980; b. May 24, 1909, Salt Lake City, Utah; m. Nada Rich (d. 1967), six children; m. Frances Morgan; building contractor; mission president.

BROUGH, Monte J. (James). Seventy, Oct. 1, 1988; b. June 11, 1939, Randolph, Utah; m. Lanette Barker, seven children; businessman; regional representative, mission president.

BROWN, Hugh B. (Brown). Asst. to the Twelve, Oct. 4, 1953; Apostle, April 10, 1958–Dec. 2, 1975; Second counselor to President McKay, Oct. 12, 1961; First counselor, Oct. 4, 1963; released at the death of President McKay, Jan. 18, 1970, and returned to the Quorum of the Twelve; b. Oct. 24, 1883, Granger, Utah; d. Dec. 2, 1975, Salt Lake City; m. Zina Young Card, eight children; attorney, educator; mission and stake president.

BROWN, Victor L. (Lee). Second counselor to Presiding Bishop John H. Vandenberg, Sept. 30, 1961; Presiding Bishop, April 6, 1972; Seventy, April 6, 1985; Emeritus General Authority, Oct. 1, 1989; b. July 31, 1914, Cardston, Alberta, Canada; m. Lois Kjar, five children; business executive; temple president.

BUEHNER, Carl W. (William). Second counselor to Presiding Bishop Joseph L. Wirthlin, April 6, 1952–Sept. 30, 1961; Second assistant to general superintendent Joseph T. Bentley, Young Men, Oct. 25, 1961–Oct. 1967; b. Dec. 27, 1898, Stuttgart, Germany; d. Nov. 18, 1974, Salt Lake City, Utah; m. Lucile Thurman, three children; business executive; regional representative, stake president.

BURTON, Robert T. (Taylor). Second counselor to Presiding Bishop Edward Hunter, Oct. 9, 1874; First counselor to Presiding Bishop William B. Preston, Oct. 5, 1884–Nov. 11, 1907; b. Oct. 25, 1821, Amherstburg, Ontario, Canada; d. Nov. 11, 1907, Salt Lake City, Utah; m. Maria Susan Haven; practiced plural marriage, twenty-seven children on record; sheriff.

BURTON, Theodore M. (Moyle). Asst. to the Twelve, Oct. 8, 1960; Seventy, Oct. 1, 1976; Emeritus General Authority, Oct. 1, 1989; b. Mar. 27, 1907, Salt Lake City, Utah; d. Dec. 22, 1989, Salt Lake City; m. Minnie Susan Preece, one child; educator; mission president.

BUSCHE, F. (Friedrich) Enzio. Seventy, Oct. 1, 1977; b. April 5, 1930, Dortmund, Germany; m. Jutta Baum, four children; business executive; regional representative, temple and mission president.

BUTTERFIELD, Josiah. Seventy, April 6, 1837; excommunicated, Oct. 7, 1844; b. Mar. 13 or 18, 1795, Saco, Maine; d. April 1871, Watsonville, California; m. Polly Mouton, one child.

CALL, Waldo P. (Pratt). Seventy, April 6, 1985–Oct. 6, 1990; b. Feb. 5, 1928, Colonia Juárez, Mexico; m. Beverly Johnson, seven children (d. 1986); m. LaRayne Whetten; farmer; regional representative, stake president.

CALLIS, Charles A. (Albert). Apostle, Oct. 12, 1933–Jan. 21, 1947; b. May 4, 1865, Dublin, Ireland; d. Jan. 21, 1947, Jacksonville, Florida; m. Grace E. Pack, eight children, attorney; mission president.

CAMARGO, Helio R. (da Rocha). Seventy, April 6, 1985–Oct. 6, 1990; b. Feb. 1, 1926, Resende, Brazil; m. Nair Belmira de Gouvea, six children; farmer and ret. Brazilian Army officer; regional representative, stake president.

CANNON, Abraham H. (Hoagland). Seventy, Oct. 8, 1882; Apostle, Oct. 7, 1889–July 19, 1896; b. Mar. 12, 1859, Salt Lake City, Utah; d. July 19, 1896, Salt Lake City; m. Sarah Ann Jenkins; practiced plural marriage, seventeen children on record.

CANNON, Clare Cordelia Moses. Second counselor to general president Louie B. Felt, Primary, June 19, 1880–Oct. 4, 1895; b. April 21, 1839, Westfield, Massachusetts; d. Aug. 21, 1926, Centerville, Utah; m. William H. Mason (d. 1860), two children; m. Angus M. Cannon, three children.

CANNON, Elaine Anderson. General president, Young Women, July 12, 1978–April 7, 1984; b. April 9, 1922, Salt Lake City, Utah; m. D. James Cannon, six children; editor "Era for Youth" in *Improvement Era.*

CANNON, George I. (Ivins). Seventy, April 6, 1986–Oct. 5, 1991; b. Mar. 9, 1920, Salt Lake City, Utah; m. Isabel Hales, seven children; businessman; regional representative, mission and stake president.

CANNON, George Q. (Quayle). Apostle, Aug. 26, 1860; Counselor to President Young, April 8, 1873; Asst. counselor to President Young, May 9, 1874; released at death of President Young, Aug. 29, 1877; First counselor to President John Taylor, Oct. 10, 1880; released at the death of President Taylor, July 25, 1887; First counselor to President Woodruff, April 7, 1889; First counselor to President Snow, Sept. 13, 1898–April 12, 1901;

b. Jan. 11, 1827, Liverpool, England; d. April 12, 1901, Monterey, California; m. Elizabeth Hoagland; practiced plural marriage, thirty-four children on record; businessman, editor.

CANNON, Janath Russell. First counselor to general president Barbara B. Smith, Relief Society, Oct. 3, 1974–April 7, 1984; b. Oct. 28, 1918, Ogden, Utah; m. Edwin Q. Cannon, six children; educator and writer; temple matron.

CANNON, John Q. (Quayle). Second counselor to Presiding Bishop William B. Preston, Oct. 5, 1884; excommunicated, Sept. 5, 1886; rebaptized May 6, 1888; b. April 19, 1857, San Francisco, California; d. Jan. 14, 1931, Salt Lake City, Utah; m. Elizabeth Ann Wells; practiced plural marriage, twelve children on record.

CANNON, Joseph J. First asst. to general superintendent George Q. Morris, Young Men, 1937–1945; b. May 22, 1877, Salt Lake City, Utah; d. Nov. 4, 1945, Salt Lake City; m. Ramona Wilcox, five children; newspaper editor; mission president.

CANNON, Lucy Grant. Second counselor to general president Martha Horne Tingey, Young Women, July 15, 1923–Mar. 28, 1929; First counselor to general president Ruth May Fox, Mar. 28, 1929–Oct. 1937; general president, Nov. 1937–April 6, 1948; b. Oct. 22, 1880, Salt Lake City, Utah; d. May 27, 1966, Salt Lake City; m. George J. Cannon, seven children.

CANNON, Sylvester Q. (Quayle). Presiding Bishop, June 4, 1925; Assoc. to the Twelve, April 6, 1938; Apostle, April 14, 1938; member of the Twelve, April 6, 1939–May 29, 1943; b. June 10, 1877, Salt Lake City, Utah; d. May 29, 1943, Salt Lake City; m. Winnifred Seville, two children; mission and stake president.

CANNON, Virginia Beesley. First counselor to general president Dwan J. Young, Primary, April 5, 1980–April 2, 1988; b. Feb. 5, 1925, Salt Lake City, Utah; m. H. Stanley Cannon, six children; homemaker; Primary general board member.

CARMACK, John K. (Kay). Seventy, April 7, 1984; b. May 10, 1931, Winslow, Arizona; m. Shirley Fay Allen, five children; attorney; regional representative, mission president.

CARRINGTON, Albert. Apostle, July 3, 1870; Counselor to President Brigham Young, April 8, 1873; Asst. counselor to President Young, May 9, 1874; released, Aug. 29, 1877 at the death of President Young; excommunicated, Nov. 7, 1885; rebaptized, Nov. 1, 1887; b. Jan. 8, 1813, Royalton, Vermont; d. Sept. 19, 1889, Salt Lake City, Utah; m. Rhoda Maria Woods; practiced plural marriage, fifteen children on record; attorney, educator; mission president.

CHILD, Hortense Hogan. First counselor to general president Ruth H. Funk, Young Women, Nov. 9, 1972–July 12, 1978; b. May 6, 1919, Thatcher, Idaho; m.

Romel Child, two children; civic worker; Young Women general board member.

CHILD, Julia Alleman. Second counselor to general president Louise Yates Robison, Relief Society, Oct. 7, 1928–Jan. 23, 1935; b. Sept. 8, 1873, Springville, Utah; d. Jan. 23, 1935, Salt Lake City, Utah; m. George N. Child, three children; educator; Relief Society general board member.

CHOULES, Albert, Jr. Seventy, Oct. 1, 1988; b. Feb. 15, 1926, Driggs, Idaho; m. Rosemary Phillips (d. 1984), three children; m. Marilyn Jeppson; businessman; regional representative, mission president.

CHRISTENSEN, Joe J. (Junior). Seventy, April 8, 1989; b. July 21, 1929, Banida, Idaho; m. Barbara Kohler, six children; president of Ricks College, Rexburg, Idaho; regional representative, mission president.

CHRISTIANSEN, ElRay L. (LaVar). Asst. to the Twelve, Oct. 11, 1951–Dec. 1, 1975; b. July 13, 1897, Mayfield, Utah; d. Dec. 1, 1975, Salt Lake City; m. Lewella Rees, three children; educator; temple and stake president.

CLAPP, Benjamin L. (Lynn). Seventy, Dec. 2, 1845; excommunicated, April 7, 1859; b. Aug. 19, 1814, West Huntsville, Alabama; d. 1860, Liberty, California; m. Mary Shultz; practiced plural marriage, twelve children; farmer.

CLARK, J. (Joshua) Reuben, Jr. Second counselor to President Grant, April 6, 1933; First counselor to President Grant, Oct. 6, 1934; Apostle, Oct. 11, 1934; First counselor to President George Albert Smith, May 21, 1945; Second counselor to President David O. McKay, April 9, 1951; First counselor to President McKay, June 12, 1959–Oct. 6, 1961; b. Sept. 1, 1871, Grantsville, Utah; d. Oct. 6, 1961, Salt Lake City; m. Luacine Savage, five children; U.S. ambassador to Mexico, attorney.

CLARKE, J. (John) Richard. Second counselor to Presiding Bishop Victor L. Brown, Oct. 1, 1976; Seventy, Oct. 1, 1988; b. April 4, 1927, Rexburg, Idaho; m. Barbara Jean Reed, eight children; businessman; regional representative, mission and stake president.

CLAWSON, Rudger. Apostle, Oct. 10, 1898–June 21, 1943; Second counselor to President Lorenzo Snow, Oct. 6, 1901; President of the Quorum of the Twelve Apostles, Mar. 17, 1921; b. Mar. 12, 1857, Salt Lake City, Utah; d. June 21, 1943, Salt Lake City; m. Florence Dinwoodey; practiced plural marriage, eleven children on record; businessman; mission and stake president.

CLEVELAND, Sarah Marietta Kingsley. First counselor to general president Emma Hale Smith, Relief Society, Mar. 17, 1842–Mar. 16, 1844; b. Oct. 20, 1788, Berkshire, Massachusetts; m. John Cleveland.

CLYDE, Aileen Hales. Second counselor to general president Elaine L. Jack, Relief Society, Mar. 31, 1990;

children on record; businessman; mission and stake president.

CLEVELAND, Sarah Marietta Kingsley. First counselor to general president Emma Hale Smith, Relief Society, Mar. 17, 1842–Mar. 16, 1844; b. Oct. 20, 1788, Berkshire, Massachusetts; m. John Cleveland.

CLYDE, Aileen Hales. Second counselor to general president Elaine L. Jack, Relief Society, Mar. 31, 1990; b. May 18, 1928, Springville, Utah; m. Hal M. Clyde, three children; homemaker, educator; Young Women general board member.

COLTRIN, Zebedee. Seventy, Feb. 28, 1835; released April 6, 1837, having previously been ordained high priest; b. Sept. 7, 1804, Ovid, New York; d. July 20, 1887, Spanish Fork, Utah; m. Julia Ann Jennings; practiced plural marriage, sixteen children on record; farmer.

CONDIE, Spencer J. (Joel). Seventy, April 7, 1989; b. Aug. 27, 1940, Preston, Idaho; m. Bridgitte Dorothea Speth, five children; educator; regional representative, mission and stake president.

COOK, Gene R. (Raymond). Seventy, Oct. 3, 1975; b. Sept. 1, 1941, Lehi, Utah; m. Janelle Schlink, eight children; management; regional representative, mission president.

CORRILL, John. Second counselor to Presiding Bishop Edward Partridge, June 3, 1831; released Aug. 1, 1837; excommunicated Mar. 17, 1839; b. Sept. 17, 1794, Worcester Co., Massachusetts; m. Margaret, five children.

COWDERY, Oliver. Apostle, May–June 1829; Second Elder of the Church, April 6, 1830; Asst. president of the High Priesthood, Dec. 5, 1834; Asst. counselor to President Joseph Smith, Sept. 3, 1837; excommunicated April 11, 1838; rebaptized Nov. 12, 1848; b. Oct. 3, 1806, Wells, Vermont; d. Mar. 3, 1850, Richmond, Missouri; m. Elizabeth Ann Whitmer, six children; attorney, educator.

COWLEY, Matthew. Apostle, Oct. 11, 1945; b. Aug. 2, 1897, Preston, Idaho; d. Dec. 13, 1953, Los Angeles, California; m. Elva Taylor, three children; attorney; mission president.

COWLEY, Matthias F. (Foss). Apostle, Oct. 7, 1897; resigned, Oct. 28, 1905; priesthood suspended, May 11, 1911; restored to full membership, April 3, 1936; b. Aug. 25, 1858, Salt Lake City, Utah; d. June 16, 1940, Salt Lake City; m. Abbie Hyde; practiced plural marriage, thirteen children on record.

CRAVEN, Rulon G. (Gerald). Seventy, Dec. 5, 1990; b. Nov. 11, 1924, Murray, Utah; m. Donna Lunt, six children; secretary to Council of the Twelve; regional representative, Sunday School general board member, mission president.

CRITCHLOW, William J. (James), Jr. Asst. to the Twelve, Oct. 16, 1958–Aug. 29, 1968; b. Aug. 21, 1892,

Brigham City, Utah; d. Aug. 29, 1968, Ogden; m. Anna Marie Taylor, three children; business executive; stake president.

CULLIMORE, James A. (Alfred). Asst. to the Twelve, April 6, 1966; Seventy, Oct. 1, 1976; Emeritus General Authority, Sept. 30, 1978; b. Jan. 17, 1906, Lindon, Utah; d. June 14, 1986, Salt Lake City; m. Grace Gardner, three children; businessman; stake president.

CURTIS, Elbert R. (Raine). General superintendent, Young Men, 1948–1958; b. April 24, 1901, Salt Lake City, Utah; m. Luceal Rockwood, three children; mission and stake president.

CURTIS, LeGrand R. (Raine). First counselor to general president Robert L. Backman, Young Men, Nov. 1972–June 23, 1974; Seventy, Mar. 31, 1990; b. May 22, 1924, Salt Lake City, Utah; m. Patricia Glade, eight children; dentist; regional representative, mission and stake president.

CUTHBERT, Derek A. (Alfred). Seventy, April 1, 1978–April 7, 1991; b. Oct. 5, 1926, Nottingham, England; d. April 7, 1991, Salt Lake City, Utah; m. Muriel Olive Mason, ten children; business executive; regional representative, mission and stake president.

CUTLER, Clinton L. (Louis). Seventy, Mar. 31, 1990; b. Dec. 27, 1929, Salt Lake City, Utah; m. Hellie Helena Sharp, six children; retired business management; regional representative, mission and stake president.

DARGER, Arlene Barlow. First counselor to general president Elaine A. Cannon, Young Women, July 12, 1978–April 7, 1984; b. July 14, 1925, Salt Lake City, Utah; m. Stanford P. Darger, five children; Tabernacle Choir member.

DÁVILA PEÑALOZA, Julio E. (Enrique). Seventy, April 6, 1991; b. May 23, 1932, Bucaramanga, Colombia; m. Mary Zapata, two children; education administration; regional representative, stake president.

DE JAGER, Jacob. Seventy, April 3, 1976; b. Jan. 16, 1923, The Hague, Netherlands; m. Bea Lim, two children; business executive; regional representative.

DELLENBACH, Robert K. (Kent). Seventy, Mar. 31, 1990; b. May 10, 1937, Salt Lake City, Utah; m. Mary-Jane Broadbent, three children; scientific education management; regional representative, mission and stake president.

DERRICK, Royden G. (Glade). Seventy, Oct. 1, 1976; Emeritus General Authority, Oct. 1, 1989; b. Sept. 7, 1915, Salt Lake City, Utah; m. Allie Jean Olson, four children; businessman; temple and mission president.

DIDIER, Charles A. (Amand) A. (Andre). Seventy, Oct. 3, 1975; b. Oct. 5, 1935, Ixelles, Belgium; m. Lucie Lodomez, two children; business executive; regional representative, mission president.

DOUGALL, Maria Young. First counselor to general president Elmina Shepherd Taylor, Young Women,

1877–Dec. 6, 1904; b. Dec. 10, 1849, Salt Lake City, Utah; d. April 30, 1935, Salt Lake City; m. William B. Dougall, three children.

DOXEY, Graham W. (Watson). First counselor to general president Neil D. Schaerrer, Young Men, April 7, 1977–Oct. 1979; Seventy, April 6, 1991; b. Mar. 30, 1927, Salt Lake City, Utah; m. Mary Louise Young, twelve children; business executive; mission and stake president.

DOXEY, Joanne Bushman. Second counselor to general president Barbara W. Winder, Relief Society, May 21, 1984–Mar. 31, 1990; b. April 17, 1932, Salt Lake City, Utah; m. David W. Doxey, eight children; Primary general board member.

DOXEY, Leone B. Watson. Second counselor to general president LaVern Watts Parmley, Primary, Sept. 10, 1953–April 6, 1962; First counselor, April 6, 1962–Oct. 23, 1969; b. Sept. 3, 1899, Salt Lake City, Utah; m. Graham H. Doxey, four children; Primary general board member.

DUNN, Loren C. (Charles). Seventy, April 6, 1968; b. June 12, 1930, Tooele, Utah; m. Sharon Longden; five children; business executive; stake and mission president.

DUNN, Paul H. (Harold). Seventy, April 6, 1964; Emeritus General Authority, Oct. 1, 1989; b. April 24, 1924, Provo, Utah; m. Jeanne Alice Cheverton, three children; educator.

DUNYON, O. (Olive) Eileen Robinson. Second counselor to general president LaVern Watts Parmley, Primary, April 6, 1962–June 3, 1963; b. June 3, 1917, Preston, Idaho; m. Joy F. Dunyon, three children; school librarian.

DURHAM, G. (George) Homer. Seventy, April 2, 1977–Jan. 10, 1985; b. Feb. 4, 1911, Parowan, Utah; d. Jan. 10, 1985, Salt Lake City; m. Eudora Widtsoe, three children; former president of Arizona State University, and former Commissioner of Higher Education for State of Utah; regional representative, stake president.

DUSENBERRY, Ida Smoot. Second counselor to general president Bathsheba W. Smith, Relief Society, Nov. 10, 1901–Sept. 20, 1910; b. May 5, 1873, Salt Lake City, Utah; d. April 25, 1955; m. George Albert Dusenberry, two children; educator.

DYER, Alvin R. (Rulon). Asst. to the Twelve, Oct. 11, 1958; Apostle, Oct. 5, 1967–Mar. 6, 1977; Counselor to President David O. McKay, April 6, 1968; released, Jan. 18, 1970, at the death of President McKay; resumed position as Asst. to the Twelve, Jan. 23, 1970; Seventy, Oct. 1, 1976; b. Jan. 1, 1903, Salt Lake City, Utah; d. Mar. 6, 1977, Salt Lake City; m. May Elizabeth Jackson, two children; businessman; mission president.

ELDREDGE, Horace S. (Sunderlin). Seventy, Oct. 7, 1854–Sept. 6, 1888; b. Feb. 6, 1816, Brutus, New York; d. Sept. 6, 1888, Salt Lake City, Utah; m. Sarah Gibbs; practiced plural marriage, twenty-eight children on record; businessman, superintendent of ZCMI; mission president.

ELDREDGE, W. Jay. General superintendent, Young Men, Sept. 17 1969–June 25, 1972; general president, Young Men, June 25, 1972–Nov. 9, 1972; b. April 27, 1913, Salt Lake City, Utah; m. Marjory Hyde, five children; businessman; mission and stake president.

EVANS, Joy Frewin. First counselor to general president Barbara W. Winder, Relief Society, May 21, 1984–Mar. 31, 1990; b. Jan. 31, 1926, Salt Lake City; m. David C. Evans, ten children; homemaker; Relief Society general board member.

EVANS, Richard L. (Louis). Seventy, Oct. 7, 1938; Apostle, Oct. 8, 1953–Nov. 1, 1971; b. Mar. 23, 1906, Salt Lake City, Utah; d. Nov. 1, 1971, Salt Lake City; m. Alice Ruth Thornley, four children; voice of the "Spoken Word" in weekly Mormon Tabernacle Broadcast, 1930-1971; editor, *Improvement Era*.

EYRING, Henry B. (Bennion). First counselor to Presiding Bishop Robert D. Hales, April 6, 1985; b. May 31, 1933, Princeton, New Jersey; m. Kathleen Johnson, six children; Commissioner of Church Education, former president of Ricks College, Rexburg, Idaho; regional representative, Sunday School general board member.

FARNSWORTH, Burton K. (Kent). Asst. to general superintendent George Q. Morris, Young Men, 1937-1945; b. Mar. 6, 1890, Beaver, Utah; d. Oct. 27, 1945, Seattle, Washington; m. Mabel Pearce, six children; educator; Young Men general board member.

FAUST, James E. (Esdras). Asst. to the Twelve, Oct. 6, 1972; Seventy, Oct. 1, 1976; Apostle, Oct. 1, 1978; b. July 31, 1920, Delta, Utah; m. Ruth Wright, five children; attorney; regional representative, mission and stake president.

FEATHERSTONE, Vaughn J. Second counselor Presiding Bishop Victor L. Brown, April 6, 1972; Seventy, Oct. 1, 1976; b. Mar. 26, 1931, Stockton, Utah; m. Merlene Miner, seven children; business executive; mission and stake president.

FELT, Louie Bouton. General president, Primary, June 19, 1880–Oct. 6, 1925; b. May 5, 1850, Norwalk, Connecticut; d. Feb. 13, 1928, Salt Lake City, Utah; m. Joseph H. Felt.

FJELSTED, Christian D. (Daniel). Seventy, April 6, 1884–Dec. 23, 1905; b. Feb. 20, 1829, Sundbyvester, (near) Copenhagen, Denmark; d. Dec. 23, 1905, Salt Lake City, Utah; m. Karen Olsen; practiced plural marriage, fifteen children on record; mission president.

FOSTER, James. Seventy, April 6, 1837–Dec. 21, 1841; b. April 1, 1786, Hillsborough County, New Hampshire; d. Dec. 21, 1841, Morgan County, Illinois; m. Abigail Glidden, six children.

FOX, Ruth May. First counselor to general president Martha Horne Tingey, Young Women, April 5, 1905–

Mar. 28, 1929; general president, Mar. 28, 1929–Oct. 1937; b. Nov. 16, 1853, Willshire, England; d. April 12, 1958; m. Jesse W. Fox, Jr., twelve children.

FREEZE, Lillie Tuckett. First counselor to general president Louie B. Felt, Primary, Dec. 29, 1905–Oct. 6, 1925; b. Mar. 26, 1855, Salt Lake City, Utah; d. Mar. 23, 1937, Salt Lake City; m. James Perry Freeze, four children; Primary and Young Women general board member.

FUNK, Ruth Hardy. General president, Young Women, June 23, 1974–July 12, 1978; b. Feb. 11, 1917, Chicago, Illinois; m. Marcus C. Funk, four children; high school choral director; Young Women general board member.

FYANS, J. (John) Thomas. Asst. to the Twelve, April 6, 1974; Seventy 1976–1985; Emeritus General Authority, Oct. 1, 1989; b. May 17, 1918, Moreland Idaho; m. Helen Cook, five children; business executive; regional representative, mission president.

GARFF, Gertrude Ryberg. Second counselor to general president Belle S. Spafford, Relief Society, April 6, 1945–Sept. 30, 1947; b. Nov. 2, 1910, Hyrum, Utah; m. Mark Brimhall Garff; Relief Society general board member.

GATES, Jacob. Seventy, April 6, 1860–April 14, 1892; b. Mar. 9, 1811, Saint Johnsbury, Vermont; d. April 14, 1892, Provo, Utah; m. Mary Minerva Snow; practiced plural marriage, thirteen children on record; farmer.

GAUSE, Jesse. Counselor to President Joseph Smith, Mar. 8, 1832; sent on mission from which he never returned; excommunicated, Dec. 3, 1832; b. about 1784, East Marlborough, Virginia; d. about 1836; m. Martha Cuntry, five children.

GAYLORD, John. Seventy, April 6, 1837; excommunicated, Jan. 13, 1838; rebaptized Oct. 5, 1839; b. July 12, 1797, Pennsylvania; d. July 17, 1878; m. Elvira Edmonds.

GEE, Salmon. Seventy, April 6, 1837; fellowship withdrawn, Mar. 6, 1838; b. Oct. 16, 1792, Lyme, Connecticut; d. Sept. 13, 1845, Ambrosia, Iowa; posthumously reinstated, Sept. 14, 1967; m. Sarah Watson Crane, two children.

GEORGE, Lloyd P. (Preal). Seventy, Oct. 1, 1988; b. Sept. 17, 1920, Kanosh, Utah. m. Leola Stott, three children; real estate broker; regional representative, mission and stake president.

GIBBONS, Francis M. (Marion). Seventy, April 6, 1986–Oct. 5, 1991; secretary to First Presidency for 16 years; b. April 10, 1921, St. Johns, Arizona; m. Helen Bay, four children; attorney; stake president.

GILES, John D. (Davis). First asst. to general superintendent George Q. Morris, Young Men, 1937–1948; b. Aug. 1, 1883, Salt Lake City, Utah; d. Sept. 23, 1955, Salt Lake City; m. Una Pratt, four children; businessman, Boy Scout official.

GOASLIND, Jack H., Jr. Seventy, Sept. 30, 1978; b. April 18, 1928, Salt Lake City, Utah; m. Gwen Caroline Bradford, six children; business executive; counselor Young Men, regional representative, mission and stake president.

GODDARD, George. First asst. to general superintendent George Q. Cannon, Sunday School, June 1872–Jan. 1899; b. Dec. 5, 1813, Leicester, England; d. Jan. 12, 1899, Salt Lake City, Utah; m. Elizabeth Harrison; practiced plural marriage, eighteen children on record.

GODDARD, Verna Wright. Second counselor to general president Lucy Grant Cannon, Young Women, Nov. 1937–July 1944; First counselor, July 1944–April 6, 1948; b. Nov. 24, 1889, Salt Lake City, Utah; d. Nov. 26, 1949; m. J. Percy Goddard, four children.

GOULD, John. Seventy, April 6, 1837–May 9, 1851; b. May 11, 1808, Ontario, Canada; d. May 9, 1851, Cooley's Mill, Iowa; m. Abigail Harrington, two children.

GRANT, Heber J. (Jeddy). Apostle, Oct. 16, 1882; President of the Quorum of the Twelve Apostles, Nov. 23, 1916; President of the Church, Nov. 23, 1918–May 14, 1945; b. Nov. 22, 1856, Salt Lake City, Utah; d. May 14, 1945, Salt Lake City; m. Lucy Stringham; practiced plural marriage, twelve children; businessman. (*See biography,* Grant, Heber J.)

GRANT, Jedediah M. (Morgan). Seventy, Dec. 2, 1845; Apostle, April 7, 1854; Second counselor to President Brigham Young, April 7, 1854–Dec. 1, 1856; b. Feb. 21, 1816, Windsor, New York; d. Dec. 1, 1856, Salt Lake City, Utah; m. Caroline Van Dyke; practiced plural marriage, eight children (including one adopted child) on record; his seventh wife, Rachel Ridgeway Ivins, was the mother of President Heber J. Grant; farmer, civil servant.

GRASSLI, Michaelene Packer. General president, Primary, April 2, 1988; b. June 19, 1940, Salt Lake City, Utah; m. Leonard M. Grassli, three children; homemaker; stake Primary president.

GROBERG, John H. (Holbrook). Seventy, April 3, 1976; b. June 17, 1934, Idaho Falls, Idaho; m. Jean Sabin, eleven children; business executive; regional representative, mission president.

HAIGHT, David B. (Bruce). Asst. to the Twelve, April 6, 1970; Apostle, Jan. 8, 1976; b. Sept. 2, 1906, Oakley, Idaho; m. Ruby Olsen, three children; business executive; regional representative, mission and stake president.

HALE, Arta Matthews. First counselor to general president LaVern Watts Parmley, Primary, May 16, 1951–April 6, 1962; b. Oct. 24, 1898, Oakley, Idaho; d. July 11, 1990, Salt Lake City, Utah; m. Dewey Hale, two children; Primary general board member.

HALES, Janette Callister. Second counselor to general president Ardeth G. Kapp, Young Women, Mar. 31,

1990; b. June 7, 1933, Springville, Utah; m. Robert H. Hales, five children; homemaker, legislator; Primary general board member.

HALES, Robert D. (Dean). Asst. to the Twelve, April 4, 1975; Seventy, Oct. 1, 1976; First counselor to general president Hugh W. Pinnock, Sunday School, July 1981–July 1985; Presiding Bishop, April 6, 1985; b. Aug 24, 1932, New York City, New York; m. Mary Elene Crandall, two children; business executive; regional representative, mission and stake president.

HAMMOND, F. (Frank) Melvin. Seventy, April 7, 1989; b. Dec. 19, 1933, Blackfoot, Idaho; m. Bonnie Sellers, six children; educator, legislator; mission and stake president.

HAN, In Sang. Seventy, June 1, 1991; b. Dec. 9, 1939, Seoul, Korea; m. Lee Hyn In, five children; business management; regional representative and mission president.

HANCOCK, Levi W. (Ward). Seventy, Feb. 28, 1835; released April 6, 1837, having supposedly previously been ordained a high priest; restored to place in First Council of the Seventy, Sept. 3, 1837; b. April 7, 1803, Springfield, Massachusetts; d. June 10, 1882, Washington, Utah; m. Clarissa Reed; practiced plural marriage, nineteen children on record; cabinet maker.

HANKS, Marion D. (Duff). Seventy Oct. 4, 1953; Asst. to the Twelve, April 6, 1968; b. Oct. 13, 1921, Salt Lake City, Utah; m. Maxine Christensen, five children; educator; temple and mission president.

HANSEN, W. (Warren) Eugene. Seventy, April 8, 1989; b. Aug. 23, 1928, Tremonton, Utah; m. Jeanine Showell, six children; attorney; stake president.

HARBERTSON, Robert B. Seventy, April 7, 1984–Oct. 1, 1989; b. April 19, 1932, Ogden, Utah; m. Norma Creer, five children; business executive; regional representative, mission president.

HARDY, Leonard W. (Wilford). First counselor to Presiding Bishop Edward Hunter, Oct. 6, 1856–Oct. 16, 1883, and to Bishop William B. Preston April 6, 1884–July 31, 1884; b. Dec. 31, 1805, Bradford, Massachusetts; d. July 31, 1884, Salt Lake City, Utah; m. Elizabeth Harriman Nichols; practiced plural marriage, eighteen children on record; farmer, businessman.

HARDY, M. (Milton) H. First asst. to general superintendent Junius F. Wells, Young Men, 1876–1880; b. Sept. 26, 1844, Groveland, Massachusetts; d. Aug. 23, 1905, Provo, Utah; m. Elizabeth Smoot, five children.

HARDY, Ralph W. (Williams). Second asst. to general superintendent Elbert R. Curtis, Young Men, 1948–1957; b. May 6, 1916, Salt Lake City, Utah; d. Aug. 6, 1957, Ogden; m. Maren Eccles, four children; radio executive.

HARDY, Rufus K. (Kay). Seventy, Oct. 6, 1934–Mar. 7, 1945; b. May 28, 1878, Salt Lake City, Utah; d. Mar. 7, 1945, Salt Lake City; m. Alelade Underwood Eldredge; business executive; mission president.

HARRIMAN, Henry. Seventy, Feb. 6, 1838–May 17, 1891; b. June 9, 1804, Rowley (Georgetown), Massachusetts; d. May 17, 1891, Huntington, Utah; m. Clarissa Boynton; practiced plural marriage, nine children on record.

HARRIS, Devere. Seventy, April 7, 1984–Oct. 1, 1989; b. May 30, 1916, Portage, Utah; m. Velda Gibbs, five children; businessman; regional representative, temple and stake president.

HART, Charles H. (Henry). Seventy, April 9, 1906–Sept. 29, 1934; b. July 5, 1866, Bloomington, Idaho; d. Sept. 29, 1934, Salt Lake City, Utah; m. Adelia Greenhalgh (d. 1913), ten children; m. LaLene Hendricks.

HATCH, Lorenzo H. (Hill). Second asst. to general superintendent George Q. Morris, Young Men, 1937–1948; b. Feb. 23, 1893, Franklin, Idaho; d. Nov. 27, 1971, Salt Lake City, Utah; m. Ina Porter, four children; stake president.

HIGBEE, Elias. Church historian, April 6, 1838–June 8, 1843; b. Oct. 23, 1795, Galloway, New Jersey; d. June 8, 1843, Nauvoo, Illinois; m. Sarah Elizabeth Ward, eight children; judge.

HILL, George R. (Richard), III. Seventy, April 4, 1987; b. Nov. 24, 1921, Ogden, Utah; m. Melba Parker, seven children; educator; regional representative.

HILLAM, Harold G. (Gordon). Seventy, Mar. 31, 1990; b. Sept. 1, 1934, Sugar City, Idaho; m. Carol Lois Rasmussen, seven children; orthodontist; regional representative, mission and stake president.

HINCKLEY, Alonzo A. (Arza). Apostle, Oct. 11, 1934–Dec. 22, 1936; b. April 23, 1870, Cove Fort, Utah; d. Dec. 22, 1936, Salt Lake City; m. Rose May Robison, 14 children; stake president; (christened Arza Alonzo Hinckley, but signed his name Alonzo A. Hinckley).

HINCKLEY, Gordon B. (Bitner). Asst. to the Twelve, April 6, 1958; Apostle Oct. 5, 1961; Counselor to President Spencer W. Kimball, July 23, 1981; Second counselor, Dec. 2, 1982; First counselor to President Ezra Taft Benson, Nov. 10, 1985; b. June 23, 1910, Salt Lake City, Utah; m. Marjorie Pay, five children; business executive; stake president.

HINCKLEY, May Green. General president, Primary, Jan. 1, 1940–May 2, 1943; b. May 1, 1885, Brampton, England; d. May 2, 1943, Salt Lake City, Utah; m. Bryant S. Hinckley; nurse; stake Young Women president.

HOLLAND, Jeffrey R. (Roy). Seventy, April 7, 1989; b. Dec. 3, 1940; m. Patricia Terry, three children; educator, President of BYU and former Commissioner of Church Education; regional representative.

HOLLAND, Patricia Terry. First counselor to general president Ardeth G. Kapp, Young Women, May 11, 1984–April 6, 1986; b. Feb. 16, 1942, St. George, Utah;

m. Jeffrey R. Holland, three children; homemaker; Young Women general board member.

HOLT, Dorothy Martha Porter. Second counselor to general president Florence S. Jacobsen, Young Women, Sept. 30, 1961–Nov. 9, 1972; b. Feb, 5, 1912, Salt Lake City, Utah; m. A. Palmer Holt, five children; homemaker.

HOWARD, F. (Fred) Burton. Seventy, Sept. 30, 1978; b. Mar. 24, 1933, Logan, Utah; m. Caroline Heise, five children; attorney; stake president.

HOWELLS, Adele Cannon. First counselor to general president May Green Hinckley, Primary, Jan. 1, 1940– May 2, 1943; general president, July 29, 1943–April 14, 1951; b. Jan. 12, 1886, Salt Lake City, Utah; d. Apr. 14, 1951, Salt Lake City; m. David P. Howells, three children; homemaker, educator.

HOWELLS, Marcia Knowlton. First counselor to general president Amy Brown Lyman, Relief Society, April 1940–April 6, 1945; b. May 28, 1888, Farmington, Utah; d. June 10, 1976, Salt Lake City; m. Thomas J. Howells, one child; homemaker; Relief Society general board member.

HUNTER, Edward. Presiding Bishop of the Church, April 7, 1851–Oct. 16, 1883; b. June 22, 1793, Newton, Pennsylvania; d. Oct. 16, 1883, Salt Lake City, Utah; m. Ann Standly (Stanley); practiced plural marriage, thirteen children on record; farmer.

HUNTER, Howard W. (William). Apostle, Oct. 15, 1959; Acting president of the Quorum of the Twelve, Nov. 10, 1985; President of the Quorum, June 2, 1988; b. Nov. 24, 1907, Boise, Idaho; m. Clara May Jeffs (d. 1983), three children; m. Inis Egan; attorney; stake president.

HUNTER, Milton R. (Reed). Seventy, April 6, 1945– June 27, 1975; b. Oct. 25, 1902, Holden, Utah; d. June 27, 1975, Salt Lake City; m. Ferne Gardner, six children; educator.

HYDE, Annie M. Taylor. First counselor to general president Bathsheba W. Smith, Relief Society, Nov. 10, 1901–Mar. 12, 1909; b. Oct. 20, 1849, Salt Lake City, Utah; d. Mar. 12, 1909; m. Alonzo E. Hyde, eight children.

HYDE, Orson. Apostle, Feb. 15, 1835; dropped from the Quorum, May 4, 1839; restored to the Quorum, June 27, 1839; President of the Quorum of Twelve Apostles, Dec. 27, 1847; seniority adjusted to date of second entry into the Quorum, April 10, 1875; b. Jan. 8, 1805, Oxford, Connecticut; d. Nov. 28, 1878, Spring City, Utah; m. Marinda Nancy Johnson; practiced plural marriage, thirty-two children on record; editor.

ISAACSON, H. (Henry) Thorpe B. (Beal). Second counselor to Presiding Bishop LeGrand Richards, Dec. 12, 1946; First counselor to Presiding Bishop Joseph L. Wirthlin, April 6, 1952; Asst. to the Twelve, Sept. 30, 1961; Counselor to President David O. McKay, Oct. 28,

1965; released at death of President McKay, Jan. 18, 1970; resumed position as Asst. to the Twelve, Jan. 23, 1970–Nov. 9, 1970; b. Sept. 6, 1898, Ephraim, Utah; d. Nov. 9, 1970, Salt Lake City; m. Lula Maughn Jones, two children; businessman.

IVINS, Anthony W. (Woodward). Apostle, Oct. 6, 1907; Second counselor to President Heber J. Grant, Mar. 10, 1921; First counselor to President Grant, May 28, 1925– Sept. 23, 1934; b. Sept. 16, 1852, Toms River, New Jersey; d. Sept. 23, 1934, Salt Lake City, Utah; m. Elizabeth Ashby Snow, nine children; rancher, businessman; Young Men general board member.

IVINS, Antoine R. (Ridgeway). Seventy, Oct. 8, 1931– Oct. 18, 1967; b. May 11, 1881, St. George, Utah; d. Oct. 18, 1967, Salt Lake City; m. Vilate Romney; farm manager; mission president.

JACK, Elaine Low. Second counselor to general president Ardeth G. Kapp, Young Women, April 4, 1987– Mar. 31, 1990; general president, Relief Society, Mar. 31, 1990; b. Mar. 22, 1928, Cardston, Alberta, Canada; m. Joseph E. Jack, four children; homemaker; Relief Society general board member, stake Relief Society president.

JACOBSEN, Florence Smith. General president, Young Women, Sept. 30, 1961–Nov. 9, 1972; b. April 7, 1913, Salt Lake City, Utah; m. Theodore C. Jacobsen, three children; homemaker, businesswoman; Church curator of museums.

JENSEN, Marlin K. (Keith). Seventy, April 7, 1989; b. May 18, 1942, Ogden, Utah; m. Kathleen Bushnell, eight children; attorney; regional representative, stake president.

JEPPSEN, Malcolm S. (Seth). Seventy, April 7, 1989; b. Nov. 1, 1924, Mantua, Utah; m. Marian Davis, five children; physician; regional representative, stake president.

JEPSEN, Betty Jo Nelson. First counselor to general president Michaelene P. Grassli, Primary, April 2, 1988; b. Dec. 3, 1940, Boise, Idaho; m. Glen F. Jepsen, four children; educator, homemaker; Primary general board member, stake Primary president.

JOHNSON, Kenneth. Seventy, May 31, 1990; b. July 5, 1940; Norwich, England; m. Pamela Wilson, one child; business executive; regional representative, stake president.

JOHNSON, Luke S. Apostle, Feb. 15, 1835; excommunicated, April 13, 1838; rebaptized in 1846; b. Nov. 2, 1807, Pomfret, Vermont; d. Dec. 9, 1861, Salt Lake City, Utah; m. Susan Poteet; practiced plural marriage, fifteen children on record; educator, doctor.

JOHNSON, Lyman E. (Eugene). Apostle, Feb. 14, 1835; excommunicated, April 13, 1838; b. Oct. 24, 1811; Pomfret, Vermont; d. Dec. 20, 1856, Prairie du Chien, Wisconsin; m. Sarah Land (Lang, Long), two children; attorney.

JUDD, Margaret Romney Jackson. First counselor to general president Florence S. Jacobsen, Young Women, Sept. 30, 1961–Nov. 9, 1972; b. Sept. 7, 1909, Colonia Juárez, Mexico; m. Junius M. Jackson (d. 1981), five children; m. George E. Judd; homemaker; Young Women general board member.

KAPP, Ardeth Greene. Second counselor to general president Ruth H. Funk, Young Women, Nov. 9, 1972– July 12, 1978; general president, Young Women, April 7, 1984; b. Mar. 19, 1931, Glenwood, Alberta, Canada; m. Heber B. Kapp; educator; Church Correlation Committee member.

KAY, F. (Ferril) Arthur. Seventy, Oct. 6, 1984; Emeritus General Authority, Oct. 1, 1989; b. July 15, 1916, Annabella, Utah; m. Eunice D. Nielsen, six children; dentist; temple president.

KENDRICK, L. (Larry) Lionel. Seventy, April 2, 1988; b. Sept. 19, 1931, Baton Rouge, Louisiana; m. Myrtis Lee Noble, four children; educator; regional representative, mission and stake president.

KIKUCHI, Yoshihiko. Seventy, Oct. 1, 1977; b. July 25, 1941, Horoizumi, Japan; m. Toshiko Koshiya, four children; business executive; mission and stake president.

KIMBALL, Heber C. (Chase). Apostle, Feb. 14, 1835; First counselor to President Brigham Young, Dec. 27, 1847–June 22, 1868; b. June 14, 1801, Sheldon, Vermont; d. June 22, 1868, Salt Lake City, Utah; m. Vilate Murray; practiced plural marriage, sixty-five children on record; potter, businessman. (*See biography*, Kimball, Heber C.)

KIMBALL, J. (Jonathan) Golden. Seventy, April 5, 1892–Sept. 2, 1938; b. June 9, 1853, Salt Lake City, Utah; d. Sept. 2, 1938, Reno, Nevada; m. Jennie Knowlton, six children; Young Men general board member, mission president.

KIMBALL, Spencer W. (Woolley). Apostle, Oct. 7, 1943; President of the Quorum of Twelve Apostles, 1970; President of the Church, Dec. 30, 1973–Nov. 5, 1985; b. Mar. 28, 1895, Salt Lake City, Utah; d. Nov. 5, 1985, Salt Lake City; m. Camilla Eyring, four children; businessman; stake president. (*See biography*, Kimball, Spencer W.)

KING, David S. (Sjodahl). Second asst. to general superintendent Elbert R. Curtis, Young Men, 1948–1958; b. June 20, 1917, Salt Lake City, Utah; m. Rosalie Lehner, three children; former United States Congressman.

KIRKHAM, Oscar A. (Ammon). Seventy, Oct. 5, 1941– Mar. 10, 1958; b. Jan. 22, 1880, Lehi, Utah; d. Mar. 10, 1958, Salt Lake City; m. Ida Murdock, eight children; Young Men general board member, Boy Scouts of America executive.

KNIGHT, Lucy Jane (Jennie) Brimhall. First counselor to general president Clarissa Smith Williams, Relief Society, April 2, 1921–Oct. 7, 1928; b. Dec. 13, 1875, Spanish Fork, Utah; d. Mar. 31, 1957, Provo, Utah; m. Jesse William Knight, two children; executive for Utah County Red Cross.

KOFFORD, Cree-L. Seventy, April 6, 1991; b. July 11, 1933, Santaquin, Utah; m. Ila Macdonald, five children; attorney; regional representative, mission and stake president.

KOMATSU, Adney Y. (Yoshio). Asst. to the Twelve, April 4, 1975; Seventy, Oct. 1, 1976; b. Aug. 2, 1923, Honolulu, Hawaii; m. Judy Nobue Fujitani, four children; businessman; regional representative, temple and mission president.

LAMBERT, Edith Elizabeth Hunter. Second counselor to general president May Anderson, Primary, Dec. 11, 1933–Dec. 31, 1939; b. Mar. 14, 1878, Salt Lake City, Utah; d. Mar. 3, 1964, Salt Lake City; m. James N. Lambert, three children.

LANE, Florence Reece. Second counselor to general president LaVern Watts Parmley, Primary; Jan. 8, 1970– Oct. 5, 1974; b. Feb. 24, 1915; m. Perry L. Lane, three children; educator; Primary general board member.

LARSEN, Dean L. (LeRoy). Seventy, Feb. 22, 1980; b. May 24, 1927, Hyrum, Utah; m. Geneal Johnson, five children; coach, educator; regional representative, mission president, Young Men general board member.

LASATER, John R. (Roger). Seventy, April 4, 1987; b. Dec. 8, 1931, Farmington, Utah; m. Marily Jones, five children; USAF ret.; regional representative, mission and stake president.

LAW, William. Second counselor to President Joseph Smith, Jan. 24, 1841; excommunicated, April 18, 1844; b. Sept. 8, 1809, Tyrone County, North Ireland; d. Jan. 19, 1892, Shullsburg, Wisconsin; m. Jane Silverthorn, eight children; businessman, doctor.

LAWRENCE, W. (William) Mack. Seventy, Dec. 5, 1990; b. Oct. 28, 1926, Salt Lake City, Utah; m. Jacqueline Young, three children; business executive; regional representative.

LEE, George P. (Patrick). Seventy, Oct. 3, 1975; excommunicated, Sept. 1, 1989; b. Mar. 23, 1943, Towaoc, Colorado; m. Katherine Hettich, three children; educator; mission president.

LEE, Harold B. (Bingham). Apostle, April 10, 1941; President of the Quorum of the Twelve and first counselor to President Joseph Fielding Smith, Jan. 23, 1970; President of the Church, July 7, 1972–Dec. 26, 1973; b. Mar. 28, 1899, Clifton, Idaho; d. Dec. 26, 1973, Salt Lake City, Utah; m. Fern Lucinda Tanner (d. 1962), two children; m. Freda Joan Jensen; educator, civil servant; stake president. (*See biography*, Lee, Harold B.)

LEMMON, Colleen Bushman. Second counselor to general president Naomi M. Shumway, Primary, Oct. 5, 1974–April 2, 1977; First counselor, April 2, 1977–April 5, 1980; b. July 14, 1927, Salt Lake City, Utah; m. George Van Lemmon, four children; president New

Louis, Missouri; d. July 20, 1899; m. Martha J. Coray; practiced plural marriage, sixteen children on record.

LINDSAY, Richard P. (Powell). Seventy, April 7, 1989; b. Mar. 18, 1926; m. Marian Bangerter, six children; managing director Special Affairs/Public Communication Dept. of the Church; stake president.

LONGDEN, John. Asst. to the Twelve, Oct. 6, 1951–Aug. 30, 1969; b. Nov. 4, 1898, Oldham, England; d. Aug. 30, 1969, Salt Lake City, Utah; m. Frances LaRue Carr, three children; businessman; stake president.

LONGDEN, Frances LaRue Carr. Second counselor to Bertha S. Reeder, Young Women, June 13, 1948–Sept. 30, 1961; b. April 2, 1901; d. May 16, 1991, Salt Lake City, Utah; m. John Longden, three children; stake Young Women president.

LUND, Anthon H. (Henrik). Apostle, Oct. 7, 1889; Second counselor to President Joseph F. Smith, Oct. 17, 1901; First counselor, April 7, 1910; First counselor to President Heber J. Grant, Nov. 23, 1918–Mar. 2, 1921; b. May 15, 1844, Ålborg, Denmark; d. Mar. 2, 1921, Salt Lake City, Utah; m. Sarah Ann Peterson; practiced plural marriage, nine children on record; Young Men general board member, mission president, president of the Genealogical Society of Utah.

LYBBERT, Merlin R. (Rex). Seventy, April 1, 1989; b. Jan. 31, 1926, Cardston, Alberta, Canada; m. Nola Cahoon, seven children; attorney; regional representative, stake president.

LYMAN, Amasa M. (Mason). Apostle, Aug. 20, 1842; Counselor to President Joseph Smith, Feb. 4, 1843; released at the death of President Joseph Smith, June 27, 1844; returned to Quorum of the Twelve Apostles, Aug. 12, 1844; deprived of apostleship, Oct. 6, 1867; excommunicated, May 12, 1870; b. Mar. 30, 1813, Lyman, New Hampshire; d. Feb. 4, 1877, Fillmore, Utah; blessings restored after death; m. Louisa Maria Tanner; practiced plural marriage, thirty-seven children on record; farmer.

LYMAN, Amy Brown. General president, Relief Society, Jan. 1, 1940–April 6, 1945; b. Feb. 7, 1872, Pleasant Grove, Utah; d. Dec. 5, 1959; m. Richard R. Lyman, two children. (*See biography,* Lyman, Amy Brown.)

LYMAN, Francis M. (Marion). Apostle, Oct. 27, 1880; President of the Quorum of the Twelve Apostles, Oct. 6, 1903–Nov. 18, 1916; b. Jan. 12, 1840, Good Hope, Illinois; d. Nov. 18, 1916, Salt Lake City, Utah; m. Rhoda Ann Taylor; practiced plural marriage; twenty-two children on record; businessman; mission president.

LYMAN, Richard R. (Roswell). Apostle, April 7, 1918; excommunicated, Nov. 12, 1943; rebaptized Oct. 27, 1954; b. Nov. 23, 1870, Fillmore, Utah; d. Dec. 31, 1963, Salt Lake City, Utah; m. Amy Brown, two children; asst. superintendent in Young Men.

MADSEN, Louise Wallace. Second counselor to general president Belle S. Spafford, Relief Society, Aug. 1958–Oct. 3, 1974; b. April 25, 1909, Salt Lake City, Utah; d. Oct. 4, 1987, Salt Lake City; m. Francis A. Madsen, five children.

MAESER, Karl G. (Gottfried). Second asst. to general superintendent George Q. Cannon, Sunday School, July 1894–Jan. 1899; First asst., Jan. 1899–Feb. 1901; b. Jan. 16, 1828, Meiszen, Saxony, Germany; d. Feb. 15, 1901, Salt Lake City, Utah; m. Anna Meith; practiced plural marriage, nine children on record; educator, mission president.

MALAN, Jayne Broadbent. First counselor to Ardeth G. Kapp, Young Women, April 4, 1987; b. April 18, 1924, Heber City, Utah; m. Terry Malan, two children; professional writer; Relief Society and Young Women general board member.

MARSH, Thomas B. (Baldwin). Apostle, April 26, 1835; President of the Quorum of Twelve Apostles, May 2, 1835; excommunicated for apostasy, Mar. 17, 1839; rebaptized, July 16, 1857; b. Nov. 1, 1799, Acton, Massachusetts; d. Jan. 1866, Ogden, Utah; m. Elizabeth Godkin; practiced plural marriage, one child on record; educator, physician to the Church.

MARTIN, Douglas J. (James). Seventy, April 4, 1987; b. April 20, 1927, Hastings, New Zealand; m. Amelia Wati Crawford, four children; business executive; regional representative, stake president.

MARTINS, Helvécio. Seventy, Mar. 31, 1990; b. July 27, 1930, Rio de Janeiro, Brazil; m. Ruda Tourinho de Assis, four children; educator, business management; mission president.

MAXWELL, Neal A. (Ash). Asst. to the Twelve, April 6, 1974; Seventy, Oct. 1, 1976; Apostle, July 23, 1981; b. July 6, 1926, Salt Lake City, Utah; m. Colleen Hinckley, four children; educator, Commissioner of Church Education; regional representative, Young Men general board member.

MCCONKIE, Bruce R. (Redd). Seventy, Oct. 6, 1946; Apostle, Oct. 12, 1972–April 19, 1985; b. July 29, 1915, Ann Arbor, Michigan; d. April 19, 1985, Salt Lake City; m. Amelia Smith, eleven children; attorney; mission president.

MCKAY, David Lawrence. Second asst. to general superintendent George R. Hill, Sunday School, Sept. 1949–Oct. 1952; First asst., Oct. 1952–Nov. 1966; general superintendent, Nov. 1966–June 1971; b. Sept. 30, 1901, Ogden, Utah; m. Mildred Dean Calderwood, four children; attorney; mission president.

MCKAY, David O. (Oman). Apostle, April 9, 1906; Second counselor to President Heber J. Grant, Oct. 6, 1934; Second counselor to President George Albert Smith, May 21, 1945; President of the Quorum of Twelve Apostles, Sept. 30, 1950; President of the Church, April 9, 1951–Jan. 18, 1970; b. Sept. 8, 1873, Huntsville, Utah; d. Jan. 18, 1970, Salt Lake City; m. Emma Ray Riggs, seven children; educator. (*See biography*, McKay, David O.)

MCKAY, Quinn G. (Gunn). Second counselor to general president Neil D. Schaerrer, Young Men, April 7, 1977–Oct. 1979; b. Oct. 30, 1926; m. Shirley Frame, five children; management consultant; mission president.

MCKAY, Thomas E. (Evans). Asst. to the Twelve, April 6, 1941–Jan. 15, 1958; b. Oct. 29, 1875, Huntsville, Utah; d. Jan. 15, 1958, Salt Lake City; m. Faun Brimhall, five children; businessman, educator; mission president.

MCLELLIN, William E. Apostle, Feb. 15, 1835; excommunicated May 11, 1838; b. Jan. 18, 1806, Smith County, Tennessee; d. April 24, 1883, Independence, Missouri; m. Cynthia Ann; three children; educator.

MCMURRIN, Joseph W. (William). Seventy, Oct. 5, 1897–Oct. 24, 1932; b. Sept. 5, 1858, Tooele, Utah; d. Oct. 24, 1932, Los Angeles, California; m. Mary Ellen Hunter, seven children; teamster, stone cutter; mission president.

MELCHIN, Gerald E. (Eldon). Seventy, Oct. 1, 1988; b. May 24, 1921, Kitchener, Canada; m. Evelyn Knowles, seven children; businessman; regional representative, mission president.

MERRILL, Joseph F. (Francis). Apostle, Oct. 8, 1931–Feb. 3, 1952; b. Aug. 24, 1868, Richmond, Utah; d. Feb. 3, 1952, Salt Lake City; m. Annie Laura Hyde, two children.

MERRILL, Marriner W. (Wood). Apostle, Oct. 1889–Feb. 6, 1906; b. Sept. 25, 1835, Sackville, New Brunswick; d. Feb. 6, 1906, Richmond, Utah; m. Sarah A. Atkinson; practiced plural marriage, forty-five children.

MICKELSEN, Lynn A. (Alvin). Seventy, Mar. 31, 1990; b. July 21, 1935, Idaho Fall, Idaho; m. Jeanine Andersen, nine children; farmer; regional representative, mission and stake president.

MILES, Daniel S. (Sanborn). Seventy, April 6, 1837–Oct. 12, 1845; b. July 23, 1772, Sanbornton, New Hampshire; d. Oct. 12, 1845, Hancock Co., Illinois; m. Electa Chamberlin, one child.

MILLER, George. Sustained in Nauvoo as Second Bishop of the Church, Oct. 7, 1844; dropped prior to 1847; disfellowshipped, Oct. 20, 1848; b. Nov. 25, 1794, Orange County, Virginia; d. 1856, Meringo County, Illinois; m. Mary Catherine Fry; practiced plural marriage, four children on record; carpenter-lumberman, farmer.

MILLER, Orrin Porter. Seventy, Feb. 10, 1884–July 7, 1918; Second counselor to Presiding Bishop Charles W. Nibley, Oct. 24, 1901; First counselor, Dec. 4, 1907–July 7, 1918; b. Sept. 11, 1858, Mill Creek, Utah; d. July 7, 1918, Salt Lake City; m. Elizabeth M. Morgan, nine children; businessman, rancher; stake president.

MONSON, Thomas S. (Spencer). Apostle, Oct. 4, 1963; Second counselor to President Ezra Taft Benson, Nov. 10, 1985; b. Aug. 21, 1927, Salt Lake City, Utah; m. Frances Beverly Johnson, three children; business executive; mission president.

MORGAN, John. Seventy, Oct. 8, 1884–Aug. 14, 1894; b. Aug. 8, 1842, Greensburg, Indiana; d. Aug. 14, 1894, Preston, Idaho; m. Helen M. Groesbeck, eleven children.

MORLEY, Isaac. First counselor to Presiding Bishop Edward Partridge, June 6, 1831; released at death of Bishop Partridge; b. Mar. 11, 1786, Montague, Massachusetts; d. June 24, 1865, Fairview, Utah; m. Lucy Gunn Blakeslee; practiced plural marriage, ten children; civic leader.

MORRIS, George Q. (Quayle). Asst. to the Twelve, Oct. 6, 1951; Apostle, April 8, 1954–April 23, 1962; b. Feb. 20, 1874, Salt Lake City, Utah; d. April 23, 1962, Salt Lake City; m. Emma Ramsey, three children; Young Men general board member, mission president.

MORRISON, Alexander B. (Baillie). Seventy, April 4, 1987; b. Dec. 22, 1930, Edmonton, Alberta, Canada; m. Shirley E. Brooks, eight children; educator; regional representative.

MOYLE, Henry D. (Dinwoodey). Apostle, April 10, 1947; Second counselor to President David O. McKay, June 12, 1959; First counselor, Oct. 12, 1961–Sept. 18, 1963; b. April 22, 1889, Salt Lake City, Utah; d. Sept. 18, 1963, Deer Park, Florida; m. Clara Alberta Wright, six children; attorney, business executive; stake president.

MURDOCK, Dorthea Lou Christiansen. Second counselor to general president Naomi M. Shumway, Primary, April 2, 1977–April 5, 1980; b. May 23, 1929; m. Robert Murdock, five children; homemaker; Primary general board member.

MUREN, Joseph C. (Carl). Seventy, April 6, 1991; b. Feb. 5, 1936, Richmond, California; m. Gladys Smith, six children; Church administration; mission and stake president.

NADAULD, Stephen D. (Douglas). Seventy, June 1, 1991; b. May 31, 1942, Idaho Falls, Idaho; m. Margaret Dyreng, seven children; business management, former president Weber State College; regional representative.

NELSON, Russell M. (Marion). Apostle, April 12, 1984; b. Sept. 9, 1924, Salt Lake City, Utah; m. Dantzel White, ten children; heart surgeon; regional representative, stake president.

NEUENSCHWANDER, Dennis B. (Bramwell). Seventy, April 6, 1991; b. Oct. 6, 1939, Salt Lake City, Utah; m. LeAnn Clement, four children; Church administration; mission president.

Utah; m. LeAnn Clement, four children; Church administration; mission president.

NIBLEY, Charles W. (Wilson). Presiding Bishop of the Church, Dec. 4, 1907; Second counselor to President Heber J. Grant, May 28, 1925–Dec. 11, 1931; b. Feb. 5, 1849, Hunterfield, Scotland; d. Dec. 11, 1931, Salt Lake City, Utah; m. Rebecca Neibaur; practiced plural marriage, twenty-four children on record.

NYSTROM, Mae Taylor. Second counselor to general president Martha Horne Tingey, Young Women, April 5, 1905–July 15, 1923; b. Aug. 11, 1891, Salt Lake City, Utah; m. Theodore Nystrom, two children; Young Women general board member.

OAKS, Dallin H. (Harris). Apostle, May 3, 1984; b. Aug. 12, 1932, Provo, Utah; m. June Dixon, six children; Utah Supreme Court Justice, former President of BYU; regional representative.

OKAZAKI, Chieko Nishimura. First counselor to general president Elaine L. Jack, Relief Society, Mar. 31, 1990; b. Oct. 26, 1926, Kohala, Hawaii; m. Edward Yulio Okazaki, two children; homemaker, educator; Primary and Young Women general board member.

ORTON, Roger. Seventy, April 7, 1845, sustained but was never set apart and did not function; dropped from this position, Oct. 6, 1845; m. Clarissa Bicknell.

OSBORN, Spencer H. (Hamlin). Seventy, April 7, 1984–Oct. 1, 1989; b. July 8, 1921, Salt Lake City, Utah; m. Avanelle Richards, seven children; businessman; regional representative, mission and stake president.

OSWALD, William D. (Duncan). Second counselor to general president Russell M. Nelson, Sunday School, May 1978–Aug. 1979; b. Dec. 26, 1935; m. Mavis Morris, six children; attorney; Sunday School general board member.

PACE, Glenn L. (Leroy). Second counselor to Presiding Bishop Robert D. Hales, April 6, 1985; b. Mar. 21, 1940, Provo, Utah; m. Jolene Clayson, six children; certified public accountant; managing director of Welfare Services.

PACK, Sadie Grant. First counselor to general president May Anderson, Primary, Oct. 6, 1925–Sept. 11, 1939; b. Dec. 20, 1877, Bountiful, Utah; d. Aug. 23, 1960, Salt Lake City; m. Frederick J. Pack, four children.

PACKER, Boyd K. (Kenneth). Asst. to the Twelve, Sept. 30, 1961; Apostle, April 9, 1970; b. Sept. 10, 1924, Brigham City, Utah; m. Donna Smith, ten children; educator, assistant administrator of Seminaries and Institutes of Religion; mission president.

PAGE, John E. (Edward). Apostle, Dec. 19, 1838; disfellowshipped, Feb. 9, 1846; excommunicated, June 27, 1846; b. Feb. 25 or 26, 1799, Trenton Township, New York; d. Oct. 14, 1867, near Sycamore, De Kalb Co., Illinois; m. Lorain Stevens; practiced plural marriage, three children on record.

PARAMORE, James M. (Martin). Seventy, April 2, 1977; b. May 6, 1928, Salt Lake City, Utah; m. Helen Heslington, six children; executive secretary to the Quorum of the Twelve Apostles; regional representative, mission president.

PARMLEY, LaVern Watts. Second counselor to general president May Green Hinckley, Primary, May 1942–May 2, 1943; First counselor to general president Adele Cannon Howells, July 20, 1943–April 14, 1951; general president, May 16, 1951–Oct. 5, 1974; b. Jan. 1, 1900, Murray, Utah; d. Jan. 27, 1980; m. Thomas J. Parmley, three children; educator; Primary general board member.

PARTRIDGE, Edward. First Bishop of the Church, Feb. 4, 1831–May 27, 1840; b. Aug. 27, 1793, Pittsfield, Massachusetts; d. May 27, 1840, Nauvoo, Illinois; m. Lydia Clisbee, seven children; businessman.

PATTEN, David W. (Wyman). Apostle, Feb. 15, 1835–Oct. 25, 1838; b. Nov. 14, 1799, Theresa, New York; d. Oct. 25, 1838, at the Battle of Crooked River, Missouri; m. Phoebe Ann Babcock. (*See biography*, Patten, David W.)

PAULSEN, Sara Broadbent. First counselor to general president Naomi M. Shumway, Primary, Oct. 5, 1974–April 2, 1977; b. Sept. 15, 1920, Heber City, Utah; m. Finn B. Paulsen, five children; stake Primary president, Primary general board member, temple matron.

PENROSE, Charles W. (William). Apostle, July 7, 1904; Second counselor to President Joseph F. Smith, Dec. 7, 1911; Second counselor to President Heber J. Grant, Mar. 10, 1921–May 16, 1925; b. Feb. 4, 1832, London, England; d. May 16, 1925, Salt Lake City, Utah; m. Lucetta Stratford, three children; mission president.

PERRY, L. (Lowell) Tom. Asst. to the Twelve, Oct. 6, 1972; Apostle, April 11, 1974; b. Aug. 5, 1922, Logan, Utah; m. Virginia Lee (d. 1974), three children; m. Barbara Dayton; business executive; stake president.

PETERSEN, Mark E. (Edward). Apostle, April 20, 1944–Jan. 11, 1974; b. Nov. 7, 1900, Salt Lake City, Utah; d. Jan. 11, 1974, Salt Lake City; m. Emma Marr McDonald, two children; newspaper editor.

PETERSON, H. (Harold) Burke. First counselor to Presiding Bishop Victor L. Brown, April 6, 1972; Seventy, April 6, 1985; b. Sept. 19, 1923, Salt Lake City, Utah; m. Brookie Cardon, five children; civil engineer; regional representative, temple and stake president.

PINEGAR, Rex D. (Dee). Seventy, Oct. 1, 1976; b. Sept. 18, 1931, Orem, Utah; m. Bonnie Lee Crabb, six children; educator; mission president.

PINNOCK, Hugh W. (Wallace). Seventy, Oct. 1, 1977; b. Jan. 15, 1934, Salt Lake City, Utah; m. Anne Hawkins, six children; business executive; regional representative, mission president.

POELMAN, B. (Byron) Lloyd. First counselor to general president Russell M. Nelson, Sunday School, April

1975–May 1978; b. July 1, 1934, Salt Lake City, Utah; m. Catherine Edwards, eight children; attorney; mission president.

POELMAN, Ronald E. (Eugene). Seventy, April 1, 1978; b. May 10, 1928, Salt Lake City, Utah; m. Claire Howell Stoddard (d. 1979), four children; m. Anne G. Osborn; business executive.

PORTER, L. (Lloyd) Aldin. Seventy, April 4, 1987; b. June 30, 1931, Salt Lake City, Utah; m. Shirley Palmer, six children; business executive; regional representative, mission and stake president.

PRATT, Orson. Apostle, April 26, 1835; excommunicated Aug. 20, 1842; rebaptized and reordained an Apostle, June 20, 1943–Oct. 3, 1881; seniority adjusted to date of second entry into the Quorum; b. Sept. 19, 1811, New York; d. Oct. 3, 1881, Salt Lake City, Utah; m. Sarah Marinda Bates; practiced plural marriage, forty-five children on record. (*See biography* Pratt, Orson.)

PRATT, Parley P. (Parker). Apostle, Feb. 21, 1835–May 13, 1857; b. April 12, 1807, Burlington, New York; assassinated, May 13, 1857, near Van Buren, Arkansas; m. Thankful Halsey; practiced plural marriage, thirty-one children on record. (*See biography* Pratt, Parley P.)

PRATT, Rey L. (Lucero). Seventy, Jan. 29, 1925–April 14, 1931; b. Oct. 11, 1878, Salt Lake City, Utah; d. April 14, 1931, Salt Lake City; m. Mary Stark, 13 children; mission president.

PRESTON, William B. (Bowker). Presiding Bishop, April 6, 1884; released due to ill health, Dec. 4, 1907; b. Nov. 24, 1830, Halifax, Virginia; d. Aug. 2, 1908, Salt Lake City, Utah; m. Harriet A. Thatcher; stake president.

PULSIPHER, Zera. Seventy, Mar. 6, 1838; released, April 12, 1862; b. June 24, 1789, Rockingham, Vermont; d. Jan. 1, 1872, Hebron, Utah; m. Polly Randall (d.); m. Mary Brown; practiced plural marriage, sixteen children on record; farmer; stake patriarch.

PYPER, George D. (Dollinger). Second asst. to general superintendent David O. McKay, Sunday School, Dec. 1918–Oct. 1934; general superintendent, Dec. 1934–Jan. 1943; b. Nov. 21, 1860, Salt Lake City, Utah; d. Jan. 16, 1943, Salt Lake City; m. Emmaretta S. Whitney, two children; manager of Tabernacle choir.

RANDALL, Naomi H. Ward. First counselor to general president LaVern Watts Parmley, Primary, Oct. 4, 1970– Oct. 5, 1974; b. Oct. 5, 1908, Pleasantville, Utah; m. Earl A. Randall, one child; author; Primary general board member (author of "I Am A Child of God," *Hymns*, no. 301).

READING, Lucile Cardon. Second counselor to general president LaVern Watts Parmley, Primary, July 23, 1963– Jan. 8, 1970; First counselor, Jan. 8, 1970–Aug. 6, 1970; b. Aug. 16, 1909, Logan, Utah; d. Mar. 22, 1982, Centerville; m. Keith E. Reading, two children; editor of the *Friend*.

RECTOR, Hartman, Jr. Seventy, April 6, 1968; b. Aug. 20, 1924, Moberly, Missouri; m. Constance Kirk Daniel, nine children; analyst, U.S. Department of Agriculture.

REEDER, Bertha Stone. General president, Young Women, April 6, 1948–Sept. 30, 1961; b. Oct. 28, 1893; m. William H. Reeder, Jr., three children.

REEVE, Rex C. (Cropper), Sr. Seventy, April 1, 1978; Emeritus General Authority Oct. 1, 1989; b. Nov. 23, 1914, Hinckley, Utah; m. Phyllis Mae Nielson, seven children; business executive; regional representative, mission president.

REISER, A. (Albert) Hamer. First asst. to general superintendent George R. Hill, Sunday School, May 1943–Sept. 1949; b. Aug. 31, 1897, Salt Lake City, Utah; d. April 25, 1981, Salt Lake City; m. Elizabeth Baxter, seven children; business management; mission and stake president.

REYNOLDS, George. Seventy, April 5, 1890–Aug. 9, 1909; b. Jan. 1, 1842, London, England; d. Aug. 9, 1909, Salt Lake City, Utah; m. Mary Ann Tuddenham; practiced plural marriage, thirty-two children on record.

RICH, Charles C. (Coulsen). Apostle, Feb. 12, 1849–Nov. 17, 1883; b. Aug. 21, 1809, Campbell Co., Kentucky; d. Nov. 17, 1883, Paris, Idaho; m. Sarah DeArmen Pea; practiced plural marriage, fifty-one children on record; legislator.

RICH, Leonard. Seventy, Feb. 28, 1835; released April 6, 1837, having previously been ordained a high priest; m. Keziah.

RICHARDS, Florence Holbrook. Second counselor to general president LaVern Watts Parmley, Primary, May 16, 1951–June 11, 1953; b. July 7, 1905, Logan, Utah; m. Lorin L. Richards, three children; Primary general board member.

RICHARDS, Franklin D. (Dewey). Apostle, Feb. 12, 1849; President of the Quorum of Twelve Apostles, Sept. 13, 1898–Dec. 9, 1899; b. April 2, 1821, Richmond, Massachusetts; d. Dec. 9, 1899, Ogden, Utah; m. Jane Snyder; practiced plural marriage, twenty-two children on record; judge.

RICHARDS, Franklin D. (Dewey). Asst. to the Twelve, Oct. 8, 1960; Seventy, Oct. 1, 1976–Nov. 13, 1987. b. Nov. 17, 1900, Ogden, Utah; d. Nov. 13, 1987, Salt Lake City; m. Helen Kearnes, four children; temple and mission president.

RICHARDS, George F. (Franklin). Apostle, April 9, 1906; Acting patriarch to the Church, Oct. 8, 1937–Oct. 3, 1942; President of the Quorum of the Twelve Apostles, May 21, 1945–Aug. 8, 1950; b. Feb. 23, 1861, Farmington, Utah; d. Aug. 8, 1950, Salt Lake City; m. Alice A. Robinson, fifteen children; mission president.

RICHARDS, Jane Snyder. First counselor to general president Zina Diantha Young, Relief Society, Oct. 11, 1888–Nov. 10, 1901; b. Jan. 31, 1823, Pamelia, New

York; d. Nov. 17, 1912, Ogden, Utah; m. Franklin D. Richards, six children.

RICHARDS, LeGrand. Presiding Bishop, April 6, 1938; Apostle, April 10, 1952–Jan. 11, 1983; b. Feb. 6, 1886, Farmington, Utah; d. Jan. 11, 1983, Salt Lake City; m. Ina Jane Ashton, six children; businessman; mission and stake president.

RICHARDS, Lynn S. (Stephen). Second asst. to general superintendent George R. Hill, Sunday School, Oct. 1952–Nov. 1966; First asst. to general superintendent David Lawrence McKay, Nov. 1966–June 1971; b. Feb. 3, 1901, Salt Lake City, Utah; m. Lucille Janet Covey, four children; attorney.

RICHARDS, Stayner. Asst. to the Twelve, Oct. 6, 1951–May 28, 1953; b. Dec. 20, 1885, Salt Lake City, Utah; d. May 28, 1953, Salt Lake City; m. Jane Foote Taylor, six children; real estate, home construction; mission and stake president.

RICHARDS, Stephen L. Apostle, Jan. 18, 1917; First counselor to President David O. McKay, April 9, 1951–May 19, 1959; b. June 18, 1879, Mendon, Utah; d. May 19, 1959, Salt Lake City; m. Irene Merrill, nine children; attorney; Sunday School general board member.

RICHARDS, Willard. Apostle, April 14, 1840; Second counselor to President Brigham Young, Dec. 27, 1847–Mar. 11, 1954; b. June 24, 1804, Hopkinton, Massachusetts; d. Mar. 11, 1854, Salt Lake City, Utah; m. Jennetta Richards; practiced plural marriage, twenty children on record; physician, editor, historian.

RIGDON, Sidney. First counselor to President Joseph Smith, Mar. 18, 1833; excommunicated, Sept. 8, 1844; b. Feb. 19, 1793, Saint Clair Township, Pennsylvania; m. Phebe Brook, eleven children; d. July 14, 1876, Friendship, New York; preacher. (*See biography*, Rigdon, Sidney.)

RINGGER, Hans B. (Benjamin). Seventy, April 6, 1985; b. Nov. 2, 1925, Zurich, Switzerland; m. Helene Suzy Zimmer, four children; architect, industrial designer; regional representative, stake president.

ROBERTS, B. (Brigham) H. (Henry). Seventy, Oct. 7, 1888–Sept. 27, 1933. b. Mar. 13, 1857, Warrington, England; d. Sept. 27, 1933, Salt Lake City, Utah; m. Sarah Louise Smith; practiced plural marriage, eight children on record; mission president.

ROBINSON, George W. Church historian, 1837–1840; b. May 14, 1814, Pawlet, Vermont; d. 1878, Friendship, New York; m. Athalia Rigdon.

ROBISON, Louise Yates. General president, Relief Society, Oct. 7, 1928–Dec. 1939; b. May 27, 1866, Scipio, Utah; d. Mar. 30, 1946, San Francisco, California; m. Joseph Lyman Robison, six children.

ROCKWOOD, Albert P. (Perry). Seventy, Dec. 2, 1845–Nov. 25, 1879. b. June 5, 1805, Holliston, Massa-

chusetts; d. Nov. 25, 1879; m. Nancy Haven; practiced plural marriage, twenty-two children on record.

ROJAS ORNELAS, Jorge A. (Alfonso). Seventy, April 6, 1991; b. Sept. 27, 1940, Delicias, Mexico; m. Marcela Burgos, five children; businessman; regional representative, mission and stake president.

ROMNEY, Marion G. (George). Asst. to the Twelve, April 6, 1941; Apostle, Oct. 11, 1951; Second counselor to President Harold B. Lee, July 7, 1972; Second counselor to President Spencer W. Kimball, Dec. 30, 1973; First counselor to President Kimball, Dec. 2, 1982; President of the Quorum of the Twelve, Nov. 10 1985–May 20, 1988; b. Sept. 19, 1897, Colonia Juárez, Mexico; d. May 20, 1988, Salt Lake City, Utah; m. Ida Jensen, two children; attorney; stake president, managing director of the Church Welfare Program.

ROSS, Isabelle Salmon. Second counselor to general president May Anderson, Primary, Oct. 6, 1925–Sept. 11, 1929; First counselor, Sept. 11, 1929–Dec. 31, 1939; b. Nov. 1, 1867, Percy, Utah; d. Dec. 28, 1947, Salt Lake City; m. Charles James Ross, three children; educator; Primary general board member.

RUDD, Glen L. (Larkin). Seventy, April 4, 1987; b. May 18, 1918, Salt Lake City, Utah; m. Marva Sperry, eight children; director of Welfare Square; regional representative, temple and mission president.

RUSSELL, Gardner H. (Hale). Seventy, April 6, 1986–Oct. 5, 1991; b. Aug. 12, 1920, Salt Lake City, Utah; m. Dorothy Richardson, four children; businessman; regional representative, mission president.

SACKLEY, Robert E. (Edward). Seventy, April 2, 1988; b. Dec. 17, 1922, Lismore, New South Wales, Australia; m. Marjorie Orth, five children; educator; mission president.

SCHAERRER, Neil D. (Dean). General president, Young Men, April 7, 1977–Oct. 1979; b. Apr. 12, 1930, Payson, Utah; d. Jan. 18, 1985, Salt Lake City; m. June Coon, four children; attorney; mission president.

SCOTT, Richard G. (Gordon). Seventy, April 2, 1977; Apostle, Oct. 6, 1988; b. Nov. 7, 1928, Pocatello, Idaho; m. Jeanene Watkins, seven children; nuclear engineer; regional representative, mission president.

SCOTT, Verl F. (Franklin). Second asst. to general superintendent G. Carlos Smith, Young Men, June 9, 1961–Oct. 4, 1961; b. July 8, 1919, Hinckley, Utah; d. April 17, 1989, Salt Lake City; m. Arline Martindale, seven children; *Improvement Era* business manager; stake president, Young Men general board member.

SHARP, Marianne Clark. First counselor to general president Belle S. Spafford, Relief Society, April 6, 1945–Oct. 3, 1974; b. Oct. 28, 1901, Grantsville, Utah; d. Jan. 2, 1990, Salt Lake City; m. Ivor Sharp, three children; editor of *Relief Society Magazine*.

SHERMAN, Lyman R. (Royal). Seventy, Feb. 28, 1835; released, April 6, 1837, having previously been ordained a high priest; b. May 22, 1804, Salem, Massachusetts; d. Jan. 27, 1839, Far West, Missouri; m. Delcena Didamia Johnson, six children.

SHIMABUKURO, Sam K. (Koyei) Seventy, July 5, 1991; b. June 7, 1925, Waipahu, Hawaii; m. Amy Michiko Hirose, one child; retired state employee; mission and stake president.

SHUMWAY, Naomi Maxfield. General president, Primary, Oct. 5, 1974–April 5, 1980; b. Oct 3, 1922, Provo, Utah; m. Roden Grant Shumway, three children; stake Primary president, Primary general board member.

SILL, Sterling W. (Welling). Asst. to the Twelve, April 6, 1954; Seventy, Oct. 1, 1976; Emeritus General Authority, Sept. 30, 1978; b. Mar. 31, 1903, Layton, Utah; m. Doris Mary Thornley, three children; business executive.

SIMONSEN, Velma Nebeker. Second counselor to general president Belle S. Spafford, Relief Society, Oct. 3, 1947–Dec. 17, 1956; b. July 15, 1896; m. John O. Simonsen, four children; Relief Society general board member.

SIMPSON, Robert L. (Leatham). First counselor to Presiding Bishop John H. Vandenberg, Sept. 30, 1961; Asst. to the Twelve, April 6, 1972; Seventy, Oct. 1, 1976; Emeritus General Authority, Oct. 1, 1989; b. Aug. 8, 1915, Salt Lake City, Utah; m. Jelaire Chandler, four children; business executive; mission president.

SLOAN, James. Church historian, 1841–1843; b. Oct. 28, 1792, Donaghmore, Ireland; d. Salt Lake City, Utah; m. Mary Magill.

SMITH, Barbara Bradshaw. General president, Relief Society, Oct. 3, 1974–April 7, 1984; b. Jan. 22, 1922, Salt Lake City, Utah; m. Douglas H. Smith, seven children; Relief Society general board member.

SMITH, Bathsheba Wilson. Second counselor to general president Zina Diantha Young, Relief Society, Oct. 11, 1888–Nov. 10, 1901; general president, Nov. 10, 1901–Sept. 20. 1910; b. May 3, 1822, Shinnston, West Virginia; d. Sept. 20, 1910, Salt Lake City, Utah; m. George A. Smith, three children. (*See biography,* Smith, Bathsheba W.*)

SMITH, David A. (Asael). Second counselor to Presiding Bishop Charles W. Nibley, Dec. 4, 1907; First counselor, July 18, 1918; First counselor to Presiding Bishop Sylvester Q. Cannon, June 4, 1925; released April 6, 1938, when Bishop Sylvester Q. Cannon was ordained an apostle; b. May 24, 1879, Salt Lake City, Utah; d. April 6, 1952, Salt Lake City; m. Emily Jenkins, nine children.

SMITH, Douglas H. (Hill). Seventy, April 4, 1987; b. May 11, 1921, Salt Lake City, Utah; m. Barbara Jean Bradshaw, seven children; business executive; regional representative, stake president.

SMITH, Eldred G. (Gee). Patriarch to the Church, April 10, 1947; Emeritus General Authority, Oct. 4, 1980; b. Jan. 9, 1907, Lehi, Utah. m. Jeanne Ness (d. 1977), five children; m. Hortense Child.

SMITH, Emma Hale. First general president of the Relief Society, May 17, 1842–Mar. 16, 1844; b. July 10, 1804, Harmony, Pennsylvania; d. April 30, 1879, Nauvoo, Illinois; m. Joseph Smith, Jr. (d. 1844), eleven children; m. Lewis Crum Bidamon. (*See biography* Smith, Emma Hale).

SMITH, G. (George) Carlos, Jr. general superintendent, Young Men, 1963–1969; b. Aug. 23, 1910, Salt Lake City, Utah; d. Mar. 29, 1987, Salt Lake City; m. La Von Petersen, five children; regional representative, mission and stake president.

SMITH, George A. (Albert). Apostle, April 26, 1839; First counselor to President Brigham Young, Oct. 7, 1868–Sept. 1, 1875; b. June 26, 1817, Potsdam, New York; d. Sept. 1, 1875, Salt Lake City, Utah; m. Bathsheba Wilson Bigler; practiced plural marriage, thirty children on record; farmer, legislator; Church historian and recorder.

SMITH, George Albert. Apostle, Oct. 8, 1903; President of the Quorum of the Twelve Apostles, July 1, 1943; President of the Church, May 21, 1945–April 4, 1951; b. April 4, 1870, Salt Lake City, Utah; d. April 4, 1951, Salt Lake City; m. Lucy Emily Woodruff, three children; businessman; mission president. (*See biography,* Smith, George Albert.)

SMITH, Hyrum. Second counselor to the First Presidency, Sept. 3, 1837; Second counselor to President Joseph Smith, Nov. 7, 1837; given all priesthood that had been originally held by Oliver Cowdery including Apostle; Patriarch to the Church and Assistant President of the Church, Jan. 24, 1841–June 27, 1844; b. Feb. 9, 1800, Tunbridge, Vermont; martyred June 27, 1844, at Carthage Jail, Carthage, Illinois; m. Jerusha Barden (d. 1836), six children; m. Mary Fielding, two children; practiced plural marriage, no other children on record; farmer. (*See biography,* Smith, Hyrum.)

SMITH, Hyrum Gibbs. Patriarch to the Church, May 9, 1912–Feb. 4, 1932; b. July 8, 1879, South Jordan, Utah; d. Feb. 4, 1932, Salt Lake City; m. Martha Gee, six children; dentist.

SMITH, Hyrum Mack. Apostle, Oct. 24, 1901–Jan. 23, 1918; b. Mar. 21, 1872, Salt Lake City, Utah; d. Jan. 23, 1918, Salt Lake City; m. Ida Bowman, five children; business executive; mission president.

SMITH, John. Asst. counselor in the First Presidency, Sept. 3, 1837; released at death of Joseph Smith, June 27, 1844; Patriarch to the Church, Jan. 1, 1849–May 23, 1854; b. July 16, 1781, Derryfield, New Hampshire; d. May 23, 1854, Salt Lake City, Utah; m. Clarissa Lyman; practiced plural marriage, four children on record; stake president.

SMITH, John Henry. Apostle, Oct. 27, 1880; Second counselor to President Joseph F. Smith, April 7, 1910–

Oct. 13, 1911; b. Sept. 18, 1848, Carbunca (now Council Bluffs), Iowa; d. Oct. 13, 1911, Salt Lake City, Utah; m. Sarah Farr; practiced plural marriage, nineteen children on record; railroad businessman, legislator; mission president.

SMITH, Joseph, Jr. Apostle, May-June 1829, by Peter, James and John; First Elder and President of the Church, April 6, 1830–June 27, 1844; President of the High priesthood, Jan. 25, 1832; b. Dec. 23, 1805, Sharon, Vermont; martyred June 27, 1844, at Carthage Jail, Carthage, Illinois; m. Emma Hale, eleven children (including two adopted); practiced plural marriage, no other children on record; farmer. (*See biography,* Smith, Joseph.)

SMITH, Joseph F. (Fielding). Apostle and counselor to President Brigham Young, July 1, 1866; released at the death of President Young, Aug. 29, 1877; Second counselor to President John Taylor, Oct. 10, 1880; released at President Taylor's death, July 25, 1887; Second counselor to President Wilford Woodruff, April 7, 1899; Second counselor to President Lorenzo Snow, Sept. 13, 1898; First counselor to President Snow Oct. 6, 1901; President of the Church, Oct. 17, 1901–Nov. 19, 1918; b. Nov. 13, 1838, Far West, Missouri; d. Nov. 19, 1918, Salt Lake City, Utah; m. Levira Annett Clark; practiced plural marriage, forty-eight children on record; farmer, civic official. (*See biography,* Smith, Joseph F.)

SMITH, Joseph F. (Fielding). Patriarch to the Church, Sept. 17, 1942–Oct. 6, 1946; b. Salt Lake City, Utah, Jan. 30, 1899; d. Salt Lake City, Aug. 29, 1964; married Ruth Pingree, seven children; educator; Young Men's General Board.

SMITH, Joseph Fielding. Apostle, April 7, 1910; Acting president of the Quorum of the Twelve Apostles, Sept. 30, 1950; President of the Quorum of the Twelve Apostles, April 9, 1951; Counselor in the First Presidency, Oct. 29, 1965; President of the Church, Jan. 23, 1970–July 2, 1972; b. July 19, 1876, Salt Lake City, Utah; d. July 2, 1972, Salt Lake City, Utah; m. Louie E. Shurtliff (d. 1908), two children; m. Ethel G. Reynolds (d. 1937), nine children; m. Jessie Ella Evans; historian. (*See biography,* Smith, Joseph Fielding.)

SMITH, Joseph, Sr. Patriarch to the Church, Dec. 18, 1833; Asst. counselor to the First Presidency, Sept. 3, 1837–Sept. 14, 1840; b. July 12, 1771, Topsfield, Massachusetts; d. Sept. 14, 1840, Nauvoo, Illinois; m. Lucy Mack, ten children; farmer. (*See biography,* Smith, Joseph, Sr.)

SMITH, Julina Lambson. Second counselor to general president Emmeline B. Wells, Relief Society, Oct. 3, 1910–April 2, 1921; b. June 18, 1849, Salt Lake City, Utah; d. Jan. 10, 1936, Salt Lake City; m. Joseph F. Smith, eleven children; homemaker.

SMITH, Nicholas G. (Groesbeck). Asst. to the Twelve, April 6, 1941–Oct. 27, 1945; b. June 20, 1881, Salt Lake City, Utah; d. Oct. 27, 1945, Salt Lake City; m. Florence Gay, four children; business executive, mission president.

SMITH, Norma Broadbent. Second counselor to general president Elaine A. Cannon, Young Women, July 12, 1978–April 7, 1984; b. May 24, 1923, Heber City, Utah; m. Lowell D. Smith, eight children; Primary general board member.

SMITH, Sylvester. Seventy, Feb. 28, 1835; released April 6, 1837; having previously been ordained a high priest; b. approximately 1805; left the Church by 1838; m. Elizabeth.

SMITH, William. Apostle, Feb. 15, 1835; dropped from the Quorum, May 4, 1839; restored to Quorum, May 25, 1839; dropped from the Quorum, Oct. 6, 1845; excommunicated, Oct. 19, 1845; b. Mar. 13, 1811, Royalton, Vermont; d. Nov. 13, 1894, Osterdock, Iowa; m. Caroline Amanda Grant; practiced plural marriage, seven children on record.

SMOOT, Reed. Apostle, April 8, 1900–Feb. 9, 1941; b. Jan. 10, 1862, Salt Lake City, Utah; d. Feb. 9, 1941, St. Petersburg, Florida; m. Alpha M. Eldredge, six children; business executive, U.S. Senator 1903-1932. (*See* Smoot Hearings).

SNOW, Eliza R. (Roxcy, most often spelled Roxey). General president, Relief Society, 1866–Dec. 5, 1887; b. Jan. 21, 1804, Becket, Massachusetts; d. Dec. 5, 1887, Salt Lake City, Utah; m. Joseph Smith, Jr. (d. 1844); m. Brigham Young; writer, poet. (*See biography,* Snow, Eliza R.)

SNOW, Erastus. Apostle, Feb. 12, 1849–May 27, 1888; b. Nov. 9, 1818, Saint Johnsbury, Vermont; d. May 27, 1888, Salt Lake City, Utah; m. Artimesia Beaman; practiced plural marriage, thirty-six children on record; mission president.

SNOW, Lorenzo. Apostle, Feb. 12, 1849; Counselor to President Brigham Young, April 8, 1873; Asst. counselor, May 9, 1874; President of the Quorum of the Twelve Apostles, April 7, 1889; President of the Church, Sept. 13, 1898–Oct. 10, 1901; b. April 3, 1814, Mantua, Ohio; d. Oct. 10, 1901, Salt Lake City, Utah; m. Mary Adaline Goddard; practiced plural marriage, forty-two children on record; educator. (*See biography,* Snow, Lorenzo.)

SONNE, Alma. Asst. to the Twelve, April 6, 1941; Seventy, Oct. 1, 1976–Nov. 27, 1977. b. Mar. 5, 1884, Logan, Utah; d. Nov. 27, 1977, Logan; m. Geneva Ballantyne (d. 1941), five children; m. Leona Ballantyne Woolley; businessman; mission and stake president.

SONNENBERG, John. Seventy, Oct. 6, 1985–Oct. 1, 1989; b. April 11, 1922, Schneidemuhle, Germany; m. Joyce C. Dalton, seven children; dentist; regional representative, stake president.

SONNTAG, Philip T. (Tadje). Seventy, April 7, 1984; Second counselor to general president Robert L. Simpson, Sunday School, Aug. 1987–Aug. 1988; b. July 13, 1921; m. Voloy Andreasen, three children; jeweler; regional representative, director of Temple Square.

SORENSEN, Donna Durrant. Second counselor to general president Amy Brown Lyman, Relief Society,

April 1940–Oct. 12, 1942; b. Dec. 24, 1904, Spanish Fork, Utah; d. June 4, 1990, Salt Lake City; m. Wesley A. Sorensen, three children.

SORENSEN, Lynn A. (Andrew). Seventy, April 4, 1987; b. Sept. 25, 1919, Salt Lake City, Utah; m. Janet Elaine Weech, nine children; management; mission president.

SPAFFORD, Belle Smith. General president, Relief Society, April 6, 1945–Oct. 3, 1974; b. Oct. 8, 1895, Salt Lake City, Utah; d. Feb. 2, 1982, Salt Lake City; m. Willis Earl Spafford, two children; writer. (*See biography,* Spafford, Belle S.)

STAPLEY, Delbert L. (Leon). Apostle, Oct. 5, 1950–Aug. 19, 1978; b. Dec. 11, 1896, Mesa, Arizona; d. Aug 19, 1978, Salt Lake City, Utah; m. Ethel Davis, three children; business executive; stake president.

STEVENSON, A. (Alfred) Walter. First asst. to general superintendent Elbert R. Curtis, Young Men, 1948–1958; b. Oct. 6, 1900, Ogden, Utah; d. Nov. 27, 1974; m. Effie Peck, four children.

STEVENSON, Edward. Seventy, Oct. 7, 1894–Jan. 27, 1897; b. May 1, 1820, Gibraltar, Spain; d. Jan. 27, 1897, Salt Lake City, Utah; m. Nancy Arede Porter; practiced plural marriage, twenty-four children on record; tinsmith.

STONE, O. (Oscar) Leslie. Asst. to the Twelve, Oct. 6, 1972; Seventy, Oct. 1, 1976; Emeritus General Authority, Oct. 4, 1980; b. May 28, 1903, Chapin, Idaho; d. April 26, 1986, Salt Lake City, Utah; m. Dorothy Cobbley, four children; business executive; regional representative, temple and stake president.

TALMAGE, James E. (Edward). Apostle, Dec. 8, 1911–July 27, 1933; b. Sept. 21, 1862, Hungerford, England; d. July 27, 1933, Salt Lake City, Utah; m. Mary May Booth, eight children; writer, former president of the University of Utah.

TANNER, Joseph Marion. Second asst. to general superintendent Lorenzo Snow, Sunday School, May 1901–Oct. 1901; Second asst. to general superintendent Joseph F. Smith, Sunday School, Nov. 1901–April 1906; b. Mar. 26, 1859, Payson, Utah; d. Aug. 19, 1927, Lethbridge, Alberta, Canada; m. Josephine Snow; practiced plural marriage, seventeen children on record; former president of Utah Agricultural College (now Utah State University).

TANNER, N. (Nathan) Eldon. Asst. to the Twelve, Oct. 8, 1960; Apostle, Oct. 11, 1962; Second counselor to President David O. McKay, Oct. 4, 1963; Second counselor to President Joseph Fielding Smith, Jan. 23, 1970; First counselor to President Harold B. Lee, July 7, 1972; First counselor to President Spencer W. Kimball, Dec. 30, 1973–Nov. 27, 1982; b. May 9, 1898, Salt Lake City, Utah; d. Nov. 27, 1982, Salt Lake City; m. Sara Isabelle Merrill, five children; businessman and educator.

TAYLOR, Anstis Elmina Shepherd. General president, Young Women, June 19, 1880–Dec. 6, 1904; b. Sept. 12, 1830, Middlefield, New York; d. Dec. 6, 1904, Salt Lake City, Utah; m. George Hamilton Taylor. (*See biography,* Taylor, Elmina Shepherd.)

TAYLOR, Henry D. (Dixon). Asst. to the Twelve, April 6, 1958; Seventy, Oct. 1, 1976; Emeritus General Authority, Sept. 30, 1978; b. Nov. 22, 1903, Provo, Utah; d. Feb. 24, 1987, Salt Lake City; m. Alta Hansen (d. 1967), four children; m. Ethelyn Peterson; business executive; mission and stake president.

TAYLOR, John. Apostle, Dec. 19, 1838; President of the Quorum of the Twelve Apostles, Oct. 6, 1877; President of the Church, Oct. 10, 1880–July 25, 1887; b. Nov. 1, 1808, Milnthrope, England; d. July 25, 1887, Kaysville, Utah; m. Leonora Cannon; practiced plural marriage, thirty-five children on record; farmer. (*See biography,* Taylor, John.)

TAYLOR, John H. (Harris). Seventy, Oct. 6, 1933–May 28, 1946; b. June 28, 1875, Salt Lake City, Utah; d. May 28, 1946, Salt Lake City; m. Susan Rachel Grant, two children; dentist; mission president.

TAYLOR, John W. (Whittaker). Apostle, April 9, 1884; resigned Oct. 28, 1905; excommunicated for polygamy Mar. 28, 1911; b. May 15, 1858, Provo, Utah; d. Oct. 10, 1916, Salt Lake City; m. May Leona Rich; practiced plural marriage, twenty-nine children on record.

TAYLOR, Margaret Young. First counselor to general president Elmina Shepherd Taylor, Young Women, June 19 1880–1887; b. April 24, 1837, Westport, Connecticut; d. May 3, 1919, Salt Lake City, Utah; m. John Taylor, nine children.

TAYLOR, Russell C. (Carl). Seventy, April 7, 1984–Oct, 1, 1989; b. Nov. 25, 1925, Red Mesa, Colorado; m. Joyce Elaine Mortensen, six children; business executive; regional representative, mission and stake president.

TAYLOR, William W. (Whittaker). Seventy, April 7, 1880–Aug. 1, 1884; b. Sept. 11, 1853, Salt Lake City, Utah; d. Aug. 1, 1884, Salt Lake City; m. Sarah Taylor Hoagland; practiced plural marriage, eight children on record.

TEASDALE, George. Apostle, Oct. 16, 1882–June 9, 1907; b. Dec. 8, 1831, London, England; d. June 9, 1907, Salt Lake City, Utah; m. Emily Emma Brown; mission president.

TENORIO, Horacio A. (Antonio). Seventy, April 1, 1989; b. Mar. 6, 1935, Mexico, D.F., Mexico; m. Maria Teresa de Tenorio, three children; businessman; regional representative, mission and stake president.

THATCHER, Moses. Apostle, April 9, 1879; dropped from the Quorum, April 6, 1896; b. Feb. 2, 1842, Springfield, Illinois; d. Aug. 21, 1909, Logan, Utah; m. Celestia Ann Farr; practiced plural marriage, eleven children on record; businessman; mission president.

THOMAS, Edna Harker. Second counselor to general president May Anderson, Primary, Sept. 11, 1929–Dec. 11, 1933; b. April 11, 1881, Taylorsville, Utah; d. Apr. 29, 1942, Washington, D.C.; m. Elbert D. Thomas, three children.

THOMAS, Shirley Wilkes. Second counselor to general president Barbara B. Smith, Relief Society, Nov. 28, 1978–April 7, 1984; b. Feb. 26, 1925, Englewood, California; m. Robert K. Thomas, three children; Relief Society general board member, stake Relief Society president.

THOMPSON, Robert B. (B[l]ashel). Church historian, 1840–1841; b. Oct. 1, 1811, Great Driffield, England; d. Aug. 27, 1841, Nauvoo, Illinois; m. Mercy Rachel Fielding, one child.

THOMPSON, Janet Lennox Murdock. Second counselor to general president May Green Hinckley, Primary, Jan. 1, 1940–May 2, 1943; b. Aug. 8, 1884, Salt Lake City, Utah; d. April 24, 1953, Salt Lake City; m. Jerrold E. Thompson.

TINGEY, Earl C. (Carr). Seventy, Dec. 5, 1990; b. June 11, 1934, Bountiful, Utah; m. Joanne Wells, four children; attorney; regional representative, mission president.

TINGEY, Martha Jane Horne. General president, Young Women, April 5, 1905–Mar. 28, 1929; b. Oct. 15, 1857, Salt Lake City, Utah; d. Mar. 11, 1938, Salt Lake City; m. Joseph S. Tingey, seven children.

TURLEY, Maurine Johnson. Second counselor to general president Ardeth G. Kapp, Young Women, May 11, 1984–April 6, 1986; First counselor, April 6, 1986–April 4, 1987; b. May 2, 1931; m. Robert S. Turley, Jr., five children; educator.

TUTTLE, A. (Albert) Theodore. Seventy, Oct. 1, 1976–Nov. 28, 1986; b. Mar. 2, 1919, Manti, Utah; d. Nov. 28, 1986, Salt Lake City; m. Marné Whitaker, seven children; educator; mission and temple president.

VAN COTT, John. Seventy, Oct. 8. 1862–Feb. 18, 1883; b. Sept. 7, 1814, Canaan, New York; d. Feb. 18, 1883, Salt Lake City, Utah; m. Lucy Sackett; practiced plural marriage, twenty-eight children on record; businessman, legislator, farmer.

VANDENBERG, John H. (Henry). Presiding Bishop, Sept. 30, 1961; Asst. to Twelve, April 6, 1972; Emeritus General Authority, Sept. 30, 1978; b. Dec. 18, 1904, Ogden, Utah; m. Ariena Stok, two children; rancher, businessman; mission president.

WARNER, Richard L. (Longstroth). Second counselor to general president Russell M. Nelson, Sunday School, June 1971–April 1975; m. Marian Nelson, nine children; businessman; regional representative, stake president.

WASHBURN, J Ballard. Seventy, Mar. 31, 1990; b. Jan. 18, 1929, Blanding, Utah; m. Barbara Harries, ten children; physician; regional representative, mission and stake president.

WELLS, Daniel H. (Hanmer). Second counselor to President Brigham Young, Jan. 4, 1857; released at the death of President Young, Aug. 29, 1877; Counselor to the Twelve, Oct. 6, 1877–Mar. 24, 1891; b. Oct. 27, 1814, Trenton, New Jersey; d. Mar. 24, 1891, Salt Lake City, Utah; m. Eliza Rebecca Robinson; practiced plural marriage, thirty-five children on record; public servant, educator, farmer; mission president.

WELLS, Emmeline B. (Blanche) Woodward. General president, Relief Society, Oct. 3, 1910–April 2, 1921; b. Feb. 29, 1828, Petersham, Massachusetts; d. April 25, 1921, Salt Lake City, Utah; m. James Harvey Harris (d. 1845), two children; m. Newel K. Whitney (d. 1850), two children, m. Daniel H. Wells, three children; writer and editor. (*See biography*, Wells, Emmeline B.)

WELLS, John. Second counselor to Presiding Bishop Charles W. Nibley, July 18, 1918; Second counselor to Presiding Bishop Sylvester Q. Cannon, June 4, 1925; released, April 6, 1938, when Bishop Cannon was ordained an apostle; b. Sept. 16, 1864, Carlton, England; d. April 18, 1941, Salt Lake City, Utah; m. Almena Thorpe, seven children; hospital administrator.

WELLS, Junius F. (Free). Seventy, Oct. 1875–Mar. 24, 1891; general superintendent, Young Men, 1876–1880; b. June 1, 1854, Salt Lake City, Utah; d. April 15, 1930, Salt Lake City; m. Helena Middleton Fobes, two children; asst. Church historian. (*See biography*, Wells, Junius F.)

WELLS, Robert E. (Earl). Seventy, Oct. 1, 1978; b. Dec. 28, 1927, Las Vegas, Nevada; m. Meryl Leavitt (d. 1960); m. Helen Walser, seven children; banking executive; regional representative, mission and stake president; father of Sharlene Wells Hawkes, Miss America, 1985.

WELLS, Rulon S. (Seymour). Seventy, April 5, 1893–May 7, 1941. b. July 7, 1854, Salt Lake City, Utah; d. May 7, 1941, Salt Lake City; m. Josephine E. Beatie, seven children; businessman; Young Men general board member, mission president.

WEST, Franklin L. (Lorenzo). Second asst. to general superintendent Albert E. Bowen, Young Men, 1935–1937; b. Feb. 1, 1885, Ogden, Utah; d. Oct. 21, 1966, Salt Lake City; m. Violet Madsen, six children; educator; Commissioner of Church Education.

WEST, Josephine Richards. Second counselor to general president Louie B. Felt, Primary, Dec. 15, 1896–Nov. 24, 1905; b. May 25, 1853, Salt Lake City, Utah; d. April 23, 1933, Logan; m. Joseph A. West, six children; stake Primary president.

WHITMER, John. Church historian 1831–1835; excommunicated, Mar. 10, 1838; b. Aug. 27, 1802; d. July 11, 1878, Far West, Missouri; m. Sarah Jackson, five children; farmer.

WHITNEY, Elizabeth Ann Smith. Second counselor to general president Emma Hale Smith, Relief Society,

May 17, 1842–Mar. 16, 1844; Second counselor to general president Eliza R. Snow, Relief Society, June 19, 1880–Feb. 15, 1882; b. Dec. 26, 1800, Derby, Connecticut; d. Feb. 15, 1883, Salt Lake City, Utah; m. Newel K. Whitney, eleven children.

WHITNEY, Newel K. (Kimball). First Bishop of Kirtland Oct. 7, 1844; Presiding Bishop, April 6, 1847–Sept. 23, 1850; b. Feb. 5, 1795, Marlborough, Vermont; d. Sept. 23, 1850, Salt Lake City, Utah; m. Elizabeth Ann Smith; practiced plural marriage, fourteen children on record; merchant.

WHITNEY, Orson F. (Ferguson). Apostle April 9, 1906–May 16, 1931; b. July 1, 1855, Salt Lake City, Utah; d. May 16, 1931, Salt Lake City; m. Zina Beal Smoot; practiced plural marriage, twelve children on record.

WIDTSOE, John A. (Andreas). Apostle, Mar. 17, 1921–Nov. 29, 1952; b. Jan. 31, 1872, Daloe, Island of Fröyen, Norway; d. Nov. 29, 1952, Salt Lake City, Utah; m. Leah Eudora Dunford, seven children; educator, former president of Utah State Agricultural College and of the University of Utah; Young Men general board member.

WIGHT, Lyman. Apostle, April 8, 1841; excommunicated Dec. 3, 1848; b. May 9, 1796, Fairfield, New York; d. Mar. 31, 1858, Dexter, Texas; m. Harriet Benton, six children.

WILCOX, Keith W. (Wilson). Seventy, Oct. 6, 1984–Oct. 1, 1989; b. May 15, 1921, Hyrum, Utah; m. Viva May Gammell, six children; architect; regional representative, temple, mission, and stake president. (Architect of the Washington, D.C. Temple.)

WILLIAMS, Clarissa Smith. First counselor to general president Emmeline B. Wells, Relief Society, Oct. 3, 1910–April 2, 1921; general president, Relief Society, April 2, 1921–Oct. 7, 1928; b. April 21, 1859, Salt Lake City, Utah; d. Mar. 8, 1930; m. William N. Williams, eleven children.

WILLIAMS, Frederick G. (Granger). Second counselor to President Joseph Smith, Mar. 18, 1833; rejected Nov. 7, 1837; excommunicated, Mar. 17, 1839; restored to fellowship, April 8, 1840; b. Oct. 28, 1787, Suffield, Connecticut; d. Oct. 25, 1842, Quincy, Illinois; m. Rebecca Swain, four children; businessman.

WILLIAMS, Helen Spencer. First counselor to general president Lucy Grant Cannon, Young Women, Nov. 1937–May 17, 1944; b. Nov. 29, 1896, Salt Lake City, Utah; d. Aug. 10, 1965, Salt Lake City; m. Rex W. Williams, three children.

WINDER, Barbara Woodhead. General president, Relief Society, April 7, 1984–Mar. 31, 1990; b. May 9, 1931, Midvale, Utah; m. Richard W. Winder, four children; homemaker; Relief Society general board member.

WINDER, John R. (Rex). Second counselor to Presiding Bishop William B. Preston, April 8, 1887; First counselor to President Joseph F. Smith, Oct. 17, 1901–

Mar. 27, 1910; b. Dec. 11, 1821, Biddenham, England; d. Mar. 27, 1910, Salt Lake City, Utah; m. Ellen Walters Winder (d. 1892), ten children; m. Maria Burnham; business executive.

WIRTHLIN, Joseph B. (Bitner). First counselor to general president Russell M. Nelson, Sunday School, June 1971–April 1975; Asst. to the Twelve, April 4, 1975; Seventy, Oct. 1, 1976; Apostle, Oct. 9, 1986; b. June 11, 1917, Salt Lake City, Utah; m. Elisa Young Rogers, eight children; businessman.

WIRTHLIN, Joseph L. (Leopold). Second counselor to Presiding Bishop LeGrand Richards, April 6, 1938; First counselor, Dec. 12, 1946; Presiding Bishop, April 6, 1952–Sept. 30 1961; b. Aug 14, 1893, Salt Lake City, Utah; d. Jan. 25, 1963, Salt Lake City; m. Madeline Bitner, five children; businessman; stake president.

WOODRUFF, Abraham O. (Owens). Apostle, Oct. 7, 1897–June 20, 1904; b. Nov. 23, 1872, Salt Lake City, Utah; d. June 20, 1904, El Paso, Texas; m. Helen May Winters.

WOODRUFF, Wilford. Apostle, April 26, 1839; President of the Quorum of the Twelve Apostles, Oct. 10, 1880; President of the Church, April 7, 1889–Sept. 2, 1898; b. Mar. 1, 1807, Avon (now Farmington), Connecticut; d. Sept. 2, 1898, San Francisco, California; m. Phoebe Whittemore Carter; practiced plural marriage, thirty-three children on record; miller. (*See biography,* Woodruff, Wilford)

WOOLSEY, Durrel A. (Arden). Seventy, Mar. 31, 1990; b. June 12, 1926, Stockton, California; m. LaRae Wood, three children; businessman; mission and stake president.

WRIGHT, Ruth Broadbent. Second counselor to general president Michaelene P. Grassli, Primary, April 2, 1988; b. Bingham, Utah; m. Gary E. Wright, five children; educator; stake Primary president, stake Young Women president.

YOUNG, Brigham. Apostle, Feb. 14, 1835; President of the Quorum of the Twelve Apostles, April 14, 1840; President of the Church, Dec. 27, 1847–Aug. 29, 1877; b. June 1, 1801, Whitingham, Vermont; d. Aug. 29, 1877, Salt Lake City, Utah; m. Miriam Words (d. 1824), two children; m. Mary Ann Angell; practiced plural marriage, sixty-one children on record (including four adopted children); carpenter-glazier. (*See biography,* Young, Brigham.)

YOUNG, Brigham, Jr. Apostle, Feb. 4, 1864; Member of the Quorum of the Twelve Apostles, Oct. 9, 1868; Counselor to President Young, April 8, 1873; Asst. counselor to President Young, May 9, 1874; released, Aug. 29, 1877, at the death of President Young; President of the Quorum of Twelve Apostles, Oct. 17, 1901–April 11, 1903; b. Dec. 18, 1836, Kirtland, Ohio; d. April 11, 1903, Salt Lake City, Utah; m. Catherine Curtis Spencer; practiced plural marriage, eighteen children on record; mission president.

YOUNG, Clifford E. (Earle). Asst. to the Twelve, April 6, 1941–Aug. 21, 1958; b. Dec. 7, 1883, Salt Lake City, Utah; d. Aug. 21, 1958, Salt Lake City; m. Edith Grant, four children; businessman, civic leader; stake president.

YOUNG, Dwan Jacobsen. General president, Primary, April 5, 1980–April 2, 1988; b. May 1, 1931, Salt Lake City, Utah; m. Thomas Young, Jr., five children; homemaker; Primary general board member.

YOUNG, John W. (Willard). Counselor to President Brigham Young, April 8, 1873; Asst. counselor May 9, 1874; First counselor, Oct. 7, 1876; released at death of President Young; Counselor to the Twelve, Oct. 6, 1877–Oct. 6, 1891; b. Oct. 1, 1844, Nauvoo, Illinois; d. Feb. 11, 1924, New York City, New York; m. Lucy Maria Canfield; practiced plural marriage, ten children on record; builder of Utah railroads.

YOUNG, Joseph. Seventy, Feb. 28, 1835–July 16, 1881; b. April 7, 1797, Hopkinton, Massachusetts; d. July 16, 1881, Salt Lake City, Utah; m. Jane A. Bicknell; practiced plural marriage, twenty children on record.

YOUNG, Joseph Angell. Ordained an Apostle, Feb. 4, 1864, but never served in the Quorum of the Twelve Apostles; b. Oct. 14, 1834, Kirtland, Ohio; d. Aug. 5, 1875, Manti, Utah; m. Clara Federata Stenhouse; practiced plural marriage, eleven children on record.

YOUNG, Levi Edgar. Seventy, Oct. 6, 1909–Dec. 13, 1963; b. Feb. 2, 1874, Salt Lake City, Utah; d. Dec. 13, 1963, Salt Lake City; m. Valeria Brinton, three children; mission president.

YOUNG, Seymour B. (Bicknell). Seventy, Oct. 14, 1882–Dec. 15, 1924; b. Oct. 3, 1837, Kirtland, Ohio; d. Dec. 15, 1924, Salt Lake City, Utah; m. Ann Elizabeth Riter; practiced plural marriage, thirteen children on record; physician.

YOUNG, S. (Seymour) Dilworth. Seventy, Oct. 1, 1976–July 9, 1981; Emeritus General Authority, Sept. 30, 1978; b. Sept. 7, 1897, Salt Lake City, Utah; d. July 9, 1981, Salt Lake City; m. Gladys Pratt (d. 1964), two children; m. Huldah Parker; Boy Scouts of America official; mission president.

YOUNG, Zina Diantha Huntington. First counselor to general president Eliza R. Snow, Relief Society, June 19, 1880–April 1888; general president, Relief Society, April 8, 1888–Aug. 28, 1901; b. Jan. 31, 1821, Watertown, New York; d. Aug. 28, 1901, Salt Lake City, Utah; m. Henry B. Jacobs (div. 1841), m. Joseph Smith, Jr. (d. 1844); m. Brigham Young, four children.

Appendix 2

A Chronology of Church History

The following are significant events in the history of The Church of Jesus Christ of Latter-day Saints. Words in small capitals refer to articles in the *Encyclopedia*.

1771, July 12. Joseph SMITH, Sr. (1771–1840) b. Topsfield, Essex Co., MA.

1775, July 8. Lucy Mack SMITH (1775–1856) b. Gilsum, Cheshire Co., NH.

1796, January 24. Joseph SMITH, Sr., and Lucy Mack SMITH m. in Tunbridge, VT.

1801, June 1. Brigham YOUNG (1801–1877) b. Whitingham, Windham Co., VT.

1804, July 10. Emma Hale SMITH (1804–1879) b. to Isaac Hale and Elizabeth Lewis Hale, HARMONY, Susquehanna Co., PA.

1805, December 23. Joseph SMITH (1805–1844) b. to Joseph Smith, Sr., and Lucy Mack Smith, Sharon, Windsor Co., VT.

1807, March 1. Wilford WOODRUFF (1807–1898) b. Farmington, Hartford Co., CT.

1808, November 1. John TAYLOR (1808–1887) b. Milnthorpe, Westmoreland, England.

1814, April 3. Lorenzo SNOW (1814–1901) b. Mantua, Portage Co., OH.

1816. The "year without a summer." Crops failed throughout New England. Joseph SMITH, Sr., left Norwich, VT, settled his family in Palmyra, NY.

1820, Early spring. Joseph SMITH received FIRST VISION in a grove near his home in Palmyra, NY.

1823, September 21–22. Joseph SMITH visited by ANGEL MORONI and told of Book of Mormon record. Joseph viewed GOLD PLATES buried in nearby hill (CUMORAH). [*See* Book of Mormon Plates & Records; Moroni, Visitations of.]

1825, October. Joseph SMITH hired by Josiah Stowell to work at HARMONY, PA. Boarded at Isaac Hale's and met Emma Hale.

1826, March 20. Joseph SMITH tried and acquitted on charge of being a disorderly person at SOUTH BAINBRIDGE, NY. [*See* Smith, Joseph: Legal Trials of Joseph Smith.]

1827, January 18. Joseph SMITH m. Emma Hale in SOUTH BAINBRIDGE, NY. [*See* Smith, Emma Hale.]

September 22. Joseph SMITH obtained GOLD PLATES from hill CUMORAH.

December. Joseph and Emma SMITH moved to HARMONY, PA, where plates could be safely translated.

1828, February. Martin HARRIS took a transcript of characters from the GOLD PLATES to Charles Anthon in New York City. [*See* Anthon Transcript.]

April 12–June 14. First 116 translated manuscript pages stolen from the Harris home (June–July). [*See* Book of Mormon Translation by Joseph Smith; Manuscript, Lost 116 Pages.]

1829, April 7. Joseph SMITH resumed translation of the record assisted by Oliver COWDERY as scribe.

May 15. JOHN THE BAPTIST conferred AARONIC PRIESTHOOD on Joseph SMITH, and Oliver COWDERY near HARMONY, PA.

May–June. Joseph SMITH and Oliver COWDERY received MELCHIZEDEK PRIESTHOOD from PETER, JAMES, AND JOHN, near the Susquehanna River between HARMONY, PA, and COLESVILLE, NY.

June. Translation of Book of Mormon completed and copyright applied for (June 11). The Three Witnesses shown the plates and other Nephite artifacts by Moroni in FAYETTE, NY. The Eight Witnesses shown the GOLD PLATES by Joseph SMITH in Manchester, NY. [*See* Book of Mormon Witnesses.]

August. Egbert B. Grandin began printing the Book of Mormon at PALMYRA, NY. Martin HARRIS guaranteed payment.

1830, March 26. First copies of Book of Mormon available at Grandin Bookstore.

April 6. The "Church of Christ" organized, Fayette township, NY, and "Articles and Covenants of the Church" revealed (D&C 20). [*See* April 6; Fayette, NY.]

June. "Visions of Moses" received by Joseph SMITH as part of Bible translation (now chapter 1 of the BOOK OF MOSES, PEARL OF GREAT PRICE). [*See* Joseph Smith Translation of the Bible.]

June 9. First CONFERENCE of the Church held in Whitmer log home, FAYETTE, NY.

September–October. First missionaries called to preach to the LAMANITES (NATIVE AMERICANS). [*See* Lamanite Mission.]

October–November. "Lamanite missionaries" converted some 130 non-Indians in KIRTLAND, OH, area en route to western border of Missouri.

December. Sidney RIGDON called as scribe to assist Joseph SMITH in Bible translation (D&C 35:20).

December. First revelation on gathering given. Command for Church to move to Ohio (D&C 37). Reiterated (D&C 38).

1831, February 1. Joseph SMITH arrived at Newel K. WHITNEY STORE in KIRTLAND, OH, and commenced ministry there.

February 4. Edward Partridge called and ordained first BISHOP of Church.

February 9. Revelation on Church government and LAW OF CONSECRATION received (D&C 42).

May. Fayette, Colesville, and Manchester branches of Church in New York arrived in KIRTLAND-Thompson areas, OH.

June 3–6. Fourth general CONFERENCE of Church held, Kirtland township. Brethren first ordained to the High Priesthood. [*See* High Priest; Conferences: General Conference.]

July 20. Site for city of ZION in Independence, MO, revealed to Joseph SMITH (D&C 57).

August 2. Saints laid first log for a schoolhouse as a foundation of ZION, Kaw Township, Jackson Co., MO. Sidney RIGDON consecrated land of ZION by prayer.

August 3. Temple site, Independence, MO, dedicated by Joseph SMITH.

November 1. CONFERENCE, at HIRAM, OH. Decision made to print revelations received by Joseph SMITH. [*See* Book of Commandments.]

1832, January 25. Joseph SMITH sustained President of High Priesthood at CONFERENCE, Amherst, OH. [*See* High Priest; Presiding High Priest.]

February 16. Revelation known as "The Vision" (D&C 76) received by Joseph SMITH, HIRAM, OH. [*See* Visions of Joseph Smith; Degrees of Glory.]

March 24. Joseph SMITH and Sidney RIGDON beaten, tarred, feathered by mob, HIRAM, OH.

June. First issue of THE EVENING AND THE MORNING STAR, Independence, MO.

December 25. Revelation and Prophecy on War (D&C 87) received by Joseph SMITH. [*See* Civil War Prophecy.]

December 27. Revelation known as The Olive Leaf (D&C 88) received by Joseph SMITH, calling for

building a temple in Kirtland and establishing SCHOOL OF THE PROPHETS.

1833, February 27. Revelation known as the WORD OF WISDOM (D&C 89) received by Joseph SMITH.

March 18. Sidney RIGDON and Frederick G. Williams set apart as Counselors in Presidency of the Church (D&C 81 headnote).

July 2. Joseph SMITH concluded first draft of Bible translation.

July 20. Mob at INDEPENDENCE demanded removal of Saints from Jackson Co. Printing office destroyed, halting printing of BOOK OF COMMANDMENTS.

July 23. Saints at INDEPENDENCE made treaty with mob to leave Jackson Co. KIRTLAND TEMPLE cornerstones laid.

November 7. Saints fled from Jackson Co. mobs across Missouri River into Clay Co. [SEE Missouri Conflict.]

December 18. Joseph SMITH, Sr., ordained first CHURCH PATRIARCH.

1834, February 17. First STAKE and HIGH COUNCIL of Church organized, KIRTLAND, OH.

May 5. Joseph SMITH left KIRTLAND for Missouri as leader of ZION'S CAMP to bring relief to Saints expelled from Jackson Co.

July 3. Presidency and HIGH COUNCIL organized, Clay Co., MO, David WHITMER, president.

October. First issue of MESSENGER AND ADVOCATE published, Kirtland, OH.

December 5. Oliver COWDERY made Assistant (Associate) President of Church.

1835, February 14. QUORUM OF THE TWELVE APOSTLES organized, Kirtland, OH.

February 28. FIRST COUNCIL OF THE SEVENTY organized, KIRTLAND, OH.

March 28. Revelation on priesthood (D&C 107) given through Joseph SMITH.

July 3. Michael Chandler exhibited Egyptian mummies and papyrus, KIRTLAND, OH. [*See* Papyri (Joseph Smith).]

July 6. Mummies and papyrus purchased, and Joseph SMITH commenced translation. [*See* Book of Abraham, Translation.]

August 17. DOCTRINE AND COVENANTS adopted as STANDARD WORK of the Church, KIRTLAND.

September. DOCTRINE AND COVENANTS issued from press in KIRTLAND.

September 14. Emma Smith appointed to select HYMNS according to previous revelation (D&C 25).

1836, January 21. In KIRTLAND TEMPLE, Joseph SMITH, received vision of CELESTIAL KINGDOM and revelation concerning salvation of the dead (D&C 137). [*See* Visions of Joseph Smith.]

March 27. KIRTLAND TEMPLE dedicated. Outpouring of Spirit of the Lord and presence of angels reported.

April 3. Jesus Christ appeared to Joseph Smith and Oliver COWDERY, KIRTLAND TEMPLE. MOSES, ELIAS, and ELIJAH appeared and conveyed priesthood KEYS. (D&C 110).

November 2. Kirtland Safety Society Bank organized. [*See* Kirtland, Ohio: Economy.]

1837, July 19. Heber C. KIMBALL and others arrived in Liverpool, England, on first overseas mission. [*See* Missions of Twelve to British Isles.]

July 30. Nine persons baptized in river Ribble, Preston, England. First converts in BRITISH ISLES.

September. *A Voice of Warning* published, New York City, by Parley P. PRATT.

October. The *Elders' Journal* first published in Kirtland, OH.

1838, March 14. Joseph SMITH established headquarters of Church in FAR WEST, MO.

April 26. Name of the Church—THE CHURCH OF JESUS CHRIST OF LATTER-DAY SAINTS—specified by revelation (D&C 115).

May 19. ADAM-ONDI-AHMAN selected as settlement site in Daviess Co., MO.

July 4. Temple cornerstones, FAR WEST, MO, laid. Sidney RIGDON delivered July 4 oration.

July 8. Revelation on TITHING received (D&C 119).

August 6. Election-day fight, Gallatin, MO. [*See* Missouri Conflict.]

October 25. Battle of Crooked River, between Missouri State militia and Saints. David W. PATTEN, apostle, slain.

October 27. Missouri Governor Lilburn W. Boggs issued EXTERMINATION ORDER, Jefferson City, MO. (Rescinded June 25, 1976, by Governor Christopher S. Bond.)

October 30. HAUN'S MILL MASSACRE, Caldwell Co., MO.

October 31. Joseph SMITH and other leaders of the Church arrested by Missouri State militia, FAR WEST.

November 9. Joseph SMITH and fellow prisoners arrived at Richmond, MO, and put in chains. Joseph rebuked guards. [*See* Richmond Jail.]

November 13. Joseph F. SMITH (1838–1918) b. FAR WEST, Caldwell Co., MO.

December 1. Joseph SMITH and others imprisoned, LIBERTY JAIL, Liberty, Clay Co., MO.

1839, February 23. Many refugee Saints arrived at Quincy, IL, and local citizens adopted relief measures.

March 20–25. Joseph SMITH still imprisoned in LIBERTY JAIL, wrote epistle to Saints (D&C 121, 122, 123).

April 26. Apostles (at great personal risk) gathered at Far West Temple site, to fulfill revelation regarding second apostolic mission to BRITISH ISLES (D&C 118).

May 9–10. Joseph SMITH moved from Quincy to Commerce (later renamed NAUVOO), IL.

August 8. John TAYLOR and Wilford WOODRUFF, the first Apostles to leave Commerce on British mission.

October 29. Joseph SMITH left Commerce for Washington, D.C., to petition U.S. Government for redress of losses in Missouri.

November. First issue of TIMES AND SEASONS published, Commerce, IL.

1840, May. First number of MILLENNIAL STAR published, Manchester, England.

August 15. BAPTISM FOR THE DEAD publicly announced by Joseph SMITH.

September 14. Joseph SMITH, Sr., d. Nauvoo, age 69.

December 16. Nauvoo charter signed by Illinois Governor Thomas Carlin.

1841, January 19. Saints commanded to build NAUVOO TEMPLE and NAUVOO HOUSE (D&C 124).

April 6. Nauvoo Temple cornerstones laid.

October 24. Orson HYDE dedicated Palestine for return of Jews.

1842, March 1. Publication of BOOK OF ABRAHAM commenced in TIMES AND SEASONS.

March 1. WENTWORTH LETTER published in TIMES AND SEASONS. [*See* Appendix 12.]

March 17. Female Relief Society organized, Nauvoo, IL. [*See* Relief Society in Nauvoo.]

May 4. First ENDOWMENT ordinances given, Red Brick Store, Nauvoo. [*See* Temple Ordinances.]

August 6. Joseph SMITH prophesied Saints would be driven to Rocky Mountains.

1843, July 12. Revelation on celestial marriage received (D&C 132).

1844, March 11. The General Council (COUNCIL OF FIFTY) organized in Nauvoo.

April 7. KING FOLLETT DISCOURSE delivered by Joseph SMITH.

June 7. NAUVOO EXPOSITOR, anti-Mormon newspaper, published.

June 10. NAUVOO EXPOSITOR declared public nuisance and destroyed.

June 27. Joseph SMITH and Hyrum SMITH martyred in Carthage jail. [*See* Martyrdom of Joseph & Hyrum Smith.]

August 8. At Church meeting, Nauvoo, mantle of Prophet fell upon senior apostle, Brigham YOUNG. Apostles sustained by people to lead Church. [*See* Succession in the Presidency; Quorum of the Twelve.]

1845, April 6. The Twelve Apostles issue "Proclamation . . . To all the Kings of the World; To the President of the United States of America; To the Governors of the Several States, And to the Rulers and People of all Nations." [*See* Proclamations of the First Presidency and the Quorum of the Twelve Apostles.]

1846, February 4. Nauvoo Saints commenced crossing Mississippi river to move to the Great Basin.

February 4. Ship *Brooklyn* sailed from New York for California with 238 Saints, Samuel Brannan, leader.

May 1. NAUVOO TEMPLE publicly dedicated by Orson HYDE. [*See* Temples: Latter–day Saint Temples.]

June 30. U.S. Army asked Church at COUNCIL BLUFFS, IA, to raise 500 volunteers to fight in war with Mexico.

July 16. MORMON BATTALION mustered into U.S. service.

September 10–17. Battle of Nauvoo fought between remaining Saints and Illinois mob.

1847, January 14. Brigham YOUNG received revelation concerning organization of Saints for move west (D&C 136).

April 5. First element of Brigham YOUNG's Pioneer company left WINTER QUARTERS on the journey west.

July 21. Orson PRATT and Erastus Snow made first LDS reconnaissance of SALT LAKE VALLEY.

July 24. Brigham YOUNG entered SALT LAKE VALLEY.

July 28. SALT LAKE TEMPLE site selected by Brigham YOUNG.

December 5. Brigham YOUNG unanimously sustained as President of Church by council of Apostles, Kanesville, Pottawattamie Co., IA.

December 27. CONFERENCE of Church at Kanesville sustained Brigham YOUNG, Heber C. KIMBALL, Willard Richards as FIRST PRESIDENCY.

1848, June. Crickets came from mountains into Salt Lake Valley, devastating crops. Fields saved as flocks of SEAGULLS devoured crickets.

1849, Fall. PERPETUAL EMIGRATING FUND company established.

December 9. SUNDAY SCHOOL organized by Richard BALLANTYNE.

1850, June 15. DESERET NEWS began publication in SALT LAKE CITY.

September 20. Brigham YOUNG appointed governor of UTAH TERRITORY by U.S. President Millard Fillmore.

1851, July 11. PEARL OF GREAT PRICE first published, Liverpool, England.

November 1. First issue of JOURNAL OF DISCOURSES published, Liverpool, England.

November 11. "UNIVERSITY OF DESERET" opened, SALT LAKE CITY, UTAH.

1852, August 29. Public announcement of PLURAL MARRIAGE made, SALT LAKE CITY.

1853, February 14. Temple Block consecrated and ground broken, SALT LAKE CITY. [*See* Temple Square.]

April 6. SALT LAKE TEMPLE cornerstones laid under direction of FIRST PRESIDENCY.

1855, May 5. ENDOWMENT HOUSE on Temple Block dedicated at SALT LAKE CITY. [*See* Temple Ordinances.]

Fast day inaugurated as first Thursday of each month. [*See* Fast and Testimony Meeting.]

1856, May 14. Lucy Mack SMITH, mother of the Prophet Joseph Smith, d. Nauvoo, age 81.

September 26. First two handcart companies arrived at SALT LAKE CITY, led by Edmund L. Ellsworth and Daniel D. McArthur.

October 28. HANDCART COMPANY of Captain Edward Martin detained by early snow storms. Found by members of rescue company from SALT LAKE VALLEY.

November 9. Captain James G. Willie's HANDCART COMPANY arrived in SALT LAKE CITY. Suffered 67 deaths of a company of 500.

November 22. Heber J. GRANT (1856–1945) b. SALT LAKE CITY.

November 30. Martin HANDCART COMPANY arrived, SALT LAKE CITY. Suffered between 135 and 150 deaths.

1856–1857. "Mormon Reformation." [*See* Reformation (LDS) of 1856–1857.]

1857, May 13. Elder Parley P. PRATT murdered near Van Buren, AK.

July 24. Word received of UTAH EXPEDITION.

August 5. Governor Brigham YOUNG placed UTAH TERRITORY under martial law and forbade U.S. troops to enter Salt Lake Valley.

September 7–11. Emigrating party led by John T. Baker and Alexander Fancher besieged by Indians at Mountain Meadows; killed by Indians and Mormon militia. [*See* Mountain Meadows Massacre.]

1858, May. "Move South" began evacuation of all northern Utah settlements in preparation for war with U.S. troops.

June 11. Peaceful settlement to "Utah War" negotiated through efforts of Brigham YOUNG, Governor Alfred Cumming, Thomas L. KANE, and government peace commissioners.

1862, July 8. Morrill antibigamy bill became law, designed to prevent practice of POLYGAMY in U.S. territories. [See Anti–Polygamy Legislation.]

1867, October 6. First General Conference held in new Tabernacle, SALT LAKE CITY.

December 8. Relief Society program reemphasized by President Brigham YOUNG, under President Eliza R. SNOW.

1869, March 1. Zion's Cooperative Mercantile Institution (ZCMI), a cooperative business system, began in SALT LAKE CITY.

May 10. Great Pacific Railroad completed by junction of Union Pacific and Central Pacific Railroads, Promontory Summit, UT.

November 28. Young Ladies' RETRENCHMENT ASSOCIATION organized by Brigham YOUNG, forerunner of modern YOUNG WOMEN organization.

1870, April 4. George Albert SMITH (1870–1951) b. SALT LAKE CITY.

August 30. Martin HARRIS (age 88) arrived in SALT LAKE CITY and bore TESTIMONY to truth of Book of Mormon at GENERAL CONFERENCE.

1872, June. First issue of WOMAN'S EXPONENT published, SALT LAKE CITY, UTAH.

1873, September 8. David O. MCKAY (1873–1970) b. Huntsville, UT.

1873–1874, Winter. UNITED ORDERS movement established under direction of President Brigham YOUNG.

1875, June 10. Young Men's Mutual Improvement Association organized, forerunner of YOUNG MEN program.

July 10. Martin HARRIS, one of Three Witnesses to the Book of Mormon, d. Clarkston, Cache Co., UT, age 92.

October 16. Brigham Young Academy organized, Provo, UT, first Church academy. [See Academies.]

1876, July 19. Joseph Fielding SMITH (1876–1972) b. SALT LAKE CITY.

1877, April 6. St. George Temple dedicated. [See Temples: Latter–day Saint Temples.] President Brigham YOUNG received revelation to set in order the Church priesthood organization and stakes of ZION.

August 29. President Brigham YOUNG d. SALT LAKE CITY, age 76.

1878, August 25. Aurelia Spencer ROGERS founded PRIMARY organization, Farmington, UT.

1879, January 6. U.S. Supreme Court upheld 1862 antibigamy law in George Reynolds case. [See Antipolygamy Legislation; Reynolds v. United States.]

April 30. Emma Hale SMITH Bidamon d. Nauvoo, IL., age 74.

1880, April 6. Fiftieth year since organization of Church declared Year of Jubilee. [See April 6.]

October 10. John TAYLOR sustained President of Church. PEARL OF GREAT PRICE accepted as standard work.

1882, March 22. Edmunds bill signed into law by President Chester A. Arthur. [See Antipolygamy Legislation.]

1887, March 3. Edmunds-Tucker bill became law without signature of President Grover Cleveland. [See Antipolygamy Legislation.]

July 25. President John TAYLOR d. in exile, Kaysville, Davis Co., UT.

1889, April 7. Wilford WOODRUFF sustained President of Church.

1890, September 24. President Wilford WOODRUFF received the vision which led to his issuance of the "MANIFESTO" stating PLURAL MARRIAGE officially discontinued in the Church.

October 6. "MANIFESTO" accepted in General Conference.

1893, April 6. SALT LAKE TEMPLE, forty years in construction, dedicated by President Wilford WOODRUFF. [See Temples: Latter-day Saint Temples.]

1894, April 5. President Wilford WOODRUFF presented to his counselors and QUORUM OF THE TWELVE a revelation concerning ENDOWMENTS and adoptions. [See Law of Adoption.]

November 13. GENEALOGICAL SOCIETY OF UTAH organized.

1895, March 28. Spencer W. KIMBALL (1895–1985) b. SALT LAKE CITY.

1896, January 4. Utah became U.S. 45th state, proclamation signed by President Grover Cleveland. [See Utah Statehood.]

April 6. LDS "Political Manifesto" issued at General Conference.

December 6. Fast Day changed from first Thursday of month to first Sunday. [See Fast and Testimony Meeting.]

1897, November. First issue of IMPROVEMENT ERA published.

1898, September 2. President Wilford WOODRUFF d. San Francisco, CA, age 91.

September 13. Lorenzo SNOW became President of Church.

Publication of first serial CONFERENCE REPORT.

1899, March 28. Harold B. LEE (1899–1973) b. Clifton, Oneida Co., ID.

May 17. President Lorenzo SNOW received revelation in St. George prompting him to emphasize TITHING.

August 4. Ezra Taft BENSON (1899–) b. Whitney, Oneida Co., ID.

1901, October 10. President Lorenzo SNOW d. SALT LAKE CITY, age 87.

October 17. Joseph F. SMITH became President of Church.

1902, January. First issue of CHILDREN'S FRIEND published.

1903, October 15. Brigham Young Academy became BRIGHAM YOUNG UNIVERSITY.

1904, April 5. President Joseph F. SMITH issued "Second Manifesto."

1904–1906. U.S. Senate hearings regarding seating of Reed Smoot, an apostle, elected to Senate in 1902. [*See* Smoot Hearings.]

1909, November. FIRST PRESIDENCY issued statement on "Origin of Man." [*See* Origin of Man].

1911. Church adopted Boy Scout program. [*See* Scouting.]

1912, Fall. First LDS seminary opened at Granite High School, SALT LAKE CITY. [*See* Seminaries.]

1915, January. RELIEF SOCIETY MAGAZINE began publication.

1916, June 30. FIRST PRESIDENCY and QUORUM OF THE TWELVE APOSTLES issued statement on "The Father and the Son." [*See* Appendix 4.]

1917, October 2. Church Administration Building completed.

1918, October 3. President Joseph F. SMITH received "Vision of the Redemption of the Dead" (D&C 138).

November 19. President Joseph F. SMITH d. SALT LAKE CITY, age 80.

November 23. Heber J. GRANT became President of Church.

1922, 6 May. Restored gospel taught by radio for first time as station KZN broadcast message from President Heber J. Grant. [*See* KSL Radio.]

1926, Fall. First Institute of Religion, Moscow, ID.

1929, July 15. Tabernacle Choir began weekly network radio broadcasts. [*See* Mormon Tabernacle Choir Broadcasts.]

1930, April 6. CENTENNIAL of Church organization.

1931, April 4. CHURCH NEWS section of DESERET NEWS began publication.

1936, April 7. Church Security Program instituted to assist poor during Great Depression; became Church Welfare Program. [*See* Welfare.]

1938. DESERET INDUSTRIES Program established.

Inauguration of microfilming of genealogical records by Genealogical Society.

1941, April 6. ASSISTANTS TO THE TWELVE first called.

1945, May 14. President Heber J. GRANT d. SALT LAKE CITY, age 88.

May 21. George Albert SMITH became President of Church.

1946, February. Elder Ezra Taft BENSON left to administer to physical and spiritual needs of European Saints after World War II.

1947. Church membership reached 1 million.

July 24. CENTENNIAL of Pioneer entry into SALT LAKE VALLEY.

1951, April 4. President George Albert SMITH d. SALT LAKE CITY, age 81.

April 9. David O. MCKAY sustained President of Church.

1952, November 25. Elder Ezra Taft BENSON, apostle, appointed U.S. secretary of agriculture by President Dwight D. Eisenhower.

1955, February 12. President David O. McKay broke ground for Church College of Hawaii.

1961, October. All–Church Coordinating Council established to correlate CURRICULUM and activities for children, youth, and adults. [*See* Correlation.]

1963. Church membership reached 2 million.

March 7. Stake Presidencies also became presidencies of stake high priests quorums. [*See* High Priest.]

1964, October. Observance of Family Home Evening reemphasized.

1965, January. Home Evening program manual placed in homes.

1966. Uniform Church Curriculum year inaugurated; all organizations begin curriculum year at same time.

1967, September 29. First REGIONAL REPRESENTATIVES called, to begin January 1, 1968.

1969, August 3–8. First World Conference on Records held, SALT LAKE CITY.

1970, January 18. President David O. MCKAY d. SALT LAKE CITY, age 96.

January 23. Joseph Fielding Smith became President of Church.

1971. Church membership reached 3 million.

January. New Church magazines, ENSIGN, NEW ERA, and FRIEND commenced publication.

August 27–29. First Area Conference held, Manchester, England.

1972, July 2. President Joseph Fielding SMITH d. SALT LAKE CITY, age 95.

July 7. Harold B. LEE became President of the Church.

1973, December 26. President Harold B. LEE d. SALT LAKE CITY, age 74.

December 30. Spencer W. KIMBALL became President of the Church.

1974. Church–owned hospitals divested.

1975, July 24. The 28-story Church Office Building dedicated, SALT LAKE CITY.

October 3. President Spencer W. KIMBALL announced organization of First Quorum of SEVENTY.

1976, April 3. Two revelations added to Pearl of Great Price. Later became D&C 137 and D&C 138, 1981.

October 1. ASSISTANTS TO THE TWELVE made Seventies.

1978. Church membership reached 4 million.

June 8. FIRST PRESIDENCY issued letter announcing revelation granting the priesthood to worthy men of all races.

September 16. First annual women's meeting held.

September 30. June 8 revelation on priesthood sustained by Church (D&C: OFFICIAL DECLARATION —2); "emeritus" status announced for GENERAL AUTHORITIES other than FIRST PRESIDENCY and Twelve.

1979, February 18. The 1,000th stake of the Church organized, Nauvoo, IL, by Ezra Taft BENSON, President of the Twelve.

August. LDS edition of King James Bible with study helps published. [See Bible, LDS Publication of.]

1980, March 2. Consolidated ward meeting schedule inaugurated in Church units in U.S., Canada.

April 6. Church sesquicentennial General Conference held, with commemorative activities.

1981, September 26. New editions of BOOK OF MORMON, DOCTRINE AND COVENANTS, PEARL OF GREAT PRICE published.

Announcement made of network of satellite receiving dishes for stake centers outside Utah for receiving Church broadcasts. [See Satellite Communication System.]

1982. Church membership reached 5 million.

1983. Stake welfare properties placed under general Church control.

1984, April. Genealogical management system for home computers, Personal Ancestral File, made available. [See Ancestral File.]

June. Area presidencies inaugurated, with members called from the Seventies. [See Area, Area Presidency.]

April 4. Museum of Church History and Art dedicated, SALT LAKE CITY, UTAH.

October 28. The 1,500th Church stake organized, Ciudad Obregon Mexico Yaqui Stake.

1985, August 2. Revised LDS Hymnbook published.

October 23. The Family History Library dedicated.

November 5. President Spencer W. KIMBALL d. SALT LAKE CITY, age 90.

November 10. Ezra Taft BENSON became President of Church.

1986. Church membership reached 6 million.

October 4. Seventies quorums in stakes were discontinued.

1987, February 15. Tabernacle Choir performed 3,000th radio broadcast.

July 24–26. 150th anniversary of first missionary labors in Britain celebrated.

1989. Church membership reached 7 million.

April 1. Second Quorum of SEVENTY organized.

May 16. BYU Jerusalem Center dedicated by Howard W. Hunter, President of the Twelve.

1990, September 13. Registration of Leningrad Branch of Church approved by Soviet government.

December. Number of missionaries serving reached 43,651. [See Missionary; Missionary Life.]

1991, June. Mormon Tabernacle Choir toured Eastern Europe.

June 24. The Russian Republic, the largest republic in the Soviet Union, granted official recognition to the Church.

In 1991, Church membership exceeded 8 million members.

Appendix 3

Church Periodicals

YEAR	TITLE	FIRST EDITOR OR ORGANIZATION	PLACE
1832–1834	*Evening and the Morning Star, The*	W. W. Phelps	Independence, Missouri, and Kirtland, Ohio
1832–1834 [1835–1836]	*Evening and Morning Star*	Oliver Cowdery	Kirtland, Ohio
1834–1837	*Latter Day Saints' Messenger and Advocate*	Oliver Cowdery	Kirtland, Ohio
1837–1838	*Elders' Journal*	Joseph Smith, Jr.	Kirtland and Far West, Missouri
1839–1846	*Times and Seasons*	E. Robinson and Don Carlos Smith	Commerce (Nauvoo), Illinois
1840–1970	*Millennial Star, The*	European Mission	Manchester, Liverpool and London, England
1841	*Gospel Reflector, The*	Benjamin Winchester	Philadelphia, Pennsylvania
1845–1865	*Prophetic Almanac*	Orson Pratt	New York City, New York
1853–1856	*Zion's Watchman, The*	Agustus A. Farnham	Sydney, Australia
1853–1854	*Seer, The*	Orson Pratt	Washington, D.C. and Liverpool, England
1854–1886	*Journal of Discourses*	George D. Watt	Liverpool, England
1854	*LDS Millennial Star and Monthly Visitor, The*	Richard Ballantyne	Madras, India
1866–1970	*Juvenile Instructor* (Changed to *The Instructor* 1929)	George Q. Cannon Sunday School	Salt Lake City, Utah
1872–1914	*Woman's Exponent*	Louisa Lula Green Relief Society	Salt Lake City, Utah
1879–1896	*Contributor, The*	Junius F. Wells	Salt Lake City, Utah
1886–1890	*Historical Record*	Andrew Jenson	Salt Lake City, Utah
1889–1929	*Young Woman's Journal, The*	Susa Young Gates	Salt Lake City, Utah
1897–1970	*Improvement Era, The*	YMMIA	Salt Lake City, Utah
1898–1900	*Southern Star*	Southern States Mission	Chattanooga, Tennessee
1899–1901	*Truth's Reflex*	Southwestern States Mission	St. Johns, Kansas
1902–1970	*Children's Friend, The*	Primary	Salt Lake City, Utah
1903–1907	*Elder's Journal, The*	Southern States Mission	Atlanta, Georgia and Chattanooga, Tennessee

1907–1945	*Liahona, The* (Changed to *Liahona the Elders' Journal* 1907)	B.F. Cummings	Independence, Missouri
1907–1913	*Elder's Messenger* (Changed to *Messenger* 1908)	New Zealand Mission	Auckland, New Zealand
1917–1956	*Truth*	Northern States Mission	Chicago, Illinois
1910–1940	*Utah Genealogical and Historical Magazine*	Genealogical Society of Utah	Salt Lake City, Utah
1912–1975	*Messenger to the Sightless* (Braille) (Changed to *New Messenger* 1953)		Provo, Utah Louisville, Kentucky
1914–1970	*Relief Society Magazine*	Susa Young Gates	Salt Lake City, Utah
1924–1947	*Genealogical and Historical Magazine of Arizona Temple District*	Arizona Temple District	Mesa, Arizona
1925–1937, 1959–	*BYU Studies*	BYU	Provo, Utah
1927–1970	*Cumorah Monthly Bulletin* (Changed to *Cumorah's Southern Cross* 1929; *Cumorah's Southern Messenger* 1933)	South African Mission	Mowbray, South Africa
1965-	*Priesthood Bulletin* (Changed to *Bulletin*)		Salt Lake City, Utah
1963–1971	*Liahona, The* (for American Indians)	Indian Committee	Salt Lake City, Utah
1971–	*Ensign of The Church of Jesus Christ of Latter-day Saints, The*	The Church of Jesus Christ of Latter-day Saints	Salt Lake City, Utah
1971–	*New Era*	The Church of Jesus Christ of Latter-day Saints	Salt Lake City, Utah
1971–	*Friend, The*	The Church of Jesus Christ of Latter-day Saints	Salt Lake City, Utah
1977–	*Tambuli*	International Magazines	Manila and Makati, Philippines
1976–	*Ensign Talking Book*		Salt Lake City, Utah

International Magazines

YEAR	TITLE	ORGANIZATION OR FIRST EDITOR	PLACE
		CHINESE	
1959–	*Sheng te jr sheng* (Changed to *Shentao che sheng* 1986; changed to *Sheng tu chih sheng* 1988; Unified 1967)	Southern Far East Mission	Hong Kong Taiwan
		CZECH	
1929–1939	*Hvezdika*	Czechoslovakian Mission	Prague, Czechoslovakia
1945–1949	*Novy Hlas*	Czechoslovakian Mission	Prague, Czechoslovakia
		DANISH	
1851–1984 1985–	*Skandinaviens Stjerne* (Changed to *Den Danske Stjerne* 1957; changed to *Sjernen* 1985) (Unified 1967)	Scandinavian Mission	Copenhagen, Denmark Frankfurt, Germany
1880–1887	*Ungdommens Raadgiver*	N. Wilhelmse	Copenhagen, Denmark
1882–1885	*Morgenstjernen*	Andrew Jenson	Salt Lake City, Utah
		DUTCH	
1896–	*De Ster* (Unified 1967)	Netherlands Mission	Rotterdam, and The Hague, Holland Frankfurt, Germany
		FINNISH	
1950–	*Valkeus* (Unified 1967)	Finnish Mission	Helsinki, Finland Frankfurt, Germany
		FRENCH	
1851–1852	*Etoile Du Deseret*	John Taylor	Paris, France
1853	*Le Reflecteur*	T.B.H. Stenhouse	Geneva, Switzerland
1928–	*L'Etoile* (Changed to *La Nouvelle Etoile* 1963; changed to *L'Etoile* 1967; (Unified 1967)	French Mission	Geneva, Switzerland Liege, Belgium, and Lyon, France Frankfurt, Germany
		GERMAN	
1851–1852	*Zion's Panier*	German Mission	Hamburg, Germany
1855–1861	*Der Darsteller der Heiligen der Letzten Tage*	German Mission	Geneva and Zurich, Switzerland
1862–1863	*Die Reform der Heiligen der Letzten Tage*	John L. Smith	Geneva, Switzerland

1869–	*Der Stern* (Unified 1967)	German Mission	Zurich, Bern, and Basel, Switzerland Frankfurt, Germany
1927–1936	*Der Wegweiser*	Swiss-German and German-Austrian Mission	Basel, Switzerland

HAWAIIAN

1908–1911	*Ka Elele Oiaio*	Hawaiian Mission	Honolulu, Hawaii

ITALIAN

1967–	*La Stella* (Unified)	Italian Mission	Florence, Italy, and Frankfurt, Germany

JAPANESE

1967–	*Seito No Michi* (Unified 1968)	Northern Far East Mission	Tokyo, Japan

KOREAN

1965–	*Songdo Wi Bot*, (Changed to *Songdo ui pot*, 1988; Unified 1967)	Korean Mission	Seoul, South Korea

MAORI

1907–1955	*Te Karere*	New Zealand Mission	Auckland, New Zealand

NORWEGIAN

1922–1925	*Morgenstjernen*	Norwegian Mission	Oslo, Norway
1937–	*Lys Over Norge* (Unified 1967)	Norwegian Mission	Oslo, Norway and Lynge, Denmark Frankfurt, Germany

PORTUGUESE

1948–	*A Gaivota* (Changed to *A Liahona* 1951) (Unified 1968)	Brazilian Mission	São Paulo, Brazil

SAMOAN

1968–	*O Le Liahona* (Unified)	Samoan Mission	Auckland, New Zealand

SPANISH

1927–1930	*Evangelio Restaurado*	Mexican Mission	El Paso, Texas, and
1937–	*El Atalaya* (Changed to *In Yaotlapiyoui* 1937; changed to *Atalaya* 1944; changed to *Liahona* 1945; Unified 1967)	Mexican Mission	Los Angeles, California Mexico City, Mexico
1937–1955	*El Mensajero* (Changed to *El Mensajero Deseret* 1941)	Argentine Mission	Buenos Aires, Argentina
1951–1961	*El Candil*	Uruguayan Mission	Montevideo, Uruguay
1954–1955	*El Deseret Oriental*	Uruguayan Mission	Montevideo, Uruguay

SWEDISH

1877–	*Nordstjernan* (Changed to *Nordstjärnan* 1894) (Unified 1967)		Copenhagen, Denmark and Stockholm, Sweden Frankfurt, Germany

TAHITIAN

1907–1961	*Te Heheuraa Api*	Tahitian Mission	Papeeti, Tahiti
1968–1970	*Te Tiarama* (Unified 1968)	French-Polynesian Mission	Auckland, New Zealand

THAI

1984–	*Khaawaansidthichon*	International Magazines	Bangkok, Thailand

TONGAN

1954–	*Ko E Tuhulu* (Changed to *Tuhulu* 1980; Unified 1968)	Tongan Mission	Auckland, New Zealand

WELSH

1846–1858	*Prophwyd y Jubili* (Changed to *Udgorn Seion* 1849)	Dan Jones and John Davis	Methyr Tydifil, Caerfyrddin and Abertawy, Wales

Church Newspapers

DATE	TITLE	FIRST EDITOR	PLACE
1832–1833	*Upper Missouri Advertiser, The*	W.W. Phelps	Independence, Missouri
1835–1836	*Northern Times, The*	Frederick G. Williams	Kirtland, Ohio
1842–1843	*Wasp, The*	William Smith	Nauvoo, Illinois
1843–1845	*Nauvoo Neighbor, The*	John Taylor	Nauvoo, Illinois
1844–1845	*Prophet, The*	William Smith	New York City, New York
1845	*New York Messenger, The*	Parley P. Pratt	New York City, New York
1847–1848	*California Star, The*	E.P. Jones	Yerba Buena (San Francisco), California
1849–1852	*Frontier Guardian, The*	Orson Hyde	Kanesville, Iowa
1850–	*Deseret News*	Willard Richards	Salt Lake City, Utah
1852	*Western Bugle*	Almon W. Babbitt	Kanesville, Iowa
1854–1855	*Saint Louis Luminary, The*	Erastus Snow	St. Louis, Missouri
1855–1857	*Mormon, The*	John Taylor	New York City, New York
1856–1857	*Western Standard, The*	George Q. Cannon	San Francisco, California
1931–	"Church Section" in *Deseret News* (Changed to *Church News*, 1943)		Salt Lake, City, Utah
1944–1948	*Church News, LDS Servicemen's Edition*		Salt Lake City, Utah

Foreign Language Newspapers Published in Salt Lake City, Utah

DANISH		
1876–1935	*Bikuben*	Local Danish-Norwegian groups
1873–1874	*Utah Posten*	Local Danish-Norwegian groups
1874–1877	*Utah Skandinav*	Local Danish groups
DUTCH		
1914–1935	*De Utah Nederlander*	Local Dutch groups
GERMAN		
1890–1935	*Salt Lake City, Beobacher*	Local German groups
SWEDISH		
1885–1892	*Svenska Hardden*	Local Swedish groups
1900–1935	*Utah-Posten*	Local Swedish groups

Appendix 4

Doctrinal Expositions of the First Presidency

From time to time the First Presidency (sometimes accompanied by the Council of the Twelve Apostles) has issued official clarifications and pronouncements on doctrinal themes. Three such documents are included here. The first two are on the same subject: the first was published in 1909 and is titled "The Origin of Man," the second is dated 1925 and is titled "'Mormon' View of Evolution." The third document was published in June 1916 and is titled "The Father and the Son," being a detailed statement of the distinctive roles of God the Father and of his Son Jesus Christ.

THE ORIGIN OF MAN
By The First Presidency of the Church

"God created man in his own image."

Inquiries arise from time to time respecting the attitude of the Church of Jesus Christ of Latter-day Saints upon questions which, though not vital from a doctrinal standpoint, are closely connected with the fundamental principles of salvation. The latest inquiry of this kind that has reached us is in relation to the origin of man. It is believed that a statement of the position held by the Church upon this important subject will be timely and productive of good.

In presenting the statement that follows we are not conscious of putting forth anything essentially new; neither is it our desire so to do. Truth is what we wish to present, and truth—eternal truth—is fundamentally old. A restatement of the original attitude of the Church relative to this matter is all that will be attempted here. To tell the truth as God has revealed it, and commend it to the acceptance of those who need to conform their opinions thereto, is the sole purpose of this presentation.

"God created man in his own image, in the image of God created he him; male and female created he them." In these plain and pointed words the inspired author of the book of Genesis made known to the world the truth concerning the origin of the human family. Moses, the prophet-historian, "learned," as we are told, "in all the wisdom of the Egyptians," when making this important announcement, was not voicing a mere opinion, a theory derived from his researches into the occult lore of that ancient people. He was speaking as the mouthpiece of God, and his solemn declaration was for all time and for all people. No subsequent revelator of the truth has contradicted the great leader and lawgiver of Israel. All who have since spoken by divine authority upon this theme have confirmed his simple and sublime proclamation. Nor could it be otherwise. Truth has but one source, and all revelations from heaven are harmonious with each other. The omnipotent Creator, the maker of heaven and earth—had shown unto Moses everything pertaining to this planet, including the facts relating to man's origin, and the authoritative pronouncement of that mighty prophet and seer to the house of Israel, and through Israel to the whole world, is couched in the simple clause: "God created man in his own image" (Genesis 1:27; Pearl of Great Price—Book of Moses, 1:27–41).

The creation was two-fold—firstly spiritual, secondly temporal. This truth, also, Moses plainly taught—much more plainly than it has come down to us in the imperfect translations of the Bible that are now in use. Therein the fact of a spiritual creation, antedating the temporal creation, is strongly implied, but the proof of it is not so clear and conclusive as in other records held by the Latter-day Saints to be of equal authority with the Jewish scriptures. The partial obscurity of the latter upon the point in question is owing, no doubt, to the loss of those "plain and precious" parts of sacred writ, which, as the Book of Mormon informs us, have been taken away from the Bible during its passage down the centuries (1 Nephi 13:24–29). Some of these missing parts the Prophet Joseph Smith undertook to restore when he revised those scriptures by the spirit of revelation, the result being that more complete account of the creation which is found in the book of Moses, previously cited. Note the following passages:

And now, behold, I say unto you, that these are the generations of the heaven and of the earth, when they were created, in the day that I, the Lord God, made the heaven and the earth;

And every plant of the field before it was in the earth, and every herb of the field before it grew.

For I, the Lord God, created all things of which I have spoken, spiritually, before they were naturally upon the face of the earth. For I, the Lord God, had not caused it to rain upon the face of the earth.

And I, the Lord God, had created all the children of men, and not yet a man to till the ground; for in heaven created I them, and there was not yet flesh upon the earth, neither in the water, neither in the air.

But, I, the Lord God, spake, and there went up a mist from the earth, and watered the whole face of the ground.

And I, the Lord God, formed man from the dust of the ground, and breathed into his nostrils the breath of life; and man became a living soul, the first flesh upon the earth, the first man also.

Nevertheless, all things were before created, but spiritually were they created and made, according to my word (Pearl of Great Price—Book of Moses, 3:4–7. See also chapters 1 and 2, and compare with Genesis 1 and 2).

These two points being established, namely, the creation of man in the image of God, and the two-fold character of the creation, let us now inquire: What was the form of man, in the spirit and in the body, as originally created? In a general way the answer is given in the words chosen as the text of this treatise. "God created man in his own image." It is more explicitly rendered in the Book of Mormon thus: "All men were created in the beginning after mine own image" (Ether 3:15). It is the Father who is speaking. If, therefore, we can ascertain the form of the "Father of spirits," "The God of the spirits of all flesh," we shall be able to discover the form of the original man.

Jesus Christ, the Son of God, is "the express image" of His Father's person (Hebrews 1:3). He walked the earth as a human being, as a perfect man, and said, in answer to a question put to Him: "He that hath seen me hath seen the Father" (John 14:9). This alone ought to solve the problem to the satisfaction of every thoughtful, reverent mind. The conclusion is irresistible, that if the Son of God be the express image (that is, likeness) of His

Father's person, then His Father is in the form of a man; for that was the form of the Son of God, not only during His mortal life, but before His mortal birth, and after His resurrection. It was in this form that the Father and the Son, as two personages, appeared to Joseph Smith, when, as a boy of fourteen years, he received his first vision. Then if God made man—the first man—in His own image and likeness, he must have made him like unto Christ, and consequently like unto men of Christ's time and of the present day. That man was made in the image of Christ is positively stated in the Book of Moses: "And I, God, said unto mine Only Begotten, which was with me from the beginning, Let us make man in our image, after our likeness; and it was so. . . . And I, God, created man in mine own image, in the image of mine Only Begotten created I him, male and female created I them" (2:26, 27).

The Father of Jesus is our Father also. Jesus Himself taught this truth, when He instructed His disciples how to pray: "Our Father which art in heaven," etc. Jesus, however, is the firstborn among all the sons of God— the first begotten in the spirit, and the only begotten in the flesh. He is our elder brother, and we, like Him, are in the image of God. All men and women are in the similitude of the universal Father and Mother, and are literally the sons and daughters of Deity.

"God created man in His own image." This is just as true of the spirit as it is of the body, which is only the clothing of the spirit, its complement; the two together constituting the soul. The spirit of man is in the form of man, and the spirits of all creatures are in the likeness of their bodies. This was plainly taught by the Prophet Joseph Smith (Doctrine and Covenants 77:2).

Here is further evidence of the fact. More than seven hundred years before Moses was shown the things pertaining to this earth, another great prophet, known to us as the brother of Jared, was similarly favored by the Lord. He was even permitted to behold the spirit-body of the foreordained Savior, prior to His incarnation; and so like the body of a man was gazing upon a being of flesh and blood. He first saw the finger and then the entire body of the Lord—all in the spirit. The Book of Mormon says of this wonderful manifestation:

And it came to pass that when the brother of Jared had said these words, behold the Lord stretched forth His hand and touched the stones one by one with His finger; and the veil was taken from off the eyes of the brother of Jared, and he saw the finger of the Lord; and it was as the finger of a man, like unto flesh and blood; and the brother of Jared fell down before the Lord, for he was struck with fear.

And the Lord saw that the brother of Jared had fallen to the earth; and the Lord said unto him, Arise, why hast thou fallen?

And he saith unto the Lord, I saw the finger of the Lord, and I feared lest he should smite me; for I knew not that the Lord had flesh and blood.

And the Lord said unto him, Because of thy faith thou hast seen that I shall take upon me flesh and blood; and never has man come before me with such exceeding faith as thou hast; for were it not so, ye could not have seen my finger. Sawest thou more than this?

And he answered, Nay, Lord, show thyself unto me.

And the Lord said unto him, Believest thou the words which I shall speak?

And he answered, Yea, Lord, I know that thou speakest the truth, for thou art a God of truth and canst not lie.

And when he had said these words, behold, the Lord showed himself unto him, and said, Because thou knowest these things ye are redeemed from the fall; therefore ye are brought back into my presence; therefore I show myself unto you.

Behold, I am He who was prepared from the foundation of the world to redeem my people. Behold, I am Jesus Christ, I am the Father and the Son. In me shall all mankind have light, and that eternally, even they who shall believe on my name; and they shall become my sons and my daughters.

And never have I shewed myself unto man whom I have created, for never hath man believed in me as thou hast. Seest thou that ye are created after mine own image? Yea, even all men were created in the beginning after mine own image.

Behold, this body, which ye now behold, is the body of my spirit, and man have I created after the body of my spirit; and even as I appear unto thee to be in the spirit, will I appear unto my people in the flesh. (Ether 3:6–16.)

What more is needed to convince us that man, both in spirit and in body, is the image and likeness of God, and that God Himself is in the form of man?

When the divine Being whose spirit-body the brother of Jared beheld, took upon Him flesh and blood, He appeared as a man, having "body, parts and passions," like other men, though vastly superior to all others, because He was God, even the Son of God, the Word made flesh: in Him "dwelt the fulness of the Godhead bodily." And why should He not appear as a man? That was the form of His spirit, and it must needs have an appropriate covering, a suitable tabernacle. He came unto the world as He had promised to come (III Nephi 1:13), taking an infant tabernacle, and developing it gradually to the fulness of His spirit stature. He came as man had been coming for ages, and as man has continued to come ever since. Jesus, how-ever, as shown, was the only begotten of God in the flesh.

Adam, our progenitor, "the first man," was, like Christ, a pre-existent spirit, and like Christ he took upon him an appropriate body, the body of a man, and so became a "living soul." The doctrine of the pre-existence, —revealed so plainly, particularly in latter days, pours a wonderful flood of light upon the otherwise mysterious problem of man's origin. It shows that man, as a spirit, was begotten and born of heavenly parents, and reared to maturity in the eternal mansions of the Father, prior to coming upon the earth in a temporal body to undergo an experience in mortality. It teaches that all men existed in the spirit before any man existed in the flesh, and that all who have inhabited the earth since Adam have taken bodies and become souls in like manner.

It is held by some that Adam was not the first man upon this earth, and that the original human being was a development from lower orders of the animal creation. These, however, are the theories of men. The word of the Lord declares that Adam was "the first man of all men" (Moses 1:34), and we are therefore in duty bound to regard him as the primal parent of our race. It was shown to the brother of Jared that all men were created in the *beginning* after the image of God; and whether we take this to mean the spirit or the body, or both, it commits us to the same conclusion: Man began life as a human being, in the likeness of our heavenly Father.

True it is that the body of man enters upon its career as a tiny germ embryo, which becomes an infant, quickened at a certain stage by the spirit whose tabernacle it is, and the child, after being born, develops into a man. There is nothing in this, however, to indicate that the original man, the first of our race, began life as anything less than a man, or less than the human germ or embryo that becomes a man.

Man, by searching, cannot find out God. Never, unaided, will he discover the truth about the beginning of human life. The Lord must reveal Himself, or remain unrevealed; and the same is true of the facts relating to the origin of Adam's race—God alone can reveal them. Some of these facts, however, are already known, and what has been made known it is our duty to receive and retain.

The Church of Jesus Christ of Latter-day Saints, basing its belief on divine revelation, ancient and modern, proclaims man to be the direct and lineal offspring of Deity. God Himself is an exalted man, perfected, enthroned, and supreme. By His almighty power He organized the earth, and all that it contains, from spirit and element, which exist co-eternally with Himself. He formed every plant that grows, and every animal that breathes, each after its own kind, spiritually and temporally—"that which is spiritual being in the likeness of that which is temporal, and that which is temporal in the likeness of that which is spiritual." He made the tadpole and the ape, the lion and the elephant but He did not make them in His own image, nor endow them with Godlike reason and intelligence. Nevertheless, the whole animal creation will be perfected and perpetuated in the Hereafter, each class in its "distinct order or sphere," and will enjoy "eternal felicity." That fact has been made plain in this dispensation (Doctrine and Covenants 77:3).

Man is the child of God, formed in the divine image and endowed with divine attributes, and even as the infant son of an earthly father and mother is capable in due time of becoming a man, so the undeveloped offspring of celestial parentage is capable, by experience through ages and aeons, of evolving into a God.

> Joseph F. Smith,
> John R. Winder,
> Anthon H. Lund,
>   First Presidency of The Church of Jesus Christ
>   of Latter-day Saints

"MORMON" VIEW OF EVOLUTION

A Statement by the First Presidency of
The Church of Jesus Christ of Latter-day Saints

"God created man in his own image, in the image of God created he him; male and female created he them."

In these plain and pointed words the inspired author of the book of Genesis made known to the world the truth concerning the origin of the human family. Moses, the prophet-historian, who was "learned" we are told, "in all the wisdom of the Egyptians," when making this important announcement, was not voicing a mere opinion. He was speaking as the mouthpiece of God, and his solemn declaration was for all time and for all people. No subsequent revelator of the truth has contradicted the great leader and lawgiver of Israel. All who have since spoken by divine authority upon this theme have confirmed his simple and sublime proclamation. Nor could it be otherwise. Truth has but one source, and all revelations from heaven are harmonious one with the other.

Jesus Christ, the Son of God, is "the express image" of his Father's person (Hebrews 1:3). He walked the earth as a human being, as a perfect man, and said, in answer to a question put to him: "He that hath seen me hath seen the Father" (John 14:9). This alone ought to solve the problem to the satisfaction of every thoughtful, reverent mind. It was in this form that the Father and the Son, as two distinct personages, appeared to Joseph Smith, when, as a boy of fourteen years, he received his first vision.

The Father of Jesus Christ is our Father also. Jesus himself taught this truth, when he instructed his disciples how to pray: "Our Father which art in heaven," etc. Jesus, however, is the first born among all the sons of God—the first begotten in the spirit, and the only begotten in the flesh. He is our elder brother, and we, like him, are in the image of God. All men and women are in the similitude of the universal Father and Mother, and are literally sons and daughters of Deity.

Adam, our great progenitor, "the first man," was, like Christ, a pre-existent spirit, and, like Christ, he took upon him an appropriate body, the body of a man, and so became a "living soul." The doctrine of pre-existence pours a wonderful flood of light upon the otherwise mysterious problem of man's origin. It shows that man, as a spirit, was begotten and born of heavenly parents, and reared to maturity in the eternal mansions of the Father, prior to coming upon the earth in a temporal body to undergo an experience in mortality.

The Church of Jesus Christ of Latter-day Saints, basing its belief on divine revelation, ancient and modern, proclaims man to be the direct and lineal offspring of Deity. By his Almighty power God organized the earth, and all that it contains, from spirit and element, which exist co-eternally with himself.

Man is the child of God, formed in the divine image and endowed with divine attributes, and even as the infant son of an earthly father and mother is capable in due time of becoming a man, so that undeveloped offspring of celestial parentage is capable, by experience through ages and aeons, of evolving into a God.

> HEBER J. GRANT
> ANTHONY W. IVINS
> CHARLES W. NIBLEY
> First Presidency

THE FATHER AND THE SON: A DOCTRINAL EXPOSITION BY THE FIRST PRESIDENCY AND THE TWELVE

The scriptures plainly and repeatedly affirm that God is the Creator of the earth and the heavens and all things that in them are. In the sense so expressed the Creator is an Organizer. God created the earth as an organized sphere; but He certainly did not create, in the sense of bringing into primal existence, the ultimate elements of the materials of which the earth consists, for "the elements are eternal" (D&C 93:33).

So also life is eternal, and not created; but life, or the vital force, may be infused into organized matter, though the details of the process have not been revealed unto man. For illustrative instances see Genesis 2:7; Moses 3:7; and Abraham 5:7. Each of these scriptures states that God breathed into the body of man the breath of life. See further Moses 3:19, for the statement that God breathed the breath of life into the bodies of the beasts and birds. God showed unto Abraham "the intelligences that were organized before the world was"; and by "intelligences" we are to understand personal "spirits" (Abraham 3:22, 23); nevertheless, we are expressly told that "Intelligence" that is, "the light of truth was not created or made, neither indeed can be" (D&C 93:29).

The term "Father" as applied to Deity occurs in sacred writ with plainly different meanings. Each of the four significations specified in the following treatment should be carefully segregated.

1. *"Father" as Literal Parent*

Scriptures embodying the ordinary signification—literally that of Parent—are too numerous and specific to require citation. The purport of these scriptures is to the effect that God the Eternal Father, whom we designate by the exalted name-title "Elohim," is the literal Parent of our Lord and Savior Jesus Christ, and of the spirits of the human race. Elohim is the Father in every sense in which Jesus Christ is so designated, and distinctively He is the Father of spirits. Thus we read in the Epistle to the Hebrews: "Furthermore we have had fathers of our flesh which corrected us, and we gave them reverence; shall we not much rather be in subjection unto the Father of spirits, and live?" (Hebrews 12:9). In view of this fact we are taught by Jesus Christ to pray: "Our Father which art in heaven, Hallowed be thy name."

Jesus Christ applies to Himself both titles, "Son" and "Father." Indeed, he specifically said to the brother of Jared: "Behold, I am Jesus Christ. I am the Father and the Son" (Ether 3:14). Jesus Christ is the Son of Elohim both as spiritual and bodily offspring; that is to say, Elohim is literally the Father of the spirit of Jesus Christ and also of the body in which Jesus Christ performed His mission in the flesh, and which body died on the cross and was afterward taken up by the process of resurrection, and is now the immortalized tabernacle of the eternal spirit of our Lord and Savior. No extended explanation of the title "Son of God" as applied to Jesus Christ appears necessary.

2. *"Father" as Creator*

A second scriptural meaning of "Father" is that of Creator, e.g., in passages referring to any one of the Godhead as "The Father of the heavens and of the earth and all things that in them are" (Ether 4:7; see also Alma 11:38, 39 and Mosiah 15:4).

God is not the Father of the earth as one of the worlds in space, nor of the heavenly bodies in whole or in part, nor of the inanimate objects and the plants and the animals upon the earth, in the literal sense in which He is the Father of the spirits of mankind. Therefore, scriptures that refer to God in any way as the Father of the heavens and the earth are to be understood as signifying that God is the Maker, the Organizer, the Creator of the heavens and the earth.

With this meaning, as the context shows in every case, Jehovah, who is Jesus Christ the Son of Elohim, is called "the Father," and even "the very eternal Father of heaven and of earth" (see passages before cited, and also Mosiah 16:15). With analogous meaning Jesus Christ is called "The Everlasting Father" (Isaiah 9:6; compare 2 Nephi 19:6). The descriptive titles "Everlasting" and "Eternal" in the foregoing texts are synonymous.

That Jesus Christ, whom we also know as Jehovah, was the executive of the Father, Elohim, in the work of creation is set forth in the book "Jesus the Christ" chapter 4. Jesus Christ, being the Creator, is consistently called the Father of heaven and earth in the sense explained above; and since His creations are of eternal quality He is very properly called the Eternal Father of heaven and earth.

3. *Jesus Christ the "Father" of Those Who Abide in His Gospel*

A third sense in which Jesus Christ is regarded as the "Father" has reference to the relationship between Him and those who accept His Gospel and thereby become heirs of eternal life. Following are a few of the scriptures illustrating this meaning.

In the fervent prayer offered just prior to His entrance into Gethsemane, Jesus Christ supplicated His Father in behalf of those whom the Father had given unto Him, specifically the apostles, and, more generally, all who would accept and abide in the Gospel through the ministry of the apostles. Read in the Lord's own words the solemn affirmation that those for whom He particularly prayed were His own, and that His Father had given them unto Him: "I have manifested thy name unto the men which thou gavest me out of the world: thine they were, and thou gavest them me; and they have kept thy word. Now they have known that all things whatsoever thou hast given me are of thee. For I have given unto them the words which thou gavest me; and they have received them, and have known surely that I came out from thee, and they have believed that thou didst send me. I pray for them: I pray not for the world, but for them which thou hast given me; for they are thine. And all mine are thine, and thine are mine; and I am glorified in them. And now I am no more in the world, but these are in the world, and I come to thee. Holy Father, keep through thine own name those whom thou hast given me, that they may be one as we are. While I was with them in the world, I kept them in thy name: those that thou gavest me I have kept, and none of them is lost, but the son of perdition; that the scripture might be fulfilled" (John 17:6–12).

And further: "Neither pray I for these alone, but for them also which shall believe on me through their word; That they all may be one; as thou, Father, art in me, and I in thee, that they also may be one in us: that the world may believe that thou hast sent me. And the glory which thou gavest me I have given them; that they may be one, even as we are one: I in them, and thou in me, that they may be made perfect in one; and that the world may know that thou hast sent me, and hast loved them, as thou hast loved me. Father, I will that they also, whom thou hast given me, be with me where I am; that they may behold my glory, which thou hast given me: for thou lovedst me before the foundation of the world" (John 17:20–24).

To His faithful servants in the present dispensation the Lord has said: "Fear not, little children; for you are mine, and I have overcome the world, and you are of them that my Father hath given me" (D&C 50:41).

Salvation is attainable only through compliance with the laws and ordinances of the Gospel; and all who are thus saved become sons and daughters unto God in a distinctive sense. In a revelation given through Joseph the Prophet to Emma Smith the Lord Jesus addressed the woman as "My daughter," and said: "for verily I say unto you, all those who receive my gospel are sons and daughters in my kingdom" (D&C 25:1). In many instances the Lord has addressed men as His sons (e.g. D&C 9:1; 34:3; 121:7).

That by obedience to the Gospel men may become sons of God, both as sons of Jesus Christ, and, through Him, as sons of His Father, is set forth in many revelations given in the current dispensation. Thus we read in an utterance of the Lord Jesus Christ to Hyrum Smith in 1829: "Behold, I am Jesus Christ, the Son of God. I am the life and light of the world. I am the same who came unto mine own and mine own received me not; but verily, verily, I say unto you, that as many as receive me, to them will I give power to become the sons of God, even to them that believe on my name. Amen" (D&C 11:28–30). To Orson Pratt the Lord spoke through Joseph the Seer, in 1830: "My son Orson, hearken and hear and behold what I, the Lord God, shall say unto you, even Jesus Christ your Redeemer; the light and the life of the world; a light which shineth in darkness and the darkness comprehendeth it not; who so loved the world that he gave his own life, that as many as would believe might become the sons of God: wherefore you are my son" (D&C 34:1–3). In 1830 the Lord thus addressed Joseph Smith and Sidney Rigdon: "Listen to the voice of the Lord your God, even Alpha and Omega, the beginning and the end, whose course is one eternal round, the same today as yesterday, and forever. I am Jesus Christ, the Son of God, who was crucified for the sins of the world, even as many as will believe on my name, that they may become the sons of God, even one in me as I am one in the Father, as the Father is one in me, that we may be one" (D&C 35:1–2). Consider also the following given in 1831: "Hearken and listen to the voice of him who is from all eternity to all eternity, the Great I am, even Jesus Christ, the light and the life of the world; a light which shineth in darkness and the darkness comprehendeth it not: the same which came in the meridian of time unto mine own, and mine own received me not; but to as many as received me, gave I power to become my sons, and even so will I give unto as many as will receive me, power to become my sons" (D&C 39:1–4). In a revelation given through Joseph Smith in March, 1831, we read: "For verily I say unto you that I am Alpha and Omega, the beginning and the end, the light and the life of the world—a light that shineth in darkness and the darkness comprehendeth it not. I came unto mine own, and mine own received me not; but unto as many as received me, gave I power to do many miracles, and to become the sons of God, and even unto them that believed on my name gave I power to obtain eternal life" (D&C 45:7–8).

A forceful exposition of this relationship between Jesus Christ as the Father and those who comply with the requirements of the Gospel as His children was given by Abinadi, centuries before our Lord's birth in the flesh: "And now I say unto you. Who shall declare his generation? Behold, I say unto you, that when his soul has been made an offering for sin, he shall see his seed. And now what say ye? And who shall be his seed? Behold I say unto you, that whosoever has heard the words of the prophets, yea, all the holy prophets who have prophesied concerning the coming of the Lord; I say unto you, that all those who have hearkened unto their words, and believed that the Lord would redeem his people, and have looked forward to that day for a remission of their sins; I say unto you, that these are his seed, or they are the heirs of the kingdom of God: for these are they whose sins he has borne; these are they for whom he has died to redeem them from their transgressions. And now, are they not his seed? Yea, and are not the prophets, every one that has opened his mouth to prophesy, that has not fallen into transgression; I mean all the holy prophets ever since the world began? I say unto you that they are his seed" (Mosiah 15:10–13).

In tragic contrast with the blessed state of those who become children of God through obedience to the Gospel of Jesus Christ is that of the unregenerate, who are specifically called the children of the devil. Note the words of Christ, while in the flesh, to certain wicked Jews who boasted of their Abrahamic lineage: "If ye were Abraham's children, ye would do the works of Abraham. . . . Ye do the deeds of your father. . . . If God were your Father, ye would love me. . . . Ye are of your father the devil, and the lusts of your father ye will do" (John 8:39, 41, 42, 44). Thus Satan is designated as the father of the wicked, though we cannot assume any personal relationship of parent and children as existing between him and them. A combined illustration showing that the righteous are the children of God and the wicked the children of the devil appears in the parable of the Tares: "The good seed are the children of the kingdom; but the tares are the children of the wicked one" (Matt. 13:38).

Men may become children of Jesus Christ by being born anew—born of God, as the inspired word states: "He that committeth sin is of the devil; for the devil sinneth from the beginning. For this purpose the Son of God was manifested, that he might destroy the works of the devil. Whosoever is born of God doth not commit sin; for his seed remaineth in him: and he cannot sin, because he is born of God. In this the children of God are manifest, and the children of the devil: whosoever doeth not righteousness is not of God, neither he that loveth not his brother" (1 John 3:8–10).

Those who have been born unto God through obedience to the Gospel may by valiant devotion to righteousness obtain exaltation and even reach the status of godhood. Of such we read: "Wherefore, as it is written, they are gods, even the sons of God" (D&C 76:58; compare 132:20, and contrast paragraph 17 in same section; see also paragraph 37). Yet, though they be gods they are still subject to Jesus Christ as their Father in this exalted relationship; and so we read in the paragraph following the above quotation: "and they are Christ's, and Christ is God's" (76:59).

By the new birth—that of water and the Spirit—mankind may become children of Jesus Christ, being through the means by Him provided "begotten sons and daughters unto God" (D&C 76:24). This solemn truth is further emphasized in the words of the Lord Jesus Christ given through Joseph Smith in 1833: "And now, verily I say unto you, I was in the beginning with the Father, and am the firstborn; and all those who are begotten through me are partakers of the glory of the same, and are the church of the firstborn" (D&C 93:21, 22). For such figurative use of the term "begotten" in application to those who are born unto God see Paul's explanation: "for in Christ Jesus I have begotten you through the gospel" (1 Cor. 4:15). An analogous instance of sonship attained by righteous service is found in the revelation relating to the order and functions of Priesthood, given in 1832: "For whoso is faithful unto the obtaining of these two priesthoods of which I have spoken, and the magnifying their calling, are sanctified by the Spirit unto the renewing of their bodies: they become the sons of Moses and of Aaron and the seed of Abraham, and the church and kingdom, and the elect of God" (D&C 84:33, 34).

If it be proper to speak of those who accept and abide in the Gospel as Christ's sons and daughters—and upon this matter the scriptures are explicit and cannot be gainsaid nor denied—it is consistently proper to speak of Jesus Christ as the Father of the righteous, they having become His children and He having been made their Father through the second birth—the baptismal regeneration.

4. *Jesus Christ the "Father" By Divine Investiture of Authority*

A fourth reason for applying the title "Father" to Jesus Christ is found in the fact that in all His dealings with the human family Jesus the Son has represented and yet represents Elohim His Father in power and authority. This is true of Christ in His preexistent, antemortal, or unembodied state, in the which He was known as Jehovah; also during His embodiment in the flesh; and during His labors as a disembodied spirit in the realm of the dead; and since that period in His resurrected state. To the Jews He said: "I and my Father are one" (John 10:30; see also 17:11, 22); yet He declared "My Father is greater than I" (John 14:28); and further, "I am come in my Father's name" (John 5:43; see also 10:25). The same truth was declared by Christ Himself to the Nephites (see 3 Nephi 20:35 and 28:10), and has been reaffirmed by revelation in the present dispensation (D&C 50:43). Thus the Father placed His name upon the Son; and Jesus Christ spoke and ministered in and through the Father's name; and so far as power, authority, and Godship are concerned His words and acts were and are those of the Father.

We read, by way of analogy, that God placed His name upon or in the Angel who was assigned to special ministry unto the people of Israel during the exodus. Of that Angel the Lord said: "Beware of him, and obey his voice, provoke him not; for he will not pardon your transgressions: for my name is in him" (Exodus. 23:21).

The ancient apostle, John, was visited by an angel who ministered and spoke in the name of Jesus Christ. As we read: "The Revelation of Jesus Christ, which God gave unto him, to shew unto his servants things which must shortly come to pass; and he sent and signified it by his angel unto his servant John" (Revelation 1:1). John was about to worship the angelic being who spoke in the name of the Lord Jesus Christ, but was forbidden: "And I John saw these things, and heard them. And when I had heard and seen, I fell down to worship before the feet of the angel which showed me these things. Then saith he unto me, See thou do it not: for I am thy fellowservant, and of thy brethren the prophets, and of them which keep sayings of this book: worship God" (Revelation 22:8, 9). And then the angel continued to speak as though he were the Lord Himself: "And, behold, I come quickly; and my reward is with me, to give every man according as his work shall be. I am Alpha and Omega, the beginning and the end, the first and the last" (verses 12, 13). The resurrected Lord, Jesus Christ, who had been exalted to the right hand of God His Father, had placed His name upon the angel sent to John, and the angel spoke in the first person, saying "I come quickly," "I am Alpha and Omega," though he meant that Jesus Christ would come, and that Jesus Christ was Alpha and Omega.

None of these considerations, however, can change in the least degree the solemn fact of the literal relationship of Father and Son between Elohim and Jesus Christ. Among the spirit children of Elohim the firstborn was and is Jehovah or Jesus Christ to whom all others are juniors. Following are affirmative scriptures bearing upon this great truth. Paul, writing to the Colossians, says of Jesus Christ: "Who is the image of the invisible God, the firstborn of every creature: for by him were all things created, that are in heaven, and that are in earth, visible and invisible, whether they be thrones, or dominions, or principalities, or powers; all things were created by him, and for him: and he is before all things, and by him all things consist. And he is the head of the body, the church: who is the beginning, the firstborn from the dead; that in all things he might have the preeminence. For it pleased the Father that in him should all fullness dwell" (Colossians 1:15–19). From this scripture we learn that Jesus Christ was "the firstborn of every creature" and it is evident that the seniority here expressed must be with respect to antemortal existence, for Christ was not the senior of all mortals in the flesh. He is further designated as "the firstborn from the dead" this having reference to Him as the first to be resurrected from the dead, or as elsewhere written "the firstfruits of them that slept" (1 Corinthians 15:20, see also verse 23); and "the first begotten of the dead" (Revelation 1:5; compare Acts 26:23). The writer of the Epistle to the Hebrews affirms the status of Jesus Christ as the firstborn of the spirit children of His Father, and extols the preeminence of the Christ when tabernacled in flesh: "And again, when he bringeth in the firstbegotten into the world, he saith, And let all the angels of God worship him" (Hebrews 1:6; read the preceding verses). That the spirits who were juniors to Christ were predestined to be born in the image of their Elder Brother is thus attested by Paul: "And we know that all things work together for good to them that love God, to them who are the called according to his purpose. For whom he did foreknow, he also did predestinate to be conformed to the image of his Son, that he might be the firstborn among many brethren" (Romans 8:28, 29). John the Revelator was commanded to write to the head of the Laodicean church, as the words of the Lord Jesus Christ: "These things saith the Amen, the faithful and true witness, the beginning of the creation of God" (Revelation 3:14). In the course of a revelation given through Joseph Smith in May, 1833, the Lord Jesus Christ said as before cited: "And now, verily I say unto you, I was in the beginning with the Father, and am the Firstborn" (D&C 93:21). A later verse makes plain the fact that human beings generally were similarly existent in spirit state prior to their embodiment in the flesh: "Ye were also in the beginning with the Father; that which is Spirit, even the Spirit of truth" (verse 23).

There is no impropriety, therefore, in speaking of Jesus Christ as the Elder Brother of the rest of human kind. That He is by spiritual birth Brother to the rest of us is indicated in Hebrews: "Wherefore in all things it behoved him to be made like unto his brethren, that he might be a merciful and faithful high priest in things pertaining to God, to make reconciliation for the sins of the people" (Hebrews 2: 17). Let it not be forgotten, however, that He is essentially greater than any and all others, by reason (1) of His seniority as the oldest or firstborn; (2) of His unique status in the flesh as the offspring of a mortal mother and of an immortal, or resurrected and glorified, Father; (3) of His selection and foreordination as the one and only Redeemer and Savior of the race; and (4) of His transcendent sinlessness.

Jesus Christ is not the Father of the spirits who have taken or yet shall take bodies upon this earth, for He is one of them. He is The Son, as they are sons and daughters of Elohim. So far as the stages of eternal progression and attainment have been made known through divine revelation, we are to understand that only resurrected and glorified beings can become parents of spirit offspring. Only such exalted souls have reached maturity in the appointed course of eternal life; and the spirits born to them in the eternal worlds will pass in due sequence through the several stages or estates by which the glorified parents have attained exaltation.

The First Presidency and the Council
of the Twelve Apostles of the Church
of Jesus Christ of Latter-day Saints
(June 1916)

Appendix 5
General Church Officers, A Chronology

Presidents of the Church

Joseph Smith (April 1830–June 1844)
Brigham Young (Dec. 1847–Aug. 1877)
John Taylor (Oct. 1880–July 1887)
Wilford Woodruff (April 1889–Sept. 1898)
Lorenzo Snow (Sept. 1898–Oct. 1901)
Joseph F. Smith (Oct. 1901–Nov. 1918)
Heber J. Grant (Nov. 1918–May 1945)
George Albert Smith (May 1945–April 1951)
David O. McKay (April 1951–Jan. 1970)
Joseph Fielding Smith (Jan. 1970–July 1972)
Harold B. Lee (July 1972–Dec. 1973)
Spencer W. Kimball (Dec. 1973–Nov. 1985)
Ezra Taft Benson (Nov. 1985–   )

Assistant Presidents of the Church

Oliver Cowdery (1834–1837)
Hyrum Smith (1841–1844)

First Counselors in the First Presidency

Sidney Rigdon (1833–1844)
Heber C. Kimball (1847–1868)
George A. Smith (1868–1875)
John W. Young (1876–1877)
George Q. Cannon (1880–1887; 1889–1901)
Joseph F. Smith (1901–1901)
John R. Winder (1901–1910)
Anthon H. Lund (1910–1921)
Charles W. Penrose (1921–1925)
Anthony W. Ivins (1925–1934)
J. Reuben Clark, Jr. (1934–1951; 1959–1961)
Stephen L Richards (1951–1959)
Henry D. Moyle (1961–1963)
Hugh B. Brown (1963–1970)
Harold B. Lee (1970–1972)
N. Eldon Tanner (1972–1982)
Marion G. Romney (1982–1985)
Gordon B. Hinckley (1985–   )

Second Counselors in the First Presidency

Frederick G. Williams (1833–1837)
Hyrum Smith (1837–1841)
William Law (1841–1844)
Willard Richards (1847–1854)
Jedediah M. Grant (1854–1856)
Daniel H. Wells (1857–1877)
Joseph F. Smith (1880–1887; 1889–1901)
Rudger Clawson (1901)

Anthon H. Lund (1901–1910)
John Henry Smith (1910–1911)
Charles W. Penrose (1911–1921)
Anthony W. Ivins (1921–1925)
Charles W. Nibley (1925–1931)
J. Reuben Clark, Jr. (1933–1934; 1951–1959)
David O. McKay (1934–1951)
Henry D. Moyle (1959–1961)
Hugh B. Brown (1961–1963)
N. Eldon Tanner (1963–1972)
Marion G. Romney (1972–1982)
Gordon B. Hinckley (1982–1985)
Thomas S. Monson (1985–   )

Other Counselors in the First Presidency

Jesse Gause (1832)
John C. Bennett (1841–1842)
Amasa M. Lyman (1843–1844)
Joseph F. Smith (1866–1877)
Lorenzo Snow (1873–1874)
Brigham Young, Jr. (1873–1874)
Albert Carrington (1873–1874)
John W. Young (1873–1874)
George Q. Cannon (1873–1874)
Hugh B. Brown (1961)
Joseph Fielding Smith (1965–1970)
H. Thorpe B. Isaacson (1965–1970)
Alvin R. Dyer (1968–1970)
Gordon B. Hinckley (1981–1982)

Assistant Counselors in the First Presidency

Oliver Cowdery (1837–1838)
Joseph Smith, Sr. (1837–1840)
Hyrum Smith (1837)
John Smith (1837–1844)
Lorenzo Snow (1874–1877)
Brigham Young, Jr. (1874–1877)
Albert Carrington (1874–1877)
John W. Young (1874–1876)
George Q. Cannon (1874–1877)

Apostles in the Quorum of the Twelve

Thomas B. Marsh (1835–1839)
David W. Patten (1835–1838)
Brigham Young (1835–1847)
Heber C. Kimball (1835–1847)
Orson Hyde (1835–1839; 1839–1878)

William E. McLellin (1835–1838)
Parley P. Pratt (1835–1857)
Luke S. Johnson (1835–1838)
William Smith (1835–1839; 1839–1845)
Orson Pratt (1835–1842; 1843–1881)
John F. Boynton (1835–1837)
Lyman E. Johnson (1835–1838)
John E. Page (1838–1846)
John Taylor (1838–1880)
Wilford Woodruff (1839–1889)
George Albert Smith (1839–1868)
Willard Richards (1840–1847)
Lyman Wight (1841–1848)
Amasa M. Lyman (1842–1843; 1844–1867)
Ezra T. Benson (1846–1869)
Charles C. Rich (1849–1883)
Lorenzo Snow (1849–1898)
Erastus Snow (1849–1888)
Franklin D. Richards (1849–1899)
George Q. Cannon (1860–1880)
Brigham Young, Jr. (1868–1903)
Joseph F. Smith (1867–1880)
Albert Carrington (1870–1885)
Moses Thatcher (1879–1896)
Francis M. Lyman (1880–1916)
John Henry Smith (1880–1910)
George Teasdale (1882–1907)
Heber J. Grant (1882–1918)
John W. Taylor (1884–1905)
Marriner W. Merrill (1889–1906)
Anthon H. Lund (1889–1901)
Abraham H. Cannon (1889–1896)
Matthias F. Cowley (1897–1905)
Abraham O. Woodruff (1897–1904)
Rudger Clawson (1898–1943)
Reed Smoot (1900–1941)
Hyrum Mack Smith (1901–1918)
George Albert Smith (1903–1945)
Charles W. Penrose (1904–1911)
George F. Richards (1906–1950)
Orson F. Whitney (1906–1931)
David O. McKay (1906–1934)
Anthony W. Ivins (1907–1921)
Joseph Fielding Smith (1910–1970)
James E. Talmage (1911–1933)
Stephen L Richards (1917–1951)
Richard R. Lyman (1918–1943)
Melvin J. Ballard (1919–1939)
John A. Widtsoe (1921–1952)
Joseph F. Merrill (1931–1952)
Charles A. Callis (1933–1947)
Alonzo A. Hinckley (1934–1936)
Albert E. Bowen (1937–1953)
Sylvester Q. Cannon (1938–1943)
Harold B. Lee (1941–1970)
Spencer W. Kimball (1943–1973)
Ezra Taft Benson (1943–1985)

Mark E. Petersen (1944–1984)
Matthew Cowley (1945–1953)
Henry D. Moyle (1947–1959)
Delbert L. Stapley (1950–1978)
Marion G. Romney (1951–1972; 1985–1988)
LeGrand Richards (1952–1983)
Adam S. Bennion (1953–1958)
Richard L. Evans (1953–1971)
George Q. Morris (1954–1962)
Hugh B. Brown (1958–1961; 1970–1975)
Howard W. Hunter (1959–   )
Gordon B. Hinckley (1961–1981)
N. Eldon Tanner (1962–1963)
Thomas S. Monson (1963–1985)
Boyd K. Packer (1970–   )
Marvin J. Ashton (1971–   )
Bruce R. McConkie (1972–1985)
L. Tom Perry (1974–   )
David B. Haight (1976–   )
James E. Faust (1978–   )
Neal A. Maxwell (1981–   )
Russell M. Nelson (1984–   )
Dallin H. Oaks (1984–   )
M. Russell Ballard, Jr. (1985–   )
Joseph B. Wirthlin (1986–   )
Richard G. Scott (1988–   )

Patriarchs to the Church

Joseph Smith, Sr. (1833–1840)
Hyrum Smith (1841–1844)
William Smith (1845–1845)
John Smith (1849–1854)
John Smith (1855–1911)
Hyrum Gibbs Smith (1912–1932)
George F. Richards (1937–1942) (Acting Patriarch)
Joseph Fielding Smith (1942–1946)
Eldred G. Smith (1947–1979)

Assistants to the Twelve

Marion G. Romney (1941–1951)
Thomas E. McKay (1941–1958)
Clifford E. Young (1941–1958)
Alma Sonne (1941–1976)
Nicholas G. Smith (1941–1945)
George Q. Morris (1951–1954)
Stayner Richards (1951–1953)
ElRay L. Christiansen (1951–1975)
John Longden (1951–1969)
Hugh B. Brown (1953–1958)
Sterling W. Sill (1954–1976)
Gordon B. Hinckley (1958–1961)
Henry D. Taylor (1958–1976)
William J. Critchlow, Jr. (1958–1968)
Alvin R. Dyer (1958–1967; 1970–1976)
N. Eldon Tanner (1960–1962)

Franklin D. Richards (1960–1976)
Theodore M. Burton (1960–1976)
H. Thorpe B. Isaacson (1961–1965; 1970)
Boyd K. Packer (1961–1970)
Bernard P. Brockbank (1962–1976)
James A. Cullimore (1966–1976)
Marion D. Hanks (1968–1976)
Marvin J. Ashton (1969–1971)
Joseph Anderson (1970–1976)
David B. Haight (1970–1976)
William H. Bennett (1970–1976)
John H. Vandenberg (1972–1976)
Robert L. Simpson (1972–1976)
O. Leslie Stone (1972–1976)
James E. Faust (1972–1976)
L. Tom Perry (1972–1974)
J. Thomas Fyans (1974–1976)
Neal A. Maxwell (1974–1976)
William Grant Bangerter (1975–1976)
Robert D. Hales (1975–1976)
Adney Y. Komatsu (1975–1976)
Joseph B. Wirthlin (1975–1976)

Seventies

First Council of the Seventy

Hazen Aldrich (1835–1837)
Joseph Young (1835–1881)
Levi W. Hancock (1835–1882)
Leonard Rich (1835–1837)
Zebedee Coltrin (1835–1837)
Lyman R. Sherman (1835–1837)
Sylvester Smith (1835–1837)
John Gould (1837–1837)
James Foster (1837–1841)
Daniel S. Miles (1837–1845)
Josiah Butterfield (1837–1844)
Salmon Gee (1837–1838)
John Gaylord (1837–1838)
Henry Harriman (1838–1891)
Zera Pulsipher (1838–1862)
Roger Orton (1845–1845)
Albert P. Rockwood (1845–1879)
Benjamin L. Clapp (1845–1859)
Jedediah M. Grant (1845–1854)
Horace S. Eldredge (1854–1888)
Jacob Gates (1860–1892)
John Van Cott (1862–1883)
William W. Taylor (1880–1884)
Abraham H. Cannon (1882–1889)
Theodore B. Lewis (1882–1882) (sustained but never
    set apart)
Seymour B. Young (1882–1924)
Christian D. Fjelsted (1884–1905)
John Morgan (1884–1894)
B. H. Roberts (1888–1933)
George Reynolds (1890–1909)

J. Golden Kimball (1892–1938)
Rulon S. Wells (1893–1941)
Edward Stevenson (1894–1897)
Joseph W. McMurrin (1897–1932)
Charles H. Hart (1906–1934)
Levi E. Young (1909–1963)
Rey L. Pratt (1925–1931)
Antoine R. Ivins (1931–1967)
Samuel O. Bennion (1933–1945)
John H. Taylor (1933–1946)
Rufus K. Hardy (1934–1945)
Richard L. Evans (1938–1953)
Oscar A. Kirkham (1941–1958)
S. Dilworth Young (1945–1975)
Milton R. Hunter (1945–1975)
Bruce R. McConkie (1946–1972)
Marion D. Hanks (1953–1968)
A. Theodore Tuttle (1958–1975)
Paul H. Dunn (1964–1975)
Hartman Rector, Jr. (1968–1975)
Loren C. Dunn (1968–1975)
Rex D. Pinegar (1972–1975)
Gene R. Cook (1975–1975)

First and Second Quorums of the Seventy (1975–1991)

Angel Abrea (1981–   )
Carlos H. Amado (1989–   )
H. Verlan Andersen (1986–1991)
Joseph Anderson (1976–1978)
Carlos E. Asay (1976–   )
Eduardo Ayala (1990–   )
Robert L. Backman (1978–   )
M. Russell Ballard, Jr. (1976–1985)
William Grant Bangerter (1976–1989)
Ben B. Banks (1989–   )
William H. Bennett (1976–1978)
William R. Bradford (1975–   )
Ted E. Brewerton (1978–   )
Bernard P. Brockbank (1976–1980)
Monte J. Brough (1988–   )
Victor L. Brown (1985–1989)
Theodore M. Burton (1976–1989)
F. Enzio Busche (1977–   )
Waldo P. Call (1985–1990)
Helio R. Camargo (1985–1990)
George I. Cannon (1986–1991)
John K. Carmack (1984–   )
Albert Choules, Jr. (1988–   )
Joe J. Christensen (1989–   )
J. Richard Clarke (1985–   )
Spencer J. Condie (1989–   )
Gene R. Cook (1975–   )
Rulon G. Craven (1990–   )
James A. Cullimore (1976–1978)
LeGrand R. Curtis (1990–
Derek A. Cuthbert (1978–1991)
Clinton L. Cutler (1990–   )

Julio E. Davila (1991–   )
Jacob de Jager (1976–   )
Robert K. Dellenback (1990–   )
Royden G. Derrick (1976–1989)
Charles A. Didier (1975–   )
Graham W. Doxey (1991–   )
Loren C. Dunn (1975–   )
Paul H. Dunn (1975–1989)
G. Homer Durham (1977–1985)
Alvin R. Dyer (1976–1977)
James E. Faust (1976–1978)
Vaughn J. Featherstone (1976–   )
J. Thomas Fyans (1976–1989)
Lloyd P. George, Jr. (1988–   )
Francis M. Gibbons (1986–1991)
Jack H. Goaslind, Jr. (1978–   )
John H. Groberg (1976–   )
Robert D. Hales (1976–1985)
F. Melvin Hammond (1989–   )
In Sang Han (1991–   )
Marion D. Hanks (1976–   )
W. Eugene Hansen (1989–   )
Robert B. Harbertson (1984–1989)
Devere Harris (1984–1989)
George R. Hill, III (1987–   )
Harold G. Hillam (1990–   )
Jeffrey R. Holland (1989–   )
F. Burton Howard (1978–   )
Marlin K. Jensen (1989–   )
Malcolm S. Jeppsen (1989–   )
Kenneth Johnson (1990–   )
F. Arthur Kay (1984–1989)
L. Lionel Kendrick (1988–   )
Yoshihiko Kikuchi (1977–   )
Cree-L Kofford (1991–   )
Adney Y. Komatsu (1976–   )
Dean L. Larsen (1976–   )
John R. Lasater (1987–   )
W. Mack Lawrence (1990–   )
George P. Lee (1975–1989)
Richard P. Lindsay (1989–   )
Merlin R. Lybbert (1989–   )
Douglas J. Martin (1987–   )
Helvecio Martins (1990–   )
Neal A. Maxwell (1976–1981)
Gerald E. Melchin (1988–   )
Lynn A. Mickelsen (1990–   )
Alexander B. Morrison (1987–   )
Joseph C. Muren (1991–   )
Stephen D. Nadauld (1991–   )
Dennis B. Neuenschwander (1991–   )
Spencer H. Osborn (1984–1989)
James M. Paramore (1977–   )
H. Burke Peterson (1985–   )
Rex D. Pinegar (1975–   )
Hugh W. Pinnock (1977–   )
Ronald E. Poelman (1978–   )

L. Aldin Porter (1987–   )
Hartman Rector, Jr. (1975–   )
Rex C. Reeve, Sr. (1978–1989)
Franklin D. Richards (1976–1987)
Hans B. Ringger (1985–   )
Jorge A. Rojas (1991–   )
Glen L. Rudd (1987–   )
Gardner H. Russell (1986–1991)
Robert E. Sackley (1988–   )
Richard G. Scott (1977–1988)
Sam K. Shimabukuro (1991–   )
Sterling W. Sill (1976–1978)
Robert L. Simpson (1976–1989)
Douglas H. Smith (1987–   )
Alma Sonne (1976–1977)
John Sonnenberg (1984–1989)
Philip T. Sonntag (1984–1989)
Lynn A. Sorensen (1987–   )
O. Leslie Stone (1976–1980)
Henry D. Taylor (1976–1978)
Russell C. Taylor (1984–1989)
Horacio A. Tenorio (1989–   )
Earl C. Tingey (1990–   )
A. Theodore Tuttle (1975–1986)
John H. Vandenberg (1976–1978)
J Ballard Washburn (1990–   )
Robert E. Wells (1976–   )
Keith W. Wilcox (1984–1989)
Joseph B. Wirthlin (1976–1986)
Durrel A. Woolsey (1990–   )
S. Dilworth Young (1975–1978)

Presiding Bishops of the Church

Edward Partridge (1831–1840)
Newel K. Whitney (1847–1850)
Edward Hunter (1851–1883)
William B. Preston (1884–1907)
Charles W. Nibley (1907–1925)
Sylvester Q. Cannon (1925–1938)
LeGrand Richards (1938–1952)
Joseph L. Wirthlin (1952–1961)
John H. Vandenberg (1961–1972)
Victor L. Brown (1972–1985)
Robert D. Hales (1985–   )

First Counselors in the Presiding Bishopric

Isaac Morley (1831–1840)
Leonard W. Hardy (1856–1884)
Robert T. Burton (1884–1907)
Orrin P. Miller (1907–1918)
David A. Smith (1918–1938)
Marvin O. Ashton (1938–1946)
Joseph L. Wirthlin (1946–1952)
H. Thorpe B. Isaacson (1952–1961)
Robert L. Simpson (1961–1972)

H. Burke Peterson (1972–1985)
Henry B. Eyring (1985–   )

Second Counselors in the Presiding Bishopric

John Corrill (1831–1837)
Titus Billings (1837–1840)
Jesse C. Little (1856–1874)
Robert T. Burton (1874–1884)
John Q. Cannon (1884–1886)
John R. Winder (1887–1901)
Orrin P. Miller (1901–1907)
David A. Smith (1907–1918)
John Wells (1918–1938)
Joseph L. Wirthlin (1938–1946)
H. Thorpe B. Isaacson (1946–1952)
Carl W. Buehner (1952–1961)
Victor L. Brown (1961–1972)
Vaughn J. Featherstone (1972–1976)
J. Richard Clarke (1976–1985)
Glenn L. Pace (1985–   )

Church Historians

Oliver Cowdery (1830–1831; 1835–1837)
John Whitmer (1831–1835)
George W. Robinson (1837–1840)
John Corrill (1838–1839)
Elias Higbee (1838–1843)
Robert B. Thompson (1840–1841) (General Clerk)
James Sloan (1841–1843) (General Clerk)
Willard Richards (1842–1854)
George A. Smith (1854–1870)
Albert Carrington (1870–1874)
Orson Pratt (1874–1881)
Wilford Woodruff (1883–1889)
Franklin D. Richards (1889–1899)
Anthon H. Lund (1900–1921)
Joseph Fielding Smith (1921–1970)
Howard W. Hunter (1970–1972)
Leonard J. Arrington (1972–1980)
Alvin R. Dyer (1972–1975) (Managing Director)
Joseph Anderson (1975–1977) (Managing Director)
G. Homer Durham (1977–1985) (Managing Director and Historian)
Dean L. Larsen (1985–1989) (Executive Director and Historian)
John K. Carmack (1989–1991) (Executive Director and Historian)
Loren C. Dunn (1991–   ) (Executive Director and Historian)

Sunday School General Superintendencies and Presidencies

George Q. Cannon, Superintendent (1867–1901)
    First Assistants
        George Goddard (1872–1899)
        Karl G. Maeser (1899–1901)
    Second Assistants
        John Morgan (1883–1894)
        Karl G. Maeser (1894–1899)
        George Reynolds (1899–1901)
Lorenzo Snow, Superintendent (1901–1901)
    First Assistant
        George Reynolds (1901–1901)
    Second Assistant
        J. M. Tanner (1901–1901)
Joseph F. Smith, Superintendent (1901–1918)
    First Assistants
        George Reynolds (1901–1909)
        David O. McKay (1909–1918)
    Second Assistants
        J. M. Tanner (1901–1906)
        David O. McKay (1907–1909)
        Stephen L Richards (1909–1918)
David O. McKay, Superintendent (1918–1934)
    First Assistant
        Stephen L Richards (1918–1934)
    Second Assistant
        George D. Pyper (1918–1934)
George D. Pyper, Superintendent (1934–1943)
    First Assistant
        Milton Bennion (1934–1943)
    Second Assistant
        George R. Hill (1934–1943)
Milton Bennion, Superintendent (1943–1949)
    First Assistant
        George R. Hill (1943–1949)
    Second Assistant
        A. Hamer Reiser (1943–1949)
George R. Hill, Superintendent (1949–1966)
    First Assistants
        A. Hamer Reiser (1949–1952)
        David Lawrence McKay (1952–1966)
    Second Assistants
        David Lawrence McKay (1949–1952)
        Lynn S. Richards (1952–1966)
David Lawrence McKay, Superintendent (1966–1971)
    First Assistant
        Lynn S. Richards (1966–1971)
    Second Assistant
        Royden G. Derrick (1966–1971)
Russell M. Nelson, Superintendent (1971–1972)
    First Assistant
        Joseph B. Wirthlin (1971–1972)
    Second Assistant
        Richard L. Warner (1971–1972)
Russell M. Nelson, President (1972–1979)
    First Counselors
        Joseph B. Wirthlin (1972–1975)
        B. Lloyd Poelman (1975–1978)
        Joe J. Christensen (1978–1979)
        William D. Oswald (1979–1979)
    Second Counselors
        Richard L. Warner (1972–1975)

Joe J. Christensen (1975–1978)
William D. Oswald (1978–1979)
J. Hugh Baird (1979–1979)
Hugh W. Pinnock, President (1979–1986)
First Counselors
Ronald E. Poelman (1979–1981)
Robert D. Hales (1981–1985)
Adney Y. Kamatsu (1985–1986)
Second Counselors
Jack H. Goaslind, Jr. (1979–1981)
James M. Paramore (1981–1983)
Loren C. Dunn (1983–1985)
Ronald E. Poelman (1985–1986)
Robert L. Simpson, President (1986–1989)
First Counselors
Adney Y. Komatsu (1986–1987)
Devere Harris (1987–1989)
Second Counselors
A. Theodore Tuttle (1986–1986)
Devere Harris (1987–1987)
Phillip T. Sonntag (1987–1988)
Derek A. Cuthbert (1988–1989)
Hugh W. Pinnock, President (1989–   )
First Counselor
Derek A. Cuthbert (1989–1991)
H. Verlan Andersen (1990–1991)
Hartman Rector, Jr. (1991–   )
Second Counselor
Ted E. Brewerton (1989–1990)
H. Verlan Andersen (1990–1991)
Rulon G. Craven (1991–1991)
Clinton L. Cutler (1991–   )

Young Men General Superintendencies and Presidencies

Junius F. Wells, Superintendent (1876–1880)
First Counselor
M. H. Hardy
Second Counselor
Rodney C. Badger
Wilford Woodruff, Superintendent (1880–1898)
First Assistant
Joseph F. Smith
Second Assistant
Moses Thatcher
Lorenzo Snow, Superintendent (1898–1901)
First Assistant
Joseph F. Smith
Second Assistant
Heber J. Grant
Assistant
B. H. Roberts
Joseph F. Smith, Superintendent (1901–1918)
First Assistant
Heber J. Grant
Second Assistant
B. H. Roberts

Anthony W. Ivins, Superintendent (1918–1921)
First Assistant
B. H. Roberts
Second Assistant
Richard R. Lyman
George Albert Smith, Superintendent (1921–1935)
First Assistant
B. H. Roberts
Second Assistants
Richard R. Lyman
Melvin J. Ballard
Albert E. Bowen, Superintendent (1935–1937)
First Assistant
George Q. Morris
Second Assistant
Franklin West
George Q. Morris, Superintendent (1937–1948)
First Assistants
Joseph J. Cannon
John D. Giles
Second Assistants
Burton K. Farnsworth
Lorenzo H. Hatch
Elbert R. Curtis, Superintendent (1948–1958)
First Assistant
A. Walter Stevenson
Second Assistants
Ralph W. Hardy
David S. King
Joseph T. Bentley, Superintendent (1958–1962)
First Assistants
Alvin R. Dyer (1958–1958)
G. Carlos Smith (1958–1961)
Marvin J. Ashton (1961–1962)
Second Assistants
Marvin J. Ashton (1958–1961)
Verl F. Scott (1961–1961)
Carl W. Buehner (1961–1962)
G. Carlos Smith, Superintendent (1962–1969)
First Assistant
Marvin J. Ashton (1962–1969)
Second Assistants
Carl W. Beuhner (1962–1967)
George R. Hill (1967–1969)
W. Jay Eldredge, Superintendent (1969–1972)
First Assistant
George R. Hill (1969–1972)
Second Assistant
George I. Cannon (1969–1972)
W. Jay Eldredge, President (1972–1972)
First Counselor
George I. Cannon (1972–1972)
Second Counselor
Robert L. Backman (1972–1972)
Robert L. Backman, President (1972–1974)
First Counselor
LeGrand R. Curtis (1972–1974)

Second Counselor
Jack H. Goaslind, Jr. (1972–1974)
Neil D. Schaerrer, President (1977–1979)
First Counselor
Graham W. Doxey (1977–1979)
Second Counselor
Quinn G. McKay (1977–1979)
Robert L. Backman, President (1979–1985)
First Counselor
Vaughn J. Featherstone (1979–1985)
Second Counselor
Rex D. Pinegar (1979–1985)
Vaughn J. Featherstone, President, (1985–1990)
First Counselors
Rex D. Pinegar (1985–1989)
Jeffrey R. Holland (1989–1990)
Second Counselors
Robert L. Simpson (1985–1986)
Hartman Rector, Jr. (1986–1988)
Robert B. Harbertson (1988–1989)
Monte J. Brough (1989–1990)
Jack H. Goaslind, Jr., President (1990–   )
First Counselor
LeGrand R. Curtis (1990–1991)
Robert K. Dellenbach (1991–   )
Second Counselor
Robert K. Dellenbach (1990–1991)
Stephen D. Nadauld (1991–   )

Primary General Presidencies

Louie Bouton Felt, President (1880–1925)
First Counselors
Matilda W. Barrett (1880–1888)
Lillie T. Freeze (1888–1905)
May Anderson (1905–1925)
Second Counselors
Clare C. M. Cannon (1880–1895)
Josephine R. West (1896–1905)
Clara W. Beebe (1905–1925)
May Anderson, President (1925–1939)
First Counselors
Sadie Grant Pack (1925–1929)
Isabelle Salmon Ross (1929–1939)
Second Counselors
Isabelle Salmon Ross (1925–1929)
Edna Harker Thomas (1929–1933)
Edith Hunter Lambert (1933–1939)
May Green Hinckley, President (1940–1943)
First Counselor
Adele Cannon Howells (1940–1943)
Second Counselors
Janet Murdock Thompson (1940–1942)
LaVern Watts Parmley (1942–1943)
Adele Cannon Howells, President (1943–1951)
First Counselor
LaVern Watts Parmley (1943–1951)

Second Counselor
Dessie Grant Boyle (1943–1951)
LaVern Watts Parmley, President (1951–1974)
First Counselors
Arta M. Hale (1951–1962)
Leone W. Doxey (1962–1969)
Lucille C. Reading (1970–1970)
Naomi W. Randall (1970–1974)
Second Counselors
Florence H. Richards (1951–1953)
Leone W. Doxey (1953–1962)
Eileen R. Dunyon (1962–1963)
Lucille C. Reading (1963–1970)
Florence R. Lane (1970–1974)
Naomi M. Shumway, President (1974–1980)
First Counselors
Sara B. Paulsen (1974–1977)
Colleen B. Lemmon (1977–1980)
Second Counselors
Colleen B. Lemmon (1974–1977)
Dorthea C. Murdock (1977–1980)
Dwan J. Young, President (1980–1988)
First Counselor
Virginia B. Cannon (1980–1988)
Second Counselor
Michaelene P. Grassli (1980–1988)
Michaelene P. Grassli, President (1988–   )
First Counselor
Betty Jo Jepsen (1988–   )
Second Counselor
Ruth B. Wright (1988–   )

Young Women General Presidencies

Elmina Shephard Taylor, President (1880–1904)
First Counselors
Margaret Young Taylor (1880–1887)
Maria Young Dougall (1887–1904)
Second Counselor
Martha Horne Tingey (1880–1904)
Martha Horne Tingey, President (1905–1929)
First Counselor
Ruth May Fox (1905–1929)
Second Counselors
Mae Taylor Nystrom (1905–1923)
Lucy Grant Cannon (1923–1929)
Ruth May Fox, President (1929–1937)
First Counselor
Lucy Grant Cannon (1929–1937)
Second Counselor
Clarissa A. Beesley (1929–1937)
Lucy Grant Cannon, President (1937–1948)
First Counselors
Helen S. Williams (1937–1944)
Verna W. Goddard (1944–1948)
Second Counselors
Verna W. Goddard (1937–1944)
Lucy T. Anderson (1944–1948)

Bertha S. Reeder, President (1948–1961)
  First Counselor
    Emily H. Bennett (1948–1961)
  Second Counselor
    LaRue C. Longden (1948–1961)
Florence S. Jacobsen, President (1961–1972)
  First Counselor
    Margaret R. Jackson (1961–1972)
  Second Counselor
    Dorothy P. Holt (1961–1972)
Ruth H. Funk, President (1972–1978)
  First Counselor
    Hortense H. Child (1972–1978)
  Second Counselor
    Ardeth G. Kapp (1972–1978)
Elaine A. Cannon, President (1978–1984)
  First Counselor
    Arlene B. Darger (1978–1984)
  Second Counselor
    Norma B. Smith (1978–1984)
Ardeth G. Kapp, President (1984–   )
  First Counselors
    Patricia T. Holland (1984–1986)
    Maurine J. Turley (1986–1987)
    Jayne B. Malan (1987–   )
  Second Counselors
    Maurine J. Turley (1984–1986)
    Jayne B. Malan (1986–1987)
    Elaine L. Jack (1987–1990)
    Janette C. Hales (1990–   )

Relief Society General Presidencies

Emma Hale Smith, President (1842–1844)
  First Counselor
    Sarah M. Cleveland (1842–1844)
  Second Counselor
    Elizabeth Ann Whitney (1842–1844)
Eliza Roxcy Snow, President (1866–1887)
  First Counselor
    Zina Diantha Young (1880–1888)
  Second Counselor
    Elizabeth Ann Whitney (1880–1882)
Zina Diantha Young, President (1888–1901)
  First Counselor
    Jane S. Richards (1888–1901)
  Second Counselor
    Bathsheba W. Smith (1888–1901)
Bathsheba W. Smith, President (1901–1910)
  First Counselor
    Annie Taylor Hyde (1901–1909)

  Second Counselor
    Ida Smoot Dusenberry (1901–1910)
Emmeline B. Wells, President (1910–1921)
  First Counselor
    Clarissa Smith Williams (1910–1921)
  Second Counselor
    Julina L. Smith (1910–1921)
Clarissa Smith Williams, President (1921–1928)
  First Counselor
    Jennie Brimhall Knight (1921–1928)
  Second Counselor
    Louise Yates Robison (1921–1928)
Louise Yates Robison, President (1928–1939)
  First Counselor
    Amy Brown Lyman (1928–1939)
  Second Counselors
    Julia A. Child (1928–1935)
    Kate M. Barker (1935–1939)
Amy Brown Lyman, President (1940–1945)
  First Counselor
    Marcia K. Howells (1940–1945)
  Second Counselors
    Donna D. Sorensen (1940–1942)
    Belle S. Spafford (1942–1945)
Belle S. Spafford, President (1945–1974)
  First Counselor
    Marianne C. Sharp (1945–1974)
  Second Counselors
    Gertrude R. Garff (1945–1947)
    Velma Simonsen (1947–1956)
    Helen W. Anderson (1957–1958)
    Louise W. Madsen (1958–1974)
Barbara B. Smith, President (1974–1984)
  First Counselors
    Janath R. Cannon (1974–1978)
    Marian R. Boyer (1978–1984)
  Second Counselors
    Marian R. Boyer (1974–1978)
    Shirley W. Thomas (1978–1984)
    Ann S. Reese (1983–1984)
Barbara W. Winder, President, (1984–1990)
  First Counselor
    Joy F. Evans (1984–1990)
  Second Counselor
    Joanne B. Doxey (1984–1990)
Elaine L. Jack, President (1990–   )
  First Counselor
    Chieko N. Okazaki (1990–   )
  Second Counselor
    Aileen H. Clyde (1990–   )

Appendix 6

A Selection of LDS Hymns

#1 THE MORNING BREAKS

This hymn in praise of the Restoration was published as Hymn #1 in the Manchester Hymnal in 1840; it is also the first hymn in the 1985 hymnal. Parley P. Pratt's text is a Latter-day Saint meditation upon a line from Charles Wesley's "Wrestling Jacob," from which he borrowed the first line of the hymn. George Careless composed the hymn tune in 1864 as he and a group of other Latter-day Saint converts from the British Isles sailed into New York on the ship *Hudson*.

The Morning Breaks

Triumphantly ♩=88-100

1. The morn - ing breaks, the shad - ows flee; Lo, Zi - on's
2. The clouds of er - ror dis - ap - pear Be - fore the
3. The Gen - tile ful - ness now comes in, And Is - rael's
4. Je - ho - vah speaks! Let earth give ear, And Gen - tile
5. — An-gels from heav'n and truth from earth Have met, and

stan - dard is un - furled! The dawn - ing of a
rays of truth di - vine; The glo - ry burst - ing
bless - ings are at hand. Lo, Ju - dah's rem - nant,
na - tions turn and live. His might - y arm is
both have rec - ord borne; Thus Zi - on's light is

bright - er day, The dawn - ing of a bright - er
from a - far, The glo - ry burst - ing from a -
cleansed from sin, Lo, Ju - dah's rem - nant, cleansed from
mak - ing bare, His might - y arm is mak - ing
burst - ing forth, Thus Zi - on's light is burst - ing

day Ma - jes - tic ris - es on the world.
far Wide o'er the na - tions soon will shine.
sin, Shall in their prom - ised Ca - naan stand.
bare His cov - 'nant peo - ple to re - ceive.
forth To bring her ran - somed chil - dren home.

Text: Parley P. Pratt, 1807-1857
Music: George Careless, 1839-1932

Isaiah 60:1-3
3 Nephi 16:7-20

#2 THE SPIRIT OF GOD

Linked to important events in Church history such as the dedication of the Kirtland Temple in 1836, this hymn has been part of Latter-day Saint hymn tradition since its inclusion in Emma Smith's hymnal in 1835. Today it is sung at all temple dedications, as well as in Sunday meetings and on other joyous occasions. The origin of the hymn tune is uncertain. Its first known publication was in a small hymnal printed in 1844 for the use of Latter-day Saint missionaries in New England.

The Spirit of God

1. The Spir - it of God like a fire is burn - ing! The
2. The Lord is ex - tend - ing the Saints' un - der - stand - ing, Re-
3. We'll call in our sol - emn as - sem - blies in spir - it, To
4. How bless - ed the day when the lamb and the li - on Shall

lat - ter - day glo - ry be - gins to come forth; The vi - sions and
stor - ing their judg - es and all as at first. The knowl - edge and
spread forth the king - dom of heav - en a - broad, That we through our
lie down to - geth - er with - out an - y ire, And E - phraim be

bless - ings of old are re - turn - ing, And an - gels are com - ing to
pow - er of God are ex - pand - ing; The veil o'er the earth is be-
faith may be - gin to in - her - it The vi - sions and bless - ings and
crowned with his bless - ing in Zi - on, As Je - sus de - scends with his

vis - it the earth.
gin - ning to burst.
glo - ries of God.
char - iot of fire!

We'll sing and we'll shout with the

ar - mies of heav - en, Ho - san - na, ho - san - na to

God and the Lamb! Let glo - ry to them in the high - est be

giv - en, Hence - forth and for - ev - er, A - men and a - men!

Text: William W. Phelps, 1792-1872. Included in the first
LDS hymnbook, 1835. Sung at the Kirtland Temple dedication in 1836.
Music: Anon., ca. 1844

Doctrine and Covenants
109:79-80
Doctrine and Covenants 110

#5 HIGH ON THE MOUNTAIN TOP

Many Latter-day Saint hymn writers, among them Joel H. Johnson, made use of the parallels between the mountainous Utah landscape of the latter-day Zion and biblical prophecies such as Isaiah 2:2: "The Lord's house shall be established in the top of the mountains, and shall be exalted above the hills; and all nations shall flow unto it." The text of this hymn was first published in 1856, and the tune in the 1889. The tune is similar to an earlier L. Mason tune "Stow."

High on the Mountain Top

Resolutely ♩=56-72

1. High on the moun-tain top   A ban-ner is un-furled.
2. For God re-mem-bers still   His prom-ise made of old
3. His house shall there be reared,   His glo-ry to dis-play,
4. For there we shall be taught   The law that will go forth,

Ye na-tions, now look up;   It waves to all the world.
That he on Zi-on's hill   Truth's stan-dard would un-fold!
And peo-ple shall be heard   In dis-tant lands to say:
With truth and wis-dom fraught,   To gov-ern all the earth.

In Des - er - et's sweet, peace - ful land,
Her light should there at-tract the gaze
We'll now go up and serve the Lord,
For-ev-er there his ways we'll tread,

On Zi - on's mount be-hold it stand!
Of all the world in lat-ter days.
O-bey his truth and learn his word.
And save our - selves with all our dead.

Text: Joel H. Johnson, 1802-1882
Music: Ebenezer Beesley, 1840-1906

Isaiah 2:2-3
Isaiah 5:26

#19 WE THANK THEE, O GOD, FOR A PROPHET
Written by English Latter-day Saint convert William Fowler before his emigration to Utah, this hymn text was first printed in 1863. Its first two lines are particularly meaningful as a declaration of the distinctive Latter-day Saint belief in a living prophet. The tune is by Caroline Sheridan Norton, a well-known English poet and social activist, who composed it as a setting for a poem she had written in honor of an officer killed in the Crimean War.

We Thank Thee, O God, for a Prophet

bless - ing Be - stowed by thy boun-te - ous hand. We feel it a
good-ness. We've proved him in days that are past. The wick-ed who
fec - tion The hon - est and faith-ful will go, While they who re-

plea - sure to serve thee, And love to o - bey thy com-mand.
fight a-gainst Zi - on Will sure - ly be smit - ten at last.
ject this glad mes - sage Shall nev - er such hap - pi - ness know.

Text: William Fowler, 1830-1865
Music: Caroline Sheridan Norton, 1808-ca. 1877

Doctrine and Covenants 21:1-5
Mosiah 2:41

#26 JOSEPH SMITH'S FIRST PRAYER

This hymn text is a narrative, summarizing in some detail the story of Joseph Smith's First Vision in the Sacred Grove, as given in Joseph Smith–History 1:14-20, 25. The text of this hymn was first printed in the *Juvenile Instructor* in 1878. Two composers share credit for the hymn tune: American composer Sylvanus Billings Pond wrote the first two lines, and Latter-day Saint composer A. C. Smyth wrote the last two lines.

Joseph Smith's First Prayer

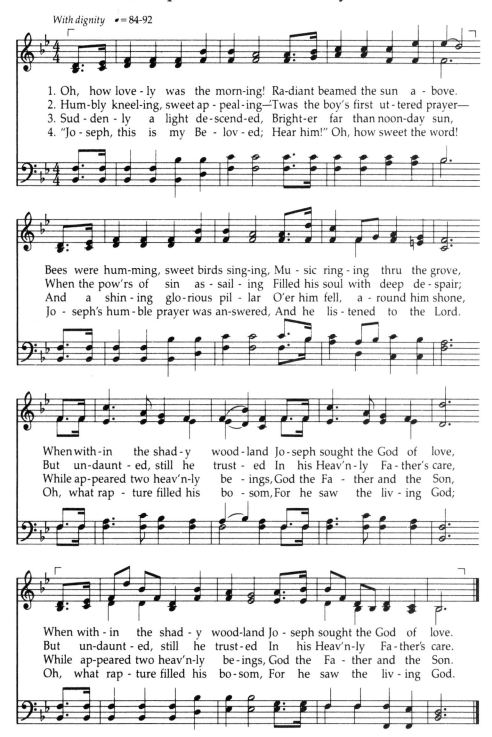

With dignity ♩ = 84-92

1. Oh, how love-ly was the morn-ing! Ra-diant beamed the sun a-bove.
2. Hum-bly kneel-ing, sweet ap-peal-ing—Twas the boy's first ut-tered prayer—
3. Sud-den-ly a light de-scend-ed, Bright-er far than noon-day sun,
4. "Jo-seph, this is my Be-lov-ed; Hear him!" Oh, how sweet the word!

Bees were hum-ming, sweet birds sing-ing, Mu-sic ring-ing thru the grove,
When the pow'rs of sin as-sail-ing Filled his soul with deep de-spair;
And a shin-ing glo-rious pil-lar O'er him fell, a-round him shone,
Jo-seph's hum-ble prayer was an-swered, And he lis-tened to the Lord.

When with-in the shad-y wood-land Jo-seph sought the God of love,
But un-daunt-ed, still he trust-ed In his Heav'n-ly Fa-ther's care,
While ap-peared two heav'n-ly be-ings, God the Fa-ther and the Son,
Oh, what rap-ture filled his bo-som, For he saw the liv-ing God;

When with-in the shad-y wood-land Jo-seph sought the God of love.
But un-daunt-ed, still he trust-ed In his Heav'n-ly Fa-ther's care.
While ap-peared two heav'n-ly be-ings, God the Fa-ther and the Son.
Oh, what rap-ture filled his bo-som, For he saw the liv-ing God.

Text: George Manwaring, 1854-1889
Music: Sylvanus Billings Pond, 1792-1871; adapted by
   A.C. Smyth, 1840-1909

Joseph Smith—History 1:14-20, 25
James 1:5

#30 COME, COME, YE SAINTS

Written in 1846 while William Clayton was traveling westward with the first company of Mormons forced out of Nauvoo, this hymn text reflects the strength and devotion of the Mormon pioneers. Along with its accompanying English folk tune, this historically significant text has become today the hymn most readily identified with The Church of Jesus Christ of Latter-day Saints. It has appeared in every Latter-day Saint hymnal since 1851.

Come, Come, Ye Saints

With conviction ♩ = 66-84

1. Come, come, ye Saints, no toil nor la-bor fear; But with joy
2. Why should we mourn or think our lot is hard? 'Tis not so;
3. We'll find the place which God for us pre-pared, Far a-way
4. And should we die be-fore our jour-ney's through, Hap-py day!

wend your way. Though hard to you this jour-ney may ap-pear,
all is right. Why should we think to earn a great re-ward
in the West, Where none shall come to hurt or make a-fraid;
All is well! We then are free from toil and sor-row, too;

Grace shall be as your day. 'Tis bet-ter far for
If we now shun the fight? Gird up your loins; fresh
There the Saints will be blessed. We'll make the air with
With the just we shall dwell! But if our lives are

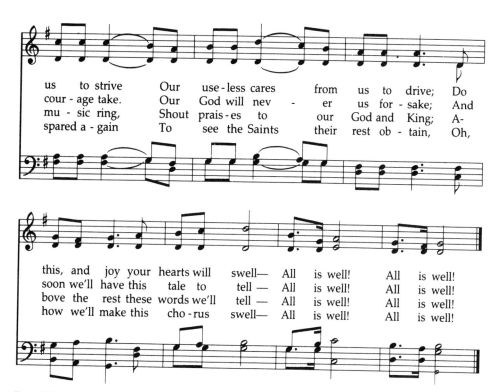

us to strive   Our use-less cares   from   us to drive;   Do
cour-age take. Our God will nev - er   us for-sake;   And
mu-sic ring,   Shout prais-es to   our God and King;   A-
spared a-gain   To   see the Saints   their rest ob-tain,   Oh,

this, and joy your hearts will swell— All is well! All is well!
soon we'll have this tale to   tell — All is well! All is well!
bove the rest these words we'll tell — All is well! All is well!
how we'll make this cho-rus swell— All is well! All is well!

Text: William Clayton, 1814-1879
Music: English folk song

Doctrine and Covenants 61:36-39
Doctrine and Covenants 59:1-4

#134 I BELIEVE IN CHRIST

Among the forty-four new Latter-day Saint contributions added to the 1985 hymnal is this hymn text closely paraphrasing the Book of Mormon text of 2 Nephi 31:20. The words have broad Christian relevance, and the tune was written specifically for this text. Both the text and tune were by contemporary Latter-day Saints.

I Believe in Christ

Fervently ♩ = 88-104

1. I be-lieve in Christ; he is my King! With all my
2. I be-lieve in Christ; oh, bless - ed name! As Ma - ry's
3. I be-lieve in Christ — my Lord, my God! My feet he
4. I be-lieve in Christ; he stands su - preme! From him I'll

heart to him I'll sing; I'll raise my voice in
Son he came to reign 'Mid mor - tal men, his
plants on gos - pel sod. I'll wor - ship him with
gain my fond - est dream; And while I strive through

praise and joy, In grand a - mens my tongue em - ploy.
earth - ly kin, To save them from the woes of sin.
all my might; He is the source of truth and light.
grief and pain, His voice is heard: "Ye shall ob - tain."

I be-lieve in Christ; he is God's Son. On earth to
I be-lieve in Christ, who marked the path, Who did gain
I be-lieve in Christ; he ran - soms me. From Sa - tan's
I be-lieve in Christ; so come what may, With him I'll

dwell his soul did come. He healed the sick; the
all his Fa - ther hath, Who said to men: "Come,
grasp he sets me free, And I shall live with
stand in that great day When on this earth he

dead he raised. Good works were his; his name be praised.
fol - low me, That ye, my friends, with God may be."
joy and love In his e - ter - nal courts a - bove.
comes a - gain To rule a - mong the sons of men.

Text: Bruce R. McConkie, 1915-1985. © 1972 LDS
Music: John Longhurst, b. 1940. © 1985 LDS

2 Nephi 25:23, 26, 29
Mormon 7:5-7

#136 I KNOW THAT MY REDEEMER LIVES

Many composers have written music to accompany this well-known text by Protestant writer Samuel Medley. This setting by Welsh-born Latter-day Saint composer Lewis D. Edwards is a well-established part of Mormon hymnody today and is much loved by members of the Church. The tune was first published in 1901.

I Know That My Redeemer Lives

He lives to bless me with his love. He lives to
He lives to si-lence all my fears. He lives to
He lives and grants me dai - ly breath. He lives, and
He lives! All glo - ry to his name! He lives, my

plead for me a - bove. He lives my hun-gry soul to
wipe a - way my tears. He lives to calm my trou-bled
I shall con-quer death. He lives my man-sion to pre-
Sav - ior, still the same. Oh, sweet the joy this sen-tence

feed. He lives to bless in time of need.
heart. He lives all bless-ings to im - part.
pare. He lives to bring me safe - ly there.
gives: "I know that my Re - deem - er lives!"

Text: Samuel Medley, 1738-1799. Included in the first
  LDS hymnbook, 1835.
Music: Lewis D. Edwards, 1858-1921

Job 19:25
Psalm 104:33-34

#149 AS THE DEW FROM HEAVEN DISTILLING

    This hymn is familiar to people throughout the world because it serves as the traditional closing organ postlude music for the weekly broadcast of the Mormon Tabernacle Choir. Latter-day Saint musician Joseph J. Daynes wrote the setting for this Protestant text by Thomas Kelly based on Deuteronomy 32:2. The text appeared in 1806, and the Latter-day Saint tune was first published in the 1889 *Latter-day Saints' Psalmody*.

As the Dew from Heaven Distilling

Earnestly ♩ = 60-72

1. As the dew from heav'n dis - till - ing Gent - ly
2. Let thy doc - trine, Lord, so gra - cious, Thus de -
3. Lord, be - hold this con - gre - ga - tion; Pre - cious
4. Let our cry come up be - fore thee. Thy sweet

on the grass de - scends And re - vives it,
scend - ing from a - bove, Blest by thee, prove
prom - is - es ful - fill. From thy ho - ly
Spir - it shed a - round, So the peo - ple

thus ful - fill - ing What thy prov - i - dence in - tends,
ef - fi - ca - cious To ful - fill thy work of love.
hab - i - ta - tion Let the dews of life dis - till.
shall a - dore thee And con - fess the joy - ful sound.

Text: Thomas Kelly, 1769-1854
Music: Joseph J. Daynes, 1851-1920

Deuteronomy 32:2
Isaiah 55:10-11

#193 I STAND ALL AMAZED

In addition to the opening and closing hymns in each Sunday sacrament meeting, the LDS congregation sings a hymn known as the sacrament hymn. This example is a borrowed hymn that entered Latter-day Saint hymnody by way of *Deseret Sunday School Songs* in 1909, ten years after its first publication in a gospel-song collection.

I Stand All Amazed

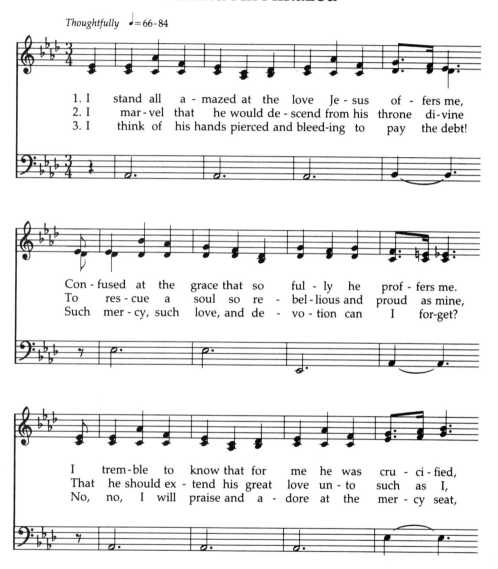

Thoughtfully ♩ = 66-84

1. I stand all a - mazed at the love Je - sus of - fers me,
2. I mar - vel that he would de - scend from his throne di - vine
3. I think of his hands pierced and bleed-ing to pay the debt!

Con - fused at the grace that so ful - ly he prof - fers me.
To res - cue a soul so re - bel - lious and proud as mine,
Such mer - cy, such love, and de - vo - tion can I for-get?

I trem - ble to know that for me he was cru - ci - fied,
That he should ex - tend his great love un - to such as I,
No, no, I will praise and a - dore at the mer - cy seat,

That for me, a sin - ner, he suf - fered, he bled and died.
Suf - fi - cient to own, to re - deem, and to jus - ti - fy.
Un - til at the glo - ri - fied throne I kneel at his feet.

Oh, it is won - der - ful that he should care for me E-nough to

die for me! Oh, it is won - der - ful, won - der-ful to me!

Text and music: Charles H. Gabriel, 1856-1932

Mosiah 3:5-8
John 15:13

#195 HOW GREAT THE WISDOM AND THE LOVE

The text of this sacrament hymn by Eliza R. Snow was first published in 1871. The tune, composed as a setting for this text and first published in 1884, is by Scottish-born Latter-day Saint composer Thomas McIntyre, who emigrated to Utah in 1859.

How Great the Wisdom and the Love

1. How great the wis - dom and the love That
2. His pre - cious blood he free - ly spilt; His
3. By strict o - be - dience Je - sus won The
4. He marked the path and led the way, And

filled the courts on high And sent the Sav - ior
life he free - ly gave, A sin - less sac - ri -
prize with glo - ry rife: "Thy will, O God, not
ev - 'ry point de - fines To light and life and

from a - bove To suf - fer, bleed, and die!
fice for guilt, A dy - ing world to save.
mine be done," A - dorned his mor - tal life.
end - less day Where God's full pres - ence shines.

5. In mem'ry of the broken flesh
   We eat the broken bread,
   And witness with the cup, afresh,
   Our faith in Christ, our Head.

6. How great, how glorious, how complete,
   Redemption's grand design,
   Where justice, love, and mercy meet
   In harmony divine!

Text: Eliza R. Snow, 1804-1887
Music: Thomas McIntyre, 1833-1914
Verses 1, 2, 5, and 6 are especially appropriate for the sacrament.

Moses 4:1-2
Alma 42:14-15

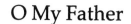

#292 O MY FATHER

First published in 1845, Eliza R. Snow's hymn text sets forth the distinctive Latter-day Saint doctrines of a pre-earth life and of a Heavenly Mother. Many Latter-day Saint composers have written musical settings for these words, but the favorite tune today is by a non-Latter-day Saint composer, James McGranahan, who originally wrote this melody to accompany a text by Philip Paul Bliss.

O My Father

hab - i - ta - tion, Did my spir - it once re - side? In my
se - cret some-thing Whis-pered, "You're a strang - er here," And I
par - ents sin - gle? No, the thought makes rea - son stare! Truth is
I've com - plet - ed All you sent me forth to do, With your

first pri - me - val child-hood, Was I nur - tured near thy side?
felt that I had wan-dered From a more ex - alt - ed sphere.
rea - son; truth e - ter - nal Tells me I've a moth - er there.
mu - tual ap - pro - ba - tion Let me come and dwell with you.

Text: Eliza R. Snow, 1804-1887
Music: James McGranahan, 1840-1907

Romans 8:16-17
Acts 17:28-29 (22-31)

1707

#301 I AM A CHILD OF GOD

Children along with adults attend sacrament meeting, the principal Latter-day Saint worship service, and the 1985 hymnal includes ten children's songs. This song, written in 1957, was well known among Primary children prior to its appearance in the hymnal, and it is a favorite among many adults as well.

I Am a Child of God

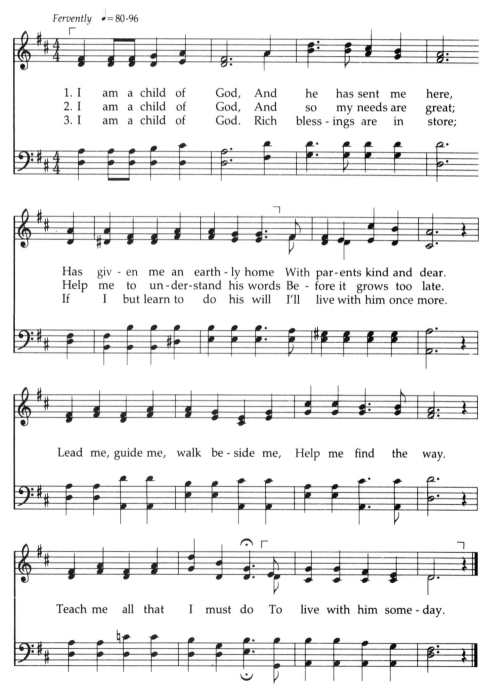

Text: Naomi W. Randall, b. 1908. © 1957 LDS
Music: Mildred T. Pettit, 1895-1977. © 1957 LDS

Psalm 82:6; Mosiah 4:15
Doctrine and Covenants 14:7

Joseph Smith Translation of the Bible
(Selections)

The Joseph Smith Translation of the Bible (JST) contains several thousand verses that are different from the King James Version. As space limitations prevent a complete presentation in this Appendix, the texts below were selected for their doctrinal value; variations from the King James Version are shown in italics. Extracts of the Joseph Smith Translation published in the PEARL OF GREAT PRICE (Book of Moses and Joseph Smith—Matthew) are readily available; therefore, the texts of these extracts are not included here, although reference is made to them. Also, excerpts that are used in the *Encyclopedia* article JOSEPH SMITH TRANSLATION OF THE BIBLE are not repeated here. The excerpts included here are used by permission of the Reorganized Church of Jesus Christ of Latter Day Saints.

VISIONS OF MOSES 1:1–42
(No equivalent in KJV.) The full text can be found in Moses chapter 1 of the Pearl of Great Price.

GENESIS 1:1–8:18 (KJV 1:1–6:13)
This material is not included here because it is reproduced in Moses chapters 2–8 of the Pearl of Great Price. It is greatly expanded over the King James text.

GENESIS 9:21–25
21 And the bow shall be in the cloud; and I will look upon it, that I may remember the everlasting covenant, *which I made unto thy father Enoch; that, when men should keep all my commandments, Zion should again come on the earth, the city of Enoch which I have caught up unto myself.*
22 *And this is mine everlasting covenant, that when thy posterity shall embrace the truth, and look upward, then shall Zion look downward, and all the heavens shall shake with gladness, and the earth shall tremble with joy;*
23 *And the general assembly of the church of the first-born shall come down out of heaven, and possess the earth, and shall have place until the end come. And this is mine everlasting covenant, which I made with thy father Enoch.*
24 And the bow shall be in the cloud, and I will *establish my covenant unto thee, which I have made* between *me* and *thee,* for every living creature of all flesh that *shall be* upon the earth.
25 And God said unto Noah, This is the token of

the covenant which I have established between me and *thee; for* all flesh that *shall be* upon the earth.

GENESIS 14:17–18 (KJV 14:18–19)
17 And Melchizedek, king of Salem, brought forth bread and wine; and he *break bread and blest it; and he blest the wine, he being* the priest of the most high God,
6 *But have turned from the commandment and taken unto themselves the washing of children, and the blood of sprinkling;*

GENESIS 14:25–40
25 *And Melchizedek lifted up his voice and blessed Abram.*
26 *Now Melchizedek was a man of faith, who wrought righteousness; and when a child he feared God, and stopped the mouths of lions, and quenched the violence of fire.*
27 *And thus, having been approved of God, he was ordained an high priest after the order of the covenant which God made with Enoch,*
28 *It being after the order of the Son of God; which order came, not by man, nor the will of man; neither by father nor mother; neither by beginning of days nor end of years; but of God;*
29 *And it was delivered unto men by the calling of his own voice, according to his own will, unto as many as believed on his name.*
30 *For God having sworn unto Enoch and unto his seed with an oath by himself; that every one being ordained after this order and calling should have*

power, by faith, to break mountains, to divide the seas, to dry up waters, to turn them out of their course;

31 To put at defiance the armies of nations, to divide the earth, to break every band, to stand in the presence of God; to do all things according to his will, according to his command, subdue principalities and powers; and this by the will of the Son of God which was from before the foundation of the world.

32 And men having this faith, coming up unto this order of God, were translated and taken up into heaven.

33 And now, Melchizedek was a priest of this order; therefore he obtained peace in Salem, and was called the Prince of peace.

34 And his people wrought righteousness, and obtained heaven, and sought for the city of Enoch which God had before taken, separating it from the earth, having reserved it unto the latter days, or the end of the world;

35 And hath said, and sworn with an oath, that the heavens and the earth should come together; and the sons of God should be tried so as by fire.

36 And this Melchizedek, having thus established righteousness, was called the king of heaven by his people, or, in other words, the King of peace.

37 And he lifted up his voice, and he blessed Abram, being the high priest, and the keeper of the storehouse of God;

38 Him whom God had appointed to receive tithes for the poor.

39 Wherefore, Abram paid unto him tithes of all that he had, of all the riches which he possessed, which God had given him more than that which he had need.

40 And it came to pass, that God blessed Abram, and gave unto him riches, and honor, and lands for an everlasting possession; according to the covenant which he had made, and according to the blessing wherewith Melchizedek had blessed him.

GENESIS 15:9–12

9 And Abram said, Lord God, how wilt thou give me this land for an everlasting inheritance?

10 And the Lord said, Though thou wast dead, yet am I not able to give it thee?

11 And if thou shalt die, yet thou shalt possess it, for the day cometh, that the Son of Man shall live; but how can he live if he be not dead? he must first be quickened.

12 And it came to pass, that Abram looked forth

and saw the days of the Son of Man, and was glad, and his soul found rest, and he believed in the Lord; and the Lord counted it unto him for righteousness.

GENESIS 17:3–7

3 And it came to pass, that Abram fell on his face, and called upon the name of the Lord.

4 And God talked with him, saying, My people have gone astray from my precepts, and have not kept mine ordinances, which I gave unto their fathers;

5 And they have not observed mine anointing, and the burial, or baptism wherewith I commanded them;

6 But have turned from the commandment, and taken unto themselves the washing of children, and the blood of sprinkling;

7 And have said that the blood of the righteous Abel was shed for sins; and have not known wherein they are accountable before me.

GENESIS 17:11–12

11 And I will establish a covenant of circumcision with thee, and it shall be my covenant between me and thee, and thy seed after thee, in their generations; that thou mayest know for ever that children are not accountable before me until they are eight years old.

12 And thou shalt observe to keep all my covenants wherein I covenanted with thy fathers; and thou shalt keep the commandments which I have given thee with mine own mouth, and I will be a God unto thee and thy seed after thee.

GENESIS 19:9–15

9 And they said unto him, Stand back. And they were angry with him.

10 And they said among themselves, This one man came in to sojourn among us, and he will needs now make himself to be a judge; now we will deal worse with him than with them.

11 Wherefore they said unto the man, We will have the men, and thy daughters also; and we will do with them as seemeth us good.

12 Now this was after the wickedness of Sodom.

13 And Lot said, Behold now, I have two daughters which have not known man; let me, I pray you, plead with my brethren that I may not bring them out unto you; and ye shall not do unto them as seemeth good in your eyes;

14 For God will not justify his servant in this thing; wherefore, let me plead with my brethren, this

once only, *that* unto these men ye do nothing, *that they may have peace in my house;* for therefore came they under the shadow of my roof.

15 *And they were angry with Lot* and came near to break the door, but the *angels of God, which were holy men,* put forth their hand and pulled Lot into the house unto them, and shut the door.

GENESIS 21:5 (KJV 21:6)
5 And Sarah said, God has made me to *rejoice; and also* all that *know me* will *rejoice* with me.

GENESIS 48:5–11
5 And now, of thy two sons, Ephraim and Manasseh, which were born unto thee in the land of Egypt, before I came unto thee into Egypt; *behold, they* are mine, *and the God of my fathers shall bless them; even as Reuben and Simeon they shall be blessed, for they are* mine; *wherefore they shall be called after my name.* (Therefore they were called Israel.)

6 And thy issue which thou begettest after them, shall be thine, and shall be called after the name of their brethren in their inheritance, *in the tribes; therefore they were called the tribes of Manasseh and of Ephraim.*

7 And Jacob said unto Joseph when the God of my fathers appeared unto me in Luz, in the land of Canaan; he sware unto me that he would give unto me, and unto my seed, the land for an everlasting possession.

8 Therefore, O my son, he hath blessed me in raising thee up to be a servant unto me, in saving my house from death;

9 In delivering my people, thy brethren, from famine which was sore in the land; wherefore the God of thy fathers shall bless thee, and the fruit of thy loins, that they shall be blessed above thy brethren, and above thy father's house;

10 For thou hast prevailed, and thy father's house hath bowed down unto thee, even as it was shown unto thee, before thou wast sold into Egypt by the hands of thy brethren; wherefore thy brethren shall bow down unto thee, from generation to generation, unto the fruit of thy loins for ever;

11 For thou shalt be a light unto my people, to deliver them in the days of their captivity, from bondage; and to bring salvation unto them, when they are altogether bowed down under sin.

GENESIS 50:24–38
24 And Joseph said unto his brethren, I die, *and go unto my fathers; and I go down to my grave with*

joy. *The God of my father Jacob be with you, to deliver you out of affliction in the days of your bondage; for the Lord hath visited me, and I have obtained a promise of the Lord, that out of the fruit of my loins, the Lord God will raise up a righteous branch out of my loins; and unto thee, whom my father Jacob hath named Israel, a prophet; (not the Messiah who is called Shilo;) and this prophet shall deliver my people out of Egypt in the days of thy bondage.*

25 *And it shall come to pass that they shall be scattered again; and a branch shall be broken off, and shall be carried into a far country; nevertheless they shall be remembered in the covenants of the Lord, when the Messiah cometh; for he shall be made manifest unto them in the latter days, in the Spirit of power; and shall bring them out of darkness into light; out of hidden darkness, and out of captivity unto freedom.*

26 *A seer shall the Lord my God raise up, who shall be a choice seer unto the fruit of my loins.*

27 *Thus saith the Lord God of my fathers unto me, A choice seer will I raise up out of the fruit of thy loins, and he shall be esteemed highly among the fruit of thy loins; and unto him will I give commandment that he shall do a work for the fruit of thy loins, his brethren.*

28 *And he shall bring them to the knowledge of the covenants which I have made with thy fathers; and he shall do whatsoever work I shall command him.*

29 *And I will make him great in mine eyes, for he shall do my work; and he shall be great like unto him whom I have said I would raise up unto you, to deliver my people, O house of Israel, out of the land of Egypt; for a seer will I raise up to deliver my people out of the land of Egypt; and he shall be called Moses. And by this name he shall know that he is of thy house; for he shall be nursed by the king's daughter, and shall be called her son.*

30 *And again, a seer will I raise up out of the fruit of thy loins, and unto him will I give power to bring forth my word unto the seed of thy loins; and not to the bringing forth of my word only, saith the Lord, but to the convincing them of my word, which shall have already gone forth among them in the last days;*

31 *Wherefore the fruit of thy loins shall write, and the fruit of the loins of Judah shall write; and that which shall be written by the fruit of thy loins, and also that which shall be written by the fruit of the loins of Judah, shall grow together unto the confounding of false doctrines, and laying down of*

contentions, and establishing peace among the fruit of thy loins, and bringing them to a knowledge of their fathers in the latter days; and also to the knowledge of my covenants, saith the Lord. 32 *And out of weakness shall he be made strong, in that day when my work shall go forth among all my people, which shall restore them, who are of the house of Israel, in the last days.*

33 *And that seer will I bless, and they that seek to destroy him shall be confounded; for this promise I give unto you; for I will remember you from generation to generation; and his name shall be called Joseph, and it shall be after the name of his father; and he shall be like unto you; for the thing which the Lord shall bring forth by his hand shall bring my people unto salvation.*

34 *And the Lord sware unto Joseph that he would preserve his seed forever, saying, I will raise up Moses, and a rod shall be in his hand, and he shall gather together my people, and he shall lead them as a flock, and he shall smite the waters of the Red Sea with his rod.*

35 *And he shall have judgment, and shall write the word of the Lord. And he shall not speak many words, for I will write unto him my law by the finger of mine own hand. And I will make a spokesman for him, and his name shall be called Aaron.*

36 *And it shall be done unto thee in the last days also, even as I have sworn.* Therefore, Joseph said unto his brethren, God will surely visit you, and bring you out of this land, unto the land which he sware unto Abraham, and unto Isaac, and to Jacob.

37 And Joseph *confirmed many other things unto his brethren*, and took an oath of the children of Israel, saying unto them, God will surely visit you, and ye shall carry up my bones from hence.

38 So Joseph died *when he was* an hundred and ten years old; and they embalmed him, and *they* put him in a coffin in Egypt; *and he was kept from burial by the children of Israel, that he might be carried up and laid in the sepulchre with his father. And thus they remembered the oath which they sware unto him.*

EXODUS 6:2–3

2 And God spake unto Moses, and said unto him, I am the Lord;

3 And I appeared unto Abraham, unto Isaac, and unto Jacob. *I am the Lord* God Almighty; *the Lord* JEHOVAH. *And was not my name* known unto them?

EXODUS 18:1

1 When Jethro, the *high* priest of Midian, Moses' father-in-law, heard . . .

EXODUS 22:28

28 Thou shalt not revile *against God*, nor curse the ruler of thy people.

EXODUS 23:3

3 Neither shalt thou countenance a *wicked* man in his cause.

EXODUS 32:14

14 And the Lord *said unto Moses, If they will repent of the evil which they have done, I will spare them, and turn away my fierce wrath; but, behold, thou shalt execute judgment upon all that will not repent of this evil this day. Therefore, see thou do this thing that I have commanded thee, or I will execute all that which I had* thought to do unto *my* people.

EXODUS 33:20

20 And he said *unto Moses,* Thou canst not see my face *at this time, lest mine anger be kindled against thee also, and I destroy thee, and thy people; for there shall no man among them see me at this time, and live, for they are exceeding sinful. And no sinful man hath at any time, neither shall there be any sinful man at any time, that shall see my face and live.*

EXODUS 34:1–2

1 And the Lord said unto Moses, Hew thee two *other* tables of stone, like unto the first, and I will write upon *them* also, the words *of the law, according as they were written at the first on the* tables which thou brakest; *but it shall not be according to the first, for I will take away the priesthood out of their midst; therefore my holy order, and the ordinances thereof, shall not go before them; for my presence shall not go up in their midst, lest I destroy them.*

2 *But I will give unto them the law as at the first, but it shall be after the law of a carnal commandment; for I have sworn in my wrath, that they shall not enter into my presence, into my rest, in the days of their pilgrimage. Therefore do as I have commanded thee,* and be ready in the morning, and come up in the morning unto mount Sinai, . . .

LEVITICUS 22:9

9 They shall therefore keep mine ordinance, lest they bear sin for it, and die; therefore, if they profane *not mine ordinances*, I the Lord *will* sanctify them.

NUMBERS 16:10

10 And he hath brought thee near to him, and all thy brethren the sons of Levi with thee; and seek ye the *high* priesthood also?

DEUTERONOMY 10:1–2

1 At that time the Lord said unto me, Hew thee two *other* tables of stone like unto the first, and come up unto me *upon* the mount, and make thee an ark of wood.

2 And I will write on the tables the words that were *on* the first tables, which thou breakest, *save the words of the everlasting covenant of the holy priesthood*, and thou shalt put them in the ark.

DEUTERONOMY 34:6

6 *For the Lord took him unto his fathers*, in a valley in the land of Moab, over against Beth-peor; *therefore* no man knoweth of his sepulcher unto this day.

1 SAMUEL 16:14–16, 23

14 But the Spirit of the Lord departed from Saul, and an evil spirit *which was not of* the Lord troubled him.

15 And Saul's servants said unto him, Behold now, an evil spirit *which is not of* God troubleth thee.

16 Let our lord now command thy servants, which are before thee, to seek out a man, who is a cunning player on a harp; and it shall come to pass, when the evil spirit, *which is not of* God, is upon thee, that he shall play with his hand, and thou shalt be well.

. . .

23 And it came to pass, when the evil spirit, *which was not of* God, was upon Saul, that David took a harp and played with his hand; so Saul was refreshed, and was well, and the evil spirit departed from him.

1 SAMUEL 19:9

9 And the evil spirit *which was not of* the Lord was upon Saul . . .

2 SAMUEL 12:13

13 And David said unto Nathan, I have sinned against the Lord. And Nathan said unto David, The Lord also hath *not* put away thy sin *that* thou shalt not die.

1 KINGS 3:14

14 And if thou wilt walk in my ways to keep my statutes, and my commandments, then I will lengthen thy days, *and thou shalt not walk in unrighteousness*, as did thy father David.

1 KINGS 14:8

8 And rent the kingdom away from the house of David and gave it thee, *because he kept not my commandments. But* thou hast not been as my servant David, *when he* followed me with all his heart only to do right in mine eyes.

2 CHRONICLES 18:20–22

20 Then there came out a *lying* spirit and stood before *them*, and said, I will entice him. And the Lord said unto him, Wherewith?

21 And he said, I will go out, and be a lying spirit in the mouth of all his prophets. And the Lord said, Thou shalt entice him, and thou shalt also prevail; go out, and do even so; *for all these have sinned against me.*

22 Now therefore, behold, the Lord hath *found* a lying spirit in the mouth of these thy prophets, and the Lord hath spoken evil against thee.

PSALM 11:1–5

1 *In that day thou shalt come, O Lord; and* I will put my trust *in thee. Thou shalt say unto thy people, for mine ear hath heard thy voice; thou shalt say unto every* soul, Flee unto *my* mountain; *and the righteous shall flee like* a bird *that is let go from the snare of the fowler.*

2 For the wicked bend their bow; lo, they make ready their arrow upon the string, that they may privily shoot at the upright in heart, *to destroy their foundation.*

3 *But the foundations of the wicked shall be destroyed, and what can they do?*

4 *For the Lord, when he shall come into* his holy temple, *sitting upon God's* throne in heaven, his *eyes shall pierce the wicked.*

5 Behold his eyelids *shall* try the children of men, *and he shall redeem the righteous, and they shall be tried.* The Lord *loveth* the righteous, but the wicked, and him that loveth violence, his soul hateth.

PSALM 14:1–7

1 The fool hath said in his heart, *There is no man that hath seen God. Because he showeth himself*

not unto us, therefore there is no God. *Behold,* they are corrupt; they have done abominable works, *and none of them* doeth good.

2 *For* the Lord looked down from heaven upon the children of men, *and by his voice said unto his servant, Seek ye among the children of men,* to see if there *are* any that *do* understand God. *And he opened his mouth unto the Lord, and said, Behold, all these who say they are thine.*

3 *The Lord answered and said,* They are all gone aside, they are together become filthy, *thou canst behold* none of them that *are doing* good, no, not one.

4 *All they have for their teachers are* workers of iniquity, *and there is* no knowledge *in them. They are they* who eat up my people. They eat bread and call not upon the Lord.

5 They are in great fear, for God *dwells* in the generation of the righteous. *He is the counsel of the poor, because they are ashamed of the wicked, and flee unto the Lord, for their refuge.*

6 *They are ashamed* of the counsel of the poor because the Lord is his refuge.

7 Oh that *Zion were established out of heaven,* the salvation of Israel. *O Lord, when wilt thou establish Zion?* When the Lord bringeth back the captivity of his people, Jacob shall rejoice, Israel shall be glad.

PSALM 22:12

12 Many *armies* have compassed me; strong *armies* of Bashan have beset me around.

PSALM 24:7–10

7 Lift up your heads, O ye *generations of Jacob;* and be ye lifted up; and the Lord strong and mighty; the Lord mighty in battle, who is the king of glory, *shall establish you forever.*

8 *And he will roll away the heavens; and will come down to redeem his people; to make you an everlasting name; to establish you upon his everlasting rock.*

9 Lift up your heads, O ye *generations of Jacob;* lift up your *heads,* ye everlasting *generations,* and the *Lord of hosts, the king of kings;*

10 *Even* the king of glory shall come *unto you; and shall redeem his people, and shall establish them in righteousness.* Selah.

PSALM 30:5, 9

5 For his anger *kindleth against the wicked; they repent, and in* a moment *it is turned away, and they are* in his favor, *and he giveth them* life; there-

fore, weeping may endure for a night, but joy cometh in the morning.

. . .

9 When I go down to the pit, *my blood shall return to* the dust. *I will* praise thee; *my soul* shall declare thy truth; *for what profit am I, if I do it not?*

PSALM 32:1

Blessed *are they* whose transgressions *are* forgiven, and who have *no* sins *to be* covered.

PSALM 36:1

The wicked, *who live in* transgression, saith in *their* hearts, *There is no condemnation; for* there is no fear of God before *their* eyes.

PSALM 138:8

8 The Lord will perfect me *in knowledge, concerning his kingdom. I will praise thee* O Lord, forever; *for thou art merciful, and wilt* not forsake the works of thine own hands.

PSALM 141:5

5 *When* the righteous smite me *with the word of the Lord* it is a kindness; and *when they* reprove me, it shall be an excellent oil, *and* shall not *destroy* my *faith;* for yet my prayer also shall be *for them. I delight not* in their calamities.

ISAIAH 42:19–23

19 *For I will send my servant unto you who are blind; yea, a messenger to open the eyes of the blind, and unstop the ears of the deaf;*

20 *And they shall be made perfect notwithstanding their blindness, if they will hearken unto the messenger, the Lord's servant.*

21 *Thou art a people,* seeing many things, but thou observest not; opening the ears *to hear, but thou hearest not.*

22 The Lord is *not* well pleased *with such a people, but* for his righteousness' sake he will magnify the law and make it honorable.

23 *Thou art* a people robbed and spoiled; *thine enemies,* all of them, *have snared thee* in holes, and they have hid thee in prison houses; they have taken thee for a prey, and none delivereth; for a spoil, and none saith, Restore.

ISAIAH 52:15

15 So shall he *gather* many nations . . .

AMOS 3:6–7

6 . . . shall there be evil in a city, and the Lord hath not *known* it?

7 Surely the Lord God will do nothing, *until*

he revealeth *the* secret unto his servants the prophets.

MATTHEW 3:45–46 (KJV 3:16–17)

45 And Jesus, when he was baptized, went up straightway out of the water; *and John saw,* and lo, the heavens were opened unto him, and he saw the Spirit of God descending like a dove and lighting upon *Jesus.*

46 And lo, *he heard* a voice from heaven, saying, This is my beloved Son, in whom I am well pleased. *Hear ye him.*

MATTHEW 5:21 (KJV 5:19)

21 Whosoever, therefore, shall break one of these least commandments, and shall teach men so *to do,* he shall in no wise be saved in the kingdom of heaven; but whosoever shall do and teach *these commandments of the law until it be fulfilled,* the same shall be called great, *and shall be saved* in the kingdom of heaven.

MATTHEW 6:38 (KJV 6:33)

38 *Wherefore, seek not the things of this world but* seek ye first *to build up* the kingdom of God, and *to establish* his righteousness, and all these things shall be added unto you.

MATTHEW 7:4–11

4 *And again, ye shall say unto them, Why is it that thou* beholdest the mote that is in thy brother's eye, but considerest not the beam that is in thine own eye?

5 Or how wilt thou say to thy brother, Let me pull out the mote out of thine eye; *and canst not behold* a beam in thine own eye?

6 *And Jesus said unto his disciples, Beholdest thou the Scribes, and the Pharisees, and the Priests, and the Levites? They teach in their synagogues, but do not observe the law, nor the commandments; and all have gone out of the way, and are under sin.*

7 *Go thou and say unto them, Why teach ye men the law and the commandments, when ye yourselves are the children of corruption?*

8 *Say unto them,* Ye hypocrites, first cast out the beam out of thine own eye; and then shalt thou see clearly to cast out the mote out of thy brother's eye.

9 *Go ye into the world, saying unto all, Repent, for the kingdom of heaven has come nigh unto you.*

10 *And the mysteries of the kingdom ye shall keep within yourselves; for it is not meet to* give that which is holy unto the dogs; neither cast ye your pearls *unto* swine, lest they trample them under their feet.

11 *For the world cannot receive that which ye, yourselves, are not able to bear; wherefore ye shall not give your pearls unto them, lest they* turn again and rend you.

MATTHEW 9:18–21

18 *Then said the Pharisees unto him, Why will ye not receive us with our baptism, seeing we keep the whole law?*

19 *But Jesus said unto them, Ye keep not the law. If ye had kept the law, ye would have received me, for I am he who gave the law.*

20 *I receive not you with your baptism, because it profiteth you nothing.*

21 *For when that which is new is come, the old is ready to be put away.*

MATTHEW 13:10–11, 49–50 (KJV 13:12, 30, 49)

10 For whosoever *receiveth,* to him shall be given, and he shall have more abundance;

11 But whosoever *continueth* not *to receive,* from him shall be taken away even that he hath.

. . .

29 Let both grow together until the harvest, and in the time of harvest, I will say to the reapers, Gather ye together first the *wheat into my barn;* and the tares are *bound* in bundles to *be burned.*

. . .

49 So shall it be at the end of the world.

50 *And the world is the children of the wicked.*

MATTHEW 16:26–29

26 *And now for a man to take up his cross, is to deny himself all ungodliness, and every worldly lust, and keep my commandments.*

27 *Break not my commandments for to save your lives;* for whosoever will save his life *in this world,* shall lose it *in the world to come.*

28 And whosoever will lose his life *in this world,* for my sake, shall find it *in the world to come.*

29 *Therefore, forsake the world, and save your souls;* for what is a man profited, if he shall gain the whole world, and lose his own soul? Or what shall a man give in exchange for his soul?

MATTHEW 17:10–14

10 And Jesus answered and said unto them, Elias truly shall first come, and restore all things, *as the prophets have written.*

11 *And again* I say unto you that Elias has come already, *concerning whom it is written, Behold, I*

will send my messenger, and he shall prepare the way before me; and they knew him not, and have done unto him, whatsoever they listed.

12 Likewise shall also the Son of Man suffer of them.

13 *But I say unto you, Who is Elias? Behold, this is Elias, whom I send to prepare the way before me.*

14 Then the disciples understood that he spake unto them of John the Baptist, *and also of another who should come and restore all things, as it is written by the prophets.*

MATTHEW 21:47–56

47 And when the chief priests and Pharisees had heard his parables, they perceived that he spake of them.

48 *And they said among themselves, Shall this man think that he alone can spoil this great kingdom? And they were angry with him.*

49 But when they sought to lay hands on him, they feared the multitude, because they learned that the multitude took him for a prophet.

50 *And now his disciples came to him, and Jesus said unto them, Marvel ye at the words of the parable which I spake unto them?*

51 *Verily, I say unto you, I am the stone, and those wicked ones reject me.*

52 *I am the head of the corner. These Jews shall fall upon me, and shall be broken.*

53 *And the kingdom of God shall be taken from them, and shall be given to a nation bringing forth the fruits thereof; (meaning the Gentiles.)*

54 *Wherefore, on whomsoever this stone shall fall, it shall grind him to powder.*

55 *And when the Lord therefore of the vineyard cometh, he will destroy those miserable, wicked men, and will let again his vineyard unto other husbandmen, even in the last days, who shall render him the fruits in their seasons.*

56 *And then understood they the parable which he spake unto them, that the Gentiles should be destroyed also, when the Lord should descend out of heaven to reign in his vineyard, which is the earth and the inhabitants thereof.*

MATTHEW 24:1–56 (KJV 24:1–51)

This expanded text is reproduced in Joseph Smith–Matthew 1:1–55 in the Pearl of Great Price.

MATTHEW 25:11 (KJV 25:12)

11 But he answered and said, Verily I say unto you, *Ye* know *me* not.

MARK 2:26–27

26 *Wherefore the Sabbath was given unto man for a day of rest; and also that man should glorify God, and not that man should not eat;*

27 *For the Son of Man made the Sabbath day,* therefore the Son of Man is Lord also of the Sabbath.

MARK 8:37–38

37 For whosoever will save his life, shall lose it; *or whosoever will save his life, shall be willing to lay it down for my sake; and if he is not willing to lay it down for my sake, he shall lose it.*

38 But whosoever shall *be willing to* lose his life for my sake, and the *gospel,* the same shall save it.

MARK 9:40–48

40 *Therefore,* if thy hand offend thee, cut it off; *or if thy brother offend thee and confess not and forsake not, he shall be cut off.* It is better for thee to enter into life maimed, than having two hands, to go into hell.

41 *For it is better for thee to enter into life without thy brother, than for thee and thy brother to be cast into hell;* into the fire that never shall be quenched, where their worm dieth not, and the fire is not quenched.

42 *And again,* if thy foot offend thee, cut it off; *for he that is thy standard, by whom thou walkest, if he become a transgressor, he shall be cut off.*

43 It is better for thee, to enter halt into life, than having two feet to be cast into hell; into the fire that never shall be quenched.

44 *Therefore, let every man stand or fall, by himself, and not for another; or not trusting another.*

45 *Seek unto my Father, and it shall be done in that very moment what ye shall ask, if ye ask in faith, believing that ye shall receive.*

46 And if thine eye *which seeth for thee, him that is appointed to watch over thee to show thee light, become a transgressor and offend thee, pluck him out.*

47 It is better for thee to enter into the kingdom of God, with one eye, than having two eyes to be cast into hell fire.

48 *For it is better that thyself should be saved, than to be cast into hell with thy brother,* where their worm dieth not, and where the fire is not quenched.

MARK 14:20–25

20 And as they did eat, Jesus took bread and blessed it, and brake, and gave to them, and said, *Take it, and eat.*

21 *Behold, this is for you to do in remembrance of my body; for as oft as ye do this ye will remember this hour that I was with you.*

22 And he took the cup, and when he had given thanks, he gave it to them; and they all drank of it.

23 *And he said unto them, This is in remembrance of my blood which is shed for many, and the new testament which I give unto you; for of me ye shall bear record unto all the world.*

24 *And as oft as ye do this ordinance, ye will remember me in this hour that I was with you and drank with you of this cup, even the last time in my ministry.*

25 Verily I say unto you, *Of this ye shall bear record; for* I will no more drink of the fruit of the vine *with you,* until that day that I drink it new in the kingdom of God.

MARK 14:36–38 (KJV 14:32–34)

36 And they came to a place which was named Gethsemane, *which was a garden; and the disciples began to be sore amazed, and to be very heavy, and to complain in their hearts, wondering if this be the Messiah.*

37 *And Jesus knowing their hearts, said* to his disciples, Sit ye here, while I shall pray.

38 And he taketh with him Peter, and James, and John, *and rebuked them,* and said unto them, My soul is exceeding sorrowful, *even* unto death; tarry ye here and watch.

LUKE 3:4–11

4 As it is written in the book of the *prophet* Esaias; *and these are the words,* saying, The voice of one crying in the wilderness, Prepare ye the way of the Lord, and make his paths straight.

5 *For behold, and lo, he shall come, as it is written in the book of the prophets, to take away the sins of the world, and to bring salvation unto the heathen nations, to gather together those who are lost, who are of the sheepfold of Israel;*

6 *Yea, even the dispersed and afflicted; and also to prepare the way, and make possible the preaching of the gospel unto the Gentiles;*

7 *And to be a light unto all who sit in darkness, unto the uttermost parts of the earth; to bring to pass the resurrection from the dead, and to ascend up on high, to dwell on the right hand of the Father,*

8 *Until the fulness of time, and the law and the testimony shall be sealed, and the keys of the kingdom shall be delivered up again unto the Father;*

9 *To administer justice unto all; to come down in judgment upon all, and to convince all the ungodly of their ungodly deeds, which they have committed; and all this in the day that he shall come;*

10 *For it is a day of power; yea,* every valley shall be filled, and every mountain and hill shall be brought low; . . .

LUKE 5:23

23 *Does it require more power to* forgive sins *than to make the sick* rise up and walk?

LUKE 6:29–30

29 And unto him who smiteth thee on the cheek, offer also the other; *or, in other words, it is better to offer the other, than to revile again.* And him who taketh away thy cloak, forbid not to take thy coat also.

30 *For it is better that thou suffer thine enemy to take these things, than to contend with him. Verily I say unto you, Your heavenly Father who seeth in secret, shall bring that wicked one into judgment.*

LUKE 8:23

23 But as they sailed he fell asleep; and there came down a storm of wind on the lake; and they were filled with *fear,* and were in *danger.*

LUKE 9:31

31 Who appeared in glory, and spake of his *death, and also his resurrection,* which he should accomplish at Jerusalem.

LUKE 10:22 (KJV 10:21)

22 In that hour Jesus rejoiced in spirit, and said, I thank thee, O Father, Lord of heaven and earth, that thou hast hid these things from *them who think they are* wise and prudent, and hast revealed them unto babes; even so, Father; for so it seemed good in thy sight.

LUKE 11:53 (KJV 11:52)

53 Woe unto you, lawyers! For ye have taken away the key of knowledge, *the fulness of the scriptures;* ye enter not in yourselves *into the kingdom;* and *those who* were entering in, ye hindered.

LUKE 12:9–12

9 But he *who* denieth me before men, shall be denied before the angels of God.

10 *Now his disciples knew that he said this, because they had spoken evil against him before the people; for they were afraid to confess him before men.*

11 *And they reasoned among themselves, saying, He knoweth our hearts, and he speaketh to our condemnation, and we shall not be forgiven. But he answered them, and said unto them,*

12 Whosoever shall speak a word against the Son of Man, *and repenteth*, it shall be forgiven him; but unto him *who* blasphemeth against the Holy Ghost, it shall not be forgiven him.

LUKE 12:34 (KJV 12:31)

34 *Therefore* seek ye to *bring forth* the kingdom of God, and all these things shall be added unto you.

LUKE 12:41–57

41 *For, behold, he cometh in the first watch of the night, and he shall also come in the second watch, and again he shall come in the third watch.*

42 *And verily I say unto you, He hath already come, as it is written of him; and again when he shall come in the second watch, or come in the third watch, blessed are those servants when he cometh,* that he shall find so *doing;*

43 *For the Lord of those servants shall gird himself, and make them to sit down to meat, and will come forth and serve them.*

44 *And now, verily I say these things unto you, that ye may know this, that the coming of the Lord is as a thief in the night.*

45 *And it is like unto a man who is an householder, who, if he watcheth not his goods, the thief cometh in an hour of which he is not aware, and taketh his goods, and divideth them among his fellows.*

46 *And they said among themselves,* If the good man of the house had known what hour the thief would come, he would have watched, and not have suffered his house to be broken through *and the loss of his goods.*

47 *And he said unto them,* Verily I say unto you, be ye therefore ready also; for the Son of Man cometh at an hour when ye think not.

48 Then Peter said unto him, Lord, speakest thou this parable unto us, or unto all?

49 And the Lord said, *I speak unto those whom the Lord shall make rulers* over his household, to give *his children* their portion of meat in due season.

50 *And they said, Who then is that faithful and wise servant?*

51 *And the Lord said unto them, It is that servant who watcheth, to impart his portion of meat in due season.*

52 Blessed *be* that servant whom his Lord *shall* find, when he cometh, so doing.

53 Of a truth I say unto you, that he will make him ruler over all that he hath.

54 *But the evil servant is he who is not found watching. And if that servant is not found watching, he will say* in his heart, My Lord delayeth his coming; and shall begin to beat the menservants, and the maidens, and to eat, and drink, and to be drunken.

55 The *Lord* of that servant will come in a day he looketh not for, and at an hour when he is not aware, and will cut him *down*, and will appoint him his portion with the unbelievers.

56 And that servant who knew his Lord's will, and prepared not *for his Lord's coming*, neither did according to his will, shall be beaten with many stripes.

57 But he that knew not *his Lord's will*, and did commit things worthy of stripes, shall be beaten with few. For unto whomsoever much is given, of him shall much be required; and to whom *the Lord* has committed much, of him *will men* ask the more.

LUKE 13:36 (KJV 13:35)

36 Behold, your house is left unto you desolate. And verily I say unto you, Ye shall not *know* me, *until ye have received from the hand of the Lord a just recompense for all your sins;* until the time come when ye shall say, Blessed is he who cometh in the name of the Lord.

LUKE 14:35–37

35 *Then certain of them came to him, saying, Good Master, we have Moses and the prophets, and whosoever shall live by them, shall he not have life?*

36 *And Jesus answered, saying, Ye know not Moses, neither the prophets; for if ye had known them, ye would have believed on me; for to this intent they were written. For I am sent that ye might have life. Therefore I will liken it unto salt which is good;*

37 But if the salt *has* lost *its* savor, wherewith shall it be seasoned?

LUKE 16:16–23

16 *And they said unto him, We have the law, and the prophets; but as for this man we will not receive him to be our ruler; for he maketh himself to be a judge over us.*

17 *Then said Jesus unto them,* The law and the prophets *testify of me; yea, and all the prophets*

who have written, even until John, *have foretold of these days.*

18 Since that time, the kingdom of God is preached, and every man *who seeketh truth* presseth into it.

19 And it is easier for heaven and earth to pass, than for one tittle of the law to fail.

20 *And why teach ye the law, and deny that which is written; and condemn him whom the Father hath sent to fulfil the law, that ye might all be redeemed?*

21 *O fools! for you have said in your hearts, There is no God. And you pervert the right way; and the kingdom of heaven suffereth violence of you; and you persecute the meek; and in your violence you seek to destroy the kingdom; and ye take the children of the kingdom by force. Woe unto you, ye adulterers!*

22 *And they reviled him again, being angry for the saying, that they were adulterers.*

23 *But he continued, saying,* Whosoever putteth away his wife, and marrieth another, committeth adultery; and whosoever marrieth her who is put away from her husband, committeth adultery. *Verily I say unto you, I will liken you unto the rich man.*

LUKE 17:36–40

36 And they answered and said unto him, Where, Lord, *shall they be taken.*

37 And he said unto them, Wheresoever the body is *gathered; or, in other words, whithersoever the saints are gathered,* thither will the eagles be gathered together; *or, thither will the remainder be gathered together.*

38 *This he spake, signifying the gathering of his saints; and of angels descending and gathering the remainder unto them; the one from the bed, the other from the grinding, and the other from the field, whithersoever he listeth.*

39 *For verily there shall be new heavens, and a new earth, wherein dwelleth righteousness.*

40 *And there shall be no unclean thing; for the earth becoming old, even as a garment, having waxed in corruption, wherefore it vanisheth away, and the footstool remaineth sanctified, cleansed from all sin.*

LUKE 21:24–25

24 *And then his disciples asked him, saying, Master, tell us concerning thy coming?*

25 *And he answered them, and said, In the genera-* tion in which the times of the Gentiles shall be fulfilled, there shall be signs in the sun, and in the moon, and in the stars; and upon the earth distress of nations with perplexity, *like* the sea and the waves roaring. *The earth also shall be troubled, and the waters of the great deep;*

JOHN 1:1–34

1 In the beginning was the *gospel preached through the Son. And the gospel was the word, and the word was with the Son, and the Son was with God, and the Son was of God.*

2 The same was in the beginning with God.

3 All things were made by him; and without him was not anything made which was made.

4 In him was *the gospel, and the gospel was the life,* and the life was the light of men;

5 And the light shineth *in the world,* and the *world perceiveth* it not.

6 There was a man sent from God, whose name was John.

7 The same came *into the world* for a witness, to bear witness of the light, *to bear record of the gospel through the Son, unto all,* that through him *men* might believe.

8 He was not that light, but *came* to bear witness of that light,

9 *Which* was the true light, which lighteth every man *who* cometh into the world;

10 *Even the Son of God.* He *who* was in the world, and the world was made by him, and the world knew him not.

11 He came unto his own, and his own received him not.

12 But as many as received him, to them gave he power to become the sons of God; *only* to them *who* believe on his name.

13 *He was* born, not of blood, nor of the will of the flesh, nor of the will of man, but of God.

14 And the *same* word was made flesh, and dwelt among us, and we beheld his glory, the glory as of the Only Begotten of the Father, full of grace and truth.

15 John *bear* witness of him, and cried, saying, This *is* he of whom I spake; He *who* cometh after me, is preferred before me; for he was before me.

16 *For in the beginning was the Word, even the Son, who is made flesh, and sent unto us by the will of the Father, And as many as believe on his name shall receive of his fulness.* And of his fulness have all we received, *even immortality and eternal life, through his grace.*

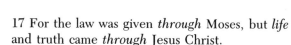

17 For the law was given *through* Moses, but *life* and truth came *through* Jesus Christ.

18 *For the law was after a carnal commandment, to the administration of death; but the gospel was after the power of an endless life, through Jesus Christ, the Only Begotten Son, who is in the bosom of the Father.*

19 *And* no man hath seen God at any time, *except he hath borne record of the Son; for except it is through him no man can be saved.*

20 And this is the record of John, when the Jews sent priests and Levites from Jerusalem, to ask him; Who art thou?

21 And he confessed, and denied not *that he was Elias*; but confessed, *saying*; I am not the Christ.

22 And they asked him, saying; *How then art thou Elias? And he said, I am not that Elias who was to restore all things. And they asked him, saying,* Art thou that prophet? And he answered, No.

23 Then said they unto him, Who art thou? that we may give an answer to them that sent us. What sayest thou of thyself?

24 He said, I am the voice of one crying in the wilderness, Make straight the way of the Lord, as saith the prophet Esaias.

25 And they who were sent were of the Pharisees.

26 And they asked him, and said unto him; Why baptizest thou then, if thou be not the Christ, nor Elias *who was to restore all things*, neither that prophet?

27 John answered them, saying; I baptize with water, but there standeth one among you, whom ye know not;

28 *He it is of whom I bear record. He is that prophet, even Elias,* who, coming after me, is preferred before me, whose shoe's latchet I am not worthy to unloose, *or whose place I am not able to fill; for he shall baptize, not only with water, but with fire, and with the Holy Ghost.*

29 The next day John seeth Jesus coming unto him, and said; Behold the Lamb of God, who taketh away the sin of the world!

30 *And John bare record of him unto the people, saying,* This is he of whom I said; After me cometh a man who is preferred before me; for he was before me, and I knew him, *and* that he should be made manifest to Israel; therefore am I come baptizing with water.

31 And John bare record, saying; *When he was baptized of me,* I saw the Spirit descending from heaven like a dove, and it abode upon him.

32 And I knew him; *for* he *who* sent me to baptize with water, the same said unto me; Upon whom thou shalt see the Spirit descending, and remaining on him, the same is he who baptizeth with the Holy Ghost.

33 And I saw, and bare record that this is the Son of God.

34 *These things were done in Bethabara, beyond Jordan, where John was baptizing.*

JOHN 4:26 (KJV 4:24)

26 *For unto such hath God promised his* Spirit. And they *who* worship him, must worship in spirit and in truth.

JOHN 6:44

44 No man can come unto me, except *he doeth the will of my Father who hath sent me. And this is the will of him who hath sent me, that ye receive the Son; for the Father beareth record of him; and he who receiveth the testimony, and doeth the will of him who sent me,* I will raise up *in the resurrection of the just.*

JOHN 9:32

32 Since the world began was it not heard that any man opened the eyes of one that was born blind, *except he be of God.*

JOHN 10:8

8 All that ever came before me *who testified not of me* are thieves and robbers; but the sheep did not hear them.

JOHN 13:8–10

8 Peter saith unto him, *Thou needest not to* wash my feet. Jesus answered him, If I wash thee not, thou hast no part with me.

9 Simon Peter saith unto him, Lord, not my feet only, but also my hands and my head.

10 Jesus saith to him, He that *has* washed *his hands and his head,* needeth not save to wash his feet, but is clean every whit; and ye are clean, but not all. *Now this was the custom of the Jews under their law; wherefore, Jesus did this that the law might be fulfilled.*

ROMANS 3:24

24 *Therefore* being justified *only* by his grace through the redemption that is in Christ Jesus;

ROMANS 7:5–27

5 For when we were in the flesh, the motions of sins, which were *not according to* the law, did work in our members to bring forth fruit unto death.

6 But now we are delivered from the law wherein we were held, *being dead to the law*, that we should serve in newness of spirit, and not in the oldness of the letter.

7 What shall we say then? Is the law sin? God forbid. Nay, I had not known sin, but by the law; for I had not known lust, except the law had said, Thou shalt not covet.

8 But sin, taking occasion by the commandment, wrought in me all manner of concupiscence. For without the law sin was dead.

9 For *once* I was alive without *transgression of* the law, but when the commandment *of Christ* came, sin revived, and I died.

10 And *when I believed not* the commandment *of Christ which came*, which was ordained to life, I found *it condemned me* unto death.

11 For sin, taking occasion, *denied* the commandment, *and* deceived me and by it *I was slain*.

12 *Nevertheless, I found* the law *to be* holy, and the commandment *to be* holy, and just, and good.

13 Was then that which is good made death unto me? God forbid. But sin, that it might appear sin by that which is good *working death in me*; that sin, by the commandment, might become exceeding sinful.

14 For we know that the *commandment* is spiritual; but *when I was under the law*, I *was yet* carnal, sold under sin.

15 *But now I am spiritual*; for that which *I am commanded to do, I do; and that which I am commanded not to allow*, I allow not.

16 *For what I know is not right I would* not *do; for that which is sin*, I hate.

17 If then I do *not* that which I would not *allow*, I consent unto the law, that it is good; *and I am not condemned*.

18 Now then, it is no more I that do *sin*; but I *seek to subdue that* sin *which* dwelleth in me.

19 For I know that in me, that is, in my flesh, dwelleth no good thing; for to will is present with me, but to perform that which is good I find not, *only in Christ*.

20 For the good that I would *have done when under the law, I find not to be good; therefore*, I do it not.

21 But the evil which I would not *do under the law, I find to be good*; that, I do.

22 Now if I do that, *through the assistance of Christ*, I would not *do under the law, I am not under the law; and* it is no more *that I seek to do wrong*, but to *subdue* sin that dwelleth in me.

23 I find then that *under the* law, that when I would do good evil *was* present with me; for I delight in the law of God after the inward man.

24 *And now I see another law, even the commandment of Christ, and it is imprinted in my mind.*

25 *But* my members *are* warring against the law of my mind, and bringing me into captivity to the law of sin which is in my members.

26 *And if I subdue not the sin which is in me, but with the flesh serve the law of sin*; O wretched man that I am! who shall deliver me from the body of this death?

27 I thank God through Jesus Christ our Lord, then, that so with the mind I myself serve the law of God.

ROMANS 8:8–10, 13

8 So then they that are *after* the flesh cannot please God.

9 But ye are not *after* the flesh, but *after* the Spirit, if so be that the Spirit of God dwell in you. Now if any man have not the Spirit of Christ, he is none of his.

10 And if Christ be in you, *though* the body *shall die* because of sin, *yet* the Spirit is life, because of righteousness.

. . .

13 For if ye live after the flesh, *unto sin*, ye shall die; but if ye through the Spirit do mortify the deeds of the body, ye shall live *unto Christ*.

1 CORINTHIANS 7:1, 5, 9, 29–33

1 Now concerning the things whereof ye wrote unto me, *saying*, It is good for a man not to touch a woman.

. . .

5 *Depart* ye not one *from* the other, except it be with consent for a time, that ye may give yourselves to fasting and prayer.

. . .

9 But if they cannot *abide*, let them marry; for it is better to marry than *that any should commit sin*.

. . .

29 But *I speak unto you who are called unto the ministry. For* this I say, brethren, the time that remaineth is but short, *that ye shall be sent forth unto the ministry*. Even they who have wives, shall be as though they had none; *for ye are called and chosen to do the Lord's work*.

30 And it shall be with them who weep, as though they wept not; and them who rejoice, as though

they rejoiced not, and them who buy, as though they possessed not;

31 And *them who* use this world, as not using it; for the fashion of this world passeth away.

32 But *I would, brethren, that ye magnify your calling.* I would have you without carefulness. For he who is unmarried, careth for the things that belong to the Lord, how he may please the Lord; *therefore he prevaileth.*

33 But he who is married, careth for the things that are of the world, how he may please his wife; *therefore there is a difference, for he is hindered.*

2 THESSALONIANS 2:7–9

7 For the mystery of iniquity doth already work, *and he it is who now worketh, and Christ suffereth him to work, until the time is fulfilled that he shall* be taken out of the way.

8 And then shall that wicked *one* be revealed, whom the Lord shall consume with the spirit of his mouth, and shall destroy with the brightness of his coming.

9 *Yea, the Lord, even Jesus,* whose coming is *not until* after *there cometh a falling away, by* the working of Satan with all power, and signs and lying wonders . . .

2 TIMOTHY 4:2

2 Preach the word; be instant in season; *those who are* out of season, reprove, rebuke, exhort with all long-suffering and doctrine.

HEBREWS 7:19–20, 25–26

19 For the law *was administered without an oath* and made nothing perfect, but *was only* the bringing in of a better hope; by the which we draw nigh unto God.

20 Inasmuch as *this high priest* was not without an oath, *by so much was Jesus made the surety of a better testament.*

. . .

25 For such an high priest became us, who is holy, harmless, undefiled, separate from sinners, and made *ruler over* the heavens;

26 *And not* as those high priests *who* offered up sacrifice *daily,* first for *their* own sins, and then for the *sins of the people; for he needeth not offer sacrifice for his own sins, for he knew no sins; but for the sins of the people. And* this he did once, when he offered up himself.

HEBREWS 11:1

1 Now faith is the *assurance* of things hoped for, the evidence of things not seen.

1 PETER 4:2

2 For *you who have* suffered in the flesh *should cease* from sin, that *you* no longer the rest of *your* time in the flesh, should live to the lusts of men, but to the will of God.

1 JOHN 4:12

12 No man hath seen God at any time, *except them who believe.*

REVELATION 1:1–8

1 The Revelation of *John, a servant of God,* which *was given* unto him *of Jesus Christ,* to show unto his servants things which must shortly come to pass, *that* he sent and signified by his angel unto his servant John,

2 Who *bore* record of the word of God, and of the testimony of Jesus Christ, and of all things that he saw.

3 Blessed *are they* who read, and they who hear *and understand* the words of this prophecy, and keep those things which are written therein, for the time *of the coming of the Lord draweth nigh.*

4 *Now this is the testimony of* John to *the seven servants who are over* the seven churches in Asia. Grace unto you, and peace from him *who* is, and *who* was, and *who* is to come; *who hath sent forth his angel from* before his throne, *to testify unto those who are the seven servants over the seven churches.*

5 *Therefore, I, John,* the faithful witness, *bear record of the things which were delivered me of the angel,* and from Jesus Christ the first begotten of the dead, and the Prince of the kings of the earth.

6 *And* unto him *who* loved us, *be glory;* who washed us from our sins in his own blood, and hath made us kings and priests unto God, his Father. To him be glory and dominion, forever and ever. Amen.

7 *For* behold, he cometh *in the* clouds *with ten thousands of his saints in the kingdom, clothed with the glory of his Father.* And every eye shall see him; and they *who* pierced him, and all kindreds of the earth shall wail because of him. Even so, Amen.

8 *For he saith,* I am Alpha and Omega, the beginning and the ending, the Lord, who is, and who was, and who is to come, the Almighty.

REVELATION 2:26–27

26 And *to him who* overcometh, and keepeth my *commandments* unto the end, will I give power over *many kingdoms;*

27 And he shall rule them with *the word of God; and they shall be in his hands* as the vessels *of clay in the hands of* a potter; *and he shall govern them by faith, with equity and justice,* even as I received of my Father.

REVELATION 12:1–8

1 And there appeared a great *sign* in heaven, *in the likeness of things on the earth*; a woman clothed with the sun, and the moon under her feet, and upon her head a crown of twelve stars.

2 And *the woman* being with child, cried, travailing in birth, and pained to be delivered.

3 *And she brought forth a man child, who was to rule all nations with a rod of iron; and her child was caught up unto God and his throne.*

4 And there appeared another *sign* in heaven; and behold, a great red dragon, having seven heads and ten horns, and seven crowns upon his heads. And his tail drew the third part of the stars of heaven, and did cast them to the earth. And the dragon stood before the woman which was delivered, ready to devour her child *after* it was born.

5 And the woman fled into the wilderness, where she *had* a place prepared of God, that they should feed her there a thousand two hundred and threescore *years.*

6 And there was war in heaven; Michael and his angels fought against the dragon; and the dragon and his angels *fought against Michael*;

7 And *the dragon* prevailed not *against Michael, neither the child, nor the woman which was the church of God, who had been delivered of her pains, and brought forth the kingdom of our God and his Christ.*

8 Neither was *there* place found in heaven *for* the great dragon, *who* was cast out; that old serpent called the devil, and *also called* Satan, which deceiveth the whole world; he was cast out into the earth; and his angels were cast out with him.

Appendix 8

Letters of the First Presidency

The following letters of the First Presidency of The Church of Jesus Christ of Latter-day Saints were selected to illustrate some of the many interests of the Presidency in the leadership of the Church. Letters included here are of a regulatory and directive nature and represent only one facet of a wide range of responsibilities and activities.

Examples of other types of documents emanating from the First Presidency are contained in additional Appendices under the titles of Doctrinal Expositions, and Temple Dedicatory Prayers. Members of the First Presidency also deliver formal messages at General Conferences and other conferences, and publish an annual Christmas Message and statements on other occasions when needed.

Letters from the First Presidency carry the official letterhead:

The Church of Jesus Christ of Latter-day Saints
OFFICE OF THE FIRST PRESIDENCY
Salt Lake City, Utah

To conserve space in this Appendix the letterhead does not appear with the individual selections. A brief notation indicates the general subject matter of each letter.

Cub Scout Program Encouraged

December 19, 1960

To the Priesthood, Primary Workers, and Cub Scout Leaders

It is the desire of the First Presidency that Latter-day Saint boys have the full advantage of the Scouting program, including Cub Scouting, Boy Scouting, and Exploring. It is also the desire of the First Presidency that Latter-day Saint boys have this experience in units sponsored by the Church, under the direction of Church leaders, and according to Church policies and standards. When we do not accept this responsibility but leave it to the school, the community, or another church, we do two things: we place our boys in a situation where their activities may not be conducted according to Church standards; we may be sowing the seeds of Church inactivity at a most impressionable age.

The Cub Scout program was adopted by the Church in 1953. That year 114 Packs were organized. At the close of 1960 there were about 1,075 Packs and 28,000 Cub Scouts.

The Latter-day Saint belief in the eternal nature of the family places special emphasis on the value of this home-centered program.

Cub Scouting is a potent and effective part of the youth program of the Church and must have the enthusiastic support of the priesthood and Primary workers.

We extend congratulations and commendation for the outstanding success of this program to date, and pray that the blessings of the Lord will ever be with you as you continue willingly to give of yourselves for the protection and guidance of our youth.

Sincerely yours,

THE FIRST PRESIDENCY
David O. McKay
J. Reuben Clark, Jr.
Henry D. Moyle

For the Strength of Youth

June 2, 1965

Preface "For the Strength of Youth"

The general officers of the Young Men's and Young Women's Mutual Improvement Associations, together with the Brigham Young University and the Church School System and a large group of representative youth of the Church, have prepared an excellent treatise on Latter-day Saint standards and entitled it "For the Strength of Youth," with sub-titles on Dress, Manners, Dating, Dancing, and Clean Living.

We wish to endorse what has been here written, commend all responsible for their efforts, and express the hope that all members of the Church, not only the youth, will familiarize themselves with the suggestions herein contained and conform to the regulations set forth.

All rules and regulations, in fact all laws, especially the laws of God, are made for the benefit of the people. It is, of course, of the utmost importance that we become familiar therewith and conform thereto that we may have the blessings which were intended.

Let us never lose sight of the eternal principle enunciated by the Master that while free agency will not be trammeled by our Heavenly Father, conformity to established rules of conduct is a necessary prerequisite to the blessings promised to those who obey and keep his commandments.

THE FIRST PRESIDENCY
David O. McKay
Hugh B. Brown
N. Eldon Tanner

National Family Week

May 3, 1967

Presidents of Stakes and Bishops of Wards in the United States

Dear Brethren:

The Family Service Association of America has recommended the observance of Family Week, May 7–14. The Church of Jesus Christ of Latter-day Saints is pleased to join with all other religious and with civic organizations in the observance of this occasion.

We urge that the true spirit of the home be emphasized in church meetings, in bulletins, by the family home teachers as they visit the homes of the people, and by the families in their home evening gatherings. We cannot emphasize too strongly the need for a concerted effort to strengthen the relationship between husband and wife and parents and children, and the respect that should be maintained for moral, ethical and spiritual values.

Sincerely yours,

THE FIRST PRESIDENCY
David O. McKay
Hugh B. Brown
N. Eldon Tanner
Joseph Fielding Smith

Home Beautification Encouraged

September 20, 1974

To Stake and Mission Presidents, Bishops, Branch Presidents, and District Presidents

Dear Brethren:

Attached is a statement regarding a cleanup and beautification effort which we ask you to implement immediately.

We suggest that you organize these and other methods of implementation which you feel will be effective:

1. Ask home teachers to stress in their messages to families the need to clean up and beautify their homes and surroundings. . . .

2. Assign elders quorums . . . to clean up and beautify our meetinghouse buildings and grounds. Also, make arrangements for the upkeep of our meetinghouses and grounds so that they are always neat and attractive. Aaronic Priesthood quorum members may be asked to assist in this effort where desired.

3. Encourage Young Adult and Special Interest groups to organize themselves to assist the elderly, the fatherless, and the needy in improving the appearance of their homes and surroundings and in properly maintaining them. . . .

4. Request that Sunday School and Primary teachers, in the course of their lesson presentations, instruct class members in orderliness, in respecting buildings and property generally, in taking care of their belongings, and in keeping them in their proper places.

5. Encourage the leadership of the Relief Society to provide "how to" suggestions to women in keeping with the spirit of this effort. . . .

May the Lord bless you in this and your other leadership responsibilities in building the kingdom of God on earth.

Sincerely yours,

THE FIRST PRESIDENCY
Spencer W. Kimball
N. Eldon Tanner
Marion G. Romney

American Woman's Movement

October 7, 1974

To Stake Presidents, Stake Relief Society Presidents

Dear Brethren and Sisters:

We are enclosing a pamphlet containing a copy of the talk given by President Belle S. Spafford at the Lochinvar Club in New York on the subject "The American Woman's Movement."

This talk is an excellent presentation of the history of the women's movement in the United States and the world. It also emphasizes the efforts of the Church to give status to women and to enhance the role of motherhood.

We hope you will take the opportunity in future talks to share with the membership in your stake the pertinent information contained in this pamphlet.

Sincerely,

THE FIRST PRESIDENCY
Spencer W. Kimball
N. Eldon Tanner
Marion G. Romney

Support for Boy Scout Programs

June 20, 1975

To all Regional Representatives, Stake and Mission Presidents, Bishops, District and Branch Presidents in the United States

Dear Brethren:

For the past 62 years the Church has enjoyed a rewarding relationship with the Boy Scouts of America. The ideals of Scouting fostering citizenship training, physical fitness, and moral integrity, based upon a firm belief in God, are in harmony with the objectives of the Church.

We are pleased to support Scouting in the Church. The attached letter from the Presiding Bishopric is included to give you information regarding a policy change concerning the Church's relationship with the Venturing and Exploring programs. We urge the support of local priesthood leaders in the Scouting program as explained in the letter from the Presiding Bishopric.

We encourage priesthood leaders to do all possible in strengthening the young men of the Church through the Aaronic Priesthood and the use of the Scouting program.

Sincerely yours,

THE FIRST PRESIDENCY
Spencer W. Kimball
N. Eldon Tanner
Marion G. Romney

National Bible Week

November 1, 1975

To all Stake and Mission Presidents in the United States

Dear Brethren:

As we approach National Bible Week, November 23–30, we suggest that you ask all bishops and branch presidents under your leadership to read at sacrament meeting the following statement on this observance:

> "America continues to be shaken by rising crime, widespread permissiveness, and the breakdown of far too many marriages and homes.
> "One positive way to combat these destructive forces is to lead our youth into a new appreciation of the scriptures.
> "In them they will find ways to build greater strengths in the home and in the individual. Also in the scriptures are time-tested keys to a personal happiness which endures.

"We therefore urge Latter-day Saints to fully support National Bible Week, November 23–30.

"Read the scriptures together as a family. Ponder them as individuals. Enjoy the scriptures at Family Home Evenings and otherwise.

"What a treasure of wisdom, inspiration, and practical suggestions for more abundant living are found in our Standard Works: the Bible, Book of Mormon, Doctrine and Covenants, and Pearl of Great Price!

"'For my soul delighteth in the scriptures . . .' wrote Nephi. (2 Nephi 4:15)

"Teach your family, beginning with yourself, to love the scriptures, to delight in them, and to realize that in them are the answers to most of the problems besetting this great nation today."

Encourage our people to turn more to the Lord's words. All of us so much need them to meet the daily challenges of today's world.

Sincerely yours,

THE FIRST PRESIDENCY
Spencer W. Kimball
N. Eldon Tanner
Marion G. Romney

Proper Conversion to the Gospel

January 3, 1977

To all Mission Presidents

Dear Brethren:

We are pleased with the great number of stable and sound converts who are coming into the Church, and we extend our highest commendation to you, your missionaries, and all who labor with you. Your devotion, sacrifice, and achievements are deeply appreciated. We hope and pray that through your continued labors, additional worthy and honest truth seekers will receive the blessings of the gospel.

As we begin this new year of missionary efforts, we might review the revealed requirements that our Heavenly Father's children should attain to qualify for baptism:

All those who humble themselves before God, and desire to be baptized, and come forth with broken hearts and contrite spirits, and witness before the Church that they have truly repented of all their sins, and are willing to take upon them the name of Jesus Christ, having a determination to serve him to the end, and truly manifest by their works that they have received of the Spirit of Christ unto the remission of their sins, shall be received by baptism into His Church. (D&C 20:37)

As part of the necessary preparation for baptism, investigators should come to a knowledge of Christ and the first principles of the gospel; they should have attended Church meetings and should feel a unity and oneness with Church members; and they should desire to love and serve God with all their hearts.

New members should be carefully fellowshipped and involved in suitable activity and service in Church programs to encourage their continued growth and understanding of the gospel.

We pray that the Lord will continue to bless and prosper you, your missionaries, and all those who labor with you, that the great harvest now underway will continue, all to the honor and glory of His name.

Sincerely,

THE FIRST PRESIDENCY
Spencer W. Kimball
N. Eldon Tanner
Marion G. Romney

Fast Day and Donation to the Needy of Africa

January 11, 1985

To General Authorities, Regional Representatives, Stake Presidents, Bishops and Branch Presidents in the United States and Canada

Dear Brethren:

People throughout the world have been touched by the portrayal in the media of the plight of many thousands of starving people in Africa. There are others in similar circumstances in other areas. We have sent funds to assist those in need. We now feel that our people would like to participate more extensively in the great humanitarian effort to assist those in Ethiopia, other areas of Africa, and perhaps in other parts of the world.

The First Presidency and the Council of the Twelve have accordingly determined that Sunday, January 27, should be designated as a special fast day when our people will be invited to refrain from partaking of two meals and contribute the equivalent value, or more, to the Church to assist those in need. All fast offering funds contributed on this day will be dedicated for the use of the victims of famine and other causes resulting in hunger and privation among people of Africa, and possibly in some other areas. They will be placed through agencies of unquestioned integrity.

The regular February fast day will be held on the first Sunday of the month as usual and funds contributed on that day will be used in the customary way to assist those in need in the Church. We repeat, however, that all funds contributed on January 27 will be earmarked particularly to assist the hungry and needy in distressed areas regardless of Church membership.

We shall appreciate your advising the people of your wards and stakes accordingly. This letter may be read in the Sacrament meetings of all wards and branches. We are confident that there will be a great outpouring from this effort.

Sincerely, your brethren,

THE FIRST PRESIDENCY
Spencer W. Kimball
Marion G. Romney
Gordon B. Hinckley

National Day of Fasting To Be Observed

November 15, 1985

To Area Presidencies in the United States

Dear Brethren:

Attached is a letter to priesthood leaders outlining the First Presidency's desire to have Church members participate in a National Day of Fasting and prayer for hunger relief on Sunday, November 24, 1985, as declared by Congress and the President of the United States. This letter will be sent from Church headquarters today. . . .

Priesthood leaders should be advised that—

1. Sunday, November 24, has been designated as a National Day of Fasting and prayer for hunger relief.

2. The First Presidency is encouraging Church members to join in this special day by fasting two meals on November 24 and contributing the equivalent value, or more, to hunger relief. It will be administered to the needy regardless of their church membership.

3. Instructions for forwarding contributions to Church headquarters are in the mail and will be received by priesthood leaders on November 18 or 19.

Thank you for your assistance in this very special undertaking.

Sincerely your brethren,

THE FIRST PRESIDENCY
Ezra Taft Benson
Gordon B. Hinckley
Thomas S. Monson

An Invitation to Come Back

December 23, 1985

To: All Stake Presidents

Dear Brethren:

There are members of the Church who have become inactive, or who have been disciplined, or who otherwise have become alienated from the Church. At this time of the year it is important that we reach out to all such persons to encourage them to return to full activity and thereby to enjoy all the blessings the Church affords.

You will find the enclosed statement from the First Presidency which was published in the December 22 issue of the Church News which elaborates on this theme. We request that you make copies of this statement available to all bishops and that you ask them to read the statement at a sacrament meeting. At that time the bishops should also encourage the members of the Church in attendance to reach out and to endeavor to reactivate those who may have become alienated.

Sincerely your brethren,

THE FIRST PRESIDENCY
Ezra Taft Benson
Gordon B. Hinckley
Thomas S. Monson

December 25, 1985

AN INVITATION

FROM THE FIRST PRESIDENCY OF THE CHURCH OF JESUS CHRIST OF LATTER-DAY SAINTS

Come back, Come back and

feast at the table of the Lord, and taste again

the sweet and satisfying fruits of

fellowship with the Saints.

We rejoice in the blessings that come of membership and activity in this Church whose head is the Son of God, the Lord Jesus Christ. In deep sincerity we express our love and gratitude for our brethren and sisters everywhere.

We are aware of some who are less active, of others who have become critical and are prone to find fault, and of those who have been disfellowshipped or excommunicated because of serious transgressions.

To all such we reach out in love. The Lord said: "I, the Lord, will forgive whom I will forgive, but of you it is required to forgive all men." (D&C 64:10)

We encourage members to forgive those who may have wronged them. To those who have ceased activity and to those who have become critical, we say, "Come back. Come back and feast at the table of the Lord, and taste again the sweet and satisfying fruits of fellowship with the saints."

We are confident that many have longed to return, but have felt awkward about doing so. We assure you that you will find open arms to receive you and willing hands to assist you.

We know there are many who carry heavy burdens of guilt and bitterness. To such we say, "Set them aside and give heed to the words of the Savior, who gave His life for the sins of all. 'Come unto me, all ye that are heavy laden, and I will give you rest.

"'Take my yoke upon you, and learn of me; for I am meek and lowly in heart; and ye shall find rest unto your souls.

"'For my yoke is easy, and my burden is light.'" (Matt. 11:28–30)

We plead with you. We pray for you. We invite and welcome you with love and appreciation.

Sincerely your brethren,

Ezra Taft Benson
Gordon B. Hinckley
Thomas S. Monson

Political Neutrality and Non-Use of Church Buildings

June 9, 1988

To General Authorities and the following priesthood leaders in the United States: Regional Representatives; Stake, Mission and District Presidents; Bishops; and Branch Presidents

Dear Brethren:

Political Neutrality (To be read in sacrament meeting.)

In this election year, we reiterate the long-standing policy of the Church of strict political neutrality, of not endorsing political candidates or parties in elections, and of not using Church facilities for political purposes, including voter registration.

The Church of Jesus Christ of Latter-day Saints does not favor one political party over another. We have no candidates for political office and we do not undertake to tell people how to vote.

We do urge all voters to involve themselves in the political process and to study carefully and prayerfully candidates' positions on issues and to vote for those who will most nearly carry out their views of government and its role.

The use of branch, ward, or stake premises, chapels or other Church facilities or equipment in any way for voter registration or political campaign purpose is contrary to our counsel and advice. This stricture applies to speech-making, class discussion, fund-raising, or preparation or distribution of campaign literature. Church directories or mailing lists should not be made available for any purpose to candidates for distribution of campaign literature or fund solicitation or to those involved in voter registration.

Those who attempt to use Church meetings or facilities or equipment to further their own or another's political ambitions injure their own cause and do the Church a disservice. We appeal, therefore, to all candidates for public office to take notice of this instruction and to conduct their campaigns in strict compliance with this requirement pertaining to use of Church facilities, equipment, meetings and membership lists.

We also call on all political candidates who are members of The Church of Jesus Christ of Latter-day Saints neither to state nor imply the endorsement of their candidacy by the Church or its leaders.

Sincerely your brethren,

THE FIRST PRESIDENCY
Ezra Taft Benson
Gordon B. Hinckley
Thomas S. Monson

Appendix 9

Letters of the Presiding Bishopric

The role and duties of the Presiding Bishopric of The Church of Jesus Christ of Latter-day Saints change as the Church grows and needs dictate. The following excerpts were selected from many available documents to illustrate a few of the responsibilities of the Presiding Bishopric.

Consecration of Property, 1832

Following is an excerpt from a formal document labeled a "Lease of inheritance in Jackson Co. and loan of property there." It is dated October 12, 1832, and signed by Edward Partridge, Bishop. A printed form was used; words in brackets indicate the handwritten parts. Spelling and punctuation are preserved as in the original.

BE IT KNOWN, THAT I, [Edward Partridge—]
Of Jackson county, and state of Missouri, bishop of the church of Christ, organized according to law, and established by the revelations of the Lord, on the 6th day of April, 1830, have leased, and by these presents do lease unto [Joseph Knight Junr] of Jackson county, and state of Missouri, a member of said church, the following described parcel of land, being a part of section No. [thirty three] township No. [forty nine] range No. [thirty three] situated in Jackson county, and state of Missouri, and is bounded as follows, viz:—
[Beginning forty two rods E. from the N. W. corner of S*d*. Sec. thence E. on the N. line of the S*d*. Sec ten rods, thence S. 5½″ W. thirty rods twenty one L. thence W. six rods to land leased to N. Knight, thence N. thirty six rods to the place of beginning, containing one acre and eighty one hundredths be the same more or less.]

And also have loaned the following described property, viz:— [Sundry articles of crockery, tinware, knives, forks and spoons valued nine dollars forty three cents,— Sundry articles of iron ware and household furniture valued twelve dollars ninety two cents,—one bed and bedding, valued nineteen dollars,—Sundry articles of clothing valued twenty two dollars thirteen cents,—grain valued seven dollars,—Sundry articles of joiner tools valued twenty dollars forty four cents,—one cow valued twelve dollars.

TO HAVE AND TO HOLD the above described property by him the said [Joseph Knight Junr.—] to be used and occupied as to him shall seem meet and proper. And as a consideration for the use of the above described property unto the said [Edward Partridge—] bishop of said church, or his successor in office, of myself and family. . . .

Spiritual Welfare of Young Men Ages 18 and Over

August 31, 1973

To all Stake Presidents, Mission and District Presidents, Bishops and Branch Presidents

Dear Brethren:

The October 1972 *Priesthood Bulletin* (item No. 1) contained the following policy statement:

> At the age of eighteen, Aaronic Priesthood bearers may be ordained to the office of an Elder in the Melchizedek Priesthood or transferred to the prospective elders program. If, in the judgment of the bishop, such qualifying circumstances as date of graduation from high school, individual maturation, or peer group association seem to indicate a need for a postponement, a young man may remain in the priests quorum until such circumstances change, or until the young man becomes nineteen.

This policy should be applied in the new correlated reporting system when determining the organization that is responsible for reporting the activities of eighteen-year-old men. If the eighteen-year-old is not ordained to the office of an elder, or transferred to the prospective elders program, he continues to be the responsibility of the priests quorum and is listed on the Priests Quorum roll. As soon as he reaches nineteen, he should either be ordained an elder, if worthy, or transferred to the prospective elders program. . . .

The prime concern of all leaders must be the welfare, spirituality and improvement of the individual.

Sincerely,

THE PRESIDING BISHOPRIC
Victor L. Brown
H. Burke Peterson
Vaughn J. Featherstone

Utah Flood Disaster Aid

14 June 1983

To Executive Administrators, Regional Representatives, Stake Presidents and Bishops in Utah

Dear Brethren:

As a result of the flood disaster in Utah each stake president and bishop should carefully apply the concepts outlined in the First Presidency's letter of 10 June 1983 entitled "Rebuilding and Giving Service Following Disasters." Give particular attention to:

"The responsibility for each members's spiritual, social, emotional, physical or economic well-being rests first with the member, second upon the family, and third, upon the Church."

When disaster assistance is requested by members, the bishop and stake president should handle these requests using normal procedures for obtaining and handling fast-offering funds as outlined in the *Church Financial Records* booklet. . . .

We trust this will help priesthood leaders administer fast-offering assistance where required and needed.

Sincerely your brethren,

THE PRESIDING BISHOPRIC
Victor L. Brown
H. Burke Peterson
J. Richard Clarke

Implementing the Budget Allowance Program; Sacred Nature of Tithing Funds

5 December 1989

To General Authorities, Regional Representatives, and Stake Presidents in the United States and Canada

Dear Brethren:

Local Unit Budget Allowance Program

On 15 November 1989 the First Presidency announced a new method of providing financial support for wards and stakes in the United States and Canada. This plan provides a budget allowance for stakes and wards from general Church funds and eliminates the need for local units to receive or to seek budget contributions from their members.

The announcement letter indicated additional instructions concerning the plan would be forthcoming. Attached are the materials priesthood leaders will need in order to implement the budget allowance program. . . .

Any questions concerning the program should first be directed to the stake president. In the event a question remains, stake presidents may make inquiry at Church headquarters. . . .

Church members should be reminded of the blessings associated with the payment of an honest tithe. They should also be encouraged to care for the poor by being generous in their fast offering contributions and should feel their responsibility to financially support missionary activities.

Tithing funds, by their very nature, are sacred. Priesthood and auxiliary leaders must be wise stewards over the budget allowance given them to ensure sacred funds are used to bless people and further gospel purposes. . . .

As this new program is implemented, all priesthood leaders are asked to be sensitive to the broad interests of the entire Church rather than the provincial concerns of a local unit.

May our Father in Heaven's blessings be with you as you implement this important new program and apply the principles associated with it.

Sincerely your brethren,

THE PRESIDING BISHOPRIC
Robert D. Hales
Henry B. Eyring
Glenn L. Pace

Guidelines for New Meetinghouse Projects

1 February 1991

To General Authorities, Regional Representatives, Stake and District Presidents, Bishops and Branch Presidents

Dear Brethren:

Approval has been given to new guidelines for local units to qualify for a meetinghouse project. These new guidelines are attached and are effective with the receipt of this letter.

Because of budget limitations, it is possible some requests for projects which fully meet the guidelines may not be undertaken when requested. Area Presidencies will give priority to projects within approved budgets. In some areas, Area Presidencies may also use additional requirements to assist in establishing priorities. . . .

These guidelines are designed to encourage priesthood leaders to use meetinghouse facilities more fully in meeting the Church's ever-expanding needs.

Sincerely your brethren,

THE PRESIDING BISHOPRIC
Robert D. Hales
Henry B. Eyring
Glenn L. Pace

Appendix 10

Lines of Priesthood Authority

This compilation shows the line of highest priesthood authority and date of ordination for those persons who have served as **Presidents of the Church, Counselors in the First Presidency,** and members of **The Quorum of the Twelve Apostles.** Everyone in the Church today holding the holy priesthood will be able to trace his line of authority to one or more of these persons.

The Three Witnesses to the Book of Mormon—Oliver Cowdery, David Whitmer, and Martin Harris—were appointed by revelation to choose the Twelve Apostles (D&C 18:37). The Three Witnesses were set apart for this purpose by the First Presidency—Joseph Smith, Sidney Rigdon, and Frederick G. Williams—on February 14, 1835 (HC 2:187).

Oliver Cowdery was with the Prophet Joseph Smith in 1829, when Peter, James and John conferred the Melchizedek Priesthood upon them and ordained them apostles. An 1829 revelation verifies that Oliver Cowdery and David Whitmer both held the apostolic office (D&C 18:9). Martin Harris was ordained to the High Priesthood on June 3, 1831 by Lyman Wight, who had been ordained to the High Priesthood that same day by Joseph the Prophet. President Rigdon was ordained to the High Priesthood by Lyman Wight, and President Williams by Joseph Smith and Oliver Cowdery.

Peter, James and John had been ordained apostles by Jesus Christ (John 15:16).

The three Witnesses were subsequently set apart by the First Presidency to ordain the Twelve. After the Three Witnesses had ordained the Twelve "to the apostleship," the First Presidency then laid their hands on the Twelve and confirmed the blessings and ordinations (from Heber C. Kimball's journal, published in T&S, vol. 6, #7, April 15, 1845, p. 868).

Tracing the Line of Authority. The person named in bold print identifies the person ordained. Regular type identifies the person who performed the ordination on the date indicated. Code: (A) = Apostle; (HP) = High Priest

Ashton, Marvin Jeremy (A)
Harold B. Lee, **December 2, 1971**

Ballard, Melvin Joseph (A)
Heber J. Grant, **January 7, 1919**

Ballard, Melvin Russell, Jr. (A)
Gordon B. Hinckley, **October 10, 1985**

Bennett, John Cook
Presented as assistant president with the First Presidency, **April 8, 1841**

Bennion, Adam Samuel (A)
David O. McKay, **April 9, 1953**

Benson, Ezra T. (A)
Brigham Young, **July 16, 1846**

Benson, Ezra Taft (A)
Heber J. Grant, **October 7, 1943**

Bowen, Albert Ernest (A)
Heber J. Grant, **April 8, 1937**

Boynton, John Farnham (A)
The Three Witnesses, **February 15, 1835**

Brown, Hugh Brown (A)
David O. McKay, **April 10, 1958**

Callis, Charles Albert (A)
Heber J. Grant, **October 12, 1933**

Cannon, Abraham Hoagland (A)
Joseph F. Smith, **October 7, 1889**

Cannon, George Quayle (A)
Brigham Young, **August 26, 1860**

Cannon, Sylvester Quayle (A)
Heber J. Grant, **April 14, 1938**

Carrington, Albert (A)
Brigham Young, **July 3, 1870**

Clark, Joshua Reuben, Jr. (HP) (A)
Called to First Presidency **April 6, 1933**, ordained
High Priest by Heber J. Grant, **April 13, 1933**, ordained Apostle by Heber J. Grant, **October 11,
1934**

Clawson, Rudger (A)
Lorenzo Snow, **October 10, 1898**

Cowdery, Oliver (A)
Peter, James, and John, **May-June 1829**

Cowley, Matthew (A)
George Albert Smith, **October 11, 1945**

Cowley, Matthias Foss (A)
George Q. Cannon, **October 7, 1897**

Dyer, Alvin Rulon (A)
David O. McKay, **October 5, 1967**
(Never served in the Quorum of the Twelve)

Evans, Richard Louis (A)
David O. McKay, **October 8, 1953**

Faust, James Esdras (A)
Spencer W. Kimball, **October 1, 1978**

Gause, Jesse
Ordained a counselor in the Presidency of the High
Priesthood by Joseph Smith, **March 8, 1832**

Grant, Heber Jeddy (A)
George Q. Cannon, **October 16, 1882**

Grant, Jedediah Morgan (A)
Brigham Young, **April 7, 1854**
(Never served in Quorum of the Twelve)

Haight, David Bruce (A)
Spencer W. Kimball, **January 8, 1976**

Hinckley, Alonzo Arza (A)
Heber J. Grant, **October 11, 1934**

Hinckley, Gordon Bitner (A)
David O. McKay, **October 5, 1961**

Hunter, Howard William (A)
David O. McKay, **October 15, 1959**

Hyde, Orson (A)
The Three Witnesses, **February 15, 1835**

Isaacson, Henry Thorpe Beal (HP)
Charles A. Callis, **October 1, 1941**

Ivins, Anthony Woodward (A)
Joseph F. Smith, **October 6, 1907**

Johnson, Luke S. (A)
The Three Witnesses, **February 15, 1835**

Johnson, Lyman Eugene (A)
The Three Witnesses, **February 14, 1835**

Kimball, Heber Chase (A)
The Three Witnesses, **February 14, 1835**

Kimball, Spencer Woolley (A)
Heber J. Grant, **October 7, 1943**

Law, William
Set apart as second counselor to President Joseph
Smith, **January 24, 1841**

Lee, Harold Bingham (A)
Heber J. Grant, **April 10, 1941**

Lund, Anthon Henrik (A)
George Q. Cannon, **October 7, 1889**

Lyman, Amasa Mason (A)
Brigham Young, **August 20, 1842**

Lyman, Francis Marion (A)
John Taylor, **October 27, 1880**

Lyman, Richard Roswell (A)
Joseph F. Smith, **April 7, 1918**

Marsh, Thomas Baldwin (A)
The Three Witnesses, **April 26, 1835**

Maxwell, Neal Ash (A)
Nathan Eldon Tanner, **July 23, 1981**

McConkie, Bruce Redd (A)
Harold B. Lee, **October 12, 1972**

McKay, David Oman (A)
Joseph F. Smith, **April 9, 1906**

McLellin, William E. (A)
Oliver Cowdery and David Whitmer, **February 15,
1835**

Merrill, Joseph Francis (A)
Heber J. Grant, **October 8, 1931**

Merrill, Marriner Wood (A)
Wilford Woodruff, **October 7, 1889**

Monson, Thomas Spencer (A)
Joseph Fielding Smith, **October 10, 1963**

Morris, George Quayle (A)
David O. McKay, **April 8, 1954**

Moyle, Henry Dinwoodey (A)
George Albert Smith, **April 10, 1947**

Nelson, Russell Marion (A)
Gordon B. Hinckley, **April 12, 1984**

Nibley, Charles Wilson (HP)
Joseph F. Smith, **June 9, 1901**

Oaks, Dallin Harris (A)
Gordon B. Hinckley, **May 3, 1984**

Packer, Boyd Kenneth (A)
Joseph Fielding Smith, **April 9, 1970**

Page, John Edward (Edmonds?) (A)
Brigham Young and Heber C. Kimball, **December
19, 1838**

Patten, David Wyman (A)
The Three Witnesses, **February 15, 1835**

Penrose, Charles William (A)
Joseph F. Smith, **July 7, 1904**

Perry, Lowell Tom (A)
Spencer W. Kimball, **April 11, 1974**

Petersen, Mark Edward (A)
Heber J. Grant, **April 20, 1944**

Pratt, Orson (A)
The Three Witnesses, **April 26, 1835**

Pratt, Parley Parker (A)
Joseph Smith, Oliver Cowdery, David Whitmer, **February 21, 1835**

Rich, Charles Coulsen (A)
Brigham Young, **February 12, 1849**

Richards, Franklin Dewey (A)
Heber C. Kimball, **February 12, 1849**

Richards, George Franklin (A)
Joseph F. Smith, **April 9, 1906**

Richards, LeGrand (A)
David O. McKay, **April 10, 1952**

Richards, Stephen L (A)
Joseph F. Smith, **January 18, 1917**

Richards, Willard (A)
Brigham Young, **April 14, 1840**

Rigdon, Sidney (HP)
Lyman Wight, **June 3, 1831**

Romney, Marion George (A)
David O. McKay, **October 11, 1951**

Scott, Richard Gordon (A)
Thomas S. Monson, **October 6, 1988**

Smith, George A. (A)
Heber C. Kimball, **April 26, 1839**

Smith, George Albert (A)
Joseph F. Smith, **October 8, 1903**

Smith, Hyrum (HP) (A)
Ordained HP by Joseph Smith, **June 3, 1831**; given all priesthood callings formerly held by Oliver Cowdery by Joseph Smith, about **January 19, 1841** (D&C 124:94–95)

Smith, Hyrum Mack (A)
Joseph F. Smith, **October 24, 1901**

Smith, John (HP)
Sidney Rigdon, **June 6, 1833**

Smith, John Henry (A)
Wilford Woodruff, **October 27, 1880**

Smith, Joseph (A)
Peter, James, and John, **May-June 1829**

Smith, Joseph, Sr. (HP)
Lyman Wight, **June 3, 1831**

Smith, Joseph F. (A)
Brigham Young, **July 1, 1866,**
sustained to Quorum of Twelve **October 8, 1867**

Smith, Joseph Fielding (A)
Joseph F. Smith, **April 7, 1910**

Smith, William (A)
The Three Witnesses, **February 15, 1835**

Smoot, Reed (A)
Lorenzo Snow, **April 8, 1900**

Snow, Erastus (A)
Brigham Young, **February 12, 1849**

Snow, Lorenzo (A)
Heber C. Kimball, **February 12, 1849**

Stapley, Delbert Leon (A)
George Albert Smith, **October 5, 1950**

Talmage, James Edward (A)
Joseph F. Smith, **December 8, 1911**

Tanner, Nathan Eldon (A)
David O. McKay, **October 11, 1962**

Taylor, John (A)
Brigham Young and Heber C. Kimball, **December 19, 1838**

Taylor, John Whittaker (A)
John Taylor, **April 9, 1884**

Teasdale, George (A)
John Taylor, **October 16, 1882**

Thatcher, Moses (A)
John Taylor, **April 9, 1879**

Wells, Daniel Hanmer (A)
Brigham Young, **January 4, 1857**
(Never served in Quorum of the Twelve)

Whitney, Orson Ferguson (A)
Joseph F. Smith, **April 9, 1906**

Widtsoe, John Andreas (A)
Heber J. Grant, **March 17, 1921**

Wight, Lyman (A)
Joseph Smith, **April 8, 1841**

Williams, Frederick Granger (HP)
Oliver Cowdery, **October 25, 1831**

Winder, John Rex (HP)
Edward Hunter, **March 4, 1872**

Wirthlin, Joseph Bitner (A)
Thomas S. Monson, **October 9, 1986**

Woodruff, Abraham Owen (A)
Wilford Woodruff, **October 7, 1897**

Woodruff, Wilford (A)
Brigham Young, **April 26, 1839**

Young, Brigham (A)
The Three Witnesses, **February 14, 1835**

Young, Brigham, Jr. (A)
Brigham Young, **February 4, 1864,**
sustained to Quorum of the Twelve **October 9, 1868**

Young, John Willard (A)
Brigham Young, **February 4, 1864**
(Never served in Quorum of the Twelve)

Young, Joseph Angell (A)
Brigham Young, **February 4, 1864**
(Never served in Quorum of the Twelve)

Appendix 11

Temple Dedicatory Prayers
(Excerpts)

The dedicatory prayers of the temples are inspired statements and sup- plications. The following selections illustrate important points of LDS doc- trine, especially related to the nature and importance of temples. The first LDS Temple in Kirtland, Ohio, was dedicated by the Prophet Joseph Smith and because the entire text is given as Doctrine and Covenants section 109, it is not included in this Appendix. Spelling and punctuation of the printed sources are preserved.

St. George Temple (First Temple in Utah)

Dedicatory prayer by President Daniel H. Wells, April 6, 1877

We thank Thee, O Lord, that Thy people . . . have been enabled to gather together the materials of which this building is composed; to put together and erect the same, even a Temple, which we dedicate and now consecrate to Thee that it may be holy unto Thee the Lord our God, for sacred and holy purposes and that the blessing, even life for evermore, may be commanded here from heaven, even from Thy presence, and may flow through the ordinances which appertain unto Thy holy place, unto us Thy children. We pray that the blessings pertaining to our eternal salvation and to the establishing of Thy Kingdom upon this, Thine earth, may be poured out upon Thy holy Priesthood and Thy people, who shall worship and offici- ate in this Thy Holy House. . . .

We pray that Thy blessing may attend those of Thy servants who admin- ister and who may officiate in the ordinances that may be performed therein in behalf of Thy people, and in behalf of those our progenitors, our relatives and friends, who have gone before us to the spirit world, so far as we may be enabled and permitted to officiate for them. We dedicate also to Thee the rooms of this building...for the purposes for which they may be used, by the Priesthood, for prayer, for worship, for councils or meetings, or for adminis- tering the Holy Ordinances of Thy House, that they may be holy unto Thee, the Lord Our God. . . .

Accept, O God, of this tribute of our hearts, and let Thy peace and blessing dwell and abide here in this Holy Temple, which we now, with uplifted hearts and hands, present and consecrate and dedicate entire as a sacred offering unto Thee for Thine acceptance. May it stand as a monument of purity and holiness as long as the earth shall remain, commemorative of Thy great goodness toward us, Thy People, and Thy name shall have the honor, the praise and glory, for we ask all in Jesus' name, and unto Thee and our blessed Lord and Savior, and to the Holy Spirit be all power, might and dominion worlds without end. Amen. [N. B. Lundwall, *Temples of the Most High*, pp. 79–83, Salt Lake City, 1947.]

Salt Lake Temple

Dedicated by President Wilford Woodruff, April 6, 1893

We thank Thee, O Thou Great Eloheim, that Thou didst raise up Thy servant, Joseph Smith through the loins of Abraham, Isaac and Jacob, and made him a Prophet, Seer, and Revelator, and through the assistance and administrations of angels from heaven Thou didst enable him to bring forth the Book of Mormon, the stick of Joseph, in the hand of Ephraim, in fulfillment of the prophecies of Isaiah and other prophets, which record has been translated and published in many languages. We also thank Thee, our Father in heaven, that Thou didst inspire Thy servant and give him power on the earth to organize Thy Church in this goodly land in all its fullness, power and glory, with Apostles, Prophets, Pastors and Teachers with all the gifts and graces belonging thereto and all this by the power of the Aaronic and Melchizedek Priesthood, which Thou didst bestow upon him by the administration of holy angels, who held that Priesthood in the days of the Savior. We thank Thee, our God, that Thou didst enable Thy servant Joseph to build two Temples, in which ordinances were administered for the living and the dead; that he also lived to send the Gospel to the nations of the earth and to the islands of the sea, and labored exceedingly until he was martyred for the word of God and the testimony of Jesus Christ.

We also thank Thee, O our Father in Heaven, that Thou didst raise up Thy servant Brigham Young, who held the keys of the Priesthood on the earth for many years, and who led Thy people to these valleys of the mountains, and laid the corner-stone of this great Temple. . . .

O Lord, we regard with intense and indescribable feelings the completion of this sacred house. Deign to accept this the fourth Temple which Thy covenant children have been assisted by Thee in erecting in these mountains. In past ages Thou didst inspire with Thy Holy Spirit Thy servants, the prophets, to speak of the time in the latter days when the mountain of the Lord's house should be established in the tops of the mountains, and should be exalted above the hills. We thank Thee that we have had the glorious opportunity of contributing to the fulfillment of these visions of Thine ancient Seers, and that Thou hast condescended to permit us to take part in the great work. And as this portion of Thy servants' words has thus so marvelously been brought to pass, we pray Thee, with increased faith and renewed hope, that all their words with regard to Thy great work in gathering Thine Israel and building up Thy kingdom on earth in the last days may be as amply fulfilled, and that, O Lord, speedily. . . .

And today we dedicate the whole [temple] unto Thee, with all that pertains unto it, that it may be holy in Thy sight; that it may be a house of prayer, a house of praise and of worship; that Thy glory may rest upon it; that Thy holy presence may be continually in it; that it may be the abode of Thy Well-Beloved Son, our Savior; that the angels who stand before Thy face may be the hallowed messengers who shall visit it, bearing to us Thy wishes and Thy will, that it may be sanctified and consecrated in all its parts holy unto Thee, the God of Israel, the Almighty Ruler of Mankind. And we pray Thee that all people who may enter upon the threshold of this, Thine House, may feel Thy power and be constrained to acknowledge that Thou hast sanctified it, that it is Thy House, a place of Thy holiness. . . .

O Thou God of our fathers Abraham, Isaac, and Jacob, whose God Thou delightest to be called, we thank Thee with all the fervor of overflowing gratitude that Thou hast revealed the powers by which the hearts of the children are being turned to their fathers, and the hearts of the fathers to the children, that the sons of men, in all their generations can be made partakers of the glories and joys of the kingdom of heaven. Confirm upon us the spirit of Elijah, we pray Thee, that we may thus redeem our dead and also connect ourselves with our fathers who have passed behind the veil, and furthermore seal up our dead to come forth in the first resurrection, that we who dwell on the earth may be bound to those who dwell in heaven. We thank Thee for their sake who have finished their work in mortality, as well as for our own, that the prison doors have been opened, that deliverance has been proclaimed to the captive, and the bonds have been loosened from those who were bound. We praise Thee that our fathers from last to first, from now, back to the beginning, can be united with us in indissoluble links, welded by the Holy Priesthood and that as one great family united in Thee and cemented by Thy power, we shall together stand before Thee, and by the power of the atoning blood of Thy Son be delivered from all evil, be saved and sanctified, exalted and glorified. Wilt Thou also permit holy messengers to visit us within these sacred walls and make known unto us with regard to the work we should perform in behalf of our dead. And, as Thou has inclined the hearts of many who have not yet entered into covenant with Thee to search out their progenitors, and in so doing they have traced the ancestry of many of Thy Saints, we pray Thee that Thou wilt increase this desire in their bosoms, that they may in this way aid in the accomplishment of Thy work. Bless them, we pray Thee, in their labors, that they may not fall into errors in preparing their genealogies; and furthermore, we ask Thee to open before them new avenues of information and place in their hands the records of the past, that their work may not only be correct but complete also. . . .

And now, our Father, we bless Thee, we praise Thee, we glorify Thee, we worship Thee, day by day we magnify Thee, and give Thee thanks for Thy great goodness towards us, Thy children, and we pray Thee, in the name of Thy Son Jesus Christ, our Savior, to hear these our humble petitions, and answer us from heaven, Thy holy dwelling place where Thou sittest enthroned in glory, might, majesty, and dominion, and with an infinitude of power which we, Thy mortal creatures, cannot imagine, much less comprehend. Amen and Amen. [Lundwall, *Temples of the Most High*, pp. 126–36, Salt Lake City, 1947.]

Hawaii Temple (First Outside of North America)

Dedicated by President Heber J. Grant, November 27, 1919

We thank Thee, O God, the Eternal Father, that Thou and Thy Son, Jesus Christ, didst visit the boy, Joseph Smith, Jr., and that he was instructed by Thee and Thy beloved Son.

We thank Thee that Thou didst send Thy servant, John the Baptist, and that he did lay his hands upon Joseph Smith and Oliver Cowdery and ordain them to the Aaronic, or Lesser, Priesthood.

We thank Thee for sending Thy servants Peter, James and John, Apostles of the Lord Jesus Christ who ministered with the Savior in the flesh and after His crucifixion, and that they did ordain Thy servants Joseph Smith and Oliver Cowdery apostles of the Lord Jesus Christ, and bestowed upon them the Holy Melchizedek Priesthood, by which Authority and Apostleship we do dedicate unto Thee, this day, this holy edifice.

We thank Thee for the integrity and devotion of Thy servants, the Prophet and the Patriarch, Joseph Smith and Hyrum Smith. We thank Thee that they labored all the days of their lives, from the time of the restitution of the Gospel of Jesus Christ until the day of their martyrdom, and that they sealed their testimony with their blood. . . .

We thank Thee that the plates containing the Book of Mormon were preserved so that they could be translated, and that Thy words to the Prophet Joseph Smith might be fulfilled; namely, That the Lamanites might come to the knowledge of their fathers, and that they might know the promises of the Lord, and that they may believe the Gospel and rely upon the merits of Jesus Christ, and be glorified through faith in His name, and that through their repentance, they might be saved.

We thank Thee, that thousands and tens of thousands of the descendants of Lehi, in this favored land, have come to a knowledge of the gospel, many of whom have endured faithfully to the end of their lives. We thank Thee, our Father and our God, that those who are living and who have embraced the gospel are now to have the privilege of entering into this holy house and laboring for the salvation of the souls of their ancestors. . . .

We also thank Thee for sending Thy servants, Moses, and Elias, and Elijah, to the Kirtland temple, and delivering to Thy servants, Joseph and Oliver the keys of every dispensation of the gospel of Jesus Christ from the days of Father Adam down to the present dispensation, which is the dispensation of the fulness of times.

We thank Thee, that Elijah has appeared and that the prophecy of Thy servant Malachi, that the hearts of the fathers should be turned to the children, and the hearts of the children to the fathers, lest the earth be smitten with a curse, has been fulfilled in our day, and that our hearts in very deed, go out to our fathers; and we rejoice beyond our ability to express that we can, through the ordinances of the gospel of Jesus Christ, become saviors of our ancestors. . . .

. . . We have dedicated this House unto Thee, by virtue of the Priesthood of the Living God which we hold, and we most earnestly pray that this sacred building may be a place in which Thou shalt delight to pour out Thy Holy Spirit in great abundance, and in which Thy Son may see fit to manifest Himself and to instruct Thy servants. In the name of Jesus Christ, our Redeemer. Amen and Amen. [Lundwall, *Temples of the Most High*, pp. 151–59, Salt Lake City, 1947.]

Swiss Temple (First Temple in Europe)

Dedicated by President David O. McKay, September 11, 1955

O Father, we sense that the crying need of the world today is acceptance of Jesus Christ and his Gospel to counteract false teachings that now disturb the peace of honest men and women, and which undermine the faith of millions whose belief in Thee has been faltering and unstable, because they have not yet had presented unto them the eternal Plan of Salvation.

Guide us, O God, in our efforts to hasten the day when humanity will renounce contention and strife, when nation shall not lift up sword against nation, neither shall they learn war any more.

To this end bless the leaders of nations that their hearts may be cleared of prejudices, suspicion, and avarice, and filled with a desire for peace and righteousness.

As one means of uniting the children in the bond of peace and love, this Temple and other Holy Houses of the Lord are erected in thy Name.

Help Thy people to realize that only by Obedience to the eternal principles and ordinances of the Gospel may loved ones who died without baptism be permitted the glorious privilege of entrance into the Kingdom of God. Increase our desire, O Father, to put forth even greater effort toward the consummation of Thy purpose to bring to pass the immortality and eternal life of all thy children. This edifice is one more means to aid in bringing about this divine consummation. . . .

May this building ever be held sacred, that all who enter may feel a peaceful and hallowed influence, and may those who pass the grounds whether members or non-members of the Church feel a hallowed influence and substitute for a doubt or possible sneer in their minds, a prayer in their hearts.

Now, O God, Our Heavenly Eternal Father, the faithful membership of thy Church, through love for Thee and thy children, have erected to Thee by tithes and offerings this Holy House in which shall be performed ordinances and ceremonies pertaining to the happiness and salvation of thy children living in mortality and in the Spirit World.

Accept of our offering, hallow it by Thy Holy Spirit and protect it from destructive elements and the bitterness of ignorance and wickedness of bigoted hearts until its divine purposes shall have been consummated; and Thine be the glory, honor, and praise forever, through Jesus Christ, our Lord and Savior, Amen and Amen! [*Church News*, p. 4, September 17, 1955.]

New Zealand Temple (First Temple in South Pacific)

Dedicated by President David O. McKay, April 20, 1958

We express gratitude that to these fertile islands Thou didst guide descendants of Father Lehi, and hast enabled them to prosper, to develop, and to become associated in history with leading and influential nations among mankind. [*Church News*, pp. 2, 6, May 10, 1958.]

London Temple

Dedicated by President David O. McKay, September 7, 1958

O God, our Heavenly Father, Thou who hast created all things, whose Plans Infinite and Progressive, ever serve to foster closer relationship between Thee and the human family. We, Thy children assemble before Thee this day in gratitude and praise. Thou hast said that Thy work and Thy Glory is "to bring to pass the immortality and eternal life of man."

Therefore, human beings are engaged in life's highest activity when they cooperate with Thee in bringing about this consummation. . . . Temples are but one means of man's cooperation with Thee in accomplishing this divine purpose. . . .

When in the Middle Ages the Church departed from Christ's teachings, Thou didst inspire honest, upright men here in Great Britain to raise their voices against corrupt practices. Mingling with the denunciatory messages of Luther and Melanchthon in Germany, and Zwingli in Switzerland, were the voices of George Wishart, and later John Knox of Scotland. We thank Thee that before the scorching flames silenced his tongue and reduced his body to ashes Thou didst permit George Wishart to glimpse that: "This Realm shall be illuminated with the light of Christ's Evangel as clearly as ever was any Realm since the days of the Apostles. The house of God shall be builded in it; yea, it shall not lack the very capstone."

Much clearer was the inspiration given President Wilford Woodruff, and President Joseph F. Smith, and other more recent Apostles, who stated prophetically that: "Temples of God . . . will be erected in the divers countries of the earth," and that "Temples will appear all over the land of Joseph—North and South America—and also in Europe and elsewhere; and all the descendants of Shem, Ham, and Japheth, who received not the Gospel in the flesh, must be officiated for in the temples of God, before the Savior can present the kingdom to the Father, saying, "It is finished." [*Church News*, p. 3, September 13, 1958.]

Provo Utah Temple

Dedicated by President Harold B. Lee, February 9, 1972

O God, the Eternal Father, the Creator of heaven and earth and all things that in them are; Thou Man of Holiness who hast created us, Thy children in Thine own image and likeness, and endowed us with power and agency to follow Thee; Thou who knowest all things and hast all power, all might, and all dominion; Thou who created the universe and ruleth with justice and equity and mercy over all the works of Thy hands—hallowed be Thy great and holy name! . . .

O our Father, we seek to be like Thee; we seek to pattern our lives after the life of Thy Son; we desire righteousness, for ourselves and our children and our children's children; we turn our faces to this holy house; and we plead with Thee to make us worthy to inherit the fulness of those blessings found only in Thy holy temples—even those blessings which grow out of the continuation of the family unit forever.

Thou knowest, O Father, that we seek these blessings, not only for ourselves and our descendants, but also for our forebears; for Thou hast said that we, as saviors on Mount Zion, have power to save and redeem our worthy dead; we seek so to do, and we plead for Thy guidance and directing light as we go forward in this work—one of the greatest ever revealed to the children of men in any age of the earth. . . .

We thank Thee, O our God, that Thou didst ordain and establish the Constitution of the United States "by the hands of wise men whom" Thou didst raise up unto this very purpose. We thank Thee for the freedoms and "rights and privileges" which are guaranteed to us in this sacred document and pray that they may be established forever. . . .

Let that great temple of learning, The Brigham Young University, and all that is associated with it, and all other church schools, institutes, and seminaries—be prospered to the full. . . .

May those who teach and study in all academic fields have their souls enlightened with spiritual knowledge, so they will turn to Thy house for blessings and knowledge and learning that surpass all that may be found elsewhere.

. . . acting in the authority of that priesthood which is after the order of Thy Son and in His Holy Name, we dedicate this Temple unto Thee, the Lord.

We dedicate it as a house of baptism, a house of endowment, a house of marriage, and a house of righteousness, for the living and the dead. . . .

O Lord God of our fathers, who sitteth upon Thy throne, and who liveth, and reigneth over all things—blessed be Thy Holy Name, both now and forever.

In the name of the Lord Jesus Christ, Thine Only Son, even so, amen and amen. [*Church News*, pp. 4–5, February 12, 1972.]

Washington [D.C.] Temple

Dedicated by President Spencer W. Kimball, November 19, 1974

Father, we are concerned with the political world of today, and that nations seem to need only the lighting of a match to bring war and desolation and destruction. Bless, we pray Thee, the leaders of nations, that they may rule wisely and righteously, and give Thy people freedom to worship Thee in truth and righteousness. Stay the powers, our Father, that would bring us to the brink of annihilation. . . .

Our Gracious Father, there are national gates which seemingly need to be unlocked and doors that need to be opened, and hearts of kings, presidents, emperors, and ministers, which need to be softened, that they may permit the gospel to be taken to their people.

Our Father, bless the countless millions in the world, that they may receive Thy truth, and bless the missionaries on whom the sun never sets, that nothing will prevail against them in their faithful presentation of Thy gospel to the world, and bless especially, our Father, the children of Thy people in overseas countries, that they may devote their sons to this holy work. Wherein we have failed, help us to see our duties; wherein we have been prevented, open the doors, we pray, and swing the gates wide open and let Thy servants cover the earth with their testimonies. [*Church News*, p. 5, November 23, 1974.]

Mexico City Temple

Dedicated by President Gordon B. Hinckley, December 2, 1983

Bless thy saints in this great land and those from other lands who will use this temple. Most have in their veins the blood of Father Lehi. Thou hast kept thine ancient promise. Many thousands "that walked in darkness have seen a great light." (Isaiah 9:2) May the harvest that we have witnessed here foreshadow greater things to come as Thy work rolls on in power and majesty in this, the dispensation of the fulness of times. [*Church News,* pp. 4–5, December 11, 1983.]

Freiberg Germany Temple (First in Eastern Europe)

Dedicated by President Gordon B. Hinckley, June 29, 1985

We are met here today as people of various nations bound by a common love for thee our Father and thy Son, the Redeemer of all mankind. We thank Thee for the peace which makes this possible and for the hospitality of this nation in permitting us to join together in this house of sacred worship. Our hearts are touched by the bond of fellowship we feel one with another. Strengthen that bond, and may we reach out in a spirit of love and appreciation and respect for one another. This gospel, which so deeply touches our lives, is the gospel of peace. May we grow in knowledge and understanding of thine everlasting plan for thy children, thy sons and daughters of all nations. . . .

Father, we thank thee for the measure of peace to be found in the world, and pray that it may continue and grow that men and women everywhere may use their time, their talents, and their means for good. May understanding and respect increase between the nations of the earth. [*Church News,* p. 5, June 30, 1985.]

Johannesburg South Africa Temple

Dedicated by President Gordon B. Hinckley, August 24, 1985

We thank thee for the dimensions of thy Church in this nation of South Africa. We thank thee for men and women of great strength who constitute its membership, for the goodness of their lives, for the manner in which thou hast enlightened their minds and quickened their understanding of thy ways and thy purposes. Many of them, dear Father, sacrificed much in years past to travel afar to partake of those blessings which are available only in the Lord's House. . . .

Wilt thou whisper peace to thy people by the power of thy Spirit when they come here with burdened hearts to seek direction in their perplexities. Wilt thou comfort and sustain them when they come in times of sorrow. Wilt thou give them courage, direction, and faith, when they gather, as to a refuge, from the turmoil of the world. Wilt thou reassure them of thy reality and divinity, and of the reality and divinity of thy resurrected Son. Wilt Thou endow them with love in their hearts for their ancestors who have gone before and with a great desire to labor in behalf of these their forebears.

Almighty God, wilt thou overrule for the blessing and safety of thy faithful saints. We pray for peace in this troubled land. Bless this nation which has befriended thy servants. May those who rule in the offices of government be inspired to find a basis for reconciliation among those who now are in conflict one with another. May the presence of thy house on the soil of this land bring blessings to the entire nation. [*Church News,* p. 5, 1 September 1985.]

Appendix 12

The Wentworth Letter

The Prophet Joseph Smith explained the origin of the WENTWORTH LETTER as follows:

> At the request of Mr. John Wentworth, Editor and Proprietor of the *Chicago Democrat*, I have written the following sketch of the rise, progress, persecution, and faith of the Latter-day Saints, of which I have the honor, under God, of being the founder. Mr. Wentworth says that he wishes to furnish Mr. Bastow [Barstow?], a friend of his, who is writing the history of New Hampshire, with this document. As Mr. Bastow has taken the proper steps to obtain correct information, all that I shall ask at his hands, is, that he publish the account entire, ungarnished, and without misrepresentation. [*Times and Seasons*, III, #9, p. 706.]

Following is the complete text of the letter as published in the *Times and Seasons*, III, 9, 706–710, March 1, 1842, Nauvoo, Illinois. (Original spelling and punctuation are preserved; however, obvious errors are corrected in brackets.)

> I was born in the town of Sharon Windsor co., Vermont, on the 23d of December, A.D. 1805. When ten years old my parents removed to Palmyra New York, where we resided about four years, and from thence we removed to the town of Manchester.
>
> My father was a farmer and taught me the art of husbandry. When about fourteen years of age, I began to reflect upon the importance of being prepared for a future state, and upon inquiring the plan of salvation, I found that there was a great clash in religious sentiment; if I went to one society they referred me to one plan, and another to another; each one pointing to his own particular creed as the summum bonum of perfection: considering that all could not be right, and that God could not be the author of so much confusion I determined to investigate the subject more fully, believing that if God had a church it would not be split up into factions, and that if he taught one society to worship one way, and administer in one set of ordinances, he would not teach another, principles which were diametrically opposed. Believing the word of God I had confidence in the declaration of James; "If any man lack wisdom let him ask of God who giveth to all men liberally and upbraideth not and it shall be given him," I retired to a secret place in a grove and began to call upon the Lord, while fervently engaged in supplication my mind was taken away from the objects with which I was surrounded, and I was enwrapped in a heavenly vision, and saw two glorious personages, who exactly resembled each other in features and likeness, surrounded with a brilliant light which eclipsed the sun at noon-day. They told me that all religious denominations were believing in incorrect doctrines, and that none of them was acknowledged of God as his Church and kingdom. And I was expressly commanded to "go not after them," at the same time receiving a promise that the fulness of the Gospel should at some future time be made known unto me.

On the evening on the 21st of September, A.D. 1823, while I was praying unto God, and endeavoring to exercise faith in the precious promises of scripture on a sudden a light like that of day, only of a far purer and more glorious appearance and brightness burst into the room, indeed the first sight was as though the house was filled with consuming fire; the appearance produced a shock that affected the whole body; in a moment a personage stood before me surrounded with a glory yet greater than that with which I was already surrounded. This messenger proclaimed himself to be an angel of God, sent to bring the joyful tidings, that the covenant which God made with ancient Israel was at hand to be fulfilled, that the preparatory work for the second coming of the Messiah was speedily to commence; that the time was at hand for the gospel in all its fulness to be preached in power, unto all nations that a people might be prepared for the millennial reign.

I was informed that I was chosen to be an instrument in the hands of God to bring about some of his purposes in this glorious dispensation.

I was also informed concerning the aboriginal inhabitants of this country, and shown who they were, and from whence they came; a brief sketch of their origin, progress, civilization, laws, governments, of their righteousness and iniquity, and the blessings of God being finally withdrawn from them as a people, was made known unto me; I was also told where were deposited some plates on which were engraven an abridgment of the records of the ancient prophets that had existed on this continent. The angel appeared to me three times the same night and unfolded the same things. After having received many visits from the angels of God unfolding the majesty, and glory of the events that should transpire in the last days, on the morning of the 22d of September, A.D. 1827, the angel of the Lord delivered the records into my hands.

These records were engraven on plates which had the appearance of gold, each plate was six inches wide and eight inches long, and not quite so thick as common tin. They were filled with engravings, in Egyptian characters and bound together in a volume as the leaves of a book with three rings running through the whole. The volume was something near six inches in thickness, a part of which was sealed. The characters on the unsealed part were small, and beautifully engraved. The whole book exhibited many marks of antiquity in its construction and much skill in the art of engraving. With the records was found a curious instrument which the ancients called "Urim and Thummim," which consisted of two transparent stones set in the rim of a bow fastened to a breast plate.

Through the medium of the Urim and Thummim I translated the record by the gift and power of God.

In this important and interesting book the history of ancient America is unfolded, from its first settlement by a colony that came from the Tower of Babel, at the confusion of languages to the beginning of the fifth century of the Christian era. We are informed by these records that America in ancient times has been inhabited by two distinct races of people. The first were called Jaredites, and came directly from the tower of Babel. The second race came directly from the city of Jerusalem, about six hundred years before Christ. They were principally Israelites, of the descendants of Joseph. The Jaredites were destroyed about the time that the Israelites came from Jerusalem, who succeeded them in the inheritance of the country. The principal nation of the second race fell in battle towards the close of the fourth century. The remnant are the Indians that now inhabit this country. This book also tells us that our Saviour made his appearance upon this continent after his resurrection, that he planted the gospel here in all its fulness, and richness, and power, and blessing; that they had apostles, prophets, pastors, teachers, and evangelists; the same order, the same priesthood, the same ordinances, gifts, powers, and blessings, as was enjoyed on the eastern continent, that the people were cut off in consequence of their transgressions, that the last of their prophets who existed among them was commanded to write an abridgment of their prophecies, history, &c., and to hide it up in the earth, and that it should come forth and be united with the bible for the accomplishment of the purposes of God in the last days. For a more particular account I would refer to the Book of Mormon, which can be purchased at Nauvoo, or from any of our traveling elders.

As soon as the news of this discovery was made known, false reports, misrepresentation and slander flew as on the wings of the wind, in every direction, the house was frequently beset by mobs, and evil designing persons, several times I was shot at, and very narrowly escaped, and every device was made use of to get the plates away from me, but the power and blessing of God attended me, and several began to believe my testimony.

On the 6th of April, 1830, the "Church of Jesus Christ of Latter-Day Saints," was first organized in the town of Manchester, Ontario co., [Fayette, Seneca County] state of New York. Some few were called and ordained by the Spirit of revelation, and prophecy, and began to preach as the spirit gave them utterance, and though weak, yet were they strengthened by the power of God, and many were brought to repentance, were immersed in the water, and were filled with the Holy Ghost by the laying on of hands. They saw visions and prophesied, devils were cast out, and the sick healed by the laying on of hands. From that time the work rolled forth with astonishing rapidity, and churches were soon formed in the states of New York, Pennsylvania, Ohio, Indiana, Illinois, and Missouri; in the last named state a considerable settlement was formed in Jackson co.; numbers joined the Church and we were increasing rapidly; we made large purchases of land, our farms teemed with plenty, and peace and happiness was enjoyed in our domestic circle and throughout our neighborhood; but as we could not associate with our neighbors who were, many of them, of the basest of men, and had fled from the face of civilized society, to the frontier country to escape the hand of justice, in their midnight revels, their sabbath breaking, horse-racing and gambling; they commenced at first ridicule, then to persecute and finally an organized mob assembled and burned our houses, tarred, and feathered, and whipped many of our brethren and finally drove them from their habitations; who, houseless, and homeless, contrary to law, justice and humanity, had to wander on the bleak prairies till the children left the tracks of their blood on the prairie, this took place in the month of November, and they had no other covering but the canopy of heaven, in this inclement season of the year; this proceeding was winked at by the government, and although we had warrantee deeds for our land, and had violated no law we could obtain no redress.

There were many sick, who were thus inhumanly driven from their houses, and had to endure all this abuse and to seek homes where they could be found. The result was, that a great many of them being deprived of the comforts of life, and the necessary attendances, died; many children were left orphans, wives, widows and husbands, widowers. Our farms were taken possession of by the mob, many thousands of cattle, sheep, horses and hogs were taken and our household goods, store goods, and printing press and type were broken, taken, or otherwise destroyed.

Many of our brethren removed to Clay where they continued until 1836, three years; there was no violence offered, but there were threatenings of violence. But in the summer of 1836 these threatenings began to assume a more serious form; from threats, public meetings were called, resolutions were passed, vengeance and destruction were threatened, and affairs again assumed a fearful attitude, Jackson County was a sufficient precedent, and as the authorities in that county did not interfere, they boasted that they would not in this, which on application to the authorities we found to be too true, and after much violence, privation and loss of property we were again driven from our homes.

We next settled in Caldwell, and Daviess counties, where we made large and extensive settlements, thinking to free ourselves from the power of oppression, by settling in new counties, with very few inhabitants in them; but here we were not allowed to live in peace, but in 1838 we were again attacked by mobs, an exterminating order was issued by Gov. Boggs, and under the sanction of law an organized banditti ranged through the country, robbed us of our cattle, sheep, hogs, &c., many of our people were murdered in cold blood, the chastity of our women was violated, and we were forced to sign away our property at the point of the sword, and after enduring every indignity that could be heaped upon us by an inhuman, ungodly band of marauders, from twelve to fifteen thousand souls, men, women, and children were driven from their own fire sides, and from lands that they had warrantee deeds of, houseless, friendless, and homeless (in the depths of winter,) to wander as exiles on the earth or to seek an asylum in a more genial clime, and among a less barbarous people.

Many sickened and died, in consequence of the cold, and hardships they had to endure; many wives were left widows, and children orphans, and destitute. It would take more time than is allotted me here to describe the injustice, the wrongs, the murders, the bloodshed, the theft, misery and woe that have been caused by the barbarous, inhuman, and lawless proceedings of the state of Missouri.

In the situation before alluded to we arrived in the state of Illinois in 1839, where we found a hospitable people and a friendly home; a people who were willing to be governed by the principles of law and humanity. We have commenced to build a city called "Nauvoo," in Hancock co., we number from six to eight thousand here, besides vast numbers in the county around and in almost every county of the state. We have a city charter granted us and charter for a legion the troops of which now number 1500. We have also a charter for a university, for an agricultural and manufacturing society, have our own laws and administrators, and possess all the privileges that other free and enlightened citizens enjoy.

Persecution has not stopped the progress of truth, but has only added fuel to the flame, it has spread with increasing rapidity, proud of the cause which they have espoused, and conscious of our innocence, and of the truth of their system, amidst calumny and reproach have the elders of this church gone forth, and planted the gospel in almost every state in the Union; it has penetrated our cities, it has spread over our villages, and has caused thousands of our intelligent, noble, and patriotic citizens to obey its divine mandates, and be governed by its sacred truths. It has also spread into England, Ireland, Scotland, and Wales: in the year of 1839 [1840] where a few of our missionaries were sent, and over five thousand joined the standard of truth; there are numbers now joining in every land.

Our missionaries are going forth to different nations, and in Germany, Palestine, New Holland, the East Indies, and other places, the standard of truth has been erected; no unhallowed hand can stop the work from progressing; persecutions may rage, mobs may combine, armies may assemble, calumny may defame, but the truth of God will go forth boldly, nobly, and independent, till it has penetrated every continent, visited every clime, swept every country, and sounded in every ear, till the purposes of God shall be accomplished and the great Jehovah shall say the work is done.

We believe in God the Eternal Father, and in his son Jesus Christ, and in the Holy Ghost.

We believe that men will be punished for their own sins and not for Adam's transgression.

We believe that through the atonement of Christ all mankind may be saved by obedience to the laws and ordinances of the Gospel.

We believe that these ordinances are: 1st, Faith in the Lord Jesus Christ; 2d, Repentance; 3d, Baptism by immersion for the remission of sins; 4th, Laying on of hands for the gift of the Holy Ghost.

We believe that a man must be called of God by "prophesy and by the laying on hands" by those who are in authority to preach the gospel and administer in the ordinances thereof.

We believe in the same organization that existed in the primitive Church, viz: apostles, prophets, pastors, teachers, evangelists &c.

We believe in the gift of tongues, prophecy, revelation, visions, healing, interpretation of tongues, &c.

We believe the Bible to be the word of God as far as it is translated correctly; we also believe the Book of Mormon to be the word of God.

We believe all that God has revealed, all that he does now reveal, and we believe that he will yet reveal many great and important things pertaining to the kingdom of God.

We believe in the literal gathering of Israel and in the restoration of the Ten Tribes. That Zion will be built upon this continent. That Christ will reign personally upon the earth, and that the earth will be renewed and receive its paradasaic glory.

We claim the privilege of worshiping Almighty God according to the dictates of our conscience, and allow all men the same privilege let them worship how, where, or what they may.

We believe in being subject to kings, presidents, rulers and magistrates, in obeying honoring, and sustaining the law.

We believe in being honest, true, chaste, benevolent, virtuous, and in doing good to *all men*; indeed we may say that we follow the admonition of Paul, "we believe all things, we hope all things," we have endured many things, and hope to be able to endure all things. If there is anything virtuous, lovely, or of good report, or praiseworthy, we seek after these things. Respectfully, &c.,

JOSEPH SMITH.

See also: Jessee, Dean C. (comp. and ed.). *The Personal Writings of Joseph Smith*, pp. 212–220, Salt Lake City, 1984. Jessee also includes other background information to the letter.

Appendix 13

Church Membership Figures
as of January 1, 1991

THE CHURCH IN THE WORLD

Geographical Area	Members	Missions	Stakes/Districts	Wards and Branches
Africa	52,000	9	7/24	232
Asia	443,000	31	84/87	1,267
Canada	128,000	6	34/8	378
Europe	148,000	30	39/44	735
Mexico and Central America	869,000	27	166/79	2,053
Oceania	266,000	12	59/32	739
Scandinavia	21,000	5	7/11	117
South America	1,359,000	43	217/164	2,823
United Kingdom and Ireland	152,000	8	40/2	325
United States	4,267,000	79	1,123/17	9,202
West Indies	56,000	6	7/11	182
Other Countries	900	0	1/0	17
Totals:	7,762,000	256	1,784/479	18,070

(Asterisks indicate fewer than 100 members. Subtotals may not agree due to rounding.)

THE CHURCH IN AFRICA

Countries	Members	Missions	Stakes/Districts	Wards and Branches
Egypt	*	0	0/1	1
Ghana	9,000	1	0/5	39
Ivory Coast	600	0	0/1	6
Kenya	*	0	0/0	0
Lesotho	100	0	0/0	1
Liberia	1,100	1	0/1	10
Mauritius	200	0	0/0	1
Morocco	*	0	0/0	1
Namibia	*	0	0/0	1
Nigeria	17,000	2	2/9	77
Reunion	400	1	0/1	3

THE CHURCH IN AFRICA (*continued*)

Countries	Members	Missions	Stakes/Districts	Wards and Branches
Sierra Leone	200	0	0/0	3
Somalia	*	0	0/0	1
South Africa	19,000	2	5/2	57
Swaziland	300	0	0/0	1
Tunisia	*	0	0/0	1
Zaire	2,000	1	0/2	13
Zimbabwe	2,300	1	0/2	16
Totals:	52,000	9	7/24	232

THE CHURCH IN ASIA

Countries	Members	Missions	Stakes/Districts	Wards and Branches
Burma	*	0	0/0	1
China	*	0	0/0	3
Cyprus	*	0	0/0	1
Diego Garcia	*	0	0/0	1
Hong Kong	18,000	1	4/0	27
India	900	0	0/3	9
Indonesia	4,200	0	0/3	18
Japan	96,000	10	23/15	265
Korea, Republic	59,000	4	14/4	147
Macau	300	0	0/0	1
Malaysia	400	0	0/1	5
Pakistan	*	0	0/0	2
Papua New Guinea	2,500	0	0/1	13
Philippines	237,000	12	40/52	694
Singapore	1,600	1	0/1	5
Soviet Union	*	0	0/0	3
Sri Lanka	100	0	0/0	1
Taiwan	18,000	2	3/3	47
Thailand	4,200	1	0/3	19
Turkey	200	0	0/1	5
Totals:	443,000	31	84/87	1,267

THE CHURCH IN CANADA

Provinces or Territories	Members	Missions	Stakes/Districts	Wards and Branches
Alberta	56,000	1	16/1	159
British Columbia	24,000	1	5/3	68
Manitoba	3,700	1	1/0	9
New Brunswick	2,100	0	1/0	10
Newfoundland	500	0	0/0	3
Northwest Terr.	100	0	0/0	1
Nova Scotia	3,800	1	1/0	14
Ontario	28,000	1	7/2	76
Prince Edward Island	300	0	0/0	2
Quebec	6,800	1	2/1	19
Saskatchewan	4,200	0	1/1	16
Yukon	200	0	0/0	1
Totals:	128,000	6	34/8	378

THE CHURCH IN EUROPE

Area	Members	Missions	Stakes/Districts	Wards and Branches
Austria	3,700	2	1/0	19
Belgium	4,400	2	1/1	23
Bulgaria	*	0	0/1	0
Czechoslovakia	*	1	0/1	0
France	23,000	2	5/5	98
Germany, United	38,100	5	16/1	181
Greece	200	1	0/1	3
Hungary	600	1	0/1	5
Italy	14,000	4	2/9	90
Luxembourg	*	0	0/0	1
Malta	*	0	0/0	1
Netherlands	7,000	1	3/0	33
Poland	200	1	0/1	2
Portugal	28,000	3	5/8	109
Romania	*	0	0/1	0
Spain	21,000	5	3/13	135
Switzerland	6,300	2	3/0	32
Yugoslavia	*	0	0/1	3
Totals:	148,000	30	39/44	735

THE CHURCH IN MEXICO AND CENTRAL AMERICA

Countries	Members	Missions	Stakes/Districts	Wards and Branches
Mexico	617,000	17	122/45	1,380
Belize	1,500	0	0/1	5
Costa Rica	16,000	1	3/4	58
El Salvador	35,000	2	8/0	94
Guatemala	125,000	3	20/15	323
Honduras	43,000	2	9/6	98
Nicaragua	8,600	1	0/6	38
Panama	20,000	1	4/2	57
Totals:	869,000	27	166/79	2,053

THE CHURCH IN OCEANIA

Countries	Members	Missions	Stakes/Districts	Wards and Branches
Australia	76,000	5	18/13	208
Belau	300	0	0/1	4
Cook Islands	700	0	0/1	6
Fiji	8,600	1	1/2	19
French Polynesia (Tahiti)	12,000	1	3/3	46
Guam	1,800	1	0/1	3
Kiribati	2,300	0	0/1	17
Marshall Islands	1,700	0	0/1	7
Micronesia Federated States	2,200	0	0/5	19
Nauru	*	0	0/0	1
New Caledonia	800	0	0/1	4
New Zealand	76,000	2	16/2	168
Niue	300	0	0/1	2
Northern Mariiana Islands	500	0	0/0	2
Samoa, American	6,900	0	2/0	21
Tonga	35,000	1	10/0	116
Tuvalu	*	0	0/0	1
Vanuatu	200	0	0/0	1
Western Samoa	41,000	1	9/0	94
Totals:	266,000	12	59/32	739

THE CHURCH IN SCANDINAVIA

Countries	Members	Missions	Stakes/Districts	Wards and Branches
Denmark	4,300	1	2/0	23
Finland	4,200	2	2/3	29
Greenland	*	0	0/0	0
Iceland	200	0	0/1	3
Norway	3,700	1	1/3	23
Sweden	7,900	1	2/4	39
Totals:	21,000	5	7/11	117

CHURCH IN SOUTH AMERICA

Area	Members	Missions	Stakes/Districts	Wards and Branches
Argentina	171,000	9	25/39	511
Bolivia	64,000	2	10/9	136
Brazil	368,000	12	56/31	649
Chile	298,000	6	51/19	577
Colombia	83,000	3	9/16	130
Ecuador	81,000	2	9/9	121
French Guiana	*	0	0/0	2
Guyana	*	0	0/0	1
Paraguay	12,000	1	2/6	49
Peru	178,000	5	37/20	410
Suriname	*	0	0/0	1
Uruguay	52,000	1	10/8	111
Venezuela	53,000	2	8/7	123
S. America Total	1,360,000	43	£17/164	2,821

THE CHURCH IN THE UNITED KINGDOM AND IRELAND

Countries	Members	Missions	Stakes/Districts	Wards and Branches
England	117,000	6	32/0	232
Ireland	1,800	1	0/2	10
Northern Ireland	5,300	0	1/0	15
Scotland	22,000	1	5/0	49
Wales	6,500	0	2/0	19
Totals:	152,000	8	40/2	325

THE CHURCH IN THE UNITED STATES

States	Members	Missions	Stakes/Districts	Wards and Branches
Alabama	23,000	1	6/0	66
Alaska	21,000	1	5/3	59
Arizona	241,000	3	59/0	470
Arkansas	14,000	1	3/0	41
California	725,000	12	155/0	1,320
Colorado	89,000	1	25/0	193
Connecticut	10,000	1	3/0	23
Delaware	3,200	0	1/0	7
District of Columbia	400	0	0/0	1
Florida	86,000	4	17/0	161
Georgia	42,000	2	10/0	90
Hawaii	51,000	1	13/0	109
Idaho	297,000	1	94/0	663
Illinois	39,000	2	10/0	84
Indiana	26,000	1	8/0	71
Iowa	12,000	1	3/0	35
Kansas	20,000	0	4/1	53
Kentucky	17,000	1	4/1	49
Louisiana	22,000	1	7/0	56
Maine	7,300	0	2/0	23
Maryland	28,000	1	8/0	54
Massachusetts	14,000	1	3/0	33
Michigan	28,000	2	8/1	75
Minnesota	17,000	1	4/1	46
Mississippi	13,000	1	3/0	41
Missouri	35,000	2	10/0	89
Montana	34,000	1	10/1	106
Nebraska	13,000	0	3/1	36
Nevada	110,000	1	26/0	195
New Hampshire	6,400	1	3/0	19
New Jersey	16,000	1	4/0	34
New Mexico	48,000	1	12/0	107
New York	40,000	2	10/0	98
North Carolina	46,000	2	12/0	112
North Dakota	4,600	0	1/1	14
Ohio	38,000	2	10/1	94
Oklahoma	27,000	2	8/0	66
Oregon	114,000	2	32/0	227

THE CHURCH IN THE UNITED STATES *(continued)*

States	Members	Missions	Stakes/Districts	Wards and Branches
Pennsylvania	29,000	3	9/1	83
Rhode Island	1,700	0	0/0	6
South Carolina	24,000	1	5/0	51
South Dakota	7,700	1	2/3	34
Tennessee	23,000	1	7/0	55
Texas	154,000	6	34/0	331
Utah	1,329,000	3	387/0	2,924
Vermont	2,800	0	1/0	9
Virginia	56,000	2	14/1	119
Washington	190,000	3	46/0	368
West Virginia	10,000	1	3/0	31
Wisconsin	13,000	1	3/1	43
Wyoming	52,000	0	16/0	128
Totals:	4,267,000	79	1,123/17	9,202

THE CHURCH IN THE WEST INDIES

Countries	Members	Missions	Stakes/Districts	Wards and Branches
Antigua	*	0	0/0	1
Aruba	*	0	0/0	1
Bahamas	300	0	0/0	2
Barbados	400	1	0/0	4
Bermuda	*	0	0/0	1
Bonaire	*	0	0/0	1
Cayman Islands	*	0	0/0	1
Cuba	*	0	0/0	1
Curacao	300	0	0/0	1
Dominican Republic	31,000	2	3/7	76
Grenada	*	0	0/0	1
Guadeloupe	*	0	0/0	1
Haiti	4,500	1	0/2	18
Jamaica	1,900	1	0/2	13
Martinique	*	0	0/0	1
Netherlands/Antilles	*	0	0/0	1
Puerto Rico	16,000	1	4/0	50
St. Kitts-Nevis	*	0	0/0	1
Saint Lucia	*	0	0/0	1
Saint Martin	*	0	0/0	1

THE CHURCH IN THE WEST INDIES *(continued)*

Countries	Members	Missions	Stakes/Districts	Wards and Branches
Saint Vincent and Grenadines	200	0	0/0	1
Trinidad and Tobago	300	0	0/0	2
Virgin Islands	200	0	0/0	2
Totals:	56,000	6	7/11	182

Glossary

The following words are frequently encountered when reading or listening to discussions about The Church of Jesus Christ of Latter-day Saints. Entries marked with an asterisk have a separate article in the *Encyclopedia*.

Aaronic Priesthood* The lesser priesthood of the Church, consisting of the offices of deacon, teacher, priest, and bishop. Holders of this priesthood attend to temporal affairs of the Church (cf. Melchizedek Priesthood).

active in the Church Refers to regular attendance at meetings, observance of the principles of the gospel, and acceptance of Church callings.

Adam* The first man. Latter-day Saints view him as one of the greatest and noblest of all men.

Adamic language* A perfect spoken and written language given by God to Adam.

Adam-ondi-Ahman* The place (in what is now Daviess County, Missouri) where Adam gathered and blessed his posterity before his death; a locale where a future priesthood meeting will be held just previous to Christ's second coming.

added upon A phrase indicating that the faithful receive additional blessings in the life to follow. Those who were faithful in premortal life had blessings "added upon" them in mortality. Those who are faithful in this life will have "glory added upon their heads for ever and ever" (Abr. 3:26).

administer To perform an ordinance, such as anointing the sick with oil or saying the set prayers to bless the bread and water of the sacrament.

agency* (often called free agency) The granted right to choose good or evil, and the responsibility for the choices made.

age of accountability The age at which a child becomes personally responsible for motives, attitudes, desires, and actions. Designated by revelation to begin at eight years of age (D&C 68:25).

Ancestral File™* A computerized system of genealogical information that links names of individuals into pedigrees, showing their ancestors and descendants.

Ancient of Days A term used in Daniel 7:9, identified by revelation to Joseph Smith as Adam.

angel, fallen Specifically, the devil.* Generally, all who followed the devil in the premortal existence.

angels* Literally, messengers; usually referring to messengers from God.

anointing(s) The placing of a drop or two of consecrated olive oil on a person's head as part of a special blessing, under the direction of the Melchizedek Priesthood.

apostates* Members who seriously oppose or ignore cardinal teachings of the Church, publicly or privately.

apostle* An office in the Melchizedek Priesthood; usually a member of the Quorum of the Twelve Apostles.

apostolic Church The Church presided over by the Twelve Apostles following the resurrection and ascension of Jesus Christ.

area* A geographical ecclesiastical unit of the Church consisting of several regions and presided over by a president, who is a General Authority.

archives A general description for the record-keeping facilities of the Church in Salt Lake City. The archives hold a wide variety of records, including Church membership information, historical accounts, and the largest collection of genealogical data in the world.

Articles of Faith* Thirteen concise statements of LDS belief written by Joseph Smith in the Wentworth Letter.*

assistants to the twelve* Persons who at one time in the Church were specifically called to be General Authorities to assist the Quorum of the Twelve Apostles.

authority* Duly conferred priesthood power or delegated responsibility associated with position or function.

auxiliary organizations* The Primary (children), Relief Society (adult women), Sunday School, and Young Men and Young Women organizations of the Church. Auxiliary organizations exist primarily to assist the priesthood government of the Church.

Babylon A term symbolic of worldliness.

baptism for the dead* The practice of vicarious baptism for the deceased.

bear testimony To express one's personal convictions of the truthfulness of the gospel of Jesus Christ.

bear the priesthood To possess or hold duly conferred priesthood authority.

beehive symbol* A logo representing industry and harmony, appearing frequently on objects associated with the LDS Church and Utah.

beyond the veil A metaphorical expression for the spirit world or for life after death.

bind on earth, bind in heaven Through the priesthood sealing power, to make an ordinance performed on earth valid throughout eternity.

bishop* A priesthood office whose bearer has been ordained and set apart to preside over a ward.

bishop's court A term used until recent years to indicate a disciplinary council conducted by a bishop.

bishopric* A bishop and his two counselors.

board (general, auxiliary) A small group of Church members called to help leaders of Church auxiliary organizations, such as Relief Society or Sunday School, at both the stake and the general Church administrative levels.

blood atonement* The doctrine that the shedding of blood atones for sin.

Book of Abraham* Writings of Abraham, revealed to Joseph Smith. The Book of Abraham is one of the books in the Pearl of Great Price.

Book of Commandments* The earliest published collection of revelations to Joseph Smith; a predecessor to the Doctrine and Covenants.

Book of Mormon* An account of ancient inhabitants of the Western Hemisphere, recorded on gold plates and translated by Joseph Smith. The record contains both a history of the people and the fulness of the everlasting gospel as revealed by the Savior to the ancient inhabitants.

Book of Moses* A record from the creation of the world and mankind to the flood at Noah's time, revealed to Joseph Smith while he was translating the Bible. Selections from the Book of Moses are now part of the Pearl of Great Price.

book of remembrance* (1) A record begun by Adam and his immediate posterity; (2) a personal book containing genealogy and significant family history.

born in the covenant* All children born to a couple after they have been married (sealed) in a temple.

branch* Generally the smallest organized congregation of Latter-day Saints.

brass plates A record spoken of in the Book of Mormon, which was similar to the Old Testament, written on plates of brass, containing many writings of the prophets (1 Ne. 5:10–16); brought by Lehi and his family to the Western Hemisphere.

brethren (1) All male members of the Church; (2) "The Brethren," a designation of the General Authorities of the Church.

burning in the bosom A metaphorical description of the feeling that sometimes attends the enveloping Spirit of the Lord, particularly when one understands God's words through the influence of the Holy Ghost (Luke 24:32; D&C 9:3–8).

callings* Invitations to accept an office or assignment; offices or assignments themselves.

celestial kingdom* The highest of three degrees of glory in the kingdom of heaven.

center place of Zion The "center place," Independence, Missouri, the future site of the City of Zion (the New Jerusalem) and the temple (D&C 57:3); sometimes incorrectly called "center stake."

chapel The room or hall in a Church meetinghouse used for worship services.

child of God The Latter-day Saint belief that all persons are spirit children of God in the premortal existence and that this parent–child relationship continues on this earth and through eternity.

Children's Friend* The Church's children's magazine, 1902–1970.

chosen people Specifically those selected by God for special responsibilities, often requiring service and sacrifice; participants in the covenant of the gospel.

Church News* A weekly news supplement published by the *Deseret News*, the Church-owned newspaper.

Church of Jesus Christ of Latter-day Saints, The* The official name of the Church.

church of the Firstborn* Those who are exalted or assured of receiving exaltation.

collection of fast offerings The collection of voluntary offerings on fast day, usually the first Sunday of each month.

Comforter* The scriptures speak of two Comforters. The First Comforter is the Holy Ghost. The Second Comforter is Jesus Christ (John 14:16–23; see also *TPJS*, pp. 150–51).

common consent* The principle whereby Church members vote to sustain and approve those called to serve in the Church and decisions made by leaders.

common judge The bishop of each ward, who has the responsibility to judge the spiritual and temporal condition of members of his ward. The stake president of each stake serves as a common judge for all members of his stake.

companion, missionary A missionary's partner. Missionaries in the Church always work in pairs.

compassionate service* Aid or comfort rendered to others, in particular by members of the Relief Society.

conference reports* The published proceedings of the general conferences of the Church.

confirmation* The bestowal of the gift of the Holy Ghost to newly baptized members by holders of the Melchizedek Priesthood; also official recognition of Church membership.

consecration, law of* A divine principle whereby men and women voluntarily dedicate their time, talents, and material wealth to the establishment and building up of God's kingdom.

convert (noun) A person who has chosen to join The Church of Jesus Christ of Latter-day Saints by being baptized and confirmed.

correlation* A process by which all programs of the Church are identified and placed in proper relationship to each other: teachings, organizations, programs, meetings, and instructional materials.

council in heaven* The meeting in the premortal life of the Godhead and spirits designated for this earth, in which the plan of salvation was presented.

counselor A person called to serve as an adviser, assistant, and occasional substitute for an officer or leader in the Church.

court (Church) A term formerly used to mean a Church disciplinary council.

crickets (Mormon) A type of cricket that threatened the crops of early Mormon pioneers. The crops were saved when large flocks of seagulls came and devoured the crickets.

Cumorah* (1) A hill in which the Book of Mormon prophet Mormon concealed sacred records before the annihilation of his people; (2) the hill in New York State, near the town of Palmyra, where Joseph Smith unearthed the gold plates from which he translated the Book of Mormon.

damnation* (1) The opposite of salvation; (2) to be stopped in one's spiritual progress; (3) the suffering of various degrees of penalty at the final judgment by those who have not accepted the gospel of Jesus Christ and repented of their sins.

Danites* A small and briefly organized band of Mormon militia men in 1838 who became the source for anti-Mormon legends.

deacon* An office in the Aaronic Priesthood.

degrees of glory* The celestial, terrestrial, and telestial kingdoms in heaven.

denying the Holy Ghost (1) In general terms, rejecting a spiritual witness given by the Holy Ghost; (2) another term for blasphemy against the Holy Ghost, which is an unpardonable sin.

deseret* A Book of Mormon word meaning "honey bee," often used in titles of LDS institutions or by businesses in areas with concentrated LDS populations.

devils* Those spirits who chose to follow Lucifer in his revolt against God in the premortal existence.

disciplinary procedures* The process of bringing a Church member before a priesthood officer or disciplinary council to account for alleged transgressions against Church standards and to take necessary steps toward repentance.

discussion (missionary term) A structured lesson on basic gospel principles presented to interested nonmembers.

disfellowshipment A disciplinary action against a Church member that severely restricts participation in Church activity but falls short of excommunication.

dispensation (of the gospel, of the fulness of times) A period of time in which priesthood authority and keys are established among mankind. The present dispensation, the last before the second coming of Christ, is called the "fulness of times."

distribution centers* Centrally located outlets from which Church publications and other supplies are distributed.

district* (1) An ecclesiastical unit consisting of several branches of the Church in a geographic area where stakes are not organized; (2) a unit of organization in missions, consisting of missionaries and presided over by an experienced missionary called the *district leader.*

Doctrine and Covenants* A volume of Latter-day Saint scripture containing selected revelations given to Joseph Smith and his successors in the presidency of the Church.

early morning seminary LDS religion courses for high school students offered before the normal school day begins.

elder* An office in the Melchizedek Priesthood; a title designating a holder of this priesthood, a General Authority, or a male missionary.

elder brother A name or title of Jesus Christ, the firstborn of all Heavenly Father's spirit children.

elders quorum A group consisting of men holding the office of elder in the Melchizedek Priesthood.

Elohim* God the Father.

endowment* Ordinances of instruction and covenant performed by and for individuals in temples.

enduring to the end* The doctrine that converted individuals must continue to show their faith through good works till the end of mortal life.

Enoch, book of A record kept by Enoch, yet to be revealed (D&C 107:57).

Ensign* Since 1971, the official monthly periodical published by the Church.

Ephraim* The son of Joseph who was sold into Egypt, and heir to the birthright. The patriarchal blessings of many Latter-day Saints declare them to be of the lineage of Ephraim.

eternal life* Exaltation in the highest degree of the celestial kingdom; often spoken of as "eternal lives."

eternal progression* Endless increase in glory and dominion.

eternity A synonym for "endless" as contrasted to things of mortality.

evangelist* The office of patriarch in the Melchizedek Priesthood.

Eve* The first woman. Latter-day Saints view her as one of the greatest and noblest of all women.

exaltation* Attainment of the highest degree of glory in the celestial kingdom.

excommunication A disciplinary action against a Church member in which membership is withdrawn.

family history, genealogy* Activity in the LDS Church that involves tracing one's lineage and composing ancestral histories.

Family History Library* The Church's repository of genealogical and historical data, the largest of its kind in the world, with branch libraries in more than 1,400 stake centers.

family home evening* A program in which families gather (usually on Monday evening) for family-centered spiritual training and social activities.

Family Registry™ A service provided by the Family History Department of the Church to help people who are doing research on the same family lines to cooperate and share results.

FamilySearch™ An automated computer system designed to simplify the task of family history research.

fast offerings* Donations of at least the value of meals not eaten on fast Sunday, given to the bishop for the relief of the needy.

Fast Sunday Usually the first Sunday of each month, on which Church members refrain from food or drink for two meals and donate the equivalent cost to the Church to assist the poor and needy. The sacrament meeting on each fast Sunday, called fast and testimony meeting, is devoted to the voluntary bearing of testimony by members.

fellowshipping members* The activity of encouraging established Church members to help new or inactive members to participate in Church practices.

firesides* Informal gatherings of Church members and friends, often in homes and usually on Sundays, that feature a speaker or program of a spiritual theme. Occasionally Churchwide firesides are held under the direction of the First Presidency.

First Presidency* The President of the Church and his counselors; the highest ranking quorum in the Church.

first principles and ordinances of the gospel* Faith in Jesus Christ, repentance, baptism by immersion in water for the remission of sins, and the laying on of hands for the gift of the Holy Ghost.

First Vision* The initial appearance of God the Father and Jesus Christ to Joseph Smith in the spring of 1820 near Palmyra, New York, marking the beginning of the restoration of the gospel.

following the brethren* Heeding the counsel of local and general leaders of the Church.

food storage A supply of food necessary to sustain life for a year. Church leaders encourage members, where possible, to store food, clothing, fuel, and other items in preparation for emergencies.

foreordination* The doctrine that individuals were called and set apart in the premortal existence to perform certain roles in mortal life, should they so choose.

free agency (*See* agency.)

Friend, The Since 1971, the Church periodical for children.

fulness of the gospel* The doctrine, ordinances, authority, and organization necessary to enable individuals to attain salvation.

Gabriel A person spoken of in Daniel 8:16 and Luke 1:11–19, identified as Noah by the Prophet Joseph Smith.

garments* Sacred ceremonial undergarments associated with temple covenants.

General Authorities* Members of the presiding lay leadership of the Church: the First Presidency, Quorum of the Twelve Apostles, Quorums of the Seventy, and Presiding Bishopric.

general conference General assemblies of Church members in Salt Lake City, regularly convened every April and October.

Gentile(s)* According to the context in which it is used, the following meanings are possible for Latter-day Saints: (1) one not of the lineage of Israel; (2) a non–Latter-day Saint; (3) one who is not Jewish; (4) one who is not a Lamanite.

gold plates* The anciently engraved metal plates from which Joseph Smith translated the Book of Mormon.

gospel* The "good news" of redemption through Jesus Christ; the principles and ordinances of the plan of salvation.

grace* Divine help given through the mercy of Jesus Christ. It is an enabling power that allows men and women to receive eternal life and exaltation after they have expended their own best efforts.

great and abominable church* All assemblies, congregations, or associations of people not authorized by God and that fight against God and his purposes

heaven* (1) The dwelling place of God; (2) any kingdom of glory.

hell* (1) The condition of misery one may feel after sinning; (2) the temporary dwelling place of the unrepentant till the judgment day.

high council (high councilor)* A group of twelve high priests (and sometimes alternates) who help direct the affairs of a stake.

high priest* An office in the Melchizedek Priesthood.

Holy Ghost* The third member of the Godhead, a personage of Spirit.

homemaking One of three areas of emphasis in the Relief Society of the Church.

home teaching* A Church program in which priesthood holders regularly visit assigned homes of members.

Improvement Era, The An official publication of the Church, 1897–1970.

Indian student placement* The practice of bringing LDS American Indian children to live in LDS homes during the school year.

Inspired Version of the Bible Another name for the Joseph Smith Translation of the Bible.

institutes of religion* Weekday religious instruction for students attending colleges, universities, and other postsecondary schools.

investigator (missionary term) A person who is interested in the Church and is receiving missionary instruction.

iron rod An image from Lehi's dream in the Book of Mormon, meaning "the word of God"—suggesting straitness and security.

Israel* (1) Members of the Church; (2) the Old Testament patriarch Jacob and his descendants.

Jehovah* Another name for Jesus Christ, particularly in the Old Testament.

Joseph Smith Translation of the Bible (JST)* The translation of the Bible by Joseph Smith, begun in 1830, which resulted in his receiving many doctrinal revelations.

Journal of Discourses A collection of sermons by LDS leaders, 1854–1886 (26 volumes); it is not an official source for Church doctrine.

keys of the priesthood* The right to exercise or direct authority, perform ordinances, or to preside over a priesthood function, quorum, or Church organization.

kingdom of God* (1) God's dominion; (2) the Church; (3) the political government of God.

Lamanites* (1) An Israelite people in the Book of Mormon, descendants of Joseph of Egypt through Lehi and Ishmael; (2) today, many American Indians.

Latter-day Saint* A member of The Church of Jesus Christ of Latter-day Saints.

laying on of hands* The placing of hands by those holding priesthood authority on the head of a member to confer authority, office, calling, or blessing.

Levitical Priesthood* The lesser priesthood. (*See also* Aaronic Priesthood.)

Light of Christ.* The power of Christ infused in all creation.

line of authority (1) A priesthood bearer's "priesthood lineage," that is, a sequential listing of ordinations tracing one's own priesthood authority through priesthood leaders to the apostles and Jesus Christ. [*See* Appendix 10.]

magnifying one's calling* Measuring up to the duties to which one may be called.

Manifesto of 1890* The pronouncement that the Church had officially ended the solemnization of new plural marriages.

marriage, eternal* The doctrine that the bonds of marriage may continue into the eternities if a man and a woman are sealed in a temple and continue faithful to their covenants.

martyrdom of Joseph and Hyrum Smith* The murder of Joseph and Hyrum Smith by a mob in Carthage, Illinois, on June 27, 1844.

marvelous work and a wonder A reference to a prophecy of Isaiah (29:1–14) concerning the restoration of the gospel and the coming forth of the Book of Mormon.

Melchizedek Priesthood* The higher priesthood, including the offices of elder, seventy, high priest, patriarch, and apostle, and focused upon the spiritual things of the gospel (cf. with Aaronic Priesthood).

membership record* The official certificate of membership in the Church kept at Church headquarters.

Michael The archangel, identified in LDS teachings as Adam.*

Millennial Star The official publication of the Church in the United Kingdom, 1840–1970.

missionary discussions Basic gospel lessons missionaries use to teach interested people about the Church and its doctrines.

missionary training centers (MTC)* Centers where formally called missionaries are instructed and trained before departure to assigned missions.

Mormonism, Mormons* Unofficial terms for The Church of Jesus Christ of Latter-day Saints and its members; members prefer to use the official name of the Church and to be referred to as Latter-day Saints.

Mormon Tabernacle Choir* The large lay choir that broadcasts weekly from Temple Square in Salt Lake City.

Moroni* (1) A Nephite military leader, c. 60 BC; (2) a Book of Mormon prophet, c. AD 420 who in 1827, as a resurrected being, gave Joseph Smith the gold plates from which Joseph translated the Book of Mormon. A statue of Moroni is placed atop some LDS temples and on the hill Cumorah.

Mother in Heaven* The teaching that spirits born on this earth have their premortal origins with a literal Heavenly Mother as well as a Heavenly Father.

Mountain Meadows Massacre* An incident in which certain Indian and Southern Utah Mormons participated in the massacre of a wagon train of immigrants passing through the Territory of Utah, 1857.

Mutual The Church's auxiliary organization for youth ages twelve through eighteen, for many years called the Mutual Improvement Association, or MIA.

Name Extraction Program* Systematic transcription of genealogical information from original vital records.

New Era* Since 1971, the Church periodical for young people.

new and everlasting covenant* The gospel of Jesus Christ. All covenants between God and mankind are part of the new and everlasting covenant.

New Jerusalem* The administrative headquarters of the kingdom of God in the Western Hemisphere during Christ's millennial reign.

office (1) A position of authority, duty, or trust in the Church organization; (2) an ordained calling or assignment to serve in the priesthood.

ordinances* A performance or prescribed ceremony related to the reception of a blessing, covenant, or ordination, such as baptism, confirmation, endowment, marriage, etc., performed by one who has been ordained to the priesthood and authorized to perform the ordinance.

outer darkness A region totally removed from the light and glory of God, to which Satan and his followers will be consigned.

paradise* The dwelling place of the spirits of the righteous dead who await resurrection and judgment.

patriarch* (1) An office in the Melchizedek Priesthood; (2) a holder of that office in the Melchizedek Priesthood who gives patriarchal blessings; (3) an evangelist; (4) the father of a family.

patriarchal blessing* A formal blessing given by an ordained patriarch in which the recipient's lineage from one of the tribes of Israel is usually

declared, exhortations are given, and spiritual gifts and life-missions are specified.

Pearl of Great Price* One of the standard works of the Church, containing the book of Moses, the book of Abraham, Joseph Smith—Matthew (a translation of Matthew 24), the Joseph Smith–History, and the Articles of Faith.

Personal Ancestral File® (PAF)* A genealogical software package produced by the Church.

Pioneer Day* July 24, celebration of the anniversary of the arrival of the Latter-day Saints in Salt Lake Valley in 1847.

plan of salvation* The plan presented in the premortal existence providing for the creation, fall, probation, death, resurrection, judgment, salvation, and exaltation of mankind.

plural marriage* The doctrine that a man may be authorized by revelation from God through the living prophet to have more than one living wife.

polygamy The practice of having more than one wife; more accurately, polygyny.

preexistence* (*See* premortal life.)

premortal life* The doctrine of life as a spirit being before mortality. It is also called pre-earthly existence or antemortal life.

Presiding Bishop* A General Authority under the First Presidency who directs the temporal affairs of the Church, assisted by two counselors; together they compose the Presiding Bishopric.

priest* An office in the Aaronic Priesthood.

priestcraft* Misuse of priesthood authority or spiritual gifts to gain personal influence or money.

priesthood* (1) The power of God; (2) the authority to act in God's name; (3) the right and responsibility to preside within the Church organization; (4) a term referring to the men of the Church in general.

priesthood blessings* Blessings of counsel and divine influence conferred by the authority of the priesthood.

priesthood offices* Specific appointments to positions of authority or of responsibility in the priesthood.

priesthood quorum* An organized body of male members who hold the same priesthood office.

Primary* The auxiliary organization in the Church for children from ages eighteen months through eleven years.

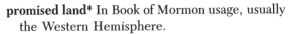

promised land* In Book of Mormon usage, usually the Western Hemisphere.

prophet* (1) When capitalized, often refers to Joseph Smith; (2) when not capitalized, it can refer to the President of the Church, or any authorized spokesman for God; (3) one who has a testimony of Jesus Christ by the Holy Ghost has the "spirit of prophecy" (Rev. 19:10).

prophet, seer, and revelator* The special powers and functions held by members of the First Presidency and the Quorum of the Twelve Apostles.

proselyte (verb) An LDS variant of "proselytize," that is, to invite others to convert to The Church of Jesus Christ of Latter-day Saints.

quorum (*See* priesthood quorum.)*

Quorum of the Twelve Apostles* The body of twelve men who, under the direction of the First Presidency, constitute the second-highest presiding quorum of the Church.

Quorums of the Seventy General Authorities organized in bodies of up to seventy members. Under supervision of the First Presidency and the Quorum of the Twelve, they direct missionary and other administrative activities of the Church.

reformed Egyptian A set of characters used by Book of Mormon writers on metal plates because of their conciseness.

Regional Representative* A specially called priesthood leader who serves in a teaching and training capacity between stake leaders and an Area Presidency. Each region consists of several stakes.

Relief Society* The adult women's auxiliary organization of the Church.

Reorganized Church of Jesus Christ of Latter Day Saints* A church that arose in response to the schism that followed the June 27, 1844, murder of Joseph Smith. Formally organized on April 6, 1860, at Amboy, Illinois.

restoration* (1) The reestablishment of the ancient gospel of Jesus Christ through Joseph Smith in the latter days; (2) the culmination of God's work on the earth in the latter days, including the restoration of the gospel, the gathering of Israel, and the renewal of the earth; (3) the returning of good for good, or evil for evil, in the last judgment (Alma 41:13).

returned missionary One who has completed a full-time mission for the Church.

roadshow A brief, original dramatic production, often presented at two or more locations within a stake.

sacrament* The water and bread blessed and distributed as emblems of the body and blood of Jesus Christ to Church members in ward or branch sacrament meetings.

sacrament meeting* The principal worship meeting of the Church, during which the sacrament of the Lord's supper is blessed and distributed to members of the Church. The members also pray, sing, and hear sermons.

Sacred Grove* The grove of trees near Palmyra/Manchester, New York, in which in 1820 Joseph Smith received his First Vision of God the Father and Jesus Christ.

Saints* Faithful members of the Church.

salvation* Resurrection to a kingdom of glory; sometimes used to signify exaltation in the celestial kingdom.

saved (1) To be delivered from physical death by the grace of God, through the death and resurrection of Jesus Christ; (2) to be delivered from the consequences of personal sin by the grace of God through faith in Jesus Christ, repentance, and obedience to the commandments of God.

scriptures (*See* Standard Works.)

sealed portion of the plates A segment of the gold plates that Joseph Smith obtained from the hill Cumorah, containing a revelation from the beginning to the end of the world. This segment was not translated by Joseph Smith.

sealing* (1) Through the power of the priesthood, making valid in heaven an action performed on earth; (2) the temple ordinance joining husband and wife or children and parents for time and eternity.

Second Comforter A name-title for Jesus Christ. (*See* Comforter.)

seer* A person endowed with a special gift of seeing spiritually the past, present, and the future.

seer stones* Sacred stones that, when used by a person with the gift of seership, reveal the past, present, and future. (*See* Urim and Thummim.)

self-reliance The principle that individual Church members and families should, to the extent possible, provide and plan for their own necessities.

seminaries* The weekday religious instruction program of the Church for secondary-school students.

setting apart* The authorization of an individual, by the laying on of hands to serve in a calling in the Church.

Seventy* An office in the Melchizedek Priesthood, with a special calling to missionary service or to administrative duties. Today all the Seventy are General Authorities.

sick, blessing the* An ordinance in which ill persons are anointed with consecrated olive oil and blessed by Melchizedek Priesthood holders, to the end that healing may take place. (See Anointing.)

single adults* Adult Church members who are not married.

Social Services* A separate corporation from the Church (called LDS Social Services) which serves as a resource for meeting special social and emotional needs of Church members.

solemn assemblies* Special assemblies of priesthood holders, generally held in temples.

sons of perdition* Individuals who have sinned against the Holy Ghost and have thus committed the unpardonable sin.

soul* The united spirit and body. All living things on earth are souls, meaning they consist of a spirit body and a physical body.

spirit body* A being formed of refined element, with which a physical body of earthly element unites to form a soul. Human spirits are literally children of God.

spirit prison* The place where the spirits of the dead, particularly the untaught and nonrighteous, await resurrection and judgment.

spirit world* The place where the spirits of the dead await resurrection and judgment; it consists of paradise, prison, and hell.

stake* A geographical-ecclesiastical unit of the Church, composed of several wards and sometimes branches.

stake center A meetinghouse of the Church in which the administrative offices of stake leaders are also located.

stake president* The presiding authority of a stake.

standard works* The canonized Latter-day Saint scriptures: Bible, Book of Mormon, Doctrine and Covenants, and Pearl of Great Price. (The latter three, when bound under one cover, are often called the "Triple Combination.")

Stick of Joseph* A biblical term having reference to the Book of Mormon, which is a record of a remnant of the posterity of Joseph who was sold into Egypt (Ezek. 37:15–19).

Stick of Judah* A biblical term having reference to the Bible, being a record of the Jews and preserved by the prophets of Judah and by the apostles (Ezek. 37:15–19).

tabernacle (1) The physical body in which a person's spirit dwells during earth life; (2) a special building used for assemblies, such as the Tabernacle on Temple Square.

teacher* An office in the Aaronic Priesthood.

telestial kingdom* The lowest of three degrees of glory; inherited by the wicked after they have suffered for their sins.

temple* A sacred building, the "House of the Lord," in which Latter-day Saints perform sacred ceremonies and ordinances of the gospel for themselves and for the dead.

temple marriage A term for a marriage solemnized by an eternal covenant in a Latter-day Saint temple.

temple ordinances* Sacred ceremonies performed in Latter-day Saint temples.

temple recommend* A certificate of worthiness to participate in temple ordinances.

Temple Square* A ten-acre city block in Salt Lake City on which the Salt Lake Temple, Tabernacle, and adjacent buildings are located.

ten tribes Those tribes of the house of Israel carried captive into Assyria c. 721 BC; known as the lost tribes of Israel because they became lost to the people and records of the Bible. Prophecy proclaims their return in the latter days.

terrestrial kingdom* The middle of the three degrees of glory; inherited by "honorable" people of the earth who did not accept the fulness of the gospel of Jesus Christ.

testimony* A personal expression of one's convictions or beliefs about the gospel of Jesus Christ.

time and eternity* A term suggesting that gospel ordinances and blessings are valid forever, both on earth and in the heavens.

tithing* The donation of one-tenth of one's increase (gross income) to the Church.

topical guide* An index and concordance to the standard works of the Church; contained in the LDS publication of the Bible.

translated beings* Individuals who are changed in mortality so that they do not experience physical pain and whose death and resurrection will be in a "twinkling of the eye"; Enoch, Elijah, and John the Beloved are examples.

triple combination (*See* Standard Works.)

united orders* Social and economic orders in which Church members, in an act of consecration, deed their property to a bishop, who allots stewardships and resources according to need. It is not currently being practiced in the Church.

unpardonable sin* The sin against the Holy Ghost.

Urim and Thummim* Two stones set in "silver bows," and often associated with a breastplate, given to Joseph Smith to aid in the translation of the Book of Mormon and in receiving other revelations. The Urim and Thummim mentioned in the Bible are probably not the same as those possessed by Joseph Smith.

visiting teaching* A Church program in which members of the Relief Society are assigned to visit regularly other sisters to give brief instruction and support.

visitors centers* Reception centers of the Church, at temples and historic sites, to introduce visitors to the history and doctrine of the Church.

war in heaven* The conflict between Lucifer and Jesus Christ, and their followers, in the premortal existence.

ward* A geographic ecclesiastical unit in the Church, consisting of several hundred members presided over by a bishop.

washings and anointings* Initiatory temple ordinances, preliminary to endowment.

welfare* A plan and program in the Church administered by priesthood officers and the Relief Society which attends to the temporal well-being of needy members and admonishes all members to become self-reliant.

welfare square* A geographic block in Salt Lake City reflecting the emphasis in the Church on storing food and other commodities for emergencies.

word of wisdom* The revealed health code of the Church, as set forth in section 89 of the Doctrine and Covenants.

year's supply A supply of food, clothing, and, where possible, fuel and other items necessary to sustain life for a year. Church leaders encourage members, where possible, to store such items as a principle of management and in preparation for an emergency.

young adult The program in the Church for young single members.

young men* The instruction and activity program in the Church for young men ages twelve to eighteen.

young women* The instruction and activity program in the Church for young women ages twelve to eighteen.

Zion* A word meaning the "pure in heart"; also a geographic location where the righteous are gathered by obedience to the gospel.

zone A unit of organization within the boundaries of a mission. Typically, several zones compose a mission.

Index

Page numbers in **bold** indicate a major discussion. <u>Underlined</u> page numbers indicate illustrations.

Aaron, brother of Moses, **1**, 312, 718, 828, 1139–40, 1143
Aaronic Priesthood, **1–4**, 278, 335, 882, 937, 1275
  angels, 41
  baptism, 98
  bishop, 117, 118
  Catholicism and Mormonism, 257
  deacon, 361
  dispensation of the fulness of times, 388
  Doctrine and Covenants, 411, 414, 418
  Elias, 449
  Elias, spirit of, 449
  first principles of the Gospel, 514
  high council, 587
  high priest, 588
  home teaching, 654
  Joseph of Egypt, 761
  laying on of hands, 813
  Levitical Priesthood, 828
  missions, 919
  Moses, 959
  motion pictures, 965
  Nauvoo Temple, 1001
  ordinances, 1033
  ordination to, 1034–35
  organization, 1036
  powers and offices of, 1–3
  presiding bishopric, 1128
  priest, 1–4, 514, 635, 1132–33, 1139
  priesthood offices, 1143
  religious experience, 1209
  remission of sins, 1211
  restoration of, **3–4**, 210, 574, 602, 755, 763, 781, 1034, 1132, 1135, 1209, 1335
  restoration of all things, 1219
  sacrament, 1244
  sculptors, 1286
  Smith, Joseph, 1335
  Taylor, John, 1439
  teacher, 1441
  values, 1508
  Young Men, 1613
  youth, 1620

  see also Bishop, history of the office; Priest, Aaronic priesthood
Abbott, Sheldon L., 1025
Abel, **5**, 125, 245, 1299
  Cain, 245–46, 1391
Abinadi, **5–7**, 149, 161, 198, 265, 701, 739, 748
  martyrs, 863
  natural man, 985
  Old Testament, 1028
  prophecy, 1163, 1164
  prophets, 1166
  scripture, 1283
Abortion, **7**, 20, 365, 645, 971, 1096, 1102, 1158, 1376, <u>1377</u>, 1418
Abraham, **7–9**, 582, 780
  altar, 37
  astronomy, 82
  covenant Israel, 330
  creation accounts, 341–42
  Doctrine and Covenants, 422
  elect of God, 448
  Enoch, 462
  foreordination, 522
  Israel, 711
  Jesus Christ, 753
  Melchizedek, 879
  mother in Israel, 963
  Nauvoo, 991
  papyri, 1059
  Restoration of the Gospel of Jesus Christ, 1220
  scripture, 1283
  second estate, 1290
  seed of, 1292
  Smith, Joseph, 1343
  see also Abrahamic covenant; Book of Abraham; Gospel of Abraham; Sarah
Abraham, Gospel of. *See* Gospel of Abraham
Abrahamic covenant, **9–10**, 334, 419
  Book of Abraham, 135
  Elias, 449
  gathering, 536
  Gospel of Abraham, 555

  hope of Israel, 657
  implementation, 9–10
  Israel, 706
  mother in Israel, 963
  Native Americans, 982
  Old Testament, 1028
  perpetuation, 10
  Polynesians, 1110
  Restoration of the Gospel of Jesus Christ, 1220
  seed of Abraham, 1292
  see also Covenant Israel, Latter-day
Abravanel, Maurice, 951
Abrea, Angel, 1399, 1631, 1680
Abrea, Maria Victoria Chiapparino, 1399
Abstinence
  alcoholic beverages, 30, 416, 417, 1584
  birth control, 116
  celibacy, 260
  coffee and tea, 289, 416, 417, 1584
  see also Chastity, law of; Prohibition movement
Abuse, spouse and child, **11**, 1096, 1158
Abuse, substance. *See* Alcoholic beverages and alcoholism; Drugs, abuse of
Academia Juárez, 13
Academies, **11–13**, 274, 444, 627, 628, 634, 637, 684, 1379
  see also specific name, e.g., Brigham Young Academy
Accountability, **13**
  agency, 26
  children, 267
  confirmation, 310
  consecration, 312
  death and dying, 365
  Doctrine and Covenants, 418
  Ezekiel, 480
  freedom, 525
  infant baptism, 682
  law, 808
  life and death, spiritual, 833

Accountability *(Cont'd)*
  plan of salvation, 1090
  politics, 1104
  Smith, Joseph, 1341
Acquired immune deficiency syn-
  drome. *See* AIDS
Activity in the Church, **13–15**, 59,
  1054
  values, transmission of, 1508
  see also Callings; Conversion;
    Temples, worship and activity;
    Ward
Adair, James, 1509
Adam, **15–18**, 636
  altar, 37
  ancient sources, 17–18
  atonement of Jesus Christ, 83, 84
  children, 268
  confession of sins, 309
  covenants, 334
  creation accounts, 341
  dispensations of the Gospel, 388
  Doctrine and Covenants, 422
  Enoch, 457
  Garden of Eden, 533–34
  garments, 534
  LDS sources, 15–17
  Lehi, 828
  mankind, 853
  Moses, 959
  obedience, 1021
  opposition, 1031
  origin of man, 1053
  patriarchal blessings, 1066
  record keeping, 1195
  see also Adamic language; Eve;
    Fall of Adam; Michael; Mortal-
    ity; Original Sin; Plan of Salva-
    tion
Adam-God. *See* God
Adamic language, **18–19**, 751, 1194
Adam-ondi-Ahman, 16, **19–20**, 355,
  458, 460, 534, 551, 593, 845,
  931, 1299, 1365
Adams, L. LaMar, 704
Adams, Maude, 634, 1380
Adamsen, Peter, 1262
Administration of Ordinances. *See*
  Ordinances, administration of
Adoption, law of. *See* Law of Adop-
  tion
Adoption of children, **20–21**, 1386,
  1445
Adultery, **21**, 1158, 1305, 1307,
  1443
Adversary. *See* Devil
Advocate with the Father. *See* Jesus
  Christ, names and titles of

Affirmation organization, 1389
A fortiori, 183
Africa, the Church in, **22–26**, 1756–
  57
  diplomatic relations, 383
  economic aid, 434
  humanitarian service, 662, 663
  interfaith relationships, 696
  missions, 917
  see also South Africa
Afro-American Oral History Project,
  126
Afterlife, **26**
  celestial kingdom, 259–60
  David, King, 360
  exaltation, 479
  life and death, spiritual, 833
  telestial kingdom, 1443
  terrestrial kingdom, 1470
  work, role of, 1586–87
  see also Heaven
Afton, New York. *See* South Bainbridge (Afton), New York
Agency, **26–27**, 596
  abuse, spouse and child, 11
  accountability, 13
  Articles of Faith, 67
  atonement of Jesus Christ, 83
  baptism, 96
  birth control, 116
  business, 240
  children, 267
  church and state, 281
  civil rights, 286
  commandments, 297
  consecration, 312
  Constitution, U.S., 318
  constitutional law, 315
  Council in Heaven, 329
  degrees of glory, 369
  doctrine, 402–403
  Doctrine and Covenants, 418
  drugs, abuse of, 419
  Ezekiel, 480
  family, 488
  fate, 503
  father's blessings, 504
  freedom, 525
  Garden of Eden, 534
  grace, 561
  intelligence, 692
  law, 808
  mankind, 853
  mortality, 958
  opposition, 1031
  plan of salvation, 1088
  politics, 1104
  purpose of earth life, 1181

  temptation, 1468
  war in heaven, 1546
  war and peace, 1547
Agriculture, **27–29**, 636
  Book of Mormon, 173
  Brigham Young University, 223
  business, 242
  Canada, 253, 254
  humanitarian service, 662
  material culture, 864
  pioneer economy, 1084
  see also Farm Management Com-
    panies; specific organizations
    and products
AgriNorthwest Company, 242
Ahah, 718
Ahlstrom, Sydney, 938
Ahman, **29**, 548, 551, 751
  see also Adam-ondi-Ahman
Ah Mu, 1023
Aid, economic. *See* Economic aid
AIDS, **29–30**, 131, 1051, 1096
Air Force, U.S., Brigham Young
  University, 224
Alberta Stake, 251, 625
Alberta Temple. *See* Cardston Tem-
  ple
Alcoholic beverages and alcoholism,
  30–31, 416, 417, 580, 1097,
  1375, 1584
  see also Drugs, abuse of; Prohibi-
    tion movement
Aldrich, Hazen, 1631, 1680
Aldrich, Mark, 48
Alexander, Sarah, 1255
Alger, Fanny, 1092
Allegory, Book of Mormon, 183–84
Allegory of Zenos, **31–32**, 57, 1623–
  24
Allen, James B., 935, 1176
Allen, Joseph L., 172
Allen, Rufus, 1117
ALMA. *See* Associated Latter-day
  Media Artists
Allopathic medicine, 374
Allred, Rulon, 531
Alma₁ (c. 174–92 b.c.), **32–33**, 960
  Abinadi, 6
  conversion, 321
  death and dying, 366
  people of, 194
  prophecy, 1164
  record of, 149
Alma₂ (c. 90–73 b.c.), **33–35**, 584,
  960
  Amulek, 38
  Antichrists, 45
  book of, 150–52, 164

Book of Mormon, 150–52, 161
chastity law, 265
conversion, 321
cursings, 352
death and dying, 364
Deuteronomy, 378
foreordination, 522
holiness, 649
Jesus Christ, 748
martyrs, 863
Melchizedek, 879
Messiah, 894
miracles, 908
premortal life, 1124
prophecy, 1163
prophets, 1166, 1167
tree of life, 1486
Almanacs, **35–36**, 1176
Alpha and Omega, 741–42
see also Jesus Christ
Altamirano, Ignacio Manuel, 899
Altar, **36–37**, <u>188</u>, <u>189</u>
Amado, Carlos H., 902, 1631, 1680
Amaleki, 148
Amalekites, 194
Amalickiah, 165
AMCAP. *See* Association of Mormon Counselors and Psychotherapists
Amen, **38**, 1020, 1180
see also Hosanna shout
American Indian Services, 984–85
American Indians. *See* American Indian Services; Indian Relief Society; Indian Student Placement Services; Native Americans
"America's Witness for Christ" (pageant), 346, 347
Amlicites, 194
Amlici war, 164–65
AML. *See* Association of Mormon Letters
Ammon, 6
Ammonihah, 165
Ammonites, 195, 584
Amnigaddah, 718
Amulek, **38–39**, 677, 748, 772, 863, 1315
Amulonites, 194
Amussen, Carl Christian, 101
Amussen, Flora Smith. *See* Benson, Flora Smith Amussen
Anabaptists, 683
Ancestral File™, 39, 304, 493, 495, 500
Andersen, H. Verlan, 1631, 1680, 1683

Anderson, Charlotte, 72
Anderson, Edward H., 678
Anderson, Edward O., 64
Anderson, Elizabeth, 86
Anderson, F. I., 881
Anderson, George, 1381, 1561
Anderson, Joseph, 591, 1631, 1680, 1682
Anderson, May, 231, 270, 660, 1147, 1631, 1684
Anderson, Nephi, 838–39, 842
Anderson, Robert, 86
Andrus, Hyrum L., 137
Andrus, Paul, 77
Angell, Truman O., 64, 1253, 1433
Angel Moroni statue, **39–40**, 346, 347, 755, 1254, 1286
Angels, **40–42**, 405, 414
see also Devils; Moroni, visitations of
Animals, **42–43**, 163, 186
Anointings. *See* Washings and anointings
Anthon, Charles, 43, 44, 159, 210, 575
Anthon Transcript, **43–44**, 159, 575, 602
see also Book of Mormon language
Anthony, Susan B., 536, 785, 1313, 1560, <u>1573</u>
Anti-Bigamy Act of 1862, 625
Antichrists, **44–45**, 148, 151
Anti-Mormonism. *See* Anti-Mormon publications; Persecution
Anti-Mormon publications, **45–52**, 206, 589, 619, 633, 647, 1179
clergy, 288
early criticisms (1829–1846), 46–48
psychology (1897–1945), 49–50
Reformation (1856–1857), 1197
revival (1946–1990), 50–51
stereotyping and polygamy (1847–1896), 48–49
see also Persecution
Anti-Nephi-Lehies, 194
Antipolygamy legislation, **52–53**
anti-Mormonism, 48
bishops, 121
Canada, 253
economic history, 436, 439
history, 623, 625, 630
immigration and emigration, 675–76
legal and judicial history, 825
Manifesto (1890), 852
Mexico, 896

Perpetual Emigrating Fund, 1075
persecution, 1076
plural marriage, 1091
politics, 1101
Retrenchment Association, 1224
Reynolds v. *United States*, 1229–30
Seventy, 1302
social and cultural history, 1383
Utah statehood, 1502
Utah Territory, 1505
woman suffrage, 1572
Woodruff, Wilford, 1583
see also Edmunds Act; Edmunds-Tucker Act; Morrill Act; Poland Act
Anti-Semitism, 695
Apache tribe, 896
Apocalypse of Adam, 18
Apocalyptic texts, **54**, 184
Apocrypha and pseudepigrapha, **55–56**, 343, 687, 718, 735, 742
Apollonarianism, 272
Apostasy, **56–58**
authority, 89
Book of Mormon, 152, 155
celibacy, 260
covenant Israel, 330
Daniel, prophecies of, 355
disciplinary procedures, 386
dispensation of the fulness of times, 388
dispensations of the Gospel, 389
doctrine, 395, 400
Elias, spirit of, 449
infant baptism, 682
kingdom of heaven, 790
Melchizedek Priesthood, 884
parables, 1061
priesthood, 1135
prophets, 1169
Restoration of the Gospel of Jesus Christ, 1220
true and living Church, 1489
see also Organization of the Church in New Testament times
Apostate, **59**, 996
Apostles, **59–61**, 278, 1126, 1678–79
Book of Mormon, 159
British Isles, 228
Christians and Christianity, 271
dispensation of the fulness of times, 388
doctrine, 401
Doctrine and Covenants, 410
history, 602

Apostles *(Cont'd)*
  keys of the priesthood, 780
  Kimball, Spencer W., 786
  Melchizedek Priesthood, 883
  New Testament, 1013
  ordination, 1034, 1035
  Paul, 1068
  priesthood quorums, 1146
  Seventy, 1301
  testimony of Jesus Christ, 1472
  see also Quorum of the Twelve
    Apostles; specific name, e.g.,
    John the Apostle
Appropriations Committee, 508–509
April 6, **61–62**, 171, 259, 261, 262,
  505, 1050, 1253, 1254
Aquinas, Thomas, 561, 809, 986,
  1182, 1193
Arbaugh, George, 46
Archaeological Research Institute,
  209
Archaeology, **62–63**, 173, 209, 1388
Archangels, 41–42
Architecture, **63–65**
  ·cross, 344
  folk art, 517
  Kirtland Temple, 798
  meetinghouse, 876–77
  Salt Lake Temple, 1253, 1254
  social and cultural history, 1381
  symbolism, 1429
Archives. *See* Libraries and archives
Area, area presidency, **65–66**, 279,
  325, 539, 1045, 1198
  diplomatic relations, 384
  district, district presidency, 391
  finances of the Church, 508
  Kimball, Spencer W., 788
  presiding bishopric, 1130
Argentina, the Church in, 873, 917,
  1399–1400
Arianism, 272
Aristotle, 1193
Arizona, pioneer settlements in,
  66–67
  antipolygamy legislation, 52, 53
Armageddon, **67**
Armenia, the Church in, 434, 518
Army ROTC, U.S., Brigham Young
  University, 224
Arrington, James, 838
Arrington, Leonard J., 114, 308,
  591, 937, 983, 1176, 1631,
  1682
Arteaga, Silviano, 899
Articles of Faith, **67–69**, 941, 1054
  baptism, 92

children, 267
church and state, 281
creeds, 343
discipleship, 384
education, 441
evangelists, 475
gift of the Holy Ghost, 1090
Jesus Christ, 753
Joseph Smith Translation of the
  Bible, 764
Nauvoo, 991
New Jerusalem, 1009
New Testament, 1013
ordinances, 1033
Pearl of Great Price, 1071
values, 1508
Wentworth letter, 1561
Artificial insemination, **70**, 1096
Artists, visual, **70–73**, 946–47, 1381
Art in Mormonism, **73–75**, 1381,
  1389
  see also Architecture; Artists, vis-
    ual; Dance; Drama; Fine arts;
    Folk art; Folklore; Material cul-
    ture; Mormons, image of; Mu-
    sicians; Sculptors; Symbols,
    cultural and artistic
Asay, Carlos E., 461, 1592, 1631,
  1680
Asceticism, 58
Ashton, Marvin J., 81, 110, 1187,
  1577, 1631, 1679, 1680, 1683,
  1739
Ashton, Marvin O., 1631, 1681
Ashton, Wendell J., 1177
Asia, the Church in, **75–81**, 1757
  conversion, 323
  East Asia, 75–79
  interfaith relationships, 696
  missions, 917
  South and Southeast Asia, 79–81
  see also specific country names
Asper, Frank, 976, 1435
Assembly Hall, The, 65
Assistants to the Twelve, **81–82**,
  635, 642, 1037, 1302, 1679
Associated Latter-day Media Artists,
  1389
Association of Mormon Counselors
  and Psychotherapists (AMCAP),
  1388
Association of Mormon Letters
  (AML), 1388
Astronomy, scriptural references to,
  82, 135
Atchison, David R., 929, 931
Atiya, Aziz S., 137, 1060

Atkins, W. H., 1583
Atonement, blood. *See* Blood atonement
Atonement of Jesus Christ, **82–86**,
  389, 581, 732, 752
  Alma, 35
  animals, 42
  Articles of Faith, 67–68
  birth, 116
  Book of Mormon, 140, 147, 152
  Catholicism and Mormonism, 257
  children, 269
  death and dying, 366
  degrees of glory, 367
  disciplinary procedures, 386
  doctrine, 401
  Doctrine and Covenants, 408
  Easter, 433
  fall of Adam, 486, 534
  Gethsemane, 542
  gift of the Holy Ghost, 1210
  Gospel of Jesus Christ, 556
  heirs, 583
  hell, 485
  holiness, 648
  humility, 664
  immaculate conception, 673
  immortality, 676
  infant baptism, 682
  joy, 771
  judgment, 772
  justice and mercy, 775
  justification, 776
  law of Moses, 811
  life and death, spiritual, 833
  love, 846
  miracles, 910
  Mormon, 933
  mortality, 958
  natural man, 985
  origin of man, 1053
  plan of salvation, 1088, 1089–90
  reverence, 1229
  righteousness, 1236
  salvation, 1256
  Samuel the Lamanite, 1259
  sanctification, 1259
  second estate, 1290
  sexuality, 1307
  sin, 1315
  Smith, Joseph, 1341
  suffering in the world, 1422
  see also Blood atonement; Resur-
    rection
Audiovisual Department, 965
Auditing Department, 509
August, Carl, 1263

Augustine, 477, 561, 683, 1052, 1193
Australia, the Church in, **86–88**, 229, 685, 873
Austral Star, 87
Austria, the Church in, 471, 474
Authority, **88–89**, 277
  baptismal prayer, 95
  Book of Mormon, 202
  born in the covenant, 218
  Catholicism and Mormonism, 257
  Christians and Christianity, 270
  clergy, 288
  confirmation, 310
  covenants, 332
  doctrine, 399
  elder, Melchizedek Priesthood, 447
  First Presidency, 512
  fulness of the Gospel, 530
  gift of the Holy Ghost, 543
  Holy Ghost, 649
  Jesus Christ, 730
  laying on of hands, 814
  ordinances, 1032
  organization of the Church, 1050
  politics, 1106
  priesthood offices, 1143
  priests, 1132
  Quorum of the Twelve Apostles, 1185
  sealing, 1288
  setting apart, 1300
  Smith, Joseph, 1342
Authorship, Book of Mormon, 166–67
Autobiography. *See* Biography and autobiography
Automobile industry in Utah, 439
Autopsy, 89
Auxiliary organizations, **89–90**, 279, 539, 685, 1045, 1682–85
  bishops, 120, 123
  Brigham Young University, 221
  callings, 249
  celebrations, 259
  community, 302
  correlation of the Church, 324
  curriculum, 347
  history, 623, 635
  magazines, 849
  meetinghouse, 876
  missions, 919
  presidency, 1126
  priesthood councils, 1141
  priesthood executive committee, 1142

Primary, 1146
Relief Society, 1202
Sunday School, 1426
ward council, 1544
Young Men, 1613
Young Women, 1616
see also specific name, e.g., Relief Society
Avard, Sampson, 356–57
Avila, Juan Carlos, 1399
Ayala, Eduardo, 1400, 1631, 1680
Azevedo, Lex de, 837

Babbitt, Almon W., 371
Babcock, Phoebe Ann, 1068
Babies. *See* Children; Infant baptism
Babylon. *See* Worldliness
Backman, Robert L., 1277, 1631, 1680, 1683
Baden-Powell, Robert, 1275
Badger, Rodney C., 1631, 1683
Bagley, Pat, 665
Bailey, Lydia, 545
  see also Knight, Lydia
Bailey, Mary, 1360
Bailey, Paul Drayton, 839
Bailey, Rozella, 1436
Baird, J. Hugh, 1632, 1683
Baird, Robert, 938
Baker, Fred A., 238
Baker, John T., 966
Baker, Zina, 1611
Baldwin, Caleb, 830
Ballantyne, David, 91
Ballantyne, Jane, 1440
Ballantyne, Richard, **91–92**, 231, 1424
Ballard, Melvin J., 540, 917, 1145, 1246, 1397, 1399, 1679, 1683, 1739
Ballard, M. Russell, 461, 647, 1187, 1397, 1632, 1679, 1680, 1739
Ballif, Arta Romney, 1015
Ballo, Domenico, 1380
Bamberger, Simon, 695
Bancroft, George, 317
Bancroft, Hubert H., 590, 625
Bangerter, Geri, 1396
Bangerter, William Grant, 1632, 1680
Banks, Ben B., 1632, 1680
Bannerman, Ann, 91
Bannock Stake Academy, 12
Baptism, **92–94**, 310, 389
  Aaronic Priesthood, 4
  Abraham, 8

Alma, 32
blessings, 129
Book of Mormon, 158, 203
Born of God, 218
Catholicism and Mormonism, 258
celebrations, 258
children, 267
conversion, 321
covenant Israel, 331
cross, 345
Doctrine and Covenants, 408, 411, 414, 421
dove, sign of the, 428
elect of God, 448
endowment, 455
enduring to the end, 457
Enoch, 462
faith in Jesus Christ, 483
first principles of the Gospel, 514
gift of the Holy Ghost, 543
Gospel of Jesus Christ, 557
history, 602
Holy Ghost, 649
humility, 663
interviews, 697
Israel, 710
Jesus Christ, 93, 546, 730, 735, 744
joining the Church, 758
law of Moses, 812
life and death, spiritual, 833
membership, 887
Noah, 1017
ordinances, 1032
ordination, 1034
original sin, 1052
plan of salvation, 1090
priesthood, 1138
remission of sins, 1210
repentance, 1217
salvation, 1257
sanctification, 1259
Scandinavia, 1262
scripture, 1283
signs of the true Church, 1311
Smith, Joseph, 1342
symbolism, 1428, 1430
vital statistics, 1526
women, roles of, 1575
see also Infant baptism; Rebaptism
Baptismal covenant, **94–95**, 332
  death and dying, 366
  individuality, 681
  Primary, 1149
Baptismal prayer, 92, **95**, 202, 1118
  scripture, 1280

Baptism for the dead, 94, **95–97**, 421
  ancient sources, 97
  endowment, 456
  family history, genealogy, 493
  freemasonry, 529
  history, 612
  LDS practice, 95–96
  marriage, 859
  Nauvoo, 991
  Nauvoo Temple, 1001
  New Testament, 1013
  Paul, 1070
  record keeping, 1196
  salvation, 1257
  Smith, Joseph, 1342
  social and cultural history, 1379
  temple ordinances, 1445
  temples, 1447, 1454
  see also Salvation of the dead
Baptism of fire and the Holy Ghost, 92, **97–98**, 543, 730, 1208
Baptist church, 168, 169, 683, 687
Barber, George, 79
Barber, Phyllis, 844
Barden, Jerusha. *See* Smith, Jerusha Barden
Barfoot, Joseph, 972
Barker, Kate Montgomery, 1632, 1685
Barratt, Matilda Morehouse, 1632, 1684
Barratt, William James, 86
Barrows, Nancy, 1312
Barsch, Wulf, 72, 74
Barstow, George, 1562
Basketball, 1410
Battle of the Bulls, 936
Bawden, Henry, 597
Beadel, John H., 49
Beaman, Louisa, 1337
Bean, Orestes Utah, 837
Bean, Willard W., 592
Beardsley, Harry M., 50
Beatitudes, **98–99**, 1012, 1283, 1298
Beauchamp, Robert, 86
Beauregard, Donald, 71
Beebe, Clara M. Woodruff, 1632, 1684
Beehive Clothing Mills, 826
Beehive House, 64, 371, 595, 1605
Beehive symbol, **99**, 371, 517, 1431
Beesley, Clarissa, 1615, 1632, 1684
Beesley, Ebenezer, 232, 667, 950, 976
Beet sugar industry. *See* Sugar beet industry

Begay, Harrison, 1286
Belgium, 471
Belief and conduct, 316
Belisle, Orvilla S., 49, 949
Bell, Alfreda Eva, 49
Bell, Eloise, 840
Bell, Terrell H., 286
Belle S. Spafford Endowed Chair in Social Work, 1402
Benbow, Jane, 230
Benbow, John, 230
Benchley, Julius, 1087
Beneficial Development Company, 242
Beneficial Life Insurance Company, 242
Benjamin, **99–100**, 584, 959, 960
  Book of Mormon, 160, 164, 166–67, 197, 203
  Gethsemane, 542
  Jesus Christ, 744, 748, 750
  manuscript, lost 116 pages, 855
  Messiah, 894
  natural man, 985
  obedience, 1021
  poverty, 1113
  prophecy, 1164
  sanctification, 1260
  signs as divine witness, 1320
  speech, 149
Bennett, Archibald F., 537
Bennett, Emily Higgs, 1632, 1685
Bennett, John C., 46, 47, 48, 1093, 1235, 1632, 1678, 1739
Bennett, William H., 1632, 1680
Bennion, Adam S., 1043, 1632, 1679, 1739
Bennion, Lowell, 840
Bennion, Milton, 1426, 1632, 1682
Bennion, M. Lynn, 441
Bennion, Samuel O., 1632, 1680
Bens, Mariana Comb, 1313
Benson, Barbara, 101
Benson, Beth, 101
Benson, Beverly, 101
Benson, Bonnie, 101
Benson, Ezra T. (Ezra Taft's great-grandfather), 101, 1036, 1632, 1679, 1739
Benson, Ezra Taft, 60, **100–104**, 286, 513, 597, 787, 1126, 1131, 1632, 1678, 1679, 1739
  Adamic language, 18
  adoption of children, 20
  agriculture, 29
  Asia, 79, 80
  Book of Mormon, 142

British Isles, 231
  callings, 249
  compassionate service, 303
  contention, 320
  Europe, 472
  family prayer, 498
  fulness of the Gospel, 530
  Gethsemane, 542
  Gospel of Jesus Christ, 558
  history, 639, 646
  home teaching, 655
  humanitarian service, 661
  inspiration, 683
  Jesus Christ, 725, 737
  marriage, 857, 859
  motherhood, 962
  organization, 1043
  politics, 1108
  pride, 1131
  prophets, 1165
  Quorum of the Twelve Apostles, 1186
  Scandinavia, 1263, 1264
  scouting, 1276
  senior citizens, 1297
  sin, 1316
  single adults, 1318
  sports, 1410
  stake, 1412
  temples, 1454
  West Indies, 1562
Benson, Flora Smith Amussen, 101
Benson, George Taft, Jr. (Ezra's father), 100-101
Benson, John, Jr., 101
Benson, John, Sr., 101
Benson, Mark, 101
Benson, Orval, 101
Benson, Purnell, 1082
Benson, Reed, 101
Benson Institute. *See* Ezra Taft Benson Agriculture and Food Institute
Bentin, Johan, 72
Bentley, Adamson, 1233
Bentley, Joseph T., 1632, 1683
Berge, Dale, 63
Berlin, Adele, 182
Bernhisel, John M., 766
Berrett, William E., 425
Bertola, Francesco, 1059
B. H. Roberts Society, 1389
Bible, **104–111**, 278, 325
  Book of Mormon, 106, 139–40, 158–60, 168–69, 179
  Book of Moses, 216
  commandments, 296

completeness, 106–107
covenants in, 333–35
doctrine, 399
importance, 104–108
Jesus Christ in, 745–48
King James Version, 109–110,
179, 393, 427, 585
LDS belief, 108, 598, 941
LDS publication, 110–11, 766
priesthood in, 1138–40
prophecy, 1162–63
prophets, 1167–70
reading, 107
sacrifice, 1248–49
Seventy, 1301
teachings and practices, 105–106
Topical Guide, 1483–84
Urim and Thummim, 1499
see also Joseph Smith Translation
of the Bible; New Testament;
Old Testament; Scripture
Bible, LDS, 111
Bible Aids committee, 110
Bible dictionary, 110, 646, 111–12,
1484
Bible scholarship, 112–13, 689
scripture, 1279
BIC. See Bonneville International
Corporation
Bidamon, Emma Smith. See Smith,
Emma Hale
Bidamon, Lewis C., 186, 997, 1326
Bierstadt, Albert, 947, 1381
Biesinger, Thomas, 471
Bigamy. See Antipolygamy legisla-
tion; Plural marriage
Big Horn Basin, Wyoming, 294
Bigler, Bathsheba. See Smith, Bath-
sheba Bigler
Bigler, Henry W., 247, 578
Bigler, Mark, 1320
Billings, Alfred, 66
Billings, Titus, 1632, 1682
Bill of Rights, 315–16
Bingham, Louisa Emiline, 821
Biography and autobiography, 113–
15, 304
Biology, College of (BYU), 223
Birth, 115–16
foreordination, 522
plan of salvation, 1088
premortal life, 1123
second estate, 1290
see also Born of God; Death and
dying; First estate; Life and
death, spiritual; Mortality; Premortal life; Purpose of earth
life

Birth, spiritual. See Born of God;
Premortal life
Birth control, 116–17, 488, 645,
1306, 1418
see also Abortion; Fertility; Procreation; Sterilization; Vasectomy
Birth of a Nation, The (film), 947
Birth rates. See Fertility; Vital statistics
Bishop, 117–18, 288, 520, 609, 617,
643, 1050
Aaronic Priesthood, 3
callings, 249
calamities and disasters, 246
chastity law, 266
common consent, 298
community, 300
confession of sins, 309
consecration, 313
deacon, Aaronic Priesthood, 361
death and dying, 366
disciplinary procedures, 385
Doctrine and Covenants, 412,
418
elder, Melchizedek Priesthood,
447
fast offerings, 501
finances of the Church, 508
high priest, 587
meetinghouse libraries, 878
Melchizedek Priesthood, 883
New Testament, 1013
presidency, 1125
presiding bishopric, 1128
priest, 1132
priesthood, 1137, 1140
priesthood blessings, 1140
priesthood quorums, 1144
Relief Society, 1200
social services, 1386
tithing, 1481
types, 119
ward, 1541
Bishop, history of the office, 119–
22, 1128
Bishopric, 117, 122–23, 1126,
1681–82
burial, 239
deacon, Aaronic Priesthood, 361
disciplinary procedures, 386
fast and testimony meeting, 502
fellowshipping members, 506
high council, 586
ordination, 1035
organization, 1048
priesthood quorums, 1144
see also Presiding bishopric

Bishop's storehouse, 118, 119, 120,
123–25, 313, 367, 454, 501,
1113, 1553, 1555, 1558, 1567
Bitton, Davis, 114, 770
Black, Adam, 1346
Black, Joseph S., 831
Black Hawk War (1865–1868), 999
Blackmore, John, 254
Blacks, 125–27, 423, 642, 645, 789,
873, 1530
see also Africa, the Church in;
Doctrine and Covenants Official Declaration—2; Race,
racism
Blasphemy, 127–28, 352, 1499
see also Profanity
Blessing of children, 129, 267, 268
Blessing on food, 128
Blessings, 128–30
bishops, 120
callings, 250
celebrations, 258–59
children, 129, 267, 268
death and dying, 365
elder, Melchizedek priesthood,
447
elect of God, 448
fathers', 504
food, 128
gift of the Holy Ghost, 543
grace, 562
laying on of hands, 814
mission president, 914
obedience, 1021
patriarchal, 1066–67
priesthood, 1140–41
temples, 1454–55
see also Cursings; Ordinances
Blind, materials for the, 130–31
Blood atonement, 48, 131, 633,
1197
Blood Indians (Canada), 253
Blood sacrifices, 332, 390
Blood transfusions, 131–32
Blumenbach, Johann Friedrich,
1191
Bodden, Rodolfo, 1562
Boggs, Lilburn W., 46, 421, 480,
577, 611, 830, 927, 929, 931,
1018, 1347
Bolivia, the Church in, 1396
Bolton, Curtis E., 213
Bond, Christopher S., 480
Bonhoeffer, Dietrich, 561
Bonneville International Corpora-
tion (BIC), 132, 241, 242, 800
broadcasting, 233–34

Bonneville International Corporation (BIC) (Cont'd)
  interfaith relationships, 694
  politics, 1108
Book of Abraham, **132–38**, 609
  astronomy, 82
  blacks, 126
  contents, 135
  covenants, 334
  creation accounts, 340
  dove, sign of the, 428
  facsimiles, 135–37, 1479, 1480
  intelligences, 692
  Jesus Christ, 743
  origin, 132–34, 1058
  papyri, 1058
  RLDS Church, 1213
  scripture, 1283
  studies, 137–38
  time and eternity, 1479
  translation and publication, 134
Book of Breathings, 136, 137
Book of Commandments (Smith), **138**, 406, 409, 411, 412, 425, 1173
Book of the Dead, 135, 136, 137
Book of Joseph of Egypt. *See* Joseph of Egypt, writings of
Book of Life, **138–39**
Book of Mormon, **139–58**, 278, 325
  Africa, 25
  Alma, book of, 34, 150–52
  Angel Moroni statue, 40
  Asia, 77, 78, 79, 80, 81
  charity, 264
  chastening, 265
  Christians and Christianity, 271
  circumcision, 283
  commandments, 296
  consecration, 314
  deaf, materials for the, 364
  Deuteronomic teachings in, 378
  distribution centers, 390
  doctrine, 394
  education, 441
  Enos, book of, 148
  Ether, book of, 156–57, 190, 378, 717–18
  fall of Adam, 485
  freedom, 525
  Helaman, book of, 152–53, 1291
  hope, 657
  humanitarian service, 661
  Isaiah, 700–702
  Jacob, book of, 147–48, 714, 1624
  Jarom, book of, 148
  Jesus Christ, 748–50

  John, revelations of, 754
  Lamanites, 804–805
  law of Moses, 811
  laying on of hands, 814
  military and the Church, 903
  Mormon, book of, 156
  Mormon, words of, 149
  Moroni, book of, 157–58, 956, 957
  Moses, 958
  Mosiah, book of, 149–50
  mysteries of God, 977
  Native Americans, 981
  Nephi, first book of, 144–46, 749, 828
  Nephi, second book of, 146–47
  Nephi, book of third, 153–55, 1291, 1477
  Nephi, book of fourth, 155–56
  obedience, 1021
  Omni, book of, 148
  overview, 139–43
  politics, 1098
  prophecy in, 1163–64
  revelation, 1225
  scripture, 1283
  Sermon on the Mount, 1298
  Smith, Joseph, 1333
  standard works, 1415–16
  title page, 144, 462, 707, 933
  tree of life, 1487
  View of the Hebrews, 1510
  visions of Joseph Smith, 1514
  "voice from the dust," 1538
  women in, 1577–80
  see also Doctrine and Covenants
Book of Mormon, biblical prophecies about, **158–60**, 481, 707
Book of Mormon, government and legal history in the, **160–62**
Book of Mormon, history of warfare in, **162–66**, 956, 1547–49
Book of Mormon authorship, **166–67**
Book of Mormon in a biblical culture, 106, **168–69**
Book of Mormon chronology, **169–71**, 730
Book of Mormon commentaries, **171–72**
Book of Mormon economy and technology, **172–75**, 718
Book of Mormon editions, **175–76**
Book of Mormon geography, **176–79**, 347, 1270
Book of Mormon language, **179–81**
Book of Mormon literature, **181–85**, 1004

Book of Mormon manuscripts, **185–86**
Book of Mormon names, **186–87**
Book of Mormon Near Eastern background, **187–90**
Book of Mormon peoples, **191–95**, 760, 805, 959, 969, 1160, 1163, 1270, 1452
Book of Mormon personalities, **195**
Book of Mormon plates and records, **195–201**, 346, 555, 1004, 1284
Book of Mormon religious teachings and practices, **201–205**
Book of Mormon studies, **205–209**
Book of Mormon translation by Joseph Smith, **210–13**, 602, 1226, 1335
Book of Mormon translations, **213–14**, 555, 1264
Book of Mormon witnesses, **214–16**, 335, 505, 555, 575, 602–603, 1335, 1348, 1514, 1564
Book of Moses, 138, **216–17**, 505, 766, 958
  creation accounts, 340
  Enoch, 457
  Jesus Christ, 743
  Rigdon, Sidney, 1234
  scripture, 1283
Book of Remembrance, **217**, 845, 1194
Booth, Ezra, 46, 48
Booth, Joseph, 902
Boren, Clara Lorenzi, 1398
Boren, Samuel, 1398
Born again. *See* Born of God
Born in the covenant, **218**, 1289, 1445
Born of God, **218–19**
  Alma, 34
  baptism, 93, 97
  gift of the Holy Ghost, 544
  heirs, 583
  righteousness, 1236
  salvation of the dead, 1258
  see also Conversion
Bountiful, Utah, <u>64</u>, 177
Bousquet, Georges, 1592
Bowden, Robert C., 953
Bowen, Albert E., <u>637</u>, <u>1186</u>, 1632, 1679, 1683, <u>1739</u>
Bowen, Emma Lucy Gates, 535, 977
Boyer, Marian Richards, 1632, 1685
Boyle, Dessie, 1632, 1684
Boynton, John F., 1185, 1633, 1679, 1739

Boy scouts. *See* Scouting
Bradford, Mary Lythgoe, 840
Bradford, William R., 1633, 1680
Bradley, Ian, 230
Bradshaw, Merrill, 974
Bramall, William, 229
Branch, branch president, **219**, 279, 288, 390
 elder, Melchizedek Priesthood, 447
 finances of the Church, 508
 membership records, 887
 organization, 1037
 priesthood quorums, 1144
 scouting, 1276
 see also specific branch name, e.g., Colesville, New York
Brandley, Elsie Talmage, 1615, 1616
Brannan, Sam, 247
Brazil, the Church in, 873, 914, 1393–96, 1760
Bresil, Henri-Robert, 72
Brewerton, Ted E., 1398, 1633, 1680, 1683
Briant, Nancy, 1233
Bridgeforth, Ruffin, 125
Bridger, Jim, 1599
Bridgman, Peter G., 1400
Briggs, Jason, 1212, 1266
Brigham City Cooperative, 621
Brigham Young (film), 567, 633, 948
Brigham Young Academy, 12, 219, 221, 222, 275, <u>442</u>, 444, 913, 1608
Brigham Young College (BYC), 12, **219–20**
Brigham Young University (BYU), 12, **220–27**, 274, 275, 444, 539, 643, 1267
 accreditation, 225
 architecture, 64
 Benson, Ezra Taft, 103
 blacks, 126
 Book of Mormon, 172, 208
 broadcasting, 234
 colleges and programs, 223–25
 dating and courtship, 359
 drama, 429
 economic aid, 434
 faculty, 221
 general and honors education, 223
 Hawaii campus, 226–27, 274, 275, 444, 579, 645, 1109
 historians, 591
 history, 221–22

intellectual history, 688
interfaith relationships, 694, 696
Jerusalem Center for Near Eastern Studies, 225–26, 695, 902
LDS Foundation, 816
legal and judicial history, 825
libraries and archives, 832
Middle East, 902
mission, 221
Missionary Training Centers, 913–14
motion pictures, 964–65
motto, 1193–94
museums, 973
Native Americans, 984–85
organization, 1040
Polynesian Cultural Center, 1109–10
Provo, Utah, campus, 220–25
religion and religious education, 222–23
satellite communications system, 1261
science and scientists, 1272
senior citizens, 1298
social and cultural history, 1379
societies and organizations, 1389
sports, 1411
students, 221
values, 1509
see also Brigham Young Academy
Brimhall, George H., 222
British Isles, the Church in, **227–32**, 576, 1760
 Book of Mormon, 168
 centennial observances, 262
 diplomatic relations, 382
 Doctrine and Covenants, 426
 history, 616, 634
 hymns, 667
 immigration and emigration, 674, 676
 institutes of religion, 685
 Kimball, Heber C., 782
 legal and judicial history, 826
 McKay, David O., 871, 872, 873
 Millennial Star, 906
 missions, 916, 920–22
 Nauvoo, 990, 992
 occupations, 1022
 Quorum of the Twelve Apostles, 1186
 temples, 1453
 vital statistics, 230, 1525, <u>1533</u>
 see also Missions of the Twelve to the British Isles

Broadcasting, <u>232–34</u>, 800
 business, <u>241</u>, 242
 centennial observances, 261, 262
 children, 270
 conferences, 308
 deaf, materials for the, 364
 public relations, 1178
 satellite communications system, 1261
 see also KSL broadcasting; Mormon Tabernacle Choir Broadcast; Radio; Television
Brockbank, Bernard P., 1633, 1680
Brodie, Fawn M., 50, 114, 597, 939, 1403
Brooks, Juanita, 114, 115, 966
Brooks, Phebe, 1233
Brossard, Edgar B., 29, 634
Brotherhood, **234–35**, 506, 815
Brother of Jared, 157, 197, **235–36**, 717, 748, 956, 1162, 1490
Brough, Monte J., 1633, 1680, 1684
Brown, Edward, 78
Brown, Francis A., <u>53</u>
Brown, Hannah, 1601
Brown, Harold, 900
Brown, Hugh B., 81, 252, 253, 287, <u>1045</u>, 1109, 1633, 1678, 1679, <u>1739</u>
Brown, James, 66, 935, 936
Brown, John, 847
Brown, Lenore Jesperson, 900
Brown, Margaret Zimmerman, 847
Brown, Moroni, <u>53</u>
Brown, Peter, 58
Brown, Sarah, 1582
Brown, Victor L., 1129, 1633, 1680, 1681, 1682
Brown, William, 1601
Browne, Charles Farrer, 949
Browning, Orville H., 1000
Brunson, Seymour, 95
Buber, Martin, 1280
Buchanan, Golden, 679
Buchanan, James, 619, 779, 783, 825, 1101, 1500, 1501, 1505, 1608
Buddhism, 1407, 1589
Budget Committee, 508
Buehner, Carl W., 1633, 1682, 1683
Buffetings of Satan, **236**
Builders, The (pageant), 347
Building program, **236–38**, 510, 537, 644, 1042
Bulgaria, the Church in, 474
Bulletin, The (periodical), **238**, 1148

Bullock, Thomas, 590, 647, 791
Burial, **238–39**, 366, 367, 1097, 1422
  see also Cremation
Burma, the Church in, 79, 1757
Burnings, everlasting, **239**
Burton, Francis, 1592
Burton, Harold W., 64, 877
Burton, Robert T., 1633, 1681, 1682
Burton, Theodore M., 1633, 1680
Busche, F. Enzio, 473, 1633, 1680
Bush, George, 952
Bushman, Richard L., 114, 597
Business, **239–43**
  Church participation, 240–43, 509, 1048, 1107
  LDS attitudes, 239–40
  Salt Lake City, Utah, 1252
  see also Agriculture; Deseret Industries; Economic history of the Church; Finances of the Church; LDS Business College; Mormon Handicraft
Butler, Alva J., 1025
Butterfield, Josiah, 1633, 1680
BYU. *See* Brigham Young University
BYU Studies (periodical), 849

Cable television, 234
Caffeine, 289
Cain, 5, **245–46**, 1391
  see also Abel
Calamities and disasters, **246**, 265
  see also Bishop's storehouse; Emergency preparedness
Calder, David, 976
Caldwell, C. Max, 425
Caldwell County. *See* Missouri, LDS communities in Caldwell and Daviess counties
California, pioneer settlements in, **246–48**, 633
  see also Gold Rush; Mormon Battalion
California Intermountain News (periodical), 1011
Call, Anson, 1313
Call, Waldo P., 1633, 1680
Calling and election, 248, 583, 652
  see also Elect of God
Callings, **248–50**, 1054
  blessings, 130
  business, 240
  colonization, 291
  common consent, 298

Deseret Industries, 376
discernment, gift of, 384
Doctrine and Covenants, 415, 423
eternal life, 464
family, 491
fear of God, 506
fellowshipping members, 506
following the brethren, 520
gifts of the spirit, 545
history, 618
humility, 663
individuality, 681
interviews, 697
Jesus Christ, 743
laying on of hands, 814
lay participation, 814
lifestyle, 834
magnifying one's calling, 850
meetings, 878
Melchizedek Priesthood, 883
membership, 887
missionaries, 910–11, 918–19
oaths, 1020
ordination, 1034
patriarchal blessings, 1066
presidency, 1125
priesthood offices, 1143
senior citizens, 1297
setting apart, 1300
social and cultural history, 1378
stewardship, 1418
ward, 1541
  see also Calling and election; General authorities; Leadership training; Ward organization
Callis, Charles A., 637, 1186, 1145, 1633, 1679, 1739
Callister, Marion J., 826
Calvin, John, 561, 1052, 1221
Calvinism, 168
Camargo, Helio R., 1396, 1633, 1680
Cambodia, the Church in, 662
Cambridge University Press, 111, 112
Cameron, Mae, 1286
Camp, Walter, 1410
Campbell, Alexander, 46, 47, 48, 166, 169, 205–206, 665, 1475, 1221, 1233
Campbell, Thomas, 1221
Camp Floyd, Utah, 63
Canada, the Church in, **251–52**, 634, 1758
  immigration and emigration, 676
  marriage, 856

Missionary Training Centers, 913, 914
  Nauvoo, 990
  occupations, 1022
  ward, 1452
Canada, LDS pioneer settlements in, **252–54**, 625
Cannon, Abraham H., 320, 1633, 1679, 1680, 1739
Cannon, Ann M., 1615
Cannon, Clare Cordelia Moses, 1633, 1684
Cannon, David H., Jr., 1452
Cannon, Donald Q., 114
Cannon, Elaine Anderson, 678, 1617, 1618, 1619, 1633, 1685
Cannon, Frank J., 633
Cannon, George I., 1633, 1680, 1683
Cannon, George Q., 233, 328, 512, 578, 1633, 1678, 1679, 1682, 1740
  books by, 114, 213
  British Isles, 231
  Canada, 253
  Deseret Book Company, 374
  Deseret News, 377
  Doctrine and Covenants, 426
  history, 624, 626, 627
  intellectual history, 688
  Juvenile Instructor, 777
  Manifesto (1890), 853
  Polynesians, 1110
  priesthood, 1136
  Smith, Joseph F., 1351
  Sunday School, 1425
  Utah statehood, 1502
Cannon, Hugh J., 678, 1617
Cannon, Janath Russell, 1634, 1685
Cannon, John Q., 1634, 1682
Cannon, Joseph, 471, 1634, 1683
Cannon, Leonora, 1438, 1440
Cannon, Lucy Grant, 1617, 1618, 1634, 1684
Cannon, Marsena, 1381
Cannon, Mattie Hughes Paul, 285
Cannon, Sylvester Q., 637, 1129, 1634, 1679, 1681, 1740
Cannon, Tracy Y., 976
Cannon, Virginia Beesley, 1634, 1684
Cannon Publishing Company, 320
Canon, 166, **254**, 401, 1282
Capital punishment, **255**, 971, 1376, 1377
Card, Charles Ora, 251, 252, 253, 625

Card, Orson Scott, 347, 665, 838, 839, 844
Card, Zina, 253
Cardon, Paul, 1312
Cardon, Phillip V., 29
Cardon, Susanna, 1312
Cardston Company, 253
Cardston Temple (Alberta), 64, 251, 254
Careless, George, 232, 667, 950, 976
Carlin, Thomas, 999
Carmack, John K., 592, 1634, 1680, 1682
Carmichael, Sarah Elizabeth, 1381
Carr, Gail E., 78
Carrington, Albert, 590, 1136, 1634, 1678, 1679, 1682, 1740
Carroll, Sarah Jane, 1092
Carson Valley, Nevada, 290
Carter, Charles W., 1381
Carter, Gary, 73
Carter, Jared, 793
Carter, Mary, 1313
Carter, Phoebe Whittemore, 1582
Carthage Jail, **255–56**, 595, 613, 635, 824, 860, 997, 998, 999
  politics, 1100
  Smith, Hyrum, 1331
  Smith, Joseph, 1338
  Smith, Joseph F., 1352
  Taylor, John, 1438
Carver, Wayne, 842
Caswell, Henry, 46, 47–48
Catholicism and Mormonism, **257–58**
  apocrypha, 55
  Bible, 109
  cross, 344
  deification, early Christian, 370
  doctrine, 400, 401
  Elijah, 451
  epistemology, 463
  Europe, 469, 473
  grace, 560–61
  interfaith relationships, 693–95
  marriage and divorce, 856, 857
  purpose of earth life, 1182
  reason and revelation, 1193
  sacrament, 1243
Cave of Treasures (Syriac work), 18
CBS. *See* Columbia Broadcasting System
Ceciliato, Ana Gláucia, 1396
Celebrations, **258–59**
  see also specific celebration, e.g., Pioneer Day

Celestial kingdom, **259–60**
  afterlife, 479
  baptism, 92
  burnings, everlasting, 239
  celibacy, 260
  Church and state, 281
  consecration, 313
  damnation, 353
  death and dying, 365
  degrees of glory, 367, 368–69
  doctrine, 401
  Doctrine and Covenants, 414, 422
  Enoch, 458
  equality, 463
  eternal life, 464
  eternal progression, 466
  heirs, 583
  kingdom of heaven, 790
  light of Christ, 835
  marriage, 856, 858
  paradise, 1062
  Pearl of Great Price, 1072
  plan of salvation, 1090
  priesthood, 1137
  salvation, 1257
  scripture, 1278
  Smith, Joseph, 1343
  see also Heaven; Telestial kingdom; Terrestrial kingdom
Celestial law, 463
Celestial living, 312
Celibacy, 258, **260**, 401
Censorship. *See* Confidential records
Centennial observances, 260–62
Central America. *See* Mexico and Central America, the Church in
Central Pacific Mission (Hawaii), 579
Ceremonies, **262–63**, 746
  see also Centennial observances; Cumorah pageant; General Conference; Pioneer Day
Cezoram, 165
Chamberlain, Joseph, 1401
Chamberlain, Mary W., 285
Chambers, Samuel, 125
Chandler, Michael H., 132, 133, 1058, 1059
Chandler, Neal, 844
Chang I–Ch'ing, 79
Channing, William E., 169
Chaplains, **263–64**
Chapman, William A., 1247
Charity, **264**, 684
  gifts of the spirit, 546

Mormon, 933
New Testament, 1013
religious experience, 1208
see also Lectures on Faith
Charles Redd Center for Western Studies (BYU), 223
Chastening, **264–65**, 582, 1260
  see also Wrath of God
Chastity, law of, **265–66**, 1054, 1096, 1158
  adultery, 21
  Book of Mormon, 147
  dating and courtship, 358
  disciplinary procedures, 386
  family, 487
  health, 580
  homosexuality, 656
  joining the Church, 759
  law of Moses, 812
  modesty in dress, 932
  Old Testament, 1028
  physical body, 1080
  pornography, 1112
  premarital sex, 1123
  sex education, 1305
  sexuality, 1307
  socialization, 1385
Cheesman, Paul R., 172
Cherry, William, 1627
Chiasmus, 167, 181, 182–83
Chicago World's Fair (1893), 479, 628
Child, Hortense Hogan, 1634, 1685
Child, Julia Alleman, 1634, 1685
Children, **266–69**
  abuse of, 11
  adoption of, 20–21, 1386, 1445
  Articles of Faith, 69
  artificial insemination, 70
  blessing of, 129, 267, 268
  Book of Mormon, 142
  born in the covenant, 218
  celebrations, 258
  civil rights, 287
  conferences, 306
  death and dying, 365–66
  divorce, 392
  eternal lives, eternal increase, 465
  Europe, 473
  history, 626
  hospitals, 660
  hymns, 669
  Joseph Smith Translation of the Bible, 767, 768
  lay participation and leadership, 818

Children *(Cont'd)*
  sacrament, 1244
  salvation of, 268–69, 682, 1052, 1244
  single adults, 1317
  social characteristics, 1372, 1375
  social services, 1386
  stillborn, 1419
  temple ordinances, 1445
  vital statistics, 1521–24, 1526, 1529–30, 1533
  see also Family; Fatherhood; Infant baptism; Maternity and child health care; Motherhood; Primary; Youth
Children's Convalescent Hospital, 660
Children's Friend, The (periodical), **269–70**, 635, 1064, 1147
  see also Friend, The
"Children's Friend of the Air, The" (radio show), 270
Chile, the Church in, 917, 1399, 1760
China, the Church in, 75–77, 78–79, 917, 1757
Choirs. *See* Mormon Tabernacle Choir; Music
Choules, Albert, Jr., 1634, 1680
Christ, 740
  see also Jesus Christ
Christensen, C. C. A., 70, 71, 517, 573, 947, 1381
Christensen, James, 72
Christensen, Joe J., 1634, 1680, 1682, 1683
Christensen, P. A., 840
Christians and Christianity, **270–71**
  Apocrypha, 55
  apostasy, 58
  Book of Mormon, 166, 168
  Brigham Young University, 224
  civic duties, 285
  conversion, 322
  covenants, 333
  creation accounts, 341, 342
  cross, 344–45
  cult, 345
  damnation, 353
  deification, early Christian, 369–70
  doctrine, 399–402
  Easter, 433
  enduring to the end, 457
  Enoch, 459, 460
  ethics, 467
  foreknowledge of God, 521
  grace, 560–61

historical sites, 592
infant baptism, 682
interfaith relationships, 693–95
law, 808
Matthew, Gospel of, 869
Melchizedek, 880–81, 882
opposition, 1031
purpose of earth life, 1182
reason and revelation, 1192–93
resurrection, 1223
sacrament, 1243
scripture, 1277
spiritual death, 1407
Sunday, 1423
symbolism, 1428
temples, 1464
Christiansen, Clay, 976
Christiansen, ElRay L., 1634, 1679
Christmas, 61–62, **271–72**, 730
  see also April 6
Christmas, R. A., 842
Christology, **272–73**
  deification, early Christian, 370
  doctrine, 401
  Godhead, 553
  Godhood, 553
  Jesus Christ, 748
  light and darkness, 836
  time and eternity, 1478
Christus Statue, **273–74**, 479, 1466
Christy, Epanaia, 1286
Chronology, Book of Mormon, 169–71
Church Almanac, 35
Church Building Committee, 64
Church of Christ, 1265, 1266
Church College of Hawaii, 226, 579
  see also Brigham Young University, Hawaii campus
Church College of New Zealand, 1016
Church Educational System (CES), **274–76**, 444, 539, 643–44
  academies, 12–13
  Bible, 110, 111
  British Isles, 230
  history, 274–75
  institutes of religion, 684
  interfaith relationships, 694
  LDS Foundation, 816
  LDS Student Association, 817
  organization, 275, 1040, 1046
  philosophy, 274
  seminaries, 1295
  social and cultural history, 1383
  values, 1508–1509
  see also specific school, e.g., Brigham Young University

Church of England, 168
Church of the Firstborn, **276**, 479, 583–84, 728
Church of the Firstborn of the Fulness of Times, 531
Church government, 349
  see also Church and state
Church growth. *See* Vital statistics
Church headquarters building, 64
Churchill, Winston, 382
Church of Jesus Christ of the Children of Zion, 1266
Church of Jesus Christ of Latter-day Saints, The, **276–80**
  Mormonism, an independent interpretation, 937–41
  Mormonism, Mormons, 941–42
  name of the Church, 979, 1249
  schismatic groups, 1266
  vital statistics, 1519–37
  vocabulary, 1537–38
  see also History of the Church; Reorganized Church of Jesus Christ of Latter Day Saints (RLDS Church); Saints
Church of the Lamb of God, 531
Church News (periodical), 36, **280–81**, 1011
Church schools. *See* Church Educational System (CES)
Church Security Program, 567
  see also Welfare services
Church and state, **281–83**, 942, 1097
  education, 444
  Europe, 470
  politics, 1098, 1103
  United States of America, 1495
  war and peace, 1549
  see also Civic duties
Church trains, 674
Church in the World, **283**
Church of Zion, 1266
Cifuentes, Carlos, 1399–1400
Circumcision, 9, **283**, 332, 390, 1008, 1052
City of Joseph, 991
  see also Nauvoo
City planning, **283–85**, 435, 537
  material culture, 864
  Missouri, 924
  Nauvoo, 995
  organization, 1038
  pioneer economy, 1084
  Salt Lake City, Utah, 1251
  social and cultural history, 1378, 1381
  united orders, 1494

City of Zion. *See* Zion
Civic duties, 281, **285–86**, 1018, 1097, 1107; 1547
see also Humanitarian service
Civil rights, **286–87**, 645, 826, 1097, 1101, 1105
see also Constitutional law; Constitution of the United States of America; Legal and judicial history
Civil Rights Act (1964), 826
Civil War prophecy, **287–88**, 1549
Clapp, Benjamin L., 1634, 1680
Clapp, Julia, 1324
Clark, Dennis, 841
Clark, Ezra T., religious experience, 1209
Clark, Geraldine Merkley, 25
Clark, Harlan W., 25
Clark, Hulda Meriah, 91
Clark, John A., 47
Clark, John B., 480
Clark, J. Reuben, Jr., 81, 568, 638, 822, 1634, 1678, 1740
  Bible, 110
  biography and autobiography, 114
  callings, 250
  consecration, 313
  Constitution (U.S.), 318
  First Presidency, 1678
  history, 634
  intellectual history, 689
  military and the Church, 904
  museums, 972
  priesthood quorums, 1145
  Quorum of the Twelve Apostles, 1185
  war and peace, 1550
Clark, Levira Annett, 1352, 1360
Clark, Marden J., 844
Clark, William, 803
Clark, Wycam, 1265
Clarke, John L., 1232
Clarke, J. Richard, 1634, 1680, 1682
Clawson, Chester, 964
Clawson, Hiram, 1255, 1503
Clawson, John W., 71
Clawson, Rudger, 53, 261, 540, 637, 1329, 1145, 1634, 1678, 1679, 1740
Clawson, Shirley Young, 964
Clay, Henry, 999
Clay county. *See* Missouri, LDS communities in Jackson and Clay counties
Clayton, William, 231, 421, 422, 517, 791

Clebsch, William A., 938
Clergy, **288**, 1134
  see also Priesthood
Clerk, **288–89**, 814, 1125, 1541
Cleveland, Grover, 628, 1502, 1505
Cleveland, Sarah M., 1207, 1634, 1685
Clissold, Edward L., 77
Cluff, Benjamin, Jr., 222, 442
Clyde, Aileen Hales, 1634, 1685
Coal industry, 438, 440
Cocco, Jorge, 72
Cody, Milli, 985
Coffee, **289**, 416, 417, 580, 1097, 1441, 1584
Cole, Abigale (Edith), 1968
Cole, Abner, 46
Coleman, Michael, 73
Colesville, New York, **289–90**, 313, 337, 603, 922
Colfax, Schuyler, 1502
College Lantern (periodical), 535
Colleges. *See* specific names, e.g., Brigham Young University; Ricks College
Collegium Aesculapium, 1389
Collings, Michael R., 842
Colombia, the Church in, 434, 1396–97, 1760
Colonization, **290–94**, 469
  academies, 11
  Arizona settlements, 66–67
  California settlements, 248
  Canada settlements, 252
  centennial observances, 260
  Colorado settlements, 294
  economic history, 437
  history, 616, 633
  Idaho settlements, 671–72
  material culture, 864
  Mexico and Central America, 899–900
  Mexico settlements, 895–97
  museums, 972
  Nevada settlements, 1006–1007
  New Mexico settlements, 1010–11
  organization, 1038
  pioneer economy, 1083
  united orders, 1494
  westward migration, 1563
  Wyoming settlements, 1599
  Young, Brigham, 1607
  see also City planning; Community; Gathering; Immigration and emigration; Missions; Pioneer settlements
Colorado, pioneer settlements in, **294**

Coltrin, Zebedee, 416, 737, 1635, 1680
Columbia Broadcasting System (CBS), 232, 234
Columbus, Christopher, **294–96**, 597, 1495
Com, 717, 718
Combs, Abel, 134, 1060
"Come, Come, Ye Saints" (hymn), 232, 1696–97
Comforter. *See* Holy Ghost; Jesus Christ, second comforter
Commandments, **296–97**, 547
  agency, 26
  born of God, 218
  Doctrine and Covenants, 427
  eternal life, 464
  gifts of the Spirit, 544
  joy, 772
  law, 808
  love, 846
  metaphysics, 895
  obedience, 1020
  Old Testament, 1027, 1028
  remission of sins, 1210
  Word of Wisdom, 1584
  world religions, 1590
Commentaries, Book of Mormon, 171–72
Commerce, Illinois. *See* Nauvoo
Common consent, **297–99**, 539
  authority, 89
  callings, 250
  conferences, 307
  doctrine, 395
  Doctrine and Covenants, 407, 408, 423
  equality, 463
  First Presidency, 513
  history, 603
  Melchizedek Priesthood, 883
  organization, 1035
  presidency, 1125
  President of the Church, 1128
  prophet, seer, and revelator, 1170
  Quorum of the Twelve Apostles, 1188
  revelations, unpublished, 1228
  scripture, 1281
  setting apart, 1300
  stake president, 1415
  succession in the presidency, 1420
Communications. *See* Broadcasting; Public communications; Public relations; Satellite Communications System

Communications, College of, 224
Communion, **299**
　Easter, 433
　pioneer life, 1087
Communism
　diplomatic relations, 383
　Europe, 474
Community, **299–302**
　city planning, 283
　civic duties, 285
　eternal perspectives, 302
　intellectual history, 687–88
　Intermountain West settlement,
　　300–301
　life in, 301–302
　material culture, 864
　meetinghouse, 876
　politics, 1105
　social and cultural history, 1379
　teachings, 299–300
　twentieth century, 301
　volunteerism, 1539
　worship, 1596–97
　see also Brotherhood; Lifestyle;
　　Sisterhood; Society; Unity
Compassionate service, **303**, 1199,
　1608
*Comprehensive History of the
　Church* (B. H. Roberts), 303–
　304, 591, 633
Compromise of 1850, 1100
Computer systems, **304–305**
　see also Family History Library;
　　FamilySearch[R]; Personal Ances-
　　tral File[R]; Record keeping
Computing Research, Center for
　(BYU), 224
Condescension of God, **305**, 729
Condie, Richard P., 950
Condie, Spencer J., 1635, 1680
Conference Reports (periodical),
　305–306
Conferences, 279, **306–309**, 643,
　878
　home industries, 653
　oaths, 1020
　pioneer life, 1085
　region, 1198
　satellite communications system,
　　1261
　sports, 1410
　stake, 308–309
　see also General Conference;
　　World conferences on records
Confession of sins, **309**, 1217
Confidential records, **309–310**

Confirmation, 96, **310–11**
　blessings, 129
　Catholicism and Mormonism, 258
　celebrations, 258
　Enoch, 462
　Israel, 710
　laying on of hands, 813
　life and death, spiritual, 833
　priesthood blessings, 1140
Confucianism, 1590
Congregational church, 168, 169
Congregation. *See* Ward
Congress, U.S., 49, 52, 631
Connor, Patrick Edward, 619
Conscientious objection, **311–12**
Consecrated oil. *See* Oil, conse-
　crated
Consecration, **312–15**, 605, 621
　bishops, 119
　community, 300
　Doctrine and Covenants, 408–
　　409, 412
　economic history, 439
　freemasonry, 529
　home industries, 652
　intellectual history, 687–88
　law of, 312–14, 1006
　in Ohio and Missouri, 314–15
　patriarchal blessings, 1067
　pioneer economy, 1084
　politics, 1098
　poverty, 1113
　presiding bishopric, 1129
　Smith, Joseph, 1336, 1343
　tithing, 1481
　united orders, 1493
　washings and anointings, 1551
Constitutional law, **315–17**, 526,
　1097, 1496
　see also Civil rights; Constitution
　　of the United States of Amer-
　　ica; Council of Fifty
Constitution of the United States of
　America, **317–19**, 597, 1496
　civic duties, 285
　freedom, 526
　legal and judicial history, 826
　politics, 1099, 1104
　see also Civil rights
Contention, 32, **319–20**, 1498
Continuing education, Brigham
　Young University, 224–25
Contraception. *See* Birth control
Contributor, The (periodical), **320**,
　624, 678, 1560
Contributor Company, The, 320

Conversion, **320–23**, 423, 1729–30
　activity in the Church, 15
　Book of Mormon, 152
　colonization, 291
　Israel, 710
　lifestyle, 834
　missionary work, 322–23
　nature of, 320–21
　Nauvoo, 990, 992
　process of, 321–22
　religious experience, 1208
　vital statistics, 1525–27
　see also Born of God; Fellowship-
　　ping; Joining the Church; Mis-
　　sionary, missionary life; Testi-
　　mony
Cook, Gene R., 1635, 1680
Cook, Lyndon W., 424
Cooke, Philip St. George, 935
Cooke, William, 1014
Coolidge, Calvin, 634
Cooperative movement, 438–39,
　621, 688
Cooperative Retrenchment Associa-
　tion, 90
Coray, Martha Jane Knowlton, 1357
Coriantor, 718
Coriantum, 717, 718
Cornwall, J. Spencer, 950
Corom, 718
Correlation of the Church, adminis-
　tration, 90, 122, **323–25**, 635,
　1064
　meetinghouse libraries, 878
　organization, 1040
　social services, 1387
　Sunday School, 1426
　see also Auxiliary organizations
Corrill, John, 590, 929, 1635, 1682
Cosmology, 688, 1458–59
Cosmopolitan magazine, 49
Costa Rica, the Church in, 901,
　1759
Cotton industry, 438
Cottonwood Maternity Hospital,
　659
Cotton and Woolen Factory (Salt
　Lake City), 438
Couch, Mormon, 865
Council, ward. *See* Ward council
Council Bluffs (Kanesville), Iowa,
　325–26, 595, 615, 935, 1379
Council on the Disposition of
　Tithes, 508, 509
Council of Fifty, **326–27**
　Church and state, 282
　history, 612, 614, 616

Smith, Joseph, 1338
Young, Brigham, 1604
Council of the First Presidency and the Quorum of the Twelve Apostles, 324, **327–328**, 513, 1127
Council in Heaven, **328–29**
  atonement of Jesus Christ, 83
  birth, 116
  Book of Abraham, 135
  creation accounts, 341
  cross, 345
  devils, 379
  hosanna shout, 659
  intelligences, 692
  Jesus Christ, 729
  plan of salvation, 1088
  spirit, 1404
  war in heaven, 1546
  see also First estate
Council House, 456
Courts. *See* Disciplinary procedures
Courts, ecclesiastical, nineteenth-century, **329–30**, 813, 824, 1505
  see also Legal and judicial history of the Church
Courtship. *See* Dating and court-ship
Covenant Israel, Latter-day, **330–31**, 462
  gathering, 536
  prophecy, 1162
  see also Abrahamic Covenant
Covenants, **331–33**
  Abrahamic, 9–10
  altar, 37
  Book of Mormon, 148
  Book of Moses, 811
  born in the, 218
  celebrations, 259
  communion, 299
  consecration, 312
  covenant Israel, latter-day, 330–31
  discipleship, 385
  elect of God, 448
  endowment, 454–46
  enduring to the end, 457
  father's blessings, 504
  following the brethren, 520
  foreordination, 522
  freemasonry, 529
  garments, 534
  heirs, 583
  Holy Spirit of Promise, 651
  humility, 663
  Israel, 709

Jesus Christ, 736
Joseph, 761
Latter-day Saints, 807
manuscript, lost 116 pages, 855
Melchizedek, 879
membership, 887
Mormon, 933
Mosiah$_2$, 960
motherhood, 963
mysteries of God, 978
Noah, 1017
oaths, 1020
Old Testament, 1027, 1028
ordinances, 1033
paradise, 1062
patriarchal order, 1067
Paul, 1069
prophets, 1168–69
restoration of all things, 1218
righteousness, 1237
sacrament, 1243
sacrifice, 1248
salvation of the dead, 1258
sealing, 1289
Ten Commandments, 1469
  see also Baptismal covenant; Doctrine and Covenants; New and Everlasting Covenant; specific type, e.g., Circumcision
Covenants in biblical times, **333–35**
Cowan, Richard O., 425
Cowdery, Elizabeth Ann Whitmer, 338, 339
Cowdery, Oliver, 289, 326, **335–40**, 573, 575, 665, 1058, 1635, 1678, 1682, 1740
  Aaronic Priesthood, 2–3
  apostasy, 57
  apostles, 61
  Articles of Faith, 68
  authority, 89
  baptism, 94
  Book of Mormon, 140, 185, 210, 212, 214
  common consent, 298
  community, 299–300
  covenants, 334
  death of, 339
  dispensation of the fulness of times, 388
  Doctrine and Covenants, 405, 408, 410, 419, 425
  elder, Melchizedek Priesthood, 447
  Elias, 449
  Elijah, 450, 452
  excommunication, 338

First Presidency, 512
forgeries of historical documents, 523
Gospel of Abraham, 555
historians, 589
history, 602, 603
Holy Ghost, 650
Israel, 706, 709, 710
James the Apostle, 716
John the Beloved, 758
Joseph of Egypt, 761
Joseph Smith—History, 762
Joseph Smith Translation of the Bible, 765
journeys, 336
keys of the priesthood, 780, 781
Kirtland Temple, 799
Lamanite mission, 802, 803
laying on of hands, 814
Lectures on Faith, 821
Malachi, 851
Melchizedek Priesthood, 884, 885–86
Messenger and Advocate, 892
missions, 916
Missouri, 923, 926
Missouri Conflict, 930
Moses, 959
Mount of Transfiguration, 968
organization of the Church, 1035, 1049, 1050
Peter, 1077
pioneer life, 1085
politics, 1104
Pratt, Parley P., 1116
prayer, 1120
President of the Church, 1127, 1128
pride, 1131
priest, 1132
priesthood, 1135
priesthood offices, 1144
prophecy, 1165
Quorum of the Twelve Apostles, 1185, 1186, 1188
restoration of all things, 1219
resurrection, 1222
scripture, 1284
sealing, 1288
Smith, Hyrum, 1330
Smith, Joseph, 1335
Temple Square, 1467
tithing, 1481
visions of Joseph Smith, 1514, 1515
Whitmer, David, 1564, 1565
Cowdery, Warren, 419

Cowles, Austin, 48
Cowles, Elvira A., 1207
Cowley, Elva Taylor, 1016
Cowley, Matthew, 859, 964, 1015, 1016, 1043, 1109, 1635, 1679, 1740
Cowley, Matthias F., 328, 631, 632, 1363, 1635, 1679, 1740
Cox, Martha Cragun, 115
Crafts, 172–73
Craven, Rulon G., 1016, 1635, 1680, 1683
Cravens, John, 20
Crawford, Vesta P., 1207
Creation, creation accounts, **340–43**, 636, 1030, 1340, 1665–70
   astronomy, 82
   doctrine, 397, 400
   Earth, 431–32
   Garden of Eden, 533–34
   intellectual history, 689
   Jesus Christ, 720, 752
   light and darkness, 835
   origin of man, 1053
   plan of salvation, 1088–89
   Salt Lake Temple, 1254
   science and, 1270, 1273
   theodicy, 1473
   worlds, 1595
   see also Pre–existence; Spirit body; War in heaven
Creeds, 272, **343**, 399, 1221
Cremation, 239, **344**, 366, 1097
Crickets. *See* Seagulls, miracle of
Critchlow, William J., Jr., 1635, 1679
Crocheron, Augusta Joyce, 842
Crooked River, battle of, 480, 931
Cross, **344–45**
Crowe, Chris, 665
Cullimore, James A., 1635, 1680
Culmer, Henry Lavender Adolphus, 70, 1381
Cult, **345–46**
   see also Sect
Cultural history. *See* Social and cultural history
Cultural symbols. *See* Symbols, cultural and artistic
Cumming, Alfred, 619, 825, 1500, 1501, 1608
Cummins, Richard W., 803
Cumorah, 140, 156, 177, 210, 260, **346–47**, 592, 763, 932, 953, 954, 1058, 1518
Cumorah pageant, 346, **347**, 1057, 1178

Cundick, Robert, 976
Currency, 435
Curriculum, **347–52**, 390, 443, 686, 1046, 1284
   see also Education
Curry, L. F. P., 1214
Cursings, **352**
Curtis, Catherine, 1238
Curtis, Elbert R., 1635, 1683
Curtis, George Ticknor, 824
Curtis, Kirk M., 1452
Curtis, LeGrand R., 1635, 1680, 1683, 1684
Curtis, Rebecca, 1361
Cuthbert, Derek A., 231, 473, 1635, 1680, 1683
Cutler, Clinton L., 1635, 1680, 1683
Cyprian (bishop of Carthage), 683
Czechoslovakia, the Church in, 473, 474, 1758

Dalebout, Marva, 72
Dallin, Cyrus E., 377, 634, 1286
Dalton, Edward M., 626
Damnation, **353–54**, 1391, 1406
Damron, Joseph W., Jr., 1022
Dance, **354–55**, 518, 635
Daniel, prophecies of, **355–56**
Daniels, William M., 1176
Danites, **356–57**, 611, 633, 926, 947, 1101
Darger, Arlene Barlow, 1635, 1685
Darley, Roy, 976, 1435
Dating and courtship, **357–59**, 1305
Daughters of Utah Pioneer Museum, 832
Davenport, E. L., 1255
David, King, **359–60**
   Jesus Christ, names and titles of, 741
David, prophetic figure of last days, **360–61**
David M. Kennedy Center (BYU), 224, 1389
Davies, W. D., 399
Daviess County, Missouri. *See* Missouri, LDS communities in Caldwell and Daviess counties
Dávila Peñaloza, Julio E., 1397, 1635, 1681
Davis, John, 213
Davis v. *Beason*, 1102
Davis v. *United States* (1990), 826
Daynes, Joseph J., 232, 976, 1426
Deacon, Aaronic Priesthood, **361**, 501, 635, 1013, 1034, 1131, 1144, 1441, 1275

Dead Sea Scrolls, **361–64**
   LDS perspective, 363–64, 807
   Messiah, 893
   opposition, 1031
   overview, 361–63
Deaf, materials for the, **364**
Dean, Florence Ridges, 1023
Dean, Joseph Harry, 1023
Death and dying, 277, **364–66**
   children, 269, 365–66
   dedications, 367
   doctrine, 398
   funerals, 366
   graveside services, 366
   nature of, 365
   raising the dead, 1192
   reincarnation, 1182, 1198–99, 1591
   resurrection from, 364–65
   see also Afterlife; Autopsies, Baptism for the dead; Burial; Cremation; Judgment day, final; Life and death, spiritual; Mortality; Paradise; Prolonging life; Resurrection; Sick, blessing the; Spirit prison; Spirit world
Death penalty. *See* Capital punishment
Death rates. *See* Mortality; Vital statistics
Debtors, 161
December 25. *See* Christmas; April 6
Decker, Edward, 51
Dedications, **367**, 416, 419, 659, 1455–56, 1742–49
   Salt Lake Temple, 1254
   solemn assemblies, 1390
   temple, 1455–56
   temple recommend, 1446
Degrees of glory, **367–69**, 479, 609
   atonement of Jesus Christ, 84
   celestial glory, 368
   damnation, 353
   Doctrine and Covenants, 413, 415
   eternal progression, 466
   Joseph Smith Translation of the Bible, 767
   life and death, spiritual, 833
   Nauvoo Temple, 1001
   opportunity for, 369
   Paul, 1070
   plan of salvation, 1090–91
   salvation, 1257
   scripture, 1283
   scripture sources, 368

Smith, Joseph, 1343
 telestial glory, 369
 terrestrial glory, 368–69
 see also Celestial Kingdom; Eter-
  nal lives; Salvation of the dead;
  Telestial Kingdom; Terrestrial
  Kingdom
Deification
 Catholicism and Mormonism, 257
 doctrine, 399, 401
 Godhead, 553
 Godhood, 553
 mankind, 853
 purpose of earth life, 1182
 symbolism, 1428
 theogony, 1474
Deification, early Christian, 369–70
de Jager, Jacob, 473, 1635, 1681
DeLapp, G. L., 1214
Delaware tribe, 803
Dellenbach, Robert K., 1635, 1681,
  1684
DeMille, Cecil B., 874
Demographics. See Vital statistics
Dempsey, Jack, 294
Denmark, the Church in, 213, 624,
  697, 1262, 1264, 1760
Denndorfer, Janos, 473
Deontology, 467
De Pillis, Mario, 938
Depressions, economic, 439, 440,
  936, 1203, 1251, 1387
Depressions, mental. See Mental
  health
Derrick, Royden G., 1635, 1681,
  1682
Deseret, 246, 282, 370–71
Deseret, state of, 371–73, 616, 999,
  1100, 1438, 1404
 see also History of the Church,
  1844–77; Utah statehood; Utah
  Territory
Deseret alphabet, 373–74, 675
Deseret Book Company, 110, 242,
  374, 654, 819, 937, 1238
Deseret Gymnasium, 826, 1401
Deseret Hospital, 374–75, 624, 658,
  659, 867, 1366, 1575, 1612
Deseret Hospital, Relief Society,
  1201
Deseret Industries, 371, 375–77,
  826, 1047, 1539, 1555, 1557,
  1558
Deseret Management Corporation
  (DMC), 241, 242, 509
Deseret Museum, 972
Deseret Musical Association, 973

Deseret Musical and Dramatic Society, 355
Deseret News (newspaper), 240,
  241, 280, 377–78, 536, 631,
  647, 1011, 1039, 1174
 beehive symbol, 99
 conferences, 305, 306
 Deseret alphabet, 373
 Deseret Book Company, 374
 education, 446
 pioneer life, 1086
 social and cultural history, 1379
Deseret News Bookstore, 374
Deseret News Church Almanac, 36
Deseret News Publishing Company,
  242
Deseret Philharmonic Society, 973
Deseret Silk Association, 658, 1313,
  2264
 see also Silk culture
Deseret Store, 1481
Deseret Sunday School Union, 371,
  1425–26
Deseret Telegraph, 440, 630
Deseret Trust Company, 242
Deseret University. See University
  of Deseret
Deuteronomy, 378–79
 Book of Mormon and, 378
 Jesus' use of, 378
 LDS scriptures and, 378–79
 prophets, 1168
 see also Covenants in biblical
  times; Law of Moses; Obedi-
  ence
Devils, 379–82
 Antichrists, 45
 Cain, 245
 creation accounts, 340
 degrees of glory, 367
 discernment, gift of, 384
 freedom, 525
 Gospel of Jesus Christ, 559
 magic, 850
 physical body, 1080
 see also Fall of Adam; Satanism
De Voto, Bernard, 50
Dharmaraju, Edwin, 81
Dialogue (periodical), 1388
Dibble, Philo, 414, 971–72, 1514
Dickens, Charles, 229
Dictionary, Bible. See Bible dictionary
Didier, Charles A., 473, 1635, 1681
Dillenberger, John, 561
Diplomatic relations, 382–84
 see also specific country name,
  e. g., Africa, the Church in

Disaffiliation, vital statistics, 1527
Disasters. See Calamities and disasters
Discernment, gift of, 384, 545, 850
Disciples of Christ, 168, 169
Discipleship, 384–85, 466, 534, 546
Disciplinary Council, 266
Disciplinary procedures, 385–87,
  1055, 1097
 adultery, 21
 apostate, 59
 bishop, 118, 120
 civil rights, 287
 homosexuality, 656
 individuality, 681
 judgment, 773
 lawsuits, 813
 Melchizedek Priesthood, 884
 organization, 1045
 priesthood council, 1142
 sexuality, 1307
 stake, 1414
 Whitmer, David, 1565
 see also Justice and mercy
Disengagement, 14
Disfellowshipment. See Disciplinary
  procedures
Dispensation of the fulness of
  times, 387–88, 389
 Doctrine and Covenants, 421
 First Presidency, 512
 Gospel of Abraham, 555
 Gospel of Jesus Christ, 559
 Jesus Christ, 726, 737
 Millennium, 907
 restoration of all things, 1218
 Restoration of the Gospel of Jesus
  Christ, 1210
 sealing, 1288
 signs as divine witness, 1310
 see also Eternal progression
Dispensations of the Gospel, 388–
  90, 596
 adultery, 21
 angels, 41
 Bible, 108
 Christians and Christianity, 270
 commandments, 296
 covenants, 332, 333
 Daniel, prophecies of, 356
 doctrine, 397
 First Vision, 515
 freemasonry, 528
 Gospel of Abraham, 555
 Gospel of Jesus Christ, 559
 Holy Ghost, 649
 Jesus Christ, 736, 746

Dispensations of the Gospel (Cont'd)
John the Baptist, 756
keys of the priesthood, 780
Melchizedek Priesthood, 886
meridian of time, 892
Moses, 959
mother in Israel, 964
record keeping, 1194
restoration of all things, 1218
revelations, unpublished, 1228
Ten Commandments, 1469
see also Dispensation of the fulness of times; Fulness of the Gospel, Revelation
Distribution centers, **390**
computer systems, 304
garments, 534
meetinghouse libraries, 878
organization, 1042
District, district president, 279, **390–91**
Divine foreknowledge. See Foreknowledge of God
Divine inspiration, Bible, 112
Divine investiture, 17
Divine law, obedience, 1021
Divorce, **391–93**, 489, 645, 857, 859, 1094, 1371, 1372
see also Marriage; Sealing, cancellation of; Vital statistics
Dixie College, 12
Dixon, Maynard, 947
DMC. See Deseret Management Corporation
Dr. W.H. Groves LDS Hospital, 659, 670, 867
Doctrine, 393–404
Catholicism and Mormonism, 257
distinctive teachings, 397–99
First Presidency, 513
Gospel of Jesus Christ, 556
harmonization of paradox, 402–403
history of, 395–97
intellectual history, 686
LDS vs. other Christian, 399–402
meaning of, 393–94
publications, 1175–76
reason and revelation, 1192
source of, 394–95
treatises on, 403–404
see also Church and state; Consecration; Epistemology; Ethics; Evil; Organization; Politics; Revelation; Suffering in the world; Theodicy; Tithing; United order; War and peace; Welfare

Doctrine and Covenants, 138, 325, 337, 395, 396, **404–24**
Africa, 25
alcoholic beverages, 30
blacks, 126
Book of Abraham, 136
Civil War prophecy, 287
commandments, 296
consecration, 314
contents, 407–409
Deuteronomy, 378
dispensation of the fulness of times, 388
divorce, 391
drugs, abuse of, 429
Enoch, 458, 460
fall of Adam, 485
First Presidency, 513
foreordination, 522
Harmony, Pennsylvania, 573
Hiram, Ohio, 588
historians, 591
Isaiah, 702–703
Jesus Christ, 751–52
lawsuits, 813
Lectures on Faith, 818
Liberty Jail, 831
Malachi, 851
martyrs, 862, 863
Melchizedek, 880
overview, 405–409
presidency, 1126
quotations from, 407
revelation, 1226
scripture, 1280, 1283
section 1, 409–10
sections 20–22, 410–11, 603, 1035, 1085
section 25, 411–12
section 45, 412–13
section 76, 413–14, 588, 1225
section 84, 414–15
section 88, 415–16
section 89, 416–17, 1441, 1482, 1584
section 93, 417–18
section 107, 418–19, 885, 1146
sections 109–110, 419, 781, 885, 1037, 1135
sections 121–123, 420, 932, 1337
section 124, 421
sections 127–128, 421–22
sections 131–132, 422–23
sections 137–138, 422
Smith, Joseph, 1331
spirit body, 1405
standard works, 1416

war and peace, 1547–49
see also Book of Mormon; Book of Commandments; Unpublished revelations; Visions of Joseph Smith
Doctrine and Covenants commentaries, **424–25**
Doctrine and Covenants editions, **425–27**
1835 edition, 425
1844 Nauvoo edition, 425–26
1845 Liverpool, England, edition, 426
1876 edition, 426
1879 edition, 426
1921 edition, 426
1981 edition, 426
foreign-language, 426
Doctrine and Covenants as literature, **427**
Doctrine and Covenants official declaration—2, 383, 423–24, 426, 642, 696, 789, 918, 942, 1137
race, racism, 1192
revelations, unpublished, 1228
Dominican Republic, the Church in, 1562, 1762
Doniphan, Alexander W., 925, 929, 930, 931
Dougall, Maria Young, 1635, 1684
Douglas, Stephen A., 994, 1000, 1101, 1347, 1483
Dove, sign of the, **427–28**, 730
Doxey, Graham W., 1635, 1681, 1684
Doxey, Joanne Bushman, 1636, 1685
Doxey, Leone B. Watson, 1636, 1684
Doxey, Roy W., 424, 425
Doyle, Arthur Conan, 229, 356, 949
Drago, Pino, 72
Drama, 355, **428–29**, 518, 576, 635
Mormon writers of, 837–38
music, 974
Salt Lake Theatre, 1255
temples, 1460–61
see also Pageants
Dress, modesty in, 932
Driggs, H. Wayne, 347
Drovetti, Bernardino, 133
Druce, John, 1436
Druce-Pugsley, Nellie, 479
Drugs, abuse of, **429**, 580, 1097, 1375, 1585
see also Alcoholic beverages and alcoholism

Drummond, W. E., 1500
Duncan, Chapman, 75
Duncan, Hepera Takare, 1015
Duncan, Robert, 73
Duncan, Wiremu, 1015
Dunford, Alma Bailey, 535
Dunford, Leah Eudora, 487, 535
Dunkley, Sarah, 101
Dunklin, Daniel, 605, 929, 1627, 1629
Dunn, Loren C., 1636, 1680, 1681, 1682, 1683
Dunn, Paul H., 1636, 1680, 1681
Dunyon, O. Eileen Robinson, 1636, 1684
Durham, Alfred M., 1617
Durham, G. Homer, 424, 591, 592, 1636, 1681, 1682
Dusenberry, Ida Smoot, 1636, 1685
Dusenberry, Warren N., 222
Duty, Mary. See Smith, Mary Duty
Dyer, Alvin R., 513, 591, 1636, 1678, 1679, 1681, 1682, 1683, 1740
Dykes, George P., 213, 1262

Earth, 431–33, 552
  age of, 431
  astronomy, 82
  great flood, 432
  LDS concerns, 432–33
  marriage supper of the lamb, 860
  Millennium, 907
  new, 1009
  Noah, 1017
  opposition, 1031
  origin and destiny of, 431–32
  politics, 1105
  see also Purpose of earth life
Easter, 433
Eastern Arizona Junior College, 13
Eastern Europe, 473–75
  see also specific country name
Eastern Orthodoxy, 257–58, 344, 383, 401, 693
Easton, Robert C., 479
Eaton, Valoy, 73
Eccles, Marriner S., 634
Ecclesiastical courts. See Courts, ecclesiastical; Legal and judicial history
Eckford, Ann, 517
Economic aid, 434–35, 510, 696, 1114
  see also Emergency preparedness; Humanitarian service; Self-sufficiency

Economic history of the Church, 435–41, 629, 630, 1343
  Book of Mormon, 172–75
  equality, 439–41
  growth and independence, 436–38
  intellectual history, 688
  organization, 1039
  politics, 1102
  united orders, 1493
  unity and cooperation, 438–39
  see also Depressions, economic; Economic aid; Finances of the Church; Kirtland economy; Nauvoo economy; Pioneer economy
Ecuador, the Church in, 1397, 1760
Edgemont Stake Center (Provo, Utah), 237, 877
Edison, Thomas, 947
Editions
  Book of Mormon, 175–76
  Doctrine and Covenants, 425–27
Edmunds Act (1882), 52, 439, 625, 896, 1101, 1102, 1369, 1572
Edmunds-Tucker Act (1887), 52, 439, 444, 626, 628, 852, 999, 1007, 1075, 1101, 1102, 1225, 1370, 1572
Edsberg, Knud, 72
Edsberg, Soren, 72
Education, 441–47, 637
  attainment of, 446–47
  attitudes toward, 441–46, 686
  British Isles, 230
  civic duties, 285
  continuing, 224–25
  interfaith relationships, 694
  mankind, 854
  McKay, David O., 873
  Native Americans, 984–85
  social characteristics, 1373
  truth, 1490
  vital statistics, 1534
  see also Academies; Brigham Young University; Church Educational System; Curriculum; Intellectual history; Schools; Social and cultural history; specific field of study; specific school names
Edwards, F. Henry, 424
Egalitarianism, 490
Egypt
  language, 179–80, 370–71
  missions, 917
  mummies, 63, 132–33

papyri, 132–34, 136
pyramid texts, 528
religion, 135
spiritual death, 1407
Eight Witnesses, 214–16
Eisenhower, Dwight D., 100
Eka, David W., 24, 25
Eka-Etta, 25
Eket branch, 22
Ekland-Olson, Sheldon, 320
El, 741
  see also Jesus Christ
Elder, Melchizedek Priesthood, 447–48, 883, 884, 886, 1140
  death and dying, 365
  Doctrine and Covenants, 412, 418
  high priest, 587
  miracles, 910
  ordination, 1035
  organization of the Church, 1050
  Quorum of the Twelve Apostles, 1187
Elderly people. See Old Folks movement; Senior citizens
Elders. See Senior citizens
Elder's Journal (periodical), 830
Eldredge, Horace S., 1636, 1680
Eldredge, W. Jay, 1636, 1683
Elect of God, 448–49
Elias, 388, 449, 609
  Malachi, 851
  Melchizedek Priesthood, 886
  Mount of Transfiguration, 969
  priesthood, 1139
  restoration of all things, 1219
Elias, spirit of, 449–50
Elijah, 388, 449–50, 450–52, 609, 780, 954
  ancient sources, 451–52
  Jesus Christ, 735
  LDS sources, 450–51
  Melchizedek Priesthood, 886
  Moses, 959
  prophecy, 1163
  restoration of all things, 1219
  sealing, 1288, 1289
  translated beings, 1486
  see also Elijah, spirit of
Elijah, spirit of, 419, 452, 493
Elk Mountain Mission, Utah, 290
Elliot, Robert, 838
Elliott, Richard, 976
Ellsworth, German, 667
Elohim, 341, 452–53, 550, 741
  see also God the Father; Jesus Christ; Jehovah

El Salvador, the Church in, 901
Ely, Richard T., 633
Emer, 717
Emergency preparedness, 376, 434, **453–54**, 587
   see also Bishop's storehouse; Calamities and disasters
Emigration. *See* Immigration and emigration
Emmanuel, 741
   see also Jesus Christ
Empey, Ella V., 1616
Empey, Emma Young, 1224
Employment. *See* Occupational status
Endless and eternal, 354, **454**, 551, 586
Endowment, **454–56**
   burial, 239
   celebrations, 258
   Council of Fifty, 326
   covenants, 332
   doctrine, 399
   Elijah, 452
   exaltation, 479
   freemasonry, 528
   garments, 534
   history, 612, 622
   Jesus Christ, 735
   Nauvoo, 991
   Nauvoo Temple, 1002
   pioneer life, 1087
   priesthood, 1138
   Restoration of the Gospel of Jesus Christ, 1220
   Salt Lake Temple, 1254
   salvation, 1257
   sealing, 1289
   Smith, Joseph, 1337, 1342
   Smith, Lucy Mack, 1357
   social and cultural history, 1379
   temple, 1444–45
   temple recommend, 1447
   temple worship, 1120
   westward migration, 1563
   Young, Brigham, 1604
   see also Baptism for the dead; Endowment houses; Salvation for the dead; Temple ordinances
Endowment houses, **456**, 622, 1087, 1094, 1321, 1350, 1366
Enduring to the end, **456–57**
   born of God, 219
   eternal life, 464
   faith in Jesus Christ, 484
   Gospel of Jesus Christ, 557

repentance, 1218
   senior citizens, 1297
Engar, Keith, 837
Engineering, College of, 223
England. *See* British Isles, the Church in
England, Eugene, 840, 841
Enoch, **457–60**, 767
   ancient sources, 459–60
   Book of, 460
   Book of Moses, 216
   books of, 459–60
   covenants, 334
   Doctrine and Covenants, 458
   exit of, 460
   fall of Adam, 485
   Jesus Christ, 727, 752
   Latter-day Saints and, 458–59
   LDS sources, 457–59
   man of holiness, 852
   order of, 459
   Paul, 1069
   record keeping, 1195
   "voice from the dust," 1538
Enos, book of, 148
Ensign, Horace S., 77
Ensign, The (periodical), 305, 324, **460–61**, 678, 685, 697, 849, 906, 1042
   single adults, 1318
Ensign Peak, Utah, 456
Ensign Talking Book, 131
Ephraim, **461–62**, 481, 706, 723, 1066
Epicurus, 478
Epistemology, 403, **462–63**, 547, 1079, 1476
   see also Faith in Jesus Christ; Prophets; Reason and revelation; Science and religion
Epistles, New Testament, 1013
   see also specific name inverted, e.g., Hebrews, epistle to the
Equality, 439–41, **463–64**, 1104, 1625
   see also Common consent
Equal Rights Amendment, 646, 826–27, 1102, 1108
Era, The. See Improvement Era (periodical)
Erickson, E. E., 689
Eschatology, 1343
Espinola, Carlos, 1400
Essays, Mormon writers of, 840–41
Essays, personal, 840–41
Essenes, 343

Eternal life, **464–65**, 547, 552, 582, 582, 1030
   atonement of Jesus Christ, 83, 84
   baptism, 92, 95
   born of God, 218
   Catholicism and Mormonism, 258
   covenant Israel, 331
   degrees of glory, 368
   discipleship, 384
   equality, 463
   exaltation, 479
   family, 487
   gifts of the spirit, 546
   Holy Spirit of Promise, 652
   homosexuality, 656
   individuality, 681
   Israel, 710
   Jesus Christ, 730, 741
   love, 846
   marriage, 856
   Melchizedek, 880
   membership, 997
   paradise, 1063
   patriarchal order, 1067
   pioneer life, 1087
   plan of salvation, 1088
   priesthood, 1137
   riches of eternity, 1230
   strait and narrow, 1419
   world religions, 1590
   see also Eternal lives, eternal increase; Eternal progression; Godhood; Immortality and eternal life; Jesus Christ, second comforter; Life and death, spiritual
Eternal lives, eternal increase, 353, **465**, 466, 1137, 1158, 1198
   see also Eternal progression
Eternal marriage. *See* Marriage; Sealing
Eternal progression, 369, 390, **465–66**
   Godhood, 553
   history, 612
   lay participation, 815
   mortality, 957
   obedience, 1021
   premortal life, 1125
   Salt Lake Temple, 1254
   see also Eternal lives, eternal increase
Eternity. *See* Time and eternity
Etete, Ephraim S., <u>25</u>
Etete, Patricia, <u>25</u>
Ethem, 718

Ether
    book of, 156–57, 190, 378, 717–18
    Jesus Christ, 728
    plates of, 200–201
Ethics, **466–67**
    disciplinary procedures, 386
    doctrine, 403
    nature, law of, 986
Ethiopia, the Church in, 434, 510, 662
Ethyl alcohol, 30–31
Etoile du Déseret (periodical), 470
Euaggelion (good news), 559
Eucharist, 258
Eucharistia, 299
Europe, the Church in, **467–75**, 566, 1758
    Eastern Europe, 473–75
    history, 467–71, 625
    humanitarian service, 661
    immigration and emigration, 674–75, 676
    McKay, David O., 872, 873
    Smith, George Albert, 1327–28
    twentieth century, 471–73
    vital statistics, 470, 1525
    see also British Isles; Middle East; Scandinavia; specific country names
Euthanasia, 1096–97
    see also Death and dying; Prolonging life
Evangelists, 169, **475**, 1013, 1051, 1140
Evans, Beatrice Cannon, 115
Evans, David W., 577, 769
Evans, Edwin, 71, 1381
Evans, Jennette, 870
Evans, Jessie Ella. *See* Smith, Jessie Ella Evans
Evans, Joy Frewin, 1636, 1685
Evans, John Henry, 114, 1176
Evans, Richard L., 60, 233, 678, 854, 952, 1043, 1636, 1679, 1680, 1740
Eve, **475–76**, 490, 1577, 1578
    creation accounts, 341
    Garden of Eden, 533–34
    garments, 534
    Lehi, 828
    mankind, 853
    marriage, 858
    see also Adam; Fall of Adam
Evening and the Morning Star, The (periodical), **477**, 605, 609, 928, 929, 1011, 1173, 1379
    see also Messenger and Advocate

Evil, 340, 403, **477–78**
    Smith, Joseph, 1342
    theodicy, 1474
    see also Devils; Evil; Great and abominable church; Sin; War in heaven
Evolution, **478**, 636, 1270, 1274, 1665–70
Exaltation, **479**
    Christology, 272
    covenants, 332
    damnation, 353
    dating and courtship, 358
    deification, early Christian, 369
    eternal life, 464
    family, 490
    feminism, 507
    first estate, 511
    Godhood, 553
    heirs, 583
    immortality and eternal life, 677
    love, 846
    mankind, 853
    marriage, 858
    mortality, 957
    motherhood, 963
    mother on Israel, 963
    ordinances, 1032
    priesthood, 1137–38
    salvation, 1257
Excommunication. *See* Disciplinary procedures
Exhibitions and World's Fairs, 273, **479–80**, 854, 1178
Ex nihilo creation, 342, 397, 400, 418, 478
Exponent II (periodical), 1388
Extermination Order (1838), 46, 421, **480**, 500, 577, 611, 830, 927, 931, 1018, 1099, 1235, 1336, 1347, 1496
Eyring, Camilla. *See* Kimball, Camilla Eyring
Eyring, Henry, 689, 900, 1273, 1274
Eyring, Henry B., 1636, 1682
Ezekiel, prophecies of, 159, **480–81**
    Millennium, 907
    prophets, 1168
    temple recommend, 1446
Ezias, **481**
Ezra Taft Benson Agriculture and Food Institute (BYU), 103, 223, 434

Facer, William O., 1025
Faculty, Brigham Young University, 221

Fairbanks, Avard T., 1285, 1286
Fairbanks, John B., 71, 1381
Fairchild, James H., 1403
Fairs. *See* Exhibitions and World's Fairs
Faith in Jesus Christ, 463, **483–85**, 547, 582
    Doctrine and Covenants, 414
    first principles of the Gospel, 514
    Gospel of Jesus Christ, 557
    justification, 776
    law of Moses, 812
    Mary, mother of God, 864
    Melchizedek, 879
    Mormon, 933
    New Testament, 1013
    Noah, 1017
    plan of salvation, 1090
    public speaking, 1179
    purpose of earth life, 1181
    reason and revelation, 1192
    remission of sins, 1210
    repentance, 1216
    salvation, 1257
    sanctification, 1260
    signs of the true Church, 1311
    testimony of Jesus Christ, 1472
    truth, 1490
    see also Grace; Lectures on Faith; Visions of Joseph Smith
Fall of Adam, 389, 476, **485–86**, 490, 1665–70
    birth, 116
    Council in Heaven, 329
    Creation, creation accounts, 340
    devils, 380
    Earth, 432
    immortality, 676, 677
    infant baptism, 682
    mankind, 854
    meridian of time, 892
    Millennium, 907
    Mount of Transfiguration, 969
    opposition, 1031
    original sin, 1052
    origin of man, 1053
    paradise, 1062
    plan of salvation, 1088
    Smith, Joseph, 1341
    see also Garden of Eden; Mortality; Purpose of earth life
Family, 280, **486–92**, 1054
    adoption of children, 20–21
    Brigham Young University, 223
    celebrations, 259
    curriculum, 348
    divorce, 392

Family (Cont'd)
  doctrine, 401
  family life, 488–92
  mankind, 853
  meetinghouse libraries, 878
  Nauvoo, 992
  priesthood, 1137
  priesthood councils, 1141
  sex education, 1305
  Smith, Joseph, 1342–43
  social characteristics, 1371–77
  social services, 1386
  teachings about, 476, 486–88
  temple ordinances, 1445
  vital statistics, 488–89, 1521–24,
    1529
  see also Abuse, spouse and child;
    Birth control; Children; Family
    history, genealogy; Family
    Home Evening; Family prayer;
    Lifestyle; Marriage; Mother-
    hood; Mother in Israel
Family history, genealogy, 491,
  492–94, 536, 539, 563–64, 628,
  644–45
  biography and autobiography, 113
  Book of Abraham, 137
  computer systems, 304, 305
  death and dying, 365
  Elijah, 451, 452
  family organizations, 497
  history (LDS), 597
  journals, 770
  Malachi, 852
  organization, 1047
  record keeping, 1196
  salvation of the dead, 1258
  Smith, Emma Hale, <u>1322</u>
  Smith, Joseph, <u>1362</u>
  see also Ancestral File™; Family
    History Centers; Family His-
    tory Library; Family
    Registry™; FamilySearch^R;
    Granite Mountain Record
    Vault; International Genealogi-
    cal Index™; Salvation for the
    dead
Family History Centers, 39, 223–
  24, **492**, 499, 645, 697
  libraries and archives, 832
Family History Department, 494,
  499, 537, 644
  name extraction program, 979
Family History Library, 39, 440,
  492, 493, **494–95**, 499, 538,
  645, 697
  libraries and archives, 832

name extraction program, 980
public relations, 1179
Family home evening, 324, 488,
  495–97, 642–43, 878, 942
  Bible, 106
  bishops, 122
  celebrations, 259
  children, 267
  meetings, 878
  membership, 887
  organization, 1042
  peculiar people, 1073
  single adults, 1318
  Spafford, Belle, 1402
  stake, 1413
  teaching the Gospel, 1443
  testimony bearing, 1471
  values, 1508
Family Home Evening Resource
  Book, 496
Family organizations, **497–98**
  senior citizens, 1297
Family planning. See Birth control
Family prayer, 267, **498–99**, 1119
  values, 1508
Family Registry™, 492, 495, **499**
FamilySearch^R, 492, 493, 494, 495,
  499–500
Fancher, Alexander, 966
Farmer, Gladys Clark, 843
Farming. See Agriculture
Farm Management Companies, 241,
  242
F.A.R.M.S. See Foundation for
  Ancient Research and Mormon
  Studies
Farms Management Corporation.
  See Business, Church participa-
  tion in
Farnham, Augustus, 1014
Farnsworth, Burton K., 1636, 1683
Farnsworth, Dewey, 172
Farnsworth, Edith, 172
Farnsworth, Philo T., 634
Farr, Lorin, 1326
Farr, Sarah, 1326
Farrer, William, 578
Far West, Missouri, 284, 500, 593,
  931, 1451
Fasting, 415, **500–501**, 628, 668
  pioneer life, 1085
  prayer, 1119
  religious experience, 1209
Fast offerings, **501–502**, 1730–31
  bishops, 118, 121
  consecration, 314
  deacon, Aaronic Priesthood, 361

Far West, Missouri, 500
  finances of the Church, 508
  financial contributions, 509
  humanitarian service, 662
  poverty, 1114
  presiding bishopric, 1129
  procreation, 1157
  sacrifice, 1248
  Welfare Square, 1558
Fast and testimony meeting, 500,
  502, 1247
  children, 267, 268
  Kirtland, Ohio, 796
  prayer, 1119
  Sabbath day, 1242
  testimony bearing, 1470
Fate, **502–503**
Father in Heaven, 384, 550, 690,
  741
  see also Jesus Christ
Fatherhood, 490, **503–504**, 883,
  1342
  see also Father's blessings; Mar-
    riage; Men, roles of; Mother-
    hood
Father's blessings, 130, 263, **504**
  religious experience, 1209
Faust, James E., 81, <u>1187</u>, 1228,
  1396, 1636, 1679, 1680, 1681,
  1740
Faust, Ruth Wright, 1396
Fayette, New York, 262, **504–505**,
  593, 602, 1219, 1335
Fear of God, **505–506**
Featherstone, Vaughn J., 1277,
  1636, 1681, 1682, 1684
Federalism, 315
Feet, washing of. See Washing of
  feet
Fellowshipping members, **506**
  curriculum, 351
  see also Conversion; Joining the
    Church; Membership
Felt, Louie B., 624, 660, 1147,
  <u>1148</u>, 1636, 1684
Female Relief Society. See Relief
  Society
Feminism, **506–507**
  see also Woman suffrage
Ferguson, Ellen B., 375, 867
Ferguson, Thomas S., <u>1486</u>
Ferris, Benjamin G., <u>429</u>
Fertility, 1372, 1521–24
Fetzer, Emil, 64
Fiction. See Novels
Fidelity. See Chastity, law of
Fielding, James, 228

Ford, Thomas, 861, **1000**, 1001
Foreign-language. *See* Language
Foreknowledge of God, 466, **521–22**, 1030
  Paul, 1070
  see also Book of Mormon, biblical prophecies about
Foremaster v. *City of St. George* (1989), 826
Foreordination, 521, **522–23**, 1070, 1122
  premortal life, 1125
  purpose of earth life, 1180
  spirit, 1404
  world religions, 1591
Forgeries of historical documents, **523**, 789, 826
  Anthon Transcript, 44
  anti-Mormonism, 51
  schismatic groups, 1266
Forgiveness. *See* Remission of sins
Forsberg, William, 972
Forsgren, John Erik, 1262, 1263
Forsgren, Peter Adolf, 1262
Fort Bridger, Wyoming, 290
Fort Limhi, Idaho, 290, 671
Fort Supply, Wyoming, 290
Foster, Charles, 48
Foster, James, 1636, 1680
Foster, Robert, 48
Fotheringham, William, 1399
Foundation for Ancient Research and Mormon Studies (F.A.R.M.S.), 172, 208–209, 1389
Fourie, Johanna, 24
Fowler, William, 87
Fox, Jesse Williams, Jr., 524
Fox, Ruth May, 231, **524–25**, 1617, 1636, 1684
France, the Church in, 213, 471, 917
Franco, Ernesto, 1397
Fraternities. *See* LDS Student Association
Free, Hannah C., 1560
Freedom, **525–27**
  civic duties, 285
  Constitution, U.S., 318
  constitutional law, 316
  discipleship, 385
  evil, 478
  government and, 526–27
  human choice and, 525–26
  metaphysics, 895
  religious, 287, 316, 825, 1210, 1263–64

theodicy, 1474
  see also Civil rights
Freeman, Joseph, Jr., <u>489</u>
Freeman, Judith, 839, <u>844</u>
Freemasonry in Nauvoo, **527–28**, 529, 992, 1018
Freemasonry and the Temple, **528–29**, 1121
Freeze, Lillie T., <u>1147</u>, 1636, 1684
Frémont, John C., 1250
French, Mary, 1361
French Polynesia. *See* Polynesians
Friberg, Arnold, 71
Friend, The (periodical), 268, 270, 324, 685, **529–30**, 697, 849, 1042
Frontier Guardian (periodical), 1011
Fuller, Metta Victoria, 949
Fullmer, Nathan O., <u>233</u>
Fulness of the Gospel, **530–31**
  see also Restoration of all things; Restoration of the Gospel of Jesus Christ
Fundamentalists, **531–32**, 632, 1095, 1266
Funerals, 366, 1097
Funk, Ruth Hardy, 1617, 1618, 1637, 1685
Furnas, J. C., 949
Fyans, J. Thomas, 1637, 1680, 1681

Gabriel. *See* Angels; Noah
Gabriel, Charles H., 86
Gadianton robbers, 153, 164, 165, 585, 1291
Galland, Isaac, 987
Galt Company, 253
Gambling, **533**, 645, 1109
Garaycoa, Lorenzo, 1397
Garden of Eden, 19, 475, **533–34**
  Adam, 15–16
  Book of Moses, 216
  devils, 379
  endowment, 455
  Eve, 475
  Independence, Missouri, 679
  marriage, 858
  millenarianism, 905
  paradise, 1062
  promised land, 1160
  Restoration of the Gospel of Jesus Christ, 1220
  sacrifice, 1248
  tree of life, 1486
Garden of Gethsemane. *See* Gethsemane
Gardner, Willard, 29, 1274

Garff, Gertrude Ryberg, 1637, 1685
Garff, Louis, 899
Garff, Mark B., 238
Garments, **534–35**, 735, 1461
Gartrell, C. David, 321
Gates, B. Cecil, 535, 950, 974, 977
Gates, Crawford, 347, 974, 1618
Gates, Emma Lucy. *See* Bowen, Emma Lucy Gates
Gates, Franklin Young, 535
Gates, Harvey Harris (Hal), 535
Gates, Jacob, 535, 1637, 1680
Gates, Lydia, 1356, 1361
Gates, Susa Young, **535–36**, 838, 842, 1207, 1365, 1615
Gathering, **536–37**
  Canada, 252
  Europe, 469
  hymns, 667
  immigration and emigration, 673
  Perpetual Emigrating Fund
  pioneer life, 1087
  Smith, Joseph, 1335
  social and cultural history, 1378
  United States of America, 1497
  Young, Brigham, 1602
Gause, Jesse, 512, 1637, 1678
Gautama, Siddhartha, 1589
Gaylord, John, 1637, 1680
Geary, Edward, 840
Gee, Salmon, 1637, 1680
Gender ratios, 1527–28
Gender roles, 857, 1374–75
  see also Men, roles of; Women, roles of
Genealogical Data Communication (GEDCOM), 39
Genealogical Department, 537
Genealogical Library. *See* Family History Library
Genealogical Society of Utah, 493, 494, **537–38**, 563–64, 628, 1455, 1588
Genealogy, **538**
  restoration of all things, 1219
  see also Family history, genealogy
General Authorities, 278, 279, 327, 520, **538–40**, 579, 787, 1054, 1678–82
  almanacs, 36
  apostles, 59
  conferences, 306, 308
  correlation of the Church, 324
  Doctrine and Covenants, 423
  Europe, 470
  First Presidency, 512
  high priest, 587

Fielding, John, 1358
Fielding, Joseph, 228, 920, 1116, 1349
Fielding, Mary. *See* Smith, Mary Fielding
Fielding, Mercy. *See* Thompson, Mercy Fielding
Fiji, the Church in, 1025–26
Fillerup, Mel, 73
Fillerup, Michael, 844
Fillmore, Millard, 372, 1504, 1608
Film. *See* Motion pictures
Final Judgment. *See* Judgment Day, final
Finance and Records Department, 509
Finances of the Church, **507–509**, 539, 646
  business investments, 509
  financial administration, 508–509
  financial controls, 509
  organization, 1043
  presiding bishopric, 1129
  ward budget, 1543–44
  welfare farms, 1553–54
  see also Business; Economic history of the Church; Financial contributions; Wealth, attitudes toward
Financial contributions, **509–510**, 646
  bishop, 118
  computer systems, 304
  confidential records, 310
  LDS Foundation, 816
  presiding bishopric, 1128
Fine arts, 224, **510–11**
Finland, the Church in, 472, 697, 917, 1263
Finney, Charles G., 169, 1475
Firesides, 306, **511**, 878
  intellectual history, 686
  satellite communications system, 1261
First Amendment rights, 316
Firstborn, Church of the. *See* Church of the Firstborn
Firstborn of God. *See* Jesus Christ, names and titles of
First estate, **511–12**
  angels, 41
  damnation, 354
  Jesus Christ, 724, 752
  plan of salvation, 1088
  see also Birth; Council in Heaven; Pre-existence; Premortal life; Second estate

First Presidency, 278, 327, **512–14**, 520, 538, 609, 1125, 1126, 1678, 1724–34
  Bible, 107
  capital punishment, 253
  celebrations, 259
  chastity, 265
  correlation of the Church, 324
  courts, 329
  Deseret Industries, 375
  disciplinary procedures, 387
  doctrine, 395
  Doctrine and Covenants, 406, 418
  Family Home Evening, 495
  fast offerings, 502
  finances of the Church, 507, 508
  genealogy, 537
  high council, 586
  history, 623
  inspiration, 683
  Jesus Christ, 728
  Journal of Discourses, 770
  keys of the priesthood, 781
  Kimball, Spencer W., 786
  McKay, David O., 872
  Melchizedek Priesthood, 885
  military and the Church, 904
  missionaries, 910, 913, 914, 917
  Mother in Heaven, 961
  Mount of Transfiguration, 968
  murder, 970
  Nauvoo, 991
  New Zealand, 1015
  organization, 1037, 1045, 1046–47
  origin of man, 1053
  policies, practices, and procedures, 1095–97
  presiding bishopric, 1128
  priesthood, 1135
  priesthood offices, 1144
  priesthood quorums, 1146
  proclamations of, 285, 1151–58
  prophet, seer, and revelator, 1170
  prophets, 1165
  Quorum of the Twelve Apostles, 1185, 1187
  revelations, unpublished, 1228
  Rigdon, Sidney, 1233
  RLDS Church, 1212
  scripture, 1281
  seventy, 1300
  Smith, Joseph F., 1351
  social and cultural history, 1380
  temple president and matron, 1445
  tithing, 1481

First principles
  514–15, 12
  see also Bapti
    Christ; Gift
    Laying on
First Vision, **51**
  1058, 1114
  creeds, 343
  dispensation
    times, 388
  doctrine, 395
  Doctrine and
  fulness of the
  historical site
  intellectual h
  James, Epist
  Jesus Christ,
  King Follett
  light and dar
  name of God
  New Testame
  Old Testame
  prayer, 1118
  restoration o
  Restoration
    Christ, 12
  revelation, 1
  Sacred Grov
  Smith, Josep
  Smith, Lucy
  see also Reli
    sions of Jo
Fisher, Vardis,
Fjeldsted, Chr
  1680
Flake, Green,
Flanigan, Jame
Fletcher, Har
Flood, great,
Floyd, John B
Folk art, **516–**
  material cul
  see also Arc
    Drama; F
    hymnody
Folklore, **518–**
  see also Ma
Following the
  1127
Folsom, Willi
Food
  blessing on,
  Doctrine an
  fasting, 500
"Footprints or
  (pageant)
Forbes, Hele

history, 623
John, revelations of, 754
Melchizedek Priesthood, 883
Millennial Star, 906
motion pictures, 965
New Zealand, 1016
ordination, 1035
organization, 1037, 1044
President of the Church, 1126
presiding bishopric, 1128
profanity, 1158
Quorum of the Twelve Apostles,
  1188
Relief Society, 1200
satellite communications system,
  1261
Scandinavia, 1264
scouting, 1277
Taylor, John, 1440
volunteerism, 1539
see also Callings; Following the
  brethren
General Conference, 307–308
celebrations, 259
centennial observances, 262
historical issues, 307–308
modern objectives, 307
see also Conference Reports
General Handbook of Instructions,
  238, 386, **541**, 1045, 1096
Gentiles, **541**
Book of Mormon, 144, 146
covenant Israel, 331
Doctrine and Covenants, 413
history, 625
marriage supper of the lamb, 860
Mormon, 933
prophecy, 1163
scripture, 1283
social and cultural history, 1379
Gentiles, fulness of, **541–42**, 1013
Geography
Book of Mormon, 176–79
vital statistics, 1520–21
George, Lloyd P., 1637, 1681
George Q. Cannon and Sons, 374
see also Deseret Book Company
Germany, the Church in, 213, 471,
  472, 473, 634, 666, 697, 873
missions, 917
Gethsemane, 85, **542–543**, 716,
  723, 725, 729, 732, 746, 1120,
  1341
Gibbons, Francis M., 114, 1637,
  1681
Gibbs, George F., 770
Gibraltar, 917

Gibson, Walter Murray, 578, 1023,
  1368
Giddianhi, 165
Gift of the Holy Ghost, 389, **543–44**
Articles of Faith, 68
atonement of Jesus Christ, 84
baptism, 93, 97
birth, 116
Book of Mormon, 158
born of God, 218
covenant Israel, 331
Doctrine and Covenants, 415
elder, Melchizedek Priesthood,
  447
enduring to the end, 457
faith in Jesus Christ, 483
Gospel of Jesus Christ, 557
inspiration, 684
laying on of hands, 813
light of Christ, 835
membership, 887
ordinances, 1032
organization of the Church, 1050
plan of salvation, 1090
priesthood, 1138
religious experience, 1209
religious freedom, 1210
restoration of all things, 1219
revelation, 1226
Rigdon, Sidney, 1233
salvation, 1257
Gifts of the Spirit, **544–46**
Articles of Faith, 68
Catholicism and Mormonism, 258
Church Educational System, 275
feminism, 507
following the brethren, 520
gift of the Holy Ghost, 543
individuality, 681
miracles, 909
New Testament, 1013
religious experience, 1209
revelation, 1225
signs of the true Church, 1311
see also Discernment, gift of
Gilbert, A. Sidney, 923, 924
Gilbert, John H., 175
Gilbert Islands. *See* Kiribati
Gileadi, Avraham, 704
Giles, John D., 1637, 1683
Gitten, Alvin, 71
Glade, Earl J., 800
Glazier, Nancy, 73
Glory of God, 551
Gnosticism, 58, 880
Goaslind, Jack H., Jr., 1637, 1681,
  1683, 1684

God, **546–47**
attributes of. *See* God the Father;
  Godhood; Lectures on Faith
born of, 218–19
Catholicism and Mormonism, 257
elect of, 448–49
family of, 486–87
fear of, 505–506
foreknowledge of, 466, 521–22
Joseph Smith Translation of the
  Bible, 768
law, 809
man of holiness, 852
mysteries of, 977–78
names and titles of, 550, 980–81
omnipotence, omnipresence,
  omniscience, 1030
priesthood, 1137–38
purpose of earth life, 1181
Smith, Joseph, 1340
son of, 740
wrath of, 1310, 1598
see also Elohim; God the Father;
  Holy Ghost; Jesus Christ
Godbe, William S., 620, 1266
Godbeites, 688, 1266
Goddard, George, 1637, 1682
Goddard, Mary Adaline, 1368
Goddard, Stephen, 950
Goddard, Verna Wright, 1637, 1684
God the Father, 452, **548–52**, 729,
  730, 1670–77
atonement of Jesus Christ, 83
condescension of God, 305
glory of, 551
Godhood, 553
Holy Ghost, 649
hymns, 668
Lectures on Faith, 819
magnifying one's calling, 850
mankind, 853
marriage, 856
names and titles of, 550–51, 852,
  980
overview, 548–50
perfection, 1080
plan of salvation, 1088
work and glory of, 551–52
see also Elohim; Jehovhah; Jesus
  Christ
Godhead, 278, 546, **552–53**, 581,
  636, 1670–77
anti-Mormonism, 51
Articles of Faith, 67
birth, 116
Catholicism and Mormonism, 257
Christians and Christianity, 270

Godhead *(Cont'd)*
  Christology, 273
  community, 302
  doctrine, 397, 399
  Doctrine and Covenants, 409
  fundamentalists, 532
  gift of the Holy Ghost, 543
  history, 612
  Holy Ghost, 649
  Jesus Christ, 729, 730, 737, 753
  light and darkness, 835
  restoration of all things, 1219
  see also Deification; God the
    Father; Godhood
Godhood, 547, 549, 552, **553–55**,
    581, 596
  community, 302
  doctrine, 396
  Doctrine and Covenants, 422
  eternal life, 464
  intellectual history, 687
  mankind, 853
  obedience, 1021
  priesthood, 1137
  reason and revelation, 1193
  theogony, 1474
  world religions, 1590
  see also Christology; Deification;
    Eternal progression; Exaltion;
    God the Father; Godhead; Per-
    fection
Gold coins, 435
Gold plates, 335, **555**, 575, 601
  Anthon Transcript, 43, 44
  Book of Mormon, 157, 159, 180,
    190, 197–98, 210, 214
  centennial observances, 260
  Liahona, 830
  lost scripture, 845
  Mormon, 932
  Nephi, 1004
  New Testament, 1014
  Old Testament, 1027
  Smith, Joseph, 1334
  Smith, Joseph, Sr., 1348
  see also Kinderhook plates
Gold Rush (California), 247, 326,
    936
Goodliffe, Bonnie, 976
Goodson, John, 175
Goodwin, C. C., 633
Goshen, Utah, 63
Gospel of Abraham, 388, 419, **555–
    56**, 799
  restoration of all things, 1219
  seed of Abraham, 1292
  see also Church of the Firstborn;
    Seed of Abraham

Gospel of Jesus Christ, 277, **556–60**
  baptism, 94
  Book of Mormon, 139
  curriculum, 348–49, 351
  Daniel, prophecies of, 355
  discipleship, 384, 385
  Doctrine and Covenants, 414
  elect of God, 448
  elements of, 556–58
  enduring to the end, 456
  Enoch, 458
  eternal nature of, 558–59
  etymological considerations for,
    559–60
  exaltation, 479
  faith in Jesus Christ, 483
  family, 488
  fate, 503
  freemasonry, 528
  gift of the Holy Ghost, 543
  grace, 562
  homosexuality, 656
  Isaiah, 702
  Israel, 710
  justification, 776
  in LDS teaching, 556–59
  missions, 915
  Nephi₁, 1004
  New Jerusalem, 1010
  New Testament, 1012–13, 1050
  remission of sins, 1211
  Ricks College, 1232
  salvation of the dead, 1257
  second estate, 1290
  teaching, 1443
  telestial kingdom, 1443
  testimony of Jesus Christ, 1472
  truth, 1490
  unity, 1498
  volunteerism, 1539
  women, roles of, 1575–77
  worlds, 1595
  see also Doctrine; First principles
    of the Gospel; Preaching the
    Gospel; Restoration of the Gos-
    pel of Jesus Christ
Gould, John, 666, 1637, 1680
Gould, Priscilla, 1361
Gould, Zaccheus, 1361
Gout, Hendrik, 80
Government
  Book of Mormon, 160–61
  freedom and, 526–27
  Salt Lake City, Utah, 1252
  see also Church and state
Grace, **560–63**
  born of God, 218

faith in Jesus Christ, 484
heirs, 583
immortality and eternal life, 677
James, Epistle of, 715
law of Moses, 812
New Testament, 1013
sanctification, 1259
Graham, Billy, 58
Graham, Winifred, 49, 229, 947
Grandin, Egbert B., 48, 175, 575,
    603, 765, 1058
Granger, Lydia Dibble, 784
Granger, Oliver, 784, 793, 955
Granger, Sarah. *See* Kimball, Sarah
    Granger
Granite High School, Salt Lake
    City, Utah, 1295, 1296
Granite Mountain Record Vault,
    563–64, 1588
Grant, Anna, 565
Grant, Augusta Winters, 233, 261
Grant, Edith, 565
Grant, Florence, 565
Grant, George D., 571
Grant, Heber J., 40, 77, 102, 130,
    233, 328, 539, **564–68**, 678,
    872, 1126, 1329, 1637, 1678,
    1679, 1683, 1740
  Bible, 107
  Canada, 254
  centennial observances, 260
  consecration, 313
  Doctrine and Covenants, 417,
    426
  evolution, 478
  film, 948
  Hawaii, 579
  historical sites, 592
  history, 630, 634, 636
  interfaith relationships, 695
  journals, 770
  Millennial Star, 906
  missions, 917
  music, 974
  Polynesians, 1111
  priesthood, 1136
  priesthood quorums, 1145, 1146
  prohibition, 1159
  prophets, 1165
  scouting, 1276
  self-sufficiency, 1294
  Smith, Joseph Fielding, 1354
  social services, 1386
  temples, 1452, 1453
  tithing, 1482
  Williams, Clarissa
  Word of Wisdom, 1584
  Young Women, 1617

Grant, Jedediah M., 564, 1197, 1409, 1637, 1678, 1680, 1740
Grant, Lucy, 565
Grant, Rachel (Jedediah's daughter), 565
Grant, Rachel Ridgeway Ivins, 564
Grant, William, 1396
Grassli, Michaeline P., 1148, 1150, 1637, 1684
Graves, Daniel, 1313
Graveside services, 366
Great and abominable church, 146, 568–69
Great Basin, 438, 440, 469
  Native Americans, 982–84
Great Britain. See British Isles, the Church in
Great Depression. See Depressions, economic
Greece, the Church in, 383, 474, 662, 917
Greek Orthodox Church, 383
Greek philosophy, 58
Green, Doyle L., 461, 678
Greene, John P., 1176
Greene, Louise Lula. See Richards, Lula Greene
Greenhalgh, Joseph W., 786
Greening, Bessie, 1015
Greenwood, Alma, 1015
Gregg, Thomas, 46
Grey, Zane, 356, 947, 949
Griffith, D. W., 947
Griggs, C. Wilfred, 63
Griggs, Thomas C., 950
Groberg, John H., 1637, 1681
Grondahl, Calvin, 665
Grouard, Benjamin Franklin, 1022
Groves, Elisha H., 1068
Groves, W. H., 659
Grow, Henry, 64, 1433
Growth and atrophy, 1031–32
Guam, 77, 78, 1026
Guardian angels, 42
Guatemala, the Church in, 873, 901
Guatemala Temple, 901
Gudmundsson, Gumundur, 1263
Gurley, Zenas H., Sr., 1212, 1266

Haag, Herman H., 71
Hafen, John, 71, 1381
Haggard, Rice, 1221
Haigham, Elizabeth, 1440
Haight, David B., 81, 1187, 1637, 1679, 1680, 1740
Haight, Louisa, 1239
Haiti, the Church in, 1562–63

Hale, Alva, 602
Hale, Arta Matthews, 1637, 1684
Hale, Elizabeth (Emma's mother), 321, 574, 1321
Hale, Emma. See Smith, Emma Hale
Hale, Isaac (Emma's father), 573, 574, 602, 1321, 1400, 1401
Hale, Jannette Callister, 1637, 1685
Hale, Nathan, 838
Hale, Reuben, 210, 854
Hale, Ruth, 838
Hales, Mary Ann, 658
Hales, Mary Isabella. See Horne, Mary Isabella Hales
Hales, Robert D., 1129, 1637, 1680, 1681, 1683
Hales, Stephen, 658
Halflidasson, Thorarinn, 1263
Hall, Randall, 840
Halliday, John R., 950
Halsey, Thankful. See Pratt, Thankful Halsey
Haltern, Hagen G., 73
Hamblin, Jacob, 66, 595, 983
Hammond, Francis Asbury, 578
Hammond, F. Melvin, 1638, 1681
Hamon, Rei, 72
Han, In Sang, 78, 1638, 1681
Hancock, Levi, 802, 1638, 1680
Handbooks. See General Handbook of Instructions
Handcart companies, 571–73, 674, 943, 1039, 1075, 1286
  Relief Society, 1201
Handicapped
  blind, materials for the, 130–31
  deaf, materials for the, 364
Hanks, Knowlton F., 1022
Hanks, Marion D., 678, 1277, 1618, 1638, 1680, 1681
Hansen, Florence, 1286
Hansen, Harold I., 347
Hansen, Klaus, 939
Hansen, Peter Olsen, 213, 1262, 1264
Hansen, W. Eugene, 1638, 1681
Hanson, Benedikt, 1263
Haraguichi, Noriharu Ishigaki, 1396
Harbach, Otto, 837
Harbertson, Robert B., 1638, 1681, 1684
Harding, Mary Ann, 514
Harding, Warren G., 634
Hardy, Leonard W., 1638, 1681
Hardy, M. H., 1638, 1683
Hardy, Ralph W., 1638, 1683

Hardy, Rufus K., 1016, 1328, 1638, 1680
Hare, Deiadama, 1559
Har Megiddo, 67
Harmonization of paradox, 402–403
Harmony, Pennsylvania, 210, 215, 411, 505, 573–74, 593, 854, 1334
Harmony, Utah, 290
Harriman, Henry, 1638, 1680
Harris, Boyd L., 1025
Harris, Devere, 1638, 1681, 1683
Harris, Emer, 576
Harris, Eugene Henri, 1559
Harris, Franklin S., 29, 222, 689
Harris, George, 576
Harris, James H., 1559
Harris, Lucy, 574, 576, 603
Harris, Martin, 574–76, 1058
  Anthon Transcript, 43, 44
  apostles, 61
  Book of Mormon, 198, 199, 210, 214
  chastening, 265
  Doctrine and Covenants, 408
  Fayette, New York, 505
  historical sites, 592
  history, 602, 603
  manuscript, lost 116 pages, 854, 855
  Moroni, 955
  organization of the Church, 1050
  pageants, 1057
  play about, 576
  Quorum of the Twelve Apostles, 1185
  schismatic groups, 1266
  Smith, Joseph, 1334–35
  Temple Square, 1467
  visions of Joseph Smith, 1414
  Whitmer, David, 1564, 1565
Harris, Martin, Jr., 576
Harris, William, 47
Harrison, Benjamin, 628, 1351
Harrison, E. L. T., 1266
Harrison, G. Donald, 1435, 1436
Hart, Charles H., 1638, 1680
Hartshorn, Leon, 114
Hartshorne, Charles, 521
Harwood, James T., 71
Haskell, Thales, 66, 373
Hatch, Ira, 66
Hatch, Lorenzo, 1638, 1683
Hauck, F. Richard, 172
Haun, Jacob, 925
Haun's Mill Massacre, 577, 611, 927, 931, 998

Haven, Jesse, 22
Hawaii, the Church in, **578–79**, 1022
  Book of Mormon, 213
  Brigham Young University, 226–27
  colonization, 291
  missions, 917
Hawaii LDS News (periodical), 1011
Hawkins, James, 578
Hawkins, Paula, 285
Hawkinson, Sharon M., 844
Hawk War (1860s), 291
Hayden, William, 1233
Hay derrick, 28
Hayes, Rutherford B., 625
Hayes, Mrs. Rutherford B., 1313
Hayne, Julie Dean, 1255
Hayward, John, 68
Head of the Church, **579**, 588, 1126
Healing the sick
  elder, Melchizedek Priesthood, 447
  laying on of hands, 814
Health, attitudes toward, 286, 407, 416, **580**, 1096–97, 1375
  see also Drugs, abuse of; Maternity and child health care; Medical practices; Mental health; Physical body; Physical fitness and recreation; Prolonging life; Sick, blessing the; Word of Wisdom
Health Services Corporation, 660
Hearing impaired. *See* Deaf, materials for the
Heart, circumcision of, 283
Hearthom, 718
Heaton, Alvin F., 1092
Heaton, H. Grant, 77
Heaven, **580–81**
  degrees of glory, 367
  Earth, 432
  Jesus Christ, 730
  kingdom of God, 790
  new, 1009
  premortal life, 379
  war in, 1546–47
  see also Afterlife; Celestial kingdom; Degrees of Glory; Kingdom of God; Mother in Heaven; Paradise; Telestial kingdom; Terrestrial kingdom
Heaven Knows Why (Taylor), 664
Heavenly Father. *See* God the Father

Heavenly Mother. *See* Mother in Heaven
Heber, Reginald, 667
Heber J. Grant and Company, 242
Hebrew language, 167, 179, 180–81
Hebrew University, 226
Hebrews. *See* Hebrew language; Hebrews, Epistle to the; Jews; Old Testament
Hebrews, Epistle to the, **581–83**, 588
Hefer, Louis P., 24
Heimerdinger, Chris, 840
Heirich, Max, 321
Heirs, 581, **583–84**
  damnation, 353
  of God, 583
  joint with Christ, 583–84
  New Testament, 1013
  see also Born of God; Church of the Firstborn; Law of adoption; Salvation of the dead
Helaman₁ (c. 130 B.C.), 35, **584**
Helaman₂ (c. 100–57 B.C.), **584**
  book of, 152–53
Helaman₃ (c. 39 B.C.), **585**
Hell, 398, **585–86**
Herberg, Will, 938
Heresy. *See* Orthodoxy, heterodoxy, heresy, 1054
Herod, 171
Herod Agrippa I, 717
Heterodoxy. *See* Orthodoxy, heterodoxy, heresy
Heth, 717, 718
Hickman, William, 49
Hieroglyphics, 134
Higbee, Chauncey, 48
Higbee, Elias, 590, 1638, 1682
Higbee, Francis, 48
Higdon, William T., 1215
High council, 412, **586–87**, 609, 616, 926, 1035, 1037, 1048
  politics, 1100
  priesthood councils, 1141
  priesthood executive committee, 1142
High priest, 586, **587–88**, 635
  bishop, 117–18
  Doctrine and Covenants, 418
  Melchizedek, 879
  Melchizedek Priesthood, 883
  organization, 1037
  presiding, 885, 1034, 1037, 1130
  priesthood quorums, 1144
  Quorum of the Twelve Apostles, 1185

see also Priest, Aaronic Priesthood
Hill, Donna, 114
Hill, George R., 1426
Hill, George R. III, 1638, 1681
Hillam, Harold G., 1638, 1681
Himes, Joshua V., 47
Hinckley, Alonzo A., priesthood quorums, 1145, 1638, 1679, 1740
Hinckley, Gordon B., 60, 81, 103, 513, 539, 787, 1638, 1678, 1679, 1740
  AIDS, 30
  Asia, 78, 80
  business, 241
  cross, 345
  Mexico, 900
  Mountain Meadows Massacre, 968
  Oceania, 1023, 1025
  public communications, 1177
  reverence, 1229
  satellite communications system, 1261
  seventy, 1303
  South America, 1397, 1398
Hinckley, Ira, Jr., 1015
Hinckley, May Green, 231, 270, 1063, 1147, 1638, 1684
Hinduism, 1591–92
Hines, Jerome, 951
Hink, John, 272
Hinkle, George M., 480
Hippolytus of Rome, 682, 882
Hiram, Ohio, **588–89**, 605
Historians, Church, **589–92**, 1682
  early Church (1830–1842), 589–91, 805
  pioneer (1842–1900), 590–91
  early twentieth-century, 591
  recent, 591–92
Historical Department, 310, 591
Historical sites, 573, **592–95**, 635, 1040
  centennial observances, 260
  dedications, 367
  map of, 594
  missionaries, 911
  public relations, 1179
  Sacred Grove, 1247
  Smith, George Albert, 1328
  Smith, Joseph F., 1352
  staff of, 593
  see also Visitors Centers
History, economic. *See* Economic history of the Church

History, significance to Latter-day Saints, **595–98**, 1475
 see also Biography and autobiography; Family history, genealogy; Historical sites; Historians, Church; History of the Church; Record keeping
History, social and cultural. See Social and cultural history
History of the Church, **598–647**
 c.1820–1831, background, founding, New York period, 598–604, 1058
 c.1831–1844, Ohio, Missouri, and Nauvoo periods, 500, 604–613, 792, 1092, 1099
 c.1844–1877, Exodus and early Utah periods, 373, 613–22, 935, 1563–64
 c.1878–1898, late pioneer Utah period, 622–30, 1095
 c.1898–1945, transitions, early twentieth-century period, 630–38
 c.1945–1990, post-World War II international era period, 638–47
 Joseph Smith—History, 762
 publications, 1176
 Smith, Joseph, writings of, 1344–45
 temples, 1450–55, 1463–65
 welfare services, 1554–55
 women, roles of, 1574–75
 see also Church of Jesus Christ of Latter-day Saints, The; Doctrine, history of; Economic history; History, significance to Latter-day Saints; Intellectual history; Legal and judicial history; Lifestyle; Organization; Pioneer life and worship; Politics, political history; Social and cultural history
History of the Church (History of Joseph Smith), **647–48**
Hofmann, Mark W., 44, 51, 523, 789, 826
Hofmann forgeries, 523, 826
Hoge, Joseph P., 1000
Holder, Louisa, 1015
Holder, Martha, 1015
Holder, Thomas, 1014
Holiness, **648–49**
 see also Righteousness
Holland. See Netherlands
Holland, Jeffrey R., 222, 1638, 1681, 1684
Holland, Patricia Terry, 1638, 1685

Holmer, Paul, 561
Holt, Dorothy, 1638, 1685
Holy Ghost, **649–51**
 Abraham, 8
 Alma, 35
 blasphemy, 127
 Book of Mormon, 142, 166, 168
 commandments, 297
 confirmation, 311
 degrees of glory, 368
 dove, sign of the, 428
 Elias, spirit of, 449
 Elohim, 453
 epistemology, 463
 fathers' blessings, 504
 freedom, 526
 Godhead, 553
 Gospel of Jesus Christ, 557
 Jesus Christ, 729, 730, 742
 lay participation, 815
 Lectures on Faith, 819
 lifestyle, 834
 light of Christ, 835
 love, 846
 mysteries of God, 977
 Noah, 1017
 priesthood blessings, 1141
 Primary, 1149
 prophecy, 1160
 Protestantism, 1171
 psalms, 1172
 repentance, 1217
 righteousness, 1237
 scripture, 1281, 1284
 signs of the true Church, 1311
 suffering in the world, 1422
 testimony bearing, 1470
 truth, 1490
 unpardonable sin, 1499, 1598
 see also Gift of the Holy Ghost; Gifts of the Spirit; Holy Spirit; Holy Spirit of Promise
Holy of Holies, 37, **651**
Holy Spirit, 551, **651**
 blessings, 129
 Book of Mormon, 142, 169
 Christians and Christianity, 270
 compassionate service, 303
 conversion, 321
 devils, 381
 Doctrine and Covenants, 408
 light of Christ, 835
 plan of salvation, 1088
 revelation, 1225
 see also Holy Ghost; Holy Spirit of Promise

Holy Spirit of Promise, **651–52**
 chastity law, 266
 Church of the Firstborn, 276
 Doctrine and Covenants, 415
 endure to the end, 464
 eternal lives, eternal increase, 465
 justification, 777
 marriage, 858
 priesthood, 1137
Homans, J. E., 137
Home, **652**
 curriculum, 348
 Smith, Joseph, 1342
Home, College of the (BYU), 223
Home industries, 621, 636, **652–54**, 1575–76
 Retrenchment Association, 1224
 Snow, Eliza R., 1366
 see also Self-sufficiency; Stewardship; Welfare
Home literature, 838, 839
Homer, William H., 576
Home teaching, 461, **654–55**, 1441
 bishops, 120, 122
 brotherhood, 235
 callings, 249
 community, 302
 interviews, 698
 organization, 1042
 priesthood blessings, 1140
 priesthood executive committee, 1142
 priesthood interview, 1142
 priests, 1132
 volunteerism, 1540
 ward council, 1544
 welfare services, 1555
Homosexuality, 13, 265, 645, **655–56**, 1307
Honduras, the Church in, 901
Hong Kong, the Church in, 77, 78, 79, 80, 662, 696
Hong Kong-Taiwan Mission, 79
Hoover, Herbert, 634
Hope, **656–57**
 Mormon, 933
 see also Lectures on Faith
Hope, Len, 125
Hope, Mary, 125
Hope of Israel, **657**
 see also Covenant Israel
Hopkinson, Harold, 73
Horne, Joseph, 658
Horne, Lewis, 843
Horne, Marilyn, 951

Horne, Mary Isabella Hales, 375, **657–59**, 1224, 1437
Horner, John M., 247
Horses, 173
Hosanna shout, 261, 262, **659**, 799, 1254, 1451, 1456
Hospitals, **659–61**, 867–68, 1040, 1064
 Primary, 1148
 Relief Society, 1203
 Williams, Clarissa, 1568
 see also specific hospital names, e.g., Deseret Hospital
Hotchkiss, Horace, 987
Hotel Utah, 64, 241
Houghton, Arthur Boyd, 947
House of the Lord, The, 456
Howard, Elizabeth, 375
Howard, F. Burton, 1398, 1639, 1681
Howe, Abigail, 1601
Howe, Eber D., 46, 1235, 1403, 1592
Howells, Adele Cannon, 270, 1063, 1147, 1639, 1684
Howells, Marcia Knowlton, 1639, 1684
Humanitarian service, **661–63**
 economic aid, 434
 fast offerings, 510, 502
 interfaith relationships, 694
 poverty, 1114
 see also Civic duties; Economic aid; Welfare services
Humanities, Brigham Young University, 224
Humanities Research Center (BYU), 224
Humboldt, Alexander von, 1509
Humility, 264, **663–64**
 sanctification, 1260
Humor, **664–65**
 see also Lightmindedness
Hungary, the Church in, 471, 473, 474
Hunt, Jefferson, 935, 936
Hunter, Donnell, 842
Hunter, Edward, 120, 624, 1037, 1129, 1639, 1681
Hunter, Howard W., 60, 591, 900, 903, 1025, 1187, 1229, 1592, 1639, 1679, 1682, 1740
Hunter, Milton R., 172, 1639, 1680
Hunter, Rodello, 115
Huntington, Chauncey, 1612
Huntington, Dimmick, 983
Huntington, Elfie, 1381

Huntington, Samuel, 1611
Huntington, William, 1611
Huntington, William, Sr., 1611
Huntley, Hannah, 1361
Hurlbut, Philastus, 46, 48, 1203, 1235
Husband's blessings, 130
Hyde, Annie M. Taylor, 1639, 1685
Hyde, Marinda N., 375
Hyde, Orson, 69, 228, 326, **665–67**, 1639, 1678, 1740
 David, prophetic figure of last days, 360
 dedications, 367
 history, 611
 interfaith relationships, 695
 Israel, 711
 Lamanite mission, 802
 Middle East, 902
 missions, 916, 920
 Missouri conflict, 931
 Nevada, 1006
 organization, 1036
 publications, 1175
 Quorum of the Twelve Apostles, 1185
 Schools of the Prophets, 1269
 world religions, 1593
Hydroelectric power industry, 440, 629
Hymns and hymnody, 232, 273, 517, 524, **667–69**
 death and dying, 366
 Doctrine and Covenants, 411
 epistemology, 462
 hope of Israel, 657
 literature, 841
 publications, 1176
 sacrament meeting, 1245
 Scandinavia, 1264
 Snow, Eliza R., 1364
 social and cultural history, 1378
 Young Women, 1617
 see also Appendix; Mormon Tabernacle Choir
Hypocephalus, 133, 136

"I Am," 741
 see also Jesus Christ
"I Am a Child of God" (hymn), 273, 1708
Ibbotson, Rachel, 1358
Iceland, the Church in, 1263
Idaho, pioneer settlements in, 52, **671–72**
Idaho Falls Temple, 1460
Ignorance, 1031

Illinois, LDS communities in, **672–73**
 see also Carthage Jail; Historical Sites; Martyrdom of Joseph and Hyrum Smith; Nauvoo
Imagery, Book of Mormon, 183–84
Immaculate conception, **673**, 864, 1052
Immigration and emigration, **673–76**, 942
 bishops, 120
 British Isles, 229
 economic history, 436–37, 439
 Europe, 469–70, 471
 gathering, 537
 history, 611
 Mormon Pioneer Trail, 943
 Nauvoo, 990, 992, 994, 1000
 organization, 1039
 Salt Lake City, Utah, 1250
 Scandinavia, 1263
 social characteristics, 1376, 1377
 vital statistics, 1525
 see also Handcart companies; Perpetual Emigrating Fund; Pioneer economy; Residence and migration; Social and cultural history; Westward migration, planning and prophecy
Immortality, 552, **676–77**
 atonement of Jesus Christ, 84
 deification, early Christian, 370
 Jesus Christ, 740
 paradise, 1063
 plan of salvation, 1091
 reincarnation, 1198
 see also Immortality and eternal life; Soul; Spirit
Immortality and eternal life, **677–78**
 see also Eternal life
Improvement Era (periodical), 305, 461, 635, **678**, 965, 1040, 1616, 1617
Incense burner, 188, 189
Income and religion, 1373–74
Income tax. *See* Taxation
Independence, Missouri, 635, **678–79**, 710, 1518
India, the Church in, 79, 81, 696, 917
Indian Relief Society, 1201
Indians. *See* American Indian Services; Indian Relief Society; Indian Student Placement Services; Native Americans
Indian Student Placement Services (ISPS), 646, **679–80**, 786, 805, 984, 1041, 1205, 1387

Individuality, **680–82**
  stereotyping, 1417
  see also Lifestyle; Socialization;
    Unity; Values, transmission of
Indonesia, the Church in, 80, 696
Industry. *See* Business; Economic
    history of the Church; specific
    industry names, e.g., Deseret
    Industries
Infant baptism, 93, 158, **682–83**,
    933, 1052, 1341
Infants. *See* Children; Infant bap-
    tism
Inheritance, consecration, 313
Initchi, Sylvia, 25
Inn at Temple Square, The, 242
Inspiration, 540, 547, **683–84**
  father's blessings, 504
  scripture, 1282
Institutes. *See* Institutes of Religion;
    Seminaries and institutes; spe-
    cific institute names
Institutes of Religion, 105, 359,
    444, 637, **684–85**, 873, 1040
Instructional Development Depart-
    ment, 351
Instructor, The (periodical), 461,
    635, **685**
  see also Juvenile Instructor
Intellectual history, **685–91**
  flow of ideas, 686
  Restoration prologue, 686–87
  Restoration period (1830–1844),
    686–87
  community response (1844–1896),
    687–89
  scholarly secularism (1896–1918),
    689
  adaption and confrontation (1918–
    1945), 689
  urbanization (1945–1990), 689–91
Intelligence, **692**
  doctrine, 396
  glory of God, 551
  law, 809
  premortal life, 1123
  purpose of earth life, 1180
  reason and revelation, 1194
  see also Intelligences
Intelligences, **692–93**
  evil, 478
  Godhood, 553
  King Follett Discourse, 791
  mankind, 854
  soul, 1392
  see also First estate; Intelligence;
    Premortal life; Spirit body

Interfaith relationships, 278, **693–96**
  apostasy, 58
  Brigham Young University, 226
  Christian, 693–95
  Jewish, 695
  other faiths, 696
  see also Non-Mormons, social re-
    lations with; World religions
    and Mormonism
Intermountain Health Care, 660
Inter Mountain Republican (periodi-
    cal), 536
Intermountain Transplant Program,
    1051
Intermountain West settlement,
    300–301, 323
Internal Communications Depart-
    ment, 324, 351
International Genealogical Index™
    (IGI), 492, 493, 495, 500, 538,
    696–97
  name extraction program, 980
International Magazines (periodi-
    cals), 268, 351, 643, **697**, 1042
International Society, 1389
Interviews, **697–98**, 1054, 1142–43
Investment Policy Committee, 509
Investment Properties Division, 241
In vitro fertilization, 1096
Iowa, LDS communities in, **698**
Iran, the Church in, 902
Iron industry, 438, 440
Irrigation, 28
Isaacson, H. Thorpe B., 513, 1639,
    1678, 1680, 1681, 1682, 1740
Isaiah, 106, 159, 477, **698–704**
  authorship, 699–700, 701
  Book of Mormon, 700–702
  commentaries, 704
  Jesus Christ, 749
  Messiah, 893
  Millennium, 906
  modern scripture, 701–703
  prophecy, 1163
  prophets, 1168
Ishmael, **704–705**, 762
  Lehi, 827
Ishmaelites, 193
Islam, 283, 345, 696, 1592–93
  reason and revelation, 1192
  scripture, 1277
  spiritual death, 1407
ISPS. *See* Indian Student Place-
    ment Services
Israel, 419, **705–711**
  Book of Mormon, 160
  gathering of, 419, 462, 536, 709–

711, 714, 715, 722, 954, 1139,
    1336, 1624
  God of, 746
  land of, 707–708
  laying on of hands, 813
  lineal, 706
  lost tribes of, 461, 709
  Mormon, 933
  Mormonism, 940
  name history, 705–706
  overview, 705–708
  patriarchal blessings, 1067
  prophets, 1167
  scattering of, 462, 480, 708–709,
    714, 1624
  spiritual, 706–707
  state of (modern), 708
  temples, 1462, 1463–64
  Zenos, 1624
  see also Covenant Israel; Hope of
    Israel; Jerusalem; Jews; Mother
    in Israel; Zionism
Israelites. *See* Covenant Israel;
    Hope of Israel
Italy, the Church in, 213, 471, 472,
    917
Ivins, Anthony W., 178, 233, 478,
    539, 896, 899, 900, 1639, 1678,
    1679, 1740
Ivins, Antoine R., 1639, 1680
Ivins, Charles, 48

Jack, Elaine L., 1205, 1206, 1639,
    1685
Jackson, Carolyn, 1313
Jackson, Kent P., 172, 425
Jackson, Mary Ann, 1582
Jackson, William Henry, 947
Jackson County, Missouri. *See* Mis-
    souri, LDS communities in
    Jackson and Clay counties
Jacob, son of Lehi, **713–14**
  allegory of Zenos, 31, 148
  book of, 147–48, 714
  Isaiah, 701, 704
  Jesus Christ, 727
  lost scripture, 845
  magnifying one's calling, 850
  Messiah, 894
  prophecy, 1163, 1164
Jacobs, Henry Bailey, 1612
Jacobs, Henry Chariton, 1612
Jacobs, Zebulon William, 1612
Jacobsen, Florence S., 591, 592,
    1617, 1618, 1639, 1685
Jakeman, M. Wells, 62, 63
Jamaica, the Church in, 1563, 1762

James, Epistle of, 515, **715–16**
James, Jane Manning, 125
James the Apostle, **716–17**, 780,
  1050, 1078
  Elias, spirit of, 449
  First Presidency, 512
  prayer, 1118
  sin, 1314
  visions of Joseph Smith, 1514
Japan, the Church in, 75–77, 213,
  566, 634, 696, 873, 905, 917,
  1022, 1533, 1757
Japanese Mission (Hawaii), 579
Jardine, William M., 29
Jared. *See* Book of Mormon, Ether
  book; Brother of Jared;
  Jaredites
Jaredites, 584, **717–20**
  Adamic language, 18
  archaeology, 62
  beehive symbol, 99
  Book of Mormon, 141, 156, 157
  chronology, 169
  economy, 173–74
  government and law, 160, 161
  Mosiah₁, 959
  names, 186
  Near East, 190
  oaths, 1020
  peoples, 192
  promised land, 1160
  wrath of God, 1598
  see also Brother of Jared; Jared
Jarom, book of, 148
Jefferson, Thomas, 318
Jehovah, Jesus Christ, **720–21**, 724,
  741, 745
  Christmas, 271
  Christology, 272
  creator, 720
  cross, 345
  David, King, 360
  doctrine, 397
  in His name, 721
  Hope of Israel, 657
  Jerusalem, 722
  lawgiver, 720
  law of Moses, 811
  names and titles of, 550–51, 980
  plan of salvation, 1088
  priesthood, 1133
  prophets, 1166
  redeemer, deliverer, and advo-
    cate, 720–21
  war in heaven, 1546
  see also Elohim; God the Father;
    Jesus Christ

Jennings, Thomas, 577
Jennings, William O., 931
Jensen, Freda Johanna (Joan), 823
Jensen, Hans Peter, 1262
Jensen, Marlin K., 1639, 1681
Jensen, Miles, 679
Jenson, Andrew, 590, 591, 831,
  1476
Jeppsen, Malcolm S., 1639, 1681
Jepsen, Betty Jo Nelson, 1639, 1684
Jeremiah, prophecies of, 360, 709,
  721–22, 893, 1168
Jerusalem, 169, 179, **722–23**
  Isaiah, 702
  Israel, 710
  Melchizedek, 879
  promised land, 1160
  Smith, Joseph, 1343
  Zion, 1626
  see also Brigham Young Univer-
    sity, Jerusalem Center for Near
    Eastern Studies; New Jerusalem
Jessee, Dean, 114
Jesus Christ, 277, **723–39**, 1670–77
  Adam, 17
  angels, 40
  apostles, 60–61
  archaeology, 63
  Armageddon, 67
  baptism of, 93, 546, 730, 735,
    756
  Bible, 105
  birth of, 61–62, 171, 729–30
  blood atonement, 131
  Book of Mormon, 140, 153–55,
    159, 171, 184, 202
  brotherhood, 234
  Catholicism and Mormonism, 257
  celestial kingdom, 260
  charity, 264
  Christians and Christianity, 271
  Christmas, 271–72
  Christology, 272–73
  Church of the Firstborn, 276
  condescension of God, 305
  covenants, 334
  creation accounts, 340, 720, 752
  cross, 344–45
  crucifixion of, 171, 256, 344,
    732–33
  David, prophetic figure of last
    days, 361
  Deuteronomy, 378
  divorce, 391
  doctrine, 397
  dove, sign of the, 428
  Easter, 433

eternal life, 464
faith in, 483–85
feminism, 507
firstborn in the spirit, 728, 743,
  1404
forty-day ministry and other
  post-resurrection appearances
  of, 734–36, 1223
fulness of the Gospel, 530
Godhead, 553
head of the Church, 579
heirs, 583–84
immortality, 677
Jehovah, 720–21
Joseph Smith Translation of the
  Bible, 767
last days, 805
latter-day appearances of, 726,
  736–37, 742, 851
law of Moses, 812
lawsuits, 813
Lectures on Faith, 819
life and death, spiritual, 832
light and darkness, 836
Malachi, 851
marriage, 856
marriage supper of the lamb, 860
martyrs, 863
Matthew, Gospel of, 869–70
millenarianism, 905–906
Millennium, 907
ministry of, 730–32, 745, 1012
mortal, 724–25
only begotten in the flesh, 729,
  742, 775
overview, 724–26
physical body, 1080
plan of salvation, 1088
postmortal, 725–26
premortal, 724
priesthood, 1140
prophecies about, 726–28, 747,
  1161, 1165, 1172–73
resurrection of, 344, 725, 729,
  733–34, 738, 1222–23
sacrament, 1243–44
second coming of, 569, 737–39,
  747, 907, 1290
truth, 1489
witnesses, law of, 1570
see also Antichrists; Atonement of
  Jesus Christ; Calling and election; Jehovah, Jesus Christ;
  Mary, mother of Jesus; Second
  coming of Jesus Christ; Testimony of Jesus Christ

Jesus Christ, fatherhood and sonship of, 550, **739–40**
Jesus Christ, names and titles of, 146, 452, 550, **740–42**, 743, 751, 892–93, 980–81
Jesus Christ, second comforter, 464, 741, **742**, 777
Jesus Christ, sources for words of, **742–44**
Jesus Christ, taking the name of, upon oneself, **744**, 1312
Jesus Christ, types and shadows of, **744–45**, 1430
Jesus Christ in the Scriptures, 743, **745–53**
   Bible, 745
   Book of Mormon, 748–50
   Doctrine and Covenants, 751–52
   as God of Israel, 746–47
   historical, 745–46
   Mary, mother of Jesus, 864
   Matthew, Gospel of, 869
   Old Testament foreshadowings, 746
   Pearl of Great Price, 752–53
   portrayal through ceremony, 746
   revelation and, 747–48
   see also Jehovah, Jesus Christ
Jews, **753**
   Adam, 17
   Apocrypha, 55
   Book of Abraham, 134
   Book of Mormon, 144, 146, 162, 166, 167, 168
   circumcision, 283
   conversion, 322
   creation accounts, 342, 343
   damnation, 353
   David, prophetic figure of last days, 360
   dedications, 367
   deification, early Christian, 370
   divorce, 391
   Doctrine and Covenants, 413
   Elijah, 451–52
   Enoch, 459–60
   ethics, 467
   Europe, 469
   feminism, 507
   foreknowledge of God, 521
   Hyde, Orson, 666
   interfaith relationships, 695
   law of Moses, 811, 812
   Matthew, Gospel of, 869
   Melchizedek, 880–81, 882
   opposition, 1031
   original sin, 1052
   purpose of earth life, 1182
   reason and revelation, 1192
   resurrection, 1222
   salvation of the dead, 1257
   scripture, 1277, 1279
   Snow, Lorenzo, 1369
   spiritual death, 1497
   temples, 1464–65
   View of the Hebrews, 1509–10
   world religions and Mormonism, 1593–94
   Zionism, 1626
   see also Israel; Middle East, the Church in
Jobs. *See* Occupational status; Work, role of
Joe, Oreland, 1286
Johansen, Franz, 1286
Johansson, C. Fritz, 1263, 1264
John, Helen, 679
John the Apostle, revelations of, 138, 260, 728, **753–55**, 780, 781, 1009, 1014, 1050, 1078
   Elias, spirit of, 449
   First Presidency, 512
   great and abominable church, 568
   laying on of hands, 813
   lost scripture, 845
   New Testament, 1012
   visions of Joseph Smith, 1514
   see also John the Beloved
John the Baptist, 2, 41, 62, 98, 427, 449, **755–57**
   gift of the Holy Ghost, 543
   history, 602
   Jesus Christ, 731, 749
   laying on of hands, 813
   Lehi, 828
   Noah, 1016
   priesthood, 1139
   restoration of all things, 1219
   scripture, 1284
   visitation, 1513
John the Beloved, **757–58**, 1486
   see also John the Apostle, revelations of
Johnson, Benjamin F., 798
Johnson, Elsa, 588
Johnson, John, 588, 1514
Johnson, Kenneth, 1639, 1681
Johnson, Leroy, 531
Johnson, Luke S., 930, 1185, 1639, 1679, 1740
Johnson, Lyman E., 423, 930, 1185, 1639, 1679, 1740
Johnson, Mikel, 1263
Johnson, Marinda Nancy, 666
Johnson, Neils, 1435
Johnson, Peter N., 965
Johnson, Sonia, 51
Johnston, Albert Sidney, 619, 1500
Joining the Church, **758–60**, 1177
   see also Conversion; Fellowshipping; Lifestyle; Membership
Jonas, Abraham, 527
Jones, Abner, 1221
Jones, Ann, 1015
Jones, Daniel W., 213, 572, 697, 895, 899
Jones, Wiley, 899
Jordan, the Church in, 902
Jorgensen, Bruce, 842
Joseph of Egypt, 179–80, 706, **760–62**
   Lamanites, 804
   Moses, 958
   Nephi$_1$, 1005
   New Jerusalem, 1010
   papyri, 1059
   premortal life, 958
   prophecy, 158–159, 1163
   seed of, 762
   son of Jacob, 760–61
   "voice from the dust," 1538
   writings of, 761–62
Joseph Fielding Smith Institute for Church History (BYU), 223, 591
Josephites, 193
Joseph Smith—History, **762–63**, 957, 991, 1049, 1071, 1072, 1283
Joseph Smith—Matthew, **763**, 766, 1012, 1071, 1283
Joseph Smith Memorial, 260, 592
Joseph Smith Translation of the Bible (JST), **763–69**, 1709–1723
   authority to translate, 764–65
   Book of Moses, 216
   contributions of, 766–67
   Cowdery, Oliver, 337
   doctrine, 396, 767–69
   Doctrine and Covenants, 413
   dove, sign of the, 427
   extent of the changes, 766
   Fayette, New York, 505
   Hiram, Ohio, 588
   history, 605, 646
   intellectual history, 687
   Jesus Christ, 727, 731, 747
   John, 754
   Joseph of Egypt, 760
   Joseph Smith—History, 763
   Joseph Smith—Matthew, 763

Joseph Smith Translation of the
  Bible (JST) (Cont'd)
  Kirtland, Ohio, 796
  lost scripture, 845
  Matthew, Gospel of, 869
  Moses, 958
  New Testament, 1012
  Old Testament, 1027
  parables, 1060
  plural marriage, 1092
  procedure and time frame, 765–66
  psalms, 1172
  publication, 766
  Rigdon, Sidney, 1234
  sacrament, 1245
  scripture, 1279, 1283
  Sermon on the Mount, 1298
  Ten Commandments, 1469
  title, 766
  view of, 764
Journal of Discourses (periodical),
  306, **769–70**, 1174
Journals, 217, 305, 494, 539, 597,
  770–71, 1196
  humor, 664
  peculiar people, 1073
  seagulls, miracle of, 1287
  societies and organizations, 1388
  see also Historians, Church; Rec-
    ord keeping
Joy, **771–72**, 1260, 1342
  see also Mortality
J. Reuben Clark Law School (BYU),
  224, 1389
Juárez, Isaias, 900
Juárez Academy, 13, 274, 1267
Juárez Stake, 625
Judah, 481
Judaism. See Israel; Jews
Judd, Margaret Romney Jackson,
  1639, 1685
Judges, Book of Mormon, 161, 162
Judgment, **772–73**
  Book of Mormon, 142, 158
  degrees of glory, 367
  Millennium, 907
  Smith, Joseph, 1343
  voice of warning, 1538–39
  witnesses, law of, 1570
  see also Baptism for the dead;
    Plan of salvation; Purpose of
    earth life; Salvation of the
    dead; Temple ordinances; Voice
    of warning
Judgment Day, final, 364, **774–75**
Judicial history. See Legal and judi-
  cial history of the Church

Jury, James, 1015
Justice and mercy, **775–76**
  Book of Mormon, 152
  disciplinary procedures, 386
  judgment, 773
  law, 808
  plan of salvation, 1089
  righteousness, 1236
  Smith, Joseph, 1341
Justification, 416, 648, **776–77**,
  1236, 1260
Juvenile Instructor (periodical), 635,
  667, 685, 688, **777**, 1426
  see also Instructor
J. Willard and Alice S. Marriott
  School of Management (BYU),
  224

Kadarusman, Effian, 80
Kane, John (Thomas L.'s great-
  grandfather), 779
Kane, John Kintzing (Thomas L.'s
  father), 779
Kane, Thomas L., 66, 326, 619,
  779–80, 935, 1500
Kanesville, Iowa, 119, 325–26
Kansas-Nebraska Act (1854), 1100
Kapp, Ardeth G., 1616, 1617, 1619,
  1640, 1685
Kay, F. Arthur, 1640, 1681
Kearns, Thomas, 633
Kearny, Stephen W., 935, 936
Keeler, James, 578
Keller, Helen, 130
Kellogg, George H., 53
Kelly, Brian K., 1008
Kelly, Martin, 838
Kelsch, Louis A., 77
Kelsey, Eli B., 620, 1266
Kelsey, Texas, 294
Kendall, Amos, 935
Kendrick, L. Lionel, 1640, 1681
Kennedy, David M., 286, 642
  diplomatic relations, 382–83, 384
  Europe, 474
  politics, 1108
Kenotic theory, 272
Keys of the Priesthood, 60, 327,
  337, **780–81**, 1138
  Catholicism and Mormonism, 257
  covenants, 334
  Daniel, prophecies of, 356
  dispensations of the Gospel, 388
  Doctrine and Covenants, 414
  Elijah, 450
  First Presidency, 512
  Gospel of Abraham, 555

  history, 609
  Israel, 706, 709, 710
  John the Beloved, 757
  Kirtland Temple, 799
  Malachi, 851
  Moses, 959
  Noah, 1017
  ordinances, 1033
  organization, 1037, 1044
  President of the Church, 1126
  prophet, seer, and revelator,
    1170
  prophets, 1165
  scripture, 1278
  sealing, 1288
  Smith, Joseph, 1336, 1342
  stake president, 1415
Kib, 717
Kidder, Daniel P., 47
Kikuchi, Yoshihiko, 1640, 1681
Kim, 718
Kimball, Alice Ann, 1350
Kimball, Andrew (Spencer W.'s
  father), 786
Kimball, Anna Spaulding, 782
Kimball, Camilla Eyring (Spencer
  W.'s wife), 786, 787, 788
Kimball, Edward L. (Spencer's
  son), 786
Kimball, Edward P. (musician), 976
Kimball, Heber C., 43, 168, 175,
  228, 666, **781–84**, 786, 1640,
  1678, 1740
  British Isles, 920, 921
  endowment houses, 456
  Garden of Eden, 534
  gifts of the spirit, 545
  history, 616
  Journal of Discourses, 769
  Kirtland, Ohio, 796, 797
  missions, 916, 920, 921
  Missouri, 927
  Mormon Battalion, 935
  Moroni, 955
  organization, 1036
  plural marriage, 1094
  Quorum of the Twelve Apostles,
    1185
  religious experience, 1209
  spirit world, 1409
  temple ordinances, 1444
  temples, 1452
  "This Is the Place" monument,
    1477
  Young, Brigham, 1602
Kimball, Hiram, 784

Kimball, J. Golden, 517, 664, 665, 838, 1327, 1640, 1680

Kimball, Mary Connelly, 1207, 1615

Kimball, Olive Beth (Spencer W.'s daughter), 786

Kimball, Olive Woolley (Spencer W.'s mother), 786

Kimball, Sarah M. Granger, 784–85, 1200, 1207, 1572, 1573

Kimball, Sarah Noon, 783

Kimball, Solomon F., 782

Kimball, Spencer L. (Spencer W.'s son), 786

Kimball, Spencer W., 60, 67, 277, 530, 785–89, 873, 1126, 1640, 1678, 1679, 1740
  accountability, 13
  Africa, 24
  animals, 42
  apostasy, 58
  April 6, 62
  art, 74
  Asia, 77
  Assistants to the Twelve, 81
  biography and autobiography, 113, 114
  blacks, 126
  business, 240
  centennial observances, 262
  chastity law, 265
  Christians and Christianity, 271
  cremation, 344
  dating and courtship, 359
  diplomatic relations, 382, 383
  divorce, 392
  Doctrine and Covenants, 405, 423
  drugs, abuse of, 429
  epistemology, 462
  Europe, 474
  Eve, 476
  fast offerings, 502
  First Presidency, 512
  history, 642, 646
  Indian Student Placement Services, 679
  inspiration, 683
  intelligences, 692
  interfaith relationships, 694, 696
  Israel, 711
  journals, 770–71
  literature, 840
  Mexico and Central America, 901
  missions, 917
  modesty in dress, 932
  motherhood, 962
  motto, 788
  Native Americans, 984, 985
  Oceania, 1023, 1025
  organization, 1042, 1043
  politics, 1108
  prayer, 1119
  profanity, 1158
  prophets, 1165
  publications, 1176
  public relations, 1178
  Quorum of the Twelve Apostles, 1186
  race, racism, 1191, 1192
  record keeping, 1196
  Relief Society, 1205
  Sabbath Day, 1242
  scouting, 1276
  sealing, 487
  self-sufficiency, 1293
  Seventy, 1302
  sexuality, 1306
  South America, 1396, 1397
  temples, 1454
  true and living Church, 1489
  visiting teaching, 1517
  women, roles of, 1577
  world religions, 1592

Kimball, Vilate Murray (Heber C.'s wife), 782, 783, 1602

Kimball, Andrew E. (Spencer W.'s son), 786

Kim Ho Jik, 77

Kincaid, William, 1221

Kinderhook plates, 789–90

King, Arthur Henry, 842

King, Austin, 1347

King, David S., 1640, 1683

King, Hannah Tapfield, 1381

Kingdom of God, 259, 790–91, 879
  Book of Mormon, 147
  callings, 249
  consecration, 312
  Council of Fifty, 327
  Daniel, prophecies of, 355
  dedications, 367
  deification, early Christian, 370
  discipleship, 385
  Doctrine and Covenants, 405
  on earth, 790–91
  economic history, 435
  enduring to the end, 457
  first principles of the Gospel, 514
  in heaven, 790
  history, 630
  home industries, 653
  Jerusalem, 723
  Jesus Christ, 730
  Millennium, 907
  motherhood, 963
  Nauvoo, 1000
  Pioneer Day, 1083
  pioneer economy, 1083
  pioneer life, 1087
  sacrifice, 1248
  Smith, Joseph, 1343
  social and cultural history, 1379
  see also Heaven

King Follett Discourse, 304, 396, 465, 612, 791–92, 809, 991, 1338

King James Version. See Bible, King James Version

Kingsbury, Joseph C., 423

Kingston, Charles, 531

Kington, Thomas, 230

Kinney, Bruce, 1592

Kiribati, the Church in, 1026

Kirkham, Francis W., 172, 207

Kirkham, Oscar A., 1640, 1680

Kirtland, Ohio, 588, 593, 665, 793–98
  building program, 236
  city planning, 284
  Doctrine and Covenants, 415, 417
  economic history, 435
  fast offerings, 501
  gathering, 537
  gifts of the spirit, 545
  high council, 586
  history, 604, 605
  Kimball, Heber C., 782
  Kimball, Sarah Granger, 784
  Lamanite Mission, 802
  Lectures on Faith, 818–21
  map of, 794
  Missionary Training Centers, 913
  papyri, 1058
  pioneer life, 1085
  politics, 1099
  schools, 1268
  Smith, Joseph, 1336, 1346
  Smith, Mary Fielding, 1358
  social and cultural history, 1378
  Young, Brigham, 1602
  see also Kirtland economy; Kirtland Temple

Kirtland economy, 609, 792–93
  legal and judicial history, 823
  Smith, Emma Hale, 1324
  Smith, Joseph, 1346
  Whitmer, David, 1565

Kirtland Safety Society, 215, 576, 793, 797, 1235, 1265, 1346

Kirtland Temple, 608, 795, **798–99**, 1450
  architecture, 63
  Cowdery, Oliver, 335
  dedications, 367, 1455
  dispensation of the fulness of times, 388
  Doctrine and Covenants, 416, 419
  Elias, 449
  Elijah, 450, 452
  Ephraim, 461
  fast and testimony meeting, 502
  freemasonry, 528
  historical sites, 593
  history, 605, 609
  hosanna shout, 659
  Israel, 706, 709, 710
  Kimball, Heber C., 782
  Malachi, 851
  Melchizedek Priesthood, 886
  Moses, 959
  papyri, 1060
  pioneer life, 1085
  prophecy, 1163
  religious experience, 1210
  restoration of all things, 1219
  Rigdon, Sidney, 1235
  Smith, Joseph, 1336
  Smith, Joseph, Sr., 1349
  visions of Joseph Smith, 1514–15
  Young, Brigham, 1603
  Zionism, 1626
Kish, 718
Kishkumen war, 165
Kithtilhund, William Anderson, 803
Knaphus, Torleif S., 40, 1286
Knight, Goodwin, 285
Knight, Jesse, 253
Knight, John M., 822
Knight, Joseph, Sr., 289, 337, 408, 603, 1400, 1401, 1515
Knight, Lucy Jane Brimhall, 1640, 1685
Knight, Lydia, 536
Knight, Newel, 289, 290, 545, 604
Knowledge, **799–800**
  obedience, 1021
  opposition, 1031
  Quorum of the Twelve Apostles, 1189
  Smith, Joseph, 1341–42
  truth, 1490
Kofford, Cree-L, 1640, 1681
Kolob, 82
Komatsu, Adney Yoshio, 579, 1640, 1680, 1681, 1683

Kook, Abraham, 1593
Korea, South. *See* South Korea
Korihor (c. 74 B.C.), 45, 151, 162
KSL broadcasting, 232–33, 241, 261, 308, 631, 645, 694, 800
Kumar, Raj, 81
Kump, Eileen Gibbons, 843

Laban, 198, 1195, 1427–28
Lacerti, Giovanna, 72
Lagerberg, Karl, 1263
Laie, Hawaii, 291
Laman, 145, 704, **801–802**
  Lehi, 827
  Native Americans, 981
  Nephi₁, 1003
  record keeping, 1195
  sin, 1315
Lamanite Mission of 1830–31, 337, 604, 605, 795, **802–804**, 916
  Missouri, 922
  Missouri Conflict, 927
  Native Americans, 982
  Pratt, Parley P., 1116
  Smith, Joseph, 1336
Lamanites, 584, **804–805**
  Book of Mormon, 141, 144, 147, 148, 152–53, 156, 158, 804–805
  cursings, 352
  geography, 177
  government and law, 160, 161
  Israel, 711
  Jerusalem, 723
  Laman, 801
  LDS history, 805
  Lehi, 827
  literature, 182
  Mormon, 932
  Moroni₂, 956
  Mosiah₁, 959
  Mulek, 969
  Native Americans, 981
  peoples, 191–92
  prophecy, 1163
  Relief Society, 1201
  warfare, 162–66
  westward migration, 1564
  see also Book of Mormon peoples; Indian Student Placement Services; Lamanite Mission of 1830–1831; Native Americans; Samuel the Lamanite
Lamb, marriage supper of the. *See* Marriage supper of the lamb
Lamb, M. T., 49
Lambda Delta Sigma Sorority, 817

Lamb of God, 742
  see also Jesus Christ, names and titles of
Lambert, Edith Elizabeth Hunter, 1640, 1684
Lambourne, Alfred, 70, 1381
Lamb's book of life, 139
Lambson, Edna, 1350, 1352
Lambson, Julina, 1350, 1352, 1353
Lane, Florence Reece, 1640, 1684
Lang, William, 338
Langelund, Edna Fluge, 1265
Langelund, John, 1264
Langton, Martha, 1446
Language
  Book of Mormon, 179–81
  Doctrine and Covenants, 426
  international magazines, 697
  vocabulary, LDS, 1537–38
  see also Book of Mormon translations
Language Training Mission (LTM), 913
Lanner v. *Wimmer* (1981), 826
Laos, 662
Larsen, Dean L., 461, 592, 1640, 1681, 1682
Larsen, Svend Peter, 1262
Larson, Clinton F., 837, 841
Larson, Lynne, 843
Larson, Rolf L., 1400
Lasater, John J., 1016
Lasater, John R., 1640, 1681
Last days, 169, **805–806**
  Daniel, prophecies of, 355
  Ephraim, 461
  great and abominable church, 568
  Isaiah, 704
  Israel, 709
  Jesus Christ, 735
  Joseph, 762
  Latter-day Saints, 806
  love, 847
  marriage supper of the lamb, 860
  Moroni₂, 956
  parables, 1061
  promised land, 1160
  prophecy, 1163
  psalms, 1172
  restoration of all things, 1218
  United States of America, 1495
  see also Millennium
Lasting covenant, 761
Last Judgment. *See* Judgment Day, final
Last Supper. *See* Sacrament
Las Vegas, Nevada, 290

Latimer, Louis, 1397
Latter-day Saints (LDS), **806–807**
    see also Church of Jesus Christ of Latter-day Saints, The; Reorganized Church of Jesus Christ of Latter Day Saints (RLDS Church)
Latter-day Saint Student Association (LDSSA), 684
Latter-day Saints University, 913
Latter–day Sentinel (periodical), 1011
Lavigerie, Cardinal, 1592
Lavoisier, Antoine, 868
Law, **807–810**, 1097
    Book of Mormon, 161–62, 164
    Brigham Young University, 224
    civic duties, 285
    divine and eternal, 808–10
    ethics, 467
    Jesus Christ, 720
    Old Testament, 1028–29
    opposition, 1031
    overview, 807–808
    see also Law of Adoption; Law of Moses; Lawsuits; Legal and judicial history of the Church; Nature, law of
Law, Reuben D., 226
Law, William, 48, 421, 1000, 1640, 1678, 1740
Law, Wilson, 48
Law of adoption, **810**
    covenant Israel, 331
    elect of God, 448
    heirs, 583
    history, 628
    Israel, 706
    social and cultural history, 1379
Law of consecration. See Consecration, law of
Law of Moses, 582, **810–12**
    Aaronic Priesthood, 2
    Abinadi, 6
    blasphemy, 127
    Book of Mormon, 148, 151, 159, 160, 170
    circumcision, 283
    divorce, 391
    high priest, 588
    Jesus Christ, 746
    Levitical Priesthood, 828
    meridian of time, 892
    Nephi₁, 1004
    Paul, 1069
    poverty, 1113
    priest, 1132

priesthood, 1140
    Restoration of the Gospel of Jesus Christ, 1220
    sacrifice, 1248, 1249
    Sunday, 1423
    Ten Commandments, 1469
    see also Commandments
Law of nature. See Nature, law of
Lawsuits, **812–13**
Law of witnesses. See Witnesses, law of
Lawrence, W. Mack, 1640, 1681
Laying on of hands, 389, **813–14**
    Abraham, 8
    authority, 88
    baptism, 97
    Book of Mormon, 158
    callings, 250
    confirmation, 310, 813
    degrees of glory, 368
    elder, Melchizedek Priesthood, 447
    elect of God, 448
    enduring to the end, 457
    first principles of the Gospel, 514
    gift of the Holy Ghost, 543, 813
    healing the sick, 814
    Holy Ghost, 649
    joining the Church, 760
    law of Moses, 812
    Melchizedek Priesthood, 883, 887
    mission president, 914
    Mount of Transfiguration, 969
    New Testament, 1013
    ordinances, 1033
    ordination, 1034
    organization of the Church, 1050
    priesthood blessings, 1140
    priesthood offices, 1143
    Protestantism, 1171
    Relief Society, 1200
    remission of sins, 1210
    restoration of all things, 1219
    sacrificial ceremonies, 813
    salvation, 1257
    sealing, 1288
    setting apart, 1300
Lay participation and leadership, 279, 418, 538, **814–16**, 942
    British Isles, 231
    financial contributions, 510
    high council, 586
    history, 603
    leadership training, 817
    organization, 1035, 1044
    priesthood offices, 1143
    priesthood quorums, 1146

Seventy, 1304
    volunteerism, 1539
    see also Callings
LDS Business College, 12, 274, 275, 444, **816**, 1267
LDS Foundation, 241, **816**, 1047, 1130
LDS Hospital, 660, 867
LDSSA. See LDS Student Association
LDS Social Services, 122, 1130, 1205
LDS Student Association (LDSSA), **817**
Leach, Robert E., 680
Leadership training, 350, 815, **817–18**, 1143, 1414
    see also Callings; Values, transmission of
Leano, Jorge, 1396
Leavitt, Dudley, 983
Leavitt, Sarah Studevant, 115
LeBaron, Alma Dayer, 531
Lebolo, Antonio, 133, 1058–59
Lectures on Faith, **818–21**
    Doctrine and Covenants, 406, 425, 426
    faith in Jesus Christ, 484
    God, 547
    Godhead, 552
    Joseph Smith Translation of the Bible, 766
    Mormon, 933
    Rigdon, Sidney, 1235
    Schools of the Prophets, 1269
    theology, 1475
Lee, George P., 985, 1640, 1681
Lee, Harold B., 60, 62, 219, 351, 637, 787, **821–23**, 1126, 1640, 1678, 1679, 1740
    diplomatic relations, 382
    Doctrine and Covenants, 424
    history, 636
    intellectual history, 690
    military and the Church, 904
    motion pictures, 964
    organization, 1043, 1048
    prophets, 1165
    Quorum of the Twelve Apostles, 1186
    Relief Society, 1204
    scouting, 1276
    Smith, Joseph Fielding, 1354
    South America, 1398
    women, roles of, 1577
    Young Women, 1618
Lee, Helen, 823

Lee, J. Bracken, 873
Lee, John D., 66, 619, 966, 967
Lee, Maurine, 823
Lee, Rex E., 222, 967
Lee, Samuel Marion, 821
Legal and judicial history of the Church, 627, **823–27**, 1101, 1295, 1497
　see also Constitutional law; Constitutional history of the United States of America; Law; Politics; Smith, Joseph, legal trials of
Leggroan, Amanda, 125
Lehi, 140, 144, 158, 160, 171, 178, 186, 187–88, **827–28**
　book of, 175
　Book of Remembrance, 216
　Ezias, 481
　fall of Adam, 485, 486
　immortality, 677
　Isaiah, 701
　Israel, 706
　Jesus Christ, 748
　Joseph of Egypt, 760, 762
　Laman, 801
　Lamanites, 804
　mankind, 854
　manuscript, lost 116 pages, 854
　miracles, 908
　Native Americans, 981
　Nephites, 827
　Old Testament, 1027
　opposition, 1031
　plan of salvation, 1089
　promised land, 1160
　prophets, 1166
　record keeping, 1195
　record of, 198–99
　sacrifice, 1249
　seer, 1293
　see also Jacob, son of Lehi; Liahona
Lehi Foundation, 985
Lehites, 186
Leiper, June Duval, 779
Leipzig Relief Society, 471
Lemmon, Colleen Bushman, 1640, 1684
Lemuel, 145
Lemuelites, 193
Leonard, Glen M., 1176
Letters, Book of Mormon, 183
Levi, 718
Levitical Priesthood, 2, **828–29**, 1135, 1139–40
Lewis, C. S., 402, 560

Lewis, Elizabeth. See Hale, Elizabeth Lewis
Lewis, James, 75
Lewis, Theodore B., 1640, 1680
Liahona, 35, 584, 691, 745, 827, **829–30**, 908
Liahona (periodical), 830
Liahona the Elders' Journal (periodical), 830
Lib, 718
Liberty Jail, 265, 357, 420, 457, 593, 611, 782, **830–31**, 927, 1000
　Richmond Jail, 1231
　Rigdon, Sidney, 1235
　Smith, Joseph, 1337, 1347
　Smith, Joseph F., 1349
　Smith, Mary Fielding, 1359
Libraries and archives, **831–32**, 878
　see also Record keeping
Library of Congress, 832
Life of Adam and Eve, The, 18
Life and death, spiritual, **832–33**
　atonement of Jesus Christ, 83
　Cain, 246
　opposition, 1031
　see also Eternal life; Lifestyle; Mortality; Opposition; Spiritual death
Lifestyle, **833–35**
　humor, 665
　peculiar people, 1073
　publications, 678
　see also Civic duties; Community; Enduring to the end; Family life; Individuality; Joining the Church; Lay participation and leadership; Men, roles of; Peculiar people; Self-sufficiency; Women, roles of
Light of Christ, 546, 551, **835**
　degrees of glory, 369
　freedom, 525
　natural man, 985
　revelation, 1225
　sexuality, 1306
Light and darkness, 415, **835–36**, 1031
Light-mindedness, **836–37**
Lim, Agusto, 79
Lindsay, Richard P., 1177, 1641, 1681
Linn, William, 46
Lion House, 64, 242, 595, 1605, 1616, 1617
Literacy, 174, 1004
Literary Firm, 314

Literature
　Book of Mormon, 181–85
　Brigham Young University, 224
　Doctrine and Covenants as, 427
　Pearl of Great Price, 1072
Literature, Mormon writers of, **837–44**
　drama, 837–38
　novels, 838–40
　personal essays, 840–41
　poetry, 841–42, 1365–66
　short stories, 842–44
　see also Magazines
Little, Jesse C., 779, 935
Little Cottonwood canyon, 1253
"Living Constitution," 326
Lofland, John, 320, 321
Logan, Roger V., Jr., 967
Logan, Utah, 291
Logan temple, 624, 1449
London, Jack, 949
Longden, John, 231, 1641, 1679
Longden, Frances LaRue Carr, 1641, 1685
Longhurst, John, 976
Lord, 550–51, 741, 1455
　see also God, names and titles of; Jesus Christ, names and titles of
Lord God, 550–51
　see also God, names and titles of; Jesus Christ, names and titles of
Lord's Prayer, **844–45**
　see also Sermon on the Mount
Lord's Supper. See Sacrament
Lorenzen, Johan P., 1263
Los Angeles Stake, 633
Losee, Ferron C., 1026
Lost generation literature, 839
Lost scripture, **845–46**
　see also Manuscript, lost 116 pages
Lott, Peter, 1359
Lotteries. See Gambling
Love, **846–47**
　equality, 463
　father's blessings, 504
　God the Father, 549
　Mormon, 933
　New Testament, 1013
　Smith, Joseph, 1342
Low, Solon, 254
Lozano, Agricol, 900
LTM. See Language Training Mission
Lucas, Samuel D., 480, 931
Lucifer, 379, 1391
　see also Devils

Ludlow, Daniel H., 172, 425
Ludlow, Victor L., 704
Lund, Anthon H., 328, 478, 591, 950, 1041, 1264, 1351, 1641, 1678, 1679, 1683, 1740
Lund, Gerald, 840
Lundwall, N. B., 819
Luther, Martin, 561, 562, 668, 716, 1170, 1171, 1221
Lybbert, Merlin R., 1641, 1681
Lyman, Amasa M., 247, 1036, 1230, 1641, 1678, 1679, 1740
Lyman, Amy Brown, 636, 847–48, 1203, 1204, 1386, 1401, 1641, 1685
Lyman, Amy Kathryn, 848
Lyman, Francis M., 328, 471, 917, 1136, 1263, 1593, 1641, 1679, 1740
Lyman, Margaret, 848
Lyman, Richard R., 220, 540, 637, 847–48, 1271, 1641, 1679, 1683, 1740
    priesthood quorums, 1145
Lyman, Wendell Brown, 848
Lyman Wight's cabin. See Wight cabin
Lyne, Thomas A., 837
Lyon, T. Edgar, 424

Macao, the Church in, 78
MacArthur, John, 561
Mack, Ebenezer, 1361
Mack, John, 1361
Mack, Lucy. See Smith, Lucy Mack
Mack, Solomon, 1333, 1356, 1361, 1363
Mack, Stephen, 1348, 1356
Mack, Temperance, 1357
MacKay, Charles, 69
Madrid, Antonio, 72
Madsen, Arch L., 233
Madsen, Louise W., 1401, 1641, 1685
Maeser, Karl G., 222, 274, 442, 443–44, 777, 816, 1066, 1209, 1641, 1682
Magazines, 460–61, 643, 849, 1659–64
    anti-Mormonism, 49
    computer systems, 304
    curriculum, 351
    literature, personal essays, 840
    public relations, 1178
    Scandinavia, 1264

sisterhood, 1319
    see also Appendix 3 (1659–64); International magazines; Newspapers; specific magazine names, e.g., New Era
Magic, 849–50
Magnifying one's calling, 850, 1019, 1418
Maimonides, 521
Major, William W., 70, 1321, 1381
Malachi
    Melchizedek Priesthood, 886
    priesthood, 1139
    record keeping, 1195
    sacrifice, 1249
Malachi, prophecies of, 450, 851–52, 1163
Malan, Jayne Broadbent, 1641, 1685
Malaysia, the Church in, 696, 1757
Malta, the Church in, 917
Man
    nature of, 1340–41
    son of, 740–41
    see also Mankind; Mortality; Natural man; Origin of man
Management studies, Brigham Young University, 224
Manasseh, 1066
Manchester, New York. See History of the Church, c.1820–1831, Palmyra/Manchester, New York
Man of Holiness, 551, 852
Manifesto of 1890, 48, 52, 627, 631, 852–53, 942, 1039, 1351, 1363
    Arizona settlements, 66
    Canada, 251, 253
    Church and state, 282
    fundamentalists, 531
    persecution, 1076
    plural marriage, 1091
    politics, 1102
    social and cultural history, 1383
    Utah statehood, 1503
    Utah Territory, 1505
    ward, 1542
    war and peace, 1549
    Woodruff, Wilford, 1580
Mankind, 511, 853–54
    see also Man
Manoa, Samuela, 1023
Man's Search for Happiness (film), 479, 854, 965
Manti Temple, 625
Manuscript, lost 116 pages, 602, 854–55
    see also Lost scripture

Manuscripts, Book of Mormon, 185–86
Maori Agricultural College, 1015
Maori people, 213, 1014, 1015, 1016, 1111, 1267
Marcus, Louis, 695
Margetts, Linda, 976
Margoliouth, David, 1592
Marijuana legalization, 1376, 1377
Markow, Misha, 471
Marks, Ephraim, 365
Marks, William, 615, 1266
Marriage, 280, 332, 489, 735, 855–59, 1096
    altar, 37
    Catholicism and Mormonism, 258
    celebrations, 258
    chaplains, 263
    children, 267
    community, 302
    dating and courtship, 358
    degrees of glory, 368
    doctrine, 401
    Doctrine and Covenants, 422, 425
    eternal, 555, 857–59, 1092, 1137, 1181, 1445
    exaltation, 479
    history, 617
    Joseph Smith Translation of the Bible, 767
    mankind, 853
    Nauvoo Temple, 1002
    ordinances, 1033
    premarital sex, 1123
    priesthood, 1137
    purpose of earth life, 1181
    salvation, 1257
    sealing, 1289
    sex education, 1305
    Smith, Joseph, 1342–43
    social and behavioral perspectives, 855–57
    social characteristics, 1371, 1372
    social services, 1386
    temple ordinances, 1445
    vital statistics, 859, 1521–24, 1530–32, 1533, 1534
    see also Adultery; Divorce; Family; Plural marriage; Sealing
Marriage rates. See Vital statistics
Marriage supper of the lamb, 860, 1017
    see also Last days; Millennium
Marriott, J. Willard, 1131
Marsh, James G., 1209
Marsh, Thomas B., 604, 920, 1068, 1185, 1641, 1678, 1740

Marshall, Donald R., 840, 843, 931

Marshall, James, 936

Martial law, 164

Martin, Douglas J., 1016, 1641, 1681

Martin, Edward, 571

Martin, Thomas L., 29

Martin Company, 571, 572

Martins, Helvécio, 125, 127, 642, 1396, 1641, 1681

Martyrdom of Joseph and Hyrum Smith, 613, 647, **860–62**, 971, 991, 997, 999, 1093, 1331, 1338, 1359

Martyrs, 38, **862–63**

  see also Martyrdom of Joseph and Hyrum Smith

Mary, mother of Jesus, 673, 725, 729, 745, **863–64**, 1089, 1520, 1577, 1579

  see also Immaculate conception; Virgin birth

Masons. *See* Freemasonry in Nauvoo; Freemasonry and the Temple

Material culture, **864–66**

  see also Folk Art; Folklore

Maternity and child health care, 621, **866–68**, 1203, 1224, 1366, 1575

Mathematical sciences, Brigham Young University, 224

Matheny, Ray, 63

Matis, Henry A., 1262

Matron. *See* Temple president and matron

Matter, 402, **868–69**, 894–95, 1081

Matthew. *See* Matthew, Gospel of; Smith, Joseph—Matthew

Matthew, Gospel of, **869–70**, 1012

Mattindale, William C., 672

Maudsley, Sutcliffe, 70

Maughan, Mary Ann Weston, 115

Mauss, Vinal G., 77

Maxwell, Neal A., 25, 81, 275, 986, 1187, 1576, 1641, 1679, 1680, 1681, 1740

Maxwell automobile, 439

May, James, 524

Maya culture, 62

Mayer, Adolfo, 1398

McBride, Thomas, 577

McCleary, William, 1360

McClellan, John J., 976

McCloud, Susan Evans, 839

McColm, Reed, 838

McConkie, Bruce R., 62, 87, 110, 113, 236, 255, 1641, 1679, 1680, 1740

  doctrine, 397

  history, 639

  intellectual history, 691

  intelligences, 693

  Israel, 711

  Jesus Christ, 744

  Lectures on Faith, 821

  marriage, 858

  Peter, 1078

  prophets, 1165

  publications, 1176

  Satanism, 1261

  science and religion, 1272

  sealing, 1289

  signs as divine witness, 1310

  signs of the true Church, 1311

  South America, 1397, 1398

  spirit world, 1409

  theology, 1476

  women, roles of, 1576

  world religions, 1592, 1594

McCoy, John, 929

McCulloch, Ben, 1501

McCullough, John, 1255

McDonald, Howard S., 222

McGavin, E. Cecil, 424

McKay, David (David O.'s father), 870

McKay, David Lawrence, 1426, 1641, 1682

McKay, David O., 102, 226, 540, **870–75**, 1126, 1642, 1678, 1682, 1740

  Africa, 24

  Asia, 77

  Australia, 86

  British Isles, 229

  chastity law, 265

  conferences, 307

  Constitution, U.S., 318

  constitutional law, 315

  diplomatic relations, 383

  Europe, 472

  family home evening, 496

  First Presidency, 513

  Hawaii, 579

  history, 639

  humanitarian service, 661

  individuality, 681

  James, Epistle of, 715

  love, 847

  mankind, 853

  meetinghouse, 877

  Millennial Star, 906

  missions, 917

  motherhood, 962

  New Zealand, 1016

  Oceania, 1025

  organization, 1045

  Polynesian Cultural Center, 1109

  preaching the Gospel, 1121

  priesthood quorums, 1145

  prophets, 1165

  publications, 1178

  reverence, 1228

  scouting, 1276

  Seventy, 1302

  sex education, 1305

  South America, 1395, 1398

  Sunday School, 1425, 1426

  temple ordinances, 1444

  temples, 1453

  values, 1507

  world religions, 1593

McKay, Emma Ray Riggs (David O.'s wife), 871, 872, 873

McKay, Heber J., 1025

McKay, Quinn G., 1642, 1684

McKay, Thomas E., 472, 1642, 1679

McKean, Howard J., 237

McKelvey, Lucy, 72

McKinley, William, 1327

McLellin, William E., 930, 1185, 1269, 1641, 1679, 1740

McMurrin, Joseph W., 1642, 1680

McMurrin, Sterling M., 1476

McRae, Alexander, 830

Meadow Utah Ward, 300

Medical practices, 374, **875**, 1096–97

  see also Health, attitudes toward; Hospitals; Maternity and child health care; Mental health; Organ donations and transplants; Prolonging life; Sick, blessing the

Meetinghouse, 644, **876–78**

  architecture, 64

  buiding program, 237, 238

  calamities and disasters, 246

  dedications, 367

  lifestyle, 834

  Oceania, 1022

  social and cultural history, 1384

  symbolism, 1429

  temples, 1449

Meetinghouse libraries, **878**

Meetings, major Church, 646, **878–79**, 1085, 1097

teacher, Aaronic Priesthood, 1441
see also Sabbath Day
Meha, Stuart, 1015
Melchin, Gerald E., 1642, 1681
Melchizedek, 582, 767, **879–82**, 884
 ancient sources, 880–82
 Jerusalem, 722
 LDS sources, 879–80
 priesthood, 1138–39
 priesthood offices, 1143
 see also Melchizedek Priesthood
Melchizedek Priesthood, 278, 335,
  389, **882–87**, 937, 1139
 Aaron, brother of Moses, 1
 Aaronic Priesthood, 2, 3
 Abraham, 8
 ancient history of, 884
 angels, 41
 apostles, 59, 61
 baptism, 98
 bishops, 117, 122
 blessings, 129
 branch, branch president, 219
 burial, 239
 chaplains, 263
 children, 268
 conferences, 309
 confirmation, 310, 311
 covenants, 332
 death and dying, 366
 disciplinary procedures, 387
 dispensation of the fulness of
  times, 388
 district, district president, 390,
  391
 Doctrine and Covenants, 414,
  418, 424
 elder, 447–48
 Elias, spirit of, 449
 father's blessings, 504
 first principles of the Gospel, 514
 functioning of, 882–83
 high council, 587
 high priest, 587
 home teaching, 654
 James the Apostle, 716
 John the Baptist, 757
 John the Beloved, 758
 joining the Church, 760
 Joseph of Egypt, 761
 laying on of hands, 813
 membership, 887
 missions, 919
 modern history of, 884–85
 Moses, 958
 Mount of Transfiguration, 969
 mysteries of God, 977

Nauvoo Temple, 1001
 oil, 1027
 ordinances, 1033
 ordination to, 882–83, 1034–35
 organization, 1037, 1046
 patriarch, 1065
 patriarchal blessings, 1066
 patriarchal order, 1067
 Peter, 1078
 powers and offices in, 882–85
 President of the Church, 1127
 priesthood blessings, 1140
 priesthood executive committee,
  1142
 priesthood offices, 1143
 priesthood quorums, 1144
 prophet, seer, and revelator,
  1170
 psalms, 1172
 Quorum of the Twelve Apostles,
  1185–89
 religious experience, 1209
 remission of sins, 1211
 restoration of, 210, 289, 587, 602,
  716, 781, 885–87, 1034, 1050,
  1078, 1127, 1135, 1209, 1514
 restoration of all things, 1219
 sacrament, 1244
 sick, blessing the, 1308
 stake president, 1415
 Taylor, John, 1439
 temples, 1449
 visions of Joseph Smith, 1514
 ward, 1541
 see also Elder, Melchizedek
  Priesthood
Membership, 301, 385, 538, 543,
  887, 1217, 1756–63
 see also Conversion; Fellowshipping; Joining the Church;
  Membership records
Membership records, 289, **887–88**,
  1519–37
 see also Vital statistics
Men, roles of, **888–90**
 civil rights, 287
 fatherhood, 490, 503–504, 883,
  1342
 marriage, 857
 missionaries, 910
 social characteristics, 1371–77
 vital statistics, 1528, 1530, 1533
 see also Abuse, spouse and child;
  Brotherhood; Divorce; Family;
  Lay participation and leadership; Lifestyle; Natural man;
  Priesthood quorums; Young
  Men

Mencken, H. L., 109
Mendenhall, Wendell, 237
Mental health, **890–91**
Mercur, Utah, 63
Mercy. *See* Justice and mercy
Mercy killing. *See* Death and dying;
  Euthanasia; Murder; Prolong-
  ing life
Mere Christianity (Lewis), 402
Meridian of time, 389, 449, 541,
  547, 725, 752, **891–92**
 kingdom of heaven, 790
 marriage supper of the lamb, 860
 Restoration of the Gospel of Jesus
  Christ, 1220
 signs as divine witness, 1310
 signs of the true Church, 1311
Merrill, Harrison R., 678
Merrill, Joseph F., 637, 1145, 1186,
  1271, 1642, 1679, 1740
Merrill, Marriner W., 328, 1642,
  1679, 1740
Message of the Ages (pageant), 261
Messenger and Advocate (periodi-
  cal), 477, 589, 609, 762, **892**,
  1011, 1173
Messiah, 168, **892–94**
 Daniel, prophecies of, 356
 David, King, 360
 dove, sign of the, 428
 Gethsemane, 542
 Jerusalem, 723
 Jesus Christ, 724, 737–38, 740
 Latter-day Saints, 807
 Millennium, 906
 new heaven and new earth, 1009
 New Jerusalem, 1010
 psalms, 1172–73
 Seth, 1299
Messianic prophecies in the Old
  Testament. *See* Jesus Christ,
  prophecies about; Psalms, mes-
  sianic prophecies in
Metaphor, Book of Mormon, 183–
  84
Metaphysics, 402, 477, **894–95**,
  1079
Mete, Ere Hapati, 1015
Methodist church, 168, 169, 687
Mets, Timothy, 469
Mexico, pioneer settlements in,
  625, **895–97**, 899–900
Mexico and Central America, the
  Church in, 634, 676, 697, 873,
  897–902, 917, 1022, 1267,
  1533, 1542
Mexico City Temple, 900

Meyer, Eduard, 1592
Michael the Archangel, 42
  see also Adam; Angels
Mickelsen, Lynn A., 1642, 1681
Microfilm and microfiche, 538, 563
Micronesia, the Church in, 1026
Middle East, the Church in, 471,
  902–903
  see also Jerusalem Center for
    Near Eastern Studies
Migration. See Immigration and
  emigration; Residence and mi-
  gration; Westward migration,
  planning and prophecy
Miles, Daniel S., 1642, 1680
Military and the Church, **903–905**
  civic duties, 285
  conscientious objection, 311–12
  Danites, 357
  Extermination order, 480
  organization, 1041
  politics, 1108
  Salt Lake City, Utah, 1252
  see also Mormon Battalion; Nau-
    voo Legion; War and peace
Military Relations Committee, 264,
  905
Millenarianism, 168, **905–906**
Millennial Star (periodical), 228,
  611, **906**, 1115, 1116, 1174
Millennium, 281, 609, **906–908**
  degrees of glory, 369
  devils, 381
  dispensation of the fulness of
    times, 388
  Jesus Christ, 725, 738, 739
  marriage supper of the lamb, 860
  meridian of time, 892
  pioneer economy, 1083
  Reformation (1856–1857), 1197
  restoration of all things, 1219
  Restoration of the Gospel of Jesus
    Christ, 1221
  resurrection, 1223
  temples, 1454
  Wentworth letter, 1561
  see also Last days; New heaven
    and new earth; Time and eter-
    nity
Miller, Eleazer, 1471
Miller, George, 119, <u>517</u>, 1129,
  1642
Miller, Helen M., 1239
Miller, Henry W., 325
Miller, Orrin Porter, 1642, 1681,
  1682
Millet, Robert L., 425

Millett, Artemis, 63
Millett, Ronald A., 937
Millikin, Arthur, 1360
Millikin, Lucy Smith, 1357, 1360
Milnes, Sherrill, 951
Mining industry, 438, 440, 629
Minorities, **908**
Minto, Lord, 253
Miracle of Forgiveness (Kimball),
  787
Miracles, 545, **908–910**, 1168, 1309,
  1311
  Seagulls, Miracle of, <u>74</u>, 618,
    1287–88
Missionary, missionary life, 277,
  280, 539, 634, 645, **910–13**,
  972
  Africa, 22–25
  blacks, 126
  Book of Mormon, 142, 213
  Brigham Young University, 221
  computer systems, 304
  confidential records, 310
  conversion, 322–23
  dating and courtship, 359
  diplomatic relations, 382, 383
  elder, Melchizedek Priesthood,
    447
  endowment, 456
  Europe, 471–74
  fast offerings, 510
  humanitarian service, 662
  hymns, 668
  Israel, 710–11
  lay participation, 814
  Mexico, 899
  Nauvoo economy, 994
  preaching the Gospel, 1121
  Scandinavia, 1263
  senior citizens, 1297
  Seventy, 1302, 1304
  signs of the true Church, 1312
  true and living Church, 1489
  see also Conversion; Mission
    president; Missions; Missionary
    Training Centers; specific coun-
    try names
Missionary Training Centers (MTC),
  645, 696, **913–14**, 917, 919,
  1041, 1046
Mission president, 913, **914–15**, 918
Missions, 277, 279, 609, **915–20**
  branch, branch president, 219
  callings, 249
  chaplains, 263
  colonization, 290
  Cowdery, Oliver, 337

economic history, 438
education, 441
history of, 916–18
home industries, 652
Kirtland, Ohio, 796
Lamanite, 802–804
lifestyle, 834
marriage, 856
meetings, 879
Mexico, 900
organization, 918–19
public communications, 1177
public relations, 1177
training, 919
types of, 916
values, 1508
welfare services, 1557–58
see also Missionary, missionary
  life; Mission president; Missions of the Twelve to the British Isles; specific mission
  names, e.g., Lamanite Mission
Missions of the Twelve to the British Isles, 500, 610, 666, 675,
  782, 916, **920–22**, 990, 1114,
  1186
  Pratt, Parley P., 1116
  Smith, Joseph, 1337
  Taylor, John, 1438
  vital statistics, 1525
  Young, Brigham, 1605
Missouri, **922–27**
  consecration in, 314–15
  economic history, 435
  gathering, 537
  high council, 586
  historical sites, 593
  history, 604–613
  LDS communities in Caldwell
    and Daviess counties, 357, 534,
    609, 925–27, 1099, 1336
  LDS communities in Jackson and
    Clay counties, 534, 605, 803,
    933–25, 1099, 1336
  Ricks College, 1233
  social and cultural history, 1378
  see also Far West, Missouri
Missouri Compromise, 1100
Missouri Conflict, 46, 924, **927–32**,
  935, 994, 998, 1480
  Danites, 356
  extermination order, 480
  gathering, 537
  Haun's Mill Massacre, 577
  Liberty Jail, 830
  Richmond Jail, 1231
  Rigdon, Sidney, 1235

Smith, Emma Hale, 1324
Smith, Hyrum, 1330
Smith, Joseph, 1336
Smith, Joseph, Sr., 1349
Smith, Joseph F., 1349
war and peace, 1549
Young, Brigham, 1603
Mitchill, Samuel Latham, 575
M. L. Bean Life Science Museum
    (BYU), 223
Modesty, 812, **932**
Modesty in dress, **932**
Money. *See* Economic history of
    the Church
Monson, Thomas S., 58, 103, 110,
    513, 1026, 1277, 1399, 1642,
    1678, 1679, 1740
Monuments. *See* Statues and monu-
    ments
Moon, Harold K., 843
Moore, R. Laurence, 939
Morales, Luis Alfonzo, 1397
Moral issues, 477, 1096, 1502
    see also Ethics
Moran, Thomas, 1381
Morgan, John, 1642, 1680, 1682
Morgenstjernen (periodical), 624
Moriancumer, Mahonri, 235
Morianton, 718
Morley, Isaac, 1515, 1642, 1681
Mormon, **932–33**
    Abinadi, 6
    baptism, 93, 682
    book of, 156
    born of God, 218
    children, 269, 682
    editing, 201
    gold plates, 197, 555
    infant baptism, 682
    Jaredites, 717
    literature, 182
    lost scripture, 845
    love, 846
    Moroni₂, 956
    plates of, 200, *see also* subhead
        gold plates above
    prophecy, 1164
    sermon and letters, 158
    signs as divine witness, 1310
    warfare, 165
    war and peace, 1548
    words of, 149
    see also Book of Mormon
Mormon Arts festival, 1286
Mormon Battalion, 66, 294, 615,
    779, 903–904, **933–36**, 999
    New Mexico, 1010

politics, 1100
visitors centers, 1518
war and peace, 1549
Mormon Church. *See* Church of
    Jesus Christ of Latter-day
    Saints, The
Mormon couch, 865
Mormon crickets, 1287
Mormon Handicraft, 374, 654, **936–
    37**, 1204, 1238
Mormon hay derrick, 28
Mormon History Association, 1388
Mormonism, an independent inter-
    pretation, **937–41**
Mormonism, Mormons, **941–42**
    social characteristics, 1371
Mormonism and Catholicism. *See*
    Catholicism and Mormonism
Mormonism Unvailed (sic), 46, 47
Mormonism and World Religions.
    See World Religions and Mor-
    monism
Mormon Maid, A (film), 947
Mormon Pioneer Trail, 262, 290,
    595, 675, **942–46**, 1598
Mormons, image of, 356, **946–50**
    see also Artists, visual; Art in
        Mormonism; Folk art; "Peculiar
        People"; Stereotyping of
        Latter-day Saints
Mormon style, 877
Mormon Tabernacle Choir, 472,
    950–52, 976, 1465
    British Isles, 232
    broadcasting, 232–33, 952, 1131,
        1433
    business, 242
    exhibitions, 479
    history, 628, 633
    organization, 1046
    pioneer life, 1087
    public relations, 1178
    satellite communications system,
        1261
    social and cultural history, 1380
    stereotyping, 1417
    see also Mormon Tabernacle
        Choir Broadcast; Tabernacle
        organ
Mormon Tabernacle Choir Broad-
    cast ("The Spoken Word"),
    232–33, **952**, 1131, 1433
Mormon Trail. *See* Mormon Pioneer
    Trail
Mormon Women's Forum, 1389
Mormon Youth Symphony and Cho-
    rus (MYSC), **952–53**, 1046

Moroni
    book of, 157–58
    Melchizedek Priesthood, 886
Moroni, angel, 39–40, 140, 260,
    953, 1058
    Daniel, prophecies of, 355
    Elijah, 450
    gold plates, 555
    history, 600
    New Testament, 1014
    prophecy, 1163
    restoration of all things, 1219
    see also Angel Moroni Statue;
        Moroni₂; Moroni, visitations of
Moroni, visitations of, 601, **954–55**,
    1334, 1513
Moroni₁, **955–56**
    oaths, 1020
    war and peace, 1548
Moroni₂, 140, 159, 197, 246, 953,
    956–57
    Cain, 246
    David, prophetic figure of last
        days, 360
    enduring to the end, 457
    ethics, 467
    gifts of the spirit, 545
    gold plates, 555
    Jaredites, 1160
    Jesus Christ, 749
    lost scripture, 845
    Mormon, 933
    New Jerusalem, 1010
    prayer, 1120
    prophecy and prophets, 1164
    scripture, 1283
    Smith, Joseph, 1334
    see also Angel Moroni Statue;
        Moroni, angel; Moroni, visita-
        tions of
Moronihah war, 165
Morrill Act (1862), 52, 825, 1101,
    1229, 1230
Morris, George Q., 60, 81, 1642,
    1679, 1683, 1740
Morris, Larry E., 840
Morrison, Alexander B., 25, 1642,
    1681
Mortality, **957–58**
    agency, 26
    eternal progression, 465
    Eve, 476
    first estate, 511
    foreordination, 522
    Jesus Christ, 724–25, 740
    judgment, 772
    mankind, 854

Mortality *(Cont'd)*
  physical body, 1080
  purpose of earth life, 1180, 1181
  second estate, 1290
  spiritual death, 1407
  vital statistics, 1524–25
  see also Birth; Death and dying;
    Evil; Fall of Adam; Joy; Life
    and death, spiritual; Man; Pre-
    mortal life; Purpose of earth
    life
Mortensen, Pauline, 844
Moses, 419, 609, 780, **958–59**
  Book of. *See* Book of Moses
  endowment houses, 456
  Ephraim, 461
  following the brethren, 520
  garments, 534
  Jesus Christ, 736, 753
  Levitical Priesthood, 828
  Melchizedek Priesthood, 886
  Nephi₁, 1005
  priesthood offices, 1143
  prophets, 1167
  transfiguration, 1484
  translated beings, 1486
  see also Aaron, brother of Moses;
    Book of Moses; Law of Moses
Mosiah₁, **959**, 960
Mosiah₂, 149–50, 161, 164, **960–61**,
    1164
Moss, Robert H., 839
Mother in Heaven, 490, 549, 785,
    961
  discipleship, 384
  feminism, 507
  God the Father, 856
  intellectual history, 687, 690
  mankind, 853
  plan of salvation, 1088
  premortal life, 1124
Motherhood, **962–63**, 1096, 1342
  see also Maternity and child
    health care; Mother in Heaven;
    Mother in Israel
Mother in Israel, **963–64**, 1577
Motion pictures, LDS Productions,
    645, 947–48, **964–65**
Mountain Meadows Massacre, 290,
    304, 619, 949, **966–68**
Mount of Transfiguration, 390, 450,
    716, 735, 747, 959, **968–69**,
    1029, 1078, 1485, 1486, 1139
Mourning. *See* Death and dying
"Move South," 1500–1501
Moyle, Henry D., 1043, 1397,
    1399, 1642, 1678, 1679, 1740

Moyle, James H., 634
MTC. *See* Missionary Training Cen-
  ters
Mudget, John, 1348
Mulder, William, 597
Mulek, 706, 959, **969–70**
Mulekites, 186, 192
Mulholland, James, 647
Murder, 162, 255, **970–71**, 1028,
    1443
Murdock, Dorthea Lou Christian-
    sen, 1642, 1684
Murdock, John, 86, 414, 802, 1324,
    1424
Murphy v. *Ramsey*, 1101
Murray, Vilate. *See* Kimball, Vilate
  Murray
Muren, Joseph C., 1642, 1681
Museums, 592, **971–73**, 1060, 1179
Music, 411, 635, **973–75**, 1007,
    1086, 1686–1708
  see also Hymns and hymnody;
    Mormon Tabernacle Choir;
    Mormon Tabernacle Choir
    Broadcast; Musicians
Music Committee, 669
Musicians, **975–77**
  see also Mormon Tabernacle
    Choir; Mormon Youth Sym-
    phony and Chorus
"Music and the Spoken Word"
  (radio program). *See* Mormon
  Tabernacle Choir Broadcast
Muslims. *See* Islam.
Musselman, Mary. *See* Whitmer,
  Mary Musselman
Musser, Amos Milton, 53
Musser, Joseph, 531
Mutual Improvement Associations
  (MIA), 320, 324
  Contributor, 320
  dance, 355
  Fox, Ruth May, 524
  Improvement Era, 678
  intellectual history, 689
  New Zealand, 1015
  social and cultural history, 1383
  Wells, Junius F., 1560–61
  see also Young Men; Young
    Women
MX missile controversy, 1108
MYSC. *See* Mormon Youth Sym-
  phony and Chorus
Mysteries of God, **977–78**

Nadauld, Stephen D., 1642, 1681,
    1684
Naga, Inosi, 1026

Nag Hammadi text, 852
Naha, Helen, 72
Naifeh, Steven, 51
Name of the Church, 500, 603, **979**,
    1049, 1312
Name extraction program, 96, 493,
    494, **979–80**, 1455
Name of God, 852, **980–81**
  see also Jesus Christ, names and
    titles of
Names, Book of Mormon, 186–87
Naming. *See* Blessing of children
Napela, Jonatana, 578
Naranjo, Christina, 72
Naranjo, Terrisita, 72
Narrative texts, Book of Mormon,
    183
National Bible Press, 111
National Broadcasting Company
  (NBC), 232, 234
National Guard of Utah, 999
Native American Educational Out-
  reach Program, 984
Native Americans, **981–85**
  Arizona settlements, 66, 67
  arts, visual, 72
  Book of Mormon, 168, 180
  Canada, 253
  colonization (LDS), 290, 291
  Colorado, 1007
  Great Basin, 982–84
  history, 604, 646
  humanitarian service, 661
  Idaho, 671
  Kimball, Spencer W., 786
  Lamanite Mission, 802, 982
  Lamanites, 805
  LDS beliefs, 981–82
  Mexico, 896
  Missouri Conflict, 928
  Mountain Meadows Massacre,
    966, 967
  organization, 1041
  recent times, 984–85
  Relief Society, 1201
  Salt Lake City, Utah, 1250
  Smith, George Albert, 1329
  Smith, Joseph, 1336
  social services, 1387
  Spaulding Manuscript, 1402
  temples, 1452
  View of the Hebrews, 1509–1510
  Young, Brigham, 1608
  see also American Indian Services;
    Indian Relief Society; Indian
    Student Placement Services;
    specific tribe, e.g., Navajo

Natural man, **985–86**
  born of God, 218
  evil, 477
  metaphysics, 895
  mortality, 958
  sin, 1316
Nature, law of, 810, **986–87**
Nauvoo, 321, 782, **987–93**
  anti-Mormonism, 48
  architecture, 63
  arts, visual, 70
  Ballantyne, Richard, 91
  bishops, 119
  building program, 236
  centennial observances, 262
  city planning, 284
  community, 300
  Doctrine and Covenants, 421, 425–26
  economic history, 436
  freemasonry in, 527–28, 529, 992
  gathering, 536, 537
  historical sites, 593, 595
  history, 604–613
  martyrdom of Joseph and Hyrum Smith, 860
  Mormon Pioneer Trail, 942
  non-Mormons, 1018
  patriarchal order, 1067
  pioneer life, 1085
  Relief Society, 1199, 1207–1208
  salvation of the dead, 1257
  Seventy, 1301
  sisterhood, 1319
  Smith, Joseph, 1337, 1347
  Smith, Mary Fielding, 1359
  social and cultural history, 1379
  University of the City of, 442–43
  visitors centers, 1518
  ward, 1541
  westward migration, 1563
  Young, Brigham, 1604
Nauvoo Charter, 612, 860, 987, **993–94**, 998, 999, 1000
  Church and state, 282
  courts, 330
  education, 442
  legal and judicial history, 824
  politics, 1099
  Smith, Joseph, 1337
  social and cultural history, 1379
Nauvoo economy, 860, **994–96**
Nauvoo Expositor (periodical), 255, 824, **996–97**, 1000, 1093, 1100, 1338, 1347
Nauvoo House, 186, 421, 613, 631, 996, **997**

Nauvoo Legion, 612, 627, 860, 971, 994, **997–99**, 1000, 1018, 1099, 1500
  RLDS Church, 1213
  Smith, Joseph, 1337
  Smith, Joseph F., 1350
  Taylor, John, 1438
Nauvoo Neighbor (newspaper), **999**, 1011, 1438
Nauvoo politics, 527, 613, 860, **999–1001**, 1099, 1338
Nauvoo Temple, 63, 64, 96, 409, 421, 610, 614, 666, 995, 997, **1001–1003**, 1451, 1468
  freemasonry, 528
  history, 612, 613
  Relief Society, 1200, 1207
  Smith, Joseph, 1337
  ward, 1541
  westward migration, 1563
Navajo pot, 866
Navajo tribe, 786, 983, 984, 1329
NBC. *See* National Broadcasting Company
Near East, Book of Mormon, 187–190
  see also Middle East, the Church in the
Near Eastern studies, Jerusalem Center for, 225–26
Nebeker, George, 578
Nebuchadnezzar, 355
Necessity Committee, 303
Needlework. *See* Folk art
Neeley, Albert, 1400
Nehor, Nehorism, 45, 162, 165
  see also Antichrists; Secret combinations
Nelson, Lee, 839
Nelson, Lowry, 29
Nelson, Russell M., 1187, 1274, 1426, 1427, 1642, 1679, 1682, 1740
Neoplatonism, 402
Nephi₁, **1003–1005**
  apostasy, 57
  Book of Mormon, 140–41, 144–47, 152–56, 160, 163
  Book of Remembrance, 217
  Columbus, Christopher, 294–95
  condescension of God, 305
  enduring to the end, 457
  ethics, 467
  first book of, 144–46
  fourth book, 155–56
  fulness of the Gospel, 530
  great and abominable church, 568

history, 1003–1004
Holy Ghost, 649
Isaiah, 701, 704
Ishmael, 704
Israel, 707, 710
Jesus Christ, 726, 731, 739, 748
John, revelations of, 754
Joseph, 760
Laman, 801
messages of, 1004–1005
Messiah, 894
oaths, 1020
Old Testament, 1029
plan of salvation, 1090
plates of, 199–200
prophecy, 1163, 1164
Psalm of, 182–83
record keeping and literacy, 1004
scripture, 1280
second book of, 146–47
sin, 1315
third book of, 153–55
visions, 1004
Nephi₂, 482, **1005**
Nephi₃, 749, **1006**, 1163, 1195
Nephi₄, **1006**
Nephi (city), 177
Nephites, 584, **1006**
  archaeology, 62
  Benjamin, 99
  biblical culture, 169
  Book of Mormon, 141, 147, 148, 154, 156, 158
  chronology, 169–71
  covenants, 332
  Cumorah, 346
  economy, 173–74
  geography, 177
  government and law, 160–62
  Isaiah, 701
  Jerusalem, 723
  Jesus Christ, 726
  Laman, 801
  Lamanites, 804
  language, 179–80
  love, 846
  Mormon, 932
  Moroni₁, 955
  Mosiah₁, 959
  Native Americans, 981
  oaths, 1020
  peoples, 191
  priesthood offices, 1143
  prophecy, 1163
  sacrament, 1244
  sacrifice, 1249
  scripture, 1283

Nephites *(Cont'd)*
  warfare, 163–66
  see also Three Nephites
Neslen, C. Clarence, 233
Nestorianism, 272
Netherlands, the Church in, 213,
    469, 471, 472, 873
Neuenschwander, Dennis B., 1642,
    1681
Neum, **1006**
Nevada, pioneer settlements in,
    1006–1007
New Caledonia, the Church in,
    1026
Newel K. Whitney store. *See* Whit-
    ney store
New Era (periodical), 324, 685, 697,
    849, **1007–1008**
New and everlasting covenant, 333,
    412, **1008–1009**
  blasphemy, 127
  Covenant Israel, 330
  rebaptism, 1194
  revelation, 1227
New Heaven and New Earth, 908,
    1009
  paradise, 1062
New Hope, California, 247
New Jerusalem, 302, 605, 678,
    1009–1010
  dispensation of the fulness of
    times, 388
  Doctrine and Covenants, 409,
    412, 414
  gathering, 536
  Jerusalem, 723
  Jesus Christ, 728
  Joseph, 762
  Lamanite Mission, 802
  last days, 806
  Millennium, 907
  Missouri, 922
  Missouri Conflict, 927
  Native Americans, 981
  New Testament, 1014
  politics, 1099
  promised land, 1160
  Rigdon, Sidney, 1234
  Smith, Joseph, 1343, 1335
  suffering in the world, 1422
  United States of America, 1495
  Zion, 1626
  Zionism, 1626
  see also Zion
New Lighters, 469
New Mexico, pioneer settlements
    in, 52, **1010–11**

Newspapers, LDS, **1011**, 1659–64
  see also Magazines; Press and
    publications; specific newspa-
    per, e.g., *Deseret News*
New Testament, **1011–14**
  apostles, 1013
  epistles, 1013–14
  evangelists, 475
  gospels, 1012–13
  Jesus Christ, 734
  martyrs, 863
  organization of the Church, 1050–
    51
  psalms, 1172
  revelations, 1014
New York, early LDS sites in, 598–
    604, **1014**, 1058
  see also Palmyra/Manchester,
    New York
New York World's Fair (1964–1965),
    273, 479
New Zealand, the Church in, 685,
    826, 872, **1014–16**, 1022, 1453,
    1759
Nibley, Charles W., 478, 539, 1129,
    1643, 1678, 1681, 1740
Nibley, Hugh W., 113, 137, 166,
    171, 207–208, 370, 840, 1389,
    1464
Nibley, Preston, 114
Nicolaysen, Sterling, 1397
Nigeria, economic aid, 434
Nigeria, the Church in, 22–26
Nixon, Richard M., 383
Nnenna, Eugene, 25
Noah, 780, **1016–17**
  altar, 37
  Book of Mormon, 160–61
  Enoch, 458
  Jaredites, 718
  Jesus Christ, 752
  scripture, 1282
Non-Christian religions. *See* World
    religions (non–Christian) and
    Mormonism
Non-Mormons, social relations with,
    1017–18
  see also Interfaith relationships;
    Social and cultural history
Noon, Sarah. *See* Kimball, Sarah
    Noon
North Visitors Center, 1518
Northern Far East Mission, 77
Northern Times (newspaper), 1011
Norton, Don, 840
Norton, Jim, 73
Norway, the Church in, 1263, 1264

Novels
  Mormons, image of, 948–49
  Mormon writers of, 838–40, 842–
    44
Nuclear arms race, 646
Nursing schools, 224, 867
Nwagbara, Eugene, 25
Nyman, Monte S., 172, 704
Nystrom, Mae Taylor, 1643, 1684

Oahu Stake Samoan choir, 578
Oakley, Mary Ann, 1440
Oaks, Dallin H., 221, 222, 310,
    423, 492, 494, 744, 1187, 1643,
    1679, 1740
Oath and covenant of the priest-
    hood, 582, **1019–20**
  Doctrine and Covenants, 415
  magnifying one's calling, 850
  Melchizedek Priesthood, 883
  men, roles of, 889
Oaths, **1020**
Obedience, 547, **1020–21**
  accountability, 13
  agency, 27
  Doctrine and Covenants, 415
  garments, 534
  Jesus Christ, 732
  Mary, mother of Jesus, 864
  Ruth, 1240
Oblasser, Albano, 133
Obstetrics. *See* Maternity and child
    health care
Occupational status, 230, **1022**,
    1373, 1374, 1535, 1536, 1557
  see also Work, role of
Oceania, the Church in, **1022–26**,
    1267, 1759
  see also Hawaii; New Zealand;
    other specific country and is-
    land names
O'Dea, Thomas F., 939
O'Donnal, John (Juan), 900
Ogden, Susannah, 1320
Ogden Vinegar Works, 565
Ohio, LDS communities in, **1026–
    27**
  consecration, 314–15
  gathering, 537
  history, 604–13
  politics, 1099
  see also Kirtland, Ohio
Oil, consecrated, 367, **1027**, 1308,
    1444
Okazaki, Chieko Nishimura, 1643,
    1685
O'Kane, John. *See* Kane, John

O'Kelly, James, 1221
Okinawa, the Church in, 77
Oklahoma, antipolygamy legislation, 52
Older population. *See* Old Folks movement; Senior citizens
Old Testament, **1027–30**
   covenants and commandments, 1028
   Jesus Christ, 746
   laws, 1028
   martyrs, 862–63
   prophecies, 1029–30, 1172–73
   see also Jesus Christ, prophecies about; New Testament; specific book, e.g., Deuteronomy
Olive oil. *See* Oil, consecrated
Olmec culture, 62
Olsen, Bruce L., 1177
Olsen, Eugene F., 1400
Olsen, John, 1262
Olsen, Rae Stephens, 1400
Olson, Culbert, 285
Olson, Earl E., 591
O manuscript, Book of Mormon, 185
Omer, 717
Omni, book of, 148
Omnipotent God, Omnipresence of God, Omniscience of God 466, **1030**, 1473, 1670–77
One Hundred Years of Mormonism (film), 948
Onitchi, Lazarus, 25
Only begotten son of God. *See* Jesus Christ, only begotten in the flesh
Opposition, 478, 757, 958, **1031–32**
Ordinances, **1032–34**
   administration of, 1033–34, 1456–58
   altar, 37
   authority, 88
   bishops, 120
   Book of Mormon, 157
   ceremonies, 262
   children, 267, 268
   Christians and Christianity, 270
   Church of the Firstborn, 276
   computer systems, 304
   confirmation, 310
   covenants, 332
   discipleship, 384
   Doctrine and Covenants, 414
   endowment, 454
   enduring to the end, 456
   exaltation, 479

foreordination, 522
freemasonry, 528
garments, 534
gift of the Holy Ghost, 543
history, 602, 614, 628, 645
holiness, 648
Holy Ghost, 649
humility, 663
immortality and eternal life, 678
interviews, 697
Isaiah, 702
Israel, 710
Jesus Christ, 732
law, 809
law of Moses, 812
Melchizedek, 879
Moroni₂, 956
motherhood, 963
Mount of Transfiguration, 969
mysteries of God, 977
New Zealand, 1016
oil, 1027
overview, 1032–33
philosophy, 1079
plan of salvation, 1090
prayer, 1118
priesthood, 258–59, 1032, 1134, 1138, 1289
proxy, 1445
public speaking, 1180
record keeping, 1195–96
restoration of all things, 1218
restoration of the Gospel of Jesus Christ, 1220
sacrifice, 1248
salvation, 1257
sanctification, 1260
scripture, 1283
sealing, 1288
sick, blessing the, 1308
Smith, Joseph, 1342
temple president and matron, 1445
true and living Church, 1489
unity, 1498
see also Temple ordinances
Ordination
   priesthood offices, 1143
   Smith, Joseph, 1342
Ordination to the Priesthood, **1034–35**, 1137, 1140
Organ. *See* Tabernacle organ
Organic evolution. *See* Creation; Evolution
Organization, 538, **1035–49**
   celebrations, 259
   centennial observances, 260

contemporary, 447, 1044–49, 1130, 1198
Council of the Twelve, 1046–47
Doctrine and Covenants, 418
elder, Melchizedek Priesthood, 447
Fayette, New York, 505
First Presidency, 1046
history, 1035–44, 1144
local units, 1048–49
pioneer life, 1085
presidency, 1125
President of the Church, 1127
presiding bishopric, 1047–48, 1130
principles of, 1044–46
Quorums of the Seventy, 1047
signs of the true Church, 1311
stake, 1412–13
ward, 1036, 1544–45
Organization of the Church, 1830, 603, 885, **1049–50**, 1350, 1335, 1348
Organization of the Church in New Testament times, 884, **1050–51**, 1140, 1144, 1301, 1311
   see also Apostasy
Organizations. *See* Societies and organizations; Student organizations; specific organization names
Organ transplants and donations, **1051–52**, 1097
Origen (Greek theologian), 682–83
Original sin, 485, 673, 682, **1052–53**, 1341
Origin of man, **1053–54**, 1270
Orihah, 717
Orlob, Harold, 837
Ormandy, Eugene, 951
Orozco, Pascual, 896
Orthodoxy, heterodoxy, heresy, 272, 681, **1054–55**
Orthopraxy, 271
Orton, Roger, 1643, 1680
Osborn, Spencer M., 1643, 1681
Oswald, William D., 1643, 1682, 1683
Ottinger, George M., 71, 1381
Ottley, Jerold D., 950
Otten, Leaun G., 425
"Out of the ground", 159
Ouzounian, Mary, 518
Ouzounian, Reuben, 518

Pace, Glenn L., 1643, 1682
Pacific islands. *See* Oceania, the Church in

Pacific Publishing House, 51
Pack, Sadie Grant, 1643, 1684
Packer, Boyd K., 77, 81, 110, 639, 646, 1187, 1643, 1679, 1680, 1740
Page, Hiram, 214, 297–98, 603, 1128
Page, John E., 251, 614, 921, 1266, 1643, 1679, 1740
Pageants, 261, 246, 347, **1057**
Palawai Valley, Hawaii, 291
Palestine, the Church in, 367, 917
Palmer, A. Delbert, 1399
Palmer, Mable Johansen, 1399
Palmer, Spencer J., 78
Palmyra Celebration, 347
Palmyra/Manchester, New York, 347, 592, 599, 635, **1058**
Panama, the Church in, 901
Panics, economic, 439, 566
Papyri, Joseph Smith, 132–34, 136, 609, **1058–60**
Parables, **1060–62**
  doctrine, 395
  Israel, 710
  New Testament, 1012
  oil, 1027
Paradise, 364, 398, 422, **1062–63**
  see also Heaven
Paradox, harmonization of, 402–403
Paraguay, the Church in, 1400
Parallelisms, 182
Paramore, James M., 1643, 1681, 1683
Paris, Idaho, Tabernacle, 673
Parker, Nellie O., 936
Parmley, LaVern Watts, 270, **1063–64**, 1147, 1148, 1643, 1684
Parmley, Thomas Jennison, 1063
Parrish, Warren, 1265
Parry, Frank K., 1398
Parry, John, 232, 950, 976
Partridge, Edward, 119, 1643, 1681
  Doctrine and Covenants, 408
  history, 604
  Lamanite Mission, 802
  missions, 916
  Missouri, 923, 924, 925
  Missouri Conflict, 929
  presiding bishopric, 1129
  Rigdon, Sidney, 1234
Partridge, Emily. See Young, Emily Partridge
Passover. See Law of Moses
Patriarch, 642, 643, 1037, **1064–66**, 1679
  Church, 1065–66

Enoch, 462
evangelists, 475
father's blessings, 504
Joseph of Egypt, 761
Melchizedek Priesthood, 883
ordination, 1035
priesthood, 1137
priesthood blessings, 1140
Smith, Hyrum, 1330
Smith, Joseph, Sr., 1348
stake, 1064–65
see also Patriarchal blessings
Patriarchal blessings, 105, 129–30, **1066–67**
  ceremonies, 263
  confidential records, 310
  Enoch, 462
  Israel, 706
  Joseph, 761
  Kane, Thomas L., 779
  laying on of hands, 814
  mother in Israel, 963
  organization, 1038
  priesthood blessings, 1140
  religious experience, 1209
  values, 1508
  word religions, 1593
  youth, 1620
Patriarchal order of the priesthood, 555, 856, 885, **1067**, 1135, 1138–39
Patten, Benenio (Benoni), 1068
Patten, David W., 388, 920, 931, **1068**, 1185, 1367, 1643, 1678, 1740
Patten, John, 1068
Paul, Nicholas, 22–23
Paul the Apostle, 260, **1068–70**
  biography, 1068–69
  discipleship, 385
  dispensation of the fulness of times, 387
  enduring to the end, 457
  fear of God, 505
  foreordination, 522
  garments, 534
  gifts of the spirit, 545
  Gospel of Jesus Christ, 559
  hope, 657
  immortality, 677
  men, roles of, 889
  natural man, 986
  opposition, 1031
  original sin, 1052
  scripture, 1281
  sin, 1314
  teachings, 1069–70

worldliness, 1587
see also Joseph Smith Translation of the Bible (JST); New Testament
Paulsen, Finn B., 1395
Paulsen, Sara Broadbent, 1395, 1643, 1684
Paulsen, Vivian, 530
Pay, Mary Goble, 113
Peace. See War and Peace
Pearl of Great Price, 113, 278, 325, **1070–72**
  Africa, 25
  Articles of Faith, 67, 69
  Book of Moses, 216
  commandments, 296
  contents and publication, 762, 1071–72
  covenants, 334
  Deuteronomy, 378
  Enoch, 457
  history, 624
  Jesus Christ, 752–53
  Joseph Smith—History, 762
  Joseph Smith—Matthew, 763
  literature, 1072
  Malachi, 851
  priesthood, 1139
  revelation, 1226
  scripture, 1283
  Smith, Joseph, 1333
  standard works, 1416
  see also Book of Abraham; Jesus Christ in the Scriptures
Pearson, Carol Lynn, 665, 837
Peculiar people, 1017, **1072–74**, 1384
PEF. See Perpetual Emigrating Fund
Pelio, Kimo, 1023
Pennies by the Inch campaign, 660
Penrose, Charles W., 231, 377, 635, 1643, 1678, 1679, 1740
Penrose, Romania B. Pratt, 375
Pentateuch. See Book of Moses; Law of Moses
Peoples, Book of Mormon, 191–95
Perdition, sons of. See Sons of Perdition
Perfection, 553, 582, 648, 663, 895, **1074–75**
  physical body, 1080
  righteousness, 1236
  world religions, 1592
  see also Holiness; Sanctification
Periodicals, 1174–75
  see also Appendix 3 (1659–64); specific titles

Perpetual Emigrating Fund (PEF), 674, **1075–76**, 1439
British Isles, 229, 921
economic history, 436
Europe, 470
history, 616, 624, 627
organization, 1039
politics, 1101
Young, Brigham, 1607
Perry, Enoch Wood, Jr., 947
Perry, L. Tom, 81, 1187, 1643, 1679, 1680, 1740
Persecution, 51, 1017, **1076–77**
blood atonement, 131
British Isles, 229
Canada, 252
clergy, 288
cross, 345
economic history, 435–36
Europe, 470
history, 617, 614
interfaith relationships, 694
legal and judicial history, 823
Mexico, 895
Nauvoo, 994, 1000
Retrenchment Association, 1224
schismatic groups, 1266
signs of the true Church, 1311–12
United States of America, 1496
see also Anti-Mormon publications
Pershing, John J., 896
Personal Ancestral File^R, 39, 495, 645, **1077**
Personal computers, 305, 495
Personalities, Book of Mormon, 195
Personnel Department, 310
Peru, the Church in, 873, 1397–98
Peter the Apostle, 780, 1050, **1077–79**, 1126
callings, 248
Catholicism and Mormonism, 257
charity, 264
Elias, spirit of, 449
enduring to the end, 457
First Presidency, 512
laying on of hands, 813
New Testament, 1012
prophecy, 1163
visions of Joseph Smith, 1514
Petersen, Mark E., 60, 78, 377, 704, 964, 1043, 1186, 1397, 1486, 1643, 1679, 1741
Peterson, Hans F., 1262
Peterson, H. Burke, 1158, 1643, 1681, 1682

Peterson, Levi S., 839, 843, 844
Peterson, Ziba, 603, 802, 803, 916, 1116
Petsco, Bela, 843
Pettazzoni, 340
Pettibone, Rosetta, 1365, 1367
Phelps, William Wine, 1068
almanacs, 36
Book of Commandments, 138
hymns, 667
Messenger and Advocate, 892
Missouri, 923, 924, 925, 926
Missouri Conflict, 930
Moroni₁, 955
politics, 1104
Smith, Emma Hale, 1324
Philippines, the Church in, 77, 78, 79–80, 323, 662, 1757
Phillips, Cynthia L., 321
Philo, 17, 343
Philosophy, **1079–80**, 1192
see also Metaphysics
Phinney Bible, 765–66
Phipps, William, 58
Physical body, **1080–81**
afterlife, 26
Council in Heaven, 328
death and dying, 364
eternal progression, 466
first estate, 512
health, 580
immortality, 677
mortality, 957
plan of salvation, 1088
purpose of earth life, 1180, 1181
reincarnation, 1198
resurrection, 1223
second estate, 1290
sex education, 1305
soul, 1392
world religions, 1590
Physical fitness and recreation, 224, 351, **1081–82**
see also Sports
Physical sciences, College of (BYU), 224
Pierce, Mary, 92
Piercy, Frederick H., 70
Pietists, 169
Pinegar, Rex D., 461, 1643, 1680, 1681, 1684
Pingree, Job, 53
Pinnock, Hugh W., 461, 1427, 1643, 1681, 1683
Pioneer Day, 259, 261, 347, 615, **1082–83**, 1287

Pioneer economy, **1083–84**
home industries, 652
immigration and emigration, 674
Nauvoo, 994–96
organization, 1038
politics, 1102
united orders, 1493
see also Perpetual Emigrating Fund
Pioneer life and worship, 590–91, **1084–88**
Arizona, 66–67
bishops, 120
California, 246–48
Canada, 252–54
centennial observances, 261
Church Educational System, 274
colonization, 292, 293
Colorado, 29
Deseret, 371
Idaho, 671–72
Intermountain West, 300–301
Mormon Battalion, 936
Nevada, 1006–1007
New Mexico, 1010–11
organization, 1038–39
Salt Lake City, Utah, 1250
schools, 1268
seagulls, miracle of, 1287
temples, 1452
University of Deseret, 1498
Wyoming, 1598–99
see also Pioneer economy; Sabbath Day
Pioneer Memorial Theatre, 1255
Pitcher, Thomas L., 929
Plan of salvation, plan of redemption, 525, 547, 549, 767, 941, **1088–91**, 1596
atonement, 1089–90
creation, 1088–89
death and dying, 365
dispensation of the fulness of times, 388
dispensation of the Gospel, 388
doctrine, 394
Doctrine and Covenants, 413
endowment, 455
Eve, 476
fall, 1089
first estate, 511
Gospel of Jesus Christ, 556
history, 612
Holy Ghost, 650
immortality, 676
intelligences, 692
Jesus Christ, 752

Plan of salvation, plan of redemption (Cont'd)
joy, 772
Judgment Day, final, 774
Lehi, 827
marriage, 856
new and everlasting covenant,
1008
ordinances, 1032
premortal existence, 1088
premortal life, 1124
priesthood, 1134
procreation, 1158
Smith, Joseph, 1341
spirit world, 1090–91
symbols, 1430
temple ordinances, 1444
war in heaven, 1546
see also Salvation
Plates, metal, 481, **1091**
Isaiah, 700, 701, 704
Joseph, 760
lost scripture, 845
manuscript, lost 116 pages, 855
Mormon, 932
Moroni₂, 956
Mosiah₂, 960
Old Testament, 1027
see also Book of Mormon plates
and records; Book of Mormon
translation by Joseph Smith;
Book of Mormon witnesses;
Gold plates
Platonism, 400, 402, 1193
Pluralism, 895
Plural marriage, 942, **1091–95**
anti-Mormonism, 48–49
Arizona settlements, 66
Canada, 251
Church and state, 282
conferences, 308
constitutional law, 316
courts, 330
Cowdery, Oliver, 338, 339
diplomatic relations, 382
Doctrine and Covenants, 409,
423, 426
Europe, 470
film, 948
fundamentalists, 531
history, 609, 612, 614, 617, 631
humor, 664
Kimball, Heber C., 783
legal and judicial history, 823
Manifesto (1890), 852
Mexico, 896
Nauvoo, 993

Nauvoo Expositor, 996
politics, 1098
Pratt, Orson, 1114
press, news media, and the
Church, 1131
publications, 1174
Relief Society, 1208
Retrenchment Association, 1224
Reynolds v. *United States*, 1229
Scandinavia, 1264
schismatic groups, 1266
Smith, Emma Hale, 1325
Smith, Joseph, 1337
Smith, Joseph F., 1350, 1352
Smoot hearings, 1363
Snow, Eliza R., 1365
Snow, Lorenzo, 1368
social and cultural history, 1379
Taylor, John, 1440
Utah Expedition, 1500
Utah statehood, 1502
Utah Territory, 1505
vital statistics, 1530–31
Wells, Emmeline B., 1559
Woman's Exponent, 1571
woman suffrage, 1572
women, roles of, 1574
Woodruff, Wilford, 1580, 1582
Young, Brigham, 1604, 1606
Young, Zina D. H., 1612
see also Antipolygamy legislation;
Divorce; Polygamy
P manuscript, Book of Mormon,
186
Poelman, B. Lloyd, 1643, 1682
Poelman, Ronald E., 1644, 1681,
1683
Poetry
Book of Mormon, 182–83
Mormon writers of, 841–42,
1365–66
Polacca, Fannie Nmapeyo, 72
Polacca, Thomas, 72
Poland, the Church in, 383, 474,
917
Poland Act (1874), 330, 1101, 1102
Policies, practices, and procedures,
1095–97
Political Manifesto (1896), 1102
Politics, **1097–1109**
Articles of Faith, 68
contemporary, 1107–1109
culture, 1105, 1106–1107
Doctrine and Covenants, 425
freedom, 526
history, 617, 942, 1098–1103
mankind, 853

McKay, David O., 874
Nauvoo, 999–1001
Salt Lake City, Utah, 1251
Smith, Joseph, 1343
social characteristics, 1375–76
teachings, 1103–1105, 1343
United States of America, 1496
Utah statehood, 1502
see also Civil rights; Constitu-
tional law; Legal and judicial
history
Polk, James, 615, 779, 935
Polygamy, **1109**
see also Antipolygamy legislation;
Manifesto of 1890; Plural mar-
riage; Smoot hearings
Polynesian Cultural Center, 226,
579, **1109–1110**
Polynesians, 1022–23, **1110–12**
Pooley, Emil, 72
Poon Shiu-Tat (Sheldon), 79
Pope, Hyrum, 877
Pope, Theodore, 877
Pornography, 645, **1112–13**
Porter, L. Alden, 1644, 1681
Portugal, the Church in, 383, 473,
474, 1758
Postearth life. See Afterlife
Postmortal Jesus, 725
Potae, Henare, 1015
Potangaroa, Paora, 1015
Poverty, attitudes toward, **1113–14**
see also Wealth, attitudes toward
Powell, Lazarus, 1501
Pranoto, Hadi, 72
Pratt, Addison, 971, 1022
Pratt, Charity, 1116
Pratt, Helaman, 899
Pratt, Jared, 1116
Pratt, Lorus, 71, 1381
Pratt, Louisa Barnes, 115
Pratt, Orson, 666, **1114–15**, 1116,
1644, 1679, 1682, 1741
Adam-ondi-Ahman, 19
Ahman, 29
almanacs, 35
apostasy, 57
Articles of Faith, 69
Book of Mormon, 171, 175, 206
Canada, 251
consecration, 313
Deseret alphabet, 373
doctrine, 397
Doctrine and Covenants, 414,
423, 426
Enoch, 460
Europe, 471

God the Father, 548
historians, 590
history, 617, 624
intellectual history, 686
missions, 921
organization, 1036, 1039
plural marriage, 1094
Quorum of the Twelve Apostles, 1185
riches of eternity, 1230
Salt Lake City, Utah, 1250
science and religion, 1271
science and scientists, 1272, 1273
seer stones, 1293
westward migration, 1563, 1564
Pratt, Parley Parker, 68–69, 113, 136, 168, 175, 1114, 1115, **1116–17**, 1381, 1644, 1679, 1741
  Canada, 251
  Danites, 357
  doctrine, 397
  gifts of the spirit, 545
  history, 603, 604
  hymns, 667
  intellectual history, 686
  Lamanite Mission, 802, 803
  Lectures on Faith, 819
  light of Christ, 835
  Millennial Star, 906
  missions, 916, 920, 921
  natural man, 986
  organization, 1036
  patriarchal order, 1067
  plural marriage, 1094
  procreation, 1157
  publications, 1176
  Quorum of the Twelve Apostles, 1185
  Richmond Jail, 1230, 1231
  Rigdon, Sidney, 1233
  Schools of the Prophets, 1269
  science and religion, 1271
  sexuality, 1396
  Smith, Joseph F., 1350
  Taylor, John, 1438
  theology, 1475–76
  westward migration, 1564
  Zion's Camp, 1627
Pratt, Parley Parker, Jr., 53
Pratt, Rey L., 900, 1644, 1680
Pratt, Romania B., 375, 867
Pratt, Thankful Halsey, 545, 1116
Prayer, 1054, 1097, **1117–20**
  Doctrine and Covenants, 415, 427
  family, 498–99

Lord's Prayer, 844–45
  name of God, 980
  philosophy, 1079
  sacrament, 299, 1118, 1244–45
  scripture, 1280
  see also Blessings; Folklore;
    Prayer circle
Prayer circle, **1120–21**
  altar, 37
  endowment houses, 456
  freemasonry, 528
  intellectual history, 686
  Jesus Christ, 735
  pioneer life, 1087
  temples, 1449
Preaching the Gospel, **1121–22**
Predestination, 503, 521, 522, 561, **1122–23**
Pre-existence (pre-earthly existence), 272, **1123**, 1181
  see also Creation, creation accounts
Premarital sex, **1123**, 1307
Premortal life, 767, **1123–25**, 1665–70
  Adam, 15
  birth, 115–16
  brotherhood, 234
  covenants, 333
  creation accounts, 343
  devils, 379
  doctrine, 397
  eternal progression, 465
  family, 487
  hymns, 667
  intelligence, 692
  Jeremiah, 721
  Jesus Christ, 720, 724, 729, 735
  marriage, 856
  Moses, 958
  Mother in Heaven, 961
  opposition, 1031
  Paul, 1070
  plan of salvation, 1088
  priesthood, 1137
  purpose of earth life, 1180
  scripture, 1283
  war in heaven, 1546
  world religions, 1591
  see also First estate; Mortality;
    Pre-existence
Presbyterian church, 168
Presidency, concept of, 1044, **1125–26**
President of the Church, 327, **1126–28**, 1678
  Doctrine and Covenants, 408

First Presidency, 512
  high priest, 587
  Israel, 709, 710
  Jesus Christ, 743
  laying on of hands, 814
  Lee, Harold B., 822
  Melchizedek Priesthood, 883
  Mother in Heaven, 961
  ordination, 1035
  organization, 1035, 1044
  pioneer economy, 1074
  priesthood, 1135
  priesthood quorums, 1146
  prophets, 1164
  Quorum of the Twelve Apostles, 1187
  revelations, unpublished, 1228
  Ricks College, 1233
  scouting, 1276
  scripture, 1281
  succession, 1420
  see also specific name, e.g., Lee, Harold B.
Presiding bishopric, 120, 278, **1128–30**, 1681–82, 1735–38
  calamities and disasters, 246
  Deseret Industries, 375
  economic aid, 434
  finances of the Church, 508
  First Presidency, 513
  history, 636
  hospitals, 660
  LDS Foundation, 816
  organization, 1037, 1045, 1047–48
  Relief Society, 1202
  scouting, 1275
  tithing, 1481
Presiding high priest, 885, 1034, 1037, **1130**, 1144
Press, news media, and the Church, **1130–31**
  see also Newspapers, LDS
Press and publications, **1131**
Preston, William B., 624, 1129, 1644, 1681
Prichard, Sarah Ann, 1368
Pride, 663, **1131–32**
Priest, Aaronic Priesthood, 1–4, 50, 514, 635, **1132–33**
  see also High priest
Priestcraft, 45, **1133**
  Book of Mormon, 150
  priesthood, 1135
Priesthood, 278, 302, 581, 609, 767, **1133–38**, 1739–42
  Aaronic Priesthood, 1–4, 50, 514, 635, 1132–33

Priesthood *(Cont'd)*
  Abrahamic covenant, 9
  Adam, 15
  angels, 41, 42
  apostasy, 57
  apostles, 59–61
  authority, 88–89
  blacks, 125, 873
  Book of Mormon, 152
  callings, 249
  celebrations, 258–59
  compassionate service, 303
  correlation of the Church, 324,
    642
  Council of Fifty, 326
  covenants, 332
  curriculum, 349
  Daniel, prophecies of, 356
  dedications, 367
  definitions, 1134–35
  dispensations of the Gospel, 388
  Doctrine and Covenants, 406,
    408, 410, 414–15, 418, 421,
    423
  elder, Melchizedek Priesthood,
    447
  enduring to the end, 457
  eternal lives, eternal increase,
    465
  family and, 1137
  General Authorities, 538
  gifts of the spirit, 545
  God and, 1137–38
  high priest, 587
  history, order, and offices of,
    1135–37
  immigration and emigration, 675
  Israel, 709
  Jesus Christ, 732
  joining the Church, 759
  keys of, 780–81
  Kimball, Spencer W., 785
  law of Moses, 812
  Levitical Priesthood, 828
  magic, 850
  marriage, 857
  martyrdom of Joseph and Hyrum
    Smith, 860
  McKay, David O., 873
  meetings, 878
  Melchizedek, 447, 879
  men, roles of, 888
  Noah, 1017
  ordinances, 258–59, 1032, 1134,
    1138, 1289
  ordination to, 1034–35
  organization, 1035, 1044

  organization of the Church, 1050
  patriarchal order of, 1067
  pioneer life, 1085
  power of, 1133–34
  Primary, 1149
  quorums, 1144–46
  restoration of the Gospel of Jesus
    Christ, 1220
  Sabbath Day, 1242
  sacrifice, 1249
  sealing, 1289
  seventy, 1300
  Smith, Joseph, 1342
  women, roles of, 1574
  Young Men, 1613
Priesthood in biblical times, 1135,
    1138–40
Priesthood blessings, 128–29, 259,
    1139, **1140–41**
Priesthood councils, 1045, **1141–42**
Priesthood executive committee,
    stake and ward, **1142**
  see also Home teaching; Ward
    council
Priesthood interview, **1142–43**
Priesthood offices, **1143–44**
  apostle, 59–61
  bishop, 117–18
  deacon, Aaronic Priesthood, 361
  elder, Melchizedek Priesthood,
    447
  high priest, 587–88
  men, roles of, 889
  ordination to, 1034
  patriarch, 1064–66
  priest, Aaronic Priesthood, 1132–
    33
  seventy, 1300–1305
  teacher, Aaronic Priesthood, 1441
  see also Callings
Priesthood quorums, 520, 1137,
    1144–46
  apostles, 60
  auxiliary organizations, 89–90
  bishops, 119
  brotherhood, 234
  deacon, Aaronic Priesthood, 361
  elder, Melchizedek Priesthood,
    447
  fatherhood, 503
  high priest, 587
  history, 635
  Melchizedek Priesthood, 885
  Nauvoo, 990
  organization, 1037
  origins of, 1146
  presidency, 1126

  priest, Aaronic Priesthood, 1133
  priesthood councils, 1141
  priesthood offices, 1143
  Quorum of the Twelve Apostles,
    1189
  scouting, 1276
  single adults, 1318
  structure and purpose, 1144,
    1146
  teacher, Aaronic Priesthood, 1441
  volunteerism, 1539
  welfare services, 1555
Primary, 90, 267, 269, 279, 324,
    539, 658, **1146–50**, 1684
  Bible, taught in, 105
  community, 302
  contemporary, 1149–50
  history, 624, 635, 1146–48
  hymns, 667
  maternal and child health care,
    866
  meetings, 878
  New Zealand, 1015
  organization, 1046
  Parmley, LaVern Watts, 1063–64
  priesthood executive committee,
    1142
  Relief Society, 1202
  Rogers, Aurelia Spencer, 1238–39
  Sabbath Day, 1242
  scouting, 1275–76
  sisterhood, 1319
  Snow, Eliza R., 1364
  social and cultural history, 1383
  Sunday School, 1424
  Taylor, John, 1439
Primary Association, 90, 1684
Primary Children's Medical Center,
    660, 867–68, 1064
Prince, Walter F., 49
Privacy. *See* Confidential records
Probation. *See* Disciplinary proce-
    dures
Proclamations of the First Presi-
    dency and the Quorum of the
    Twelve Apostles, 285, **1151–57**,
    1187, 1670–77
Procreation, 487–88, 859, **1157–58**,
    1305, 1307
  see also Abortion; Artificial in-
    semination; Birth control
Production system, welfare services,
    1557
Profanity, **1158**
Progression, eternal. *See* Eternal
    progression

Prohibition movement, 636, 1102, **1158–59**, 1584
Prolonging life, 1097, **1159–60**
Promised Land, concept of a, 378, 707, **1160**
  gathering, 536
  hope of Israel, 657
  Joseph of Egypt, 761
  Liahona, 830
  Ten Commandments, 146
Promised Valley Playhouse, 429
Prophecy, **1160–62**
  of Daniel, 355
  Doctrine and Covenants, 415, 427
  gift of the Holy Ghost, 543
  Israel, 709
  Messiah, 893
  Noah, 1017
  Old Testament, 1027, 1029–30
  psalms, messianic prophecies in, 1029, 1172–73
  see also Jesus Christ, prophecies about; Prophet, prophets; Prophet Joseph Smith; Spirit of prophecy; Westward migration, planning and prophecy
Prophecy in biblical times, **1162–63**
Prophecy in the Book of Mormon, 158–60, **1163–64**
Prophet, prophets, 277, 463, 538, 932, **1164–70**
  biblical, 1167–70
  Book of Mormon, 143
  Christians and Christianity, 271
  Daniel, prophecies of, 355
  David, prophetic figure of last days, 360–61
  dispensation of the fulness of times, 387
  dispensations of the Gospel, 389
  doctrine, 401
  Doctrine and Covenants, 416
  Enoch, 457
  following the brethren, 520
  fulness of the Gospel, 530
  gifts of the Spirit, 544
  Holy Ghost, 649
  Israel, 709, 710
  Jesus Christ, 731
  joining the Church, 759
  LDS belief in, 807, 1164–67
  Melchizedek Priesthood, 883
  Moses, 958
  ordinances, 1032
  ordination, 1035
  organization, 1035, 1050

President of the Church, 1126
Protestantism, 1171
  remission of sins, 1211
  revelation, 1225
  revelations, unpublished, 1228
  Samuel the Lamanite, 1259
  scripture, 1281–82
  testimony of Jesus Christ, 1472
  see also Prophecy; Prophecy in biblical times; Prophecy in the Book of Mormon; Prophet, seer, and revelator; School of the Prophets; Seer
Prophet, seer, and revelator, 538, 1039, 1126, 1165, **1170**, 1185, 1281
  sealing, 1289
  see also First Presidency; Quorum of the Twelve Apostles
Prophetic Almanac (Pratt), 35–36
Prophet Joseph Smith, **1170**
Proselytization. *See* Conversion; Missionary, missionary life
Protestantism, **1170–71**
  Bible, 109
  Book of Mormon, 168
  covenants, 333
  doctrine, 400, 401
  ethics, 467
  Europe, 467, 469
  grace, 560–61
  interfaith relationships, 693
  marriage and divorce, 856
  original sin, 1052
  purpose of earth life, 1182
  reason and revelation, 1193
  restorationism, 1221, 1233
  sacrament, 1253
  schools, 1268
  see also Protestant Reformation; Puritans
Protestant Reformation, 561, 907, **1171–72**
Provo, Utah, Brigham Young University, 220–25
Psalm of Nephi, 182–83
Psalms, messianic prophecies in, 1029, **1172–73**
Pseudepigrapha. *See* Apocrypha and Pseudepigrapha
Psychological evil, 477
Publications, 624, **1173–77**, 1178, 1264, 1659–64
  see also Anti-Mormon publications; Journals; Magazines; Newspapers, LDS; Periodicals;

Press and publications; Scriptures; specific titles
Public communications, 51, 230, 304, 539, **1177**, 1131
Public office. *See* Civic duties
Public relations, **1177–79**
  stereotyping, 1417
  see also Anti-Mormon publications; Broadcasting; Exhibitions and World's Fairs; Magazines; Publications
Public speaking, **1179–80**
Public Works Department, 437
Publisher's Book Bindery, 111
Puerto Rico, the Church in, 1562
Pulsipher, Zera, 1644, 1680
Pure Church of Christ, 1265
Puritans, 168, 333, 442, 687, 834
Purpose of earth life, 274, 432, 596, 854, 1089, 1097, **1180–83**, 1342
  revelation, 1227
  world religions, 1590
  worlds, 1595
  see also Mortality
Pyper, George D., 1426, 1644, 1682

Quakers, 169
Quilts. *See* Folk art; Folklore
Qumran, 166
Quorums, priesthood. *See* Priesthood quorums
Quorum of the Twelve Apostles, 59, 278, 324, 327, 520, 538, 1165, **1185–89**, 1678–79
  Benson, Ezra Taft, 102
  Book of Mormon, 175
  capital punishment, 255
  celebrations, 259
  doctrine, 395
  Doctrine and Covenants, 407, 418, 423
  fast offerings, 501
  finances of the Church, 508
  First Presidency, 512
  Grant, Heber J., 566
  Harris, Martin, 576
  high council, 586
  history, 609, 614, 623
  immigration and emigration, 675
  Journal of Discourses, 769
  keys of the priesthood, 781
  Kimball, Heber C., 782
  Kimball, Spencer W., 786
  Lee, Harold B., 821
  Melchizedek Priesthood, 883
  missionaries, 910

Quorum of the Twelve Apostles
  (Cont'd)
  mission president, 914
  New Zealand, 1016
  organization, 1037, 1045, 1046,
    1047
  Pearl of Great Price, 1071
  policies, practices, and proce-
    dures, 1095–97
  Pratt, Orson, 1114
  President of the Church, 1126
  presiding bishopric, 1128
  priesthood, 1135
  priesthood councils, 1141
  priesthood quorums, 1146
  proclamations of, 1151–57
  prophet, seer, and revelator,
    1170
  publications, 1173
  Rigdon, Sidney, 1235
  RLDS Church, 1212
  scouting, 1276
  scripture, 1281, 1281
  seventy, 1300
  signs of the true Church, 1311
  tithing, 1481
  westward migration, 1563
  Woodruff, Wilford, 1581
  Young, Brigham, 1603
  see also Missions of the Twelve to
    the British Isles; Proclamations
    of the First Presidency and the
    Quorum of the Twelve Apostles
Quorum of the Twelve Apostles,
  official letters. See Appendix

Race, racism, 1191–92, 1530
  see also Doctrine and Covenants
    Official Declaration—2
Radio, 232–34, 240, 242, 261, 270,
    694
  see also KSL broadcasting; Mor-
    mon Tabernacle Choir Broad-
    cast
Railroad industry, 440, 470, 621,
    671, 1250, 1253
Raising the dead, 1192
Ramsey, Ralph, 1381
Randall, Naomi H. Ward, 1644,
    1684
Randine, Berthine, 1262
Rape, 1096
Rappeley, John, 1562
Reading, Lucile Cardon, 530, 1644,
    1684
Reagan, Ronald, 230, 1567
Real estate, 241, 242

Realistic literature, 839–40
Reason and revelation, 403, 463,
    547, 685, 1192–94, 1475
Rebachi, Aldo, 273
Rebaptism, 387, 629, 1087, 1194,
    1197
Record from the Ground, 159
Record keeping, 1194–96
  clerk, 288
  history, 597, 647
  libraries and archives, 831
  membership, 887–88
  Nephi₁, 1004
  presiding bishopric, 1128
  vital statistics, 1518
  see also Computer systems; Con-
    fidential records; Family his-
    tory, genealogy; Genealogical
    Society of Utah; Granite Moun-
    tain Record Vault; Historians,
    Church; World conferences on
    records
Recreation. See Physical fitness and
    recreation; Sports
Rector, Hartman, Jr., 1644, 1681,
    1683
Redbird, Ida, 72
Redd Center for Western Studies
    (BYU), 223
Redeemer. See Jesus Christ, names
    and titles of
Redemption. See Plan of salvation,
    plan of redemption
Reeder, Bertha Stone, 1617, 1618,
    1644, 1685
Reeve, Rex C., Sr., 1644, 1681
Reformation, Protestant. See Protes-
    tant Reformation
Reformation of 1856–1857, 120,
    619, 1087, 1197–98, 1500
Region, regional representative,
    279, 1042, 1045, 1198
Reincarnation, 1182, 1198–99, 1591
Reiser, A. Hamer, 1644, 1682
Relief Society, 279, 324, 506, 520,
    539, 1199–1206, 1685
  auxiliary organizations, 89, 90
  bishop, 120
  burial, 239
  community, 302
  compassionate service, 303
  Deseret Hospital, 374
  Doctrine and Covenants, 411
  emergency preparedness, 453
  folk art, 517
  history, 612, 621, 624, 635
  home industries, 653, 654

Horne, Mary Isabella, 657
  hospitals, 659
  humanitarian service, 661
  Kimball, Sarah Granger, 784
  lay participation, 814
  logo, 1203
  Lyman, Amy Brown, 847
  material culture, 865
  maternity and child health care,
    866, 867, 868
  meetinghouse, 876
  meetings, 878
  Mormon Handicraft, 936–37
  motto, 264, 1539
  Nauvoo, 991
  New Zealand, 1015
  organization, 1037, 1046
  origins, 1200–1201
  pioneer life, 1086
  priesthood executive committee,
    1142
  Retrenchment Association, 1224
  Robison, Louise Yates, 1237
  Sabbath Day, 1242
  silk culture, 1313
  single adults, 1317, 1318
  sisterhood, 1319
  Smith, Bathsheba Bigler, 1321
  Smith, Emma Hale, 1325
  Smith, Joseph, 1337
  Snow, Eliza R., 1364, 1365
  social and cultural history, 1379
  social services, 1386
  Spafford, Belle Smith, 1401
  stewardship, 1418
  Taylor, Elmina Shepard, 1437
  visiting teaching, 1516
  volunteerism, 1539
  welfare services, 1555
  Wells, Emmeline B., 1559
  Williams, Clarissa Smith, 1567
  Woman's Exponent, 1571
  woman suffrage, 1572
  women, roles of, 1575
  Young, Brigham, 1608
  Young, Zina D. H., 1611, 1612
  see also Ensign; Relief Society
    Magazine; Relief Society in
    Nauvoo
Relief Society Magazine, 461, 536,
    636, 964, 1203, 1204, 1206–
    1207, 1383, 1402
Relief Society in Nauvoo, 1037,
    1207–1208, 1238
Religion and science. See Science
    and religion

Religious education, 444
    Book of Mormon, 201–205
    Brigham Young University, 222–23
    see also Church Educational System; Sunday School
Religious experience, **1208–1210**
    Catholicism and Mormonism, 257
    metaphysics, 894
    Pratt, Orson, 1114
    theology, 1475
    see also Conversion
Religious freedom, 287, 316, 825, **1210**, 1263–64
Religious Studies Center (BYU), 172, 208, 694
Remarriage, 1372
    see also Marriage
Remission of sins, **1210–11**, 1316
    agency, 27
    born of God, 218
    first principles of the Gospel, 514
    gift of the Holy Ghost, 544
    humility, 663
    rebaptism, 1194
    repentance, 1218
    sacrament, 1244
    sanctification, 1259
Remy, Jules, 1087
Reorganized Church of Jesus Christ of Latter Day Saints (RLDS Church), **1211–16**, 1326, 1328
    Book of Mormon, 176, 186
    historical sites, 593
    history, 614
    Joseph Smith Translation of the Bible, 766
    Kirtland Temple, 799
    libraries and archives, 832
    Mormonism, 937, 940
    Nauvoo, 996, 997
    schismatic groups, 1266
    Smith, Joseph III, 940, 1212–14, 1266, 1324
Repentance, **1216–18**
    agency, 27
    chastening, 264
    chastity law, 266
    covenants, 332
    disciplinary procedures, 386
    Doctrine and Covenants, 414
    elect of God, 448
    enduring to the end, 457
    faith in Jesus Christ, 483
    first principles of the Gospel, 514
    Gospel of Jesus Christ, 557
    humility, 663

justification, 776
Kimball, Spencer W., 787
Melchizedek, 879
miracles, 910
mortality, 958
murder, 970
Noah, 1017
paradise, 1062
plan of salvation, 1090
premarital sex, 1123
priesthood council, 1142
prophets, 1169
remission of sins, 1210
salvation, 1257
sexuality, 1307
signs of the true Church, 1311
sin, 1316
    see also Baptism; Confession of sins; Enduring to the End
Residence and migration, 1376–77
    see also Immigration and emigration
Restoration of all things, 388, 555, 907, 1009, 1028, **1218–20**
    priesthood, 1140
    sacrifice, 1249
Restoration of the Gospel of Jesus Christ, 324, 390, 728, 737, 806, 941, **1220–21**
    angels, 41
    apocalyptic texts, 54
    apostasy, 57
    authority, 89
    Bible, 108
    Christians and Christianity, 270–71
    constitutional law, 315
    Daniel, prophecies of, 355
    Doctrine and Covenants, 410, 411
    elect of God, 448
    Elias, spirit of, 449
    Ephraim, 461
    epistemology, 463
    First Vision, 515
    following the brethren, 520
    fundamentalists, 531
    history, 599
    hope of Israel, 657
    hymns, 667
    intellectual history, 686–87
    Isaiah, 702
    keys of the priesthood, 781
    kingdom of heaven, 791
    last days, 805
    Nauvoo Expositor, 996
    New Testament, 1011

plural marriage, 1094
President of the Church, 1127
priesthood, 1138
priesthood offices, 1144
prophecy, 1162, 1163
Protestantism, 1171
raising the dead, 1192
revelation, 1227
Rigdon, Sidney, 1234
Sacred Grove, 1247
Salt Lake Temple, 1254
science and religion, 1271
Seventy, 1301
Smith, Joseph, 1334, 1340
temples, 1462–63
testimony bearing, 1470
true and living Church, 1489
United States of America, 1495
    see also Dispensation of the fulness of times; Dispensations of the Gospel; Restoration of all things
Restorationism, Protestant, **1221**, 1233
Resurrection, **1222–23**
    afterlife, 26
    angels, 41
    atonement of Jesus Christ, 83
    Book of Mormon, 152, 159
    death and dying, 364–65
    degrees of glory, 367
    deification, early Christian, 369
    devils, 380
    doctrine, 398
    eternal life, 464
    health, 580
    humility, 664
    immortality, 677
    Jesus Christ, 725, 729, 733–34, 738
    judgment, 772
    Judgment Day, final, 774
    marriage, 858, 859
    mortality, 957
    Moses, 959
    paradise, 1062
    physical body, 1080
    purpose of earth life, 1180, 1181
    Quorum of the Twelve Apostles, 1189
    reincarnation, 1198
    restoration of all things, 1219
    Samuel the Lamanite, 1259
    Smith, Joseph, 1343
    telestial kingdom, 1443
    translated beings, 1485
    witnesses, law of, 1570

Retrenchment Association, 324, 1039, **1223–25**
 history, 621, 623
 home industries, 654
 Horne, Mary Isabella, 657
 hospitals, 659
 Relief Society, 1201, 1202
 social and cultural history, 1382
 Taylor, Elmina Shepard, 1437
 Young, Zina D.H., 1612
 see also Young Women
Revelation, 540, 546, 1030, **1225–27**
 anti-Mormonism, 45
 apocalyptic texts, 54
 Articles of Faith, 68
 Book of Mormon, 156, 754
 Catholicism and Mormonism, 257
 Christians and Christianity, 271
 commandments, 296
 conferences, 307
 Council of Fifty, 326
 doctrine, 401, 403
 Doctrine and Covenants, 405, 424
 evangelists, 475
 Fayette, New York, 505
 fear of God, 505
 First Vision, 516
 following the brethren, 520
 gift of the Holy Ghost, 543
 Harmony, Pennsylvania, 573
 Holy Ghost, 650
 intellectual history, 685
 Jesus Christ, 724, 731, 747
 John, 753–55
 laying on of hands, 814
 Manifesto (1890), 852
 Melchizedek Priesthood, 883
 metaphysics, 894
 Millennial Star, 906
 Missouri, 922
 Moses, 958
 Mother in Heaven, 961
 Mount of Transfiguration, 968
 mysteries of God, 977
 nature, law of, 986
 New Testament, 1014
 Noah, 1017
 ordination, 1034
 philosophy, 1080
 physical body, 1080
 politics, 1098
 prayer, 1118
 priesthood, 1134
 prophets, 1165
 Quorum of the Twelve Apostles, 1185

 reason and, 1192–94
 religious experience, 1209
 Rigdon, Sidney, 1234
 scripture, 1278, 1281, 1283
 sick, blessing the, 1308
 signs of the true Church, 1311
 Smith, Joseph, 1331
 soul, 1392
 telestial kingdom, 1443
 Ten Commandments, 1469
 theology, 1475
 transfiguration, 1485
 truth, 1490
 types of, 1225
 worlds, 1595
 see also Prophet, prophets;
  Prophet, seer, and revelator;
  Restoration of the Gospel of
  Jesus Christ
Revelations, unpublished, 406, **1228**
Revelators. *See* Prophet, seer, and
 revelator
Reverence, 1028, **1228–29**
Rewet, Mangu, 1015
Rex, Harold M., 1396
Reynolds, Alice Louise, 1207
Reynolds, Ethel Georgina, 1353
Reynolds, George, 137, 171, 206–
 207, 231, 1229, 1644, 1680,
 1682
Reynolds, William, 577
Reynolds v. *United States* (1879),
 52, 316, 330, 619, 625, 825,
 1095, 1101, **1229–30**, 1502
Rhee Ho Nam, 78
Rhoads, Thomas, 247
Rhodakanaty, Plotino, 899
Rice, L. L., 1403
Rich, Ben E., 635
Rich, Charles C., 246, 247, 578,
 1036, 1644, 1679, 1741
Rich, Leonard, 1644, 1680
Richard L. Evans Chair of Christian
 Understanding (BYU), 694
Richards, Ezra F., 1015
Richards, Florence Holbrook, 1644,
 1684
Richards, Franklin D., 67, 328,
 537, 571, 1036, 1039, 1644,
 1679, 1741
 Book of Mormon, 175
 historians, 590
 history, 626
 Pearl of Great Price, 1071
 priesthood, 1136
 publications, 1175
 religious experience, 1209

Richards, Franklin D., 1644, 1680,
 1681, 1682
Richards, Franklin S., 824
Richards, George F., 540, 637,
 1066, 1145, 1186, 1644, 1679,
 1741
Richards, Jane S., 375, 1644, 1685
Richards, Joseph, 79
Richards, LeGrand, 60, 1043, 1129,
 1594, 1645, 1679, 1681, 1741
Richards, Lula Greene, 1366, 1571
Richards, Lynn S., 1645, 1682
Richards, Sarah Ellen, 1350, 1352
Richards, Stayner, 1645, 1679
Richards, Stephen L, 273, 516, 540,
 637, 1145, 1186, 1395, 1645,
 1678, 1679, 1682, 1741
Richards, Willard, 256, 377, 783,
 1645, 1678, 1679, 1682, 1741
 British Isles, 228
 historians, 589, 590, 591
 history, 616, 647
 King Follett Discourse, 791
 Lectures on Faith, 819
 martyrdom of Joseph and Hyrum
  Smith, 862
 medical practices, 875
 missions, 921
 museums, 972
 organization, 1036
Riches of eternity, 488, 681, **1230**,
 1551
 see also Wealth, attitudes toward
Richey, Benjamin, 79
Richmond Jail, 611, 931, **1230–31**
Ricks, Thomas E., 1232
Ricks College, 12–13, 234, 274,
 275, 444, **1232–33**, 1267
 dating and courtship, 359
 drama, 429
 Missionary Training Centers, 913
Riders of the Purple Sage (film),
 947
Ridges, Joseph, 87, 232, 1435
Rigdon, Sidney, 46, 166, 205, 337,
 665, 1221, **1233–35**, 1645,
 1678, 1741
 degrees of glory, 367
 Doctrine and Covenants, 413,
  414, 418, 421
 First Presidency, 512, 513
 freemasonry in Nauvoo, 527
 high council, 586
 Hiram, Ohio, 588
 historians, 590
 history, 604, 605, 610, 614

Joseph Smith Translation of the
  Bible, 764
Kirtland, Ohio, 797
Lamanite Mission, 802
Lectures on Faith, 819, 821
Liberty Jail, 830
Messenger and Advocate, 892
missions, 916
Missouri, 924, 926, 927, 930
politics, 1098, 1099
Pratt, Parley Parker, 1116
President of the Church, 1128
publications, 1176
Richmond Jail, 1230
schismatic groups, 1265–66
Schools of the Prophets, 1269
scripture, 1283
seer, 1293
Smith, Hyrum, 1330
Smith, Joseph, 1345
succession in the presidency,
  1420
visions, 1511
visions of Joseph Smith, 1514
Young, Brigham, 1604
Rigdon, William, 1233
Riggs, Emma Ray. *See* McKay,
  Emma Ray Riggs
Righteousness, 1054, **1235–37**
cursings, 352
degrees of glory, 368
devils, 379
enduring to the end, 457
Enoch, 457
eternal life, 464
foreordination, 522
Israel, 711
Jesus Christ, 739
joy, 772
justification, 776
politics, 1098, 1105
sanctification, 1260
world religions, 1590
see also Holiness
Riley, I. Woodbridge, 50, 1510
Ringger, Hans B., 473, 1645, 1681
Riplakish, 718
Ripplinger, Donald H., 950
Riter, William, 471
Ritual. *See* Ceremonies
Rivers, Percy John, 1023
RLDS Church, *see* Reorganized
  Church of Jesus Christ of Latter Day Saints
Roberts, B. H., 49, 172, 207, 231,
  261, 263, 678, 1645, 1680,
  1683

books by, 303–304
conversion, 322
Cumorah pageant, 347
doctrine, 397
foreordination, 522
historians, 591
history, 631, 633, 647
intellectual history, 687, 689, 690
intelligences, 693
Liberty Jail, 830
light of Christ, 835
literature, 838, 842
Nauvoo Legion, 998
publications, 1175, 1176
purpose of earth life, 1180
science and religion, 1272
scripture, 1278
"This Is the Place" monument,
  1476
View of the Hebrews, 1510
woman suffrage, 1573
Robertson, Hilton A., 77, 904
Robertson, Leroy, 974
Robinson, Ebenezer, 175, 990, 1480
Robinson, George W., 589, 1230,
  1645, 1682
Robinson, J. Frank, 662
Robison, Joseph L., 1237
Robison, Louise Yates, 636, 936,
  1204, **1237–38**, 1645, 1685
Rocha, Hélio da, 1396
Rockwell, Orrin Porter, 1050
Rockwood, Albert Perry, 356, 1645,
  1680
Rogers, Aurelia Spencer, 115, 1146,
  1147, **1238–39**
Rogers, Jacob, 577
Rogers, Noah, 1022
Rogers, Thomas F., 838, 1238, 1239
Rojas Ornelas, Jorge A., 902, 1645,
  1681
Roman Catholicism. *See* Catholicism
  and Mormonism
Romania, the Church in, 474, 1758
Romney, George W., 285, 286,
  1108, 1131
Romney, Marion G., 60, 81, 87,
  114, 323, 424, 542, 1645, 1678,
  1679, 1741
home teaching, 655
intelligences, 693
organization, 1043
South America, 1398
tree of life, 1486
Romney, Richard M., 1008
Romney, Thomas C., 830

Roosevelt, Franklin D., 102, 634,
  1107
Roosevelt, Theodore, 1327, 1364
Rose, Paul, 79
Rosenbaum, Karen, 843
Rosenblatt, Nathan, 695
Rosenvall, E. Albert, 1016
Rosenvall, Vernice, 1016
Ross, Isabelle Salmon, 1645, 1684
ROTC. *See* Army ROTC, U.S.
Roueche, Thomas F., 1440
Roundy, Lorenzo, 66
Rowland, Moses, 1347
Roxcy, Eliza. *See* Snow, Eliza R.
Roxcy, Leonora, 1365
Royle, Edwin Milton, 837
Rubio, Vincente S., 1400
Rudd, Glenn L., 1016, 1645, 1681
Ruíz, Amado, 1397
Russell, Gardner H., 1645, 1681
Russell, Isaac, 920
Russia. *See* Union of Soviet Socialist
  Republics, the Church in
Ruth, **1239–40**
Ryder, Simonds, 48

Sabbath Day, 32, 262, **1241–43**
covenant Israel, 331
Doctrine and Covenants, 409
holiness, 648
Millennium, 907
Ten Commandments, 1469
see also Sunday; Worship
Sackley, Marjorie, 25
Sackley, Robert E., 25, 87, 1645,
  1681
Sacrament, 299, 302, 334, 878,
  1243–45
Book of Mormon, 158, 159, 202
Catholicism and Mormonism, 258
children, 267
confirmation, 311
covenant Israel, 331
cross, 345
deacon, Aaronic Priesthood, 361
Doctrine and Covenants, 408,
  411
fast and testimony meeting, 502
holiness, 648
Jerusalem, 723
Jesus Christ, 735, 744
law, 809
New Testament, 1013
ordinances, 1033
pioneer life, 1085, 1087
prayer, 299, 1118, 1244–45
priesthood blessings, 1140

Sacrament *(Cont'd)*
  priests, 1132
  rebaptism, 1194
  repentance, 1218
  Sabbath Day, 1242
  Sunday School, 1426
  testimony bearing, 1471
  see also Atonement of Jesus
    Christ; Communion; Last
    Supper
Sacrament meeting, 279, 302, 646,
    878, 1244, **1245–47**
  altar, 37
  baptism, 95
  children, 267
  components, 1246
  high council, 587
  hymns, 668
  material culture, 865
  membership, 887
  organization, 1043
  Sunday School, 1242
  testimony bearing, 1471
  see also Fast and testimony meet-
    ing; Worship
Sacred Grove, 592, 599, 648, **1247–
    48**, 1431
Sacrifice, 476, 534, 1021, **1249**
  see also Consecration
Sacrifice in biblical times, **1248–49**
St. Augustine. *See* Augustine
St. George, Utah, 290, 595
St. George Stake Academy, 12
St. George Tabernacle, 1414
St. George Temple, 624, 826, 1258
St. Joseph Stake, 786
St. Joseph Stake Academy, 13
Saints, 277, 979, **1249–50**, 1259
  see also Church of Jesus Christ of
    Latter–day Saints, The
Salinas de Gortari, Carlos, 897
Salisbury, Wilkins Jenkins, 1360
Saltair Resort, 440, 630, 633, 1378
Salt covenant, 332
Salt industry, 440
Salt Lake City, Utah, 278, 321,
    1250–52, 1256
  architecture, 64
  bishops, 120
  business, 241, 242
  celebrations, 259
  city planning, 284
  civic duties, 286
  education, 443
  endowment houses, 456
  gathering, 537
  museums, 971

Schools of the Prophets, 1270
social and cultural history, 1380
world conferences on records,
    1588
Young, Brigham, 1605
see also Mormon Tabernacle
    Choir; Salt Lake Temple; Salt
    Lake Theatre; Tabernacle, Salt
    Lake City; Temple Square;
    "This Is the Place" monument;
    Welfare Square
Salt Lake Stake Academy, 12
Salt Lake Tabernacle. *See* Taberna-
    cle, Salt Lake City
Salt Lake Tabernacle Choir. *See*
    Mormon Tabernacle Choir
Salt Lake Temple, 1250, **1252–54**,
    1462, 1465
  building program, 236
  Doctrine and Covenants, 423
  endowment, 456
  history, 628, 629
  material culture, 865
  meetinghouse, 877
  organization, 1038
  Quorum of the Twelve Apostles,
    1188
  religious experience, 1210
  sculptors, 1286
  social and cultural history, 1381
  symbols, 1431
  Woodruff, Wilford, 1583
Salt Lake Theatre, 429, 437, 631,
    1255, 1380
Salt Lake Tribune (newspaper),
    377–78, 633, 1266
Salt Lake Valley, 247, 261, 274,
    1255–56
  colonization, 290
  economic history, 436
  gathering, 537
  history, 616
  museums, 972
  pioneer life, 1087
  sculptors, 1286
  seagulls, miracle of, 1287
  social and cultural history, 1380
  Temple Square, 1465
  Utah Territory, 1503
  Young, Brigham, 1605
Salvation, 277, 549, **1256–57**
  abuse, spouse and child, 11
  Adam, 16
  atonement of Jesus Christ, 83
  born of God, 219
  Catholicism and Mormonism, 258
  children, 268–69, 682, 1052, 1244

  Christians and Christianity, 270
  Council in Heaven, 328
  covenant Israel, 331
  covenants, 332
  cross, 345
  deification, early Christian, 369
  doctrine, 400
  elect of God, 448
  enduring to the end, 457
  exaltation, 479
  fall of Adam, 485
  gift of the Holy Ghost, 543
  Gospel of Jesus Christ, 557–58
  humility, 664
  repentance, 1217
  worlds, 1595
  see also Children, salvation of;
    Eternal life; Immortality; Plan
    of salvation, plan of redemp-
    tion; Salvation of the dead
Salvation of children. *See* Children,
    salvation of
Salvation of the dead, 399, 409,
    1091, **1257–59**
  degrees of glory, 369
  Elijah, 451
  endowment, 455–56
  family history, genealogy, 492,
    494, 564
  freemasonry, 529
  Gospel of Jesus Christ, 558
  hell, 586
  Jesus Christ, 725, 735
  knowledge, 799
  marriage, 859
  name extraction program, 979
  New Testament, 1014
  principles, 1257–58
  RLDS Church, 1213
  sealing, 1289
  signs of the true Church, 1312
  spirit world, 1409
  temple ordinances, 1445
  temple recommend, 1447
  see also Baptism for the dead;
    Plan of salvation, plan of re-
    demption
Samoa, the Church in, 873, 917,
    1023, 1025
Sampson-Davis, Pricilla, 25
Samuel the Lamanite, **1259**
  Book of Mormon, 152, 153, 183
  Jesus Christ, 727, 730, 748
  natural man, 986
  Nephi₂, 1005
  prophecy, 1163
San Bernardino, California, 248,
    290

Sanctification, **1259–60**
  baptism, 98
  Book of Mormon, 169
  first principles of the Gospel, 514
  holiness, 648
  righteousness, 776
  washing and anointing, 1551
  see also Born of God; Justifica-
    tion; Righteousness
Sanders, Sondra, 1015
Sandeson, Caroline, 92
Sands, Robert, 950
Sangiovanni, Guglielmo Giosue
    Rossetti, 972
San Luis Stake, 294
Sanpete Stake Academy, 13
Santa Clara, Utah, 290
Sarah, 963, **1260**, 1577
  see also Abraham
Sargent family, 125
Satanism, 379, 380, 850, **1261**
  Cain, 245
  creation accounts, 341
  Enoch, 458
  Eve, 476
  Jesus Christ, 752
  life and death, spiritual, 832
  secret combinations, 1290–91
  see also Buffetings of Satan;
    Devils
Satellite communications system,
    234, 645, **1261**
  centennial observances, 262
  conferences, 308
  economic history, 440
  organization, 1043
Sato Tatsuo, 77
Savage, Charles R., 1297, 1381
Savior, 741
  see also Jesus Christ, names and
    titles of
Scandinavia, the Church in, 382,
    616, 917, 992, **1262–65**, 1525,
    1760
  see also specific country names
Schaerrer, Neil D., 1645, 1684
Schiller, Herbert M., 695
Schismatic groups, 576, 614, 688,
    819, 832, **1265–67**
  see also Reorganized Church of
    Jesus Christ of Latter Day
    Saints
Schmidt, Donald T., 591
Schoeps, H. J., 1279
Scholarly secularism, 689
Scholarship, biblical. *See* Bible
    scholarship

School of the Elders, 1269
School and Fireside (Maeser), 444
Schools, **1267–69**
  Church and state, 282
  dedications, 367
  institutes of religion, 684
  maternity and child health care,
    867
  New Zealand, 1015–16
  see also Academies; Church Edu-
    cational System; Curriculum;
    Education; Intellectual history;
    School of the Prophets; specific
    school name
Schools of the Prophets, 274, 416,
    442, 446, 609, 620, **1269–70**
  intellectual history, 686
  Jesus Christ, 737
  Kimball, Sarah Granger, 784
  Kirtland, Ohio, 796
  Lectures on Faith, 819
  Missionary Training Centers, 913
  Pratt, Orson, 1114
  Rigdon, Sidney, 1235
  scripture, 1279
  social and cultural history, 1378
  visions of Joseph Smith, 1515
  Whitney store, 1567
  Young, Brigham, 1603
Schopenhauer, Arthur, 1181
Schreiner, Alexander, 976, 1435,
    1436
Schrödinger, Erwin, 868
Schroeder, Theodore, 50
Schwartz, Mary Taylor, 1350
Schweitzer, Albert, 272
Science and religion, 463, **1270–72**
Science and scientists, **1272–75**
  see also Intellectual history; Mat-
    ter; Metaphysics; Technology
Scotland, the Church in, 870, 871,
    873, 1760
Scott, John, 154
Scott, Richard G., 1187, 1274,
    1645, 1679, 1681, 1741
Scott, Verl F., 1645, 1683
Scott, Walter, 1233
Scott, Winfield, 1500
Scouting, 268, **1275–1277**, 1724–25,
    1728
  Aaronic Priesthood, 3, 361
  Benson, Ezra Taft, 103
  civic duties, 286
  history, 635
  organization, 1040
  Parmley, LaVern Watts, 1063
  priest, Aaronic Priesthood, 1133

  Primary, 1148
  Smith, George Albert, 1327, 1328
  values, 1508
  Young Men, 1613
Scovil, Lucius N., 527, 528
Scripture, **1277–83**
  authority of, 1281
  Catholicism and Mormonism, 257
  children, 267
  computers systems, 304, 305
  curriculum, 346–50
  Daniel, prophecies of, 355
  Deuteronomic ideas in, 378
  doctrine, 401
  equality, 463
  fear of God, 505
  following the brethren, 520
  foreknowledge of God, 521
  forthcoming, 460, 1226, 1282–83
  fulness of the Gospel, 530
  garments, 534
  God the Father, 551
  Gospel of Jesus Christ, 556
  Jesus Christ, 738, 745–53
  lay participation, 815
  lost, 845–46
  martyrs, 863
  metaphysics, 894
  New Zealand (Maori language),
    1015
  Old Testament, 1027
  publications, 1173–74
  record keeping, 1195–96
  Smith, Joseph, 1340
  stake, 1412
  standard works, 1415
  words of living prophets, 1281–82
  see also Bible; Book of Mormon;
    Doctrine and Covenants; Pearl
    of Great Price; Scripture study
Scripture, interpretation within
    scripture, **1283–84**
Scripture Publications Committee,
    110
Scripture study, 108, 444, 498,
    1284–85, 1483–84
Sculptors, **1285–86**
  see also Architecture; Kirtland
    Temple; Museums; Statues and
    monuments; Symbols
Seagulls, miracle of, 74, 618, **1287–
88**
Sealing, 389, **1288–90**
  adoption of children, 21
  artificial insemination, 70
  born in the covenant, 218
  cancellation of, 1290

Sealing *(Cont'd)*
  celebrations, 258
  celestial kingdom, 260
  ceremonies, 262
  death and dying, 365
  dispensation of the fulness of
    times, 388
  doctrine, 399
  Doctrine and Covenants, 419
  Elijah, 450, 452
  endowment houses, 456
  family, 487
  family history, genealogy, 492
  heirs, 583
  Holy Spirit of Promise, 651
  John, revelations of, 755
  keys of the priesthood, 781
  Kirtland Temple, 799
  marriage, 859
  Melchizedek Priesthood, 883
  Nauvoo, 993
  Nauvoo Temple, 1002
  ordinances, 1033
  organization, 1037
  plan of salvation, 1091
  power of, 1288–89, 1312
  priesthood, 1135, 1139
  salvation, 1257
  signs of the true Church, 1312
  Smith, Joseph, 1336, 1338, 1342
  social and cultural history, 1379
  temple ordinances, 1445
  temple recommend, 1447
  temples, 1289, 1447
  see also Marriage, eternal
Sealy, Shirley, 839, 843
Seantum, 162
Second comforter. *See* Jesus Christ,
    second comforter
Second coming of Jesus Christ, 464,
    737–39, 741, 747, **1290**, 907
  Book of Mormon, 153
  degrees of glory, 369
  dispensation of the fulness of
    times, 388
  Elias, spirit of, 449
  great and abominable church, 569
  immigration and emigration, 674
  Isaiah, 703
  Joseph Smith—Matthew, 763
  Millennium, 907
  Moroni, 954
  parables, 1061
  restoration of all things, 1219
  restoration of the Gospel of Jesus
    Christ, 1221
  signs as divine witness, 1310

Second estate, 1089, **1290**
  premortal life, 1124
  procreation, 1157
  see also First estate
Secret combinations, 585, **1290–91**
  Book of Mormon, 156, 157
  Cain, 246
  devils, 381
  Jaredites, 718
Sect, **1291–92**
  see also Cult
Seed of Abraham, **1292**
  see also Abrahamic covenant;
    Gospel of Abraham, 1292
Seegmiller, William A., 1022
Seer, 457, 458, 960, **1292–93**, 1499
  see also Prophet, prophets;
    Prophet, seer, and revelator;
    Seer stones
Seer stones, 200, 212, **1293**, 1334
  see also Urim and Thummim
SEHA. *See* Society for Early His-
    toric Archaeology
Sekaquaptewa, Wayne, 72
*Selections from the Book of Mor-
    mon*, 213
Self, Freddy, 53
Self-sufficiency (self-reliance), 434,
    438, 453, **1293–94**, 1535–36
Seminaries and institutes, 237, 274,
    275, 444, 637, 644, 684, **1295–
    96**
  Bible, 105
  computer systems, 304
  McKay, David O., 872
  Native Americans, 984
  organization, 1040, 1046
  social and cultural history, 1383
  see also Academies; Institutes of
    Religion; specific seminaries
    and institutes
Senate, U.S., 49, 631
Senior citizens, **1296–98**
Senior Cooperative Retrenchment
    Association, 658
Sermon on the Mount, **1298–99**
  Beatitudes, 98
  Book of Mormon, Third Nephi,
    153–55
  commandments, 296
  Doctrine and Covenants, 412
  Jesus Christ, 731, 736
  lawsuits, 813
  light and darkness, 836
  Matthew, Gospel of, 869
  New Testament, 1012
  riches of eternity, 1230

scripture, 1283
  Ten Commandments, 1469
  see also Lord's Prayer
Sermons, Book of Mormon, 183
Seth, 718, **1299–1300**, 1966
Setting apart, 643, **1300**
  callings, 250
  Deseret Hospital, 374
  endowment houses, 456
  laying on of hands, 814
  Melchizedek Priesthood, 883
  ordination, 1034
  priesthood blessings, 1140
  priesthood offices, 1144
  Relief Society, 1200
Settlements. *See* Colonization; Pio-
    neer life and worship
Seventy, 325, 538, 609, 624, 631,
    635, 642, **1300–1305**, 1680–81
  assistants to the Twelve, 81
  celebrations, 259
  Doctrine and Covenants, 418
  first council of, 1301
  First Presidency, 513
  Journal of Discourses, 769
  Kimball, Spencer W., 788
  Melchizedek Priesthood, 883
  Nauvoo, 991
  New Zealand, 1016
  ordination, 1035
  organization, 1037
  overview, 1300–1303
  pioneer life, 1087
  priesthood, 1140
  priesthood quorums, 1146
  quorums of, 1303–1305
  revelations, unpublished, 1228
  signs of the true Church, 1311
  Taylor, John, 1439
  Young Men, 1613
Sewing. *See* Folk art
Sex education, 1096, **1305**, 1307
Sexual abuse, 1096
Sexuality, 1096, **1306–1308**
  courts, 330
  dating and courtship, 358
  doctrine, 401
  family, 487–88, 489
  marriage, 856–57
  pornography, 1112
  premarital sex, 1123
  social characteristics, 1373
  see also Sex education; Sexual
    abuse
Shaffer, J. Wilson, 999
Shannon, Zane K., 322
Sharon, Vermont, 260, 592, 635

Sharp, Loretta Randall, 842

Sharp, Marianne Clark, 1207, <u>1401</u>, 1645, 1685

Sharp, Thomas C., 47, 48, 613

Shearman, William H., 1266

Shepard, David S., 1436

Sherem (c. 540 B.C.), 45, 148

Sherman, Lyman R., 1645, 1680

Sherwood, H. G., 527, 555

Shez, 718

Shiblon, 718

Shimabukuro, Sam K., 1646, 1681

Shinto, 1594–95

Shipp, Ellis R., 115, 375, 867

Short stories, Mormon writers of, 842–44

Shreeve, Afton Kartchner, 1399

Shule, 717

Shumway, Naomi M., 1148, 1646, 1684

Shurtliff, Louie Emily, 1353

Siam. *See* Thailand

Sick, blessing the, 129, 365, 374, 715, **1308–1309**

Sidney, Lyman, 1399

Sidon River, 177

Sigma Gamma Chi, 817
    see also LDS Student Associations

Sign of the Dove. *See* Dove, sign of the

Signs, **1309**

Signs as divine witness, **1309–1310**

Sign seeking, **1310**
    see also Miracles; Prophecy

Signs of the times, **1310–11**
    see also Jesus Christ, second coming of

Signs of the true Church, 1160, **1311–12**

Silk Culture, 621, 636, 653, 1201, **1312–14**, 1576
    see also Deseret Silk Association

Sill, Sterling W., 1646, 1679, 1681

Sillitoe, Linda, 839, 844

Simlai, Rabbi, 811

Simonsen, Velma Nebeker, 1646, 1685

Simpson, Robert L., 1016, 1646, 1680, 1681, 1683, 1684

Sims, Hester, 1401

Sin, 156, 386, **1314–16**
    plan of salvation, 1088
    remission of, 1210–11
    repentance, 1216
    sanctification, 1259
    telestial kingdom, 1443

see also Atonement of Jesus Christ; Original sin; Unpardonable sin

Singapore, the Church in, 80, 1757

Singer, John, 51

Single adults, 90, 359, **1316–19**, 1386

Sisterhood, 506, 815, 1199, **1319–20**, 1516, 1575
    see also Brotherhood

Sjodahl, Janne, 137, 171, 206–207, 424

Skousen, W. Cleon, 704

Slavery, 161, 605, 928, 1100

Sloan, James, 590, 1646, 1682

Slover, Robert H., 78

Slover, Tim, 838

Smith, Alexander Hale (Joseph's son), 1324

Smith, Alvin (Joseph's brother), 365, 422, 601, 875, 954, 1349, 1356, 1357, 1359–60, 1515

Smith, Alvin (Joseph's son), <u>574</u>

Smith, Amanda, 1209

Smith, Andrew Jackson, 935

Smith, Asael (Joseph Sr.'s father), 1333, 1348, 1361

Smith, Barbara B., 1205, 1646, 1685

Smith, Barbara McIsaac, 101

Smith, Bathsheba (daughter), 1321

Smith, Bathsheba Wilson Bigler (George A.'s wife), 316, <u>375</u>, 636, 1202, **1320–21**, <u>1567</u>, 1646, 1685

Smith, Chloe, 545

Smith, Clarissa. *See* Williams, Clarissa Smith

Smith, David A., 1646, 1681, 1682

Smith, David Hyrum (Joseph's son), <u>1324</u>, 1325

Smith, Dennis, 72, 1286

Smith, Don Carlos (Joseph's brother), 175, 365, 1356, 1357, 1360, 1480

Smith, Douglas H., 1646, 1681

Smith, Edith (George Albert's daughter), 1326

Smith, Eldred G., <u>141</u>, 1066, 1646, 1679

Smith, Elias, 1221

Smith, Eliza. *See* Snow, Eliza R.

Smith, Emily (George Albert's daughter), 1326

Smith, Emily Jane, 1326

Smith, Emma Hale (Joseph's wife), 763, **1321–26**, 1334, 1336, 1338, 1646, 1685

biography and autobiography, 114–15

Book of Mormon, 210, 214

death and dying, 365

Doctrine and Covenants, 408, 411, 412, 416, 423

Fayette, New York, 505

genealogy of, <u>1322</u>

historical sites, 593

history, 601, 604

hymns, 667, 1176

Joseph Smith Translation of the Bible, 766

manuscript, lost 116 pages, 854

Nauvoo, <u>990</u>, 997, 999

organization of the Church, 1049

Palmyra/Manchester, New York, 1058

papyri, 1060

pioneer life, 1086

plural marriage, 1093

pride, 1131

publications, 1176

Relief Society, <u>1199</u>, 1200, 1207

South Bainbridge, New York, 1400

visiting teaching, 1516

Smith, Emma Smoot, 1582

Smith, Ephraim (Joseph's brother), 1359

Smith, Ethan, 50, 1509, 1510

Smith, Frederick Granger Williams (Joseph's son), 1324

Smith, Frederick M. (Joseph III's son), 1214

Smith, Gary E., 72

Smith, G. Carlos, Jr., 80, 1646, 1683

Smith, George A., 501, 666, 1320–21, 1369, 1567, 1646, 1678, 1679, 1741
    Australia, 86
    historians, 590
    history, 647
    Kirtland Temple, 798
    missions, 921
    organization, <u>1036</u>
    standard works, <u>1416</u>
    Sunday School, 1425
    world religions, 1593

Smith, George A., Jr. (George A.'s son), 1321

Smith, George Albert (George A.'s grandson), 262, 303, <u>540</u>, 678, 786, 906, 1126, **1326–29**, 1646, 1678, 1679, 1683, 1741
    Benson, Ezra Taft, 102

Smith, George Albert (Cont'd)
  broadcasting, 233
  history, 638
  priesthood quorums, 1145
  prophets, 1165
  Quorum of the Twelve Apostles,
    1186
  scouting, 1276
  temples, 1453
  "This Is the Place" monument,
    1476, 1477
  Young, Brigham, 1607
Smith, George Albert, Jr. (George
    Albert's son), 1326
Smith, Gregory White, 51
Smith, Hyrum (Joseph's brother),
    48, 210, 211, 214, 290, 338,
    666, 963, 1329–31, 1349, 1646,
    1678, 1679, 1741
  Carthage jail, 255–56
  Doctrine and Covenants, 408,
    421, 423, 424
  history, 603
  Liberty Jail, 830
  martyrdom of, 860–62, 863
  Missouri Conflict, 932
  Nauvoo, 998, 1000
  organization of the Church, 1049
  patriarch, 1065
  persecution, 1076
  plural marriage, 1093
  prophet, seer, and revelator,
    1170
  Richmond Jail, 1230
  Rigdon, Sidney, 1235
  sacrament meeting, 1246
  Taylor, John, 1438
  tea, 1441
  Temple Square, 1467
  testator, 1470
  Wells, Junius F., 1561
  Young, Brigham, 1603, 1604
  Zion's Camp, 1627
  see also Smith, Mary Fielding
Smith, Hyrum Gibbs (Hyrum's
    great-grandson), 1065, 1646,
    1679
Smith, Hyrum Mack, 1646, 1679,
    1741
Smith, Israel A. (Joseph III's son),
    1214
Smith, Jerusha Barden (Hyrum's
    wife), 796, 1329, 1331, 1349
Smith, Jessie Ella Evans, 1353,
    1355
Smith, John (Hyrum's son), 1065,
    1350

Smith, John (Joseph's uncle), 36,
    517, 616, 779, 926, 1065, 1646,
    1678, 1679, 1741
Smith, John Gibson, 1401
Smith, John Henry (George A.'s
    son), 328, 900, 1136, 1326,
    1646, 1678, 1679, 1741
Smith, Joseph, 46, 50, 214, 1126,
    1331–47, 1647, 1678, 1741
  Aaronic Priesthood, 2–3
  Adamic language, 18
  Adam-ondi-Ahman, 19
  animals, 42
  Anthon Transcript, 43–44
  anti-Mormonism, 45–48, 49, 50
  Apocrypha, 55, 56
  apostasy, 57
  apostles, 61
  architecture, 63
  Articles of Faith, 68
  assassination, 48
  authority, 89
  baptism, 94, 95, 97
  Bible, 105, 112
  biography, 114
  Book of Abraham, 132–34, 136
  Book of Mormon, 140, 166, 178,
    185, 210–13
  born of God, 218
  burnings, everlasting, 239
  callings, 248
  Canada, 251, 253
  Carthage Jail, 255–56
  celestial kingdom, 260
  centennial observances, 260
  ceremonies, 262
  chastening, 265
  chastity law, 265
  children, 268, 269
  Christology, 273
  Church and state, 282
  city planning, 284
  Civil War prophecy, 287
  Colesville, New York, 289
  common consent, 297
  community, 299–300
  consecration, 312
  Council of Fifty, 326
  creeds, 343
  curriculum, 351
  damnation, 354
  dance, 354
  Daniel, prophecies of, 355
  Danites, 357
  David, prophetic figure of last
    days, 360
  death and dying, 365, 366

dedications, 367
degrees of glory, 367, 368
diplomatic relations, 382
dispensation of the fulness of
  times, 388
dispensations of the Gospel, 389
doctrine, 394, 396, 398, 400, 401
dove, sign of the, 428
drama, 428
Earth, 431
economic aid, 434
economic history, 435
education, 441–43
elder, Melchizedek Priesthood,
  447
Elias, 449
Elijah, 450, 451, 452
endless and eternal, 454
endowment, 455
enduring to the end, 457
Enoch, 457
epistemology, 462
eternal lives, eternal increase,
  465
eternal progression, 465
evangelists, 475
Eve, 476
exaltation, 479
extermination order, 480
faith in Jesus Christ, 484
fall of Adam, 486
family home evening, 496
Far West, Missouri, 500
fast offerings, 501
finances of the Church, 508
First Presidency, 512
first principles of the Gospel, 514
First Vision, 515–16
following the brethren, 520
foreordination, 522
forgeries of historical documents,
  523
freemasonry, 527, 528, 529
fulness of the Gospel, 530
fundamentalists, 531
Garden of Eden, 534
gathering, 536
genealogy of, 538, 1362
gift of the Holy Ghost, 544
gifts of the spirit, 545
God the Father, 549
Godhood, 553, 554
Gospel of Abraham, 555
Gospel Jesus Christ, 558
Harmony, Pennsylvania, 573
high council, 586
Hiram, Ohio, 588

historians, 589–90
history, 596, 614, 647–48, 762–63
Holy Ghost, 649, 650
humanitarian service, 661
Hyde, Orson, 666
Independence, Missouri, 679
inspiration, 683
intellectual history, 685, 686
intelligences, 692
Israel, 706, 709, 710, 711
James, Epistle of, 715
James the Apostle, 716
Jerusalem, 723
Jesus Christ, 724, 728, 736, 742, 744, 747, 753
John, revelations of, 753–54
John the Beloved, 757, 758
joining the Church, 759
Joseph of Egypt, 761
journals, 770
journeys of, 1332
joy, 771
Judgment Day, final, 774
keys of the priesthood, 780, 781
Kimball, Heber C., 782, 783
Kinderhook plates, 789
kingdom of heaven, 790
King Follett Discourse, 791, 792
Kirtland, Ohio, 795, 796, 797
Kirtland economy, 792–93
Kirtland Temple, 798
knowledge, 799
Lamanite Mission, 802, 803, 804
law, 807, 809
law of adoption, 810
lawsuits, 812
laying on of hands, 814
Lectures on Faith, 819, 821
legal trials of, 601, 647, 823, 824, 1000, 1346–48, 1400
Lehi, 828
Liahona, 829
Liberty Jail, 830, 831
libraries and archives, 831
light and darkness, 837
literature, 837
lost scripture, 845
magic, 850
Malachi, 851
manuscript, lost 116 pages, 854
martyrdom of, 860–62, 863
maternity and child health care, 866
matter, 868–69
Matthew, 753, 763
Matthew, Gospel of, 869
medical practices, 875

Melchizedek, 880
Melchizedek Priesthood, 884, 885–86
Messenger and Advocate, 892
millenarianism, 906
Millennial Star, 906
Millennium, 907
missions, 913, 915, 920, 921
Missouri, 922, 923, 924, 926
Missouri Conflict, 927, 929, 930, 931–32
Mormon, 932
Mormonism, 939–40, 941
Mormons, image of, 948, 949
Moroni₁, 956–57
Moroni₂, 953, 954–55
Moses, 959
Mother in Heaven, 961
Mount of Transfiguration, 968
music, 973
mysteries of God, 977
name of the Church, 979
name of God, 980
Native Americans, 981
natural man, 985
Nauvoo, 987, 990, 991, 995, 996, 997, 998, 999, 1000, 1001
New Jerusalem, 1009
New Testament, 1011, 1013, 1014
Noah, 1017
non-Mormons, 1018
obedience, 1021
Oceania, 1022
Old Testament, 1027, 1028, 1029, 1030
opposition, 1031
ordinances, 1032
organization, 1035, 1037, 1038
organization of the Church, 1049, 1050
Palmyra/Manchester, New York, 1058
papyri, 132–34, 136, 609, 1058–60
parables, 1060–62
paradise, 1062, 1063
patriarch, 1064, 1065
patriarchal order, 1067
Patten, David W., 1068
Paul, 1069, 1070
Pearl of Great Price, 1071, 1072
perfection, 1080
persecution, 1076
Peter, 1077, 1078
physical fitness, 1081
pioneer life, 1085
plural marriage, 1092–93

politics, 1098, 1099, 1100, 1104
poverty, 1113
Pratt, Orson, 1114, 1115
prayer, 1118, 1120
prayer circle, 1120, 1121
premortal life, 1124, 1125
President of the Church, 1127, 1128
presiding bishopric, 1129
presiding high priest, 1130
press, news media, and the Church, 1131
pride, 1131
priest, 1132
priesthood, 1134, 1135, 1137, 1139
priesthood blessings, 1141
priesthood offices, 1144
priesthood quorums, 1146
promised land, 1160
prophecy and prophets, 1161, 1162, 1163, 1164, 1165, 1167
prophet, seer, and revelator, 1170, 1331–39
Protestant Reformation, 1171, 1172
psalms, 1172
publications, 1173, 1174, 1176
purpose of earth life, 1181
Quorum of the Twelve Apostles, 1185, 1186, 1188
raising the dead, 1192
record keeping, 1194, 1196
reincarnation, 1199
Relief Society, 1199, 1200, 1201, 1207
Relief Society Magazine, 1206
religious experience, 1209
restoration of all things, 1219
restoration of the Gospel of Jesus Christ, 1220
resurrection, 1222, 1223
revelation, 1225, 1226, 1227
revelations, unpublished, 1228
Richmond Jail, 1230, 1231
Rigdon, Sidney, 1234, 1235
RLDS Church, 1211, 1213
Sabbath Day, 1242
sacrament, 1244
Sacred Grove, 1247
sacrifice, 1248
salvation of the dead, 1257, 1259
schismatic groups, 1265
Schools of the Prophets, 1269
scripture, 1278, 1281, 1283, 1284, 1285
sealing, 1288

Smith, Joseph (Cont'd)
  seer, 1293
  Sermon on the Mount, 1298
  Seventy, 1301, 1303
  Smith, Emma Hale, 1323
  Smith, Hyrum, 1330
  Snow, Eliza R., 1365
  solemn assemblies, 1390
  sons of perdition, 1391
  spirit, 1404
  sports, 1409
  succession in the presidency,
    1420
  suffering in the world, 1422
  Taylor, John, 1438, 1440
  teachers, teacher development,
    1442
  teachings of, 552, 687, 1339–43
  temples, 1447, 1450, 1451, 1454,
    1456
  Temple Square, 1467
  testator, 1470
  testimony bearing, 1471
  testimony of Jesus Christ, 1472
  theology, 1475, 1476
  tithing, 1480, 1481
  tolerance, 1483
  transfiguration, 1485, 1486
  translated beings, 1486
  true and living Church, 1489
  united orders, 1493, 1494
  United States of America, 1497
  unity, 1497
  unpardonable sin, 1499
  Urim and Thummim, 1499, 1500
  View of the Hebrews, 1509, 1510
  visions of, 647, 1001, 1349, 1412–
    16, 1511
  visiting teaching, 1517
  ward, 1541
  war in heaven, 1546
  Wells, Junius F., 1561
  Wentworth letter, 1561, 1562
  westward migration, 1563
  Whitmer, David, 1564, 1565
  Whitney store, 1566–67
  women, roles of, 1574
  worlds, 1592
  worship, 1596
  writings of, 1339, 1343–46
  Young, Brigham, 1602, 1603,
    1604
  Young, Zina D.H., 1612
  Zionism, 1626
  Zion's Camp, 1627
  see also Doctrine and Covenants;
    Historical sites; *History of the*

Church (History of Joseph
  Smith); Joseph Smith Translation of the Bible; Prophet Joseph Smith; Smith, Emma
  Hale
Smith, Joseph (Joseph's infant son),
  1324
Smith, Joseph, Jr. *See* Smith,
  Joseph
Smith, Joseph, Sr. (Joseph's father),
  408, 422, 575, 599, 603, 763,
  1058, 1065, 1247, 1329, 1333,
  1348–49, 1359, 1647, 1678,
  1679, 1741
see also Smith, Lucy Mack
Smith, Joseph III (Joseph's son),
  940, 1212–14, 1266, 1324
see also Reorganized Church of
  Jesus Christ of Latter Day
  Saints, The
Smith, Joseph F. (Hyrum's son), 42,
  328, 512, 678, 1126, 1136,
  1349–52, 1358, 1647, 1678,
  1679, 1682, 1683, 1741
  birthplace of, 500
  death of, 566
  Doctrine and Covenants, 405,
    426
  elder, Melchizedek Priesthood,
    447
  evolution, 478
  first estate, 1157
  gifts of the spirit, 545
  Hawaii, 579
  historical sites, 592
  history, 623, 624, 626, 630, 631,
    632, 635, 636
  individuality, 681
  Jesus Christ, 737
  journals, 770
  Millennial Star, 906
  Mother in Heaven, 961
  motion pictures, 964
  New Zealand, 1015
  organization, 1041
  Pearl of Great Price, 1072
  Polynesians, 1111
  priesthood quorums, 1146
  prohibition, 1159
  prophets, 1165
  Quorum of the Twelve Apostles,
    1188
Relief Society Magazine, 1206
  scripture, 1278
  Seventy, 1302
  Smoot hearings, 1363
  social services, 1386

  spirit world, 1408
  Sunday, 1424
  Sunday School, 1426
  Taylor, Elmina Shepard, 1437
  temples, 1452, 1454, 1464
  tithing, 1482
  war and peace, 1550
  welfare services, 1554
  Wells, Junius F., 1561
  Word of Wisdom, 1584
Smith, Joseph Fielding (Joseph F.'s
  son), 60, 261, 540, 637, 822,
  1126, 1352–55, 1358, 1359,
  1647, 1678, 1679, 1682, 1741
  animals, 42
  Asia, 79
  doctrine, 397
  Doctrine and Covenants, 424
  drugs, abuse of, 429
  fall of Adam, 486
  family history, genealogy, 493
  genealogy, 537
  historians, 591
  Improvement Era, 678
  intelligences, 693
  Israel, 708
  marriage, 858
  mother in Israel, 964
  murder, 970
  Oceania, 1026
  organization, 1043
  patriarch, 1066
  plan of salvation, 1089
  premortal life, 1124, 1125
  priesthood quorums, 1145
  prophets, 1165
  publications, 1176
  Quorum of the Twelve Apostles,
    1186
  record keeping, 1194
  Relief Society, 1200
  science and religion, 1272
  scripture, 1281
Smith, Joseph Fielding (Hyrum
  Mack's son), 1647, 1679
Smith, Julia (Joseph's daughter),
  1324
Smith, Julina L. (Joseph Fielding's
  mother), 1200, 1647, 1685
Smith, Katharine (Joseph's sister),
  1360
Smith, Leonard I., 22
Smith, Levira (Joseph F.'s wife),
  1350
Smith, Lot, 66
Smith, Louisa, 796

Smith, Lucy (Joseph's sister). *See* Millikin, Lucy Smith

Smith, Lucy Mack (Joseph's mother), 114, 215, 599, 763, 855, 955, 1329, 1333, 1348, **1355–58**, 1361
  mother in Israel, 963
  publications, 1176
  religious experience, 1209
  sisterhood, 1319
  Smith, Emma Hale, 1323, 1326

Smith, Martha Ann (Hyrum's daughter), 1350, 1359

Smith, Mary Duty (Joseph Sr.'s mother), 796, 1348, 1361

Smith, Mary Fielding (Hyrum's wife), 964, 1116, 1349, 1350, **1358–59**, 1360

Smith, Mother. *See* Smith, Lucy Mack

Smith, Nicholas G., 1066, 1647, 1679

Smith, Norma Broadbent, 1647, 1685

Smith, Oliver, 347

Smith, Robert, 1361

Smith, Samuel (b. 1666), 1361

Smith, Samuel, Jr. (b. 1714), 1361

Smith, Samuel Harrison (Joseph's brother), 211, 214, 322, 573, 603, 963, 1049, 1178, 1357, 1360, 1602

Smith, Sardius, 577

Smith, Sophronia (Joseph's sister), 1360

Smith, Sylvester, 1647, 1680

Smith, Thaddeus, 796

Smith, Wallace B. (William Wallace's son), 1215

Smith, Willard L., 1025

Smith, William (Joseph's brother), 212, 214, 614, 999, 1065, 1185, 1212, 1266, 1357, 1360, 1647, 1679, 1741

Smith, William Wallace (Joseph III's son), 1214, 1215

Smith family, **1359–61**
  anti-Mormonism, 46, 48–49
  arts, visual, 70
  history, 599

Smith family ancestors, **1361–63**

Smith farm, 1328

Smithies, James, 950

Smoking. *See* Tobacco

Smoot, Abraham O., 1350

Smoot, Reed, 49, 540, 567, 631, 632, 634, 1095, 1145, 1159, 1363, 1647, 1679, 1741

Smoot hearings (1903–1907), 49, 440, 631, 853, 1095, 1351, **1363–64**

Snelgrove, C. Laird, 1399

Snow, David A., 320, 321

Snow, Eliza R., 784, **1364–67**, 1381, 1647, 1685
  biography and autobiography, 115
  Deseret Hospital, 375
  history, 621, 624
  hospitals, 659
  hymns, 667
  intellectual history, 687
  Juvenile Instructor, 777
  Kirtland Temple, 798, 799
  maternity and child health care, 867
  mother in Heaven, 961
  mother in Israel, 963, 964
  Primary, 1146
  Relief Society, 1201, 1207
  religious experience, 1210
  Retrenchment Association, 1224
  Rogers, Aurelia Spencer, 1239
  Smith, Bathsheba Bigler, 1321
  social and cultural history, 1380
  visiting teaching, 1517
  woman suffrage, 1572
  Young, Zina D. H., 1612
  Young Women, 1616, 1617

Snow, Erastus, 213, 1036, 1115, 1136, 1262, 1263, 1264, 1647, 1679, 1741

Snow, Lorenzo, 42, 213, 231, 328, 1126, 1365, 1366, **1367–71**, 1647, 1678, 1679, 1682, 1683, 1741
  diplomatic relations, 382
  doctrine, 401
  economic history, 437
  Europe, 471
  finances of the Church, 508
  God the Father, 549
  Godhood, 555
  history, 621, 625, 635
  hosanna shout, 659
  intellectual history, 686, 687
  Jesus Christ, 737
  legal and judicial history, 824
  missions, 917
  organization, 1036
  plural marriage, 1093
  priesthood, 1136
  prophets, 1165
  publications, 1175
  Quorum of the Twelve Apostles, 1187

  religious experience, 1209
  Smith, Joseph F., 1351
  social and cultural history, 1380
  succession in the presidency, 1421
  Sunday School, 1426
  tithing, 1482

Snow, Oliver, 1365, 1367

Snow College, 13

Social characteristics, **1371–78**, 1507

Social Credit party (Canada), 254

Social and cultural history, 992, 1343, **1378–85**
  see also Immigration and emigration; Non-Mormons, social relations with; Socialization

Social Hall, Salt Lake City, 429

Socialization, 351, 1017, **1385–86**, 1508

Social problems, *see* Social characteristics; Social services; Welfare services; specific problem, e.g., Alcoholic beverages and alcoholism

Social sciences, College of (BYU), 223

Social services, 286, 429, 646, 679, 1041, **1386–87**
  see also Humanitarian service; Welfare services

Societies and organizations, 686, **1387–90**
  see also specific name, e.g., Relief Society

Society, **1390**

Society for Early Historic Archaelolgy (SEHA), 209, 1388

Sockyma, Michael, 72

Solemn assemblies, 262, 416, 913, **1390–91**, 1453

Son of David, 741
  see also Jesus Christ, names and titles of

Son of God, 740
  see also Jesus Christ, names and titles of

Song of Solomon, 112

Son of Man, 740–41
  see also Jesus Christ, names and titles of

Sonne, Alma, 1647, 1679, 1681

Sonnenberg, John, 1647, 1681

Sonntag, Philip T., 1016, 1647, 1681, 1683

Sorensen, Donna Durrant, 1647, 1686

Sorensen, Lynn A., 1648, 1681

Sons of perdition, **1391–92**
  damnation, 354
  degrees of glory, 367
  devils, 380
  hell, 585
  life and death, spiritual, 833
  salvation, 1256
  unpardonable sin, 1499
  wrath of God, 1598
Sonsteby, Olaf, 1264
Soper, Phebe, 1117
Sorcery. *See* Magic
Sorenson, John L., 62, 170, 172, 208
Sorenson, Virginia, 115, 839, 840, 842
Sororities, *see* LDS Student Association
Soul, 415, 1180, 1259, **1392**
South Africa, the Church in, 24, 873, 917, 1757
South America, the Church in, 323, 917, **1392–1400**, 1757
  see also specific country names
South Bainbridge (Afton), New York, 1346, **1400–1401**
Southeast Asia Mission, 80
Southern Far East Mission, 77, 79, 80
Southern States Mission (U.S.), 634
Southey, Trevor, 72, 1286
South Korea, the Church in, 77–78, 696, 905, 1757
South Pacific. *See* Oceania, the Church in
Southwest Indian Mission, 984
Southwick, Albert J., 950
Soviet Union. *See* Union of Soviet Socialist Republics, the Church in
Space industries, 1252
Spafford, Belle Smith, 1205, 1207, 1238, 1387, **1401–1402**, 1648, 1685
Spafford, Earl, 1401
Spafford, Earl, Jr., 1401
Spafford, Mary, 1401
Spain, the Church in, 213, 473, 1758
Spalding, Solomon. *See* Spaulding, Solomon
Spaulding, F. S., 137
Spaulding, Solomon, 46, 166, 206, 1235, 1402
Spaulding Manuscript, 46, 206, 1235, **1402–1403**
Speeches, Book of Mormon, 183

Spencer, Aurelia. *See* Rogers, Aurelia Spencer
Spencer, Darrell, 844
Spencer, Josephine, 842
Spencer, Lucy, 1092, 1238
Spencer, Orson, 686, 1175
Sperm donation, 1096
Sperry, Sidney B., 113, 172, 424, 704
Spirit, **1403–1405**
  afterlife, 26
  animals, 42
  children, 266
  creation accounts, 341
  doctrine, 402
  Doctrine and Covenants, 415
  Easter, 433
  Elias, 449
  Elijah, 452
  foreordination, 522
  health, 580
  metaphysics, 894–95
  patriarchal blessings, 1066
  physical body, 1081
  resurrection, 1222
  Smith, Joseph, 1340
  soul, 1392
  see also First estate; Hell; Spirit body; Spirit prison
Spirit body, **1405–1406**
  birth, 116
  Book of Mormon, 157
  premortal life, 1124
  soul, 1392
  see also Creation, creation accounts
Spirit of God. *See* Light of Christ
Spirit/matter dichotomy, 400
Spirit prison, 360, 364, 380, 585, 725, **1406**, 1409
  see also Salvation of the dead
Spirit of prophecy, 1165, 1225, 1284, **1406–1407**
Spiritual death, 833, **1407–1408**
  devils, 380
  fall of Adam, 485
  hell, 585
  physical body, 1081
  plan of salvation, 1089
  unpardonable sin, 1499
  see also Life and death, spiritual
Spirit world, 364, **1408–1409**
  angels, 41
  atonement of Jesus Christ, 85
  baptism, 95
  devils, 380
  Doctrine and Covenants, 422

  heirs, 583
  hell, 585
  Israel, 710
  marriage, 859
  paradise, 1062
  plan of salvation, 1090–91
  premortal life, 1125
  scripture, 1283
  telestial kingdom, 1443
"Spoken Word, The." *See* Mormon Tabernacle Choir Broadcast
Spori, Jacob, 471, 625, 902
Sports, 254, 635, 1383, **1409–11**
  see also Physical fitness and recreation
Spry, William, 634, 1159
Squires, Charlotte, 1368
Squires, Harriet Amelia, 1368
Sri Lanka, the Church in, 81, 696, 1757
Stafford, William, 842
Stage productions. *See* Drama; Pageants
Stake, 219, 279, 538, 872, **1411–14**
  calamities and disasters, 246
  celebrations, 259
  clerk, 288
  community, 300
  conferences, 306, 308–309
  dance, 355
  family home evening, 496
  fast offerings, 501
  home industries, 654
  Jesus Christ, 738
  Mexico, 896
  missions, 916
  music, 973
  organization, 1037, 1045
  patriarch, 1064–65
  priesthood executive committee, 1142
  promised land, 1160
  public communications, 1177
  Quorum of the Twelve Apostles, 1187
  region, 279, 1042, 1045, 1198
  Relief Society, 1199
  satellite communications system, 1261
  sick, blessing the, 1308
  Smith, Joseph, 1336
  social and cultural history, 1384
  ward, 1541
  see also Area, area presidency; Bishop, history of the office
Stake president, stake presidency, 288, 643, 1126, **1414–15**

callings, 249
conferences, 308
courts, 329
disciplinary procedures, 386
elder, Melchizedek Priesthood, 447
General Authorities, 539
high council, 586
high priest, 587
immigration and emigration, 676
lay participation, 815, 818
Melchizedek Priesthood, 883
missionaries, 910
ordination, 1035
organization, 1037, 1048
Quorum of the Twelve Apostles, 1189
Standard works, **1415–16**
fall of Adam, 485
fundamentalists, 531
Garden of Eden, 533
history, 624, 646
Jesus Christ, 751, 752
New Testament, 1011
Old Testament, 1027
Pearl of Great Price, 1071
publications, 1173
revelations, unpublished, 1228
scripture, 1278, 1280, 1281
Sunday School, 1424
Topical Guide, 1484
wealth, attitudes toward, 1552
see also specific work, e.g., Doctrine and Covenants
Standing, Joseph, 625
Stanton, Elizabeth Cady, 1560
Stapley, Delbert L., 60, 1043, 1648, 1679, 1741
Stark, Rodney, 320, 321, 345, 1520
State, church and. See Church and state
State of Deseret. See Deseret, state of
Statistical research, center for (BYU), 224
Statistics. See Vital statistics
Statues and monuments
Angel Moroni, 39–40, 346, 347, 755, 1254, 1286
Christus, 273–74, 479, 1466
Salt Lake Temple, 1254
sculptors, 1285–86
seagulls, miracle of, 1287
Temple Square, 1466–67
"This Is the Place", 262, 595, 1286, 1328, 1359, 1476–77
Wells, Junius F., 1561
see also Historical sites

Stay, Jesse E., 965
Steele, John, 1287
Stenhouse, Fanny, 49, 115
Stephens, Evan, 232, 479, 950, 974, 976, 1426
Stephens, John Lloyd, 178
Stephens, Wade N., 976
Stereotyping of Latter-day Saints, 633, 949, **1416–17**
Sterilization, 1096, **1417–18**
Sterling Scholars program, 446
Stevenson, A. Walter, 1648, 1683
Stevenson, Edward, 576, 831, 1648, 1680
Stevenson, Robert Lewis, 356, 949
Stewardship, **1418**
business, 240
community, 300
dispensations of the Gospel, 388
Doctrine and Covenants, 412
economic history, 437
family home evening, 496
intellectual history, 688
interviews, 698
lay participation, 815
magnifying one's calling, 850
prophecy, 1161
Smith, Joseph, 1343
united orders, 1493
Stewart, Doug, 837
Stewart, Isaac, 899
Stewart, James Z., 213, 899
Stewart, Joyce, 72
Stewart, LeConte, 71
Stewart, Ora Pate, 842
Stick of Joseph, **1418**
Stick of Judah, **1418**
Stillborn children, 1097, **1419**
Stoal, Josiah. See Stowell, Josiah
Stocking, Sarah Delight, 1582
Stoddard, Calvin, 1360
Stokes, Bertram, 103
Stone, Barton W., 1221
Stone, O. Leslie, 1648, 1680, 1681
Stoof, Reinhold, 1395
Storytelling, 517
see also Folklore
Stout, Hosea, 75, 373
Stowell, Josiah, 289, 601, 603, 1321, 1334, 1346, 1348, 1400, 1401
Stowell, Josiah, Jr., 1400
Strachey, Lytton, 114
Strait and narrow, **1419**
Strang, James J., 523, 1212, 1265, 1266, 1326
Strangites, 576, 1266

Straus, Roger A., 320
Stringham, Lucy, 565
Stuart, John T., 1000
Stuart, Thomas, 172
Student organizations, 684, 817
see also specific organization and school names
Studies, Book of Mormon, 205–209
Study-abroad programs, Brigham Young University, 224
Style, Mormon, 877
Style and tone, Book of Mormon, 184
Substance use, 1375
see also Alcoholic beverages and alcoholism; Drugs, abuse of; Tobacco
Succession in the presidency, 613, 635, 996, 1038, 1128, 1186, 1188, **1420–21**, 1678–79
priesthood, 1135
religious experience, 1210
Rigdon, Sidney, 1235
RLDS Church, 1212
Smith, Joseph, 1338
Young, Brigham, 1604
Sudan, the Church in, 662
Suffering in the world, 403, 1180, 1182, **1421–22**
Sugar beet industry, 240, 241, 253, 254, 438, 440, 629
Suicide, 365, 971, 1096, **1422–23**
Sunday, 878, **1423–24**
see also Sabbath Day; Sunday School
Sunday School, 89, 90, 91, 302, 324, 371, 685, 878, **1424–27**, 1682–83
Deseret alphabet, 373
Deseret News Book Company, 374
history, 624, 646
hymns, 667
McKay, David O., 871
organization, 1039, 1046
Sabbath Day, 1242
social and cultural history, 1382
welfare services, 1555
Sundström, John E., 1263
Sunstone (symbol), 1285
Sunstone Foundation, 1388
Supernatural, 895
Supreme Being. See Godhood
Supreme Court, U.S., 330
antipolygamy legislation, 52
Church and state, 281
legal and judicial history, 825–27

Supreme Court, U.S. *(Cont'd)*
politics, 1101–1102
see also specific decisions, e.g.,
Reynolds v. *United States*
Surrogate motherhood, 1096
Sweden, the Church in, 213, 473,
624, 1150, 1262, 1264, 1760
Swemer, Samuel, 1592
Swenson, May, 842
Swiss Temple, 474, 1453, 1743–44
Switzerland, the Church in, 471,
473, 872, 873, 917, 1758
Sword of Laban, 1195, **1427–28**
Syllabus. *See* Curriculum
Symbolism, 1032, **1428–30**, 1254
see also Symbols, cultural and
artistic
Symbols, cultural and artistic,
1430–31
see also Angel Moroni statue;
Architecture; Ceremonies; City
planning; Dove, sign of the;
Folk art; Historical sites; Kirt-
land Temple; Nauvoo Temple;
Sculptors; Symbolism, specific
symbol, e.g., Beehive symbol

Tabernacle, Salt Lake City, 64, 236,
307, 437, 950, 952, 1038, 1426,
1433–34, 1465, 1560
see also Mormon Tabernacle
Choir; Mormon Tabernacle
Choir Broadcast; Tabernacle
organ
Tabernacle Choir. *See* Mormon Tabernacle Choir; Mormon Tabernacle Choir Broadcast; Tabernacle organ
Tabernacle organ, 633, 950, 952,
1434–36
Tabernacles
architecture, 64
centennial observances, 261
history, 633
pioneer life, 1086
satellite communications system,
1261
see also Tabernacle, Salt Lake
City; Tabernacle organ
Taft, Chloe, 101
Tahiti, the Church in, 434, 917,
1023, 1759
Taiwan, the Church in, 77, 78, 79,
696, 1757
Talishoma, Lowell, 72, 1286
Talmage, James E., 57, 113, 175,
231, 261, 540, 635, 1648, 1679,
1741

Articles of Faith, 69
creation, 344
doctrine, 397
Earth, 432
epistemology, 463
intellectual history, 689, 690
museums, 972
patriarchal order, 1067
Pearl of Great Price, 1072
plan of salvation, 1089
premortal life, 1124
publications, 1175
science and religion, 1271, 1272
science and scientists, 1273
world religions, 1593
Talmage, May B., 1615
Talmage, Nelle, 660
Talmage, Sterling B. (James E.'s
son), 972
Talmud, 343
Tambuli (periodical), 697
Tanaka Kenji, 77
Tanner, Annie Clark, 113
Tanner, Fern Lucinda, 823
Tanner, Jerald, 51
Tanner, Joseph Marion, 1648, 1682
Tanner, Mary Jane Mount, 115
Tanner, N. Eldon, 81, 252, 254,
327, 382, 698, 1045, 1252,
1552, 1648, 1678, 1679, 1741
Tanner, Sandra, 51
Tapu, Raituia Tehina, 1023
Tarbell, Zachariah, 1401
Taxation
exemptions, 826
income tax, 1097
Taylor, Agnes, 1438
Taylor, Alma O., 77
Taylor, Elmina Shepard, 624, **1436–
37**, 1617, 1648, 1684
Taylor, George Hamilton, 1437
Taylor, Henry D., 1648, 1679, 1681
Taylor, James, 1438
Taylor, John, 666, 667, 1126, **1438–
41**, 1648, 1678, 1679, 1741
Abraham, 8
Book of Mormon, 213
British Isles, 231, 920, 921
Canada, 251, 253
Carthage jail, 256
consecration, 313
Constitution, U.S., 319
Council of Fifty, 327
Doctrine and Covenants, 417,
426
Earth, 432
Europe, 470, 471

fundamentalists, 531
Gospel of Jesus Christ, 558
history, 623, 624, 625, 626
hymns, 667
Joseph of Egypt, 761
Judgment Day, final, 774
martyrdom of Joseph and Hyrum
Smith, 862
missions, 916, 920, 921
Missouri, 927
Moroni, 955
organization, 1036, 1039, 1040,
1043
Perpetual Emigrating Fund, 1075
Pratt, Orson, 1115
Pratt, Parley P., 1116
priesthood, 1136
Primary, 1146
prophets, 1165
Schools of the Prophets, 1270
Smith, Emma Hale, 1325
Smith, Hyrum, 1331
Smith, Joseph F., 1350, 1351
Smith, Lucy Mack, 1357
succession in the presidency,
1421
Times and Seasons, 1480
Utah statehood, 1502
visions of Joseph Smith, 1515
Word of Wisdom, 1584
Young Women, 1617
Taylor, John Harris, 1648, 1680
Taylor, John W. (son), 253, 328,
631, 632, 1136, 1363, 1648,
1679, 1741
Taylor, Leonora, 1116
Taylor, Margaret Young, 1648, 1684
Taylor, Russell C., 1648, 1681
Taylor, Samuel W., 664, 839
Taylor, William W., 1648, 1680
Tea, 289, 416, 417, 1097, **1441**,
1584
Teacher, Aaronic Priesthood, 635,
1441
Teachers, teacher development,
350–51, 722, 1034, **1442**
priest, Aaronic Priesthood, 1132
priesthood, 1140
priesthood quorums, 1144
scouting, 1275
see also Education; Schools
Teaching the Gospel, **1442–43**
Teasdale, George, 231, 328, 1648,
1679, 1741
priesthood, 1136
Technology, 172–75, 223, 644–45
see also Computer systems

Teichert, Minerva Kohlhepp, 71, <u>72</u>
Telegraph system, 440, 630
Teleology, 467
Telestial kingdom, 265, **1443**
  degrees of glory, 369
  Doctrine and Covenants, 414
  hell, 585
  Salt Lake Temple, 1254
  see also Celestial kingdom;
    Heaven; Paradise; Terrestrial
    kingdom
Television, 140, 233–34, 242, 645,
  694
  see also KSL broadcasting; Satel-
    lite communications system
Temple and family history executive
  council. *See* Glossary
Temple garments. *See* Garments;
  Glossary
Temple ordinances, 1032, **1444–45**,
  1450–52
  baptism, 96
  blacks, 125
  Catholicism and Mormonism, 258
  deaf, materials for the, 364
  death and dying, 365
  district, district presidency, 391
  Doctrine and Covenants, 419,
    421, 423
  eternal life, 464
  family history, genealogy, 492–
    93, 499
  family organizations, 497
  fellowshipping members, 506
  genealogy, 538
  gift of the Holy Ghost, 543
  heirs, 583
  homosexuality, 656
  loss of, 1461–62
  name extraction program, 979
  religious experience, 1210
  restoration of all things, 1219
  reverence, 1229
  sisterhood, 1320
  world religion, 1590
Temple president and matron, 249,
  539, 1046, **1445–46**
Temple recommend, 681, 697,
  1054, **1446–47**, 1449, 1452,
  1463
  sealing, 1289
  word of wisdom, 1584
Temples, 567, **1447–65**, 1743–1749
  administration of, 1456–58
  altar, 37
  Angel Moroni statue, 40
  architecture, 64

building program, 236, 238
Catholicism and Mormonism, 258
centennial observances, 261
city planning, 283
computer systems, 304
dedications, 367, 416, 659, 1455–
  56
degrees of glory, 369
Doctrine and Covenants, 409,
  414, 416
exaltation, 479
freemasonry and, 528–29
garments, 534
Guatemala, 901
history of, 614, 622, 636, 639,
  1450–55, 1463–65
holiness, 648
immigration and emigration, 676
Israel, 706, 710
Jesus Christ, 735
Kimball, Spencer W., 785
marriage, 856, 857
meanings and functions of, 1458–
  63
membership, 887
Mexico City, 900
mysteries of God, 978
New Zealand, 1016
oaths, 1020
oil, 1027
politics, 1102
public relations, 1179
record keeping, 1196
salvation, 1257
Scandinavia, 1262, 1264–65
sculptors, 1285–86
sealings, 1289
signs of the true Church, 1312
sisterhood, 1320
Smith, Joseph, 1342
temple recommend, 1446–47
tree of life, 1486
Utah statehood, 1502
worship and activity, 389, 539,
  1120, 1201, 1297, 1444, 1447–
  50, 1597–98
see also specific temples, e.g.,
  Salt Lake Temple; Temple ordinances
Temple Square, **1465–68**
  celebrations, 259
  Christus statue, 273
  conferences, 307
  conversion, 321
  economic history, 421
  endowment houses, 593
  historical sites, 595

  history, 633
  museums, 973
  pioneer life, 1085
  public communications, 1177
  Salt Lake Temple, 1252
  sculptors, 1286
  seagulls, miracle of, 1288
  ward, 1541
  see also Mormon Tabernacle
    Choir; Tabernacle, Salt Lake
    City; Tabernacle organ
Temple Square Hotel Corporation,
  242
Temporal death, 485
Temptation, 380, 478, 1088, **1468–
69**
Ten Commandments, 296, **1469–70**
  adultery, 21
  Book of Mormon, 162
  Doctrine and Covenants, 412
  law of Moses, 811
  murder, 970
Tenorio, Horacio, 902, 1648, 1681
Teresa, Mother, 58
Terrestrial kingdom, 367, 368–69,
  414, 1254, **1470**
  see also Celestial kingdom;
    Heaven; Paradise; Telestial
    kingdom
Terry, George, 899
Testament of Abraham, 134, 137
Testator, **1470**
Testimony, 547, 1055, **1470**
  Book of Mormon, 148, 158, 214–
    16
  children, 267
  cross, 345
  humility, 663
  joining the Church, 759
  physical body, 1080
  public speaking, 1179
  scripture study, 1284
  theology, 1475
  values, 1508
  see also Conversion; Testimony
    bearing; Testimony of Jesus
    Christ
Testimony bearing, **1470–72**
Testimony of Jesus Christ, 546,
  1406, **1472**
Textiles, Book of Mormon, 173–74
Thailand, the Church in, 79, 80,
  662, 696, 1757
Thankfulness, 498, 668, **1472–73**
Thatcher, Moses, 623, 628, 899,
  <u>1136</u>, 1649, 1679, 1683, 1741
Thayer, Douglas H., 839–40, 843,
  844

Thayne, Emma Lou, 839
Theater. *See* Drama; Motion pictures; Pageants
Theodicy, 403, 478, 1030, 1182, **1473–74**
Theogony, **1474**
Theology, 400, 894, 1271, **1475–76**
Theomorphism, 273
Theophany. *See* First Vision
Thermodynamics, center for (BYU), 224
Thimme, Hans, 1592
Thiruthuvadoss, S. Paul, 81
"This Is the Place" monument, 262, 595, 1286, 1328, 1359, **1476–77**
Thomas, Charles J., 950, 973–74, 976, 1426, 1466
Thomas, Edna Harker, 1649, 1684
Thomas, Shirley Wilkes, 1649, 1685
Thompson, Mercy Fielding, 1116, 1349, 1359
Thompson, Robert B., 590, 1649, 1682
Thompson, Janet Lennox Murdock, 1649, 1684
Thompson, Una, 1015
Thorvaldsen, Bertel, 273, 1466
Thrasher, E. W., 434
Thrasher Research Fund, 434
Three Nephites, 517, 519, **1477–78,** 1486
Three Witnesses, 214–16, 1514
Thummim. *See* Urim and Thummim
Thurber, A. K., 1313
Thurman, Richard Young, 842
Thurston, Jarvis, 842
Time and eternity, **1478–79**
 born in the covenant, 218
 doctrine, 402
 law, 809
 mankind, 853
 marriage, 857
 see also Millennium; Riches of eternity
Time magazine, 633
Times and Seasons (newspaper), 178, 305, 590, 612, 647, 1011, 1379, 1438, **1479–80,** 1561
Tingey, Clarence, 87
Tingey, Earl C., 1649, 1681
Tingey, Martha Horne, 524, 1617, 1649, 1684
Tischendorf, Constantin von, 109
Tithing, 942, 1054, **1480–82**
 bishops, 121
 commandments, 297

consecration, 313, 314
economic history, 440
Far West, Missouri, 500
finances of the Church, 507–508, 509
history, 630
immigration and emigration, 674
interviews, 697
LDS Foundation, 816
lifestyle, 834
Malachi, 851
organization, 1038
presiding bishopric, 1129
priesthood, 1139
procreation, 1157
record keeping, 1196
sacrifice, 1248
Smith, Joseph, 1343
ward council, 1544
wealth, attitudes toward, 1552
Tobacco, 416, 580, 1375, **1482,** 1584
Tocqueville, Alexis de, 318
Todd, Jay M., 461
Tolerance, 693, 1177, **1482–83**
Tonga, the Church in, 382, 873, 1025, 1759
Tooele Stake, 565
Topical Guide, 110, **1483–84**
Torah. *See* Book of Moses; Law of Moses
Torres, Victor de la, 1286
Training. *See* Church Educational System; Education; Missionary Training Centers; specific school names
Transfiguration, 716, 1014, **1484–85**
 see also Mount of Transfiguration
Translated beings, 450, 753, 758, 767, **1485–86**
Translations, Book of Mormon, 213–14
Translation Services Department, 213
Transplants (medical). *See* Organ transplants and donations
Transportation, Book of Mormon, 173
Transportation industry, 440, 629
 see also specific industry, e.g., Railroad industry
Trapped by the Mormons (film), 947, 948
Treaty of Guadalupe Hidalgo, 1100
Tree of Life, 63, 184, 1004, 1062, 1419, 1431, **1486–88**
Trejo, Melitón G., 213, 899
Trials, 663, **1488**

Trials of Joseph Smith. *See* Smith, Joseph, legal trials of
Tribe, American Indian. *See* Native Americans; specific tribe, e.g., Navajo tribe
Trinity. *See* Godhead
Trip to Salt Lake City, A (film), 947
True and living Church, **1489**
Trujillo, José, 1397
Trujillo, Napoleón, 1397
Trumbo, Isaac, 1503
Truth, 534, 809, 1227, 1340, **1489–91**
Tubaloth war, 165
Tucker, Pomeroy, 46, 48
Tullidge, Edward W., 620, 976, 1266
Turkey, the Church in, 471, 625, 917, 1757
Turley, Maurine Johnson, 1649, 1685
Turner, Jonathan B., 47
Tutokohi, Te Pirihi, 1015
Tuttle, A. Theodore, 503, 1397, 1400, 1649, 1680, 1681, 1683
Twain, Mark, 664, 949
Twelve Apostles. *See* Missions of the Twelve to the British Isles; Quorum of the Twelve Apostles; specific apostle, e.g., Paul
Tyler, John, 861
Tyndale, William, 109
Typology, Book of Mormon, 183–84
Tzounis, John, 662

Udall, David K., 66
Udall, Stewart L., 286
Udoeyo, Helen Bassey Davies, 24
U and I Sugar Company, 242, 440
Unified Magazine, 697
Union Pacific (film), 567, 633
Union of Soviet Socialist Republics, the Church in, 471, 474, 917
Union Vedette (periodical), 619
Unitarian church, 169
Unitarian/Universalist church, 687
United Apostolic Brethren, 531
United Churches Ionian Relief Committee, 662
United Effort trust, 531
United Firm. *See* United orders
United orders, 66, 605, **1493–95**
 consecration, 314
 economic history, 439
 Enoch, 459, 622
 fundamentalists, 531
 history, 621, 624

home industries, 652
Horne, Mary Isabella, 658
Nephi₄, 1006
organization, 1038
politics, 1098
rebaptism, 1194
social and cultural history, 1382
Whitney store, 1567
Young, Brigham, 1608
United States of America, **1495–97**
civil rights, 286
constitutional law, 315
International Genealogical Index™, 697
vital statistics, 1533
war and peace, 1547, 1549
Unity, 279, 539, **1497–98**
common consent, 299
economic history, 438–39
family prayer, 499
following the brethren, 520
lay participation, 815
metaphysics, 895
politics, 1104
world religions, 1591
see also Common consent; Equality
Universalism, 1169
Universities, 282
see also specific name, e.g., Brigham Young University
University of the City of Nauvoo, 442–43
University of Deseret, 274, 285, 373, 443, 446, 1268, 1269, 1379, **1498–99**, 1567, 1608
see also University of Utah
University Press, 111
University of Utah, 274, 443, 832, 1255, 1402
see also University of Deseret
University of Utah Medical Complex, 660
Unpardonable sin, 586, 650, 970, 1443, **1499**, 1598
Upper Missouri Advertiser (newspaper), 605, 1011
Urim and Thummim, 1293, **1499–1500**
Book of Abraham, 136, 138
Book of Mormon, 212
history, 602
manuscript, lost 116 pages, 855
revelation, 1225
Smith, Joseph, 1335
Smith, Lucy Mack, 1357
see also Seer stones

Ursenbach, Octave, 1312
Uruguay, the Church in, 873, 1400, 1760
Utah
antipolygamy legislation, 52
Church and state, 282
civic duties, 285, 286
Deseret, state of, 371
economic history, 440
education, 446
history, 613–30
Utah Expedition, 66, 248, 578, 619, 666, **1500–1502**
colonization, 290
economic history, 439
Idaho, 671
Kane, Thomas L., 779
legal and judicial history, 825
Mountain Meadows Massacre, 966
Nauvoo Legion, 999
politics, 1101
Reformation (1856–1857), 1197
Relief Society, 1201
Salt Lake Temple, 1253
Smith, Joseph F., 1350
Snow, Eliza R., 1366
social and cultural history, 1382
Sunday School, 1425
Utah Territory, 1505
war and peace, 1549
Wyoming, 1599
Young, Brigham, 1608
see also Utah statehood
Utah Genealogical and Historical Magazine (periodical), 620, **1502**
Utah-Idaho Sugar Company, 631
Utah Lighthouse Ministry, Inc., 51
Utah Light and Railroad Company, 630
Utah Silk Commission, 1313
Utah State Archives, 832
Utah State Historical Society, 832
Utah statehood, 616, 628, 631, 779–80, 1018, **1502–1503**, 1572–73, 1583
see also Deseret, state of; Manifesto of 1890; Utah Expedition
Utah State University, 832
Utah Territory, 417, **1503–1505**
academies, 11
Church aand state, 282
courts, 330
Deseret, state of, 372
education, 443, 444
history, 616, 623

home industries, 652
legal and judicial history, 824
Nauvoo Legion, 999
politics, 1098
social and cultural history, 1382
Utah Expedition, 1500
Young, Brigham, 1608
Utah University. *See* University of Utah
Utah War (1857–1858), 1500
Utnapishtim, 718
Uto-Aztecan language, 180, 181

Values, transmission of, **1507–1509**, 1620
see also Ethics
Van Buren, Martin, 382, 590, 1337, 1496
Van Cott, John, 1649, 1680
Vandenberg, John H., 1649, 1680, 1681
Vasectomy, 1096
Vasquez, Louis, 1599
Venezuela, the Church in, 1398, 1760
Vernon, Glenn M., 320
Victor, Metta Victoria Fuller, 49
Vidal, Roberto, 1398
Video technology, 645
Vietnam, the Church in, 80–81, 662
View of the Hebrews (E. Smith), **1509–1510**
Vinson, Fred M., 100
Virgin birth, 345, 864, 1090, **1510**
Vision, The (Doctrine and Covenants), 414
Visions, 405, 427, 958, 1004, 1167, **1511–12**
see also First Vision; Visions of Joseph Smith
Visions of Joseph Smith, 647, 1001, 1349, 1511, **1512–16**
Visiting teaching, 461, 698, **1516–17**
community, 302
history, 636
Relief Society, 1201, 1208
sisterhood, 1319
welfare services, 1555
see also Compassionate service
Visitors Centers, 273, 480, 635, 645, **1517–18**
conversion, 321
dedications, 367
Fayette, New York, 505
Hiram, Ohio, 589
missionaries, 911

Visitors Centers (Cont'd)
  museums, 973
  Nauvoo, 1003
  Palmyra/Manchester, New York, 1058
  public communications, 1177
  public relations, 1179
  Temple Square, 1465
  Welfare Square, 1559
  see also Historical sites
VISN Religious Interfaith Cable Television, 694
Visual arts. See Artists, visual
Vital statistics, 288, 417, 638, 1518–37
  British Isles, the Church in, 230, 1525, 1533
  children, 1521–24, 1526, 1529–30, 1533
  demographic characteristics, 1527–37
  Europe, the Church in, 470, 1525, 1533
  family, 488–89, 1521–24, 1529
  marriage and divorce, 859, 1521–24, 1530–32, 1533
  membership size, growth, and distribution, 1519–21
  sources of population change, 1521–27
  see also International Genealogical Index; Membership records; Record keeping
Vocabulary, Latter-day Saint, 1537–38
"Voice from the Dust," 159, 1538
Voice of warning, 1122, 1282, 1538–39
Volunteerism, 286, 1105, 1252, 1539–40, 1556
Voting rights, 626
  see also Woman suffrage

Wadi Sayq, 145
Waite, Morrison W., 1230
Wales, the Church in, 213, 697, 1760
Walker, Cyrus, 1000
Walker, William H., 22
Walker War (1853–1854), 291, 999
Wallace, Irving, 949
Wandell, Charles W., 86
Ward, 279, 538, 1541–43
  bishops, 117, 120, 122
  branch, branch president, 219
  Brigham Young University, 222–23

celebrations, 259
clerk, 288
conferences, 306
dance, 355
district, district president, 390
family, 491
fast offerings, 501
finances of the Church, 508
lay participation, 814
material culture, 864
membership records, 887
motion pictures, 965
music, 973
Nauvoo, 991
priesthood executive committee, 1142
priesthood quorums, 1144
Relief Society, 1199, 1208
scouting, 1276
sick, blessing the, 1308
see also Ward budget; Ward council; Ward organization; Ward Welfare Committee
Ward, Artemus, 664
Ward, Platt, 497
Ward, William, 1253
Ward, Wilma, 497
Ward budget, 510, 1543–44
Ward council, 1048, 1142, 1141, 1544
Ward organization, 1036, 1544–45
  see also Callings; Ward
Ward Welfare Committee, 1545–46
War in Heaven, 329, 1546–47
  angels, 41
  devils, 379
  Jesus Christ, 752
  plan of salvation, 1088
  sons of perdition, 1391
  see also Creation, creation accounts
War and peace, 162–66, 638, 646, 690, 1547–50, 1549–50
  see also Conscientious objection; Military and the Church
Warner, Richard L., 1427, 1649, 1682
Warsaw Signal (newspaper), 613
Wasatch Literary Association, 565
Washburn, J Ballard, 1649, 1681
Washing of feet, 416, 659, 1550
Washings and anointings, 455, 456, 799, 812, 1357, 1444, 1447, 1551
Washington, George, 317
Washington Temple, 280
Wasp (newspaper), 1011

Watson, Wilford, 182
Watt, George D., 305, 373, 769, 1313
Watts, Isaac, 667
Waugh, Alec, 839
Wealth, attitudes toward, 1551–53
  see also Poverty, attitudes toward
Weber Stake Academy, 13
Weber State University, 13
Weeks, William, 64, 997, 1001
Weggeland, Danquart A., 71, 1381
Welch, Jay E., 950
Welch, John W., 167
Welfare, 1128, 1553, 1576
  see also Welfare farms; Welfare services
Welfare farms, 454, 826, 1553–54
Welfare services, 567, 637, 643, 1554–58
  administration, 1556–57
  calamities and disasters, 246
  consecration, 313
  Deseret Industries, 376, 1555, 1557
  elder, Melchizedek Priesthood, 448
  emergency preparedness, 454
  Europe, the Church in, 472
  high council, 587
  history of, 1554–55
  home industries, 654
  intellectual history, 688
  organization, 1047
  poverty, 1113
  principles and practices, 1555–56
  Relief Society, 1199
  Robison, Louise Yates, 1238
  self-sufficiency, 1293
  single adults, 1317
  stake, 1413
  ward, 1545–46
  see also Humanitarian service; Poverty, attitudes toward; Social services
Welfare Services Missionary Program, 662
Welfare Square, 1179, 1518, 1558–59
Wells, Daniel H., 620, 1425, 1433, 1559, 1560, 1649, 1678, 1741
Wells, Emily, 566
Wells, Emmeline B., 115, 375, 636, 658, 1200, 1203, 1366, 1559–60, 1567, 1571, 1572, 1573, 1649, 1685
Wells, Heber M., 634
Wells, John, 231, 1649, 1682

Wells, Junius F., 320, **1560–61**, 1649, 1683

Wells, Robert E., 1649, 1681

Wells, Robert W., 1627

Wells, Rulon S., 1649, 1680

Wentworth, John, 67, 1561

Wentworth letter, 67, 68, 69, 106, 343, 515, 1480, **1561–62**, 1750–55

Werner, Morris R., 633

Wesley, John, 58, 168, 668

West, Caleb, 1103

West, Franklin L., 1649, 1683

West, Josephine R., <u>1147</u>, 1649, 1684

West, Orson B., 1264

West, Ray B., 842

West, Susan Elizabeth, 1567

West Indies, the Church in, **1562–63**, 1762–63

Westward migration, planning and prophecy, 326, 537, 612, 614, 779, 861, 993, 996, 1001, **1563–64**

Weyland, Jack, 665, 839, 843

Wheatley, Kenneth, 232

Wheeler, Nathan, 665

Wheelwright, D. Sterling, 950

Whitaker, Elizabeth, 1312

Whitaker, Harriet, 1440

Whitaker, Sophia, 1440

Whitaker, Wetzel O., 964, 965

Whitaker, William F., Jr., 72

White, Hugh, 987

White, Maurice, 79

White, Orson Hyde, 1025

White, William, 987

Whitmer, Catherine, 603

Whitmer, Christian, 214

Whitmer, David, 61, 337, 338, 505, 575, 1068, **1564–66**

  Anthon Transcript, 44

  Book of Mormon, 186, 212, 214, 215

  Doctrine and Covenants, 408

  history, 602, 603

  Missouri, 925

  Missouri Conflict, 928, 930

  organization of the Church, 1049

  Quorum of the Twelve Apostles, 1185

  Smith, Joseph, 1335

  Temple Square, 1467

  visions of Joseph Smith, 1514

Whitmer, Elizabeth Ann. *See* Cowdery, Elizabeth Ann Whitmer

Whitmer, Jacob, 214

Whitmer, John, 214, 338, 408, 589, 765, 892, 925, 926, 930, 1068, 1565, 1649, 1682

Whitmer, Mary Musselman, 214, 955, 1564

Whitmer, Peter, Jr., 214, 408, 603, 802, 803, 916, 1049, 1565

  Pratt, Parley P., 1116

Whitmer, Peter, Sr., 214, 262, 505, 603, 1049, 1564

Whitmer home and farm, 63, 211, 262, 337, 505, 593, 1049

Whitney, Elizabeth Ann, 18, 1201, 1203, 1650, 1685

Whitney, Horace G. (Bud), *Deseret News*, 377

Whitney, Newel K., 119, 120, 423, <u>517</u>, 802, 1037, 1085, 1129, <u>1234</u>, 1559, 1650, 1681

  see also Whitney store

Whitney, Orson F., 58, 255, <u>540</u>, 838, 841, 842, 1573, 1650, 1679, 1741

Whitney store, 415, 593, 796, 1269, 1515, **1566–67**

Whittaker, David J., 114

Widtsoe, John A., 178, 397, 424, <u>487</u>, <u>540</u>, <u>637</u>, 678, 1650, 1679, 1741

  agriculture, 29

  consecration, 313

  Earth, 432

  Enoch, 462

  institutes of religion, 684

  intellectual history, 689

  priesthood quorums, <u>1145</u>

  Quorum of the Twelve Apostles, <u>1186</u>

  Scandinavia, 1264

  science and religion, 1271, 1272

  science and scientists, 1274

  world religions, 1593

Wight, Lyman, 614, 802, 830, 929, 1230, 1346, 1627, 1650, 1679, 1741

Wight cabin, <u>19</u>, 20

Wilcox, Jim, <u>73</u>

Wilcox, Keith W., 1650, 1681

Wilkinson, Ernest L., 222, <u>1486</u>

Willes, William, 79

Williams, Clarissa Smith, 636, <u>1200</u>, 1203, 1237, **1567–68**, 1650, 1685

Williams, Frederick G., 512, 513, 586, 802, 821, 916, 926, 1116, 1234, 1269, 1650, 1678, 1741

Williams, Frederick S., 1398, 1400

Williams, Helen Spencer, 1650, 1684

Williams, William Newjent, 1567

Williams, Zina, 1572

Willie, James G., 571

Willie Company, 572

Willing, Joseph, 1592

Winberg, Anders, 1263

Winchester, Benjamin, 57

Winder, Barbara W., 1205, 1650, 1685

Winder, John Rex, 231, 478, <u>1041</u>, 1351, 1650, 1678, 1682, <u>1741</u>

Winter, Gladys, 1238

Winter Quarters, 119, 325, 436, 595, 615, 935, 943, **1568–69**

  pioneer life, 1085, 1094

  Rogers, Aurelia Spencer, 1238

  sculptors, 1286

  Smith, Joseph F., 1350

  Smith, Mary Fielding, 1359

  social and cultural history, 1379

  ward, 1541

  Young, Brigham, 1605

Winters, Huldah Augusta, 566

Wirthlin, Joseph B., 81, 461, 1129, <u>1187</u>, 1427, 1650, 1679, 1680, <u>1681</u>, 1682, 1741

Wirthlin, Joseph L., 1650, 1681, 1682

Wisdom literature, Book of Mormon, 184

Witnesses, Book of Mormon. *See* Book of Mormon witnesses

Witnesses, law of, 1033, **1569–70**

Wolsey, Heber G., 1177

Woman's Exponent, 621, 636, 658, 689, 1207, 1224, 1366, 1383, 1559, **1571–72**

Woman suffrage, 285, 525, 621, 627, 658, 1201–1202, 1560, 1571, **1572–73**

Women, roles of, **1574–77**

  biography and autobiography, 114–15

  civic duties, 285

  civil rights, 287

  divorce, 392

  Doctrine and Covenants, 412

  feminism, 506–507

  freemasonry, 529

  handcart companies, 573

  historical and sociological development, 1574–75

  history, 646

  intellectual history, 689

  marriage, 857

Women, roles of, (Cont'd)
  missionaries, 910, 919
  Nauvoo, 992
  sculptors, 1286
  single adults, 1317
  social characteristics, 1371–77
  visiting teaching, 1516
  vital statistics, 1528, 1530, 1533, 1534–35
  see also Abuse, spouse and child; Divorce; Family; Marriage; Motherhood; Mother in Heaven; Mother in Israel; Relief Society; Retrenchment Association; Sisterhood; Woman suffrage; Women in the Book of Mormon; Women's topics; Young Women
Women in the Book of Mormon, 1577–80
Women's Cooperative Mercantile and Manufacturing Institution, 658
Women's rights. See Feminism; Woman suffrage
Women's topics, 1580
Wood, E. J., 253
Wood, Wilford C., 20, 592
Woodbury, George F., 1066
Woodford, Robert J., 424
Woodland, William West, 672
Woodruff, Abraham O., 328, 1650, 1679, 1741
Woodruff, Lucy Emily (Wilford's daughter), 1326
Woodruff, Phebe, 375
Woodruff, Wilford, 512, 666, 1126, 1580–84, 1650, 1678, 1679, 1682, 1683, 1741
  antipolygamy legislation, 48, 52
  Book of Abraham, 136
  British Isles, 228, 230, 231, 921
  constitutional law, 315
  Daniel, prophecies of, 355
  Doctrine and Covenants, 405, 426
  family history, 492
  genealogy, 537
  historians, 590
  history, 623, 626, 627, 629, 630
  inspiration, 683
  journals, 770
  King Follett Discourse, 791
  legal and judicial history, 825
  Manifesto (1890), 852–53
  Millennial Star, 906
  missions, 921

Mother in Heaven, 961
Old Testament, 1030
organization, 1036, 1040
plural marriage, 1095
politics, 1102
priesthood, 1136
prophets, 1165
Quorum of the Twelve Apostles, 1186
record keeping, 1195
Reynolds v. United States, 1239
Rogers, Aurelia Spencer, 1238
Salt Lake Temple, 1254
Smith, Emma Hale, 1326
Smith, Joseph, 1343
Smith, Joseph F., 1352
Smith, Lucy Mack, 1357
social and cultural history, 1383
succession in the presidency, 1420, 1421
Sunday School, 1425
Taylor, John, 1440
temples, 1455, 1456
"This Is the Place" monument, 1477
Times and Seasons, 1480
Utah statehood, 1503
Utah Territory, 1505
woman suffrage, 1573
Young, Zina D. H., 1613
Woodward, David, 1559
Woodward, Emmeline. See Wells, Emmeline B.
Woodworth, Lucien, 997
Wooley, Ralph E., 579
Wooley, Taylor, 877
Woolley, David, 115
Woolley, Edwin D., 786
Woolley, Lorin C., 531
Woolsey, Durrel A., 1650, 1681
Word, The, 741
  see also Jesus Christ
Wordprinting, 167
Words of Mormon, 149
Word of Wisdom, 407, 609, 620, 636, 1054, 1097, 1584–85
  alcoholic beverages, 30
  civic duties, 285
  coffee, 416–17
  commandments, 297
  disciplinary procedures, 386
  law of Moses, 812
  lifestyle, 834
  Melchizedek Priesthood, 887
  peculiar people, 1073
  physical fitness, 1081
  prohibition, 1158

Schools of the Prophets, 1269
sick, blessing the, 1308
Smith, Joseph, 1336
social and cultural history, 1383
socialization, 1385
tea, 1441
tobacco, 1482
Whitney store, 1566
see also Doctrine and Covenants, section 89; Health, attitudes toward
Work, role of, 409, 1585–87
see also Occupational status
Works, 812, 1587
Works, Miriam, 1602
World Conferences on Records, 493, 1588
Worldly, worldliness, 345, 1587–88
World religions (non-Christian) and Mormonism, 695, 696, 1052, 1483, 1588–95
  Buddhism, 1407, 1589–90
  Confucianism, 1590–91
  Hinduism, 1591–92
  Islam, 283, 345, 696, 1592–93
  Judaism, 1593–94
  overview, 1589
  reason and revelation, 1192–93
  Shinto, 1594–95
  see also Interfaith relationships; Jews; Non-Mormons, social relations with
Worlds, 82, 1340, 1595–96
  see also Creation, creation accounts
World's Fairs. See Exhibitions and World's Fairs
Worship, 499, 668, 1447–50, 1596–98
  see also Hymns and hymnody; Pioneer life and worship; Prayer; Sabbath Day; Sunday; Temples, worship and activity
Wrath of God, 1310, 1598
  see also Chastening
Wren, Christopher, 876
Wright, David L., 842
Wright, Emma E., 1015
Wright, Frank Lloyd, 877
Wright, Ruth Broadbent, 1650, 1684
Wycliffe, John, 109
Wyoming, pioneer settlements in, 1598–99

Yates, Alma, 665
Yates, Elizabeth, 1237
Yates, Thomas, 1237

Year of the Bible, 107
Year of Jubilee, 624
Yerba Buena, California, 247
YLMIA. *See* Young Ladies' Mutual
    Improvement Association
YMMIA. *See* Young Men's Mutual
    Improvement Association
Yorgason, Blaine, 839
Yorgason, Brenton, 839
Yoshihiko Kikuchi, 77
Young, Alfred D., 1209
Young, Amy Eliza, 49
Young, Brigham, 354, 536, 576,
    1068, 1126, 1365, **1601–11**,
    1650, 1678, 1741
  Adam, 17
  Adamic language, 18
  agriculture, 28
  animals, 43
  apostasy, 58
  architecture, 64
  Arizona settlements, 66
  arts, visual, 70
  Book of Mormon, 175
  British Isles, 228, 231, 921
  business, 240
  California, pioneer settlements in,
      246, 247, 248
  Canada, 251
  Church Educational System, 274
  city planning, 284
  colonization, 291
  Constitution, U.S., 318
  cursings, 352
  damnation, 354
  Deseret, state of, 371, 372
  Deseret alphabet, 373, 374
  Deseret News, 377
  divorce, 391
  Doctrine and Covenants, 405,
      414, 421, 423, 426
  Earth, 432–33
  economic history, 435, 437, 439
  education, 443–44
  endowment houses, 456
  eternal lives, eternal increase,
      465
  eternal progression, 465, 466
  Europe, 471
  family home evening, 496
  freemasonry in Nauvoo, 528
  Garden of Eden, 534
  handcart companies, 571–73
  historians, 590
  historical sites, 595
  history, 614, 615–616, 619, 620,
      621, 647

  home industries, 653, 654
  hospitals, 659
  humanitarian service, 661
  humor, 664
  Hyde, Orson, 666
  hymns, 667
  Idaho, 671
  immigration and emigration, 673
  intellectual history, 686, 688
  Journal of Discourses, 769
  Kane, Thomas L., 780
  Kimball, Heber C., 782
  Kirtland, Ohio, 797
  Kirtland Temple, 798
  legal and judicial history, 824
  literature, 837
  marriage, 858
  martyrs, 863
  maternity and child health care,
      867
  medical practices, 875
  Mexico, 895, 899
  missions, 916, 921
  Missouri, 927
  Missouri Conflict, 931
  Mormonism, 940
  Mormon Pioneer Trail, 943
  Mormon Tabernacle Choir, 950
  mother in Israel, 963
  Mountain Meadows Massacre,
      966
  museums, 972
  music, 973, 976
  Native Americans, 982
  natural man, 986
  Nauvoo, 991, 993, 996, 999
  Nevada, 1006, 1007
  organization, 1036, 1038, 1039,
      1040
  physical fitness, 1081
  Pioneer Day, 1082
  pioneer economy, 1083
  pioneer life, 1085, 1087
  plural marriage, 1094
  politics, 1100, 1101, 1105
  Polynesians, 1110
  Pratt, Orson, 1115
  President of the Church, 1128
  presiding bishopric, 1129
  priesthood offices, 1146
  prophecy and prophets, 1162,
      1165
  publications, 1173, 1174
  Quorum of the Twelve Apostles,
      1185
  Reformation (1856–1857), 1197
  Relief Society, 1201, 1208

  Retrenchment Association, 1224–
      25
  revelation, 1226
  RLDS Church, 1212, 1213
  Salt Lake City, Utah, 1250
  Salt Lake Temple, 1253
  Salt Lake Theatre, 1255
  Salt Lake Valley, 1255
  Satanism, 1261
  schismatic groups, 1265
  Schools of the Prophets, 1270
  science and scientists, 1273
  seagulls, miracle of, 1287
  silk culture, 1312–13
  Smith, Emma Hale, 1325
  Smith, Joseph, 1338
  Smith, Joseph F., 1350
  Smith, Lucy Mack, 1357
  social and cultural history, 1380
  spirit world, 1408
  sports, 1409
  stake, 1413
  stereotyping, 1417
  succession in the presidency,
      1420
  Sunday School, 1425
  Tabernacle, Salt Lake City, 1433
  Taylor, John, 1438, 1439
  teachings of, 1609–11
  temples, 1452, 1454
  Temple Square, 1465
  testimony bearing, 1471
  thankfulness, 1472–73
  "This Is the Place" monument,
      1476, 1477
  tithing, 1482
  united orders, 1493, 1494
  United States of America, 1497
  Utah Expedition, 1500
  Utah statehood, 1502
  Utah Territory, 1502, 1504
  values, 1507
  ward, 1541, 1542
  wealth, attitudes toward, 1552
  westward migration, 1563
  women, roles of, 1574
  work, role of, 1587
  world religions, 1593, 1594
  Wyoming, 1599
  Young, Zina D. H., 1612
  Young Men, 1614
  see also Brigham Young Academy;
      Brigham Young College; Brig-
      ham Young University
Young, Brigham, Jr., 328, 1136,
    1425, 1650, 1678, 1679, 1741
Young, Caroline, 576, 1224

Young, Clifford E., 1651, 1679
Young, Dwan Jacobsen, 1148, 1651, 1684
Young, Elizabeth (Brigham's daughter), 1602
Young, Emily Partridge, 1326
Young, Fanny (Brigham's sister), 1602
Young, George Cannon, 64
Young, John (Brigham's brother), 1603
Young, John (Brigham's father), 1601
Young, John W. (Brigham's son), 66, 620, 972, 1651, 1678, 1741
Young, Joseph (Brigham's brother), 68, 1086, 1602, 1603, 1651, 1680
Young, Joseph Angell, 1651, 1741
Young, Joseph Don Carlos (Brigham's son), 64, 237, 673, 877
Young, Julia, 770
Young, Levi Edgar, 1651, 1680
Young, Lorenzo (Brigham's brother), 1603
Young, Lucy Bigelow, 535
Young, Lucy Cowdery, 335
Young, Mahonri (Brigham's grandson), 71, 262, 634, 1286, 1287, 1477
Young, Margaret, 1440
Young, Phineas (Brigham's brother), 1602, 1603
Young, Phinehas H., 916
Young, Richard W., 634
Young, Seymour B. (Brigham's nephew), 875, 1651, 1680
Young, S. Dilworth, 1651, 1680, 1681
Young, Vilate (Brigham's daughter), 1602
Young, Willard, 237
Young, Zina D. H. (Brigham's wife), 375, 624, 636, 658, 867, 1201, 1202, 1209, 1313, 1326, 1573, 1611–13, 1651, 1685
Young, Zina Presendia (Brigham's daughter), 1612
Young Ladies' Mutual Improvement Association (YLMIA), 324, 524, 621, 623, 1039, 1040, 1364, 1382, 1684–85
  see also Young Women
Young Men, 90, 279, 520, 635, 643, 1613–15, 1620
  Aaronic Priesthood, 3
  bishop, 118
  dance, 355

dating and courtship, 358
organization, 1039, 1046
Parmley, LaVern Watts, 1063
presiding bishopric, 1129
priest, Aaronic Priesthood, 1133
Taylor, Elmina Shepard, 1437
teacher, Aaronic Priesthood, 1441
values, 1508
Wells, Junius F., 1560–61
Young Men's Mutual Improvement Association (YMMIA), 90, 320, 324, 565, 635, 678, 1039, 1040, 1041, 1275, 1327, 1382, 1560, 1683–84
  see also Young Men
Young Stake, 294
Young Woman's Journal (periodical), 535, 624, 635, 678, 1615–16, 1617
Young Women, 89, 90, 279, 302, 324, 506, 635, 1616–19, 1620
  Aaronic Priesthood, 3
  bishop, 118
  centennial observances, 262
  dance, 355
  dating and courtship, 358
  high council, 587
  history, 621, 624
  Horne, Mary Isabella, 658
  New Zealand, 1015
  organization, 1039, 1046
  presiding bishopric, 1129
  priest, Aaronic Priesthood, 1133
  priesthood executive committee, 1142
  Relief Society, 1202
  Retrenchment Association, 1224
  Ruth, 1240
  Sabbath Day, 1242
  sisterhood, 1319
  Taylor, Elmina Shepard, 1436
  Taylor, John, 1439
  teacher, Aaronic Priesthood, 1441
  values, 1508
Young Women's Mutual Improvement Association, 1684–85
  see also Young Ladies Mutual Improvement Association
Youth, 1007, 1619–21
  see also Children; Young Men; Young Women
Yugoslavia, the Church in, 383, 473–74, 1758

Zarahemla, 177, 186, 192, 990, 1259
ZCMI. See Zion's Cooperative Mercantile Institution

Zedekiah, 171
Zemnarihah, 162, 165
Zeniff, 149, 164, 173, 194
Zenock, 1623
Zenos, 148, 183, 714, 1163, 1164, 1623–24
Zion, 155, 169, 283, 300, 302, 1624–26
  devils, 381
  Doctrine and Covenants, 409, 414
  economic history, 435
  Enoch, 312, 457, 459
  eternal progression, 466
  Europe, 469
  gathering, 536
  history, 604
  hope of Israel, 657
  immigration and emigration, 676
  Isaiah, 702
  Jesus Christ, 738
  Lamanite Mission, 802
  Missouri, 922
  Missouri Conflict, 927
  Nauvoo, 990
  pioneer life, 1087
  politics, 1104, 1105
  poverty, 1113
  pride, 1132
  Rigdon, Sidney, 1234
  Smith, Joseph, 1335, 1343, 1346
  war and peace, 1547
  westward migration, 1563
  see also New Jerusalem
Zionism, 1626
Zion's Camp, 337, 576, 608, 666, 781, 924, 929, 1627–29
  Kirtland Temple, 798
  parables, 1061
  Pratt, Orson, 1114
  Quorum of the Twelve Apostles, 1185
  Rigdon, Sidney, 1235
  Seventy, 1300
  Smith, Joseph, 1346
  visions of Joseph Smith, 1515
  Woodruff, Wilford, 1581
  Young, Brigham, 1603
Zion's Central Board of Trade, 624
Zion's Cooperative Mercantile Institution (ZCMI), 240, 241, 242, 436, 618, 621, 631, 654, 688, 1084, 1382
Zions Savings Bank and Trust, 631
Zions Securities Corporation, 242
Zoram, 705, 1629
Zoramites, 165, 193, 1629
Zurcher, Louis A., 320